Lecture Notes in Computer Science   10982

Commenced Publication in 1973
Founding and Former Series Editors:
Gerhard Goos, Juris Hartmanis, and Jan van Leeuwen

More information about this series at http://www.springer.com/series/7407

Hana Chockler · Georg Weissenbacher (Eds.)

Computer Aided Verification

30th International Conference, CAV 2018
Held as Part of the Federated Logic Conference, FloC 2018
Oxford, UK, July 14–17, 2018
Proceedings, Part II

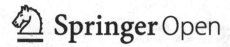

Editors
Hana Chockler
King's College
London
UK

Georg Weissenbacher
TU Wien
Vienna
Austria

ISSN 0302-9743 ISSN 1611-3349 (electronic)
Lecture Notes in Computer Science
ISBN 978-3-319-96141-5 ISBN 978-3-319-96142-2 (eBook)
https://doi.org/10.1007/978-3-319-96142-2

Library of Congress Control Number: 2018948145

LNCS Sublibrary: SL1 – Theoretical Computer Science and General Issues

This Springer imprint is published by the registered company Springer Nature Switzerland AG
The registered company address is: Gewerbestrasse 11, 6330 Cham, Switzerland

Preface

It was our privilege to serve as the program chairs for CAV 2018, the 30th International Conference on Computer-Aided Verification. CAV is an annual conference dedicated to the advancement of the theory and practice of computer-aided formal analysis methods for hardware and software systems. CAV 2018 was held in Oxford, UK, July 14–17, 2018, with the tutorials day on July 13.

This year, CAV was held as part of the Federated Logic Conference (FLoC) event and was collocated with many other conferences in logic. The primary focus of CAV is to spur advances in hardware and software verification while expanding to new domains such as learning, autonomous systems, and computer security. CAV is at the cutting edge of research in formal methods, as reflected in this year's program.

CAV 2018 covered a wide spectrum of subjects, from theoretical results to concrete applications, including papers on application of formal methods in large-scale industrial settings. It has always been one of the primary interests of CAV to include papers that describe practical verification tools and solutions and techniques that ensure a high practical appeal of the results. The proceedings of the conference are published in Springer's *Lecture Notes in Computer Science* series. A selection of papers were invited to a special issue of *Formal Methods in System Design* and the *Journal of the ACM*.

This is the first year that the CAV proceedings are published under an Open Access license, thus giving access to CAV proceedings to a broad audience. We hope that this decision will increase the scope of practical applications of formal methods and will attract even more interest from industry.

CAV received a very high number of submissions this year—215 overall—resulting in a highly competitive selection process. We accepted 13 tool papers and 52 regular papers, which amounts to an acceptance rate of roughly 30% (for both regular papers and tool papers). The high number of excellent submissions in combination with the scheduling constraints of FLoC forced us to reduce the length of the talks to 15 minutes, giving equal exposure and weight to regular papers and tool papers.

The accepted papers cover a wide range of topics and techniques, from algorithmic and logical foundations of verification to practical applications in distributed, networked, cyber-physical, and autonomous systems. Other notable topics are synthesis, learning, security, and concurrency in the context of formal methods. The proceedings are organized according to the sessions in the conference.

The program featured two invited talks by Eran Yahav (Technion), on using deep learning for programming, and by Somesh Jha (University of Wisconsin Madison) on adversarial deep learning. The invited talks this year reflect the growing interest of the CAV community in deep learning and its connection to formal methods. The tutorial day of CAV featured two invited tutorials, by Shaz Qadeer on verification of concurrent programs and by Matteo Maffei on static analysis of smart contracts. The subjects of the tutorials reflect the increasing volume of research on verification of concurrent software and, as of recently, the question of correctness of smart contracts. As every year, one of the winners of the CAV award also contributed a presentation. The tutorial day featured a workshop in memoriam of Mike Gordon, titled "Three Research Vignettes in Memory of Mike Gordon," organized by Tom Melham and jointly supported by CAV and ITP communities.

Moreover, we continued the tradition of organizing a LogicLounge. Initiated by the late Helmut Veith at the Vienna Summer of Logic 2014, the LogicLounge is a series of discussions on computer science topics targeting a general audience and has become a regular highlight at CAV. This year's LogicLounge took place at the Oxford Union and was on the topic of "Ethics and Morality of Robotics," moderated by Judy Wajcman and featuring a panel of experts on the topic: Luciano Floridi, Ben Kuipers, Francesca Rossi, Matthias Scheutz, Sandra Wachter, and Jeannette Wing. We thank May Chan, Katherine Fletcher, and Marta Kwiatkowska for organizing this event, and the Vienna Center of Logic and Algorithms for their support.

In addition, CAV attendees enjoyed a number of FLoC plenary talks and events targeting the broad FLoC community.

In addition to the main conference, CAV hosted the Verification Mentoring Workshop for junior scientists entering the field and a high number of pre- and post-conference technical workshops: the Workshop on Formal Reasoning in Distributed Algorithms (FRIDA), the workshop on Runtime Verification for Rigorous Systems Engineering (RV4RISE), the 5th Workshop on Horn Clauses for Verification and Synthesis (HCVS), the 7th Workshop on Synthesis (SYNT), the First International Workshop on Parallel Logical Reasoning (PLR), the 10th Working Conference on Verified Software: Theories, Tools and Experiments (VSTTE), the Workshop on Machine Learning for Programming (MLP), the 11th International Workshop on Numerical Software Verification (NSV), the Workshop on Verification of Engineered Molecular Devices and Programs (VEMDP), the Third Workshop on Fun With Formal Methods (FWFM), the Workshop on Robots, Morality, and Trust through the Verification Lens, and the IFAC Conference on Analysis and Design of Hybrid Systems (ADHS).

The Program Committee (PC) for CAV consisted of 80 members; we kept the number large to ensure each PC member would have a reasonable number of papers to review and be able to provide thorough reviews. As the review process for CAV is double-blind, we kept the number of external reviewers to a minimum, to avoid accidental disclosures and conflicts of interest. Altogether, the reviewers drafted over 860 reviews and made an enormous effort to ensure a high-quality program. Following the tradition of CAV in recent years, the artifact evaluation was mandatory for tool submissions and optional but encouraged for regular submissions. We used an Artifact Evaluation Committee of 25 members. Our goal for artifact evaluation was to provide friendly "beta-testing" to tool developers; we recognize that developing a stable tool on a cutting-edge research topic is certainly not easy and we hope the constructive comments provided by the Artifact Evaluation Committee (AEC) were of help to the developers. As a result of the evaluation, the AEC accepted 25 of 31 artifacts accompanying regular papers; moreover, all 13 accepted tool papers passed the evaluation. We are grateful to the reviewers for their outstanding efforts in making sure each paper was fairly assessed. We would like to thank our artifact evaluation chair,

Igor Konnov, and the AEC for evaluating all artifacts submitted with tool papers as well as optional artifacts submitted with regular papers.

Of course, without the tremendous effort put into the review process by our PC members this conference would not have been possible. We would like to thank the PC members for their effort and thorough reviews.

We would like to thank the FLoC chairs, Moshe Vardi, Daniel Kroening, and Marta Kwiatkowska, for the support provided, Thanh Hai Tran for maintaining the CAV website, and the always helpful Steering Committee members Orna Grumberg, Aarti Gupta, Daniel Kroening, and Kenneth McMillan. Finally, we would like to thank the team at the University of Oxford, who took care of the administration and organization of FLoC, thus making our jobs as CAV chairs much easier.

July 2018

Hana Chockler
Georg Weissenbacher

Organization

Program Committee

Aws Albarghouthi	University of Wisconsin-Madison, USA
Christel Baier	TU Dresden, Germany
Clark Barrett	Stanford University, USA
Ezio Bartocci	TU Wien, Austria
Dirk Beyer	LMU Munich, Germany
Per Bjesse	Synopsys Inc., USA
Jasmin Christian Blanchette	Vrije Universiteit Amsterdam, Netherlands
Roderick Bloem	Graz University of Technology, Austria
Ahmed Bouajjani	IRIF, University Paris Diderot, France
Pavol Cerny	University of Colorado Boulder, USA
Rohit Chadha	University of Missouri, USA
Swarat Chaudhuri	Rice University, USA
Wei-Ngan Chin	National University of Singapore, Singapore
Hana Chockler	King's College London, UK
Alessandro Cimatti	Fondazione Bruno Kessler, Italy
Loris D'Antoni	University of Wisconsin-Madison, USA
Vijay D'Silva	Google, USA
Cristina David	University of Cambridge, UK
Jyotirmoy Deshmukh	University of Southern California, USA
Isil Dillig	The University of Texas at Austin, USA
Cezara Dragoi	Inria Paris, ENS, France
Kerstin Eder	University of Bristol, UK
Michael Emmi	Nokia Bell Labs, USA
Georgios Fainekos	Arizona State University, USA
Dana Fisman	University of Pennsylvania, USA
Vijay Ganesh	University of Waterloo, Canada
Sicun Gao	University of California San Diego, USA
Alberto Griggio	Fondazione Bruno Kessler, Italy
Orna Grumberg	Technion - Israel Institute of Technology, Israel
Arie Gurfinkel	University of Waterloo, Canada
William Harrison	Department of CS, University of Missouri, Columbia, USA
Gerard Holzmann	Nimble Research, USA
Alan J. Hu	The University of British Columbia, Canada
Franjo Ivancic	Google, USA
Alexander Ivrii	IBM, Israel
Himanshu Jain	Synopsys, USA
Somesh Jha	University of Wisconsin-Madison, USA

Artifact Evaluation Committee

Thibaut Balabonski	Université Paris-Sud, France
Sergiy Bogomolov	The Australian National University, Australia
Simon Cruanes	Aesthetic Integration, USA
Matthias Dangl	LMU Munich, Germany
Eva Darulova	Max Planck Institute for Software Systems, Germany
Ramiro Demasi	Universidad Nacional de Córdoba, Argentina
Grigory Fedyukovich	Princeton University, USA
Johannes Hölzl	Vrije Universiteit Amsterdam, The Netherlands
Jochen Hoenicke	University of Freiburg, Germany
Antti Hyvärinen	Università della Svizzera Italiana, Lugano, Switzerland
Swen Jacobs	Saarland University, Germany
Saurabh Joshi	IIT Hyderabad, India
Dejan Jovanovic	SRI International, USA
Ayrat Khalimov	The Hebrew University, Israel
Igor Konnov (Chair)	Inria Nancy (LORIA), France
Jan Kretínský	Technical University of Munich, Germany
Alfons Laarman	Leiden University, The Netherlands
Ravichandhran Kandhadai Madhavan	Ecole Polytechnique Fédérale de Lausanne, Switzerland
Andrea Micheli	Fondazione Bruno Kessler, Italy
Sergio Mover	University of Colorado Boulder, USA
Aina Niemetz	Stanford University, USA
Burcu Kulahcioglu Ozkan	MPI-SWS, Germany
Markus N. Rabe	University of California, Berkeley, USA
Andrew Reynolds	University of Iowa, USA
Martin Suda	TU Wien, Austria
Mitra Tabaei	TU Wien, Austria

Additional Reviewers

Alpernas, Kalev	Cohen, Ernie	Friedberger, Karlheinz
Asadi, Sepideh	Costea, Andreea	Ghorbani, Soudeh
Athanasiou, Konstantinos	Dangl, Matthias	Ghosh, Shromona
Bauer, Matthew	Doko, Marko	Goel, Shilpi
Bavishi, Rohan	Drachsler Cohen, Dana	Gong, Liang
Bayless, Sam	Dreossi, Tommaso	Govind, Hari
Berzish, Murphy	Dutra, Rafael	Gu, Yijia
Blicha, Martin	Ebrahimi, Masoud	Habermehl, Peter
Bui, Phi Diep	Eisner, Cindy	Hamza, Jad
Cauderlier, Raphaël	Fedyukovich, Grigory	He, Paul
Cauli, Claudia	Fremont, Daniel	Heo, Kihong
Ceska, Milan	Freund, Stephen	Holik, Lukas

Contents – Part II

CPS, Hardware, Industrial Applications

Contents – Part I

Runtime Verification, Hybrid and Timed Systems

Tools

Probabilistic Systems

Tools

Let this Graph Be Your Witness!

An Attestor for Verifying Java Pointer Programs

Hannah Arndt, Christina Jansen, Joost-Pieter Katoen,
Christoph Matheja(✉), and Thomas Noll

Software Modeling and Verification Group,
RWTH Aachen University, Aachen, Germany
matheja@cs.rwth-aachen.de

Abstract. We present a graph-based tool for analysing Java programs operating on dynamic data structures. It involves the generation of an abstract state space employing a user-defined graph grammar. LTL model checking is then applied to this state space, supporting both structural and functional correctness properties. The analysis is fully automated, procedure-modular, and provides informative visual feedback including counterexamples in the case of property violations.

1 Introduction

Pointers constitute an essential concept in modern programming languages, and are used for implementing dynamic data structures like lists, trees etc. However, many software bugs can be traced back to the erroneous use of pointers by e.g. dereferencing null pointers or accidentally pointing to wrong parts of the heap. Due to the resulting unbounded state spaces, pointer errors are hard to detect. Automated tool support for validation of pointer programs that provides meaningful debugging information in case of violations is therefore highly desirable.

ATTESTOR is a verification tool that attempts to achieve both of these goals. To this aim, it first constructs an abstract state space of the input program by means of symbolic execution. Each state depicts both links between heap objects and values of program variables using a graph representation. Abstraction is performed on state level by means of graph grammars. They specify the data structures maintained by the program, and describe how to summarise substructures of the heap in order to obtain a finite representation. After labelling each state with propositions that provide information about structural properties such as reachability or heap shapes, the actual verification task is performed in a second step. To this aim, the abstract state space is checked against a user-defined LTL specification. In case of violations, a counterexample is provided.

H. Arndt and C. Matheja—Supported by Deutsche Forschungsgemeinschaft (DFG) Grant No. 401/2-1.

H. Chockler and G. Weissenbacher (Eds.): CAV 2018, LNCS 10982, pp. 3–11, 2018.
https://doi.org/10.1007/978-3-319-96142-2_1

In summary, ATTESTOR's main features can be characterized as follows:

- It employs context-free graph grammars as a formal underpinning for defining heap abstractions. These grammars enable local heap concretisation and thus naturally provide implicit abstract semantics.
- The full instruction set of Java Bytecode is handled. Program actions that are outside the scope of our analysis, such as arithmetic operations or Boolean tests on payload data, are handled by (safe) over-approximation.
- Specifications are given by linear-time temporal logic (LTL) formulae which support a rich set of program properties, ranging from memory safety over shape, reachability or balancedness to properties such as full traversal or preservation of the exact heap structure.
- Except for expecting a graph grammar that specifies the data structures handled by a program, the analysis is fully automated. In particular, no program annotations are required.
- Modular reasoning is supported in the form of contracts that summarise the effect of executing a (recursive) procedure. These contracts can be automatically derived or manually specified.
- Valuable feedback is provided through a comprehensive report including (minimal) non-spurious counterexamples in case of property violations.
- The tool's functionality is made accessible through the command line as well as a graphical user and an application programming interface.

Availability. ATTESTOR's source code, benchmarks, and documentation are available online at https://moves-rwth.github.io/attestor.

2   The Attestor Tool

ATTESTOR is implemented in Java and consists of about 20.000 LOC (excluding comments and tests). An architectural overview is depicted in Fig. 1. It shows the tool inputs (left), its outputs (right), the ATTESTOR backend with its processing phases (middle), the ATTESTOR frontend (below) as well as the API connecting back- and frontend. These elements are discussed in detail below.

2.1   Input

As shown in Fig. 1 (left), a verification task is given by four inputs. First, the program to be analysed. Here, Java as well as Java Bytecode programs with possibly recursive procedures are supported, where the former is translated to the latter prior to the analysis. Second, the specification has to be given by a set of LTL formulae enriched with heap-specific propositions. See Sect. 3 for a representative list of exemplary specifications.

As a third input, ATTESTOR expects the declaration of the graph grammar that guides the abstraction. In order to obtain a finite abstract state space, this grammar is supposed to cover the data structures emerging during program

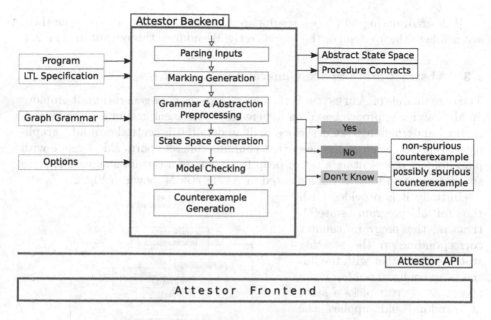

Fig. 1. The ATTESTOR tool

execution. The user may choose from a set of grammar definitions for standard data structures such as singly- and doubly-linked lists and binary trees, the manual specification in a JSON-style graph format and combinations thereof.

Fourth, additional options can be given that e.g. define the initial heap configuration(s) (in JSON-style graph format), that control the granularity of abstraction and the garbage collection behaviour, or that allow to re-use results of previous analyses in the form of procedure contracts [11,13].

2.2 Phases

ATTESTOR proceeds in six main phases, see Fig. 1 (middle). In the first and third phase, all inputs are parsed and preprocessed. The input program is read and transformed to Bytecode (if necessary), the input graphs (initial configuration, procedure contracts, and graph grammar), LTL formulae and further options are read.

Depending on the provided LTL formulae, additional markings are inserted into the initial heap (see [8] for details) in the second phase. They are used to track identities of objects during program execution, which is later required to validate visit and neighbourhood properties during the fifth phase.

In the next phase the actual program analysis is conducted. To this aim, ATTESTOR first constructs the abstract state space as described in Sect. 2.3 in detail. In the fifth phase we check whether the provided LTL specification holds on the state space resulting from the preceding step. We use an off-the-shelf tableau-based LTL model checking algorithm [2].

If desired, during all phases results are forwarded to the API to make them accessible to the frontend or the user directly. We address this output in Sect. 2.4.

2.3   Abstract State Space Generation

The core module of ATTESTOR is the abstract state space generation. It employs an abstraction approach based on hyperedge replacement grammars, whose theoretical underpinnings are described in [9] in detail. It is centred around a graph-based representation of the heap that contains concrete parts side by side with placeholders representing a set of heap fragments of a certain shape. The state space generation loop as implemented in ATTESTOR is shown in Fig. 2.

Initially it is provided with the initial program state(s), that is, the program counter corresponding to the starting statement together with the initial heap configuration(s). From these, ATTESTOR picks a state at random and applies the abstract semantics of the next statement: First, the heap configuration is locally concretised ensuring that all heap parts required for the statement to execute are accessible. This is enabled by applying rules of the input graph grammar in forward direction, which can entail branching in the state space. The resulting configurations are then manipulated according to

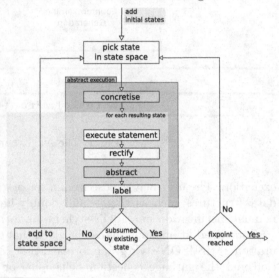

Fig. 2. State space generation.

the concrete semantics of the statement. At this stage, ATTESTOR automatically detects possible null pointer dereferencing operations as a byproduct of the state space generation. In a subsequent rectification step, the heap configuration is cleared from e.g. dead variables and garbage (if desired). Consequently, memory leaks are detected immediately. The rectified configuration is then abstracted with respect to the data structures specified by means of the input graph grammar. Complementary to concretisation, this is realised by applying grammar rules in backward direction, which involves a check for embeddings of right-hand sides. A particular strength of our approach is its robustness against local violations of data structures, as it simply leaves the corresponding heap parts concrete. Finalising the abstract execution step, the resulting state is labelled with the atomic propositions it satisfies. This check is efficiently implemented by means of heap automata (see [12,15] for details). By performing a subsumption check on the state level, ATTESTOR detects whether the newly generated state is already covered by a more abstract one that has been visited before. If not, it

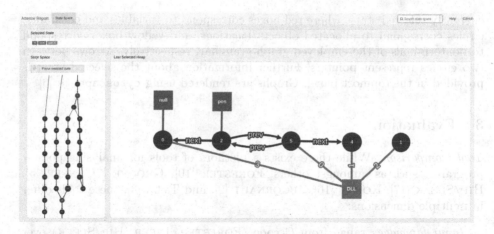

Fig. 3. Screenshot of ATTESTOR's frontend for state space exploration. (Color figure online)

adds the resulting state to the state space and starts over by picking a new state. Otherwise, it checks whether further states have to be processed or whether a fixpoint in the state space generation is reached. In the latter case, this phase is terminated.

2.4 Output

As shown in Fig. 1 (right), we obtain three main outputs once the analysis is completed: the computed abstract state space, the derived procedure contracts, and the model checking results. For each LTL formula in the specification, results comprise the possible answers "formula satisfied", "formula (definitely) not satisfied", or "formula possibly not satisfied". In case of the latter two, ATTESTOR additionally produces a counterexample, i.e. an abstract trace that violates the formula. If ATTESTOR was able to verify the non-spuriousness of this counterexample (second case), we are additionally given a concrete initial heap that is accountable for the violation and that can be used as a test case for debugging.

Besides the main outputs, ATTESTOR provides general information about the current analysis. These include log messages such as warnings and errors, but also details about settings and runtimes of the analyses. The API provides the interface to retrieve ATTESTOR's outputs as JSON-formatted data.

2.5 Frontend

ATTESTOR features a graphical frontend that visualises inputs as well as results of all benchmark runs. The frontend communicates with ATTESTOR's backend via the API only. It especially can be used to display and navigate through the generated abstract state space and counterexample traces.

A screenshot of the frontend for state space exploration is found in Fig. 3. The left panel is an excerpt of the state space. The right panel depicts the currently selected state, where red boxes correspond to variables and constants, circles correspond to allocated objects/locations, and yellow boxes correspond to nonterminals of the employed graph grammar, respectively. Arrows between two circles represent pointers. Further information about the selected state is provided in the topmost panel. Graphs are rendered using `cytoscape.js` [6].

3   Evaluation

Tool Comparison. While there exists a plethora of tools for analysing pointer programs, such as, amongst others, FORESTER [10], GROOVE [7], INFER [5], HIP/SLEEK [17], KORAT [16], JUGGRNAUT [9], and TVLA [3], these tools differ in multiple dimensions:

- *Input languages* range from C code (FORESTER, INFER, HIP/SLEEK) over Java/Java Bytecode (JUGGRNAUT, KORAT) to assembly code (TVLA) and graph programs (GROOVE).
- The *degree of automation* differs heavily: Tools like FORESTER and INFER only require source code. Others such as HIP/SLEEK and JUGGRNAUT additionally expect general data structure specifications in the form of e.g. graph grammars or predicate definitions to guide the abstraction. Moreover, TVLA requires additional program-dependent instrumentation predicates.
- *Verifiable properties* typically cover memory safety. KORAT is an exception, because it applies test case generation instead of verification. The tools HIP/SLEEK, TVLA, GROOVE, and JUGGRNAUT are additionally capable of verifying data structure invariants, so-called shape properties. Furthermore, HIP/SLEEK is able to reason about shape-numeric properties, e.g. lengths of lists, if a suitable specification is provided. While these properties are not supported by TVLA, it is possible to verify reachability properties. Moreover, JUGGRNAUT can reason about temporal properties such as verifying that finally every element of an input data structure has been accessed.

Benchmarks. Due to the above mentioned diversity there is no publicly available and representative set of standardised benchmarks to compare the aforementioned tools [1]. We thus evaluated ATTESTOR on a collection of challenging, pointer intensive algorithms compiled from the literature [3,4,10,14]. To assess our counterexample generation, we considered invalid specifications, e.g. that a reversed list is the same list as the input list. Furthermore, we injected faults into our examples by swapping and deleting statements.

Properties. During state space generation, *memory safety (M)* is checked. Moreover, we consider five classes of properties that are verified using the built-in LTL model checker:

Table 1. The experimental results. All runtimes are in seconds. Verification time includes state space generation. SLL (DLL) means singly-linked (doubly-linked) list.

Benchmark	Properties	No. states		State space gen.		Verification		Total runtime	
		Min	Max	Min	Max	Min	Max	Min	Max
SLL.traverse	M, S, R, V, N, X	13	97	0.030	0.074	0.039	0.097	0.757	0.848
SLL.reverse	M, S, R, V, X	46	268	0.050	0.109	0.050	0.127	0.793	0.950
SLL.reverse (recursive)	M, S, V, N, X	40	823	0.038	0.100	0.044	0.117	0.720	0.933
DLL.reverse	M, S, R, V, N, X	70	1508	0.076	0.646	0.097	0.712	0.831	1.763
DLL.findLast	M, C, X	44	44	0.069	0.069	0.079	0.079	0.938	0.938
SLL.findMiddle	M, S, R, V, N, X	75	456	0.060	0.184	0.060	0.210	0.767	0.975
Tree.traverse (Lindstrom)	M, S, V, N	229	67941	0.119	8.901	0.119	16.52	0.845	17.36
Tree.traverse (recursive)	M, S	91	21738	0.075	1.714	0.074	1.765	0.849	2.894
AVLTree.binarySearch	M, S	192	192	0.117	0.172	0.118	0.192	0.917	1.039
AVLTree.searchAndBack	M, S, C	455	455	0.193	0.229	0.205	0.289	1.081	1.335
AVLTree.searchAndSwap	M, S, C	3855	4104	0.955	1.590	1.004	1.677	1.928	2.521
AVLTree.leftMostInsert	M, S	6120	6120	1.879	1.942	1.932	1.943	2.813	2.817
AVLTree.insert	M, S	10388	10388	3.378	3.676	3.378	3.802	4.284	4.720
AVLTree.sllToAVLTree	M, S, C	7166	7166	2.412	2.728	2.440	2.759	3.383	3.762

- The *shape property (S)* establishes that the heap is of a specific shape, e.g. a doubly-linked list or a balanced tree.
- The *reachability property (R)* checks whether some variable is reachable from another one via specific pointer fields.
- The *visit property (V)* verifies whether every element of the input is accessed by a specific variable.
- The *neighbourhood property (N)* checks whether the input data structure coincides with the output data structure upon termination.
- Finally, we consider other functional *correctness properties (C)*, e.g. the return value is not null.

Setup. For performance evaluation, we conducted experiments on an Intel Core i7-7500U CPU @ 2.70 GHz with the Java virtual machine (OpenJDK version 1.8.0_151) limited to its default setting of 2 GB of RAM. All experiments were run using the Java benchmarking harness JMH. Our experimental results are shown in Table 1. Additionally, for comparison purpose we considered Java implementations of benchmarks that have been previously analysed for memory safety by FORESTER [10], see Table 2.

Discussion. The results show that both memory safety (M) and shape (S) are efficiently processed, with regard to both state space size and runtime. This is not surprising as these properties are directly handled by the state space generation engine. The most challenging tasks are the visit (V) and neighbourhood (N) properties as they require to track objects across program executions by means of markings. The latter have a similar impact as pointer variables: increasing their number impedes abstraction as larger parts of the heap have to be kept concrete. This effect can be observed for the Lindstrom tree traversal procedure where adding one marking (V) and three markings (N) both increase the verification effort by an order of magnitude.

Table 2. FORESTER benchmarks (memory safety only). Verification times are in seconds.

Benchmark	No. states	Verification
SLL.bubblesort	287	0.134
SLL.deleteElement	152	0.096
SLLHeadPtr (traverse)	111	0.095
SLL.insertsort	369	0.147
ListOfCyclicLists	313	0.153
DLL.insert	379	0.207
DLL.insertsort1	4302	1.467
DLL.insertsort2	1332	0.514
DLL.buildAndReverse	277	0.164
CyclicDLL (traverse)	104	0.108
Tree.construct	44	0.062
Tree.constructAndDSW	1334	0.365
SkipList.insert	302	0.160
SkipList.build	330	0.173

References

1. Abdulla, P.A., Gadducci, F., König, B., Vafeiadis, V.: Verification of evolving graph structures (Dagstuhl Seminar 15451). Dagstuhl Rep. **5**(11), 1–28 (2016)
2. Bhat, G., Cleaveland, R., Grumberg, O.: Efficient on-the-fly model checking for CTL. In: LICS 1995, pp. 388–397. IEEE (1995)
3. Bogudlov, I., Lev-Ami, T., Reps, T., Sagiv, M.: Revamping TVLA: making parametric shape analysis competitive. In: Damm, W., Hermanns, H. (eds.) CAV 2007. LNCS, vol. 4590, pp. 221–225. Springer, Heidelberg (2007). https://doi.org/10.1007/978-3-540-73368-3_25
4. Bouajjani, A., Habermehl, P., Rogalewicz, A., Vojnar, T.: Abstract regular tree model checking of complex dynamic data structures. In: Yi, K. (ed.) SAS 2006. LNCS, vol. 4134, pp. 52–70. Springer, Heidelberg (2006). https://doi.org/10.1007/11823230_5
5. Calcagno, C., Distefano, D.: Infer: an automatic program verifier for memory safety of C programs. In: Bobaru, M., Havelund, K., Holzmann, G.J., Joshi, R. (eds.) NFM 2011. LNCS, vol. 6617, pp. 459–465. Springer, Heidelberg (2011). https://doi.org/10.1007/978-3-642-20398-5_33
6. Cytoscape Consortium: Cytoscape: graph theory/network library for analysis and visualisation. http://js.cytoscape.org/
7. Ghamarian, A.H., de Mol, M.J., Rensink, A., Zambon, E., Zimakova, M.V.: Modelling and analysis using GROOVE. Int. J. Soft. Tools Technol. Transfer **14**, 15–40 (2012)
8. Heinen, J.: Verifying Java programs - a graph grammar approach. Ph.D. thesis, RWTH Aachen University, Germany (2015)
9. Heinen, J., Jansen, C., Katoen, J.P., Noll, T.: Verifying pointer programs using graph grammars. Sci. Comput. Program. **97**, 157–162 (2015)

10. Holík, L., Lengál, O., Rogalewicz, A., Simácek, J., Vojnar, T.: Fully automated shape analysis based on forest automata. CoRR abs/1304.5806 (2013)
11. Jansen, C.: Static analysis of pointer programs - linking graph grammars and separation logic. Ph.D. thesis, RWTH Aachen University, Germany (2017)
12. Jansen, C., Katelaan, J., Matheja, C., Noll, T., Zuleger, F.: Unified reasoning about robustness properties of symbolic-heap separation logic. In: Yang, H. (ed.) ESOP 2017. LNCS, vol. 10201, pp. 611–638. Springer, Heidelberg (2017). https://doi.org/10.1007/978-3-662-54434-1_23
13. Jansen, C., Noll, T.: Generating abstract graph-based procedure summaries for pointer programs. In: Giese, H., König, B. (eds.) ICGT 2014. LNCS, vol. 8571, pp. 49–64. Springer, Cham (2014). https://doi.org/10.1007/978-3-319-09108-2_4
14. Loginov, A., Reps, T., Sagiv, M.: Automated verification of the Deutsch-Schorr-Waite tree-traversal algorithm. In: Yi, K. (ed.) SAS 2006. LNCS, vol. 4134, pp. 261–279. Springer, Heidelberg (2006). https://doi.org/10.1007/11823230_17
15. Matheja, C., Jansen, C., Noll, T.: Tree-like grammars and separation logic. In: Feng, X., Park, S. (eds.) APLAS 2015. LNCS, vol. 9458, pp. 90–108. Springer, Cham (2015). https://doi.org/10.1007/978-3-319-26529-2_6
16. Milicevic, A., Misailovic, S., Marinov, D., Khurshid, S.: Korat: a tool for generating structurally complex test inputs. In: Proceedings of the 29th International Conference on Software Engineering, ICSE 2007, pp. 771–774. IEEE Computer Society, Washington, DC, USA (2007). https://doi.org/10.1109/ICSE.2007.48
17. Nguyen, H.H., David, C., Qin, S., Chin, W.-N.: Automated verification of shape and size properties via separation logic. In: Cook, B., Podelski, A. (eds.) VMCAI 2007. LNCS, vol. 4349, pp. 251–266. Springer, Heidelberg (2007). https://doi.org/10.1007/978-3-540-69738-1_18

MaxSMT-Based Type Inference
for Python 3

Mostafa Hassan[1,2], Caterina Urban[2](✉), Marco Eilers[2]iD,
and Peter Müller[2]iD

[1] German University in Cairo, Cairo, Egypt
[2] Department of Computer Science, ETH Zurich,
Zurich, Switzerland
caterina.urban@inf.ethz.ch

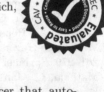

Abstract. We present TYPPETE, a sound type inferencer that auto-matically infers Python 3 type annotations. TYPPETE encodes type con-straints as a MAXSMT problem and uses optional constraints and spe-cific quantifier instantiation patterns to make the constraint solving pro-cess efficient. Our experimental evaluation shows that TYPPETE scales to real world Python programs and outperforms state-of-the-art tools.

1   Introduction

Dynamically-typed languages like Python have become increasingly popular in the past five years. Dynamic typing enables rapid development and adaptation to changing requirements. On the other hand, static typing offers early error detection, efficient execution, and machine-checked code documentation, and enables more advanced static analysis and verification approaches [15].

For these reasons, Python's PEP484 [25] has recently introduced optional type annotations in the spirit of gradual typing [23]. The annotations can be checked using MYPY [10]. In this paper, we present our tool TYPPETE, which automatically infers sound (non-gradual) type annotations and can therefore serve as a preprocessor for other analysis or verification tools.

TYPPETE performs whole-program type inference, as there are no princi-pal typings in object-oriented languages like Python [1, example in Sect. 1]; the inferred types are correct in the given context but may not be as general as possible. The type inference is constraint-based and relies on the off-the-shelf SMT solver Z3 [7] for finding a valid type assignment for the input program. We show that two main ingredients allow TYPPETE to scale to real programs: (1) a careful encoding of subtyping that leverages efficient quantifier instantiation techniques [6], and (2) the use of optional type equality constraints, which con-siderably reduce the solution search space. Whenever a valid type assignment for the input program cannot be found, TYPPETE encodes type error localization as an optimization problem [19] and reports only a minimal set of unfulfilled constraints to help the user pinpoint the cause of the error.

© The Author(s) 2018
H. Chockler and G. Weissenbacher (Eds.): CAV 2018, LNCS 10982, pp. 12–19, 2018.
https://doi.org/10.1007/978-3-319-96142-2_2

```
1  class Item(metaclass=ABCMeta):        12  class Even(Item):
2      @abstractmethod                    13      def compete(self, item):
3      def compete(self, item):           14          return item.evalEven(self)
4          pass                           15
5                                         16  class Odd(Item):
6      def evalEven(self, item):          17      def compete(self, item):
7          return "WIN"                   18          return item.evalOdd(self)
8                                         19
9      def evalOdd(self, item):           20  def match(item1, item2):
10         return "LOSE"                  21      return item1.compete(item2)
11
```

Fig. 1. A Python implementation of the *odds and evens* hand game.

TYPPETE accepts programs written in (a large subset of) Python 3. Having a static type system imposes a number of requirements on Python programs: (a) a variable can only have a single type through the whole program; (b) generic types have to be homogeneous (e.g., all elements of a set must have the same type); and (c) dynamic code generation, reflection and dynamic attribute additions and deletions are not allowed. The supported type system includes generic classes and functions. Users must supply a file and the *number* of type variables for any generic class or function. Typpete then outputs a program with type annotations, a type error, or an error indicating use of unsupported language features.

Our experimental evaluation demonstrates the practical applicability of our approach. We show that TYPPETE performs well on a variety of real-world open source Python programs and outperforms state-of-the-art tools.

2   Constraint Generation

TYPPETE encodes the type inference problem for a Python program into an SMT constraint resolution problem such that any solution of the SMT problem yields a valid type assignment for the program. The process of generating the SMT problem consists of three phases, which we describe below.

In a first pass over the input program, TYPPETE collects: (1) all globally defined names (to resolve forward references), (2) all classes and their respective subclass relations (to define subtyping), and (3) upper bounds on the size of certain types (e.g., tuples and function parameters). This pre-analysis encompasses both the input program—including all transitively imported modules—and *stub files*, which define the types of built-in classes and functions as well as libraries. TYPPETE already contains stubs for the most common built-ins; users can add custom stub files written in the format that is supported by MYPY.

In the second phase, TYPPETE declares an algebraic datatype Type, whose members correspond one-to-one to Python types. TYPPETE declares one datatype constructor for every class in the input program; non-generic classes are represented as constants, whereas a generic class with n type parameters is represented by a constructor taking n arguments of type Type. As an example, the class Odd in Fig. 1 is represented by the constant $\mathsf{class_{Odd}}$. TYPPETE also declares constructors for tuples and functions up to the maximum size determined in the pre-analysis, and for all type variables used in generic functions and classes.

The subtype relation $<:$ is represented by an uninterpreted function subtype which maps pairs of types to a boolean value. This function is delicate to define because of the possibility of *matching loops* (i.e., axioms being endlessly instanti-ated [7]) in the SMT solver. For each datatype constructor, TYPPETE generates axioms that explicitly enumerate the possible subtypes and supertypes. As an example, for the type $class_{Odd}$, TYPPETE generates the following axioms:

$$\forall t.\, subtype(class_{Odd}, t) = (t = class_{Odd}\ \lor\ t = class_{Item}\ \lor\ t = class_{object})$$
$$\forall t.\, subtype(t, class_{Odd}) = (t = class_{none}\ \lor\ t = class_{Odd})$$

Note that the second axiom allows None to be a subtype of any other type (as in Java). As we discuss in the next section, this definition of subtype allows us to avoid matching loops by specifying specific instantiation patterns for the SMT solver. A *substitution* function substitute, which substitutes type arguments for type variables when interacting with generic types, is defined in a similar way.

In the third step, TYPPETE traverses the program while creating an SMT variable for each node in its abstract syntax tree, and generating type constraints over these variables for the constructs in the program. During the traversal, a *context* maps all defined names (i.e., program variables, fields, etc.) to the corre-sponding SMT variables. The context is later used to retrieve the type assigned by the SMT solver to each name in the program. Constraints are generated for expressions (e.g., call arguments are subtypes of the corresponding parameter types), statements (e.g., the right-hand side of an assignment is a subtype of the left hand-side), and larger constructs such as methods (e.g., covariance and contravariance constraints for method overrides). For example, the (simplified) constraint generated for the call to `item1.compete(item2)` at line 21 in Fig. 1 contains a disjunction of cases depending on the type of the receiver:

$$(v_{item1} = class_{Odd} \land compete_{Odd} = f\_2(class_{Odd}, arg, ret) \land subtype(v_{item2}, arg))$$
$$\lor\ (v_{item1} = class_{Even} \land compete_{Even} = f\_2(class_{Even}, arg, ret) \land subtype(v_{item2}, arg))$$

where f_2 is a datatype constructor for a function with two parameter types (and one return type ret), and v_{item1} and v_{item2} are the SMT variables corresponding to `item1` and `item2`, respectively.

The generated constraints guarantee that any solution yields a correct type assignment for the input program. However, there are often many different valid solutions, as the constraints only impose lower or upper bounds on the types rep-resented by the SMT variables (e.g., $subtype(v_{item2}, arg)$ shown above imposes only an upper bound on the type of v_{item2}). This has an impact on performance (cf. Sect. 4) as the search space for a solution remains large. Moreover, some type assignments could be more desirable than others for a user (e.g., a user would most likely prefer to assign type int rather than object to a variable initial-ized with value zero). To avoid these problems, TYPPETE additionally generates optional type *equality* constraints in places where the mandatory constraints only demand subtyping (i.e., local variable assignments, return statements, passed function arguments), thereby turning the SMT problem into a MAXSMT opti-mization problem. For instance, in addition to $subtype(v_{item2}, arg)$ shown above,

TYPPETE generates the optional equality constraint $v_{item2} = arg$. The optional constraints guide the solver to try the specified exact type first, which is often a correct choice and therefore improves performance, and additionally leads to solutions with more precise variable and parameter types.

3   Constraint Solving

TYPPETE relies on Z3 [7] and the MaxRes [18] algorithm for solving the generated type constraints. We use *e-matching* [6] for instantiating the quantifiers used in the axiomatization of the subtype function (cf. Sect. 2), and carefully choose instantiation patterns that ensure that any choice made during the search immediately triggers the instantiation of the relevant quantifiers. For instance, for the axioms shown in Sect. 2, we use the instantiation patterns subtype(class$_{Odd}$, t) and subtype(t, class$_{Odd}$), respectively. Our instantiation patterns ensure that as soon as one argument of an application of the subtype function is known, the quantifier that enumerates the possible values of the other argument is instantiated, thus ensuring that the consequences of any type choices propagate immediately. With a naïve encoding, the solver would have to *guess* both arguments before being able to *check* whether the subtype relation holds. The resulting constraint solving process is much faster than it would be when using different quantifier instantiation techniques such as *model-based quantifier instantiation* [12], but still avoids the potential unsoundness that can occur when using e-matching with insufficient trigger expressions.

When the MAXSMT problem is satisfiable, TYPPETE queries Z3 for a model satisfying all type constraints, retrieves the types assigned to each name in the program, and generates type annotated source code for the input program. For instance, for the program shown in Fig. 1, TYPPETE automatically annotates the function evalEven with type Even for the parameter item and a str return type. Note that Item and object would also be correct type annotations for item; the choice of Even is guided by the optional type equality constraints.

When the MAXSMT problem is unsatisfiable, instead of reporting the unfulfilled constraints in the *unsatistiable core* returned by Z3 (which is not guaranteed to be minimal), TYPPETE creates a new *relaxed* MAXSMT problem where only the constraints defining the subtype function are enforced, while all other type constraints are optional. Z3 is then queried for a model satisfying as many type constraints as possible. The resulting type annotated source code for the input program is returned along with the remaining minimal set of unfulfilled type constraints. For instance, if we remove the abstract method compete of class Item in Fig. 1, TYPPETE annotates the parameters of the function match at line 20 with type object and indicates the call compete at line 21 as problematic. By observing the mismatch between the type annotations and the method call, the user has sufficient context to quickly identify and correct the type error.

	T(SMT)	T(MaxSMT)	Unfulfilled	T(Relaxed)	Pytype
adventure	2.99s / 6.30s	3.27s / 6.76s	42 / 2	1.95s / 8.83s	0 [0]
icemu	9.45s / 6.79s	9.51s / 3.63s	4 / 2	0.08s / 21.76s	18 [2]
imp	16.88s / 59.95s	16.91s / 15.87s	67 / 2	0.82s / 82.56s	3 [2]
scion	4.65s / 3.35s	4.72s / 2.97s	28 / 2	0.16s / 3.39s	0 [0]
test suite	14.66s / 1.63s	14.66s / 2.17s	-	-	55 [34]

Fig. 2. Evaluation of Typpete on small programs and larger open source projects.

4   Experimental Evaluation

In order to demonstrate the practical applicability of our approach, we evaluated our tool Typpete on a number of real-world open-source Python programs that use inheritance, operator overloading, and other features that are challenging for type inference (but not features that make static typing impossible):

adventure [21]: An implementation of the *Colossal Cave Adventure* game (2 modules, 399 LOC). The evaluation (and reported LOC) excludes the modules game.py and prompt.py, which employ dynamic attribute additions.

icemu [8]: A library that emulates integrated circuits at the logic level (8 modules, 530 LOC). We conducted the evaluation on revision 484828f.

imp [4]: A minimal interpreter for the imp toy language (7 modules, 771 LOC). The evaluation excludes the modules used for testing the project.

scion [9]: A Python implementation of a new Internet architecture (2 modules, 725 LOC). For the evaluation, we used path_store.py and scion_addr.py from revision 6f60ccc, and provided stub files for all dependencies.

We additionally ran Typpete on our test suite of manually-written programs and small programs collected from the web (47 modules and 1998 LOC).

In order to make the projects statically typeable, we had to make a number of small changes that do not impact the functionality of the code, such as adding abstract superclasses and abstract methods, and (for the **imp** and **scion** projects) introducing explicit downcasts in few places. Additionally, we made a number of other innocuous changes to overcome the current limitations of our tool, such as replacing keyword arguments with positional arguments, replacing generator expressions with list comprehensions, and replacing super calls via inlining. The complete list of changes for each project is included in our artifact.

The experiments were conducted on an 2.9 GHz Intel Core i5 processor with 8 GB of RAM running Mac OS High Sierra version 10.13.3 with Z3 version 4.5.1. Figure 2 summarizes the result of the evaluation. The first two columns show the *average running time* (over ten runs, split into constraint generation and constraint solving) for the type inference in which the use of optional type equality constraints (cf. Sect. 2) is disabled (SMT) and enabled (MaxSMT), respectively. We can observe that optional type equality constraints (considerably) reduce the search space for a solution as disabling them significantly increases the running time for larger projects. We can also note that the constraint solving time improves significantly when the type inference is run on the test suite, which consists of many independent modules. This suggests that splitting the type inference problem into independent sub-problems could further improve performance. We plan to investigate this direction as part of our future work.

The third column of Fig. 2 shows the evaluation of the *error reporting* feature of TYPPETE (cf. Sect. 3). For each benchmark, we manually introduced two type errors that could organically happen during programming and compared the size of the unsatisfiable core (left of /) and the number of remaining unfulfilled constraints (right of /) for the original and relaxed MAXSMT problems given to Z3, respectively. We also list the times needed to prove the first problem unsatisfiable and solve the relaxed problem. As one would expect, the number of constraints that remain unfulfilled for the relaxed problems is considerably smaller, which demonstrates that the error reporting feature of TYPPETE greatly reduces the time that a user needs to identify the source of a type error.

Finally, the last column of Fig. 2 shows the result of the *comparison* of TYP-PETE with the state-of-the-art type inferencer PYTYPE [16]. PYTYPE infers PEP484 [25] gradual type annotations by abstract interpretation [5] of the bytecode-compiled version of the given Python file. In Fig. 2, for the considered benchmarks, we report the number of variables and parameters that PYTYPE leaves untyped or annotated with Any. We excluded any module on which PYTYPE yields an error; in square brackets we indicate the number of modules that we could consider. TYPPETE is able to fully type all elements and thus outperforms PYTYPE *for static typing purposes*. On the other hand, we note that PYTYPE additionally supports gradual typing and a larger Python subset.

5   Related and Future Work

In addition to PYTYPE, a number of other type inference approaches and tools have been developed for Python. The approach of Maia et al. [17] has some fundamental limitations such as not allowing forward references or overloaded functions and operators. Fritz and Hage [11] as well as STARKILLER [22] infer sets of *concrete types* that can inhabit each program variable to improve execution performance. The former sacrifices soundness to handle more dynamic features of Python. Additionally, deriving valid type assignments from sets of concrete types is non-trivial. MYPY and a project by Cannon [3] can perform (incomplete) type inference for local variables, but require type annotations for function parameters and return types. PYANNOTATE [13] *dynamically* tracks variable types during execution and optionally annotates Python programs; the resulting annotations are not guaranteed to be sound. A similar spectrum of solutions exists for other dynamic programming languages like JavaScript [2,14] and ActionScript [20].

The idea of using SMT solvers for type inference is not new. Both F* [24] and LiquidHaskell [26] (partly) use SMT-solving in the inference for their dependent type systems. Pavlinovic et al. [19] present an SMT encoding of the OCaml type system. TYPPETE's approach to type error reporting can be seen as a simple instantiation of their approach.

As part of our future work, we want to explore whether our system can be adapted to infer gradual types. We also aim to develop heuristics for inferring which functions and classes should be annotated with generic types based on the reported unfulfilled constraints. Finally, we plan to explore the idea of splitting the type inference into multiple separate problems to improve performance.

Acknowledgments. We thank the anonymous reviewers for their feedback. This work was supported by an ETH Zurich Career Seed Grant (SEED-32 16-2).

References

1. Ancona, D., Zucca, E.: Principal typings for Java-like languages. In: POPL, pp. 306–317 (2004)
2. Anderson, C., Giannini, P., Drossopoulou, S.: Towards type inference for JavaScript. In: Black, A.P. (ed.) ECOOP. LNCS, vol. 3586, pp. 428–452. Springer, Heidelberg (2005). https://doi.org/10.1007/11531142_19
3. Cannon, B.: Localized type inference of atomic types in Python. Master's thesis, California Polytechnic State University (2005)
4. Conrod, J.: IMP Interpreter. https://github.com/jayconrod/imp-interpreter
5. Cousot, P., Cousot, R.: Abstract interpretation: a unified lattice model for static analysis of programs by construction or approximation of fixpoints. In: POPL, pp. 238–252 (1977)
6. de Moura, L., Bjørner, N.: Efficient E-matching for SMT solvers. In: Pfenning, F. (ed.) CADE. LNCS (LNAI), vol. 4603, pp. 183–198. Springer, Heidelberg (2007). https://doi.org/10.1007/978-3-540-73595-3_13
7. de Moura, L., Bjørner, N.: Z3: an efficient SMT Solver. In: Ramakrishnan, C.R., Rehof, J. (eds.) TACAS 2008. LNCS, vol. 4963, pp. 337–340. Springer, Heidelberg (2008). https://doi.org/10.1007/978-3-540-78800-3_24
8. Dupras, V.: Icemu. https://github.com/hsoft/icemu
9. ETH Zurich: SCION. https://github.com/scionproto/scion
10. Fisher, D., Lehtosalo, J., Price, G., van Rossum, G.: MyPy. http://mypy-lang.org/
11. Fritz, L., Hage, J.: Cost versus precision for approximate typing for Python. In: PEPM, pp. 89–98 (2017)
12. Ge, Y., de Moura, L.: Complete instantiation for quantified formulas in satisfiabiliby modulo theories. In: Bouajjani, A., Maler, O. (eds.) CAV 2009. LNCS, vol. 5643, pp. 306–320. Springer, Heidelberg (2009). https://doi.org/10.1007/978-3-642-02658-4_25
13. Grue, T., Vorobev, S., Lehtosalo, J., van Rossum, G.: PyAnnotate. https://github.com/google/pytype
14. Hackett, B., Guo, S.: Fast and precise hybrid type inference for JavaScript. In: PLDI, pp. 239–250 (2012)
15. Jensen, S.H., Møller, A., Thiemann, P.: Type analysis for JavaScript. In: SAS, pp. 238–255 (2009)
16. Kramm, M., Chen, R., Sudol, T., Demello, M., Caceres, A., Baum, D., Peters, A., Ludemann, P., Swartz, P., Batchelder, N., Kaptur, A., Lindzey, L.: Pytype. https://github.com/google/pytype

17. Maia, E., Moreira, N., Reis, R.: A static type inference for Python. In: DYLA (2012)
18. Narodytska, N. Bacchus, F.: Maximum satisfiability using core-guided maxsat resolution. In: AAAI, pp. 2717–2723 (2014)
19. Pavlinovic, Z., King, T., Wies, T.: Finding minimum type error sources. In: OOPSLA, pp. 525–542 (2014)
20. Rastogi, A., Chaudhuri, A., Hosmer, B.: The ins and outs of gradual type inference. In: POPL, pp. 481–494 (2012)
21. Rhodes, B.: Adventure. https://github.com/brandon-rhodes/python-adventure
22. Salib, M.: Starkiller : a static type inferencer and compiler for Python. Master's thesis, Massachusetts Institute of Technology (2004)
23. Siek, J., Taha, W.: Gradual typing for objects. In: Ernst, E. (ed.) ECOOP 2007. LNCS, vol. 4609, pp. 2–27. Springer, Heidelberg (2007). https://doi.org/10.1007/978-3-540-73589-2_2
24. Swamy, N., Hritcu, C., Keller, C., Rastogi, A., Delignat-Lavaud, A., Forest, S., Bhargavan, K., Fournet, C., Strub, P., Kohlweiss, M., Zinzindohoue, J.K., Béguelin, S.Z.: Dependent types and multi-monadic effects in F. In: POPL, pp. 256–270 (2016)
25. van Rossum, G., Lehtosalo, J., Langa, L.: Type hints (2014). https://www.python.org/dev/peps/pep-0484/
26. Vazou, N., Seidel, E.L., Jhala, R.: Liquidhaskell: experience with refinement types in the real world. In: Proceedings of the 2014 ACM SIGPLAN symposium on Haskell, Gothenburg, Sweden, 4–5 September 2014, pp. 39–51 (2014)

The JKind Model Checker

Andrew Gacek[1]([✉]), John Backes[1], Mike Whalen[2], Lucas Wagner[1],
and Elaheh Ghassabani[2]

[1] Rockwell Collins, Cedar Rapids, USA
andrew.gacek@gmail.com,
john.backes@gmail.com,
lucas.wagner@rockwellcollins.com
[2] University of Minnesota, Minneapolis, USA
{mwwhalen,ghass013}@umn.edu

Abstract. JKIND is an open-source industrial model checker developed
by Rockwell Collins and the University of Minnesota. JKIND uses multiple parallel engines to prove or falsify safety properties of infinite state
models. It is portable, easy to install, performance competitive with other
state-of-the-art model checkers, and has features designed to improve the
results presented to users: *inductive validity cores* for proofs and *counterexample smoothing* for test-case generation. It serves as the back-end
for various industrial applications.

1 Introduction

JKIND is an open-source[1] industrial infinite-state inductive model checker for
safety properties. Models and properties in JKIND are specified in LUSTRE [17],
a synchronous data-flow language, using the theories of linear real and integer
arithmetic. JKIND uses SMT-solvers to prove and falsify multiple properties in
parallel. A distinguishing characteristic of JKIND is its focus on the usability of
results. For a proven property, JKIND provides traceability between the property and individual model elements. For a falsified property, JKIND provides
options for simplifying the counterexample in order to highlight the root cause
of the failure. In industrial applications, we have found these additional usability
aspects to be at least as important as the primary results. Another important
characteristic of JKIND is that is it designed to be integrated directly into user-
facing applications. Written in Java, JKIND runs on all major platforms and
is easily compiled into other Java applications. JKIND bundles the Java-based
SMTINTERPOL solver and has no external dependencies. However, it can optionally call Z3, YICES 1, YICES 2, CVC4, and MATHSAT if they are available.

2 Functionality and Main Features

JKIND is structured as several parallel engines that coordinate to prove properties, mimicking the design of PKIND and KIND 2 [8,21]. Some engines are

---

[1] https://github.com/agacek/jkind.

© The Author(s) 2018
H. Chockler and G. Weissenbacher (Eds.): CAV 2018, LNCS 10982, pp. 20–27, 2018.
https://doi.org/10.1007/978-3-319-96142-2_3

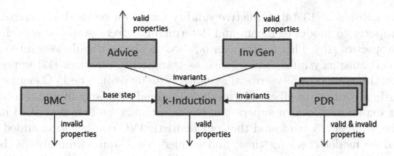

Fig. 1. JKIND engine architecture

directly responsible for proving properties, others aid that effort by generating invariants, and still others are reserved for post-processing of proof or counterexample results. Each engine can be enabled or disabled separately based on the user's needs. The architecture of JKIND allows any engine to broadcast information to the other engines (for example, lemmas, proofs, counterexamples) allowing straightforward integration of new functionality.

The solving engines in JKIND are show in Fig. 1. The **Bounded Model Checking (BMC)** engine performs a standard iterative unrolling of the transition relation to find counterexamples and to serve as the base case of k-induction. The BMC engine guarantees that any counterexample it finds is minimal in length. The k**-Induction** engine performs the inductive step of k-induction, possibly using invariants generated by other engines. The **Invariant Generation** engine uses a template-based invariant generation technique [22] using its own k-induction loop. The **Property Directed Reachability (PDR)** engine performs property directed reachability [11] using the implicit abstraction technique [9]. Unlike BMC and k-induction, each property is handled separately by a different PDR sub-engine. Finally, the **Advice** engine produces invariants based on previous runs of JKIND as described in the next section.

Invariant sharing between the solvers (shown in Fig. 1) is an important part of the architecture. In our internal benchmarking, we have found that implicit abstraction PDR performs best when operating over a single property at a time and without use of lemmas generated by other approaches. On the other hand, the invariants generated by PDR and template lemma generation often allow k-induction, which operates on all properties in parallel, to substantially reduce the verification time required for models with large numbers of properties.

2.1 Post Processing and Re-verification

A significant part of the research and development effort for JKIND has focused on post-processing results for presentation and repeated verification of models under development.

Inductive Validity Cores (IVC). For a proven property, an inductive validity core is a subset of LUSTRE equations from the input model for which the property still holds [13,14]. Inductive validity cores can be used for traceability from property to model elements and determining coverage of the model by a set of properties [15]. This facility can be used to automatically generate traceability and adequacy information (such as traceability matrices [12] important to the certification of safety-critical avionics systems [26]). The IVC engine uses a heuristic algorithm to efficiently produce minimal or nearly minimal cores. In a recent experiment over a superset of the benchmark models described in the experiment in Sect. 3, we found that our heuristic IVC computation added 31% overhead to model checking time, and yielded cores approximately 8% larger than the guaranteed minimal core computed by a very expensive "brute force" algorithm. As a side-effect, the IVC algorithm also minimizes the set of invariants used to prove a property and emits this reduced set to other engines (notably the *Advice* engine, described below).

Smoothing. To aid in counterexample understanding and in creating structural coverage tests that can be more easily explained, JKIND provides an optional post-processing step to minimize the number of changes to input variables—*smoothing* the counterexample. For example, applied to 129 test cases generated for a production avionics flight control state machine, smoothing increased runtime by 40% and removed 4 unnecessary input changes per test case on average. The smoothing engine uses a MAXSAT query over the original BMC-style unrolling of the transition relation combined with weighted assertions that each input variable does not change on each step. The MAXSAT query tries to satisfy all of these weighted assertions, but will break them if needed. This has the effect of trying to hold all inputs constant while still falsifying the original property and only allowing inputs to change when needed. This engine is only available with SMT-solvers that support MAXSAT such as YICES 1 and Z3.

Advice. The advice engine saves and re-uses the invariants that were used by JKIND to prove the properties of a model. Prior to analysis, JKIND performs model slicing and flattening to generate a flat transition-relation model. Internally, invariants are stored as a set of proven formulas (in the LUSTRE syntax) over the variables in the flattened model. An *advice* file is simply the emitted set of these invariant formulas. When a model is loaded, the formulas are loaded into memory. Formulas that are no longer syntactically or type correct are discarded, and the remaining set of formulas are submitted as an initial set of possible invariants to be proved via k-induction. If they are proved, they are passed along to other engines; if falsified, they are discarded. Names constructed between multiple runs of JKIND are stable, so if a model is unchanged, it can be usually be re-proved quickly using the invariants and k-induction. If the model is slightly changed, it is often the case that most of the invariants can be re-proved, leading to reduced verification times.

If the IVC engine is also enabled, then advice emits a (close to) minimal set of lemmas used for proof; this often leads to faster re-verification (but more expensive initial verification), and can be useful for examining which of the generated lemmas are useful for proofs.

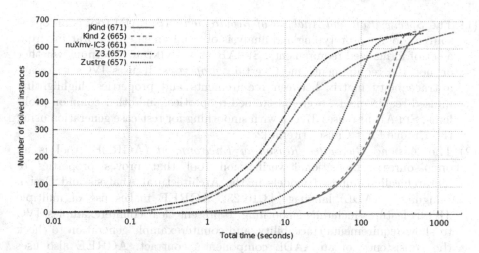

Fig. 2. Performance benchmarks

3   Experimental Evaluation

We evaluated the performance of JKIND against KIND 2 [8], ZUSTRE [20], Generalized PDR in Z3 [19], and IC3 in NUXMV [9]. We used the default options for each tool (using `check_invar_ic3` for NUXMV). Our benchmark suite comes from [9] and contains 688 models over the theory of linear integer arithmetic[2]. All experiments were performed on a 64-bit Ubuntu 17.10 Linux machine with a 12-core Intel Xeon CPU E5-1650 v3 @ 3.50 GHz, with 32 GB of RAM and a time limit of 60 s per model.

Performance comparisons are show in Fig. 2. The key describes the number of benchmarks solved for each tool, and the graph shows the aggregate time required for solving, ordered by time required per-problem, ordered independently for each tool. JKIND was able to verify or falsify the most properties, although Z3 was often the fastest tool. Many of the benchmarks in this set are quickly evaluated: Z3 solves the first 400 benchmarks in just over 12 s. Due to JKIND's use of Java, the JVM/JKIND startup time for an empty model is approximately 0.35s, which leads to poor performance on small models[3]. As always, such benchmarks should be taken with a large grain of salt. In [8], a different set of benchmarks slightly favored KIND 2, and in [9], NUXMV was the most capable tool. We believe that all the solvers are relatively competitive.

4   Integration and Applications

JKIND is the back-end for a variety of user-facing applications. In this section, we briefly highlight a few of these applications and how they employ the features discussed previously.

---

[2] https://es.fbk.eu/people/griggio/papers/tacas14-ic3ia.tar.bz2. Note that we removed 263 duplicate benchmarks from the original set.

[3] Without startup time, the curve for JKIND is close to the curve for ZUSTRE.

(1) The *Specification and Analysis of Requirements* (SPEAR) tool is an open-source tool for prototyping and analysis of requirements [12]. Starting from a set of formalized requirements, SPEAR uses JKIND to determine whether or not the requirements meet certain *properties*. It uses IVCs to create a traceability matrix between requirements and properties, highlighting unused requirements, over-constrained properties, and other common problems. SPEAR also uses JKIND with smoothing for test-case generation using the Unique First Cause criteria [28].

(2) The *Assume Guarantee Reasoning Environment* (AGREE) tool is an open-source compositional verification tool that proves properties of hierarchically-composed models in the Architectural Analysis and Design Language (AADL) language [3,10,23]. AGREE makes use of multiple JKIND features including smoothing to present clear counterexamples, IVC to show requirements traceability, and counterexample generation to check the consistency of an AADL component's contract. AGREE also uses JKIND for test-case generation from component contracts.

(3) The *Static IMPerative AnaLyzer* (SIMPAL) tool is an open-source tool for compositional reasoning over software [27]. SIMPAL is based on LIMP, a LUSTRE-like imperative language with extensions for control flow elements, global variables, and a syntax for specifying preconditions, postconditions, and global variable interactions of preexisting components. SIMPAL translates LIMP programs to an equivalent LUSTRE representation which is passed to JKIND to perform assume-guarantee reasoning, reachability, and viability analyses.

(4) JKIND is also used by two proprietary tools used by product areas within Rockwell Collins. The first is a *Mode Transition Table* verification tool used for the complex state machines which manage flight modes of an aircraft. JKIND is used to check properties and generate tests for mode and transition coverage from LUSTRE models generated from the state machines. IVCs are used to establish traceability, i.e. which transitions are covered by which properties. The second is a *Crew Alerting System* MC/DC test-case generation tool for a proprietary domain-specific language used for messages and alerts to airplane pilots. Smoothing is very important in this context as test cases need to be run on the actual hardware where timing is not precisely controllable. Thus, test cases with a minimum of changes to the inputs are ideal.

5   Related Work

JKIND is one of a number of similar infinite-state inductive model checkers including KIND 2 [8], NUXMV [9], Z3 with generalized PDR [19], and ZUSTRE [20]. They operate over a transition relation described either as a LUSTRE program (KIND 2, JKIND, and ZUSTRE), an extension of the SMV language (NUXMV), or as a set of Horn clauses (Z3). Each tool uses a portfolio-based solver approach, with NUXMV, JKIND, and KIND 2 all supporting both k-induction and a variant of PDR/IC3. NUXMV also supports guided reachability and k-liveness. Other tools such as ESBMC-DEPTHK [25], VVT [4] CPACHECKER, [5], CPROVER [7] use similar techniques for reasoning about C programs.

We believe that the JKIND IVC support is similar to *proof-core* support provided by commercial hardware model checkers: Cadence Jasper Gold and Synopsys VC Formal [1,2,18]. The proof-core provided by these tools is used for internal coverage analysis measurements performed by the tools. Unfortunately, the algorithms used in the commercial tool support are undocumented and performance comparisons are prohibited by the tool licenses, so it is not possible to compare performance on this aspect.

Previous work has been done on improving the quality of counterexamples along various dimensions similar to the JKIND notion of *smoothing*, e.g. [16,24]. Our work is distinguished by its focus on minimizing the number of deltas in the input values. This metric has been driven by user needs and by our own experiences with test-case generation.

There are several tools that support reuse or exchange of verification results, similar to our *advice* feature. Recently, there has been progress on standardized formats [6] of exchange between analysis tools. Our current advice format is optimized for use and performance with our particular tool and designed for re-verification rather than exchange of partial verification information. However, supporting a standardized format for exchanging verification information would be a useful feature for future use.

6 Conclusion

JKIND is similar to a number of other solvers that each solve infinite state sequential analysis problems. Nevertheless, it has some important features that distinguish it. First, a focus on quality of feedback to users for both valid properties (using IVCs) and invalid properties (using smoothing). Second, it is supported across all major platforms and is straightforward to port due to its implementation in Java. Third, it is small, modular, and well-architected, allowing straightforward extension with new engines. Fourth, it is open-source with a liberal distribution license (BSD), so it can be adapted for various purposes, as demonstrated by the number of tools that have incorporated it.

Acknowledgments. The work presented here was sponsored by DARPA as part of the HACMS program under contract FA8750-12-9-0179.

References

1. Cadence JasperGold Formal Verification Platform. https://www.cadence.com/
2. Synopsys VC Formal Platform. https://www.synopsys.com
3. Backes, J., Cofer, D., Miller, S., Whalen, M.W.: Requirements analysis of a quad-redundant flight control system. In: Havelund, K., Holzmann, G., Joshi, R. (eds.) NFM 2015. LNCS, vol. 9058, pp. 82–96. Springer, Cham (2015). https://doi.org/10.1007/978-3-319-17524-9_7

4. Beyer, D., Dangl, M.: SMT-based software model checking: an experimental comparison of four algorithms. In: Blazy, S., Chechik, M. (eds.) VSTTE 2016. LNCS, vol. 9971, pp. 181–198. Springer, Cham (2016). https://doi.org/10.1007/978-3-319-48869-1_14

5. Beyer, D., Dangl, M., Wendler, P.: Boosting k-Induction with continuously-refined invariants. In: Kroening, D., Păsăreanu, C.S. (eds.) CAV 2015. LNCS, vol. 9206, pp. 622–640. Springer, Cham (2015). https://doi.org/10.1007/978-3-319-21690-4_42

6. Beyer, D., et al.: Correctness witnesses: exchanging verification results between verifiers. In: FSE, pp. 326–337 (2016)

7. Brain, M., Joshi, S., Kroening, D., Schrammel, P.: Safety verification and refutation by k-invariants and k-induction. In: Blazy, S., Jensen, T. (eds.) SAS 2015. LNCS, vol. 9291, pp. 145–161. Springer, Heidelberg (2015). https://doi.org/10.1007/978-3-662-48288-9_9

8. Champion, A., Mebsout, A., Sticksel, C., Tinelli, C.: The KIND 2 model checker. In: Chaudhuri, S., Farzan, A. (eds.) CAV 2016. LNCS, vol. 9780, pp. 510–517. Springer, Cham (2016). https://doi.org/10.1007/978-3-319-41540-6_29

9. Cimatti, A., Griggio, A., Mover, S., Tonetta, S.: IC3 modulo theories via implicit predicate abstraction. In: Ábrahám, E., Havelund, K. (eds.) TACAS 2014. LNCS, vol. 8413, pp. 46–61. Springer, Heidelberg (2014). https://doi.org/10.1007/978-3-642-54862-8_4

10. Cofer, D., Gacek, A., Miller, S., Whalen, M.W., LaValley, B., Sha, L.: Compositional verification of architectural models. In: Goodloe, A.E., Person, S. (eds.) NFM 2012. LNCS, vol. 7226, pp. 126–140. Springer, Heidelberg (2012). https://doi.org/10.1007/978-3-642-28891-3_13

11. Eén, N., et al.: Efficient implementation of property directed reachability. In: FMCAD (2011)

12. Fifarek, A.W., Wagner, L.G., Hoffman, J.A., Rodes, B.D., Aiello, M.A., Davis, J.A.: SpeAR v2.0: formalized past LTL specification and analysis of requirements. In: Barrett, C., Davies, M., Kahsai, T. (eds.) NFM 2017. LNCS, vol. 10227, pp. 420–426. Springer, Cham (2017). https://doi.org/10.1007/978-3-319-57288-8_30

13. Ghassabani, E., et al.: Efficient generation of all minimal inductive validity cores. In: FMCAD (2017)

14. Ghassabani, E., et al.: Efficient generation of inductive validity cores for safety properties. In: FSE (2016)

15. Ghassabani, E., et al.: Proof-based coverage metrics for formal verification. In: ASE (2017)

16. Groce, A., Kroening, D.: Making the most of BMC counterexamples. Proc. BMC 2004 ENTCS **119**, 67–81 (2005)

17. Halbwachs, N., et al.: The synchronous dataflow programming language Lustre. IEEE (1991)

18. Hanna, Z., et al.: Formal verification coverage metrics for circuit design properties (2015). https://www.google.com/patents/US20150135150

19. Hoder, K., Bjørner, N.: Generalized property directed reachability. In: Cimatti, A., Sebastiani, R. (eds.) SAT 2012. LNCS, vol. 7317, pp. 157–171. Springer, Heidelberg (2012). https://doi.org/10.1007/978-3-642-31612-8_13

20. Kahsai, T., Bourbouh, H.: Zustre product home page. https://github.com/coco-team/zustre

21. Kahsai, T., Tinelli, C.: PKIND: a parallel k-induction based model checker. In: PDMC (2011)

22. Kahsai, T., Garoche, P.-L., Tinelli, C., Whalen, M.: Incremental verification with mode variable invariants in state machines. In: Goodloe, A.E., Person, S. (eds.) NFM 2012. LNCS, vol. 7226, pp. 388–402. Springer, Heidelberg (2012). https://doi.org/10.1007/978-3-642-28891-3_35

23. Murugesan, A., et al.: Compositional verification of a medical device system. In: HILT (2013)

24. Ravi, K., Somenzi, F.: Minimal assignments for bounded model checking. In: Jensen, K., Podelski, A. (eds.) TACAS 2004. LNCS, vol. 2988, pp. 31–45. Springer, Heidelberg (2004). https://doi.org/10.1007/978-3-540-24730-2_3

25. Rocha, H., et al.: Model checking embedded C software using k-induction and invariants. In: SBESC (2015)

26. RTCA DO-178C: Software Considerations in Airborne Systems and Equipment Certification (2011)

27. Wagner, L., et al.: SIMPAL: a compositional reasoning framework for imperative programs. In: SPIN (2017)

28. Whalen, M.W., et al.: Coverage metrics for requirements-based testing. In: ISSTA (2006)

The DEEPSEC Prover

Vincent Cheval, Steve Kremer,
and Itsaka Rakotonirina(✉)

INRIA Nancy - Grand-Est & LORIA,
Villers-lès-Nancy, France
{vincent.cheval,steve.kremer,
itsaka.rakotonirina}@inria.fr

Abstract. In this paper we describe the DEEPSEC prover, a tool for security protocol analysis. It decides equivalence properties modelled as trace equivalence of two processes in a dialect of the applied pi calculus.

1 Introduction

Cryptographic protocols ensure the security of communications. They are distributed programs that make use of cryptographic primitives, e.g. encryption, to ensure security properties, such as confidentiality or anonymity. Their correct design is quite a challenge as security is to be enforced in the presence of an *arbitrary* adversary that controls the communication network and may compromise participants. The use of symbolic verification techniques, in the line of the seminal work by Dolev and Yao [19], has proven its worth in discovering logical vulnerabilities or proving their absence.

Nowadays mature tools exist, e.g. [7,10,24] but mostly concentrate on *trace properties*, such as authentication and (weak forms of) confidentiality. Unfortunately many properties need to be expressed in terms of *indistinguishability*, modelled as behavioral equivalences in dedicated process calculi. Typically, a strong version of secrecy states that the adversary cannot distinguish the situation where a value v_1, respectively v_2, is used in place of a secret. Privacy properties, e.g., vote privacy, are also stated similarly [2,4,18].

In this paper we present the DEEPSEC prover (Deciding Equivalence Properties in Security protocols). The tool decides trace equivalence for cryptographic protocols that are specified in a dialect of the applied pi calculus [1]. DEEPSEC offers several advantages over existing tools, in terms of expressiveness, precision and efficiency: typically we do not restrict the use of private channels, allow else branches, and decide trace equivalence *precisely*, i.e., no approximations are applied. Cryptographic primitives are user specified by a set of subterm-convergent rewrite rules. The only restriction we make on protocol specifications

This work was supported by the ERC (agreement No. 645865-SPOOC) under the EU H2020 research and innovation program, and ANR project TECAP (ANR-17-CE39-0004-01).

H. Chockler and G. Weissenbacher (Eds.): CAV 2018, LNCS 10982, pp. 28–36, 2018.
https://doi.org/10.1007/978-3-319-96142-2_4

is that we forbid unbounded replication, i.e. we restrict the analysis to a finite number of protocol sessions. This restriction is similar to that of several other tools and sufficient for decidability. Note that decidability is nevertheless non-trivial as the system under study is still infinite-state due to the active, arbitrary attacker participating to the protocol.

2 Description of the Tool

2.1 Example: The Helios Voting Protocol

An input of DEEPSEC defines the cryptographic primitives, the protocol and the security properties that are to be verified. Random numbers are abstracted by *names* $(a, b, \ldots)$, cryptographic primitives by *function symbols* with arity (f/n) and messages by *terms* viewed as *modus operandi* to compute bit-string. For instance, the functions $\texttt{aenc}/3, \texttt{pk}/1$ model randomized asymmetric encryption and public-key generation: term $\texttt{aenc}(\texttt{pk}(k), r, m)$ models the plain text m encrypted with public key $\texttt{pk}(k)$ and randomness r. In DEEPSEC we write:

```
fun aenc/3. fun pk/1.
```

On the other hand, cryptographic destructors are specified by rewrite rules. For example asymmetric decryption (adec) would be defined by

```
reduc adec(k,aenc(pk(k),r,m)) -> m.
```

A plain text m can thus be retrieved from a cipher $\texttt{aenc}(\texttt{pk}(k), r, m)$ and the corresponding private key k. Such user-defined rewrite rules also allow us to describe more complex primitives such as a zero-knowledge proof (ZKP) asserting knowledge of the plaintext and randomness of a given ciphertext:

```
fun zkp/3.
const zpkok.
reduc check(zkp(r,v,aenc(p,r,v)), aenc(p,r,v)) -> zkpok.
```

Although user-defined, the rewrite system is required by DEEPSEC to be *subterm convergent*, i.e., the right hand side is a subterm of the left hand side or a ground term in normal form. Support for tuples and projection is provided by default.

Protocol Specification. Honest participants in a protocol are modeled as processes. For instance, the process Voter(auth,id,v,pkE) describes a voter in the Helios voting protocol. The process has four arguments: an authenticated channel auth, the voter's identifier id, its vote v and the public key of the tally pkE.

```
let Voter(auth,id,v,pkE) =
  new r;
  let bal = aenc(pkE,r,v) in
  out(auth,bal);
  out(c, (id, bal, zkp(r,v,bal))).

let VotingSystem(v1,v2) =
  new k; new auth1; new auth2;
  out(c,pk(k)); (
    Voter(auth1,id1,v1,pk(k)) |
    Voter(auth2,id2,v2,pk(k)) |
    Tally(k,auth1,auth2) ).
```

The voter first generates a random number r that will be used for encryption and ZKP. After that, she encrypts her vote and assigns it to the variable bal which is output on the channel auth. Finally, she outputs the ballot, id and the corresponding ZKP on the public channel c. All in all, the process VotingSystem(v1,v2) represents the complete voting scheme: two honest voters id1 and id2 respectively vote for v1 and v2; the process Tally collects the ballots, checks the ZKP and outputs the result of the election. The instances of the processes Voter and Tally are executed concurrently, modeled by the parallel operator |. Other operators supported by DEEPSEC include input on a channel (in(c,x); P), conditional (if u = v then P else Q) and non-deterministic choice (P + Q).

Security Properties. DEEPSEC focuses on properties modelled as trace equivalence, e.g. vote privacy [18] in the Helios protocol. We express it at indistinguishability of two instances of the protocol swapping the votes of two honest voters:

```
query trace_equiv(VotingSystem(yes,no),VotingSystem(no,yes)).
```

DEEPSEC checks whether an attacker, implicitly modelled by the notion of trace equivalence, cannot distinguish between these two instances. Note that all actions of dishonest voters can be seen as actions of this single attacker entity; thus only honest participants need to be specified in the input file.

2.2 The Underlying Theory

We give here a high-level overview of how DEEPSEC decides trace equivalence. Further intuition and details can be found in [14].

Symbolic Setting. Although finite-depth, even non-replicated protocols have infinite state space. Indeed, a simple input in(c,x) induces infinitely-many potential transitions in presence of an active attacker. We therefore define a *symbolic calculus* that abstracts concrete inputs by symbolic variables, and *constraints* that restrict their concrete instances. Constraints typically range over *deducibility contraints* ("the attacker is able to craft some term after spying on public channels") and *equations* ("two terms are equal"). A symbolic semantics then performs symbolic inputs and collects constraints on them. Typically, executing input in(c,x) generates a deducibility constraint on x to model the attacker being able to craft the message to be input; equations are generated by conditionals, relying on most general unifiers modulo equational theory.

Decision Procedure. DEEPSEC constructs a so-called *partition tree* to guide decision of (in)equivalence of processes P and Q. Its nodes are labelled by sets of symbolic processes and constraints; typically the root contains P and Q with empty constraints. The tree is constructed similarly to the (finite) tree of all symbolic executions of P and Q, except that some nodes may be merged or split accordingly to a constraint-solving procedure. DEEPSEC thus enforces that concrete instances of processes of a same node are indistinguishable (statically).

The final decision criterion is that P and Q are equivalent *iff* all nodes of the partition tree contain both a process originated from P and a process originated from Q by symbolic execution. The DEEPSEC prover thus returns an attack *iff* it finds a node violating this property while constructing the partition tree.

2.3 Implementation

DEEPSEC is implemented in Ocaml (16k LOC) and the source code is licensed under GPL 3.0 and publicly available [17]. Running DEEPSEC yields a terminal output summarising results, while a more detailed output is displayed graphically in an HTML interface (using the MathJax API [20]). When the query is not satisfied, the interface interactively shows how to mount the attack.

Partial-Order Reductions. Tools verifying equivalences for bounded number of sessions suffer from a combinatorial explosion as the number of sessions increases. We therefore implemented state-of-the-art partial-order reductions (POR) [8] that eliminate redundant interleavings, providing a significant speedup. This is only possible for a restricted class of processes (determinate processes) but DEEPSEC automatically checks whether POR can be activated.

Parallelism. DEEPSEC generates a partition tree (cf Sect. 2.2) to decide trace equivalence. As sibling nodes are independent, the computation on subtrees can be parallelized. However, the partition tree is not balanced, making it hard to balance the load. One natural solution would be to systematically add children nodes into a queue of pending jobs, but this would yield an important communication overhead. Consequently, we apply this method only until the size of the queue is larger than a given threshold; next each idle process fetches a node and computes the *complete* corresponding subtree. Distributed computation over n cores is activated by the option -distributed n. By default, the threshold in the initial generation of the partition tree depends on n but may be overwritten to m with the option -nb_sets m.

3   Experimental Evaluation

Comparison to Other Work. When the number of sessions is unbounded, equivalence is undecidable. Verification tools in this setting therefore have to sacrifice termination, and generally only verify the finer *diff-equivalence* [9,11,23], too fine-grained on many examples. We therefore focus on tools comparable to DEEPSEC, i.e. those that bound the number of sessions. SPEC [25,26] verifies a sound symbolic bisimulation, but is restricted to fixed cryptographic primitives (pairing, encryption, signatures, hashes) and does not allow for else branches. APTE [13] covers the same primitives but allows else branches and decides trace equivalence exactly. On the contrary, AKISS [12] allows for user-defined primitives and terminates when they form a subterm-convergent rewrite system. However AKISS only decides trace equivalence without approximation for a subclass of processes (*determinate* processes) and may perform under- and over-approximations otherwise. SAT-EQ [15] proceeds differently by reducing the equivalence problem to Graph Planning and SAT Solving: the tool is more efficient than the others by several orders of magnitude, but is quite restricted in scope (it currently supports pairing, symmetric encryption, and can only analyse a subclass of determinate processes). Besides, SAT-EQ may not terminate.

Authentication. Figure 1 displays a sample of our benchmarks (complete results can be found in [17]). DEEPSEC clearly outperforms AKISS, APTE, and SPEC, but SAT-EQ takes the lead as the number of sessions increase. However, the Otway-Rees protocol already illustrates the scope limit of SAT-EQ.

Besides, as previously mentioned, DEEPSEC includes partial-order reductions (POR). We performed experiments with and without this optimisation: for example, protocols requiring more than 12 h of computation time without POR can be verified in less than a second. Note that AKISS and APTE also implement the same POR techniques as DEEPSEC.

Protocol (# of roles)		Akiss	APTE	SPEC	Sat-Eq	DeepSec	No POR
Denning-Sacco	3	✓ <1s	✓ <1s	✓ 11s	✓ <1s	✓ <1s	✓ 1s
	6	✓ <1s	✓ 1s	(om)	✓ <1s	✓ <1s	✓ 13s
	7	✓ 6s	✓ 3s		✓ <1s	✓ <1s	✓ 9m 45s
	10	(om)	✓ 9m49		✓ <1s	✓ <1s	⏱
	12		⏱		✓ <1s	✓ <1s	
	29				✓ <1s	✓ 6s	
Yahalom-Lowe	3	✓ <1s	✓ <1s	✓ 7s	✓ <1s	✓ <1s	✓ <1s
	6	✓ 2s	✓ 41s	(om)	✓ <1s	✓ <1s	✓ 16m
	7	✓ 42s	✓ 34m38s		✓ 1s	✓ <1s	⏱
	10	(om)	⏱		✓ 1s	✓ <1s	
	17				✓ 12s	✓ 8s	
Otway-Rees	3	✓ 28s	✓ 2s	✓ 58m9s	✗	✓ <1s	✓ <1s
	6	(om)	(om)	⏱		✓ <1s	✓ 39m 41s
	7					✓ <1s	⏱
	14					✓ 5m28s	

✓ equivalence proved   ✗ out of scope   (om) out of memory/stack overflow   ⏱ timeout (12H)

Fig. 1. Benchmark results on classical authentication protocols

Protocol (# roles)		Akiss		APTE		DeepSec		Helios variant (# roles)		DeepSec	
Passive Authentication	2	✓	<1s	✓	<1s	✓	<1s	Vanilla	6	⚡	<1s
	4	✓	<1s	✓	1s	✓	<1s	No revote W	6	✓	1s
	6	✓	2m22s	✓	1m26s	✓	<1s	No revote ZKP	6	✓	2s
	7	✓	1h42m	✓	1m40s	✓	1s	Dishonest revote W	10	✓	30m 24s
	9	⏲		✓	1h55m	✓	<1s	Dishonest revote ZKP	10	✓	9m 26s
	15			⏲		✓	4s	Honest revote W	11	⚡	2s
	21					✓	8s	Honest revote ZKP	11	✓	2h 42m

✓ equivalence proved   ⚡ attack found   ⏲ timeout (12H)

Fig. 2. Benchmark results for verifying privacy type properties

Privacy. We also verified privacy properties on the private authentication protocol [2], the passive-authentication and basic-access-control protocols from the e-passport [21], AKA of the 3G telephony networks [6] and the voting protocols Helios [3] and Prêt-à-Voter [22]. DEEPSEC is the only tool that can prove vote privacy on the two voting protocols, and private authentication is out of the scope of SAT-EQ and SPEC. Besides, we analysed variants of the Helios voting protocol, based on the work of Arapinis et al. [5] (see Fig. 2). The *vanilla* version is known vulnerable to a ballot-copy attack [16], which is patched by a ballot weeding (W) or a zero-knowledge proof (ZKP). DEEPSEC proved that, (*i*) when no revote is allowed, or (*ii*) when each honest voter only votes once and a dishonest voter is allowed to revote, then both patches are secure. However, only the ZKP variant remains secure when honest voters are allowed to revote.

Parallelism. Experiments have been carried out on a server with 40 Intel Xeon E5-2687W v3 CPUs 3.10 GHz, with 50 GB RAM and 25 MB L3 Cache, using 35 cores (Server 1). However the performances of parallelisation had some unexpected behavior. For example, on the Yahalom-Lowe protocol, the use of too many cores on a same server negatively impacts performances: e.g. on Server 1, optimal results are achieved using only 20 to 25 cores. In comparison, optimal results required 40–45 cores on a server with 112 Intel Xeon vE7-4850 v3 CPUs 2.20 GHz, with 1.5 TB RAM and 35 MB L3 Cache (Server 2). This difference may be explained by cache capacity: overloading servers with processes (sharing cache) beyond a certain threshold should indeed make the hit-miss ratio drop. This is consistent with the Server 2 having a larger cache and exploiting efficiently more cores than Server 1. Using the `perf` profiling tool, we confirmed that the number of cache-references per second (CRPS) stayed relatively stable up to the optimal number of cores and quickly decreased beyond (Fig. 3).

DEEPSEC can also distribute on multiple servers, using SSH connections. Despite a communication overhead, multi-server computation may be a way to partially avoid the server-overload issue discussed above. For example, the

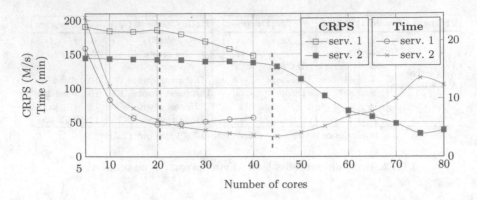

Fig. 3. Performance analysis on Yahalom-Lowe protocol with 23 roles

verification of the Helios protocol (Dishonest revote W) on 3 servers (using resp. 10, 20 and 40 cores) resulted in a running time of 18 m 14 s, while the same verification took 51 m 49 s on a 70-core server (also launched remotely via SSH).

References

1. Abadi, M., Blanchet, B., Fournet, C.: The applied pi calculus: mobile values, new names, and secure communication. J. ACM **65**(1), 1–41 (2017)
2. Abadi, M., Fournet, C.: Private authentication. Theor. Comput. Sci. **322**(3), 427–476 (2004)
3. Adida, B.: Helios: web-based open-audit voting. In: Proceedings of 17th USENIX Security Symposium, USENIX 2008, pp. 335–348. USENIX Association (2008)
4. Arapinis, M., Chothia, T., Ritter, E., Ryan, M.D.: Analysing unlinkability and anonymity using the applied pi calculus. In: Proceedings of 23rd Computer Security Foundations Symposium, CSF 2010, pp. 107–121. IEEE Computer Society Press (2010)
5. Arapinis, M., Cortier, V., Kremer, S.: When are three voters enough for privacy properties? In: Askoxylakis, I., Ioannidis, S., Katsikas, S., Meadows, C. (eds.) ESORICS 2016. LNCS, vol. 9879, pp. 241–260. Springer, Cham (2016). https://doi.org/10.1007/978-3-319-45741-3_13
6. Arapinis, M., Mancini, L., Ritter, E., Ryan, M., Golde, N., Redon, K., Borgaonkar, R.: New privacy issues in mobile telephony: fix and verification. In: Proceedings of 19th Conference on Computer and Communications Security, CCS 2012, pp. 205–216. ACM Press (2012)
7. Armando, A., et al.: The AVISPA tool for the automated validation of Internet security protocols and applications. In: Etessami, K., Rajamani, S.K. (eds.) CAV 2005. LNCS, vol. 3576, pp. 281–285. Springer, Heidelberg (2005). https://doi.org/10.1007/11513988_27

8. Baelde, D., Delaune, S., Hirschi, L.: Partial order reduction for security protocols. In: Proceedings of 26th International Conference on Concurrency Theory, CONCUR 2015. Leibniz International Proceedings in Informatics, vol. 42, pp. 497–510. Leibniz-Zentrum für Informatik, September 2015
9. Basin, D.A., Dreier, J., Sasse, R.: Automated symbolic proofs of observational equivalence. In: Proceedings of 22nd Conference on Computer and Communications Security, CCS 2015, pp. 1144–1155. ACM Press (2015)
10. Blanchet, B.: Modeling and verifying security protocols with the applied pi calculus and proverif. Found. Trends Priv. Secur. 1(1–2), 1–135 (2016)
11. Blanchet, B., Abadi, M., Fournet, C.: Automated verification of selected equivalences for security protocols. In: Proceedings of Symposium on Logic in Computer Science, LICS 2005, pp. 331–340. IEEE Computer Society Press (2005)
12. Chadha, R., Cheval, V., Ciobâcă, Ş., Kremer, S.: Automated verification of equivalence properties of cryptographic protocol. ACM Trans. Comput. Log. 23(4), 1–32 (2016)
13. Cheval, V.: APTE: an algorithm for proving trace equivalence. In: Ábrahám, E., Havelund, K. (eds.) TACAS 2014. LNCS, vol. 8413, pp. 587–592. Springer, Heidelberg (2014). https://doi.org/10.1007/978-3-642-54862-8_50
14. Cheval, V., Kremer, S., Rakotonirina, I.: DEEPSEC: deciding equivalence properties in security protocols - theory and practice. In: Proceedings of 39th IEEE Symposium on Security and Privacy, S&P 2018, pp. 525–542. IEEE Computer Society Press (2018)
15. Cortier, V., Delaune, S., Dallon, A.: Sat-equiv: an efficient tool for equivalence properties. In: Proceedings of 30th IEEE Computer Security Foundations Symposium, CSF 2017, pp. 481–494. IEEE Computer Society Press (2017)
16. Cortier, V., Smyth, B.: Attacking and fixing helios: an analysis of ballot secrecy. J. Comput. Secur. 21(1), 89–148 (2013)
17. The DeepSec Prover, January 2018. https://deepsec-prover.github.io
18. Delaune, S., Kremer, S., Ryan, M.D.: Verifying privacy-type properties of electronic voting protocols. J. Comput. Secur. 17(4), 435–487 (2009)
19. Dolev, D., Yao, A.: On the security of public key protocols. In: Proceedings of 22nd Symposium on Foundations of Computer Science, FOCS 1981, pp. 350–357. IEEE Computer Society Press (1981)
20. MathJax: Beautiful Math in All Browsers. https://www.mathjax.org
21. PKI Task Force: PKI for machine readable travel documents offering ICC read-only access. Technical report, International Civil Aviation Organization (2004)
22. Ryan, P.Y.A., Schneider, S.A.: Prêt à voter with re-encryption mixes. In: Gollmann, D., Meier, J., Sabelfeld, A. (eds.) ESORICS 2006. LNCS, vol. 4189, pp. 313–326. Springer, Heidelberg (2006). https://doi.org/10.1007/11863908_20
23. Santiago, S., Escobar, S., Meadows, C., Meseguer, J.: A formal definition of protocol indistinguishability and its verification using Maude-NPA. In: Mauw, S., Jensen, C.D. (eds.) STM 2014. LNCS, vol. 8743, pp. 162–177. Springer, Cham (2014). https://doi.org/10.1007/978-3-319-11851-2_11
24. Meier, S., Schmidt, B., Cremers, C., Basin, D.: The TAMARIN prover for the symbolic analysis of security protocols. In: Sharygina, N., Veith, H. (eds.) CAV 2013. LNCS, vol. 8044, pp. 696–701. Springer, Heidelberg (2013). https://doi.org/10.1007/978-3-642-39799-8_48

25. Tiu, A., Dawson, J.: Automating open bisimulation checking for the spi-calculus. In: Proceedings of 23rd Computer Security Foundations Symposium, CSF 2010, pp. 307–321. IEEE Computer Society Press (2010)
26. Tiu, A., Nguyen, N., Horne, R.: SPEC: an equivalence checker for security protocols. In: Igarashi, A. (ed.) APLAS 2016. LNCS, vol. 10017, pp. 87–95. Springer, Cham (2016). https://doi.org/10.1007/978-3-319-47958-3_5

SimpleCAR: An Efficient Bug-Finding Tool Based on Approximate Reachability

Jianwen Li[1(✉)], Rohit Dureja[1], Geguang Pu[2],
Kristin Yvonne Rozier[1], and Moshe Y. Vardi[3]

[1] Iowa State University, Ames, IA, USA
lijwen2748@gmail.com
[2] East China Normal University, Shanghai, China
[3] Rice University, Houston, TX, USA

Abstract. We present a new safety hardware model checker SimpleCAR
that serves as a reference implementation for evaluating Complementary Approximate Reachability (CAR), a new SAT-based model checking framework inspired by classical reachability analysis. The tool gives
a "bottom-line" performance measure for comparing future extensions
to the framework. We demonstrate the performance of SimpleCAR on
challenging benchmarks from the Hardware Model Checking Competition. Our experiments indicate that SimpleCAR is particularly suited for
unsafety checking, or *bug-finding*; it is able to solve 7 unsafe instances
within 1 h that are not solvable by any other state-of-the-art techniques,
including BMC and IC3/PDR, within 8 h. We also identify a bug (reports
safe instead of unsafe) and 48 counterexample generation errors in the
tools compared in our analysis.

1 Introduction

Model checking techniques are widely used in proving design correctness, and
have received unprecedented attention in the hardware design community [9,16].
Given a system model M and a property P, model checking proves whether or
not P holds for M. A model checking algorithm exhaustively checks all behaviors of M, and returns a counterexample as evidence if any behavior violates the
property P. The counterexample gives the execution of the system that leads to
property failure, i.e., a *bug*. Particularly, if P is a safety property, model checking
reduces to reachability analysis, and the provided counterexample has a finite
length. Popular safety checking techniques include Bounded Model Checking
(BMC) [10], Interpolation Model Checking (IMC) [21], and IC3/PDR [12,14]. It
is well known that there is no "universal" algorithm in model checking; different
algorithms perform differently on different problem instances [7]. BMC outperforms IMC on checking unsafe instances, while IC3/PDR can solve instances that
BMC cannot and vice-versa. [19]. Therefore, BMC and IC3/PDR are the most
popular algorithms in the portfolio for unsafety checking, or *bug-finding*.

© The Author(s) 2018
H. Chockler and G. Weissenbacher (Eds.): CAV 2018, LNCS 10982, pp. 37–44, 2018.
https://doi.org/10.1007/978-3-319-96142-2_5

Complementary Approximate Reachability (CAR) [19] is a SAT-based model checking framework for reachability analysis. Contrary to reachability analysis via IC3/PDR, CAR maintains two sequences of over- and under- approximate reachable state-sets. The over-approximate sequence is used for safety checking, and the under-approximate sequence for unsafety checking. CAR does not require the over-approximate sequence to be monotone, unlike IC3/PDR. Both forward (Forward-CAR) and backward (Backward-CAR) reachability analysis are permissible in the CAR framework. Preliminary results show that Forward-CAR complements IC3/PDR on safe instances [19].

We present, SimpleCAR, a tool specifically developed for evaluating and extending the CAR framework. The new tool is a complete rewrite of CARChecker [19] with several improvements and added capabilities. SimpleCAR has a lighter and cleaner implementation than CARChecker. Several heuristics that aid Forward-CAR to complement IC3/PDR are integrated in CARChecker. Although useful, these heuristics make it difficult to understand and extend the core functionalities of CAR. Like IC3/PDR, the performance of CAR varies significantly by using heuristics [17]. Therefore, it is necessary to provide a basic implementation of CAR (without code-bloating heuristics) that serves as a "bottom-line" performance measure for all extensions in the future. To that end, SimpleCAR differs from CARChecker in the following aspects:

- Eliminates all heuristics integrated in CARChecker except a configuration option to enable a IC3/PDR-like clause "propagation" heuristic.
- Uses UNSAT cores from the SAT solver directly instead of the expensive minimal UNSAT core (MUC) computation in CARChecker.
- Poses incremental queries to the SAT solver using assumptions;
- While CARChecker contributes to safety checking [19], SimpleCAR shows a clear advantage on unsafety checking.

We apply SimpleCAR to 748 benchmarks from the Hardware Model Checking Competition (HWMCC) 2015 [2] and 2017 [3], and compare its performance to reachability analysis algorithms (BMC, IMC, 4 × IC3/PDR, Avy [22], Quip [18]) in state-of-the-art model checking tools (ABC, nuXmv, IIMC, IC3Ref). Our extensive experiments reveal that Backward-CAR is particularly suited for unsafety checking: it can solve 8 instances within a 1-h time limit, and 7 instances within a 8-h time limit not solvable by BMC and IC3/PDR. We conclude that, along with BMC and IC3/PDR, CAR is an important candidate in the portfolio of unsafety checking algorithms, and SimpleCAR provides an easy and efficient way to evaluate, experiment with, and add enhancements to the CAR framework. We identify 1 major bug and 48 errors in counterexample generation in our evaluated tool set; all have been reported to the tool developers.

2   Algorithms and Implementation

We present a very high-level overview of the CAR framework (refer [19] for details). CAR is a SAT-based framework for reachability analysis. It maintains two over- and under- approximate reachable state sequences for safety and unsafety checking, respectively. CAR can be symmetrically implemented either in the forward (Forward-CAR) or backward (Backward-CAR) mode. In the forward mode, the F-sequence $(F_0, F_1, \ldots, F_i)$ is the over-approximated sequence, while the B-sequence $(B_0, B_1, \ldots, B_i)$ is under-approximated. The roles of the F- and B- sequence are reversed in the backward mode. We focus here on the backward mode of CAR, or Backward-CAR (refer [19] for Forward-CAR)

2.1 High-Level Description of Backward-CAR

A frame F_i in the F-sequence denotes the set of states that are reachable from the initial states (I) in i steps. Similarly, a frame B_i in the B-sequence denotes the set of states that

Table 1. Sequences in Backward-CAR.

	F-sequence (under)	B-sequence (over)
Init	$F_0 = I$	$B_0 = \neg P$
Constraint	$F_{i+1} \subseteq R(F_i)$	$B_{i+1} \supseteq R^{-1}(B_i)$
Safety check	-	$\exists i \cdot B_{i+1} \subseteq \bigcup_{0 < j < i} B_j$
Unsafety check	$\exists i \cdot F_i \cap \neg P \neq \emptyset$	-

can reach the bad states $(\neg P)$ in i steps. Let $R(F_i)$ represent the set of successor states of F_i, and $R^{-1}(B_i)$ represent the set of predecessor states of B_i. Table 1 shows the constraints on the sequences and their usage in Backward-CAR for safety and unsafety checking.

Let $S(F) = \bigcup F_i$ and $S(B) = \bigcup B_i$. Algorithm 1 gives a description of Backward-CAR. The B-sequence is extended exactly once in every iteration of the loop in lines 2–8, but the F-sequence may be extended multiple times in each loop iteration in lines 3–5.

Alg. 1. High-level description of Backward CAR

1: $F_0 = I$, $B_0 = \neg P$, $k = 0$;
2: **while** true **do**
3:   **while** $S(B) \wedge R(S(F)) \neq \emptyset$ **do**
4:     update F- and B- sequences.
5:     **if** $\exists i \cdot F_i \cap \neg P \neq \emptyset$ **then return** unsafe;
6:   perform propagation on B-sequence (optional),
7:   **if** $\exists i \cdot B_{i+1} \subseteq \bigcup_{0 \leq j \leq i} B_j$ **then return** safe;
8:   $k = k + 1$ and $B_k = \neg P$;

As a result, CAR normally returns counterexamples with longer depth compared to the length of the B-sequence. Due to this inherent feature of the framework, CAR is able to complement BMC and IC3/PDR on unsafety checking.

2.2 Tool Implementation

SimpleCAR is publicly available [5,6] under the GNU GPLv3 license. The tool implementation is as follows:

- **Language:** C++11 compilable under gcc 4.4.7 or above.
- **Input:** Hardware circuit models expressed as and-inverter graphs in the *aiger* 1.9 format [11] containing a single safety property.
- **Output:** "1" (unsafe) to report the system violates the property, or "0" (safe) to confirm that the system satisfies the property. A counterexample in the *aiger* format is generated if run with the -e configuration flag.

- **Algorithms:** Forward-CAR and Backward-CAR with and without the propagation heuristic (enabled using the -p configuration flag).
- **External Tools:** Glucose 3.0 [8] (based on MiniSAT [15]) is used as the underlying SAT solver. *Aiger* tools [1] are used for parsing the input aiger files to extract the model and property information, and error checking.
- **Differences with CARChecker [19]:** The Minimal Unsat Core (MUC) and Partial Assignment (PA) techniques are not utilized in SimpleCAR, which allows the implementation to harness the power of incremental SAT solving.

3 Experimental Analysis

3.1 Strategies

Tools. We consider five model checking tools in our evaluation: ABC 1.01 [13], IIMC 2.0[1], Simplic3 [17] (IC3 algorithms used by nuXmv for finite-state systems[2]), IC3Ref [4], CARChecker [19], and SimpleCAR. For ABC, we evaluate BMC (bmc2), IMC (int), and PDR (pdr). There are three different versions of BMC in ABC: bmc, bmc2, and bmc3. We choose bmc2 based on our preliminary analysis since it outperforms other versions. Simplic3 proposes different configuration options for IC3. We use the three *best candidate* configurations for IC3 reported in [17], and the Avy algorithm [22] in Simplic3. We consider CARChecker as the original implementation of the CAR framework and use it as a reference implementation for SimpleCAR. A summary of the tools and their arguments used for experiments is shown in Table 2. Overall, we consider four categories of algorithms implemented in the tools: BMC, IMC, IC3/PDR, and CAR.

Benchmarks. We evaluate all tools against 748 benchmarks in the *aiger* format [11] from the SINGLE safety property track of the HWMCC in 2015 and 2017.

Error Checking. We check correctness of results from the tools in two ways:

1. We use the aigsim [1] tool to check whether the counterexample generated for unsafe instances is a real counterexample by simulation.
2. For inconsistent results (safe and unsafe for the same benchmark by at least two different tools) we attempt to simulate the unsafe counterexample, and if successful, report an error for the tool that returns safe (surprisingly, we do not encounter cases when the simulation check fails).

Platform. Experiments were performed on Rice University's DavinCI cluster, which comprises of 192 nodes running at 2.83 GHz, 48 GB of memory and running RedHat 6.0. We set the memory limit to 8 GB with a wall-time limit of an hour. Each model checking run has exclusive access to a node. A time penalty of one hour is set for benchmarks that cannot be solved within the time/memory limits.

---

[1] We use version 2.0 available at https://ryanmb.bitbucket.io/truss/ – similar to the version available at https://github.com/mgudemann/iimc with addition of Quip [18].

[2] Personal communication with Alberto Griggio.

Table 2. Tools and algorithms (with category) evaluated in the experiments.

	Tool	Algorithm	Configuration Flags
IC3/ PDR	ABC	BMC (abc-bmc)	-c 'bmc2'
		IMC (abc-int)	-c 'int'
		PDR (abc-pdr)	-c 'pdr'
	IIMC	IC3 (iimc-ic3)	-t ic3 --ic3_stats --print_cex --cex_aiger
		Quip [18] (iimc-quip)	-t quip --quip_stats --print_cex --cex_aiger
	IC3Ref	IC3 (ic3-ref)	-b
	Simplic3	IC3 (simplic3-best1)	-s minisat -m 1 -u 4 -I 0 -O 1 -c 1 -p 1 -d 2 -G 1 -P 1 -A 100
		IC3 (simplic3-best2)	-s minisat -m 1 -u 4 -I 1 -D 0 -g 1 -X 0 -O 1 -c 0 -p 1 -d 2 -G 1 -P 1 -A 100
		IC3 (simplic3-best3)	-s minisat -m 1 -u 4 -I 0 -O 1 -c 0 -p 1 -d 2 -G 1 -P 1 -A 100 -a aic3
		Avy [22] (simplic3-avy)	-a avy
CAR	CARChecker	Forward CAR* (carchk-f)	-f
		Backward CAR* (carchk-b)	-b
	SimpleCAR	Forward CAR† (simpcar-f)	-f -e
		Backward CAR† (simpcar-b)	-b -e
		Forward CAR‡ (simpcar-fp)	-f -p -e
		Backward CAR‡ (simpcar-bp)	-b -p -e

* with heuristics for *minimal unsat core* (MUC) [20], partial assignment [23], and propagation.
† no heuristics
‡ with heuristic for PDR-like clause propagation

3.2 Results

Error Report. We identify one bug in `simplic3-best3`: reports safe instead of unsafe, and 48 errors with respect to counterexample generation in `iimc-quip` algorithm (26) and all algorithms in the Simplic3 tool (22). At the time of writing, the bug report sent to the developers of Simplic3 has been confirmed. In our analysis, we assume the results from these tools to be correct.

Coarse Analysis. We focus our analysis to unsafety checking. Figure 1 shows the total number of unsafe benchmarks solved by each category (assuming portfolio-run of all algorithms in a category). CAR **complements BMC and IC3/PDR by solving 128 benchmarks of which 8 are not solved by any other category.** Although CAR solves the least amount of total benchmarks, the count of the uniquely solved benchmarks is comparable to other categories. When the wall-time limit (memory limit does not change) is increased to 8 h, BMC and IC3/PDR can only solve one of the 8 uniquely solved

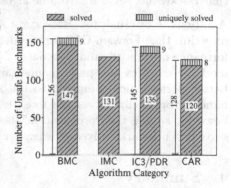

Fig. 1. Number of benchmarks solved by each algorithm category (run as a portfolio). Uniquely solved benchmarks are not solved by any other category.

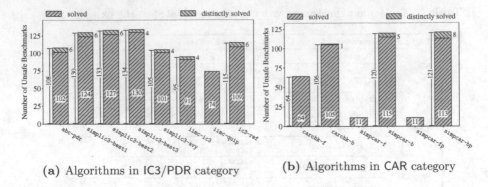

(a) Algorithms in IC3/PDR category   (b) Algorithms in CAR category

Fig. 2. Number of benchmarks solved by every algorithm in a category. Distinctly solved benchmarks by an algorithm are not solved by any algorithm in other categories. The set union of distinctly solved benchmarks for all algorithms in a category equals the count of uniquely solved for that category in Fig. 1.

benchmarks by CAR. The analysis supports our claim that CAR complements BMC/IC3/PDR on unsafety checking.

Granular Analysis. Figure 2 shows how each algorithm in the IC3/PDR (Fig. 2a) and CAR (Fig. 2b) categories performs on the benchmarks. `simpcar-bp` **distinctly solves all 8 benchmarks uniquely solved by the CAR category (Fig. 1), while no single IC3/PDR algorithm distinctly solves all uniquely solved benchmarks in the IC3/PDR category.** In fact, a portfolio including at least `abc-pdr`, `simplic3-best1`, and `simplic3-best2` solves all 8 instances uniquely solved by the IC3/PDR category. It is important to note that SimpleCAR is a very basic implementation of the CAR framework compared to the highly optimized implementations of IC3/PDR in other tools. Even then `simpcar-b` **outperforms four** IC3/PDR **implementations.** Our results show that Backward-CAR is a favorable algorithm for unsafety checking.

Analysis Conclusions. Backward-CAR presents a more promising research direction than Forward-CAR for unsafety checking. We conjecture that the performance of Forward- and Backward- CAR varies with the structure of the $aiger$ model. Heuristics and performance-gain present a trade-off. `simpcar-bp` has a better performance compared to the heuristic-heavy `carchk-b`. On the other hand, `simpcar-bp` solves the most unsafe benchmarks in the CAR category, however, adding the "propagation" heuristic effects its performance: there are several benchmarks solved by `simpcar-b` but not by `simpcar-bp`.

4 Summary

We present SimpleCAR, a safety model checker based on the CAR framework for reachability analysis. Our tool is a lightweight and extensible implementation of CAR with comparable performance to other state-of-the-art tool implementations of highly-optimized unsafety checking algorithms, and complements existing algorithm portfolios. Our empirical evaluation reveals that adding heuristics does not always improve performance. We conclude that Backward-CAR is a more promising research direction than Forward-CAR for unsafety checking, and our tool serves as the "bottom-line" for all future extensions to the CAR framework.

Acknowledgments. This work is supported by NSF CAREER Award CNS-1552934, NASA ECF NNX16AR57G, NSF CCF-1319459, and NSFC 61572197 and 61632005 grants. Geguang Pu is also partially supported by MOST NKTSP Project 2015BAG19B02 and STCSM Project No. 16DZ1100600.

References

1. AIGER Tools. http://fmv.jku.at/aiger/aiger-1.9.9.tar.gz
2. HWMCC 2015. http://fmv.jku.at/hwmcc15/
3. HWMCC 2017. http://fmv.jku.at/hwmcc17/
4. IC3Ref. https://github.com/arbrad/IC3ref
5. SimpleCAR Source. https://github.com/lijwen2748/simplecar/releases/tag/v0.1
6. SimpleCAR Website. http://temporallogic.org/research/CAV18/
7. Amla, N., Du, X., Kuehlmann, A., Kurshan, R.P., McMillan, K.L.: An analysis of SAT-based model checking techniques in an industrial environment. In: Borrione, D., Paul, W. (eds.) CHARME 2005. LNCS, vol. 3725, pp. 254–268. Springer, Heidelberg (2005). https://doi.org/10.1007/11560548_20
8. Audemard, G., Simon, L.: Predicting learnt clauses quality in modern sat solvers. In: IJCAI (2009)
9. Bernardini, A., Ecker, W., Schlichtmann, U.: Where formal verification can help in functional safety analysis. In: ICCAD (2016)
10. Biere, A., Cimatti, A., Clarke, E.M., Fujita, M., Zhu, Y.: Symbolic model checking using SAT procedures instead of BDDs (1999)
11. Biere, A.: AIGER Format. http://fmv.jku.at/aiger/FORMAT
12. Bradley, A.R.: SAT-based model checking without unrolling. In: Jhala, R., Schmidt, D. (eds.) VMCAI 2011. LNCS, vol. 6538, pp. 70–87. Springer, Heidelberg (2011). https://doi.org/10.1007/978-3-642-18275-4_7
13. Brayton, R., Mishchenko, A.: ABC: an academic industrial-strength verification tool. In: Touili, T., Cook, B., Jackson, P. (eds.) CAV 2010. LNCS, vol. 6174, pp. 24–40. Springer, Heidelberg (2010). https://doi.org/10.1007/978-3-642-14295-6_5
14. Een, N., Mishchenko, A., Brayton, R.: Efficient implementation of property directed reachability. In: FMCAD (2011)
15. Eén, N., Sörensson, N.: An extensible SAT-solver. In: Giunchiglia, E., Tacchella, A. (eds.) SAT 2003. LNCS, vol. 2919, pp. 502–518. Springer, Heidelberg (2004). https://doi.org/10.1007/978-3-540-24605-3_37
16. Golnari, A., Vizel, Y., Malik, S.: Error-tolerant processors: formal specification and verification. In: ICCAD (2015)
17. Griggio, A., Roveri, M.: Comparing different variants of the IC3 algorithm for hardware model checking. IEEE Trans. Comput-Aided Des. Integr. Circuits Syst. **35**(6), 1026–1039 (2016)
18. Ivrii, A., Gurfinkel, A.: Pushing to the top. In: FMCAD (2015)

19. Li, J., Zhu, S., Zhang, Y., Pu, G., Vardi, M.Y.: Safety model checking with complementary approximations. In: ICCAD (2017)
20. Marques-Silva, J., Lynce, I.: On improving MUS extraction algorithms. In: Sakallah, K.A., Simon, L. (eds.) SAT 2011. LNCS, vol. 6695, pp. 159–173. Springer, Heidelberg (2011). https://doi.org/10.1007/978-3-642-21581-0_14
21. McMillan, K.L.: Interpolation and SAT-based model checking. In: Hunt, W.A., Somenzi, F. (eds.) CAV 2003. LNCS, vol. 2725, pp. 1–13. Springer, Heidelberg (2003). https://doi.org/10.1007/978-3-540-45069-6_1
22. Vizel, Y., Gurfinkel, A.: Interpolating property directed reachability. In: Biere, A., Bloem, R. (eds.) CAV 2014. LNCS, vol. 8559, pp. 260–276. Springer, Cham (2014). https://doi.org/10.1007/978-3-319-08867-9_17
23. Yu, Y., Subramanyan, P., Tsiskaridze, N., Malik, S.: All-SAT using minimal blocking clauses. In: VLSID (2014)

StringFuzz: A Fuzzer for String Solvers

Dmitry Blotsky[1]([⊠]), Federico Mora[2], Murphy Berzish[1], Yunhui Zheng[3], Ifaz Kabir[1], and Vijay Ganesh[1]

[1] University of Waterloo, Waterloo, Canada
{dblotsky,vganesh}@uwaterloo.ca
[2] University of Toronto, Toronto, Canada
fmora@cs.toronto.edu
[3] IBM T.J. Watson Research Center,
Yorktown Heights, USA

Abstract. In this paper, we introduce StringFuzz: a modular SMT-LIB problem instance transformer and generator for string solvers. We supply a repository of instances generated by StringFuzz in SMT-LIB 2.0/2.5 format. We systematically compare Z3str3, CVC4, Z3str2, and Norn on groups of such instances, and identify those that are particularly challenging for some solvers. We briefly explain our observations and show how StringFuzz helped discover causes of performance degradations in Z3str3.

1 Introduction

In recent years, many algorithms for solving string constraints have been developed and implemented in SMT solvers such as Norn [6], CVC4 [12], and Z3 (e.g., Z3str2 [13] and Z3str3 [7]). To validate and benchmark these solvers, their developers have relied on hand-crafted input suites [1,4,5] or real-world examples from a limited set of industrial applications [2,11]. These test suites have helped developers identify implementation defects and develop more sophisticated solving heuristics. Unfortunately, as more features are added to solvers, these benchmarks often remain stagnant, leaving increasing functionality untested. As such, there is an acute need for a more robust, inexpensive, and automatic way of generating benchmarks to test the correctness and performance of SMT solvers.

Fuzzing has been used to test all kinds of software including SAT solvers [10]. Inspired by the utility of fuzzers, we introduce StringFuzz and describe its value as an exploratory testing tool. We demonstrate its efficacy by presenting limitations it helped discover in leading string solvers. To the best of our knowledge, StringFuzz is the only tool aimed at automatic generation of string constraints. StringFuzz can be used to mutate or transform existing benchmarks, as well as randomly generate structured instances. These instances can be scaled with respect to a variety of parameters, e.g., length of string constants, depth of concatenations (concats) and regular expressions (regexes), number of variables, number of length constraints, and many more.

© The Author(s) 2018
H. Chockler and G. Weissenbacher (Eds.): CAV 2018, LNCS 10982, pp. 45–51, 2018.
https://doi.org/10.1007/978-3-319-96142-2_6

Contributions

1. [1] **The StringFuzz tool:** In Sect. 2, we describe a modular fuzzer that can transform and generate SMT-LIB 2.0/2.5 string and regex instances. Scaling inputs (e.g., long string constants, deep concatenations) are particularly useful in identifying asymptotic behaviors in solvers, and StringFuzz has many options to generate them. We briefly document StringFuzz's components and modular architecture. We provide example use cases to demonstrate its utility as an exploratory solver testing tool.
2. **A repository of SMT-LIB 2.0/2.5 instances:** We present a repository of SMT-LIB 2.0/2.5 string and regex instance suites that we generated using StringFuzz in Sect. 3. This repository consists of two categories: one with new instances generated by StringFuzz (`generated`); and another with transformed instances generated from a small suite of industrial benchmarks (`transformed`).
3. **Experimental Results and Analysis:** We compare the performance of Z3str3, CVC4, Z3str2, and Norn on the StringFuzz suites *Concats-Balanced*, *Concats-Big*, *Concats-Extracts-Small*, and *Different-Prefix* in Sect. 4. We highlight these suites because they make some solvers perform poorly, but not others. We analyze our experimental results, and pinpoint algorithmic limitations in Z3str3 that cause poor performance.

2   StringFuzz

Implementation and Architecture. StringFuzz is implemented as a Python package, and comes with several executables to generate, transform, and analyze SMT-LIB 2.0/2.5 string and regex instances. Its components are implemented as UNIX "filters" to enable easy integration with other tools (including themselves). For example, the outputs of generators can be piped into transformers, and transformers can be chained to produce a stream of tuned inputs to a solver. StringFuzz is composed of the following tools:

`stringfuzzg`
    This tool generates SMT-LIB instances. It supports several generators and options that specify its output. Details can be found in Table 1a.
`stringfuzzx`
    This tool transforms SMT-LIB instances. It supports several transformers and options that specify its output and input, which are explained in Table 1b. Note that transformers *Translate* and *Reverse* also preserve satisfiability under certain conditions.
`stringstats`
    This tool takes an SMT-LIB instance as input and outputs its properties: the number of variables/literals, the max/median syntactic depth of expressions, the max/median literal length, etc.

---

[1] All source code, problem suites, and supplementary material referenced in this paper are available at the StringFuzz website [3].

Table 1. StringFuzz built-in (a) generators and (b) transformers.

(a) `stringfuzzg` built-in generators.

Name	Generates instances that have ...
Concats	Long concats and optional random extracts.
Lengths	Many variables (and their concats) with length constraints.
Overlaps	An expression of the form A.X = X.B.
Equality	An equality among concats, each with variables or constants.
Regex	Regexes of varying complexity.
Random-Text	Totally random ASCII text.
Random-AST	Random string and regex constraints.

(b) `stringfuzzx` built-in transformers.

Name	The transformer ...
Fuzz	Replaces literals and operators with similar ones.
Graft	Randomly swaps non-leaf nodes with leaf nodes.
Multiply[a]	Multiplies integers and repeats strings by N.
Nop	Does nothing (can translate between SMT-LIB 2.0/2.5).
Reverse[b]	Reverses all string literals and concat arguments.
Rotate	Rotates compatible nodes in syntax tree.
Translate[b]	Permutes the alphabet.
Unprintable	Replaces characters in literals with unprintable ones.

[a]Can guarantee satisfiable output instances from satisfiable input instances [3].
[b]Can guarantee input and output instances will be equisatisfiable [3].

We organized StringFuzz to be easily extended. To show this, we note that while the whole project contains 3,183 lines of code, it takes an average of 45 lines of code to create a transformer. StringFuzz can be installed from source, or from the Python PIP package repository.

Regex Generating Capabilities. StringFuzz can generate and transform instances with regex constraints. For example, the command "`stringfuzzg regex -r 2 -d 1 -t 1 -M 3 -X 10`" produces this instance:

```
(set-logic QF_S)
(declare-fun var0 () String)
(assert (str.in.re var0 (re.+ (str.to.re "R5"))))
(assert (str.in.re var0 (re.+ (str.to.re "!PC"))))
(assert (<= 3 (str.len var0)))
(assert (<= (str.len var0) 10))
(check-sat)
```

Each instance is a set of one or more regex constraints on a single variable, with optional maximum and minimum length constraints. Each regex constraint is a concatenation (`re.++` in SMT-LIB string syntax) of regex terms:

```
(re.++ T1 (re.++ T2 ... (re.++ Tn-1 Tn )))
```

and each term `Ti` is recursively defined as any one of: repetition (`re.*`), Kleene star (`re.+`), union (`re.union`), or a character literal. Nested operators are nested up to a specified (using the `--depth` flag) depth of recursion. Terms at depth 0 are regex constants. Below are 3 example regexes (in regex, not SMT-LIB, syntax) of depth 2 that can be produced this way:

$$((a|b)|(cc)+) \qquad ((ddd)*)+ \qquad ((ee)+|(fff)*)$$

Equisatisfiable String Transformations. StringFuzz can also transform problem instances. This is done by manipulating parsed syntax trees. By default most of the built-in transformers only guarantee well-formedness, however, some can even guarantee equisatisfiability. Table 1b lists the built-in transformers and notes these guarantees.

Example Use Case. In Sect. 3 we use StringFuzz to generate benchmark suites in a batch mode. We can also use StringFuzz for on-line exploratory debugging. For example, the script below repeatedly feeds random StringFuzz instances to CVC4 until the solver produces an error:

```
while stringfuzzg -r random-ast -m \
    | tee instance.smt25 | cvc4 --lang smt2.5 --tlimit=5000 --strings-exp; do
    sleep 0
done
```

3   Instance Suites

In this section, we describe the benchmark suites we generated with String-Fuzz, and on which we conducted our experimental evaluation. Table 2a lists instances that were generated by `stringfuzzg`. Table 2b lists instances derived from existing seed instances by iteratively applying `stringfuzzx`. Every transformed instance is named according to its seed and the transformations it undertook. For example, `z3-regex-1-fuzz-graft.smt2` was transformed by applying *Fuzz* and then *Graft* to `z3-regex-1.smt2`.

The *Amazon* category contains 472 instances derived from two seeds supplied by our industrial collaborators. The *Regex* category is seeded by the Z3str2 regex test suite [4], which contains 42 instances. Through cumulative transformations we expanded the 42 seeds to 7,551 unique instances. Finally, the *Sanitizer* category is obtained from five industrial e-mail address and IPv4 sanitizers.

4   Experimental Results and Analysis

We generated several problem instance suites with StringFuzz that made one solver perform poorly, but not others.[2] They are *Concats-Balanced*, *Concats-Big*, *Concats-Extracts-Small*, and *Different-Prefix*. Figure 1 shows the suites that

---

[2] Only the results that made one solver perform poorly and not others are presented, but results for all StringFuzz suites are available on the StringFuzz website [3].

Table 2. Repository of 10,258 SMT-LIB 2.0/2.5 instances.

(a) `stringfuzzg`-generated instances.

Name	Instances have a ...	Quantity
Concats-{Small,Big}	Right-heavy, deep tree of concats.	120
Concats-Balanced	Balanced, deep tree of concats.	100
Concats-Extracts-{Small,Big}	Single concat tree, with character extractions.	120
Lengths-{Long,Short}	Single, large length constraint on a variable.	200
Lengths-Concats	Tree of fixed-length concats of variables.	100
Overlaps-{Small,Big}	Formula of the form A.X = X.B.	80
Regex-{Small,Big}	Complex regex membership test.	120
Many-Regexes	Multiple random regex membership tests.	40
Regex-Deep	Regex membership test with many nested operators.	45
Regex-Pair	Test for membership in one regex, but not another.	40
Regex-Lengths	Regex membership test, and a length constraint.	40
Different-Prefix	Equality of two deep concats with different prefixes.	60

(b) `stringfuzzx`-generated instances.

Name	Seed	Quantity
Amazon	Two industrial regex membership instances.	472
Regex	Z3str2 regular expression test suite.	7,551
Sanitizer	Five e-mail and IPv4 sanitiser examples.	1,170

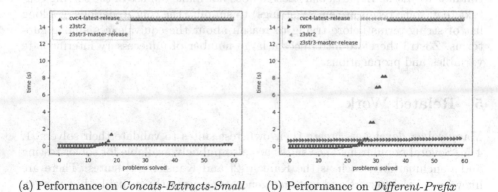

(a) Performance on *Concats-Extracts-Small*   (b) Performance on *Different-Prefix*

Fig. 1. Instances hard for CVC4

were uniquely difficult for CVC4. Figure 2 shows the suites that were uniquely difficult for Z3str3. All experiments were conducted in series, each with a timeout of 15 s, on an Ubuntu Linux 16.04 computer with 32 GB of RAM and an Intel® Core™ i7-6700 CPU (3.40 GHz).

Usefulness to Z3str3: A Case Study. StringFuzz's ability to produce scaling instances helped uncover several implementation issues and performance limitations in Z3str3. Scaling inputs can reveal issues that would normally be out of scope for unit tests or industrial benchmarks. Three different performance and

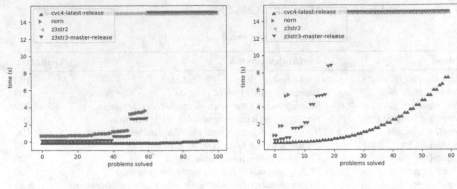

(a) Performance on *Concats-Balanced*   (b) Performance on *Concats-Big*

Fig. 2. Instances hard for Z3str3

implementation bugs were identified and fixed in Z3str3 as a result of testing with the StringFuzz scaling suites *Lengths-Long* and *Concats-Big*.

StringFuzz also helped identify a number of performance-related issues and opportunities for new heuristics in Z3str3. For example, by examining Z3str3's execution traces on the instances in the *Concats-Big* suite we discovered a potential new heuristic. In particular, Z3str3 does not make full use of the solving context (e.g. some terms are empty strings) to simplify the concatenations of a long list of string terms before trying to reason about the equivalences among subterms. Z3str3 therefore introduces a large number of unnecessary intermediate variables and propagations.

5   Related Work

Many solver developers create their own test suites to validate their solvers [1, 4,5]. Several popular instance suites are also publicly available for solver testing and benchmarking, such as the Kaluza [2] and Kausler [11] suites. There are likewise several fuzzers and instance generators currently available, but none of them can generate or transform string and regex instances. For example, the FuzzSMT [9] tool generates SMT-LIB instances with bit-vectors and arrays, but does not support strings or regexes. The SMTpp [8] tool pre-processes and simplifies instances, but does not generate new ones or fuzz existing ones.

References

1. CVC4 regression test suite. https://github.com/CVC4/CVC4/tree/master/test/regress
2. Kaluza benchmark suite. http://webblaze.cs.berkeley.edu/2010/kaluza/
3. Stringfuzz source code, benchmark suites, and supplemental material. http://stringfuzz.dmitryblotsky.com

4. Z3str2 test suite. https://github.com/z3str/Z3-str/tree/master/tests
5. Z3str3 test scripts. https://github.com/Z3Prover/z3/tree/master/src/test
6. Abdulla, P.A., et al.: Norn: an SMT solver for string constraints. In: Kroening, D., Păsăreanu, C.S. (eds.) CAV 2015. LNCS, vol. 9206, pp. 462–469. Springer, Cham (2015). https://doi.org/10.1007/978-3-319-21690-4_29
7. Berzish, M., Ganesh, V., Zheng, Y.: Z3str3: a string solver with theory-aware heuristics. In: Stewart, D., Weissenbacher, G., (eds.), 2017 Formal Methods in Computer Aided Design, FMCAD 2017, Vienna, Austria, 2–6 October 2017, pp. 55–59. IEEE (2017)
8. Bonichon, R., Déharbe, D., Dobal, P., Tavares, C.: SMTpp: preprocessors and analyzers for SMT-LIB. In: Proceedings of the 13th International Workshop on Satisfiability Modulo Theories, SMT 2015 (2015)
9. Brummayer, R., Biere, A.: Fuzzing and delta-debugging SMT solvers. In: Proceedings of the 7th International Workshop on Satisfiability Modulo Theories, SMT 2009, pp. 1–5. ACM, New York, NY, USA (2009)
10. Brummayer, R., Lonsing, F., Biere, A.: Automated testing and debugging of SAT and QBF solvers. In: Strichman, O., Szeider, S. (eds.) SAT 2010. LNCS, vol. 6175, pp. 44–57. Springer, Heidelberg (2010). https://doi.org/10.1007/978-3-642-14186-7_6
11. Kausler, S., Sherman, E.: Evaluation of string constraint solvers in the context of symbolic execution. In: Proceedings of the 29th ACM/IEEE International Conference on Automated Software Engineering, ASE 2014, pp. 259–270. ACM, New York, NY, USA (2014)
12. Liang, T., Reynolds, A., Tinelli, C., Barrett, C., Deters, M.: A DPLL(T) theory solver for a theory of strings and regular expressions. In: Biere, A., Bloem, R. (eds.) CAV 2014. LNCS, vol. 8559, pp. 646–662. Springer, Cham (2014). https://doi.org/10.1007/978-3-319-08867-9_43
13. Zheng, Y., Zhang, X., Ganesh, V.: Z3-str: a Z3-based string solver for web application analysis. In: Meyer, B., Baresi, L., Mezini, M., (eds.) Joint Meeting of the European Software Engineering Conference and the ACM SIGSOFT Symposium on the Foundations of Software Engineering, ESEC/FSE 2013, Saint Petersburg, Russian Federation, 18–26 August 2013, pp. 114–124. ACM (2013)

Static Analysis

Permission Inference for Array Programs

Jérôme Dohrau[(⊠)], Alexander J. Summers, Caterina Urban,
Severin Münger, and Peter Müller

Department of Computer Science, ETH Zurich,
Zurich, Switzerland
{jerome.dohrau,alexander.summers,
caterina.urban,peter.mueller}@inf.ethz.ch,
severin.muenger@alumni.ethz.ch

Abstract. Information about the memory locations accessed by a program is, for instance, required for program parallelisation and program verification. Existing inference techniques for this information provide only partial solutions for the important class of array-manipulating programs. In this paper, we present a static analysis that infers the memory footprint of an array program in terms of permission pre- and postconditions as used, for example, in separation logic. This formulation allows our analysis to handle concurrent programs and produces specifications that can be used by verification tools. Our analysis expresses the permissions required by a loop via maximum expressions over the individual loop iterations. These maximum expressions are then solved by a novel maximum elimination algorithm, in the spirit of quantifier elimination. Our approach is sound and is implemented; an evaluation on existing benchmarks for memory safety of array programs demonstrates accurate results, even for programs with complex access patterns and nested loops.

1 Introduction

Information about the memory locations accessed by a program is crucial for many applications such as static data race detection [45], code optimisation [16,26,33], program parallelisation [5,17], and program verification [23,30,38,39]. The problem of inferring this information statically has been addressed by a variety of static analyses, e.g., [9,42]. However, prior works provide only partial solutions for the important class of array-manipulating programs for at least one of the following reasons. (1) They approximate the entire array as one single memory location [4] which leads to imprecise results; (2) they do not produce specifications, which are useful for several important applications such as human inspection, test case generation, and especially deductive program verification; (3) they are limited to sequential programs.

In this paper, we present a novel analysis for array programs that addresses these shortcomings. Our analysis employs the notion of *access permission* from separation logic and similar program logics [40,43]. These logics associate a permission with each memory location and enforce that a program part accesses a

H. Chockler and G. Weissenbacher (Eds.): CAV 2018, LNCS 10982, pp. 55–74, 2018.
https://doi.org/10.1007/978-3-319-96142-2_7

location only if it holds the associated permission. In this setting, determining the accessed locations means to infer a sufficient precondition that specifies the permissions required by a program part.

Phrasing the problem as one of permission inference allows us to address the three problems mentioned above. (1) We distinguish different array elements by tracking the permission for each element separately. (2) Our analysis infers pre- and postconditions for both methods and loops and emits them in a form that can be used by verification tools. The inferred specifications can easily be complemented with permission specifications for non-array data structures and with functional specifications. (3) We support concurrency in three important ways. First, our analysis is sound for concurrent program executions because permissions guarantee that program executions are data race free and reduce thread interactions to specific points in the program such as forking or joining a thread, or acquiring or releasing a lock. Second, we develop our analysis for a programming language with primitives that represent the ownership transfer that happens at these thread interaction points. These primitives, `inhale` and `exhale` [31,38], express that a thread obtains permissions (for instance, by acquiring a lock) or loses permissions (for instance, by passing them to another thread along with a message) and can thereby represent a wide range of thread interactions in a uniform way [32,44]. Third, our analysis distinguishes read and write access and, thus, ensures exclusive writes while permitting concurrent read accesses. As is standard, we employ *fractional permissions* [6] for this purpose; a full permission is required to write to a location, but any positive fraction permits read access.

Approach. Our analysis reduces the problem of reasoning about permissions for array elements to reasoning about numerical values for permission fractions. To achieve this, we represent permission fractions for all array elements $q_a[q_i]$ using a *single* numerical expression $t(q_a, q_i)$ parameterised by q_a and q_i. For instance, the conditional term $(q_a=\text{a} \wedge q_i=\text{j} ? 1 : 0)$ represents full permission (denoted by 1) for array element a[j] and no permission for all other array elements.

Our analysis employs a *precise* backwards analysis for *loop-free* code: a variation on the standard notion of weakest preconditions. We apply this analysis to loop bodies to obtain a permission precondition for a single loop iteration. Per array element, the *whole loop* requires the *maximum* fraction over all loop iterations, adjusted by permissions gained and lost during loop execution. Rather than computing permissions via a fixpoint iteration (for which a precise widening operator is difficult to design), we express them as a maximum over the variables changed by the loop execution. We then use inferred numerical invariants on these variables and a novel *maximum elimination* algorithm to infer a specification for the entire loop. Permission postconditions are obtained analogously.

For the method copyEven in Fig. 1, the analysis determines that the permission amount required by a single loop iteration is $(\text{j}\%2=0?(q_a=\text{a} \wedge q_i=\text{j}?\text{rd}:0):(q_a=\text{a} \wedge q_i=\text{j} ? 1 : 0))$. The symbol rd represents a fractional read permission. Using a suitable integer invariant for the loop counter j, we obtain the loop precondition

```
method copyEven(a: Int[]) {
  var j, v: Int := 0;
  while(j < length(a)) {
    if (j % 2 == 0) { v := a[j] }
    else { a[j] := v };
    j := j + 1
  }
}
```

```
method parCopyEven(a: Int[]) {
  var j: Int := 0;
  while(j < length(a)/2) {
    exhale(a, 2*j, 1/2);
    exhale(a, 2*j+1, 1);
    j := j + 1
  }
}
```

Fig. 1. Program copyEven.

Fig. 2. Program parCopyEven.

$$e ::= n \mid x \mid n{\cdot}x \mid e_1 + e_2 \mid e_1 - e_2 \mid a[e] \mid \text{len}(a) \mid (b\,?\,e_1 : e_2)$$
$$b ::= e_1\,op\,e_2 \mid e\%n{=}0 \mid e\%n{\neq}0 \mid b_1 \wedge b_2 \mid b_1 \vee b_2 \mid \neg b$$
$$op \in \{=, \neq, <, \leq, >, \geq\}$$
$$p ::= q \mid \text{rd} \mid p_1 + p_2 \mid p_1 - p_2 \mid \min(p_1, p_2) \mid \max(p_1, p_2) \mid (b\,?\,p_1 : p_2)$$
$$s ::= \text{skip} \mid x{:=}e \mid a_1{:=}a_2 \mid x{:=}a[e] \mid a[e_1]{:=}e_2 \mid \text{exhale}(a,e,p) \mid \text{inhale}(a,e,p)$$
$$\mid\ (s_1; s_2) \mid \text{if}(b)\ \{\ s_1\ \}\ \text{else}\ \{\ s_2\ \} \mid \text{while}\ (b)\ \{\ s\ \}$$

Fig. 3. Programming Language. n ranges over integer constants, x over integer variables, a over array variables, q over non-negative fractional (permission-typed) constants. e stands for integer expressions, and b for boolean. Permission expressions p are a separate syntactic category.

$\max_{j\mid 0 \leq j < \text{len}(a)} ((j\%2{=}0\,?\,(q_a{=}a \wedge q_i{=}j\,?\,\text{rd} : 0) : (q_a{=}a \wedge q_i{=}j\,?\,1 : 0)))$. Our maximum elimination algorithm obtains $(q_a{=}a \wedge 0 \leq q_i < \text{len}(a)\,?\,(q_i\%2{=}0\,?\,\text{rd} : 1) : 0)$. By ranging over all q_a and q_i, this can be read as read permission for even indices and write permission for odd indices within the array a's bounds.

Contributions. The contributions of our paper are:

1. A novel permission inference that uses maximum expressions over parameterised arithmetic expressions to summarise loops (Sects. 3 and 4)
2. An algorithm for eliminating maximum (and minimum) expressions over an unbounded number of cases (Sect. 5)
3. An implementation of our analysis, which will be made available as an artifact
4. An evaluation on benchmark examples from existing papers and competitions, demonstrating that we obtain sound, precise, and compact specifications, even for challenging array access patterns and parallel loops (Sect. 6)
5. Proof sketches for the soundness of our permission inference and correctness of our maximum elimination algorithm (in the technical report (TR) [15])

2 Programming Language

We define our inference technique over the programming language in Fig. 3. Programs operate on integers (expressions e), booleans (expressions b), and one-dimensional integer arrays (variables a); a generalisation to other forms of arrays is straightforward and supported by our implementation. Arrays are read and updated via the statements $x := a[e]$ and $a[e] := x$; array lookups in expressions are not part of the surface syntax, but are used internally by our analysis. Permission expressions p evaluate to rational numbers; rd, min, and max are for internal use.

A full-fledged programming language contains many statements that affect the ownership of memory locations, expressed via permissions [32,44]. For example in a concurrent setting, a fork operation may transfer permissions to the new thread, acquiring a lock obtains permission to access certain memory locations, and messages may transfer permissions between sender and receiver. Even in a sequential setting, the concept is useful: in procedure-modular reasoning, a method call transfers permissions from the caller to the callee, and back when the callee terminates. Allocation can be represented as obtaining a fresh object and then obtaining permission to its locations.

For the purpose of our permission inference, we can reduce all of these operations to two basic statements that directly manipulate the permissions currently held [31,38]. An $\mathtt{inhale}(a, e, p)$ statement adds the amount p of permission for the array location $a[e]$ to the currently held permissions. Dually, an $\mathtt{exhale}(a, e, p)$ statement requires that this amount of permission is *already* held, and then removes it. We assume that for any $\mathtt{inhale}$ or $\mathtt{exhale}$ statements, the permission expression p denotes a non-negative fraction. For simplicity, we restrict $\mathtt{inhale}$ and $\mathtt{exhale}$ statements to a *single* array location, but the extension to unboundedly-many locations from the same array is straightforward [37].

Semantics. The operational semantics of our language is mostly standard, but is instrumented with additional state to track how much permission is held to each heap location; a program state therefore consists of a triple of heap H (mapping pairs of array identifier and integer index to integer values), a *permission map* P, mapping such pairs to *permission amounts*, and an environment σ mapping variables to values (integers or array identifiers).

The execution of $\mathtt{inhale}$ or $\mathtt{exhale}$ statements causes modifications to the permission map, and all array accesses are guarded with checks that *at least some* permission is held when reading and that full (1) permission is held when writing [6]. If these checks (or an $\mathtt{exhale}$ statement) fail, the execution terminates with a *permission failure*. Permission amounts greater than 1 indicate invalid states that cannot be reached by a program execution. We model run-time errors other than permission failures (in particular, out-of-bounds accesses) as stuck configurations.

3   Permission Inference for Loop-Free Code

Our analysis infers a sufficient permission precondition and a guaranteed permission postcondition for each method of a program. Both conditions are mappings from array elements to permission amounts. Executing a statement s in a state

$$pre(\textbf{skip}, p) = p \qquad pre((s_1; s_2), p) = pre(s_1, pre(s_2, p))$$
$$pre(x{:=}e, p) = p[e/x] \qquad pre(x{:=}a[e], p) = \max(p[a[e]/x], \alpha_{a,e}(\textsf{rd}))$$
$$pre(a[e]{:=}x, p) = \max(p[a'[e'] \mapsto (e = e' \wedge a = a' \; ? \; x : a'[e'])], \alpha_{a,e}(1))$$
$$pre(\textbf{exhale}(a, e, p'), p) = p + \alpha_{a,e}(p') \qquad pre(\textbf{inhale}(a, e, p'), p) = \max(0, p - \alpha_{a,e}(p'))$$
$$pre(\textbf{if}(b) \; \{ \; s_1 \; \} \; \textbf{else} \; \{ \; s_2 \; \}, p) = (b \, ? \, pre(s_1, p) : pre(s_2, p))$$

$$\Delta(\textbf{skip}, p) = p \qquad \Delta((s_1; s_2), p) = \Delta(s_1, \Delta(s_2, p))$$
$$\Delta(x{:=}e, p) = p[e/x] \qquad \Delta(x{:=}a[e], p) = p[a[e]/x]$$
$$\Delta(a[e]{:=}x, p) = p[a'[e'] \mapsto (e = e' \wedge a = a' \; ? \; x : a'[e'])]$$
$$\Delta(\textbf{exhale}(a, e, p'), p) = p - \alpha_{a,e}(p') \qquad \Delta(\textbf{inhale}(a, e, p'), p) = p + \alpha_{a,e}(p')$$
$$\Delta(\textbf{if}(b) \; \{ \; s_1 \; \} \; \textbf{else} \; \{ \; s_2 \; \}, p) = (b \, ? \, \Delta(s_1, p) : \Delta(s_2, p))$$

Fig. 4. The backwards analysis rules for permission preconditions and relative permission differences. The notation $\alpha_{a,e}(p)$ is a shorthand for $(q_a{=}a \wedge q_i{=}e \, ? \, p : 0)$ and denotes p permission for the array location $a[e]$. Moreover, $p[a'[e'] \mapsto e]$ matches all array accesses in p and replaces them with the expression obtained from e by substituting all occurrences of a' and e' with the matched array and index, respectively. The cases for inhale statements are slightly simplified; the full rules are given in Fig. 6 of the TR [15].

whose permission map P contains at least the permissions required by a *sufficient permission precondition* for s is guaranteed to not result in a permission failure. A *guaranteed permission postcondition* expresses the permissions that will at least be held when s terminates (see Sect. A of the TR [15] for formal definitions).

In this section, we define inference rules to compute sufficient permission preconditions for loop-free code. For programs which do not add or remove permissions via inhale and exhale statements, the same permissions will still be held after executing the code; however, to infer guaranteed permission postconditions in the general case, we also infer the difference in permissions between the state before and after the execution. We will discuss loops in the next section. Non-recursive method calls can be handled by applying our analysis bottom-up in the call graph and using inhale and exhale statements to model the permission effect of calls. Recursion can be handled similarly to loops, but is omitted here.

We define our permission analysis to track and generate *permission expressions* parameterised by two distinguished variables q_a and q_i; by parameterising our expressions in this way, we can use a single expression to represent a permission amount for each pair of q_a and q_i values.

Preconditions. The *permission precondition* of a loop-free statement s and a postcondition permission p (in which q_a and q_i potentially occur) is denoted by $pre(s, p)$, and is defined in Fig. 4. Most rules are straightforward adaptations of a classical weakest-precondition computation. Array lookups require some permission to the accessed array location; we use the internal expression rd to denote a non-zero permission amount; a post-processing step can later replace rd by a concrete rational. Since downstream code may require further permission for this location, represented by the permission expression p, we take the maximum of both amounts. Array updates require full permission and need to take aliasing into account. The case for `inhale` subtracts the inhaled permission amount from the permissions required by downstream code; the case for `exhale` adds the permissions to be exhaled. Note that this addition may lead to a required permission amount exceeding the full permission. This indicates that the statement is not feasible, that is, all executions will lead to a permission failure.

To illustrate our *pre* definition, let s be the body of the loop in the `parCopyEven` method in Fig. 2. The precondition $pre(s,0) = (q_a\texttt{=a} \land q_i\texttt{=2*j} ? 1/2 : 0) + (q_a\texttt{=a} \land q_i\texttt{=2*j+1} ? 1 : 0)$ expresses that a loop iteration requires a half permission for the even elements of array `a` and full permission for the odd elements.

Postconditions. The final state of a method execution includes the permissions held in the method pre-state, adjusted by the permissions that are inhaled or exhaled during the method execution. To perform this adjustment, we compute the difference in permissions before and after executing a statement. The *relative permission difference* for a loop-free statement s and a permission expression p (in which q_a and q_i potentially occur) is denoted by $\Delta(s,p)$, and is defined backward, analogously to *pre* in Fig. 4. The second parameter p acts as an accumulator; the difference in permission is represented by evaluating $\Delta(s,0)$.

For a statement s with precondition $pre(s,0)$, we obtain the postcondition $pre(s,0)+\Delta(s,0)$. Let s again be the loop body from `parCopyEven`. Since s contains `exhale` statements, we obtain $\Delta(s,0) = 0 - (q_a\texttt{=a} \land q_i\texttt{=2*j} ? 1/2 : 0) - (q_a\texttt{=a} \land q_i\texttt{=2*j+1}?1:0)$. Thus, the postcondition $pre(s,0) + \Delta(s,0)$ can be simplified to 0. This reflects the fact that all required permissions for a single loop iteration are lost by the end of its execution.

Since our Δ operator performs a backward analysis, our permission postconditions are expressed in terms of the pre-state of the execution of s. To obtain classical postconditions, any heap accesses need to refer to the pre-state heap, which can be achieved in program logics by using `old` expressions or logical variables. Formalizing the postcondition inference as a backward analysis simplifies our treatment of loops and has technical advantages over classical strongest-postconditions, which introduce existential quantifiers for assignment statements. A limitation of our approach is that our postconditions cannot capture situations in which a statement obtains permissions to locations for which no pre-state expression exists, e.g. allocation of new arrays. Our postconditions are sound; to make them precise for such cases, our inference needs to be combined with an additional forward analysis, which we leave as future work.

4   Handling Loops via Maximum Expressions

In this section, we first focus on obtaining a sufficient permission precondition for the execution of a loop in isolation (independently of the code after it) and then combine the inference for loops with the one for loop-free code described above.

4.1   Sufficient Permission Preconditions for Loops

A sufficient permission precondition for a loop guarantees the absence of permission failures for a potentially unbounded number of executions of the loop body. This concept is different from a loop invariant: we require a precondition for all executions of a particular loop, but it need not be inductive. Our technique obtains such a loop precondition by projecting a permission precondition for a single loop iteration over all possible initial states for the loop executions.

Exhale-Free Loop Bodies. We consider first the simpler (but common) case of a loop that does not contain `exhale` statements, e.g., does not transfer permissions to a forked thread. The solution for this case is also sound for loop bodies where each `exhale` is followed by an `inhale` for the same array location and at least the same permission amount, as in the encoding of most method calls.

Consider a sufficient permission precondition p for the body of a loop `while (b) { s }`. By definition, p will denote sufficient permissions to execute s once; the precise locations to which p requires permission depend on the initial state of the loop iteration. For example, the sufficient permission precondition for the body of the `copyEven` method in Fig. 1, $(j\%2=0?(q_a=\mathsf{a}\wedge q_i=j?\mathsf{rd}:0):(q_a=\mathsf{a}\wedge q_i=j?1:0))$, requires permissions to different array locations, depending on the value of j. To obtain a sufficient permission precondition for the entire loop, we leverage an *over-approximating* loop invariant $\mathcal{I}^+$ from an off-the-shelf numerical analysis (e.g., [13]) to over-approximate all possible values of the numerical variables that get assigned in the loop body, here, j. We can then express the loop precondition using the *pointwise maximum* $\max_{j|\mathcal{I}^+\wedge b}(p)$, over the values of j that satisfy the condition $\mathcal{I}^+\wedge b$. (The maximum over an empty range is defined to be 0.) For the `copyEven` method, given the invariant $0\leq j\leq \mathtt{len}(\mathsf{a})$, the loop precondition is $\max_{j|0\leq j<\mathtt{len}(\mathsf{a})}(p)$.

In general, a permission precondition for a loop body may also depend on array *values*, e.g., if those values are used in branch conditions. To avoid the need for an expensive array value analysis, we define both an over- and an under-approximation of permission expressions, denoted $p^\uparrow$ and $p^\downarrow$ (cf. Sect. A.1 of the TR [15]), with the guarantees that $p\leq p^\uparrow$ and $p^\downarrow\leq p$. These approximations abstract away array-dependent conditions, and have an impact on precision only when array values are used to determine a location to be accessed. For example, a linear array search for a particular value accesses the array only up to the (a-priori unknown) point at which the value is found, but our permission precondition conservatively requires access to the full array.

Theorem 1. *Let* `while (b) { s }` *be an exhale-free loop, let $\overline{x}$ be the integer variables modified by s, and let $\mathcal{I}^+$ be a sound over-approximating numerical loop invariant (over the integer variables in s). Then $\max_{\overline{x}|\mathcal{I}^+\wedge b}(pre(s,0)^\uparrow)$ is a sufficient permission precondition for* `while (b) { s }`.

Loops with Exhale Statements. For loops that contain `exhale` statements, the approach described above does not always guarantee a sufficient permission precondition. For example, if a loop gives away full permission to the *same* array location in every iteration, our pointwise maximum construction yields a precondition requiring the full permission once, as opposed to the *unsatisfiable* precondition (since the loop is guaranteed to cause a permission failure).

As explained above, our inference is sound if each `exhale` statement is followed by a corresponding `inhale`, which can often be checked syntactically. In the following, we present another decidable condition that guarantees soundness and that can be checked efficiently by an SMT solver. If neither condition holds, we preserve soundness by inferring an unsatisfiable precondition; we did not encounter any such examples in our evaluation.

Our soundness condition checks that the maximum of the permissions required by two loop iterations is not less than the permissions required by executing the two iterations in sequence. Intuitively, that is the case when neither iteration removes permissions that are required by the other iteration.

Theorem 2 (Soundness Condition for Loop Preconditions). *Given a loop* `while` (b) $\{\ s\ \}$, *let* $\overline{x}$ *be the integer variables modified in* s *and let* $\overline{v}$ *and* $\overline{v'}$ *be two fresh sets of variables, one for each of* $\overline{x}$. *Then* $\max_{\overline{x}|\mathcal{I}^+ \wedge b} (pre(s,0)^\uparrow)$ *is a sufficient permission precondition for* `while` (b) $\{\ s\ \}$ *if the following implication is valid in all states:*

$$(\mathcal{I}^+ \wedge b)\overline{[v/x]} \wedge (\mathcal{I}^+ \wedge b)\overline{[v'/x]} \wedge (\bigvee \overline{v \neq v'}) \Rightarrow$$
$$\max(pre(s,0)^\uparrow\overline{[v/x]}, pre(s,0)^\uparrow\overline{[v'/x]}) \geq pre(s, pre(s,0)^\uparrow\overline{[v'/x]})^\uparrow\overline{[v/x]}$$

The additional variables $\overline{v}$ and $\overline{v'}$ are used to model two arbitrary valuations of $\overline{x}$; we constrain these to represent two initial states allowed by $\mathcal{I}^+ \wedge b$ and different from each other for at least one program variable. We then require that the effect of analysing each loop iteration independently and taking the maximum is not smaller than the effect of sequentially composing the two loop iterations.

The theorem requires implicitly that no two different iterations of a loop observe exactly the same values for all integer variables. If that could be the case, the condition $\bigvee \overline{v \neq v'}$ would cause us to ignore a potential pair of initial states for two different loop iterations. To avoid this problem, we assume that all loops satisfy this requirement; it can easily be enforced by adding an additional variable as loop iteration counter [21].

For the `parCopyEven` method (Fig. 2), the soundness condition holds since, due to the $v \neq v'$ condition, the two terms on the right of the implication are equal for all values of q_i. We can thus infer a sufficient precondition as $\max_{j|0 \leq j < \mathrm{len}(a)/2} ((q_a{=}\mathtt{a} \wedge q_i{=}2{*}\mathtt{j} \ ? \ 1/2 : 0) + (q_a{=}\mathtt{a} \wedge q_i{=}2{*}\mathtt{j}{+}1 \ ? \ 1 : 0))$.

4.2   Permission Inference for Loops

We can now extend the pre- and postcondition inference from Sect. 3 with loops. $pre(\texttt{while}\ (b)\ \{\ s\ \}, p)$ must require permissions such that (1) the loop executes without permission failure and (2) at least the permissions described by p are held when the loop terminates. While the former is provided by the loop precondition as defined in the previous subsection, the latter also depends on the permissions gained or lost during the execution of the loop. To characterise these permissions, we extend the Δ operator from Sect. 3 to handle loops.

Under the soundness condition from Theorem 2, we can mimic the approach from the previous subsection and use over-approximating invariants to project out the permissions *lost* in a single loop iteration (where $\Delta(s,0)$ is negative) to those lost by the entire loop, using a maximum expression. This projection conservatively assumes that the permissions lost in a single iteration are lost by all iterations whose initial state is allowed by the loop invariant and loop condition. This approach is a sound over-approximation of the permissions *lost*.

However, for the permissions *gained* by a loop iteration (where $\Delta(s,0)$ is positive), this approach would be unsound because the over-approximation includes iterations that may not actually happen and, thus, permissions that are not actually gained. For this reason, our technique handles gained permissions via an *under-approximate*[1] numerical loop invariant $\mathcal{I}^-$ (e.g., [35]) and thus projects the gained permissions only over iterations that will surely happen.

This approach is reflected in the definition of our Δ operator below via d, which represents the permissions *possibly lost* or *definitely gained* over all iterations of the loop. In the former case, we have $\Delta(s,0) < 0$ and, thus, the first summand is 0 and the computation based on the over-approximate invariant applies (note that the negated maximum of negated values is the minimum; we take the minimum over negative values). In the latter case ($\Delta(s,0) > 0$), the second summand is 0 and the computation based on the under-approximate invariant applies (we take the maximum over positive values).

$$\Delta(\texttt{while } (b) \ \{ \ s \ \}, p) = (b\,?\,d + p' : p), \ where:$$
$$d = \max_{\overline{x}|\mathcal{I}^- \wedge b} \max(0, \Delta(s,0))^{\downarrow} - \max_{\overline{x}|\mathcal{I}^+ \wedge b} \max(0, -\Delta(s,0))^{\uparrow}$$
$$p' = \max_{\overline{x}|\mathcal{I}^- \wedge \neg b} \max(0, p)^{\downarrow} - \max_{\overline{x}|\mathcal{I}^+ \wedge \neg b} \max(0, -p)^{\uparrow}$$

$\overline{x}$ denotes again the integer variables modified in s. The role of p' is to carry over the permissions p that are gained or lost by the code following the loop, taking into account any state changes performed by the loop. Intuitively, the maximum expressions replace the variables $\overline{x}$ in p with expressions that do not depend on these variables but nonetheless reflect properties of their values right after the execution of the loop. For permissions gained, these properties are based on the under-approximate loop invariant to ensure that they hold for any possible loop execution. For permissions lost, we use the over-approximate invariant. For the loop in parCopyEven we use the invariant $0 \leq j \leq \texttt{len}(a)/2$ to obtain $d = -\max_{j|0 \leq j < \texttt{len}(a)/2} ((q_a = a \wedge q_i = 2*j\,?\,1/2:0) + (q_a = a \wedge q_i = 2*j+1\,?\,1:0))$. Since there are no statements following the loop, p and therefore p' are 0.

Using the same d term, we can now define the general case of *pre* for loops, combining (1) the loop precondition and (2) the permissions required by the code after the loop, adjusted by the permissions gained or lost during loop execution:

---

[1] An under-approximate loop invariant must be true *only* for states that will actually be encountered when executing the loop.

$$pre(\texttt{while } (b) \ \{\ s\ \}, p) = (b \ ? \max(\max_{\overline{x}|\mathcal{I}^+ \wedge b} pre(s,0)^\uparrow, \max_{\overline{x}|\mathcal{I}^+ \wedge \neg b} (p^\uparrow) - d) : p)$$

Similarly to p' in the rule for Δ, the expression $\max_{\overline{x}|\mathcal{I}^+ \wedge \neg b} (p^\uparrow)$ conservatively over-approximates the permissions required to execute the code after the loop. For method parCopyEven, we obtain a sufficient precondition that is the negation of the Δ. Consequently, the postcondition is 0.

Soundness. Our *pre* and Δ definitions yield a sound method for computing sufficient permission preconditions and guaranteed postconditions:

Theorem 3 (Soundness of Permission Inference). *For any statement s, if every* while *loop in s either is exhale-free or satisfies the condition of Theorem 2 then pre(s, 0) is a sufficient permission precondition for s, and pre(s, 0) + Δ(s, 0) is a corresponding guaranteed permission postcondition.*

Our inference expresses pre and postconditions using a maximum operator over an unbounded set of values. However, this operator is not supported by SMT solvers. To be able to use the inferred conditions for SMT-based verification, we provide an algorithm for eliminating these operators, as we discuss next.

5 A Maximum Elimination Algorithm

We now present a new algorithm for replacing maximum expressions over an unbounded set of values (called *pointwise maximum expressions* in the following) with equivalent expressions containing no pointwise maximum expressions. Note that, technically our algorithm computes solutions to $\max_{x|b \wedge p \geq 0}(p)$ since some optimisations exploit the fact that the permission expressions our analysis generates always denote non-negative values.

5.1 Background: Quantifier Elimination

Our algorithm builds upon ideas from Cooper's classic *quantifier elimination* algorithm [11] which, given a formula $\exists x.b$ (where b is a quantifier-free Presburger formula), computes an equivalent quantifier-free formula b'. Below, we give a brief summary of Cooper's approach.

The problem is first reduced via boolean and arithmetic manipulations to a formula $\exists x.b$ in which x occurs at most once per literal and with no coefficient. The key idea is then to reduce $\exists x.b$ to a disjunction of two cases: (1) there is a *smallest* value of x making b true, or (2) b is true for *arbitrarily small* values of x.

In case (1), one computes a *finite* set of expressions S (the b_i in [11]) guaranteed to include the smallest value of x. For each (in/dis-)equality literal containing x in b, one collects a *boundary expression* e which denotes a value for x

making the literal true, while the value $e - 1$ would make it false. For example, for the literal $y < x$ one generates the expression $y + 1$. If there are no (non-)divisibility constraints in b, by definition, S will include the smallest value of x making b true. To account for (non-)divisibility constraints such as $x\%2=0$, the lowest-common-multiple δ of the divisors (and 1) is returned along with S; the guarantee is then that the smallest value of x making b true will be $e + d$ for some $e \in S$ and $d \in [0, \delta - 1]$. We use $\langle\!\langle b \rangle\!\rangle_{small(x)}$ to denote the function handling this computation. Then, $\exists x.b$ can be reduced to $\bigvee_{e \in S, d \in [0, \delta - 1]} b[e + d/x]$, where $(S, \delta) = \langle\!\langle b \rangle\!\rangle_{small(x)}$.

In case (2), one can observe that the (in/dis-)equality literals in b will flip value at finitely many values of x, and so for *sufficiently small* values of x, *each* (in/dis-)equality literal in b will have a constant value (e.g., $y > x$ will be true). By replacing these literals with these constant values, one obtains a new expression b' equal to b for small enough x, and which depends on x only via (non-)divisibility constraints. The value of b' will therefore actually be determined by $x \bmod \delta$, where δ is the lowest-common-multiple of the (non-)divisibility constraints. We use $\langle\!\langle b \rangle\!\rangle_{-\infty(x)}$ to denote the function handling this computation. Then, $\exists x.b$ can be reduced to $\bigvee_{d \in [0, \delta - 1]} b'[d/x]$, where $(b', \delta) = \langle\!\langle b \rangle\!\rangle_{-\infty(x)}$.

In principle, the maximum of a function $y = \max_x f(x)$ can be defined using two first-order quantifiers $\forall x.f(x) \leq y$ and $\exists x.f(x) = y$. One might therefore be tempted to tackle our maximum elimination problem using quantifier elimination directly. We explored this possibility and found two serious drawbacks. First, the resulting formula does not yield a permission-typed expression that we can plug back into our analysis. Second, the resulting formulas are extremely large (e.g., for the copyEven example it yields several pages of specifications), and hard to simplify since relevant information is often spread across many terms due to the two separate quantifiers. Our maximum elimination algorithm addresses these drawbacks by natively working with arithmetic expression, while mimicking the basic ideas of Cooper's algorithm and incorporating domain-specific optimisations.

5.2 Maximum Elimination

The first step is to reduce the problem of eliminating general $\max_{x|b} (p)$ terms to those in which b and p come from a simpler restricted grammar. These *simple permission expressions* p do not contain general conditional expressions $(b' ? p_1 : p_2)$, but instead only those of the form $(b' ? r : 0)$ (where r is a constant or rd). Furthermore, simple permission expressions only contain subtractions of the form $p - (b' ? r : 0)$. This is achieved in a precursory rewriting of the input expression by, for instance, distributing pointwise maxima over conditional expressions and binary maxima. For example, the pointwise maximum term (part of the copyEven example): $\max_{j | 0 \leq j < \texttt{len(a)}} ((j\%2=0 ? (q_a=\texttt{a} \wedge q_i=\texttt{j} ? \texttt{rd} : 0) : (q_a=\texttt{a} \wedge q_i=\texttt{j} ? 1 : 0)))$ will be reduced to:

$$\max(\ \max_{j | 0 \leq j < \texttt{len(a)} \wedge j\%2=0} ((q_a=\texttt{a} \wedge q_i=\texttt{j} ? \texttt{rd} : 0)),$$
$$\max_{j | 0 \leq j < \texttt{len(a)} \wedge j\%2\neq0} ((q_a=\texttt{a} \wedge q_i=\texttt{j} ? 1 : 0)))$$

$$\langle\!\langle(b\,?\,p:0)\rangle\!\rangle_{smallmax(x)} = (T,\delta),\ \ where\ (S,\delta) = \langle\!\langle b\rangle\!\rangle_{small(x)}, T = \{(e,\mathsf{true})\mid e\in S\}$$
$$\langle\!\langle p_1 + p_2\rangle\!\rangle_{smallmax(x)} = (T_1\cup T_2, lcm(\delta_1,\delta_2))$$
$$where\ \ (T_1,\delta_1) = \langle\!\langle p_1\rangle\!\rangle_{smallmax(x)},\ (T_2,\delta_2) = \langle\!\langle p_2\rangle\!\rangle_{smallmax(x)}$$
$$\langle\!\langle\max(p_1,p_2)\rangle\!\rangle_{smallmax(x)} = \langle\!\langle\min(p_1,p_2)\rangle\!\rangle_{smallmax(x)} = \langle\!\langle p_1+p_2\rangle\!\rangle_{smallmax(x)}\ as\ above$$
$$\langle\!\langle p_1 - (b\,?\,p:0)\rangle\!\rangle_{smallmax(x)} = (T_1\cup T_2, lcm(\delta_1,\delta_2))$$
$$where\ \ (T_1,\delta_1) = \langle\!\langle p_1\rangle\!\rangle_{smallmax(x)},\ (S_2,\delta_2) = \langle\!\langle\neg b\rangle\!\rangle_{small(x)},$$
$$T_2' = \{(e,p_1>0)\mid e\in S_2\}$$

$$\langle\!\langle(p,b)\rangle\!\rangle_{smallmax(x)} = (T_p\cup T_b',\delta')\ where\ (T_p,\delta_p) = \langle\!\langle p\rangle\!\rangle_{smallmax(x)},\ (S_b,\delta_b) = \langle\!\langle b\rangle\!\rangle_{small(x)},$$
$$\delta' = lcm(\delta_p,\delta_b),\ (b',\delta_b) = \langle\!\langle b\rangle\!\rangle_{-\infty(x)},\ (p',\delta_p) = \langle\!\langle p\rangle\!\rangle_{-\infty(x)},$$
$$T_b' = \{(e_b,(\bigvee_{d\in[0,\delta'-1]}((\neg b'\wedge p'>0)[d/x]))\vee\bigvee_{\substack{(e_p,b_p)\in T_p\\ d_p\in[0,\delta_p-1]}}(\neg b\wedge b_p)[(e_p+d_p)/x])\mid e_b\in S_b\}$$

Fig. 5. Filtered boundary expression computation.

Arbitrarily-Small Values. We exploit a high-level case-split in our algorithm design analogous to Cooper's: given a pointwise maximum expression $\max_{x|b}(p)$, either a *smallest* value of x exists such that p has its maximal value (and b is true), or there are *arbitrarily small* values of x defining this maximal value. To handle the latter case, we define a completely analogous $\langle\!\langle p\rangle\!\rangle_{-\infty(x)}$ function, which recursively replaces all boolean expressions b' in p with $\langle\!\langle b'\rangle\!\rangle_{-\infty(x)}$ as computed by Cooper; we relegate the definition to Sect. B.3 of the TR [15]. We then use $(b'\,?\,p':0)$, where $(b',\delta_1) = \langle\!\langle b\rangle\!\rangle_{-\infty(x)}$ and $(p',\delta_2) = \langle\!\langle p\rangle\!\rangle_{-\infty(x)}$, as our expression in this case. Note that this expression still depends on x if it contains (non-)divisibility constraints; Theorem 4 shows how x can be eliminated using δ_1 and δ_2.

Selecting Boundary Expressions for Maximum Elimination. Next, we consider the case of selecting an appropriate set of boundary expressions, given a $\max_{x|b}(p)$ term. We define this first for p in isolation, and then give an extended definition accounting for the b. Just as for Cooper's algorithm, the boundary expressions must be a set guaranteed to include the *smallest* value of x defining the maximum value in question. The set must be finite, and be as small as possible for efficiency of our overall algorithm. We refine the notion of boundary expression, and compute a set of *pairs* (e,b') of integer expression e and its *filter condition* b': the filter condition represents an additional condition under which e must be included as a boundary expression. In particular, in contexts where b' is false, e can be ignored; this gives us a way to symbolically define an ultimately-smaller set of boundary expressions, particularly in the absence of contextual information which might later show b' to be false. We call these pairs *filtered boundary expressions*.

Definition 1 (Filtered Boundary Expressions). *The* filtered boundary expression computation for x in p, written $\langle\!\langle p\rangle\!\rangle_{smallmax(x)}$, returns a pair of a set T of pairs (e,b'), and an integer constant δ, as defined in Fig. 5. This definition *is also overloaded with a definition of* filtered boundary expression computation for $(x \mid b)$ *in* p, *written* $\langle\!\langle (p,b) \rangle\!\rangle_{smallmax(x)}$.

Just as for Cooper's $\langle\!\langle b \rangle\!\rangle_{small(x)}$ computation, our function $\langle\!\langle p \rangle\!\rangle_{smallmax(x)}$ computes the set T of (e, b') pairs along with a single integer constant δ, which is the least common multiple of the divisors occurring in p; the desired smallest value of x may actually be some $e + d$ where $d \in [0, \delta - 1]$. There are three key points to Definition 1 which ultimately make our algorithm efficient:

First, the case for $\langle\!\langle (b\,?\,p:0) \rangle\!\rangle_{smallmax(x)}$ only includes boundary expressions for making b *true*. The case of b being false (from the structure of the permission expression) is not relevant for trying to maximise the permission expression's value (note that this case will never apply under a subtraction operator, due to our simplified grammar, and the case for subtraction not recursing into the right-hand operand).

Second, the case for $\langle\!\langle p_1 - (b\,?\,p:0) \rangle\!\rangle_{smallmax(x)}$ dually only considers boundary expressions for making b *false* (along with the boundary expressions for maximising p_1). The filter condition $p_1 > 0$ is used to drop the boundary expressions for making b false; in case p_1 is not strictly positive we know that the evaluation of the whole permission expression will not yield a strictly-positive value, and hence is not an interesting boundary value for a non-negative maximum.

Third, in the overloaded definition of $\langle\!\langle (p,b) \rangle\!\rangle_{smallmax(x)}$, we combine boundary expressions for p with those for b. The boundary expressions for b are, however, superfluous *if*, in analysing p we have already determined a value for x which maximises p and happens to satisfy b. If all boundary expressions for p (whose filter conditions are true) make b true, *and* all non-trivial (i.e. strictly positive) evaluations of $\langle\!\langle p \rangle\!\rangle_{-\infty(x)}$ used for potentially defining p's maximum value also satisfy b, then we can safely discard the boundary expressions for b.

We are now ready to reduce pointwise maximum expressions to equivalent maximum expressions over finitely-many cases:

Theorem 4 (Simple Maximum Expression Elimination). *For any pair* (p, b), *if* $\models p \geq 0$, *then we have:*

$$\models \max_{x \mid b} p = \max\big(\max_{\substack{(e,b'') \in T \\ d \in [0, \delta-1]}} (b'' \wedge b[e+d/x]\,?\,p[e+d/x]:0)),$$

$$\max_{d \in [0, lcm(\delta_1, \delta_2)-1]} (b'[d/x]\,?\,p'[d/x]:0))$$

where $(T, \delta) = \langle\!\langle (p,b) \rangle\!\rangle_{smallmax(x)}$, $(b', \delta_1) = \langle\!\langle b \rangle\!\rangle_{-\infty(x)}$ *and* $(p', \delta_2) = \langle\!\langle p \rangle\!\rangle_{-\infty(x)}$.

To see how our filter conditions help to keep the set T (and therefore, the first iterated maximum on the right of the equality in the above theorem) small, consider the example: $\max_{x \mid x \geq 0} ((x{=}i\,?\,1:0))$ (so p is $(x{=}i\,?\,1:0)$, while b is $x \geq 0$). In this case, evaluating $\langle\!\langle (p,b) \rangle\!\rangle_{smallmax(x)}$ yields the set $T = \{(i, \text{true}), (0, i < 0)\}$ with the meaning that the boundary expression i is considered in all cases, while the boundary expression 0 is only of interest if $i < 0$. The first iterated maximum term would be $\max((\text{true} \wedge i{\geq}0\,?\,(i{=}i\,?\,1:0):0), (i{<}0 \wedge 0{\geq}0\,?\,(0{=}i\,?\,1:0):0))$. We observe that the term corresponding to the boundary

Table 1. Experimental results. For each program, we list the lines of code and the number of loops (in brackets the nesting depth). We report the relative size of the inferred specifications compared to hand-written specifications, and whether the inferred specifications are precise (a star next to the tick indicates slightly more precise than hand-written specifications). Inference times are given in ms.

Program	LOC	Loops	Size	Prec.	Time	Program	LOC	Loops	Size	Prec.	Time
addLast	12	1 (1)	1.9	✓	21	initPartBug	19	2 (1)	1.5	✓	31
append	13	1 (1)	1.9	✓	32	insertSort	21	2 (2)	2.5	✓*	35
array1	17	2 (2)	0.9	✗	28	javaBubble	24	2 (2)	2.3	✓*	32
array2	23	3 (2)	0.9	✗	35	knapsack	21	2 (2)	1.3	✗	45
array3	23	2 (2)	1.1	✓	24	lis	37	4 (2)	4.2	✓	73
arrayRev	18	1 (1)	3.2	✓*	28	matrixmult	33	3 (3)	1.5	✓	78
bubbleSort	23	2 (2)	1.8	✓*	34	mergeinter	23	2 (1)	3.4	✗	56
copy	16	2 (1)	1.6	✓	27	mergeintbug	23	2 (1)	2.6	✗	59
copyEven	17	1 (1)	1.6	✓	27	memcopy	16	2 (1)	1.6	✓	28
copyEven2	14	1 (1)	1.4	✗	20	multarray	26	2 (2)	2.1	✓	40
copyEven3	14	1 (1)	2.2	✓*	23	parcopy	20	2 (1)	1.2	✓	30
copyOdd	21	2 (1)	2.4	✓	55	pararray	20	2 (1)	1.2	✓	31
copyOddBug	19	2 (1)	7.1	✓	57	parCopyEven	22	2 (1)	5.0	✓*	79
copyPart	17	2 (1)	1.7	✓	30	parMatrix	35	4 (2)	1.1	✓	80
countDown	21	3 (2)	1.1	✓	32	parNested	31	4 (2)	0.5	✗	57
diff	31	2 (2)	2.0	✗	70	relax	33	1 (1)	1.4	✓*	55
find	19	1 (1)	3.0	✓	43	reverse	21	2 (1)	3.9	✓	42
findNonNull	19	1 (1)	3.0	✓	40	reverseBug	21	2 (1)	1.7	✓	42
init	18	2 (1)	1.1	✓	28	sanfoundry	27	2 (1)	2.1	✓	37
init2d	23	2 (2)	2.1	✓	52	selectSort	26	2 (2)	1.0	✗	38
initEven	18	2 (1)	0.9	✗	26	strCopy	16	2 (1)	0.9	✗	21
initEvenbug	18	2 (1)	1.5	✗	28	strLen	10	1 (1)	0.8	✗	15
initNonCnst	18	2 (1)	1.1	✓	27	swap	15	1 (1)	1.5	✓	19
initPart	19	2 (1)	1.1	✓	30	swapBug	15	1 (1)	1.5	✓	19

value 0 can be simplified to 0 since it contains the two contradictory conditions $i < 0$ and $0 = i$. Thus, the entire maximum can be simplified to $(i{\geq}0\ ?\ 1 : 0)$. Without the filter conditions the result would instead be $\max((i{\geq}0\ ?\ 1 : 0), (0{=}i\ ?\ 1 : 0))$. In the context of our permission analysis, the filter conditions allow us to avoid generating boundary expressions corresponding e.g. to the integer loop invariants, provided that the expressions generated by analysing the permission expression in question already suffice. We employ aggressive syntactic simplification of the resulting expressions, in order to exploit these filter conditions to produce succinct final answers.

6   Implementation and Experimental Evaluation

We have developed a prototype implementation of our permission inference. The tool is written in Scala and accepts programs written in the Viper language [38], which provides all the features needed for our purposes.

Given a Viper program, the tool first performs a forward numerical analysis to infer the over-approximate loop invariants needed for our handling of loops. The implementation is parametric in the numerical abstract domain used for the analysis; we currently support the abstract domains provided by the APRON library [24]. As we have yet to integrate the implementation of under-approximate invariants (e.g., [35]), we rely on user-provided invariants, or assume them to be false if none are provided. In a second step, our tool performs the inference and maximum elimination. Finally, it annotates the input program with the inferred specification.

We evaluated our implementation on 43 programs taken from various sources; included are all programs that do not contain strings from the array memory safety category of SV-COMP 2017, all programs from Dillig et al. [14] (except three examples involving arrays of arrays), loop parallelisation examples from VerCors [5], and a few programs that we crafted ourselves. We manually checked that our soundness condition holds for all considered programs. The parallel loop examples were encoded as two consecutive loops where the first one models the forking of one thread per loop iteration (by iteratively exhaling the permissions required for all loop iterations), and the second one models the joining of all these threads (by inhaling the permissions that are left after each loop iteration). For the numerical analysis we used the *polyhedra abstract domain* provided by APRON. The experiments were performed on a dual core machine with a 2.60 GHz Intel Core i7-6600U CPU, running Ubuntu 16.04.

An overview of the results is given in Table 1. For each program, we compared the size and precision of the inferred specification with respect to hand-written ones. The running times were measured by first running the analysis 50 times to warm up the JVM and then computing the average time needed over the next 100 runs. The results show that the inference is very efficient. The inferred specifications are concise for the vast majority of the examples. In 35 out of 48 cases, our inference inferred precise specifications. Most of the imprecisions are due to the inferred numerical loop invariants. In all cases, manually strengthening the invariants yields a precise specification. In one example, the source of imprecision is our abstraction of array-dependent conditions (see Sect. 4).

7   Related Work

Much work is dedicated to the analysis of array programs, but most of it focuses on array content, whereas we infer permission specifications. The simplest approach consists of "smashing" all array elements into a single memory location [4]. This is generally quite imprecise, as only weak updates can be performed on the smashed array. A simple alternative is to consider array elements as distinct variables [4], which is feasible only when the length of the array is statically-known. More-advanced approaches perform syntax-based [18,22,25] or semantics-based [12,34] partitions of an array into symbolic segments. These require segments to be contiguous (with the exception of [34]), and do not easily generalise to multidimensional arrays, unlike our approach. Gulwani et al. [20] propose an approach for inferring quantified invariants for arrays by lifting quantifier-free abstract domains. Their technique requires templates for the invariants.

Dillig et al. [14] avoid an explicit array partitioning by maintaining constraints that over- and under-approximate the array elements being updated by a program statement. Their work employs a technique for directly generalising the analysis of a single loop iteration (based on quantifier elimination), which works well when different loop iterations write to disjoint array locations. Gedell and Hähnle [17] provide an analysis which uses a similar criterion to determine that it is safe to parallelise a loop, and treat its heap updates as one bulk effect. The condition for our projection over loop iterations is weaker, since it allows the same array location to be updated in multiple loop iterations (like for example in sorting algorithms). Blom et al. [5] provide a specification technique for a variety of parallel loop constructs; our work can infer the specifications which their technique requires to be provided.

Another alternative for generalising the effect of a loop iteration is to use a first order theorem prover as proposed by Kovács and Voronkov [28]. In their work, however, they did not consider nested loops or multidimensional arrays. Other works rely on loop acceleration techniques [1,7]. In particular, like ours, the work of Bozga et al. [7] does not synthesise loop invariants; they directly infer post-conditions of loops with respect to given preconditions, while we additionally infer the preconditions. The acceleration technique proposed in [1] is used for the verification of array programs in the tool BOOSTER [2].

Monniaux and Gonnord [36] describe an approach for the verification of array programs via a transformation to array-free Horn clauses. Chakraborty et al. [10] use heuristics to determine the array accesses performed by a loop iteration and split the verification of an array invariant accordingly. Their non-interference condition between loop iterations is similar to, but stronger than our soundness condition (cf. Sect. 4). Neither work is concerned with specification inference.

A wide range of static/shape analyses employ tailored separation logics as abstract domain (e.g., [3,9,19,29,41]); these works handle recursively-defined data structures such as linked lists and trees, but not random-access data structures such as arrays and matrices. Of these, Gulavani et al. [19] is perhaps closest to our work: they employ an integer-indexed domain for describing recursive data structures. It would be interesting to combine our work with such separation logic shape analyses. The problems of automating biabduction and entailment checking for array-based separation logics have been recently studied by Brotherston et al. [8] and Kimura and Tatsuta [27], but have not yet been extended to handle loop-based or recursive programs.

8   Conclusion and Future Work

We presented a precise and efficient permission inference for array programs. Although our inferred specifications contain redundancies in some cases, they are human readable. Our approach integrates well with permission-based inference for other data structures and with permission-based program verification.

As future work, we plan to use SMT solving to further simplify our inferred specifications, to support arrays of arrays, and to extend our work to an inter-procedural analysis and explore its combination with biabduction techniques.

Acknowledgements. We thank Seraiah Walter for his earlier work on this topic, and Malte Schwerhoff and the anonymous reviewers for their comments and suggestions. This work was supported by the Swiss National Science Foundation.

References

1. Alberti, F., Ghilardi, S., Sharygina, N.: Definability of accelerated relations in a theory of arrays and its applications. In: Fontaine, P., Ringeissen, C., Schmidt, R.A. (eds.) FroCoS 2013. LNCS (LNAI), vol. 8152, pp. 23–39. Springer, Heidelberg (2013). https://doi.org/10.1007/978-3-642-40885-4_3
2. Alberti, F., Ghilardi, S., Sharygina, N.: Booster: an acceleration-based verification framework for array programs. In: Cassez, F., Raskin, J.-F. (eds.) ATVA 2014. LNCS, vol. 8837, pp. 18–23. Springer, Cham (2014). https://doi.org/10.1007/978-3-319-11936-6_2
3. Berdine, J., Calcagno, C., O'Hearn, P.W.: Smallfoot: modular automatic assertion checking with separation logic. In: de Boer, F.S., Bonsangue, M.M., Graf, S., de Roever, W.-P. (eds.) FMCO 2005. LNCS, vol. 4111, pp. 115–137. Springer, Heidelberg (2006). https://doi.org/10.1007/11804192_6
4. Bertrane, J., Cousot, P., Cousot, R., Feret, J., Mauborgne, L., Miné, A., Rival, X.: Static analysis and verification of aerospace software by abstract interpretation. In: AIAA (2010)
5. Blom, S., Darabi, S., Huisman, M.: Verification of loop parallelisations. In: Egyed, A., Schaefer, I. (eds.) FASE 2015. LNCS, vol. 9033, pp. 202–217. Springer, Heidelberg (2015). https://doi.org/10.1007/978-3-662-46675-9_14
6. Boyland, J.: Checking interference with fractional permissions. In: Cousot, R. (ed.) SAS 2003. LNCS, vol. 2694, pp. 55–72. Springer, Heidelberg (2003). https://doi.org/10.1007/3-540-44898-5_4
7. Bozga, M., Habermehl, P., Iosif, R., Konečný, F., Vojnar, T.: Automatic verification of integer array programs. In: Bouajjani, A., Maler, O. (eds.) CAV 2009. LNCS, vol. 5643, pp. 157–172. Springer, Heidelberg (2009). https://doi.org/10.1007/978-3-642-02658-4_15
8. Brotherston, J., Gorogiannis, N., Kanovich, M.: Biabduction (and related problems) in array separation logic. In: de Moura, L. (ed.) CADE 2017. LNCS (LNAI), vol. 10395, pp. 472–490. Springer, Cham (2017). https://doi.org/10.1007/978-3-319-63046-5_29
9. Calcagno, C., Distefano, D., O'Hearn, P.W., Yang, H.: Compositional shape analysis by means of bi-abduction. J. ACM 58(6), 26:1–26:66 (2011)
10. Chakraborty, S., Gupta, A., Unadkat, D.: Verifying array manipulating programs by tiling. In: Ranzato, F. (ed.) SAS 2017. LNCS, vol. 10422, pp. 428–449. Springer, Cham (2017). https://doi.org/10.1007/978-3-319-66706-5_21

11. Cooper, D.C.: Theorem proving in arithmetic without multiplication. Mach. Intell. **7**(91–99), 300 (1972)
12. Cousot, P., Cousot, R., Logozzo, F.: A parametric segmentation functor for fully automatic and scalable array content analysis. In: POPL, pp. 105–118 (2011)
13. Cousot, P., Halbwachs, N.: Automatic discovery of linear restraints among variables of a program. In: POPL, pp. 84–96 (1978)
14. Dillig, I., Dillig, T., Aiken, A.: Fluid updates: beyond strong vs. weak updates. In: Gordon, A.D. (ed.) ESOP 2010. LNCS, vol. 6012, pp. 246–266. Springer, Heidelberg (2010). https://doi.org/10.1007/978-3-642-11957-6_14
15. Dohrau, J., Summers, A.J., Urban, C., Münger, S., Müller, P.: Permission inference for array programs (extended version) (2018). arXiv:1804.04091
16. Ferrante, J., Ottenstein, K.J., Warren, J.D.: The program dependence graph and its use in optimization. In: Paul, M., Robinet, B. (eds.) Programming 1984. LNCS, vol. 167, pp. 125–132. Springer, Heidelberg (1984). https://doi.org/10.1007/3-540-12925-1_33
17. Gedell, T., Hähnle, R.: Automating verification of loops by parallelization. In: Hermann, M., Voronkov, A. (eds.) LPAR 2006. LNCS (LNAI), vol. 4246, pp. 332–346. Springer, Heidelberg (2006). https://doi.org/10.1007/11916277_23
18. Gopan, D., Reps, T.W., Sagiv, S.: A framework for numeric analysis of array operations. In: POPL, pp. 338–350 (2005)
19. Gulavani, B.S., Chakraborty, S., Ramalingam, G., Nori, A.V.: Bottom-up shape analysis. In: Palsberg, J., Su, Z. (eds.) SAS 2009. LNCS, vol. 5673, pp. 188–204. Springer, Heidelberg (2009). https://doi.org/10.1007/978-3-642-03237-0_14
20. Gulwani, S., McCloskey, B., Tiwari, A.: Lifting abstract interpreters to quantified logical domains. In: POPL, pp. 235–246 (2008)
21. Gupta, A., Rybalchenko, A.: InvGen: an efficient invariant generator. In: Bouajjani, A., Maler, O. (eds.) CAV 2009. LNCS, vol. 5643, pp. 634–640. Springer, Heidelberg (2009). https://doi.org/10.1007/978-3-642-02658-4_48
22. Halbwachs, N., Péron, M.: Discovering properties about arrays in simple programs. In: PLDI, pp. 339–348 (2008)
23. Jacobs, B., Smans, J., Philippaerts, P., Vogels, F., Penninckx, W., Piessens, F.: VeriFast: a powerful, sound, predictable, fast verifier for C and Java. In: Bobaru, M., Havelund, K., Holzmann, G.J., Joshi, R. (eds.) NFM 2011. LNCS, vol. 6617, pp. 41–55. Springer, Heidelberg (2011). https://doi.org/10.1007/978-3-642-20398-5_4
24. Jeannet, B., Miné, A.: APRON: a library of numerical abstract domains for static analysis. In: Bouajjani, A., Maler, O. (eds.) CAV 2009. LNCS, vol. 5643, pp. 661–667. Springer, Heidelberg (2009). https://doi.org/10.1007/978-3-642-02658-4_52
25. Jhala, R., McMillan, K.L.: Array abstractions from proofs. In: Damm, W., Hermanns, H. (eds.) CAV 2007. LNCS, vol. 4590, pp. 193–206. Springer, Heidelberg (2007). https://doi.org/10.1007/978-3-540-73368-3_23
26. Johnson, N.P., Fix, J., Beard, S.R., Oh, T., Jablin, T.B., August, D.I.: A collaborative dependence analysis framework. In: CGO, pp. 148–159 (2017)
27. Kimura, D., Tatsuta, M.: Decision procedure for entailment of symbolic heaps with arrays. In: Chang, B.-Y.E. (ed.) APLAS 2017. LNCS, vol. 10695, pp. 169–189. Springer, Cham (2017). https://doi.org/10.1007/978-3-319-71237-6_9
28. Kovács, L., Voronkov, A.: Finding loop invariants for programs over arrays using a theorem prover. In: Chechik, M., Wirsing, M. (eds.) FASE 2009. LNCS, vol. 5503, pp. 470–485. Springer, Heidelberg (2009). https://doi.org/10.1007/978-3-642-00593-0_33

29. Le, Q.L., Gherghina, C., Qin, S., Chin, W.-N.: Shape analysis via second-order bi-abduction. In: Biere, A., Bloem, R. (eds.) CAV 2014. LNCS, vol. 8559, pp. 52–68. Springer, Cham (2014). https://doi.org/10.1007/978-3-319-08867-9_4

30. Leino, K.R.M.: Dafny: an automatic program verifier for functional correctness. In: Clarke, E.M., Voronkov, A. (eds.) LPAR 2010. LNCS (LNAI), vol. 6355, pp. 348–370. Springer, Heidelberg (2010). https://doi.org/10.1007/978-3-642-17511-4_20

31. Leino, K.R.M., Müller, P.: A basis for verifying multi-threaded programs. In: Castagna, G. (ed.) ESOP 2009. LNCS, vol. 5502, pp. 378–393. Springer, Heidelberg (2009). https://doi.org/10.1007/978-3-642-00590-9_27

32. Leino, K.R.M., Müller, P., Smans, J.: Deadlock-free channels and locks. In: Gordon, A.D. (ed.) ESOP 2010. LNCS, vol. 6012, pp. 407–426. Springer, Heidelberg (2010). https://doi.org/10.1007/978-3-642-11957-6_22

33. Lerner, S., Grove, D., Chambers, C.: Composing dataflow analyses and transformations. In: POPL, pp. 270–282 (2002)

34. Liu, J., Rival, X.: An array content static analysis based on non-contiguous partitions. Comput. Lang. Syst. Struct. **47**, 104–129 (2017)

35. Miné, A.: Inferring sufficient conditions with backward polyhedral under-approximations. Electron. Not. Theor. Comput. Sci. **287**, 89–100 (2012)

36. Monniaux, D., Gonnord, L.: Cell morphing: from array programs to array-free horn clauses. In: Rival, X. (ed.) SAS 2016. LNCS, vol. 9837, pp. 361–382. Springer, Heidelberg (2016). https://doi.org/10.1007/978-3-662-53413-7_18

37. Müller, P., Schwerhoff, M., Summers, A.J.: Automatic verification of iterated separating conjunctions using symbolic execution. In: Chaudhuri, S., Farzan, A. (eds.) CAV 2016. LNCS, vol. 9779, pp. 405–425. Springer, Cham (2016). https://doi.org/10.1007/978-3-319-41528-4_22

38. Müller, P., Schwerhoff, M., Summers, A.J.: Viper: a verification infrastructure for permission-based reasoning. In: Jobstmann, B., Leino, K.R.M. (eds.) VMCAI 2016. LNCS, vol. 9583, pp. 41–62. Springer, Heidelberg (2016). https://doi.org/10.1007/978-3-662-49122-5_2

39. Piskac, R., Wies, T., Zufferey, D.: GRASShopper – complete heap verification with mixed specifications. In: Ábrahám, E., Havelund, K. (eds.) TACAS 2014. LNCS, vol. 8413, pp. 124–139. Springer, Heidelberg (2014). https://doi.org/10.1007/978-3-642-54862-8_9

40. Reynolds, J.: Separation logic: a logic for shared mutable data structures. In: Proceedings of the 17th Annual IEEE Symposium on Logic in Computer Science, LICS 2002, Washington, D.C., USA, pp. 55–74. IEEE Computer Society (2002)

41. Rowe, R.N.S., Brotherston, J.: Automatic cyclic termination proofs for recursive procedures in separation logic. In: Proceedings of the 6th ACM SIGPLAN Conference on Certified Programs and Proofs, CPP 2017, New York, NY, USA, pp. 53–65. ACM (2017)

42. Sălcianu, A., Rinard, M.: Purity and side effect analysis for Java programs. In: Cousot, R. (ed.) VMCAI 2005. LNCS, vol. 3385, pp. 199–215. Springer, Heidelberg (2005). https://doi.org/10.1007/978-3-540-30579-8_14

43. Smans, J., Jacobs, B., Piessens, F.: Implicit dynamic frames: combining dynamic frames and separation logic. In: Drossopoulou, S. (ed.) ECOOP 2009. LNCS, vol. 5653, pp. 148–172. Springer, Heidelberg (2009). https://doi.org/10.1007/978-3-642-03013-0_8

44. Summers, A.J., Müller, P.: Automating deductive verification for weak-memory programs. In: Beyer, D., Huisman, M. (eds.) TACAS 2018. LNCS, vol. 10805, pp. 190–209. Springer, Cham (2018). https://doi.org/10.1007/978-3-319-89960-2_11

45. Voung, J.W., Jhala, R., Lerner, S.: RELAY: static race detection on millions of lines of code. In: European Software Engineering Conference and Foundations of Software Engineering (ESEC-FSE), pp. 205–214. ACM (2007)

Program Analysis Is Harder Than Verification: A Computability Perspective

Patrick Cousot[1], Roberto Giacobazzi[2,3], and Francesco Ranzato[4]

[1] New York University, New York City, USA
[2] University of Verona, Verona, Italy
[3] IMDEA Software Institute, Madrid, Spain
[4] University of Padova, Padova, Italy
ranzato@math.unipd.it

Abstract. We study from a computability perspective static program analysis, namely detecting sound program assertions, and verification, namely sound checking of program assertions. We first design a general computability model for domains of program assertions and corresponding program analysers and verifiers. Next, we formalize and prove an instantiation of Rice's theorem for static program analysis and verification. Then, within this general model, we provide and show a precise statement of the popular belief that program analysis is a harder problem than program verification: we prove that for finite domains of program assertions, program analysis and verification are equivalent problems, while for infinite domains, program analysis is strictly harder than verification.

1 Introduction

It is common to assume that program analysis is harder than program verification (e.g. [1,17,22]). The intuition is that this happens because in program analysis we need to synthesize a correct program invariant while in program verification we have *just* to check whether a given program invariant is correct. The distinction between checking a proof and computing a witness for that proof can be traced back to Leibniz [18] in his *ars iudicandi* and *ars inveniendi*, respectively representing the analytic and synthetic method. In Leibniz's *ars combinatoria*, the ars inveniendi is defined as the art of discovering "correct" questions while ars iudicandi is defined as the art of discovering "correct" answers. These foundational aspects of mathematical reasoning have a peculiar meaning when dealing with questions and answers concerning the behaviour of computer programs as objects of our investigation.

Our main goal is to define a general and precise model for reasoning on the computability aspects of the notions of (sound or complete) static analyser and verifier for generic programs (viz. Turing machines). Both static analysers and verifiers assume a given domain A of abstract program assertions, that may range from synctatic program properties (e.g., program sizes or LOCs) to complexity

H. Chockler and G. Weissenbacher (Eds.): CAV 2018, LNCS 10982, pp. 75–95, 2018.
https://doi.org/10.1007/978-3-319-96142-2_8

properties (e.g., number of execution steps in some abstract machine) and all the semantic properties of the program behaviour (e.g., value range of program variables or shape of program memories). A program analyser is defined to be any total computable (i.e., total recursive) function that for any program P returns an assertion a_P in A, which is sound when the concrete meaning of the assertion a_P includes P. Instead, a program verifier is a (total) decision procedure which is capable of checking whether a given program P satisfies a given assertion a ranging in A, answering "true" or "don't know", which is sound when a positive check of a for P means that the concrete meaning of the assertion a includes P. Completeness, which coupled with soundness is here called precision, for a program analyser holds when, for any program P, it returns the strongest assertion in A for P, while a program verifier is called precise if it is able to prove any true assertion in A for a program P. This general and minimal model allows us to extend to static program analysis and verification some standard results and methods of computability theory. We provide an instance of the well-known Rice's Theorem [29] for generic analysers and verifiers, by proving that sound and precise analysers (resp. verifiers) exist only for trivial domains of assertions. This allows us to generalise known results about undecidability of program analysis, such as the undecidability of the meet over all paths (MOP) solution for monotone dataflow analysis frameworks [15], making them independent from the structure of the domain of assertions. Then, we define a model for comparing the relative "verification power" of program analysers and verifiers. In this model, a verifier $\mathcal{V}$ on a domain A of assertions is more precise than an analyser $\mathcal{A}$ on the same domain A when any assertion a in A which can be proved by $\mathcal{A}$ for a program P—this means that the output of the analyser $\mathcal{A}(P)$ is stronger than the assertion a—can be also proved by $\mathcal{V}$. Conversely, $\mathcal{A}$ is more precise than $\mathcal{V}$ when any assertion a proved by $\mathcal{V}$ can be also proved by $\mathcal{A}$. We prove that while it is always possible to constructively transform a program analyser into an equivalent verifier (i.e., with the same verification power), the converse does not hold in general. In fact, we first show that for *finite* domains of assertions, any "reasonable" verifier can be constructively transformed into an equivalent analyser, where reasonable means that the verifier $\mathcal{V}$ is: (i) nontrivial: for any program, $\mathcal{V}$ is capable to prove some assertion, possibly a trivially true assertion; (ii) monotone: if $\mathcal{V}$ proves an assertion a and a is stronger than a' then $\mathcal{V}$ is also capable of proving a'; (iii) logically meet-closed: if $\mathcal{V}$ proves both a_1 and a_2 and the logical conjunction $a_1 \wedge a_2$ is a representable assertion then $\mathcal{V}$ is also capable of proving it. Next, we prove the following impossibility result: for any *infinite* abstract domain of assertions A, no constructive reduction from reasonable verifiers on A to equivalent analysers on A is possible. This provides, to the best of our knowledge, the first formalization of the common folklore that program analysis is harder than program verification.

2   Background

We follow the standard terminology and notation for sets and computable functions in recursion theory (e.g., [12, 26, 30]). If X and Y are sets then $X \rightarrow Y$

and $X \twoheadrightarrow Y$ denote, respectively, the set of all total and partial functions from X to Y. If $f : X \twoheadrightarrow Y$ then $f(x)\!\downarrow$ and $f(x)\!\uparrow$ mean that f is defined/undefined on $x \in X$. Hence $\mathrm{dom}(f) = \{x \in X \mid f(x)\!\downarrow\}$. If $S \subseteq Y$ then $f(x) \in S$ denotes the implification $f(x)\!\downarrow \;\Rightarrow\; f(x) \in S$. If $f, g : X \twoheadrightarrow Y$ then $f = g$ means that $\mathrm{dom}(f) = \mathrm{dom}(g)$ and for any $x \in \mathrm{dom}(f) = \mathrm{dom}(g)$, $f(x) = g(x)$. The set of all partial (total) recursive functions on natural numbers is denoted by $\mathbb{N} \stackrel{r}{\twoheadrightarrow} \mathbb{N}$ ($\mathbb{N} \stackrel{r}{\to} \mathbb{N}$). Recall that $A \subseteq \mathbb{N}$ is a recursively enumerable (r.e., or semidecidable) set if $A = \mathrm{dom}(f)$ for some $f \in \mathbb{N} \stackrel{r}{\twoheadrightarrow} \mathbb{N}$, while $A \subseteq \mathbb{N}$ is a recursive (or decidable) set if both A and its complement $\bar{A} = \mathbb{N} \smallsetminus A$ are recursively enumerable, and this happens when there exists $f \in \mathbb{N} \stackrel{r}{\to} \mathbb{N}$ such that $f = \lambda n.\, n \in A \;?\; 1 : 0$.

Let Prog denote some deterministic programming language which is Turing complete. More precisely, this means that for any partial recursive function $f : \mathbb{N} \stackrel{r}{\twoheadrightarrow} \mathbb{N}$ there exists a program $P \in$ Prog such that $[\![P]\!] \cong f$, where $[\![P]\!] : D \twoheadrightarrow D$ is a denotational input/output semantics of P on a domain D of input/output values for Prog, where: undefinedness encodes nontermination and $\cong$ means equality up to some recursive encoding $\mathrm{enc} : D \stackrel{r}{\to} \mathbb{N}$ and decoding $\mathrm{dec} : \mathbb{N} \stackrel{r}{\to} D$ functions, i.e., $f = \mathrm{enc} \circ [\![P]\!] \circ \mathrm{dec}$. We also assume a small-step transition relation $\Rightarrow \;\subseteq\; (\mathrm{Prog} \times D) \times ((\mathrm{Prog} \times D) \cup D)$ for Prog defining an operational semantics which is functionally equivalent to the denotational semantics: $\langle P, i \rangle \Rightarrow^* o$ iff $[\![P]\!]i = o$. By an abuse of notation, we will identify the input/output semantics of a program P with the partial recursive function computed by P, i.e., we will consider programs $P \in$ Prog whose input/output semantics is a partial recursive function $[\![P]\!] : \mathbb{N} \stackrel{r}{\twoheadrightarrow} \mathbb{N}$, so that, by Turing completeness, $\{[\![P]\!] : \mathbb{N} \stackrel{r}{\twoheadrightarrow} \mathbb{N} \mid P \in \mathrm{Prog}\} = \mathbb{N} \stackrel{r}{\twoheadrightarrow} \mathbb{N}$.

3   Abstract Domains

Static program analysis and verification are always defined with respect to a given (denumerable) domain of program assertions, that we call here *abstract domain* [7], where the meaning of assertions is formalized by a function which induces a logical implication relation between assertions.

Definition 3.1 (Abstract Domain). An *abstract domain* is a tuple $\langle A, \gamma, \leq_\gamma \rangle$ such that:

(1) A is any denumerable set;
(2) $\gamma : A \to \wp(\mathrm{Prog})$ is any function;
(3) $\leq_\gamma \;\triangleq\; \{(a_1, a_2) \in A \times A \mid \gamma(a_1) \subseteq \gamma(a_2)\}$ is a decidable relation.

An abstract element $a \in A$ such that $\gamma(a) = \mathrm{Prog}$ is called an *abstract top*, while a is called an *abstract bottom* when $\gamma(a) = \varnothing$.   □

The elements of A are called assertions or abstract values, γ is called concretization function (this may also be a nonrecursive function, which is typical of abstract domains representing semantic program properties), and $\leq_\gamma$ is called the implication or approximation relation of A. Thus, in this general model, a program assertion $a \in A$ plays the role of some abstract representation of any program property $\gamma(a) \in \wp(\mathrm{Prog})$, while the comparison relation $a_1 \leq_\gamma a_2$ holds when a_1 is a stronger (or more precise) property than a_2. Let us also observe that, as a limit case, Definition 3.1 allows an abstract domain to be empty, that is, the tuple $\langle \varnothing, \varnothing, \varnothing \rangle$ satisfies the definition of abstract domain, where $\varnothing$ denotes both the empty set, the empty function (i.e., the unique subset of $\varnothing \times \varnothing$) and the empty relation.

Example 3.2. Let us give some simple examples of abstract domains.

(1) Consider $A = \mathbb{N}$ with $\gamma(n) \triangleq \{P \in \mathrm{Prog} \mid \mathrm{size}(P) \leq n\}$, where $\mathrm{size} : \mathrm{Prog} \to \mathbb{N}$ is some computable program size function. Here, $\leq_\gamma$ is clearly decidable and coincides with the partial order $\leq_\mathbb{N}$ on numbers.

(2) Consider $A = \mathbb{N}$ with $\gamma(n) \triangleq \{P \in \mathrm{Prog} \mid \forall i. \exists o, k.(\langle P, i \rangle \Rightarrow^k o) \ \& \ k \leq n\}$, i.e., n represents all the programs which, given any input, terminate in at most n steps. Here again, $n \leq_\gamma m$ iff $n \leq_\mathbb{N} m$, so that $\leq_\gamma$ is decidable.

(3) Consider $A = \mathbb{N}$ with $\gamma(n) \triangleq \{P \in \mathrm{Prog} \mid \forall i \in [0, n]. \exists o. \langle P, i \rangle \Rightarrow^* o\}$, that is, n represents all the programs which terminate for any input $i \leq n$. Once again, $n \leq_\gamma m$ iff $n \leq_\mathbb{N} m$.

(4) Consider $A = \mathbb{N}$ with $\gamma(n) \triangleq \{P \in \mathrm{Prog} \mid \forall i \in \mathbb{N}. [\![P]\!](i) = o \Rightarrow o \leq n\}$, that is, n represents those programs which, in case of termination, give an output o bounded by n. Again, $n \leq_\gamma m$ iff $n \leq_\mathbb{N} m$.

(5) Consider $A = \mathbb{N} \xrightarrow{\tau} \mathbb{N}$ with $\gamma(g) \triangleq \{P \in \mathrm{Prog} \mid \forall i. \big(g(i){\downarrow} \Rightarrow (\exists o, k. \langle P, i \rangle \Rightarrow^k o, k \leq g(i))\big) \wedge \big((\exists o, k. \langle P, i \rangle \Rightarrow^k o) \Rightarrow g(i){\downarrow}, k \leq g(i))\big)\}$, that is, g represents those programs whose time complexity is bounded by the function g. Here, $g \leq_\gamma g'$ iff $\forall i. g(i){\downarrow} \Rightarrow (g'(i){\downarrow} \wedge g(i) \leq g'(i))$. $\qquad \square$

Definition 3.1 does not require injectivity of the concretization function γ, thus multiple assertions could have the same meaning. Two abstract values $a_1, a_2 \in A$ are called equivalent when $\gamma(a_1) = \gamma(a_2)$. Let us observe that since $\leq_\gamma$ is required to be decidable, the equivalence $\gamma(a_1) = \gamma(a_2)$ is decidable as well. For example, for the well-known numerical abstract domain of convex polyhedra [11] represented through linear constraints between program variables, we may well have multiple representations P_1 and P_2 for the same polyhedron, e.g., $P_1 = \{x = z, z \leq y\}$ and $P_2 = \{x = z, x \leq y\}$ both represent the same polyhedron. Thus, in general, an abstract domain A is not required to be partially ordered by $\leq_\gamma$. On the other hand, the relation $\leq_\gamma$ is clearly a preorder on A. The only basic requirement is that for any pair of abstract values $a_1, a_2 \in A$, one can decide if a_1 is a more precise program assertion than a_2, i.e., if $\gamma(a_1) \subseteq \gamma(a_2)$ holds. In this sense we do not require that a partial order $\leq$ is defined a priori on A and that γ is monotone w.r.t. $\leq$, since for our purposes it is enough to consider the preorder $\leq_\gamma$ induced by γ. If instead A is endowed with a partial order $\leq_A$ and A is defined in abstract interpretation [7,8] through a Galois insertion based on the concretization map γ, then it turns out that $\gamma(a_1) \subseteq \gamma(a_2) \Leftrightarrow a_1 \leq_A a_2$ holds, so that the decidability of the relation $\leq_\gamma = \{(a_1, a_2) \in A \times A \mid \gamma(a_1) \subseteq \gamma(a_2)\}$ boils down to the decidability of the partial order relation $\leq_A$. As an example, it is well known that the abstract domain of polyhedra does not admit a Galois insertion [11], nevertheless its induced pre-order relation $\leq_\gamma$ is decidable: for example, for polyhedra represented by linear constraints, there exist algorithms for deciding if $\gamma(P_1) \subseteq \gamma(P_2)$ for any pair of convex polyhedra representations P_1 and P_2 (see e.g. [23, Sect. 5.3]).

3.1   Abstract Domains in Abstract Interpretation

An abstract domain in standard abstract interpretation [7–9] is usually defined by a poset $\langle A, \leq_A \rangle$ containing a top element $\top \in A$ and a concretization map $\gamma_A :$ $A \to \wp(\mathrm{Dom})$, where Dom denotes some concrete semantic domain (e.g., program stores or program traces), such that: (a) A is machine representable, namely the abstract elements of A are encoded by some data structures (e.g., tuples, vectors, lists, matrices, etc.), and some algorithms are available for deciding if $a_1 \leq_A a_2$ holds; (b) $a_1 \leq_A a_2 \Leftrightarrow \gamma_A(a_1) \subseteq \gamma_A(a_2)$ holds (this equivalence always holds for Galois insertions); (c) $\gamma_A(\top) = \mathrm{Dom}$. Let us point out that Definition 3.1 is very general since the concretization of an abstract value can be any program property, possibly a purely syntactic property or some space or time complexity property, as in the simple cases of Example 3.2 (1)-(2)-(5).

Let $\gamma_A : A \to \wp(\mathrm{Dom})$ and assume that Dom is defined by program stores, namely $\mathrm{Dom} \triangleq \mathrm{Var} \to \mathrm{Val}$, where Var is a finite set of program variables and Val is a corresponding denumerable set of values. Since $\mathrm{Var} \to \mathrm{Val}$ has a finite domain and a denumerable range, we can assume a recursive encoding of finite tuples of values into natural numbers $\mathbb{N}$, i.e. $\mathrm{Var} \to \mathrm{Val} \cong \mathbb{N}$, and define $\gamma_A : A \to \wp(\mathbb{N})$. This is equivalent assuming that programs have one single variable, say x, which may assume tuples of values in Val. A set of numbers $\gamma_A(a) \in \wp(\mathbb{N})$ is meant to represent a property of the values stored in the program variable x at the end of the program execution, that is, if the program terminates its execution then the variable x stores a value in $\gamma_A(a)$. Hence, as usual, the property $\varnothing \in \wp(\mathbb{N})$ means that the program does not correctly terminate its execution either by true nontermination or by some run-time error, namely, that the exit program point is not reachable. For simplicity, we do not consider intermediate program points and assertions in our semantics.

For an abstract domain $\langle A, \gamma_A, \leq_A \rangle$ in standard abstract interpretation, the corresponding concretization function $\gamma : A \to \wp(\mathrm{Prog})$ of Definition 3.1 is defined as:
$$\gamma(a) \triangleq \{P \in \mathrm{Prog} \mid \forall i \in \mathbb{N}.\ [\![P]\!](i) \in \gamma_A(a)\}$$
where we recall that $[\![P]\!](i) \in \gamma_A(a)$ means $[\![P]\!](i) = o \Rightarrow o \in \gamma_A(a)$. Hence, if A contains top $\top_A$ and bottom $\bot_A$ such that $\gamma_A(\top_A) = \mathbb{N}$ and $\gamma_A(\bot_A) = \varnothing$ then $\gamma(\top_A) = \mathrm{Prog}$ and $\gamma(\bot_A) = \{P \in \mathrm{Prog} \mid P \text{ never terminates}\}$. Moreover, since γ_A is monotonic, we have that γ is monotonic as well. The fact that all the elements in A are machine representable boils down to the requirement that A is a recursive set, while the binary preorder relation $\leq_\gamma$ is decidable because $a_1 \leq_A a_2 \Leftrightarrow \gamma(a_1) \subseteq \gamma(a_2)$ holds and $\leq_A$ is decidable. This therefore defines an abstract domain according to Definition 3.1.

In this simple view of the abstract domain A, there is no input property for the variable x, meaning that at the beginning x may store any value. It is easy to generalize the above definition by requiring an input abstract property in A for x, so that the abstract domain is a Cartesian product $A \times A$ together with a concretization $\gamma^{i/o} : A \times A \to \wp(\mathrm{Prog})$ defined as follows:

$$\gamma^{i/o}(\langle a_i, a_o \rangle) \triangleq \{P \in \mathrm{Prog} \mid \forall i \in \mathbb{N}.\, i \in \gamma_A(a_i) \Rightarrow [\![P]\!](i) \in \gamma_A(a_o)\}.$$

This is a generalization since, for any $a \in A$, we have that $\gamma(a) = \gamma^{i/o}(\langle \top_A, a \rangle)$.

Example 3.3 (Interval Abstract Domain). Let Int be the standard interval domain [7] restricted to natural numbers in $\mathbb{N}$, endowed with the standard subset ordering:

$$\mathrm{Int} \triangleq \{[a,b] \mid a, b \in \mathbb{N},\ a \leq b\} \cup \{\bot_{\mathrm{Int}}\} \cup \{[a, +\infty) \mid a \in \mathbb{N}\}$$

with concretization $\gamma_{\mathrm{Int}} : \mathrm{Int} \to \wp(\mathbb{N})$, where $\gamma_{\mathrm{Int}}(\bot_{\mathrm{Int}}) = \varnothing$, $\gamma_{\mathrm{Int}}([a,b]) = [a,b]$ and $\gamma_{\mathrm{Int}}([0,+\infty)) = \mathbb{N}$, so that $[0,+\infty)$ is also denoted by $\top_{\mathrm{Int}}$. Thus, here, for the concretization function $\gamma : \mathrm{Int} \to \wp(\mathrm{Prog})$ we have that: $\gamma(\top_{\mathrm{Int}}) = \mathrm{Prog}$, $\gamma(\bot_{\mathrm{Int}}) = \{P \in \mathrm{Prog} \mid \forall i.\, [\![P]\!](i)\!\uparrow\}$, $\gamma([a,+\infty)) = \{P \in \mathrm{Prog} \mid \forall i \in \mathbb{N}.\, [\![P]\!](i)\!\downarrow\ \Rightarrow [\![P]\!](i) \geq a\}$. We also have the input/output concretization $\gamma^{i/o} : \mathrm{Int} \times \mathrm{Int} \to \wp(\mathrm{Prog})$, where

$$\gamma^{i/o}(\langle I, J \rangle) \triangleq \{P \in \mathrm{Prog} \mid \forall i \in \mathbb{N}.\, i \in \gamma_{\mathrm{Int}}(I) \Rightarrow [\![P]\!](i) \in \gamma_{\mathrm{Int}}(J)\}. \qquad \square$$

4 Program Analysers and Verifiers

In our model, the notions of program analyser and verifier are as general as possible.

Definition 4.1 (Program Analyser). Given an abstract domain $\langle A, \gamma, \leq_\gamma \rangle$, a *program analyser* on A is any total recursive function $\mathcal{A} : \mathrm{Prog} \to A$.
The set of analysers on a given abstract domain A will be denoted by $\mathbb{A}_A$.
An analyser $\mathcal{A} \in \mathbb{A}_A$ is *sound* if for any $P \in \mathrm{Prog}$ and $a \in A$,

$$\mathcal{A}(P) \leq_\gamma a \Rightarrow P \in \gamma(a)$$

while $\mathcal{A}$ is *precise* if it is also complete, i.e., if the reverse implication also holds:

$$P \in \gamma(a) \Rightarrow \mathcal{A}(P) \leq_\gamma a. \qquad \square$$

Notice that this definition of soundness is equivalent to the standard notion of sound static analysis, namely, for any program P, $\mathcal{A}(P)$ always outputs a program assertion which is satisfied by P, i.e., $P \in \gamma(\mathcal{A}(P))$. Let us also note that on the empty abstract domain $\varnothing$, no analyser can be defined simply because there exists no function in $\mathrm{Prog} \to \varnothing$. Instead, for a singleton abstract domain $A_\bullet \triangleq \{\bullet\}$, if $\mathcal{A} \in \mathbb{A}_{A_\bullet}$ is sound then $\gamma(\bullet) = \mathrm{Prog}$, so that $\bullet$ is necessarily an abstract top. Also, if the abstract domain A contains a top abstract value

$\top_A \in A$ then, as expected, $\lambda P. \top_A$ is a trivially sound analyser on A. Finally, we observe that if $\mathcal{A}_1$ and $\mathcal{A}_2$ are both precise on the same abstract domain then we have $\mathcal{A}_1 =_\gamma \mathcal{A}_2$, meaning that $\mathcal{A}_1$ and $\mathcal{A}_2$ coincide up to equivalent abstract values, i.e., $\gamma \circ \mathcal{A}_1 = \gamma \circ \mathcal{A}_2$. In fact, for any $P \in \text{Prog}$, we have that $P \in \gamma(\mathcal{A}_2(P))$ implies $\gamma(\mathcal{A}_1(P)) \subseteq \gamma(\mathcal{A}_2(P))$ and $P \in \gamma(\mathcal{A}_1(P))$ implies $\gamma(\mathcal{A}_2(P)) \subseteq \gamma(\mathcal{A}_1(P))$, so that $\mathcal{A}_1 =_\gamma \mathcal{A}_2$.

Example 4.2. Software metrics static analysers [35] deal with nonsemantic program properties, such as the domain in Example 3.2 (1). Bounded model checking [4,34] handles program properties such as those encoded by the domains of Example 3.2 (2)-(3). Complexity bound analysers such as [32,36] cope with domains of properties such as those in Example 3.2 (4)-(5). Numerical abstract domains used in program analysis (see [23]) include the interval abstraction described in Example 3.3.   □

Definition 4.3 (Program Verifier). Given an abstract domain $\langle A, \gamma, \leq_\gamma \rangle$, a *program verifier* on A is any total recursive function $\mathcal{V} : \text{Prog} \times A \to \{\mathbf{t}, \mathbf{?}\}$. The set of verifiers on a given abstract domain A will be denoted by $\mathbb{V}_A$. A verifier $\mathcal{V} \in \mathbb{V}_A$ is *sound* if for any $P \in \text{Prog}$ and $a \in A$,

$$\mathcal{V}(P, a) = \mathbf{t} \Rightarrow P \in \gamma(a)$$

while $\mathcal{V}$ is *precise* if it is also complete, i.e., if the reverse implication also holds:

$$P \in \gamma(a) \Rightarrow \mathcal{V}(P, a) = \mathbf{t}.$$

A verifier $\mathcal{V} \in \mathbb{V}_A$ is *nontrivial* if for any program there exists at least one assertion which $\mathcal{V}$ is able to prove, i.e., for any $P \in \text{Prog}$ there exists some $a \in A$ such that $\mathcal{V}(P, a) = \mathbf{t}$. Also, a verifier is defined to be *trivial* when it is not nontrivial.
A verifier $\mathcal{V} \in \mathbb{V}_A$ is *monotone* when the verification algorithm is monotone w.r.t. $\leq_\gamma$, i.e., $(\mathcal{V}(P, a) = \mathbf{t} \wedge a \leq_\gamma a') \Rightarrow \mathcal{V}(P, a') = \mathbf{t}$.   □

Remark 4.4. Let us observe some straight consequences of Definition 4.3.
(1) Notice that for all nonempty abstract domains A, $\lambda(P, a). \mathbf{?}$ is a legal and vacuously sound verifier. Also, if $A = \varnothing$ is the empty abstract domain then the empty verifier $\mathcal{V} : \text{Prog} \times \varnothing \to \{\mathbf{t}, \mathbf{?}\}$ (namely, the function with empty graph) is trivially precise.
(2) Let us observe that if $\mathcal{V}$ is nontrivial and monotone then $\mathcal{V}$ is able to prove any abstract top: in fact, if $\top \in A$ and $\gamma(\top) = \text{Prog}$ then, for any $P \in \text{Prog}$, since there exists some $a \in A$ such that $\mathcal{V}(P, a) = \mathbf{t}$ and $a \leq_\gamma \top$, then, by monotonicity, $\mathcal{V}(P, \top) = \mathbf{t}$.
(3) Note that if a verifier $\mathcal{V}$ is precise then $\mathcal{V}(P, a) = \mathbf{?} \Leftrightarrow P \notin \gamma(a)$, so that in this case an output $\mathcal{V}(P, a) = \mathbf{?}$ always means that P does not satisfy the property a.
(4) Finally, if $\mathcal{V}_1$ and $\mathcal{V}_2$ are precise on the same abstract domain then $\mathcal{V}_1(P, a) = \mathbf{t} \Leftrightarrow P \in \gamma(a) \Leftrightarrow \mathcal{V}_2(P, a) = \mathbf{t}$, so that $\mathcal{V}_1 = \mathcal{V}_2$.   □

Example 4.5. Program verifiers abound in literature, e.g., [3,21,27]. For example, [13] aims at complexity verification on domains like that in Example 3.2 (5) while reachability verifiers like [33] can check numerical properties of program variables such as those of Example 3.3. □

5   Rice's Theorem for Static Program Analysis and Verification

Classical Rice's Theorem in computability theory [26,29,30] states that an extensional property $\Pi \subseteq \mathbb{N}$ of an effective numbering $\{\varphi_n \mid n \in \mathbb{N}\} = \mathbb{N} \xrightarrow{1} \mathbb{N}$ of partial recursive functions is a recursive set if and only if $\Pi = \varnothing$ or $\Pi = \mathbb{N}$, i.e., Π is trivial. Let us recall that $\Pi \subseteq \mathbb{N}$ is extensional when $\varphi_n = \varphi_m$ implies $n \in \Pi \Leftrightarrow m \in \Pi$. When dealing with program properties rather than indices of partial recursive functions, i.e., when $\Pi \subseteq \text{Prog}$, Rice's Theorem states that any nontrivial semantic program property is undecidable (see [28] for a statement of Rice's Theorem tailored for program properties). It is worth recalling that Rice's Theorem has been extended by Asperti [2] through an interesting generalization to so-called "complexity cliques", namely nonextensional program properties which may take into account the space or time complexity of programs: for example, the abstract domain of Example 3.2 (5) is not extensional but when logically "intersected" with an extensional domain (i.e., it is a product domain $A_1 \times A_2$ where the concretization function is the set intersection $\lambda \langle a_1, a_2 \rangle . \gamma_1(a_1) \cap \gamma_2(a_2)$) falls into this generalized version of Rice's Theorem.

In the following, we provide an instantiation of Rice's Theorem to sound static program analysis and verification by introducing a notion of extensionality for abstract domains. Abstract domains commonly used in abstract interpretation turn out to be extensional, when they are used for approximating the input/output behaviour of programs. For example, if a sound abstract interpretation of a program P in the interval abstract domain computes as abstract output a program assertion such as $x \in [1,5]$ and $y \in [2, +\infty)$ then this assertion is a sound abstract output for any other program Q having the same input/output behaviour of P.

Definition 5.1 (Extensional Abstract Domain). An abstract domain $\langle A, \gamma, \leq_\gamma \rangle$ is *extensional* when for any $a \in A$, $\gamma(a) \subseteq \text{Prog}$ is an extensional program property, namely, if $[\![P]\!] = [\![Q]\!]$ then $P \in \gamma(a) \Leftrightarrow Q \in \gamma(a)$.   □

As usual, the intuition is that an extensional program property depends exclusively on the input/output program semantics $[\![\cdot]\!]$. As a simple example, the domains of Example 3.2 (3)-(4) are extensional while the domains of Example 3.2 (1)-(2)-(5) are not.

Definition 5.2 (Trivial Abstract Domain). An abstract domain $\langle A, \gamma, \leq_\gamma \rangle$ is *trivial* when A contains abstract bottom or top elements only, i.e., for any $a \in A$, $\gamma(a) \in \{\varnothing, \text{Prog}\}$.   □

Definition 5.2 allows 4 possible types for a trivial abstract domain A: (1) $A = \varnothing$; (2) A is nonempty and consists of bottom elements only, i.e., $A \neq \varnothing$ and for all $a \in A$, $\gamma(a) = \varnothing$; (3) A is nonempty and consists of top elements only, i.e., $A \neq \varnothing$ and for all $a \in A$, $\gamma(a) = \mathrm{Prog}$; (4) A satisfies (2) and (3), i.e., A contains both bottom and top elements.

Theorem 5.3 (Rice's Theorem for Program Analysis). *Let $\langle A, \gamma, \leq_\gamma \rangle$ be an extensional abstract domain and let $\mathcal{A} \in \mathbb{A}_A$ be a sound analyser. Then, $\mathcal{A}$ is precise iff A is trivial.*

Proof. Since we assume the existence of a sound analyser $\mathcal{A} \in \mathbb{A}_A$ on the extensional abstract domain A, observe that necessarily $A \neq \varnothing$.

Assume that A is trivial. We have to show that for any $a \in A$ and $P \in \mathrm{Prog}$, $\mathcal{A}(P) \leq_\gamma a \Leftrightarrow P \in \gamma(a)$. Assume that $P \in \gamma(a)$ for some $a \in A$. Then, we have that $\gamma(a) \neq \varnothing$, so that, since A is trivial, it must necessarily be that $\gamma(a) = \mathrm{Prog}$. By soundness of $\mathcal{A}$, $P \in \gamma(\mathcal{A}(P))$, so that, since A is trivial, $\gamma(\mathcal{A}(P)) = \mathrm{Prog}$. Hence, we have that $\gamma(\mathcal{A}(P)) = \gamma(a)$, thus implying $\mathcal{A}(P) \leq_\gamma a$. On the other hand, if $\mathcal{A}(P) \leq_\gamma a$ then $\gamma(\mathcal{A}(P)) \subseteq \gamma(a)$, so that, since, by soundness of $\mathcal{A}$, $P \in \gamma(\mathcal{A}(P))$, we also have that $P \in \gamma(a)$.

Conversely, assume now that $\mathcal{A}$ is precise, namely, $P \in \gamma(a)$ iff $\mathcal{A}(P) \leq_\gamma a$. Thus, since $\mathcal{A}$ is a total recursive function and $\leq_\gamma$ is decidable, we have that, for any $a \in A$, $P \in^? \gamma(a)$ is decidable. Since $\gamma(a)$ is an extensional program property, by Rice's Theorem, $\gamma(a)$ must necessarily be trivial, i.e., $\gamma(a) \in \{\varnothing, \mathrm{Prog}\}$. This means that the abstract domain A is trivial. $\qquad\square$

Rice's Theorem for program analysis can be applied to several abstract domains. Due to lack of space, we just mention that the well-known undecidability of computing the meet over all paths (MOP) solution for a monotone dataflow analysis problem, proved by Kam and Ullman [15, Sect. 6] by resorting to undecidability of Post's Correspondence Problem, can be derived as a simple consequence of Theorem 5.3.

Along the same lines of Theorem 5.3, Rice's Theorem can be instantiated to program verification as follows.

Theorem 5.4 (Rice's Theorem for Program Verification). *Let $\langle A, \gamma, \leq_\gamma \rangle$ be an extensional abstract domain and let $\mathcal{V} \in \mathbb{V}_A$ be a sound, nontrivial and monotone verifier. Then, $\mathcal{V}$ is precise iff A is trivial.*

Proof. Let A be an extensional abstract domain and $\mathcal{V} \in \mathbb{V}_A$ be sound and nontrivial. If $A = \varnothing$ then A is trivial while the only possible verifier $\mathcal{V} : \mathrm{Prog} \times \varnothing \to \{\mathbf{t}, ?\}$ is the empty verifier, which is vacuously precise but it is not nontrivial. Thus, $A \neq \varnothing$ holds.

Assume that $\mathcal{V}$ is precise, that is, $P \in \gamma(a)$ iff $\mathcal{V}(P, a) = \mathbf{t}$. Hence, since $\mathcal{V}$ is a total recursive function, $\mathcal{V}(P, a) =^? \mathbf{t}$ is decidable, so that $P \in^? \gamma(a)$ is decidable as well. As in the proof of Theorem 5.3, since $\gamma(a)$ is an extensional program property, by Rice's Theorem, $\gamma(a) \in \{\varnothing, \mathrm{Prog}\}$. Thus, the abstract domain A is trivial.

Conversely, let $A \neq \varnothing$ be a trivial abstract domain. We have to prove that for any $a \in A$ and $P \in \text{Prog}$, $\mathcal{V}(P, a) = \mathbf{t} \Leftrightarrow P \in \gamma(a)$. Consider any $a \in A$. Since A is trivial, $\gamma(a) \in \{\varnothing, \text{Prog}\}$. If $\gamma(a) = \varnothing$ then, by soundness of $\mathcal{V}$, for any $P \in \text{Prog}$, $\mathcal{V}(P, a) = ?$, so that $\mathcal{V}(P, a) = \mathbf{t} \Leftrightarrow P \in \gamma(a)$ holds. If, instead, $\gamma(a) = \text{Prog}$, i.e. a is an abstract top, then, since $\mathcal{V}$ is assumed to be nontrivial and monotone, by Remark 4.4 (2), $\mathcal{V}$ is able to prove the abstract top a for any program, namely, for any $P \in \text{Prog}$, $\mathcal{V}(P, a) = \mathbf{t}$, so that $\mathcal{V}(P, a) = \mathbf{t} \Leftrightarrow P \in \gamma(a)$ holds. □

Let us remark a noteworthy difference of Theorem 5.4 w.r.t. Rice's theorem for static analysis. Let us consider a trivial abstract domain $A \triangleq \{\top\}$ with $\gamma(\top) = \text{Prog}$. Here, the trivially sound analyser $\lambda P.\top$ is also precise, in accordance with Theorem 5.3. Instead, the trivially sound verifier $\mathcal{V}_? \triangleq \lambda(P, a).?$ is not precise, because $P \in \gamma(\top) \Leftrightarrow \mathcal{V}_?(P, \top) = \mathbf{t}$ does not hold. The point here is that $\mathcal{V}_?$ lacks the property of being nontrivial, and therefore Theorem 5.4 cannot be applied. On the other hand, $\mathcal{V}_\mathbf{t} \triangleq \lambda(P, a).\mathbf{t}$ is nontrivial and precise, because, in this case, $P \in \gamma(\top) \Leftrightarrow \mathcal{V}_\mathbf{t}(P, \top) = \mathbf{t}$ holds. Similarly, if we consider the trivial abstract domain $A' \triangleq \{\top, \top'\}$, with $\gamma(\top) = \text{Prog} = \gamma(\top')$, then the verifier

$$\mathcal{V}'(P, a) \triangleq \begin{cases} \mathbf{t} & \text{if } a = \top \\ ? & \text{if } a = \top' \end{cases}$$

is sound and nontrivial, but still $\mathcal{V}'$ is not precise, because $P \in \gamma(\top') \Leftrightarrow \mathcal{V}'(P, \top') = \mathbf{t}$ does not hold. The point here is that $\mathcal{V}'$ is not monotone, because $\mathcal{V}'(P, \top) = \mathbf{t}$ and $\top \leq_\gamma \top'$ but $\mathcal{V}'(P, \top') \neq \mathbf{t}$, so that Theorem 5.4 cannot be applied.

6　Comparing Analysers and Verifiers

Let us now focus on a model for comparing the relative precision of program analysers and verifiers w.r.t. a common abstract domain $\langle A, \gamma, \leq_\gamma \rangle$.

Definition 6.1 (Comparison Relations). *Let* $\mathcal{V}, \mathcal{V}' \in \mathbb{V}_A$, $\mathcal{A}, \mathcal{A}' \in \mathbb{A}_A$, *and* $\mathcal{X}, \mathcal{Y} \in \mathbb{V}_A \cup \mathbb{A}_A$.

(1) $\mathcal{V} \sqsubseteq \mathcal{V}'$ *iff* $\forall P \in \text{Prog}.\forall a \in A.\ \mathcal{V}'(P, a) = \mathbf{t} \Rightarrow \mathcal{V}(P, a) = \mathbf{t}$
(2) $\mathcal{A} \sqsubseteq \mathcal{A}'$ *iff* $\forall P \in \text{Prog}.\ \mathcal{A}(P) \leq_\gamma \mathcal{A}'(P)$
(3) $\mathcal{V} \sqsubseteq \mathcal{A}$ *iff* $\forall P \in \text{Prog}.\forall a \in A.\ \mathcal{A}(P) \leq_\gamma a \Rightarrow \mathcal{V}(P, a) = \mathbf{t}$
(4) $\mathcal{A} \sqsubseteq \mathcal{V}$ *iff* $\forall P \in \text{Prog}.\forall a \in A.\ \mathcal{V}(P, a) = \mathbf{t} \Rightarrow \mathcal{A}(P) \leq_\gamma a$
(5) $\mathcal{X} \cong \mathcal{Y}$ *when* $\mathcal{X} \sqsubseteq \mathcal{Y}$ *and* $\mathcal{Y} \sqsubseteq \mathcal{X}$ □

Let us comment on the previous definitions, which intuitively take into account the relative "verification powers" of verifiers and analysers. The relation $\mathcal{V} \sqsubseteq \mathcal{V}'$ holds when every assertion proved by $\mathcal{V}'$ can be also proved by $\mathcal{V}$, while $\mathcal{A} \sqsubseteq \mathcal{A}'$ means that the output assertion provided by $\mathcal{A}$ is more precise than that produced by $\mathcal{A}'$. Also, a verifier $\mathcal{V}$ is more precise than an analyser

$\mathcal{A}$ when the verification power of $\mathcal{V}$ is not less than the verification power of $\mathcal{A}$, namely, any assertion a which can be proved by $\mathcal{A}$ for a program P, i.e. $\mathcal{A}(P) \leq_\gamma a$ holds, can be also proved by $\mathcal{V}$. Likewise, $\mathcal{A}$ is more precise than $\mathcal{V}$ when any assertion a proved by $\mathcal{V}$ can be also proved by $\mathcal{A}$, i.e., $\mathcal{V}(P,a) = \mathbf{t}$ implies $\mathcal{A}(P) \leq_\gamma a$.

Let us observe that $\langle \mathbb{V}_A, \sqsubseteq \rangle$ turns out to be a poset, while $\langle \mathbb{A}_A, \sqsubseteq \rangle$ is just a preordered set (cf. the lattice of abstract interpretations in [8]). We have that $\langle \mathbb{V}_A, \sqsubseteq \rangle$ has a greatest element $\mathcal{V}_? \triangleq \lambda(P,a).?$, which, in particular, is always sound although it is trivial. On the other hand, if A includes a top element $\top$ then $\mathcal{A}_\top \triangleq \lambda P.\top$ is a sound analyser which is a maximal element in $\langle \mathbb{A}_A, \sqsubseteq \rangle$. Also, $\mathcal{V} \cong \mathcal{V}'$ means that $\mathcal{V} = \mathcal{V}'$ as total functions, while $\mathcal{A} \cong \mathcal{A}'$ means that $\gamma \circ \mathcal{A} = \gamma \circ \mathcal{A}'$. Moreover, the comparison relation $\sqsubseteq$ is transitive even when considering analysers and verifiers together: if $\mathcal{V} \sqsubseteq \mathcal{A}$ and $\mathcal{A} \sqsubseteq \mathcal{V}'$ then $\mathcal{V} \sqsubseteq \mathcal{V}'$, and if $\mathcal{A} \sqsubseteq \mathcal{V}$ and $\mathcal{V} \sqsubseteq \mathcal{A}'$ then $\mathcal{A} \sqsubseteq \mathcal{A}'$. Also, the relation $\sqsubseteq$ shifts soundness from verifiers to analysers, and from analysers to verifiers as follows (due to lack of space the proof is omitted).

Lemma 6.2. *Let $\mathcal{V} \in \mathbb{V}_A$ and $\mathcal{A} \in \mathbb{A}_A$. If $\mathcal{V}$ is sound and $\mathcal{V} \sqsubseteq \mathcal{A}$ then $\mathcal{A}$ is sound; if $\mathcal{A}$ is sound and $\mathcal{A} \sqsubseteq \mathcal{V}$ then $\mathcal{V}$ is sound.*

As expected, any sound analyser can be used to refine a given sound verifier (cf. [19,20,24,25]) and this can be formalized and proved in our framework as follows.

Lemma 6.3. *Given $\mathcal{A} \in \mathbb{A}_A$ and $\mathcal{V} \in \mathbb{V}_A$ which are both sound, let*

$$\tau_\mathcal{A}(\mathcal{V})(P,a) \triangleq \begin{cases} \mathbf{t} & \text{if } \mathcal{A}(P) \leq_\gamma a \\ \mathcal{V}(P,a) & \text{if } \mathcal{A}(P) \not\leq_\gamma a \end{cases}$$

Then, $\tau_\mathcal{A}(\mathcal{V}) \in \mathbb{V}_A$ is sound, $\tau_\mathcal{A}(\mathcal{V}) \sqsubseteq \mathcal{V}$ and $\tau_\mathcal{A}(\mathcal{V}) = \mathcal{V} \Leftrightarrow \mathcal{V} \sqsubseteq \mathcal{A}$.

Proof. $\tau_\mathcal{A}(\mathcal{V}) \in \mathbb{V}_A$ is sound because both $\mathcal{A}$ and $\mathcal{V}$ are sound. If $\mathcal{V}(P,a) = \mathbf{t}$ then $\tau_\mathcal{A}(\mathcal{V})(P,a) = \mathbf{t}$, i.e., $\tau_\mathcal{A}(\mathcal{V}) \sqsubseteq \mathcal{V}$. Moreover, $\tau_\mathcal{A}(\mathcal{V}) = \mathcal{V}$ iff $\mathcal{A}(P) \leq_\gamma a \Rightarrow \mathcal{V}(P,a) = \mathbf{t}$ iff $\mathcal{V} \sqsubseteq \mathcal{A}$. □

6.1 Optimal and Best Analysers and Verifiers

It makes sense to define optimality by restricting to sound analysers and verifiers only. Optimality is defined as minimality w.r.t. the precision relation $\sqsubseteq$, while being the best analyser/verifier means to be the most precise.

Definition 6.4 (Optimal and Best Analysers and Verifiers). A sound analyser $\mathcal{A} \in \mathbb{A}_A$ is *optimal* if for any sound $\mathcal{A}' \in \mathbb{A}_A$, $\mathcal{A}' \sqsubseteq \mathcal{A} \Rightarrow \mathcal{A}' \cong \mathcal{A}$, while $\mathcal{A}$ is a *best* analyser if for any sound $\mathcal{A}' \in \mathbb{A}_A$, $\mathcal{A} \sqsubseteq \mathcal{A}'$.

A sound verifier $\mathcal{V} \in \mathbb{V}_A$ is *optimal* if for any $\mathcal{V}' \in \mathbb{V}_A$, $\mathcal{V}' \sqsubseteq \mathcal{V} \Rightarrow \mathcal{V}' \cong \mathcal{V}$, while $\mathcal{V}$ is the *best* verifier if for any $\mathcal{V}' \in \mathbb{V}_A$, $\mathcal{V} \sqsubseteq \mathcal{V}'$. □

Let us first observe that if a best analyser or verifier exists then this is unique, while for analysers if $\mathcal{A}_1$ and $\mathcal{A}_2$ are two best analysers on A then $\mathcal{A}_1 \cong \mathcal{A}_2$ holds. Of course, the possibility of defining an optimal/best analyser or verifier depends on the abstract domain A. For example, for a variable sign domain such as $\{\mathbb{Z}_{\leq 0}, \mathbb{Z}_{\geq 0}, \mathbb{Z}\}$ just optimal analysers and verifiers could be defined, because for approximating the set $\{0\}$ two optimal sound abstract values are available rather than a best sound abstract value. Here, the expected but interesting property to remark is that the notion of precise (i.e., sound and complete) analyser turns out to coincide with the notion of being the best analyser.

Lemma 6.5. *Let $\mathcal{A} \in \mathbb{A}_A$ be sound. Then, $\mathcal{A}$ is precise iff $\mathcal{A}$ is a best analyser.*

Proof. ($\Rightarrow$) Consider any sound $\mathcal{A}' \in \mathbb{A}_A$. Assume, by contradiction, that $\mathcal{A} \not\sqsubseteq \mathcal{A}'$, namely, there exists some $P \in$ Prog such that $\gamma(\mathcal{A}(P)) \not\subseteq \gamma(\mathcal{A}'(P))$. By soundness of $\mathcal{A}'$, $[\![P]\!] \in \gamma(\mathcal{A}'(P))$, so that, by precision of $\mathcal{A}$, $\gamma(\mathcal{A}(P)) \subseteq \gamma(\mathcal{A}'(P))$, which is a contradiction. Thus, $\mathcal{A} \sqsubseteq \mathcal{A}'$ holds. This means that $\mathcal{A}$ is a best analyser on A.

($\Leftarrow$) We have to prove that for any $P \in$ Prog and $a \in A$, $[\![P]\!] \in \gamma(a) \Rightarrow \gamma(\mathcal{A}(P)) \subseteq \gamma(a)$. Assume, by contradiction, that there exist $Q \in$ Prog and $b \in A$ such that $[\![Q]\!] \in \gamma(b)$ and $\gamma(\mathcal{A}(Q)) \not\subseteq \gamma(b)$. Then, we define $\mathcal{A}' :$ Prog $\to A$ as follows:

$$\mathcal{A}'(P) \triangleq \begin{cases} \mathcal{A}(P) & \text{if } P \not\equiv Q \\ b & \text{if } P \equiv Q \end{cases}$$

It turns out that $\mathcal{A}'$ is a total recursive function because $P \equiv Q$ is decidable. Moreover, $\mathcal{A}'$ is sound: assume that $\gamma(\mathcal{A}'(P)) \subseteq \gamma(a)$; if $P \not\equiv Q$ then $\mathcal{A}'(P) = \mathcal{A}(P)$ so that $\gamma(\mathcal{A}(P)) \subseteq \gamma(a)$, and, by soundness of $\mathcal{A}$, $[\![P]\!] \in \gamma(a)$; if $P \equiv Q$ then $\mathcal{A}'(Q) = b$ so that $\gamma(b) = \gamma(\mathcal{A}'(Q)) = \gamma(\mathcal{A}'(P)) \subseteq \gamma(a)$, hence, $[\![Q]\!] \in \gamma(b)$ implies $[\![Q]\!] \in \gamma(a)$. Since $\mathcal{A}$ is a best analyser on A, we have that $\mathcal{A} \sqsubseteq \mathcal{A}'$, so that $\gamma(\mathcal{A}(Q)) \subseteq \gamma(\mathcal{A}'(Q)) = \gamma(b)$, which is a contradiction. □

We therefore derive the following consequence of Rice's Theorem 5.3 for static analysis: the best analyser on an extensional abstract domain A exists if and only if A is trivial. This fact formalizes in our model the common intuition that, given any abstract domain, the best static analyser (where best means for any input program) cannot be defined due to Rice's Theorem. An analogous result can be given for verifiers.

Lemma 6.6. *Let $\mathcal{V} \in \mathbb{V}_A$ be sound. Then $\mathcal{V}$ is precise iff $\mathcal{V}$ is the best verifier on A.*

Proof. Assume that $\mathcal{V}$ is precise and $\mathcal{V}' \in \mathbb{V}_A$ be sound. If $\mathcal{V}'(P, a) = \mathbf{t}$ then, by soundness of $\mathcal{V}'$, $[\![P]\!] \in \gamma(a)$, and in turn, by completeness of $\mathcal{V}$, $\mathcal{V}(P, a) = \mathbf{t}$, thus proving that $\mathcal{V} \sqsubseteq \mathcal{V}'$. On the other hand, assume that $\mathcal{V}$ is the best verifier on A. Assume, by contradiction, that $\mathcal{V}$ is not complete, namely that there exist some $Q \in$ Prog and $b \in A$ such that $[\![Q]\!] \in \gamma(b)$ and $\mathcal{V}(Q, b) = ?$. We then define $\mathcal{V}' :$ Prog $\times A \to \{\mathbf{t}, ?\}$ as follows:

$$\mathcal{V}'(P,a) \triangleq \begin{cases} \mathbf{t} & \text{if } P \equiv Q \wedge a = b \\ \mathcal{V}(P,a) & \text{otherwise} \end{cases}$$

Then, $\mathcal{V}'$ is a total recursive function because $P \equiv Q$ and $a = b$ are decidable. Also, $\mathcal{V}'$ is sound because $[\![Q]\!] \in \gamma(b)$ and $\mathcal{V}$ is sound. Since $\mathcal{V}$ is the best verifier, we have that $\mathcal{V} \sqsubseteq \mathcal{V}'$, so that $\mathcal{V}'(Q,b) = \mathbf{t}$ implies $\mathcal{V}(Q,b) = \mathbf{t}$, which is a contradiction. $\square$

Thus, similarly to static analysis, as a consequence of Rice's Theorem 5.4 for verification, the best nontrivial and monotone verifier on an extensional abstract domain A exists if and only if A is trivial, which is a common belief in program verification. Let us also remark that best abstract program semantics, rather than program analysers, do exist for nontrivial domains (see e.g. [6]). Clearly, this is not in contradiction with Theorem 5.3 since these abstract program semantics are not total recursive functions, i.e., they are not program analysers.

7   Reducing Verification to Analysis and Back

As usual in computability and complexity, our comparison between verification and analysis is made through a many-one reduction, namely by reducing a verification problem into an analysis problem and vice versa. The minimal requirement is that these reduction functions are total recursive. Moreover, we require that the reduction function does not depend upon a fixed abstract domain. This allows us to be problem agnostic and to prove a reduction for all possible verifiers and analysers. Program verification and analysis are therefore equivalent problems whenever we can reduce one to the other. In the following, we prove that while it is always possible to transform a program analyser into an equivalent program verifier, the converse does not hold in general, but it can always be done for finite abstract domains.

7.1   Reducing Verification to Analysis

Theorem 7.1. *Let* $\langle A, \gamma, \leq_\gamma \rangle$ *be any given abstract domain. There exists a transform* $\sigma : \mathbb{A}_A \rightarrow \mathbb{V}_A$ *such that:*

(1) σ *is a total recursive function such that for all* $\mathcal{A} \in \mathbb{A}_A$, $\sigma(\mathcal{A}) \cong \mathcal{A}$;
(2) *if* $\mathcal{A} \in \mathbb{A}_A$ *is sound then* $\sigma(\mathcal{A})$ *is sound;*
(3) σ *is monotonic;*
(4) $\sigma(\mathcal{A}) \cong \sigma(\mathcal{A}') \Rightarrow \mathcal{A} \cong \mathcal{A}'$.

Proof. Given $\mathcal{A} \in \mathbb{A}_A$, we define $\sigma(\mathcal{A}) : \text{Prog} \times A \rightarrow \{\mathbf{t}, ?\}$ as follows:

$$\sigma(\mathcal{A})(P,a) \triangleq \begin{cases} \mathbf{t} & \text{if } \mathcal{A}(P) \leq_\gamma a \\ ? & \text{if } \mathcal{A}(P) \not\leq_\gamma a \end{cases}$$

(1) Since $\mathcal{A}$ is a total recursive function and $\leq_\gamma$ is decidable, we have that $\sigma(\mathcal{A})$ is a total recursive function, namely $\sigma(\mathcal{A}) \in \mathbb{V}_A$, and σ is a total recursive

function as well. Since, by definition, $\sigma(\mathcal{A})(P,a) = \mathbf{t} \Leftrightarrow \mathcal{A}(P) \leq_\gamma a$, we have that $\sigma(\mathcal{A}) \cong \mathcal{A}$. (2) By Lemma 6.2, if $\mathcal{A}$ is sound then the equivalent verifier $\sigma(\mathcal{A})$ is sound as well. (3) It turns out that σ is monotonic: if $\mathcal{A} \sqsubseteq \mathcal{A}'$ then $\sigma(\mathcal{A}')(P,a) = \mathbf{t} \Leftrightarrow \mathcal{A}'(P) \leq_\gamma a \Rightarrow \mathcal{A}(P) \leq_\gamma \mathcal{A}'(P) \leq_\gamma a \Leftrightarrow \sigma(\mathcal{A})(P,a) = \mathbf{t}$, so that $\sigma(\mathcal{A}) \sqsubseteq \sigma(\mathcal{A}')$ holds. (4) Assume that $\sigma(\mathcal{A}) \cong \sigma(\mathcal{A}')$, hence, for any $P \in$ Prog, $\sigma(\mathcal{A})(P,\mathcal{A}(P)) = \sigma(\mathcal{A}')(P,\mathcal{A}(P))$, namely, $\mathcal{A}(P) \leq_\gamma \mathcal{A}(P) \Leftrightarrow \mathcal{A}'(P) \leq_\gamma \mathcal{A}(P)$, so that $\mathcal{A}'(P) \leq_\gamma \mathcal{A}(P)$ holds. On the other hand, $\mathcal{A}(P) \leq_\gamma \mathcal{A}'(P)$ can be dually obtained, therefore $\gamma(\mathcal{A}(P)) = \gamma(\mathcal{A}'(P))$ holds, namely $\mathcal{A} \cong \mathcal{A}'$.   □

Intuitively, Theorem 7.1 shows that program verification on a given abstract domain A can always and unconditionally be reduced to program analysis on A. This means that a solution to the program analysis problem on A, i.e. the definition of an analyser $\mathcal{A}$, can constructively be transformed into a solution to the program verification problem on the same domain A, i.e. the design of a verifier $\sigma(\mathcal{A})$ which is equivalent to $\mathcal{A}$. The proof of Theorem 7.1 provides this constructive transform σ, which is defined as expected: an analyser $\mathcal{A}$ on any (possibly infinite) abstract domain A can be used as a verifier for any assertion $a \in A$ simply by checking whether $\mathcal{A}(P) \leq_\gamma a$ holds or not.

7.2 Reducing Analysis to Verification

It turns out that the converse of Theorem 7.1 does not hold, namely a program analysis problem in general cannot be reduced to a verification problem. Instead, this reduction can be always done for finite abstract domains. Given a verifier $\mathcal{V} \in \mathbb{V}_A$, for any program $P \in$ Prog, let us define $\mathcal{V}_\mathbf{t}(P) \triangleq \{a \in A \mid \mathcal{V}(P,a) = \mathbf{t}\}$, namely, $\mathcal{V}_\mathbf{t}(P)$ is the set of assertions proved by $\mathcal{V}$ for P. Also, given an assertion $a \in A$, we define $\uparrow a \triangleq \{a' \in A \mid a \leq_\gamma a'\}$ as the set of assertions weaker than a. The following result provides a useful characterization of the equivalence between verifiers and analysers.

Lemma 7.2. *Let $\langle A, \gamma, \leq_\gamma \rangle$ be an abstract domain, $\mathcal{A} \in \mathbb{A}_A$ and $\mathcal{V} \in \mathbb{V}_A$. Then, $\mathcal{A} \cong \mathcal{V}$ if and only if for any $P \in$ Prog, $\mathcal{V}_\mathbf{t}(P) = \uparrow\mathcal{A}(P)$.*

Proof. By Definition 6.1, it turns out that $\mathcal{A} \sqsubseteq \mathcal{V}$ iff for any P, $\mathcal{V}_\mathbf{t}(P) \subseteq \uparrow\mathcal{A}(P)$, while we have that $\mathcal{V} \sqsubseteq \mathcal{A}$ iff for any P, $\uparrow\mathcal{A}(P) \subseteq \mathcal{V}_\mathbf{t}(P)$. Thus, $\mathcal{A} \cong \mathcal{V}$ if and only if for any $P \in$ Prog, $\mathcal{V}_\mathbf{t}(P) = \uparrow\mathcal{A}(P)$.   □

A consequence of Lemma 7.2 is that, given $\mathcal{V} \in \mathbb{V}_A$, $\mathcal{V}$ can be transformed into an equivalent analyser $\tau(\mathcal{V}) \in \mathbb{A}_A$ if and only if for any program P, an assertion $a_P \in A$ exists such that $\mathcal{V}_\mathbf{t}(P) = \uparrow a_P$. In this case, one can then define $\tau(\mathcal{V})(P) \triangleq a_P$.

Lemma 7.3. *Let $\langle A, \gamma, \leq_\gamma \rangle$ be an abstract domain and $\mathcal{V} \in \mathbb{V}_A$. If $\mathcal{A} \in \mathbb{A}_A$ is such that $\mathcal{A} \cong \mathcal{V}$ then: (1) $A \neq \varnothing$; (2) $\mathcal{V}$ is not trivial; (3) $\mathcal{V}$ is monotone.*

Proof. (1) We observed just after Definition 4.1 that no analyser can be defined on the empty abstract domain. (2) If $\mathcal{V}$ is trivial then there exists a program

$Q \in \text{Prog}$ such that for any $a \in A$, $\mathcal{V}(Q, a) = ?$, so that if $\mathcal{V} \cong \mathcal{A}$ for some $\mathcal{A} \in \mathbb{A}_A$ then, from $\mathcal{V} \sqsubseteq \mathcal{A}$ we would derive $\mathcal{V}(Q, \mathcal{A}(Q)) = \mathbf{t}$, which is a contradiction. (3) Assume that $\mathcal{V}$ is not monotone. Then, there exist $Q \in \text{Prog}$ and $a, a' \in A$ such that $a \in \mathcal{V}_t(Q)$, $a \leq_\gamma a'$ but $a' \notin \mathcal{V}_t(Q)$. If $\mathcal{V} \cong \mathcal{A}$, for some $\mathcal{A} \in \mathbb{A}_A$, then, by Lemma 7.2, $\mathcal{V}_t(Q) = {\uparrow}\mathcal{A}(Q)$, so that we would have that $a \in {\uparrow}\mathcal{A}(Q)$ but $a' \notin {\uparrow}\mathcal{A}(Q)$, which is a contradiction. $\qquad\square$

We also observe that even for a nontrivial and monotone verifier $\mathcal{V} \in \mathbb{V}_A$ on a finite abstract domain A, it is not guaranteed that an equivalent analyser exists. In fact, if an equivalent analyser $\mathcal{A}$ exists then, by Lemma 7.2, for any program P, $\mathcal{V}_t(P)$ must contain the least element, namely for any program P it must be the case that there exists a strongest assertion proved by $\mathcal{V}$ for P.

Example 7.4. Consider a sign domain such as $S \triangleq \{\mathbb{Z}_{\leq 0}, \mathbb{Z}_{\geq 0}, \mathbb{Z}\}$ where $\mathbb{Z}_{\leq 0} \leq_\gamma \mathbb{Z}$ and $\mathbb{Z}_{\geq 0} \leq_\gamma \mathbb{Z}$. For a program such as $Q \equiv x := 0$, a sound verifier $\mathcal{V} \in \mathbb{V}_S$ could be able to prove all the assertions in S, namely $\mathcal{V}_t(Q) = S$. However, there exists no assertion $a_Q \in S$ such that $\mathcal{V}_t(Q) = {\uparrow}a_Q$. Hence, by Lemma 7.2, there exists no analyser in $\mathbb{A}_S$ which is equivalent to $\mathcal{V}$. Also, if $S' \triangleq \{\mathbb{Z}_{=0}, \mathbb{Z}_{\leq 0}, \mathbb{Z}_{\geq 0}, \mathbb{Z}\}$, so that S' is a meet-semilattice, and $\mathcal{V}' \in \mathbb{V}_{S'}$ is a sound verifier such that $\mathcal{V}'_t(Q) = S' \smallsetminus \{\mathbb{Z}_{=0}\}$, still, by Lemma 7.2, there exists no analyser in $\mathbb{A}_{S'}$ which is equivalent to $\mathcal{V}'$. $\qquad\square$

Definition 7.5. A verifier $\mathcal{V} \in \mathbb{V}_A$ is *finitely meet-closed* when for any $P \in \text{Prog}$ and $a, a_1, a_2 \in A$, if $\mathcal{V}(P, a_1) = \mathbf{t} = \mathcal{V}(P, a_2)$ and $\gamma(a) = \gamma(a_1) \cap \gamma(a_2)$ then $\mathcal{V}(P, a) = \mathbf{t}$. The following notation will be used: for any domain A,

$$\mathbb{V}_A^+ \triangleq \{\mathcal{V} \in \mathbb{V}_A \mid \mathcal{V} \text{ is nontrivial, monotone and finitely meet-closed}\}. \qquad \square$$

Thus, finitely meet-closed verifiers can prove logical conjunctions of provable assertions.

Theorem 7.6 (Reduction for Finite Domains). *Let $\langle A, \gamma, \leq_\gamma \rangle$ be a nonempty finite abstract domain. There exists a transform $\tau : \mathbb{V}_A^+ \to \mathbb{A}_A$ such that:*

(1) *τ is a total recursive function such that for all $\mathcal{V} \in \mathbb{V}_A^+$, $\tau(\mathcal{V}) \cong \mathcal{V}$;*
(2) *if $\mathcal{V} \in \mathbb{V}_A^+$ is sound then $\tau(\mathcal{V})$ is sound;*
(3) *τ is monotonic;*
(4) *$\tau(\mathcal{V}) \cong \tau(\mathcal{V}') \Rightarrow \mathcal{V} \cong \mathcal{V}'$.*

Proof. (1) Let $A = \{a_1, ..., a_n\}$ be any enumeration of A, with $n \geq 1$. Given $\mathcal{V} \in \mathbb{V}_A^+$, we define $\tau(\mathcal{V}) : \text{Prog} \to A$ as follows:

$$\tau(\mathcal{V})(P) \triangleq \begin{cases} r := \text{undef}; \\ \textbf{forall } i \in 1..n \textbf{ do} \\ \qquad \textbf{if } \big(a_i \in \mathcal{V}_t(P) \wedge (r = \text{undef} \vee a_i \leq_\gamma r)\big) \textbf{ then } r := a_i; \\ \textbf{output } r \end{cases}$$

Then, it turns out that τ is a total recursive function. Since $\mathcal{V}$ is a total recursive function, A is finite and $\leq_\gamma$ is decidable, we have that $\tau(\mathcal{V})$ is a total recursive function, so that $\tau(\mathcal{V}) \in \mathbb{A}_A$. Since $\mathcal{V}$ is not trivial, for any $P \in \mathrm{Prog}$, $\mathcal{V}_t(P) \neq \varnothing$. Also, since A is finite and $\mathcal{V}$ is finitely meet-closed there exists some $a_k \in \mathcal{V}_t(P)$ such that $\mathcal{V}_t(P) \subseteq \uparrow a_k$, so that $\tau(\mathcal{V})(P)$ outputs some value in A. Moreover, since $\mathcal{V}$ is monotone, $\uparrow a_k \subseteq \mathcal{V}_t(P)$, so that $\uparrow a_k = \mathcal{V}_t(P)$. Thus, the above procedure defining $\tau(\mathcal{V})(P)$ finds and outputs a_k. Hence, for any $P \in \mathrm{Prog}$ and $a \in A$, $\mathcal{V}(P, a) = t \Leftrightarrow a \in \mathcal{V}_t(P) \Leftrightarrow a \in \uparrow a_k \Leftrightarrow a_k \leq_\gamma a \Leftrightarrow \tau(\mathcal{V})(P) \leq_\gamma a$, that is, $\tau(\mathcal{V}) \cong \mathcal{V}$ holds.

(2) By Lemma 6.2, if $\mathcal{V}$ is sound then the equivalent analyser $\tau(\mathcal{V})$ is sound as well.

(3) It turns out that τ is monotonic: if $\mathcal{V} \sqsubseteq \mathcal{V}'$ then, by definition, $\mathcal{V}'_t(P) \subseteq \mathcal{V}_t(P)$, so that, since $\mathcal{V}_t(P) = \uparrow \tau(\mathcal{V})(P)$ and $\mathcal{V}'_t(P) = \uparrow \tau(\mathcal{V}')(P)$, we obtain $\tau(\mathcal{V})(P) \leq_\gamma \tau(\mathcal{V}')(P)$, namely $\tau(\mathcal{V}) \sqsubseteq \tau(\mathcal{V}')$ holds.

(4) Assume that $\tau(\mathcal{V}) \cong \tau(\mathcal{V}')$. Hence, for any $P \in \mathrm{Prog}$, $\gamma(\tau(\mathcal{V})(P)) = \gamma(\tau(\mathcal{V}')(P))$, so that, since $\mathcal{V}_t(P) = \uparrow \tau(\mathcal{V})(P)$ and $\mathcal{V}'_t(P) = \uparrow \tau(\mathcal{V}')(P)$, we obtain $\mathcal{V}_t(P) = \mathcal{V}'_t(P)$, namely $\mathcal{V} = \mathcal{V}'$. $\qquad \square$

An example of this reduction of verification to static analysis for finite domains is dataflow analysis as model checking shown in [31] (excluding Kildall's constant propagation domain [16]). Let us now focus on infinite domains of assertions.

Lemma 7.7. *There exists a denumerable infinite abstract domain $\langle A, \gamma, \leq_\gamma \rangle$ and a verifier $\mathcal{V} \in \mathbb{V}_A^+$ such that for any analyser $\mathcal{A} \in \mathbb{A}_A$, $\mathcal{A} \ncong \mathcal{V}$.*

Proof. Let us consider the infinite domain $T \triangleq \mathbb{N} \cup \{\top\}$ together with the following concretization function: $\gamma(\top) \triangleq \mathrm{Prog}$ and, for any $n \in \mathbb{N}$,

$$\gamma(n) \triangleq \{P \in \mathrm{Prog} \mid P \text{ on input } 0 \text{ converges in } n \text{ or fewer steps}\}$$

where the number of steps is determined by a small-step operational semantics $\Rightarrow$, as recalled in Sect. 2. Thus, we have that if $n, m \in \mathbb{N}$ then $n \leq_\gamma m$ iff $n \leq_\mathbb{N} m$, while $n \leq_\gamma \top$. We define a function $\mathcal{V} : \mathrm{Prog} \times T \to \{t, ?\}$ as follows:

$$\mathcal{V}(P, a) \triangleq \begin{cases} t & \text{if } a = \top \\ t & \text{if } a = n \text{ and } P \text{ on input } 0 \text{ converges in } n \text{ or fewer steps} \\ ? & \text{if } a = n \text{ and } P \text{ on input } 0 \text{ does not converge in } n \text{ or fewer steps} \end{cases}$$

Clearly, for any number $n \in \mathbb{N}$, the predicate "P on input 0 converges in n or fewer steps" is decidable, where the input 0 could be replaced by any other (finite set of) input value(s). Hence, $\mathcal{V}$ turns out to be a total recursive function, that is, a verifier on the abstract domain T. In particular, let us remark that $\mathcal{V}$ is a sound verifier. Moreover, $\mathcal{V}$ is nontrivial, since, for any $P \in \mathrm{Prog}$, $\mathcal{V}(P, \top) = t$, and monotone because if $\mathcal{V}(P, n) = t$ and $n \leq_\gamma a$ then either $a = \top$ and $\mathcal{V}(P, \top) = t$ or $a = m$, so that $n \leq_\mathbb{N} m$ and therefore $\mathcal{V}(P, m) = t$. Clearly, $\mathcal{V}$ is also finitely meet-closed, because if $\mathcal{V}(P, a_1) = t = \mathcal{V}(P, a_2)$ and $\gamma(a) = \gamma(a_1) \cap \gamma(a_2)$ then either $a = a_1$ or $a = a_2$, so that $\mathcal{V}(P, a) = \mathbf{t}$. Summing up, it turns out that $\mathcal{V} \in \mathbb{V}_\mathsf{T}^+$. Assume now, by contradiction, that there exists an analyser $\mathcal{A} \in \mathbb{A}_\mathsf{T}$ such that $\mathcal{A} \cong \mathcal{V}$. By Lemma 7.2, for any $P \in \mathrm{Prog}$, we have that $\mathcal{V}_\mathbf{t}(P) = {\uparrow}\mathcal{A}(P)$. Hence, if P on input 0 diverges then $\mathcal{V}_\mathbf{t}(P) = \{\top\}$ so that $\mathcal{A}(P) = \top$, while if P on input 0 converges in exactly n steps then $\mathcal{V}_\mathbf{t}(P) = \{m \in \mathbb{N} \mid m \geq n\} \cup \{\top\}$, so $\mathcal{A}(P) = n$, namely $\mathcal{A}$ goes as follows:

$$\mathcal{A}(P) = \begin{cases} \top & \text{if } P \text{ on input 0 diverges} \\ n & \text{if } P \text{ on input 0 converges in exactly } n \text{ steps} \end{cases}$$

Since $\mathcal{A}$ is a total recursive function, we would have defined an algorithm $\mathcal{A}$ for deciding if a program $P \in \mathrm{Prog}$ on input 0 terminates or not. Since Prog is assumed to be Turing complete with respect to the operational semantics $\Rightarrow$, this leads to a contradiction. $\qquad\square$

As a straight consequence of Lemma 7.7, the following theorem proves that for any infinite abstract domain A, no reduction from verifiers in $\mathbb{V}_A^+$ to equivalent analysers in $\mathbb{A}_A$ is possible.

Theorem 7.8 (Impossibility of the Reduction for Infinite Domains). *For any denumerable infinite abstract domain $\langle A, \gamma, \leq_\gamma \rangle$, there exists no function $\tau : \mathbb{V}_A^+ \to \mathbb{A}_A$ such that τ is a total recursive function and for all $\mathcal{V} \in \mathbb{V}_A^+$, $\tau(\mathcal{V}) \cong \mathcal{V}$.*

Proof. Assume, by contradiction, that $\tau : \mathbb{V}_A^+ \to \mathbb{A}_A$ is a total recursive function such that for all $\mathcal{V} \in \mathbb{V}_A^+$, $\tau(\mathcal{V}) \in \mathbb{A}_A$ and $\tau(\mathcal{V}) \cong \mathcal{V}$. Then, for the infinite domain A and verifier $\mathcal{V} \in \mathbb{V}_A^+$ provided by Lemma 7.7, we would be able to construct an analyser $\tau(\mathcal{V}) \in \mathbb{A}_A$ such that $\tau(\mathcal{V}) \cong \mathcal{V}$, which would be in contradiction with Lemma 7.7. $\qquad\square$

Intuitively, this result states that given any infinite abstract domain A, no general algorithm exists for constructively designing out of a reasonable (i.e., nontrivial, monotone and finitely meet-closed) verifier $\mathcal{V}$ on A an equivalent analyser on the same domain A. This can be read as a precise statement proving the folklore belief that "program analysis is harder than verification", at least for infinite domains of program assertions. It is important to remark that the verifier $\mathcal{V} \in \mathbb{V}_A^+$ on the infinite domain A defined by the proof of Lemma 7.7 is sound. Thus, even if we restrict the reduction transform $\tau : \mathbb{V}_A^{+,\mathrm{sound}} \to \mathbb{A}_A^{\mathrm{sound}}$ of Theorem 7.8 to be applied to sound verifiers—so that by Lemma 6.2 the range would be the sound analysers in $\mathbb{A}_A$—the same proof of Lemma 7.7 could still be used for proving that such transform τ cannot exist.

A further consequence of Theorem 7.8 is the fact proved in [10] that abstract interpretation-based program analysis with infinite domains and widening/narrowing operators is strictly more powerful than with finite domains.

8   Conclusion and Future Work

We put forward a general model for studying static program analysers and veri-fiers from a computability perspective. This allowed us to state and prove, with simple arguments borrowed from standard computability theory, that for infi-nite abstract domains of program assertions, program analysis is a harder prob-lem than program verification. This is, to the best of our knowledge, the first formalization and proof of this popular belief, which also includes the relation-ship between type inference and type checking. We think that this foundational model can be extended to study further properties of program analysers and verifiers. In particular, this opens interesting perspectives in reasoning about program analysis and verification in a more abstract way towards a theory of computation that may include approximate methods, such as program analysers and verifiers, as objects of investigation, as suggested in [5,14]. For instance, the precision of program analysis and program verification, as well as their computa-tional complexity, are intensional program properties. Intensionally different but extensionally equivalent programs may exhibit completely different behaviours when analysed or verified. In this perspective, new intensional versions of Rice's Theorem can be stated for program analysis, similarly to what is known for Blum's complexity in [2]. Also, new models for reasoning about the space and time complexities of program analysis and verification algorithms can be stud-ied, especially for defining a notion of complexity class of program analysers and verifiers.

References

1. Alglave, J., Donaldson, A.F., Kroening, D., Tautschnig, M.: Making software veri-fication tools really work. In: Bultan, T., Hsiung, P.-A. (eds.) ATVA 2011. LNCS, vol. 6996, pp. 28–42. Springer, Heidelberg (2011). https://doi.org/10.1007/978-3-642-24372-1_3

2. Asperti, A.: The intensional content of Rice's theorem. In: Proceedings of 35th ACM Symposium on Principles of Programming Languages (POPL 2008), pp. 113–119. ACM (2008)

3. Barnett, M., Chang, B.-Y.E., DeLine, R., Jacobs, B., Leino, K.R.M.: Boogie: a modular reusable verifier for object-oriented programs. In: de Boer, F.S., Bon-sangue, M.M., Graf, S., de Roever, W.-P. (eds.) FMCO 2005. LNCS, vol. 4111, pp. 364–387. Springer, Heidelberg (2006). https://doi.org/10.1007/11804192_17

4. Biere, A., Cimatti, A., Clarke, E., Zhu, Y.: Symbolic model checking without BDDs. In: Cleaveland, W.R. (ed.) TACAS 1999. LNCS, vol. 1579, pp. 193–207. Springer, Heidelberg (1999). https://doi.org/10.1007/3-540-49059-0_14

5. Cadar, C., Donaldson, A.F.: Analysing the program analyser. In: Proceedings of 38th International Conference on Software Engineering (ICSE 2016), pp. 765–768. ACM (2016)

6. Cousot, P.: Constructive design of a hierarchy of semantics of a transition system by abstract interpretation. Theor. Comput. Sci. **277**(1–2), 47–103 (2002)

7. Cousot, P., Cousot, R.: Abstract interpretation: a unified lattice model for static analysis of programs by construction or approximation of fixpoints. In: Proceedings of 4th ACM Symposium on Principles of Programming Languages (POPL 1977), pp. 238–252. ACM Press (1977)
8. Cousot, P., Cousot, R.: Systematic design of program analysis frameworks. In: Proceedings of 6th ACM Symposium on Principles of Programming Languages (POPL 1979), pp. 269–282. ACM Press (1979)
9. Cousot, P., Cousot, R.: Abstract interpretation frameworks. J. Logic Comp. **2**(4), 511–547 (1992)
10. Cousot, P., Cousot, R.: Comparing the Galois connection and widening/narrowing approaches to abstract interpretation. In: Bruynooghe, M., Wirsing, M. (eds.) PLILP 1992. LNCS, vol. 631, pp. 269–295. Springer, Heidelberg (1992). https://doi.org/10.1007/3-540-55844-6_142
11. Cousot, P., Halbwachs, N.: Automatic discovery of linear restraints among variables of a program. In: Proceedings of 5th ACM Symposium on Principles of Programming Languages (POPL 1978), pp. 84–96. ACM Press (1978)
12. Cutland, N.: Computability: An Introduction to Recursive Function Theory. Cambridge University Press, Cambridge (1980)
13. Flajolet, P., Salvy, B., Zimmermann, P.: Lambda-Upsilon-Omega: an assistant algorithms analyzer. In: Mora, T. (ed.) AAECC 1988. LNCS, vol. 357, pp. 201–212. Springer, Heidelberg (1989). https://doi.org/10.1007/3-540-51083-4_60
14. Giacobazzi, R., Logozzo, F., Ranzato, F.: Analyzing program analyses. In: Proceedings of 42nd ACM Symposium on Principles of Programming Languages (POPL 2015), pp. 261–273. ACM Press (2015)
15. Kam, J.B., Ullman, J.D.: Monotone data flow analysis frameworks. Acta Informatica **7**, 305–317 (1977)
16. Kildall, G.A.: A unified approach to global program optimization. In: Proceedings of 1st ACM Symposium on Principles of Programming Languages (POPL 1973), pp. 194–206 (1973)
17. Laski, J., Stanley, W.: Software Verification and Analysis: An Integrated, Hands-on Approach. Springer, Heidelberg (2009). https://doi.org/10.1007/978-1-84882-240-5
18. Leibniz, G.: Dissertatio de arte combinatoria, Habilitation Thesis in Philosophy at Leipzig University (1666). https://en.wikipedia.org/wiki/De_Arte_Combinatoria
19. Leino, K.R.M., Logozzo, F.: Loop invariants on demand. In: Yi, K. (ed.) APLAS 2005. LNCS, vol. 3780, pp. 119–134. Springer, Heidelberg (2005). https://doi.org/10.1007/11575467_9
20. Leino, K., Logozzo, F.: Using widenings to infer loop invariants inside an SMT solver, or: a theorem prover as abstract domain. In: Proceedings of International Workshop on Invariant Generation (WING 2007) (2007)
21. Leino, K.R.M.: Dafny: an automatic program verifier for functional correctness. In: Clarke, E.M., Voronkov, A. (eds.) LPAR 2010. LNCS (LNAI), vol. 6355, pp. 348–370. Springer, Heidelberg (2010). https://doi.org/10.1007/978-3-642-17511-4_20
22. Merz, F., Sinz, C., Falke, S.: Challenges in comparing software verification tools for C. In: Proceedings of 1st International Workshop on Comparative Empirical Evaluation of Reasoning Systems (COMPARE 2012), Manchester, UK, pp. 60–65 (2012)
23. Miné, A.: Tutorial on static inference of numeric invariants by abstract interpretation. Found. Trends Program. Lang. **4**(3–4), 120–372 (2017)

24. Moy, Y.: Sufficient preconditions for modular assertion checking. In: Logozzo, F., Peled, D.A., Zuck, L.D. (eds.) VMCAI 2008. LNCS, vol. 4905, pp. 188–202. Springer, Heidelberg (2008). https://doi.org/10.1007/978-3-540-78163-9_18

25. Moy, Y., Marché, C.: Modular inference of subprogram contracts for safety checking. J. Symb. Comput. **45**(11), 1184–1211 (2010)

26. Odifreddi, P.: Classical Recursion Theory. Studies in Logic and the Foundations of Mathematics. Elsevier, New York City (1999)

27. O'Halloran, C.: Where is the value in a program verifier? In: Shankar, N., Woodcock, J. (eds.) VSTTE 2008. LNCS, vol. 5295, pp. 255–262. Springer, Heidelberg (2008). https://doi.org/10.1007/978-3-540-87873-5_21

28. Reus, B.: Limits of Computation from a Programming Perspective. Springer, Heidelberg (2016). https://doi.org/10.1007/978-3-319-27889-6

29. Rice, H.G.: Classes of recursively enumerable sets and their decision problems. Trans. Amer. Math. Soc. **74**(2), 358–366 (1953)

30. Rogers, H.: Theory of Recursive Functions and Effective Computability. The MIT press, Cambridge (1992)

31. Schmidt, D.A.: Data flow analysis is model checking of abstract interpretations. In: Proceedings of 25th ACM Symposium on Principles of Programming Languages (POPL 1998), pp. 38–48. ACM (1998)

32. Sinn, M., Zuleger, F., Veith, H.: Complexity and resource bound analysis of imperative programs using difference constraints. J. Autom. Reasoning **59**(1), 3–45 (2017)

33. Stefanescu, A., Park, D., Yuwen, S., Li, Y., Rosu, G.: Semantics-based program verifiers for all languages. In: Proceedings of ACM International Conference on Object-Oriented Programming, Systems, Languages, and Applications (OOPSLA 2016), pp. 74–91. ACM (2016)

34. Shtrichman, O.: Tuning SAT checkers for bounded model checking. In: Emerson, E.A., Sistla, A.P. (eds.) CAV 2000. LNCS, vol. 1855, pp. 480–494. Springer, Heidelberg (2000). https://doi.org/10.1007/10722167_36

35. Vogelsang, A., Fehnker, A., Huuck, R., Reif, W.: Software metrics in static program analysis. In: Dong, J.S., Zhu, H. (eds.) ICFEM 2010. LNCS, vol. 6447, pp. 485–500. Springer, Heidelberg (2010). https://doi.org/10.1007/978-3-642-16901-4_32

36. Wilhelm, R., Engblom, J., Ermedahl, A., Holsti, N., Thesing, S., Whalley, D., Bernat, G., Ferdinand, C., Heckmann, R., Mitra, T., Mueller, F., Puaut, I., Puschner, P., Staschulat, J., Stenström, P.: The worst-case execution-time problem - overview of methods and survey of tools. ACM Trans. Embed. Comput. Syst. **7**(3), 361–3653 (2008)

Theory and Security

Automata vs Linear-Programming Discounted-Sum Inclusion

Suguman Bansal[✉], Swarat Chaudhuri[✉], and Moshe Y. Vardi[✉]

Rice University, Houston, TX 77005, USA
suguman@rice.edu

Abstract. The problem of *quantitative inclusion* formalizes the goal of comparing quantitative dimensions between systems such as worst-case execution time, resource consumption, and the like. Such systems are typically represented by formalisms such as weighted logics or weighted automata. Despite its significance in analyzing the quality of computing systems, the study of quantitative inclusion has mostly been conducted from a theoretical standpoint. In this work, we conduct the first empirical study of quantitative inclusion for discounted-sum weighted automata (DS-inclusion, in short).

Currently, two contrasting approaches for DS-inclusion exist: the linear-programming based DetLP and the purely automata-theoretic BCV. Theoretical complexity of DetLP is exponential in time and space while of BCV is PSPACE-complete. All practical implementations of BCV, however, are also exponential in time and space. Hence, it is not clear which of the two algorithms renders a superior implementation.

In this work we present the first implementations of these algorithms, and perform extensive experimentation to compare between the two approaches. Our empirical analysis shows how the two approaches complement each other. This is a nuanced picture that is much richer than the one obtained from the theoretical study alone.

1 Introduction

The analysis of quantitative dimensions of systems, such as worst-case execution time, energy consumption, and the like, has been studied thoroughly in recent times. By and large, these investigations have tended to be purely theoretical. While some efforts in this space [12,13] do deliver prototype tools, the area lacks a thorough empirical understanding of the relative performance of different but related algorithmic solutions. In this paper, we further such an empirical understanding for *quantitative inclusion* for *discounted-sum weighted automata*.

Weighted automata [17] are a popular choice for system models in quantitative analysis. The problem of quantitative language inclusion [15] formalizes the goal of determining which of any two given systems is more efficient under such a system model. In a discounted-sum weighted automata the value of quantitative dimensions are computed by *aggregating* the costs incurred during each step of a system execution with discounted-sum aggregation. The discounted-sum (DS) function relies on the intuition that costs incurred in the near future

H. Chockler and G. Weissenbacher (Eds.): CAV 2018, LNCS 10982, pp. 99–116, 2018.
https://doi.org/10.1007/978-3-319-96142-2_9

are more "expensive" than costs incurred later on. Naturally, it is the choice for aggregation for applications in economics and game-theory [20], Markov Decision Processes with discounted rewards [16], quantitative safety [13], and more.

The hardness of quantitative inclusion for nondeterministic DS-automata, or DS-inclusion, is evident from PSPACE-hardness of language-inclusion (LI) problem for nondeterministic Büchi automata [23]. Decision procedures for DS-inclusion were first investigated in [15], and subsequently through target discounted-sum [11], DS-determinization [10]. A comparator-based argument [9] finally established its PSPACE-completeness. However, these theoretical advances in DS-inclusion have not been accompanied with the development of efficient and scalable tools and algorithms. This is the focus of this paper; our goal is to develop practical algorithms and tools for DS-inclusion.

Theoretical advances have lead to two algorithmic approaches for DS-inclusion. The first approach, referred to as DetLP, combines automata-theoretic reasoning with linear-programming (LP). This method first determinizes the DS-automata [10], and reduces the problem of DS-inclusion for deterministic DS-automata to LP [7,8]. Since determinization of DS-automata causes an exponential blow-up, DetLP yields an exponential time algorithm. An essential feature of this approach is the separation of automata-theoretic reasoning–determinization–and numerical reasoning, performed by an LP-solver. Because of this separation, it does not seem easy to apply on-the-fly techniques to this approach and perform it using polynomial space, so this approach uses exponential time and space.

In contrast, the second algorithm for DS-inclusion, referred to as BCV (after name of authors) is purely automata-theoretic [9]. The component of numerical reasoning between costs of executions is handled by a special Büchi automaton, called the *comparator*, that enables an on-line comparison of the discounted-sum of a pair of weight-sequences. Aided by the comparator, BCV reduces DS-inclusion to language-equivalence between Büchi automata. Since language-equivalence is in PSPACE, BCV is a polynomial-space algorithm.

While the complexity-theoretic argument may seem to suggest a clear advantage for the pure automata-theoretic approach of BCV, the perspective from an implementation point of view is more nuanced. BCV relies on LI-solvers as its key algorithmic component. The polynomial-space approach for LI relies on Savitch's Theorem, which proves the equivalence between deterministic and non-deterministic space complexity [21]. This theorem, however, does not yield a practical algorithm. Existing efficient LI-solvers [3,4] are based on Ramsey-based inclusion testing [6] or rank-based approaches [18]. These tools actually use exponential time and space. In fact, the exponential blow-up of Ramsey-based approach seems to be worse than that of DS-determinization. Thus, the theoretical advantage BCV seems to evaporate upon close examination. Thus, it is far from clear which algorithmic approach is superior. To resolve this issue, we provide in this paper the first implementations for both algorithms and perform exhaustive empirical analysis to compare their performance.

Our first tool, also called DetLP, implements its namesake algorithm as it is. We rely on existing LP-solver GLPSOL to perform numerical reasoning. Our second tool, called QuIP, starts from BCV, but improves on it. The key improvement arises from the construction of an improved comparator with fewer states. We revisit the reduction to language inclusion in [9] accordingly. The new reduction reduces the transition-density of the inputs to the LI-solver (Transition density is the ratio of transitions to states), improving the overall performance of QuIP since LI-solvers are known to scale better at lower transition-density inputs [19].

Our empirical analysis reveals that theoretical complexity does not provide a full picture. Despite its poorer complexity, QuIP scales significantly better than DetLP, although DetLP solves more benchmarks. Based on these observations, we propose a method for DS-inclusion that leverages the complementary strengths of these tools to offer a scalable tool for DS-inclusion. Our evaluation also highlights the limitations of both approaches, and opens directions for further research in improving tools for DS-inclusion.

2   Preliminaries

Büchi Automata.   A *Büchi automaton* [23] is a tuple $\mathcal{A} = (S, \Sigma, \delta, Init, \mathcal{F})$, where S is a finite set of *states*, Σ is a finite *input alphabet*, $\delta \subseteq (S \times \Sigma \times S)$ is the *transition relation*, $Init \subseteq S$ is the set of *initial states*, and $\mathcal{F} \subseteq S$ is the set of *accepting states*. A Büchi automaton is *deterministic* if for all states s and inputs a, $|\{s'|(s,a,s') \in \delta\}| \leq 1$. Otherwise, it is *nondeterministic*. For a word $w = w_0 w_1 \ldots \in \Sigma^\omega$, a *run* ρ of w is a sequence of states $s_0 s_1 \ldots$ satisfying: (1) $s_0 \in Init$, and (2) $\tau_i = (s_i, w_i, s_{i+1}) \in \delta$ for all i. Let $inf(\rho)$ denote the set of states that occur infinitely often in run ρ. A run ρ is an *accepting run* if $inf(\rho) \cap \mathcal{F} \neq \emptyset$. A word w is an accepting word if it has an accepting run.

The language $\mathcal{L}(\mathcal{A})$ of Büchi automaton $\mathcal{A}$ is the set of all words accepted by it. Büchi automata are known to be closed under set-theoretic union, intersection, and complementation. For Büchi automata A and B, the *language-equivalence* and *language-inclusion* are whether $\mathcal{L}(A) \equiv \mathcal{L}(B)$ and $\mathcal{L}(A) \subseteq \mathcal{L}(B)$, resp.

Let $A = A[0], A[1], \ldots$ be a natural-number sequence, $d > 1$ be a rational number. The *discounted-sum* of A with discount-factor d is $DS(A, d) = \Sigma_{i=0}^\infty \frac{A[i]}{d^i}$. For number sequences A and B, (A, B) and $(A - B)$ denote the sequences where the i-th element is $(A[i], B[i])$ and $A[i] - B[i]$, respectively.

Discounted-Sum Automata.   A *discounted-sum automaton* with discount-factor $d > 1$, *DS-automaton* in short, is a tuple $\mathcal{A} = (\mathcal{M}, \gamma)$, where $\mathcal{M} = (S, \Sigma, \delta, Init, S)$ is a Büchi automaton, and $\gamma : \delta \rightarrow \mathbb{N}$ is the *weight function* that assigns a weight to each transition of automaton $\mathcal{M}$. *Words* and *runs* in weighted ω-automata are defined as they are in Büchi automata. Note that all states are accepting states in this definition. The *weight sequence* of run $\rho = s_0 s_1 \ldots$ of word $w = w_0 w_1 \ldots$ is given by $wt_\rho = n_0 n_1 n_2 \ldots$ where $n_i = \gamma(s_i, w_i, s_{i+1})$ for all i. The *weight of a run* ρ is given by $DS(wt_\rho, d)$. For simplicity, we denote this by $DS(\rho, d)$. The *weight of a word* in DS-automata is defined as $wt_\mathcal{A}(w) = sup\{DS(\rho, d)|\rho \text{ is a run of } w \text{ in } \mathcal{A}\}$. By convention, if a word $w \notin \mathcal{L}(\mathcal{A})$, then

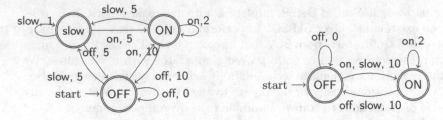

Fig. 1. System S **Fig. 2.** Specification P

$wt_{\mathcal{A}}(w) = 0$ [15]. A DS-automata is said to be *complete* if from every state there is at least one transition on every alphabet. Formally, for all $p \in S$ and for all $a \in \Sigma$, there exists $q \in S$ s.t $(p, a, q) \in \delta$. A run $\rho \in P$ of word $w \in \mathcal{L}(P)$ is a *diminished run* if there exists a run $\sigma \in Q$ over the same word w s.t. $DS(\rho, d) < DS(\sigma, d)$. We abuse notation, and use $w \in \mathcal{A}$ to mean $w \in \mathcal{L}(\mathcal{A})$ for Büchi automaton or DS-automaton $\mathcal{A}$. We limit ourselves to integer discount-factors only. Given DS-automata P and Q and discount-factor $d > 1$, the *discounted-sum inclusion problem*, denoted by $P \sqsubseteq_d Q$, determines whether for all words $w \in \Sigma^{\omega}$, $wt_P(w) \le wt_Q(w)$.

Comparator Automata.   For natural number μ, integer discount-factor $d > 1$ and inequality relation $\le$, the *discounted-sum comparator* $\mathcal{A}_{\le}^{\mu,d}$, *comparator*, in short, is a Büchi automaton that accepts (infinite) words over the alphabet $\{0, 1 \ldots, \mu - 1\} \times \{0, 1 \ldots, \mu - 1\}$ such that a pair (A, B) of sequences is in $\mathcal{L}(\mathcal{A}_d^{\mu})$ iff $DS(A, d) \le DS(B, d)$. Closure properties of Büchi automata ensure that comparator exists for all inequality relations [9].

Motivating Example.   As an example of such a problem formulation, consider the system and specification in Figs. 1 and 2, respectively [15]. Here, the specification P depicts the worst-case energy-consumption model for a motor, and the system S is a candidate implementation of the motor. Transitions in S and P are labeled by transition-action and transition-cost. The cost of an execution (a sequence of actions) is given by an *aggregate* of the costs of transitions along its run (a sequence of automaton states). In non-deterministic automata, where each execution may have multiple runs, cost of the execution is the cost of the run with maximum cost. A critical question here is to check whether implementation S is more energy-efficient than specification P. This problem can be framed as a problem of quantitative inclusion between S and P.

3   Prior Work

We discuss existing algorithms for DS-inclusion i.e. DetLP and BCV in detail.

3.1   DetLP: DS-determinization and LP-based

Böker and Henzinger studied complexity and decision-procedures for determinization of DS-automata in detail [10]. They proved that a DS-automata can be determinized if it is complete, all its states are accepting states and the discount-factor is an integer. Under all other circumstances, DS-determinization may not be guaranteed. DS-determinization extends subset-construction for automata over finite words. Every state of the determinized DS-automata is represented by an $|S|$-tuple of numbers, where $S = \{q_1, \ldots q_{|S|}\}$ denotes the set of states of the original DS-automaton. The value stored in the i-th place in the $|S|$-tuple represents the "gap" or extra-cost of reaching state q_i over a finite-word w compared to its best value so far. The crux of the argument lies in proving that when the DS-automata is complete and the discount-factor is an integer, the "gap" can take only finitely-many values, yielding finiteness of the determinized DS-automata, albeit exponentially larger than the original.

Theorem 1 [10] [DS-determinization analysis]. *Let A be a complete DS-automata with maximum weight μ over transitions and s number of states. DS-determinization of A generates a DS-automaton with at most μ^s states.*

Chatterjee et al. reduced $P \subseteq_d Q$ between non-deterministic DS-automata P and deterministic DS-automata Q to linear-programming [7,8,15]. First, the product DS-automata $P \times Q$ is constructed so that $(s_P, s_Q) \xrightarrow{a} (t_P, t_Q)$ is a transition with weight $w_P - w_Q$ if transition $s_M \xrightarrow{a} t_M$ with weight w_M is present in M, for $M \in \{P, Q\}$. $P \subseteq_q Q$ is **False** iff the weight of any word in $P \times Q$ is greater than 0. Since Q is deterministic, it is sufficient to check if the maximum weight of all infinite paths from the initial state in $P \times Q$ is greater than 0. For discounted-sum, the maximum weight of paths from a given state can be determined by a linear-program: Each variable (one for each state) corresponds to the weight of paths originating in this state, and transitions decide the constraints which relate the values of variables (or states) on them. The objective is to maximize weight of variable corresponding to the initial state.

Therefore, the DetLP method for $P \subseteq_d Q$ is as follows: Determinize Q to Q_D via DS-determinization method from [10], and reduce $P \subseteq_d Q_D$ to linear programming following [15]. Note that since determinization is possible only if the DS-automaton is complete, DetLP can be applied only if Q is complete.

Lemma 1. *Let P and Q be non-deterministic DS-automata with s_P and s_Q number of states respectively, τ_P states in P. Let the alphabet be Σ and maximum weight on transitions be μ. Then $P \subseteq_d Q$ is reduced to linear programming with $\mathcal{O}(s_P \cdot \mu^{s_Q})$ variables and $\mathcal{O}(\tau_P \cdot \mu^{s_Q} \cdot |\Sigma|)$ constraints.*

Anderson and Conitzer [7] proved that this system of linear equations can be solved in $\mathcal{O}(m \cdot n^2)$ for m constraints and n variables. Therefore,

Theorem 2 [7,15] [Complexity of DetLP]. *Let P and Q be DS-automata with s_P and s_Q number of states respectively, τ_P states in P. Let the alphabet be Σ and maximum weight on transitions be μ. Complexity of DetLP is $\mathcal{O}(s_P^2 \cdot \tau_P \cdot \mu^{s_Q} \cdot |\Sigma|)$.*

1: **Input:** Weighted automata P, Q, and discount-factor d
2: **Output:** True if $P \subseteq_d Q$, False otherwise
3: $\hat{P} \leftarrow$ AugmentWtAndLabel(P)
4: $\hat{Q} \leftarrow$ AugmentWtAndLabel(Q)
5: $\hat{P} \times \hat{Q} \leftarrow$ MakeProductSameAlpha($\hat{P}, \hat{Q}$)
6: $\mu \leftarrow$ MaxWeight(P, Q)
7: $\mathcal{A}^{\mu,d}_{\leq} \leftarrow$ MakeComparator(μ, d)
8: $DimWithWitness \leftarrow$ Intersect($\hat{P} \times \hat{Q}, \mathcal{A}^{\mu,d}_{\leq}$)
9: $Dim \leftarrow$ FirstProject($DimWithWitness$)
10: **return** $\hat{P} \equiv Dim$

Algorithm 1. BCV(P, Q, d), Is $P \subseteq_d Q$?

3.2 BCV: Comparator-based approach

The key idea behind BCV is that $P \subseteq_d Q$ holds iff every run of P is a diminished run. As a result, BCV constructs an intermediate Büchi automaton Dim that consists of all diminished runs of P. It then checks whether Dim consists of all runs of P, by determining language-equivalence between Dim and an automaton $\hat{P}$ that consists of all runs of P. The comparator $\mathcal{A}^{\mu,d}_{\leq}$ is utilized in the construction of Dim to compare weight of runs in P and Q.

Strictly speaking, BCV as presented in [9], is a generic algorithm for inclusion under a general class of aggregate functions, called ω-regular aggregate functions. Here, BCV (Algorithm 1) refers to its adaptation to DS. Procedure AugmentWtAndLabel separates between runs of the same word in DS-automata by assigning a unique transition-identity to each transition. It also appends the transition weight, to enable weight comparison afterwards. Specifically, it transforms DS-automaton $\mathcal{A}$ into Büchi automaton $\hat{\mathcal{A}}$, with all states as accepting, by converting transition $\tau = s \xrightarrow{a} t$ with weight wt and unique transition-identity l to transition $\hat{\tau} = s \xrightarrow{(a,wt,l)} t$ in $\hat{\mathcal{A}}$. Procedure MakeProductSameAlpha($\hat{P}, \hat{Q}$) takes the product of $\hat{P}$ and $\hat{Q}$ over the same word i.e., transitions $s_{\mathcal{A}} \xrightarrow{(a,n_{\mathcal{A}},l_{\mathcal{A}})} t_{\mathcal{A}}$ in $\mathcal{A}$, for $\mathcal{A} \in \{\hat{P}, \hat{Q}\}$, generates transition $(s_P, s_Q) \xrightarrow{(a,n_P,l_P,n_Q,l_Q)} (t_P, t_Q)$ in $\hat{P} \times \hat{Q}$. The comparator $\mathcal{A}^{\mu,d}_{\leq}$ is constructed with upper-bound μ that equals the maximum weight of transitions in P and Q, and discount-factor d. Intersect matches the alphabet of $\hat{P} \times \hat{Q}$ with $\mathcal{A}^{\mu,d}_{\leq}$, and intersects them. The resulting automaton $DimWithWitness$ accepts word $(w, wt_P, id_P, wt_Q, id_Q)$ iff $DS(wt_P, d) \leq DS(wt_Q, d)$. The projection of $DimWithWitness$ on the first three components of $\hat{P}$ returns Dim which contains the word (w, wt_P, id_P) iff it is a diminished run in P. Finally, language-equivalence between Dim and $\hat{P}$ returns the answer.

Unlike DetLP, BCV operates on incomplete DS-automata as well, and can be extended to DS-automata in which not all states are accepting.

4   QuIP: BCV-based Solver for DS-inclusion

We investigate more closely why BCV does not lend itself to a practical implementation for DS-inclusion (Sect. 4.1). We identify its drawbacks, and propose an improved algorithm QuIP as is described in Sect. 4.3. QuIP improves upon BCV by means of a new optimized comparator that we describe in Sect. 4.2.

4.1   Analysis of BCV

The proof for PSPACE-complexity of BCV relies on LI to be PSPACE. In practice, though, implementations of LI apply Ramsey-based inclusion testing [6], rank-based methods [18] etc. All of these algorithms are exponential in time and space in the worst case. Any implementation of BCV will have to rely on an LI-solver. Therefore, in practice BCV is also exponential in time and space. In fact, we show that its worst-case complexity (in practice) is poorer than DetLP.

Another reason that prevents BCV from practical implementations is that it does not optimize the size of intermediate automata. Specifically, we show that the size and transition-density of Dim, which is one of the inputs to LI-solver, is very high (Transition density is the ratio of transitions to states). Both of these parameters are known to be deterrents to the performance of existing LI-solvers [5], subsequently to BCV as well:

Lemma 2. *Let s_P, s_Q, s_d and τ_P, τ_Q, τ_d denote the number of states and transitions in P, Q, and $\mathcal{A}_{\leq}^{\mu,d}$, respectively. Number of states and transitions in Dim are $\mathcal{O}(s_P s_Q s_d)$ and $\mathcal{O}(\tau_P^2 \tau_Q^2 \tau_d |\Sigma|)$, respectively.*

Proof. It is easy to see that the number of states and transitions of $\hat{P}$ $\hat{Q}$ are the same as those of P and Q, respectively. Therefore, the number of states and transitions in $\hat{P} \times \hat{Q}$ are $\mathcal{O}(s_P s_Q)$ and $\mathcal{O}(\tau_P \tau_Q)$, respectively. The alphabet of $\hat{P} \times \hat{Q}$ is of the form $(a, wt_1, id_1, wt_2, id_2)$ for $a \in \Sigma$, wt_1, wt_2 are non-negative weights bounded by μ and id_i are unique transition-ids in P and Q respectively. The alphabet of comparator $\mathcal{A}_{\leq}^{\mu,d}$ is of the form (wt_1, wt_2). To perform intersection of these two, the alphabet of comparator needs to be matched to that of the product, causing a blow-up in number of transitions in the comparator by a factor of $|\Sigma| \cdot \tau_P \cdot \tau_Q$. Therefore, the number of states and transitions in $DimWithWitness$ and Dim is given by $\mathcal{O}(s_P s_Q s_d)$ and $\mathcal{O}(\tau_P^2 \tau_Q^2 \tau_d |\Sigma|)$.

The comparator is a non-deterministic Büchi automata with $\mathcal{O}(\mu^2)$ states over an alphabet of size μ^2 [9]. Since transition-density $\delta = |S| \cdot |\Sigma|$ for non-deterministic Büchi automata, the transition-density of the comparator is $\mathcal{O}(\mu^4)$. Therefore,

Corollary 1. *Let s_P, s_Q, s_d denote the number of states in P, Q, $\mathcal{A}_{\leq}^{\mu,d}$, respectively, and δ_P, δ_Q and δ_d be their transition-densities. Number of states and transition-density of Dim are $\mathcal{O}(s_P s_Q \mu^2)$ and $\mathcal{O}(\delta_P \delta_Q \tau_P \tau_Q \cdot \mu^4 \cdot |\Sigma|)$, respectively.*

The corollary illustrates that the transition-density of Dim is very high even for small inputs. The blow-up in number of transitions of $Dim\,With\,Witness$ (hence Dim) occurs during alphabet-matching for Büchi automata intersection (Algorithm 1, Line 8). However, the blow-up can be avoided by performing intersection over a substring of the alphabet of $\hat{P} \times \hat{Q}$. Specifically, if $s_1 \xrightarrow{(a,n_P,id_P,n_Q,id_Q)} s_2$ and $t_1 \xrightarrow{(wt_1,wt_2)} t_2$ are transitions in $\hat{P} \times \hat{Q}$ and comparator $\mathcal{A}^{\mu,d}_{\leq}$ respectively, then $(s_1,t_1,i) \xrightarrow{(a,n_P,id_P,n_Q,id_Q)} (s_2,t_2,j)$ is a transition in the intersection iff $n_P = wt_1$ and $n_Q = wt_2$, where $j = (i+1) \bmod 2$ if either s_1 or t_1 is an accepting state, and $j = i$ otherwise. We call intersection over substring of alphabet IntersectSelectAlpha. The following is easy to prove:

Lemma 3. *Let $\mathcal{A}_1 = \mathsf{Intersect}(\hat{P} \times \hat{Q}, \mathcal{A}^{\mu,d}_{\leq})$, and $\mathcal{A}_2 = \mathsf{IntersectSelectAlpha}(\hat{P} \times \hat{Q}, \mathcal{A}^{\mu,d}_{\leq})$. Intersect extends alphabet of $\mathcal{A}^{\mu,d}_{\leq}$ to match the alphabet of $\hat{P} \times \hat{Q}$ and IntersectSelectAlpha selects a substring of the alphabet of $\hat{P} \times \hat{Q}$ as defined above. Then, $\mathcal{L}(\mathcal{A}_1) \equiv \mathcal{L}(\mathcal{A}_2)$.*

IntersectSelectAlpha prevents the blow-up by $|\Sigma| \cdot \tau_P \cdot \tau_Q$, resulting in only $\mathcal{O}(\tau_P \tau_Q \tau_d)$ transitions in Dim Therefore,

Lemma 4 [Trans. Den. in BCV]. *Let δ_P, δ_Q denote transition-densities of P and Q, resp., and μ be the upper bound for comparator $\mathcal{A}^{\mu,d}_{\leq}$. Number of states and transition-density of Dim are $\mathcal{O}(s_P s_Q \mu^2)$ and $\mathcal{O}(\delta_P \delta_Q \cdot \mu^4)$, respectively.*

Language-equivalence is performed via tools for language-inclusion. The most effective tool for language-inclusion RABIT [1] is based on Ramsay-based inclusion testing [6]. The worst-case complexity for $A \subseteq B$ via Ramsay-based inclusion testing is known to be $2^{\mathcal{O}(n^2)}$, when B has n states. Therefore,

Theorem 3 [Practical complexity of BCV]. *Let P and Q be DS-automata with s_P, s_Q number of states respectively, and maximum weight on transitions be μ. Worst-case complexity for BCV for integer discount-factor $d > 1$ when language-equivalence is performed via Ramsay-based inclusion testing is $2^{\mathcal{O}(s_P^2 \cdot s_Q^2 \cdot \mu^4)}$.*

Recall that language-inclusion queries are $\hat{P} \subseteq Dim$ and $Dim \subseteq \hat{P}$. Since Dim has many more states than $\hat{P}$, the complexity of $\hat{P} \subseteq Dim$ dominates.

Theorems 2 and 3 demonstrate that the complexity of BCV (in practice) is worse than DetLP.

4.2   Baseline Automata: An Optimized Comparator

The $2^{\mathcal{O}(s^2)}$ dependence of BCV on the number of states s of the comparator motivates us to construct a more compact comparator. Currently a comparator consists of $\mathcal{O}(\mu^2)$ number of states for upper bound μ [9]. In this section, we introduce the related concept of *baseline automata* which consists of only $\mathcal{O}(\mu)$-many states and has transition density of $\mathcal{O}(\mu^2)$.

Definition 1 (Baseline automata). *For natural number μ, integer discount-factor $d > 1$ and relation R, for $R \in \{\leq, \geq, <, >, =\}$, the DSbaseline automata $\mathcal{B}_R^{\mu,d}$, baseline in short, is a Büchi automaton that accepts (infinite) words over the alphabet $\{-(\mu-1), \ldots, \mu-1\}$ s.t. sequences $V \in \mathcal{L}(\mathcal{B}_R^{\mu,d})$ iff $DS(V, d)$ R 0.*

Semantically, a baseline automata with upper bound μ, discount-factor d and inequality relation R is the language of all integer sequences bounded by μ for which their discounted-sum is related to 0 by the relation R. Baseline automata can also be said to be related to *cut-point languages* [14].

Since $DS(A, d) \leq DS(B, d) = DS(A - B, d) \leq 0$, $\mathcal{A}_{\leq}^{\mu,d}$ accepts (A, B) iff $\mathcal{B}_{\leq}^{\mu,d}$ accepts $(A - B)$, regularity of baseline automata follows straight-away from the regularity of comparator. In fact, the automaton for $\mathcal{B}_{\leq}^{\mu,d}$ can be derived from $\mathcal{A}_{\leq}^{\mu,d}$ by transforming the alphabet from (a, b) to $(a - b)$ along every transition. The first benefit of the modified alphabet is that its size is reduced from μ^2 to $2 \cdot \mu - 1$. In addition, it coalesces all transitions between any two states over alphabet $(a, a + v)$, for all a, into one single transition over v, thereby also reducing transitions. However, this direct transformation results in a baseline with $\mathcal{O}(\mu^2)$ states. We provide a construction of baseline with $\mathcal{O}(\mu)$ states only.

The key idea behind the construction of the baseline is that the discounted-sum of sequence V can be treated as a number in base d i.e. $DS(V, d) = \sum_{i=0}^{\infty} \frac{V[i]}{d^i} = (V[0].V[1]V[2]\ldots)_d$. So, there exists a non-negative value C in base d s.t. $V + C = 0$ for arithmetic operations in base d. This value C can be represented by a non-negative sequence C s.t. $DS(C, d) + DS(V, d) = 0$. Arithmetic in base d over sequences C and V result in a sequence of carry-on X such that:

Lemma 5. *Let V, C, X be the number sequences, $d > 1$ be a positive integer such that following equations holds true:*

1. *When $i = 0$, $V[0] + C[0] + X[0] = 0$*
2. *When $i \geq 1$, $V[i] + C[i] + X[i] = d \cdot X[i-1]$*

Then $DS(V, d) + DS(C, d) = 0$.

In the construction of the comparator, it has been proven that when A and B are bounded non-negative integer sequences s.t. $DS(A, d) \leq DS(B, d)$, the corresponding sequences C and X are also bounded integer-sequences [9]. The same argument transcends here: When V is a bounded integer sequence s.t. $DS(V, d) \leq 0$, there exists a corresponding pair of bounded integer sequence C and X. In fact, the bounds used for the comparator carry over to this case as well. Sequence C is non-negative and is bounded by $\mu_C = \mu \cdot \frac{d}{d-1}$ since $-\mu_C$ is the minimum value of discounted-sum of V, and integer-sequence X is bounded by $\mu_X = 1 + \frac{\mu}{d-1}$. On combining Lemma 5 with the bounds on X and C we get:

Lemma 6. *Let V and be an integer-sequence bounded by μ s.t. $DS(V, d) \leq 0$, and X be an integer sequence bounded by $(1 + \frac{\mu}{d-1})$, then there exists an X s.t.*

1. When $i = 0$, $0 \le -(X[0] + V[0]) \le \mu \cdot \frac{d}{d-1}$
2. When $i \ge 1$, $0 \le (d \cdot X[i-1] - V[i] - X[i]) \le \mu \cdot \frac{d}{d-1}$

Equations 1–2 from Lemma 6 have been obtained by expressing $C[i]$ in terms of $X[i]$, $X[i-1]$, $V[i]$ and d, and imposing the non-negative bound of $\mu_C = \mu \cdot \frac{d}{d-1}$ on the resulting expression. Therefore, Lemma 6 implicitly captures the conditions on C by expressing it only in terms of V, X and d for $DS(V, d) \le 0$ to hold.

In construction of the baseline automata, the values of $V[i]$ is part of the alphabet, upper bound μ and discount-factor d are the input parameters. The only unknowns are the value of $X[i]$. However, we know that it can take only finitely many values i.e. integer values $|X[i]| \le \mu_X$. So, we store all possible values of $X[i]$ in the states. Hence, the state-space S comprises of $\{(x) \| |x| \le \mu_X\}$ and a start state s. Transitions between these states are possible iff the corresponding x-values and alphabet v satisfy the conditions of Eqs. 1–2 from Lemma 6. There is a transition from start state s to state (x) on alphabet v if $0 \le -(x+v) \le \mu \cdot \frac{d}{d-1}$, and from state (x) to state (x') on alphabet v if $0 \le (d \cdot x - v - x') \le \mu \cdot \frac{d}{d-1}$. All (x)-states are accepting. This completes the construction for baseline automaton $\mathcal{B}_{\le}^{\mu,d}$. Clearly $\mathcal{B}_{\le}^{\mu,d}$ has only $\mathcal{O}(\mu)$ states.

Since Büchi automata are closed under set-theoretic operations, baseline automata is ω-regular for all other inequalities too. Moreover, baseline automata for all other inequalities also have $\mathcal{O}(\mu)$ states. Therefore for sake of completion, we extend $\mathcal{B}_{\le}^{\mu,d}$ to construct $\mathcal{B}_{<}^{\mu,d}$. For $DS(V, d) < 0$, $DS(C, d) > 0$ (implicitly generated C). Since C is a non-negative sequence it is sufficient if at least one value of C is non-zero. Therefore, all runs are diverted to non-accepting states $(x, \perp)$ using the same transitions until the value of c is zero, and moves to accepting states (x) only if it witnesses a non-zero value for c. Formally,

Construction. Let $\mu_C = \mu \cdot \frac{d}{d-1} \le 2 \cdot \mu$ and $\mu_X = 1 + \frac{\mu}{d-1}$. $\mathcal{B}_{<}^{\mu,d} = (S, \Sigma, \delta_d, Init, \mathcal{F})$

– $S = Init \cup \mathcal{F} \cup S_\perp$ where
  $Init = \{s\}$, $\mathcal{F} = \{x \| |x| \le \mu_X\}$, and
  $S_\perp = \{(x, \perp) \| |x| \le \mu_X\}$ where $\perp$ is a special character, and $x \in \mathbb{Z}$.
– $\Sigma = \{v : |v| \le \mu\}$ where v is an integer.
– $\delta_d \subset S \times \Sigma \times S$ is defined as follows:
  1. Transitions from start state s:
     i. (s, v, x) for all $x \in \mathcal{F}$ s.t. $0 < -(x + v) \le \mu_C$
     ii. $(s, v, (x, \perp))$ for all $(x, \perp) \in S_\perp$ s.t. $x + v = 0$
  2. Transitions within $S_\perp$: $((x, \perp), v, (x', \perp))$ for all $(x, \perp)$, $(x', \perp) \in S_\perp$, if $d \cdot x = v + x'$
  3. Transitions within $\mathcal{F}$: (x, v, x') for all $x, x' \in \mathcal{F}$ if $0 \le d \cdot x - v - x' < d$
  4. Transition between $S_\perp$ and $\mathcal{F}$: $((x, \perp), v, x')$ for $(x, \perp) \in S_\perp$, $x' \in \mathcal{F}$ if $0 < d \cdot x - v - x' < d$

Theorem 4 [Baseline]. *The Büchi automaton constructed above is the baseline $\mathcal{B}_{<}^{\mu,d}$ with upper bound μ, integer discount-factor $d > 1$ and relation $<$.*

The baseline automata for all inequality relations will have $\mathcal{O}(\mu)$ states, alphabet size of $2 \cdot \mu - 1$, and transition-density of $\mathcal{O}(\mu^2)$.

```
 1: Input: Weighted automata P, Q, and discount-factor d
 2: Output: True if P ⊆_d Q, False otherwise
 3: P̂ ← AugmentWtAndLabel(P)
 4: Q̂ ← AugmentWt(Q)
 5: P̂ × Q̂ ← MakeProductSameAlpha(P̂, Q̂)
 6: A ← MakeBaseline(μ, d, ≤)
 7: DimWithWitness ← IntersectSelectAlpha(P̂ × Q̂, A)
 8: Dim ← ProjectOutWt(DimWithWitness)
 9: P̂_{-wt} ← ProjectOutWt(P̂)
10: return P̂_{-wt} ⊆ Dim
```

Algorithm 2. QuIP(P, Q, d), Is $P \subseteq_d Q$?

4.3   QuIP: Algorithm Description

The construction of the universal leads to an implementation-friendly QuIP from
BCV. The core focus of QuIP is to ensure that the size of intermediate automata is
small and they have fewer transitions to assist the LI-solvers. Technically, QuIP
differs from BCV by incorporating the baseline automata and an appropriate
IntersectSelectAlpha function, rendering QuIP theoretical improvement over BCV.
Like BCV, QuIP also determines all diminished runs of P. So, it disambiguates
P by appending weight and a unique label to each of its transitions. Since,
the identity of runs of Q is not important, we do not disambiguate between
runs of Q, we only append the weight to each transition (Algorithm 2, Line 4).
The baseline automaton is constructed for discount-factor d, maximum weight
μ along transitions in P and Q, and the inequality $\leq$. Since the alphabet of the
baseline automata are integers between $-\mu$ to μ, the alphabet of the product
$P̂ \times Q̂$ is adjusted accordingly. Specifically, the weight recorded along transitions
in the product is taken to be the difference of weight in $P̂$ to that in $Q̂$ i.e. if τ_P :
$s_1 \xrightarrow{a_1, wt_1, l} s_2$ and $\tau_Q : t_1 \xrightarrow{a_2, wt_2} t_2$ are transitions in $P̂$ and $Q̂$ respectively, then
$\tau = (s_1, t_1) \xrightarrow{a_1, wt_1 - wt_2, l} (s_2, t_2)$ is a transition in $P̂ \times Q̂$ iff $a_1 = a_2$ (Algorithm 2,
Line 5). In this case, IntersectSelectAlpha intersects baseline automata A and
product $P̂ \times Q̂$ only on the weight-component of alphabet in $P̂ \times Q̂$. Specifically,
if $s_1 \xrightarrow{(a, wt_1, l)} s_2$ and $t_1 \xrightarrow{wt_2} t_2$ are transitions in $P̂ \times Q̂$ and comparator $A_{\leq}^{\mu, d}$
respectively, then $(s_1, t_1, i) \xrightarrow{a, wt_1, l} (s_2, t_2, j)$ is a transition in the intersection
iff $wt_1 = wt_2$, where $j = (i+1) \mod 2$ if either s_1 or t_1 is an accepting state,
and $j = i$ otherwise. Automaton Dim and $P̂_{-wt}$ are obtained by project out the
weight-component from the alphabet of $P̂ \times Q̂$ and $P̂$ respectively. The alphabet
of $P̂ \times Q̂$ and $P̂$ are converted from (a, wt, l) to only (a, l). It is necessary to
project out the weight component since in $P̂ \times Q̂$ they represent the difference
of weights and in $P̂$ they represent the absolute value of weight.

Finally, the language of Dim is equated with that of $P̂_{-wt}$ which is the
automaton generated from $P̂$ after discarding weights from transitions. However,
it is easy to prove that $Dim \subseteq P̂_{-wt}$. Therefore, instead of language-equivalence

between Dim and $\hat{P}_{-wt}$ and, it is sufficient to check whether $\hat{P}_{-wt} \subseteq Dim$. As a result, QuIP utilizes LI-solvers as a black-box to perform this final step.

Lemma 7 [Trans. Den. in *QuIP*]. *Let δ_P, δ_Q denote transition-densities of P and Q, resp., and μ be the upper bound for baseline $\mathcal{B}^{\mu,d}_{\leq}$. Number of states and transition-density of Dim are $\mathcal{O}(s_P s_Q \mu)$ and $\mathcal{O}(\delta_P \delta_Q \cdot \mu^2)$, respectively.*

Theorem 5 [Practical complexity of *QuIP*]. *Let P and Q be DS-automata with s_P, s_Q number of states, respectively, and maximum weight on transitions be μ. Worst-case complexity for QuIP for integer discount-factor $d > 1$ when language-equivalence is performed via Ramsay-based inclusion testing is $2^{\mathcal{O}(s_P^2 \cdot s_Q^2 \cdot \mu^2)}$.*

Theorem 5 demonstrates that while complexity of QuIP (in practice) improves upon BCV (in practice), it is still worse than DetLP.

5 Experimental Evaluation

We provide implementations of our tools QuIP and DetLP and conduct experiments on a large number of synthetically-generated benchmarks to compare their performance. We seek to find answers to the following questions: (1). Which tool has better performance, as measured by runtime, and number of benchmarks solved? (2). How does change in transition-density affect performance of the tools? (3). How dependent are our tools on their underlying solvers?

5.1 Implementation Details

We implement our tools QuIP and DetLP in C++, with compiler optimization o3 enabled. We implement our own library for all Büchi-automata and DS-automata operations, except for language-inclusion for which we use the state-of-the-art LI-solver RABIT [4] as a black-box. We enable the -fast flag in RABIT, and tune its JAVA-threads with Xss, Xms, Xmx set to 1 GB, 1 GB and 8 GB respectively. We use the large-scale LP-solver GLPSOL provided by GLPK (GNU Linear Programming Kit) [2] inside DetLP. We did not tune GLPSOL since it consumes a very small percentage of total time in DetLP, as we see later in Fig. 4.

We also employ some implementation-level optimizations. Various steps of QuIP and DetLP such as product, DS-determinization, baseline construction, involve the creation of new automaton states and transitions. We reduce their size by adding a new state only if it is reachable from the initial state, and a new transition only if it originates from such a state.

The universal automata is constructed on the restricted alphabet of only those weights that appear in the product $\hat{P} \times \hat{Q}$ to include only necessary transitions. We also reduce its size with Büchi minimization tool Reduce [4].

Since all states of $\hat{P} \times \hat{Q}$ are accepting, we conduct the intersection so that it avoids doubling the number of product states. This can be done, since it is sufficient to keep track of whether words visit accepting states in the universal.

5.2   Benchmarks

To the best of our knowledge, there are no standardized benchmarks for DS-automata. We attempted to experimented with examples that appear in research papers. However, these examples are too few and too small, and do not render an informative view of performance of the tools. Following a standard approach to performance evaluation of automata-theoretic tools [5,19,22], we experiment with our tools on *randomly generated* benchmarks.

Random Weighted-Automata Generation. The parameters for our random weighted-automata generation procedure are the number of states N, transition-density δ and upper-bound μ for weight on transitions. The states are represented by the set $\{0, 1, \ldots, N-1\}$. All states of the weighted-automata are accepting, and they have a unique initial state 0. The alphabet for all weighted-automata is fixed to $\Sigma = \{a, b\}$. Weight on transitions ranges from 0 to $\mu-1$. For our experiments we only generate complete weighted-automata. These weighted automata are generated only if the number of transitions $\lfloor N \cdot \delta \rfloor$ is greater than $N \cdot |\Sigma|$, since there must be at least one transition on each alphabet from every state. We first complete the weighted-automata by creating a transition from each state on every alphabet. In this case the destination state and weight are chosen randomly. The remaining $(N \cdot |\Sigma| - \lfloor N \cdot \delta \rfloor)$-many transitions are generated by selecting all parameters randomly i.e. the source and destination states from $\{0, \ldots N-1\}$, the alphabet from Σ, and weight on transition from $\{0, \mu-1\}$.

5.3   Design and Setup for Experimental Evaluation

Our experiments were designed with the objective to compare DetLP and QuIP. Due to the lack of standardized benchmarks, we conduct our experiments on randomly-generated benchmarks. Therefore, the parameters for $P \subseteq_d Q$ are the number of states s_P and s_Q, transition density δ, and maximum weight wt. We seek to find answers to the questions described at the beginning of Sect. 5.

Each instantiation of the parameter-tuple (s_P, s_Q, δ, wt) and a choice of tool between QuIP and DetLP corresponds to one experiment. In each experiment, the weighted-automata P and Q are randomly-generated with the parameters (s_P, δ, wt) and (s_Q, δ, wt), respectively, and language-inclusion is performed by the chosen tool. Since all inputs are randomly-generated, each experiment is repeated for 50 times to obtain statistically significant data. Each experiment is run for a total of 1000 sec on for a single node of a high-performance cluster. Each node of the cluster consists of two quad-core Intel-Xeon processor running at 2.83 GHz, with 8 GB of memory per node. The runtime of experiments that do not terminate within the given time limit is assigned a runtime of ∞. We report the median of the runtime-data collected from all iterations of the experiment.

These experiments are scaled-up by increasing the size of inputs. The worst-case analysis of QuIP demonstrates that it is symmetric in s_P and s_Q, making the algorithm impartial to which of the two inputs is scaled (Theorem 5). On the other hand, complexity of DetLP is dominated by s_Q (Theorem 2). Therefore, we scale-up our experiments by increasing s_Q only.

Since DetLP is restricted to complete automata, these experiments are conducted on complete weighted automata only. We collect data on total runtime of each tool, the time consumed by the underlying solver, and the number of times each experiment terminates with the given resources. We experiment with $s_P = 10$, δ ranges between 2.5–4 in increments of 0.5 (we take lower-bound of 2.5 since $|\Sigma| = 2$), $wt \in \{4, 5\}$, and s_Q ranges from 0–1500 in increments of 25, $d = 3$. These sets of experiments also suffice for testing scalability of both tools.

5.4 Observations

We first compare the tools based on the number of benchmarks each can solve. We also attempt to unravel the main cause of failure of each tool. Out of the 50 experiments for each parameter-value, DetLP consistently solves more benchmarks than QuIP for the same parameter-values (Fig. 3a–b)[1]. The figures also reveal that both tools solve more benchmarks at lower transition-density. The most common, in fact almost always, reason for QuIP to fail before its timeout was reported to be memory-overflow inside RABIT during language-inclusion between $\hat{P}_{-wt}$ and Dim. On the other hand, the main cause of failure of DetLP was reported to be memory overflow during DS-determinization and preprocessing of the determinized DS-automata before GLPSOL is invoked. This occurs due to the sheer size of the determinized DS-automata, which can very quickly become very large. These empirical observations indicate that the bottleneck in QuIP and DetLP may be language-inclusion and explicit DS-determinization, respectively.

We investigate the above intuition by analyzing the runtime trends for both tools. Figure 4a plots the runtime for both tools. The plot shows that QuIP fares significantly better than DetLP in runtime at $\delta = 2.5$. The plots for both the tools on logscale seem curved (Fig. 4a), suggesting a sub-exponential runtime complexity. These were observed at higher δ as well. However, at higher δ we observe very few outliers on the runtime-trend graphs of QuIP at larger inputs when just a few more than 50% of the runs are successful. This is expected since effectively, the median reports the runtime of the slower runs in these cases. Figure 4b records the ratio of total time spent inside RABIT and GLPSOL. The plot reveals that QuIP spends most of its time inside RABIT. We also observe that most memory consumptions in QuIP occurs inside RABIT. In contrast, GLPSOL consumes a negligible amount of time and memory in DetLP. Clearly, performance of QuIP and DetLP is dominated by RABIT and explicit DS-determinization, respectively. We also determined how runtime performance of tools changes with increasing discount-factor d. Both tools consume lesser time as d increases.

Finally, we test for scalability of both tools. In Fig. 5a, we plot the median of total runtime as s_Q increases at $\delta = 2.5, 3$ ($s_P = 10, \mu = 4$) for QuIP. We attempt to best-fit the data-points for each δ with functions that are linear, quadratic and cubic in s_Q using squares of residuals method. Figure 5b does the same for

---

[1] Figures are best viewed online and in color.

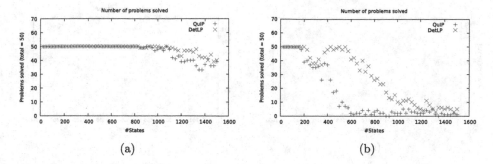

Fig. 3. Number of benchmarks solved out of 50 as s_Q increases with $s_P = 10$, $\mu = 4$. $\delta = 2.5$ and $\delta = 4$ in Fig. 3a and b, respectively.

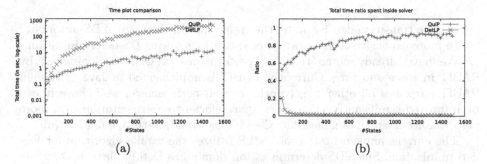

Fig. 4. Time trends: Fig. 4a plots total runtime as s_Q increases $s_P = 10, \mu = 4$, $\delta = 2.5$. Figure shows median-time for each parameter-value. Figure 4b plots the ratio of time spent by tool inside its solver at the same parameter values.

DetLP. We observe that QuIP and DetLP are best fit by functions that are linear and quadratic in s_Q, respectively.

Inferences and Discussion. Our empirical analysis arrives at conclusions that a purely theoretical exploration would not have. First of all, we observe that despite having a the worse theoretical complexity, the median-time complexity of QuIP is better than DetLP by an order of n. In theory, QuIP scales exponentially in s_Q, but only linearly in s_Q in runtime. Similarly, runtime of DetLP scales quadratically in s_Q. The huge margin of complexity difference emphasizes why solely theoretical analysis of algorithms is not sufficient.

Earlier empirical analysis of LI-solvers had made us aware of their dependence on transition-density δ. As a result, we were able to design QuIP cognizant of parameter δ. Therefore, its runtime dependence on δ is not surprising. However, our empirical analysis reveals runtime dependence of DetLP on δ. This is unexpected since δ does not appear in any complexity-theoretic analysis of DetLP (Theorem 1). We suspect this behavior occurs because the creation of each transition, say on alphabet a, during DS-determinization requires the procedure to analyze every transition on alphabet a in the original DS-automata.

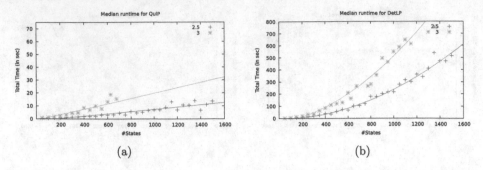

Fig. 5. Scalability of QuIP (Fig. 5a) and DetLP (Fig. 5b) at $\delta = 2.5, 3$. Figures show median-time for each parameter-value.

Higher the transition-density, more the transitions in the original DS-automata, hence more expensive is the creation of transitions during DS-determinization.

We have already noted that the performance of QuIP is dominated by RABIT in space and time. Currently, RABIT is implemented in Java. Although RABIT surpasses all other LI-solvers in overall performance, we believe it can be improved significantly via a more space-efficient implementation in a more performance-oriented language like C++. This would, in-turn, enhance QuIP.

The current implementation of DetLP utilizes the vanilla algorithm for DS-determinization. Since DS-determinization dominates DetLP, there is certainly merit in designing efficient algorithms for DS-determinization. However, we suspect this will be of limited advantage to DetLP since it will persist to incur the complete cost of explicit DS-determinization due to the separation of automata-theoretic and numeric reasoning.

Based on our observations, we propose to extract the complementary strengths of both tools: First, apply QuIP with a small timeout; Since DetLP solves more benchmarks, apply DetLP only if QuIP fails.

6 Concluding Remarks and Future Directions

This paper presents the first empirical evaluation of algorithms and tools for DS-inclusion. We present two tools DetLP and QuIP. Our first tool DetLP is based on explicit DS-determinization and linear programming, and renders an exponential time and space algorithm. Our second tool QuIP improves upon a previously known comparator-based automata-theoretic algorithm BCV by means of an optimized comparator construction, called universal automata. Despite its PSPACE-complete theoretical complexity, we note that all practical implementations of QuIP are also exponential in time and space.

The focus of this work is to investigate these tools in practice. In theory, the exponential complexity of QuIP is worse than DetLP. Our empirical evaluation reveals the opposite: The median-time complexity of QuIP is better than DetLP by an order of n. Specifically, QuIP scales linearly while DetLP scales quadratically in the size of inputs. This re-asserts the gap between theory and practice, and aserts the need of better metrics for practical algorithms. Further emprirical analysis by scaling the right-hand side automaton will be beneficial.

Nevertheless, DetLP consistently solves more benchmarks than QuIP. Most of QuIP's experiments fail due to memory-overflow within the LI-solver, indicating that more space-efficient implementations of LI-solvers would boost QuIP's performance. We are less optimistic about DetLP though. Our evaluation highlights the impediment of explicit DS-determinization, a cost that is unavoidable in DetLP's separation-of-concerns approach. This motivates future research that integrates automata-theoretic and numerical reasoning by perhaps combining implicit DS-determinzation with baseline automata-like reasoning to design an on-the-fly algorithm for DS-inclusion.

Last but not the least, our empirical evaluations lead to discovering dependence of runtime of algorithms on parameters that had not featured in their worst-case theoretical analysis, such as the dependence of DetLP on transition-density. Such evaluations build deeper understanding of algorithms, and will hopefully serve a guiding light for theoretical and empirical investigation in-tandem of algorithms for quantitative analysis

Acknowledgements. We thank anonymous reviewers for their comments. We thank K. S. Meel, A. A. Shrotri, L. M. Tabajara, and S. Zhu for helpful discussions. This work was partially supported by NSF Grant No. 1704883, "Formal Analysis and Synthesis of Multiagent Systems with Incentives".

References

1. RABIT: Ramsey-based Büchi automata inclusion testing
2. GLPK. https://www.gnu.org/software/glpk/
3. GOAL. http://goal.im.ntu.edu.tw/wiki/
4. Rabit-Reduce. http://www.languageinclusion.org/
5. Abdulla, P.A., et al.: Simulation subsumption in Ramsey-based Büchi automata universality and inclusion testing. In: Touili, T., Cook, B., Jackson, P. (eds.) CAV 2010. LNCS, vol. 6174, pp. 132–147. Springer, Heidelberg (2010). https://doi.org/10.1007/978-3-642-14295-6_14
6. Abdulla, P.A., et al.: Advanced Ramsey-based Büchi automata inclusion testing. In: Katoen, J.-P., König, B. (eds.) CONCUR 2011. LNCS, vol. 6901, pp. 187–202. Springer, Heidelberg (2011). https://doi.org/10.1007/978-3-642-23217-6_13
7. Andersen, G., Conitzer, V.: Fast equilibrium computation for infinitely repeated games. In: Proceedings of AAAI, pp. 53–59 (2013)
8. Andersson, D.: An improved algorithm for discounted payoff games. In: ESSLLI Student Session, pp. 91–98 (2006)
9. Bansal, S., Chaudhuri, S., Vardi, M.Y.: Comparator automata in quantitative verification. In: Baier, C., Dal Lago, U. (eds.) FoSSaCS 2018. LNCS, vol. 10803, pp. 420–437. Springer, Cham (2018). https://doi.org/10.1007/978-3-319-89366-2_23
10. Boker, U., Henzinger, T. A.: Exact and approximate determinization of discounted-sum automata. LMCS, **10**(1) (2014)
11. Boker, U., Henzinger, T.A., Otop, J.: The target discounted-sum problem. In Proceedings of LICS, pp. 750–761 (2015)

116   S. Bansal et al.

12. Černý, P., Chatterjee, K., Henzinger, T.A., Radhakrishna, A., Singh, R.: Quantitative synthesis for concurrent programs. In: Gopalakrishnan, G., Qadeer, S. (eds.) CAV 2011. LNCS, vol. 6806, pp. 243–259. Springer, Heidelberg (2011). https://doi.org/10.1007/978-3-642-22110-1_20
13. Cerny, P., Henzinger, T.A., Radhakrishna, A.: Quantitative abstraction refinement. ACM SIGPLAN Not. 48(1), 115–128 (2013)
14. Chatterjee, K., Doyen, L., Henzinger, T.A.: Expressiveness and closure properties for quantitative languages. In: Proceedings of LICS, pp. 199–208. IEEE (2009)
15. Chatterjee, K., Doyen, L., Henzinger, T.A.: Quantitative languages. Trans. Comput. Log. 11(4), 23 (2010)
16. Chatterjee, K., Majumdar, R., Henzinger, T.A.: Markov decision processes with multiple objectives. In: Durand, B., Thomas, W. (eds.) STACS 2006. LNCS, vol. 3884, pp. 325–336. Springer, Heidelberg (2006). https://doi.org/10.1007/11672142_26
17. Droste, M., Kuich, W., Vogler, H.: Handbook of Weighted Automata. Springer, Heidelberg (2009). https://doi.org/10.1007/978-3-642-01492-5
18. Kupferman, O., Vardi, M.Y.: Weak alternating automata are not that weak. Trans. Comput. Log. 2(3), 408–429 (2001)
19. Mayr, R., Clemente, L.: Advanced automata minimization. ACM SIGPLAN Not. 48(1), 63–74 (2013)
20. Rubinstein, A.: Finite automata play the repeated prisoner's dilemma. J. Econ. Theory 39(1), 83–96 (1986)
21. Savitch, W.J.: Relationships between nondeterministic and deterministic tape complexities. J. Comput. Syst. Sci. 4(2), 177–192 (1970)
22. Tabakov, D., Vardi, M.Y.: Experimental evaluation of classical automata constructions. In: Sutcliffe, G., Voronkov, A. (eds.) LPAR 2005. LNCS (LNAI), vol. 3835, pp. 396–411. Springer, Heidelberg (2005). https://doi.org/10.1007/11591191_28
23. Mazala, R.: Infinite games. In: Grädel, E., Thomas, W., Wilke, T. (eds.) Automata Logics, and Infinite Games. LNCS, vol. 2500, pp. 23–38. Springer, Heidelberg (2002). https://doi.org/10.1007/3-540-36387-4_2

Model Checking Indistinguishability
of Randomized Security Protocols

Matthew S. Bauer[1,4]([✉]), Rohit Chadha[2], A. Prasad Sistla[3],
and Mahesh Viswanathan[1]

[1] University of Illinois at Urbana-Champaign, Champaign, USA
msbauer2@illinois.edu
[2] University of Missouri, Columbia, USA
[3] University of Illinois at Chicago, Chicago, USA
[4] Galois Inc., Arlington, USA

Abstract. The design of security protocols is extremely subtle and vulnerable to potentially devastating flaws. As a result, many tools and techniques for the automated verification of protocol designs have been developed. Unfortunately, these tools don't have the ability to model and reason about protocols with randomization, which are becoming increasingly prevalent in systems providing privacy and anonymity guarantees. The security guarantees of these systems are often formulated by means of the indistinguishability of two protocols. In this paper, we give the first practical algorithms for model checking indistinguishability properties of randomized security protocols against the powerful threat model of a bounded Dolev-Yao adversary. Our techniques are implemented in the Stochastic Protocol ANalayzer (SPAN) and evaluated on several examples. As part of our evaluation, we conduct the first automated analysis of an electronic voting protocol based on the 3-ballot design.

1 Introduction

Security protocols are highly intricate and vulnerable to design flaws. This has led to a significant effort in the construction of tools for the automated verification of protocol designs. In order to make automation feasible [8,12,15,23,34,48,55], the analysis is often carried out in the *Dolev-Yao* threat model [30], where the assumption of perfect cryptography is made. In the Dolev-Yao model, the omnipotent adversary has the ability to read, intercept, modify and replay all messages on public channels, remember the communication history as well as non-deterministically inject its own messages into the network while remaining anonymous. In this model, messages are symbolic terms modulo

M. S. Bauer and M. Viswanathan—Partially supported by grant NSF CNS 1314485.
R. Chadha—Partially supported by grants NSF CNS 1314338 and NSF CNS 1553548.
A. Prasad Sistla—Partially supported by grants NSF CNS 1314485 and CCF 1564296.

H. Chockler and G. Weissenbacher (Eds.): CAV 2018, LNCS 10982, pp. 117–135, 2018.
https://doi.org/10.1007/978-3-319-96142-2_10

an equational theory (as opposed to bit-strings) and cryptographic operations are modeled via equations in the theory.

A growing number of security protocols employ randomization to achieve privacy and anonymity guarantees. Randomization is essential in protocols/systems for anonymous communication and web browsing such as Crowds [49], mix-networks [21], onion routers [37] and Tor [29]. It is also used in fair exchange [11, 35], vote privacy in electronic voting [6,20,52,54] and denial of service prevention [40]. In the example below, we demonstrate how randomization is used to achieve privacy in electronic voting systems.

Example 1. Consider a simple electronic voting protocol for 2 voters Alice and Bob, two candidates and an election authority. The protocol is as follows. Initially, the election authority will generate two private tokens t_A and t_B and send them to Alice and Bob encrypted under their respective public keys. These tokens will be used by the voters as proofs of their eligibility. After receiving a token, each voter sends his/her choice to the election authority along with the proof of eligibility encrypted under the public key of the election authority. Once all votes have been collected, the election authority tosses a fair private coin. The order in which Alice and Bob's votes are published depends on the result of this coin toss. *Vote privacy* demands that an adversary not be able to deduce how each voter voted.

All the existing Dolev-Yao analysis tools are fundamentally limited to protocols that are purely non-deterministic, where non-determinism models concurrency as well as the interaction between protocol participants and their environment. There are currently no analysis tools that can faithfully reason about protocols like those in Example 1, a limitation that has long been identified by the verification community. In the context of electronic voting protocols, [28] identifies three main classes of techniques for achieving vote privacy; blind signature schemes, homomorphic encryption and randomization. There the authors concede that protocols based on the latter technique are "hard to address with our methods that are purely non-deterministic." Catherine Meadows, in her summary of the over 30 year history of formal techniques in cryptographic protocol analysis [46,47], identified the development of formal analysis techniques for anonymous communication systems, almost exclusively built using primitives with randomization, as a fundamental and still largely unsolved challenge. She writes, "it turned out to be difficult to develop formal models and analyses of large-scale anonymous communication. The main stumbling block is the threat model".

In this work, we take a major step towards overcoming this long-standing challenge and introduce the first techniques for automated Dolev-Yao analysis of randomized security protocols. In particular, we propose two algorithms for determining indistinguishability of randomized security protocols and implemented them in the Stochastic Protocol ANalyzer (SPAN). Several works [7,9,28,32,41] have identified indistinguishability as the natural mechanism to model security guarantees such as anonymity, unlinkability, and privacy. Consider the protocol from Example 1, designed to preserve vote privacy. Such a property holds if the executions of the protocol in which Alice votes for candidate 1 and Bob votes for candidate 2 cannot be distinguished from the executions of the protocol in which Alice votes for candidate 2 and Bob votes for candidate 1.

Observe that in Example 1, it is crucial that the result of the election authority's coin toss is not visible to the adversary. Indeed if the adversary is allowed to "observe" the results of private coin tosses, then the analysis may reveal "security flaws" in correct security protocols (see examples in [13, 17, 19, 22, 36]). Thus, many authors [10, 13, 17–19, 22, 26, 36] have proposed that randomized protocols be analyzed with respect to adversaries that are forced to schedule the same action in any two protocol executions that are indistinguishable to them.

For randomized security protocols, [10, 18, 53] have proposed that trace equivalence from the applied π-calculus [5] serve as the indistinguishability relation on traces. In this framework, the protocol semantics are described by partially observable Markov decision processes (POMDPs) where the adversary's actions are modeled non-deterministically. The adversary is required to choose its next action based on the partial information that it can observe about the execution thus far. This allows us to model the privacy of coin tosses. Two security protocols are said to be indistinguishable [18, 53] if their semantic descriptions as POMDPs are indistinguishable. Two POMDPs $\mathcal{M}$ and $\mathcal{M}'$ are said to be indistinguishable if for any adversary $\mathcal{A}$ and trace $\bar{o}$, the probability of the executions that generate the trace $\bar{o}$ with respect to $\mathcal{A}$ are the same for both $\mathcal{M}$ and $\mathcal{M}'$.

Our algorithms for indistinguishability in randomized security protocols are built on top of techniques for solving indistinguishability in finite POMDPs. Our first result shows that indistinguishability of finite POMDPs is $\mathbf{P}$-complete. Membership in $\mathbf{P}$ is established by a reduction of POMDP indistinguishability to equivalence in probabilistic finite automata (PFAs), which is known to be $\mathbf{P}$-complete [31, 45, 57]. Further, we show that the hardness result continues to hold for acyclic POMDPs. An acyclic POMDP is a POMDP that has a set of "final" absorbing states and the only cycles in the underlying graph are self-loops on these states.

For acyclic finite POMDPs, we present another algorithm for checking indistinguishability based on the technique of translating a POMDP $\mathcal{M}$ into a fully observable Markov decision process (MDP), known as the belief MDP $\mathcal{B}(\mathcal{M})$ of $\mathcal{M}$. It was shown in [14] that two POMDPs are indistinguishable if and only if the belief MDPs they induce are bisimilar as labeled Markov decision processes. When $\mathcal{M}$ is acyclic and finite then its belief MDP $\mathcal{B}(\mathcal{M})$ is finite and acyclic and its bisimulation relation can be checked recursively.

Protocols in SPAN are described by a finite set of roles (agents) that interact asynchronously by passing messages. Each role models an agent in a protocol session and hence we only consider bounded number of sessions. An action in a role performs either a message input, or a message output or a test on messages. The adversary schedules the order in which these actions are executed and generates input recipes comprised of public information and messages previously output by the agents. In general, there are an unbounded number of input recipes available at each input step, resulting in POMDPs that are infinitely branching.

SPAN, however, searches for bounded attacks by bounding the size of attacker messages. Under this assumption, protocols give rise to finite acyclic POMDPs. Even with this assumption, protocols specified in SPAN describe POMDPs that are exponentially larger than their description. Nevertheless, we show that when considering protocols defined over subterm convergent equational theories, indistinguishability of randomized security protocols is in **PSPACE** for bounded Dolev-Yao adversaries. We further show that the problem is harder than #SAT$_D$ and hence it is both **NP**-hard and **coNP**-hard.

The main engine of SPAN translates a randomized security protocol into an acyclic finite POMDP by recursively unrolling all protocol executions and grouping states according to those that are indistinguishable. We implemented two algorithms for checking indistinguishability in SPAN. The first algorithm, called the PFA algorithm, checks indistinguishability of P and P' by converting them to corresponding PFAs A and A' as in the proof of decidability of indistinguishability of finite POMDPs. PFA equivalence can then be solved through a reduction to linear programming [31]. The second algorithm, called the on-the-fly (OTF) algorithm, is based on the technique of checking bisimulation of belief MDPs. Although asymptotically less efficient than the PFA algorithm, the recursive procedure for checking bisimulation in belief MDPs can be embedded into the main engine of SPAN with little overhead, allowing one to analyze indistinguishability on-the-fly as the POMDP models are constructed.

In our evaluation of the indistinguishability algorithms in SPAN, we conduct the first automated Dolev-Yao analysis for several new classes of security protocols including dinning cryptographers networks [38], mix networks [21] and a 3-ballot electronic voting protocol [54]. The analysis of the 3-ballot protocol, in particular, demonstrates that our techniques can push symbolic protocol verification to new frontiers. The protocol is a full scale, real world example, which to the best of our knowledge, hasn't been analyzed using any existing probabilistic model checker or protocol analysis tool.

Summary of Contributions. We showed that the problem of checking indistinguishability of POMDPs is **P**-complete. The indistinguishability problem for bounded instances of randomized security protocols over subterm convergent equational theories (bounded number of sessions and bounded adversarial nondeterminism) is shown to be in **PSPACE** and #SAT$_D$-hard. We proposed and implemented two algorithms in the SPAN protocol analysis tool for deciding indistinguishability in bounded instances of randomized security protocols and compare their performance on several examples. Using SPAN, we conducted the first automated verification of a 3-ballot electronic voting protocol.

Related Work. As alluded to above, techniques for analyzing security protocols have remained largely disjoint from techniques for analyzing systems with randomization. Using probabilistic model checkers such as PRISM [44], STORM [27] and APEX [42] some have attempted to verify protocols that explicitly employ randomization [56]. These ad-hoc techniques fail to capture powerful threat models, such as a Dolev-Yao adversary, and don't provide a general verification framework. Other works in the Dolev-Yao framework [28,43] simply abstract away essential protocol components that utilize randomization, such as anonymous channels. The first formal framework combining Dolev-Yao analysis with randomization appeared in [10], where the authors studied the conditions under which security properties of randomized protocols are preserved by protocol composition. In [53], the results were extended to indistinguishability.

Complexity-theoretic results on verifying secrecy and indistinguishability properties of bounded sessions of randomized security protocols against unbounded Dolev-Yao adverasries were studied in [18]. There the authors considered protocols with a fixed equational theory[1] and no negative tests (else branches). Both secrecy and indistinguishability were shown to be in **coNEXP-TIME**, with secrecy being **coNEXPTIME**-hard. The analogous problems for purely non-deterministic protocols are known to be **coNP**-complete [25,33,51]. When one fixes, a priori, the number of coin tosses, secrecy and indistinguishability in randomized protocols again become **coNP**-complete. In our asymptotic complexity results and in the SPAN tool, we consider a general class of equational theories and protocols that allow negative tests.

2 Preliminaries

We assume that the reader is familiar with probability distributions. For a set X, $\mathsf{Dist}(X)$ shall denote the set of all discrete distributions μ on X such that $\mu(x)$ is a rational number for each $x \in X$. For $x \in X$, δ_x will denote the Dirac distribution, i.e., the measure μ such that $\mu(x) = 1$. The *support* of a discrete distribution μ, denoted $\mathsf{support}(\mu)$, is the set of all elements x such that $\mu(x) \neq 0$.

Markov Decision Processes (MDPs). MDPs are used to model processes that exhibit both probabilistic and non-deterministic behavior. An MDP $\mathcal{M}$ is a tuple $(Z, z_s, \mathsf{Act}, \Delta)$ where Z is a countable set of states, $z_s \in Z$ is the initial state, Act is a countable set of actions and $\Delta : Z \times \mathsf{Act} \to \mathsf{Dist}(Z)$ is the probabilistic transition function. $\mathcal{M}$ is said to be finite if the sets Z and Act are finite. An execution of an MDP is a sequence $\rho = z_0 \xrightarrow{\alpha_1} z_1 \xrightarrow{\alpha_2} \cdots \xrightarrow{\alpha_m} z_m$ such that $z_0 = z_s$ and $z_{i+1} \in \mathsf{support}(\Delta(z_i, \alpha_{i+1}))$ for all $i \in \{0, \ldots, m-1\}$. The *measure* of ρ, denoted $\mathsf{prob}_{\mathcal{M}}(\rho)$, is $\prod_{i=0}^{m-1} \Delta(z_i, \alpha_{i+1})(z_{i+1})$. For the execution ρ, we write $\mathsf{last}(\rho) = z_m$ and say that the length of ρ, denoted $|\rho|$, is m. The set of all executions of $\mathcal{M}$ is denoted as $\mathsf{Exec}(\mathcal{M})$.

Partially Observable Markov Decision Processes (POMDPs). A POMDP $\mathcal{M}$ is a tuple $(Z, z_s, \mathsf{Act}, \Delta, \mathcal{O}, \mathsf{obs})$ where $\mathcal{M}_0 = (Z, z_s, \mathsf{Act}, \Delta)$ is an MDP, $\mathcal{O}$ is a countable set of observations and $\mathsf{obs} : Z \to \mathcal{O}$ is a labeling of states with observations. $\mathcal{M}$ is said to be finite if $\mathcal{M}_0$ is finite. The set of executions of $\mathcal{M}_0$ is taken to be the set of executions of $\mathcal{M}$, i.e., we define $\mathsf{Exec}(\mathcal{M})$ as the set $\mathsf{Exec}(\mathcal{M}_0)$. Given an execution $\rho = z_0 \xrightarrow{\alpha_1} z_1 \xrightarrow{\alpha_2} \cdots \xrightarrow{\alpha_m} z_m$ of $\mathcal{M}$, the trace of

---

[1] The operations considered are pairing, hashing, encryption and decryption.

ρ is $\mathrm{tr}(\rho) = \mathrm{obs}(z_0)\alpha_1\mathrm{obs}(z_1)\alpha_2 \cdots \alpha_m\mathrm{obs}(z_m)$. For a POMDP $\mathcal{M}$ and a sequence $\overline{o} \in \mathcal{O} \cdot (\mathsf{Act} \cdot \mathcal{O})^*$, the probability of $\overline{o}$ in $\mathcal{M}$, written $\mathrm{prob}_{\mathcal{M}}(\overline{o})$, is the sum of the measures of executions in $\mathsf{Exec}(\mathcal{M})$ with trace $\overline{o}$. Given two POMDPs $\mathcal{M}_0$ and $\mathcal{M}_1$ with the same set of actions Act and the same set of observations $\mathcal{O}$, we say that $\mathcal{M}_0$ and $\mathcal{M}_1$ are *distinguishable* if there exists $\overline{o} \in \mathcal{O} \cdot (\mathsf{Act} \cdot \mathcal{O})^*$ such that $\mathrm{prob}_{\mathcal{M}_0}(\overline{o}) \neq \mathrm{prob}_{\mathcal{M}_1}(\overline{o})$. If $\mathcal{M}_0$ and $\mathcal{M}_1$ cannot be distinguished, they are said to be *indistinguishable*. We write $\mathcal{M}_0 \approx \mathcal{M}_1$ if $\mathcal{M}_0$ and $\mathcal{M}_1$ are indistinguishable. As is the case in [18,53], indistinguishability can also be defined through a notion of an adversary. Our formulation is equivalent, even when the adversary is allowed to toss coins [18].

Probabilistic Finite Automata (PFAs). A PFA is like a finite-state deterministic automaton except that the transition function from a state on a given input is described as a probability distribution. Formally, a PFA A is a tuple $(Q, \Sigma, q_s, \Delta, F)$ where Q is a finite set of states, Σ is a finite input alphabet, $q_s \in Q$ is the initial state, $\Delta : Q \times \Sigma \rightarrow \mathsf{Dist}(Q)$ is the transition relation and $F \subseteq Q$ is the set of accepting states. A run ρ of A on an input word $u \in \Sigma^* = a_1a_2\cdots a_m$ is a sequence $q_0q_1\cdots q_m \in Q^*$ such that $q_0 = q_s$ and $q_i \in \mathsf{support}(\Delta(q_{i-1}, a_i))$ for each $1 \leq i \leq m$. For the run ρ on word u, its measure, denoted $\mathrm{prob}_{A,u}(\rho)$, is $\prod_{i=1}^{m} \Delta(q_{i-1}, a_i)(q_i)$. The run ρ is called *accepting* if $q_m \in F$. The probability of accepting a word $u \in \Sigma$, written $\mathrm{prob}_A(u)$, is the sum of the measures of the accepting runs on u. Two PFAs A_0 and A_1 with the same input alphabet Σ are said to be *equivalent*, denoted $A_0 \equiv A_1$, if $\mathrm{prob}_{A_0}(u) = \mathrm{prob}_{A_1}(u)$ for all input words $u \in \Sigma^*$.

3   POMDP Indistinguishability

In this section, we study the underlying semantic objects of randomized security protocols, POMDPs. The techniques we develop for analyzing POMDPs provide the foundation for the indistinguishability algorithms we implement in the SPAN protocol analysis tool. Our first result shows that indistinguishability of finite POMDPs is decidable in polynomial time by a reduction to PFA equivalence, which is known to be decidable in polynomial time [31,57].

Proposition 1. *Indistinguishability of finite POMDPs is in* **P**.

Proof (sketch). Consider two POMDPs $\mathcal{M}_i = (Z_i, z_s^i, \mathsf{Act}, \Delta_i, \mathcal{O}, \mathsf{obs}_i)$ for $i \in \{0, 1\}$ with the same set of actions Act and the set of observations $\mathcal{O}$. We shall construct PFAs A_0 and A_1 such that $\mathcal{M}_0 \approx \mathcal{M}_1$ iff $A_0 \equiv A_1$ as follows. For $i \in \{0, 1\}$, let "bad_i" be a new state and define the PFA $A_i = (Q_i, \Sigma, q_s^i, \Delta_i', F_i)$ where $Q_i = Z_i \cup \{\mathsf{bad}_i\}$, $\Sigma = \mathsf{Act} \times \mathcal{O}$, $q_s^i = z_s^i$, $F_i = Z_i$ and Δ_i' is defined as follows.

$$\Delta_i'(q, (\alpha, o))(q') = \begin{cases} \Delta_i(q, \alpha)(q') & \text{if } q, q' \in Z_i \text{ and } \mathsf{obs}(q) = o \\ 1 & \text{if } q \in Z_i, \mathsf{obs}(q) \neq o \text{ and } q' = \mathsf{bad}_i \\ 1 & \text{if } q, q' = \mathsf{bad}_i \\ 0 & \text{otherwise} \end{cases}.$$

Let $u = (\alpha_1, o_0) \ldots (\alpha_k, o_{k-1})$ be a non-empty word on Σ. For the word u, let $\overline{o}_u$ be the trace $o_0 \alpha_1 o_1 \alpha_2 \cdots \alpha_{k-1} o_{k-1}$. The proposition follows immediately from the observation that $\mathsf{prob}_{\mathsf{A}_i}(u) = \mathsf{prob}_{\mathcal{M}_i}(\overline{o}_u)$. □

An MDP $\mathcal{M} = (Z, z_s, \mathsf{Act}, \Delta)$ is said to be acyclic if there is a set of absorbing states $Z_{\mathsf{abs}} \subseteq Z$ such that for all $\alpha \in \mathsf{Act}$ and $z \in Z_{\mathsf{abs}}$, $\Delta(z, \alpha)(z) = 1$ and for all $\rho = z_0 \xrightarrow{\alpha_1} \cdots \xrightarrow{\alpha_m} z_m \in \mathsf{Exec}(\mathcal{M})$ if $z_i = z_j$ for $i \neq j$ then $z_i \in Z_{\mathsf{abs}}$. Intuitively, acyclic MDPs are MDPs that have a set of "final" absorbing states and the only cycles in the underlying graph are self-loops on these states. A POMDP $\mathcal{M} = (Z, z_s, \mathsf{Act}, \Delta, \mathcal{O}, \mathsf{obs})$ is acyclic if the MDP $\mathcal{M}_0 = (Z, z_s, \mathsf{Act}, \Delta)$ is acyclic. We have the following result, which can be shown from the $\mathbf{P}$-hardness of the PFA equivalence problem [45].

Proposition 2. *Indistinguishability of finite acyclic POMDPs is $\mathbf{P}$-hard. Hence Indistinguishability of finite POMDPs is $\mathbf{P}$-complete.*

Thanks to Proposition 1, we can check indistinguishability for finite POMDPs by reducing it to PFA equivalence. We now present a new algorithm for indistinguishability of finite acyclic POMDPs. A well-known POMDP analysis technique is to translate a POMDP $\mathcal{M}$ into a fully observable belief MDP $\mathcal{B}(\mathcal{M})$ that emulates it. One can then analyze $\mathcal{B}(\mathcal{M})$ to infer properties of $\mathcal{M}$. The states of $\mathcal{B}(\mathcal{M})$ are probability distributions over the states of $\mathcal{M}$. Further, given a state $b \in \mathcal{B}(\mathcal{M})$, if states z_1, z_2 of $\mathcal{M}$ are such that $b(z_1), b(z_2)$ are non-zero then z_1 and z_2 must have the same observation. Hence, by abuse of notation, we can define $\mathsf{obs}(b)$ to be $\mathsf{obs}(z)$ if $b(z) \neq 0$. Intuitively, an execution $\rho = b_0 \xrightarrow{\alpha_1} b_1 \xrightarrow{\alpha_2} \cdots \xrightarrow{\alpha_m} b_m$ of $\mathcal{B}(\mathcal{M})$ corresponds to the set of all executions ρ' of $\mathcal{M}$ such that $\mathsf{tr}(\rho') = \mathsf{obs}(b_0) \alpha_1 \mathsf{obs}(b_1) \alpha_2 \cdots \alpha_m \mathsf{obs}(b_m)$. The measure of execution ρ in $\mathcal{B}(\mathcal{M})$ is exactly $\mathsf{prob}_{\mathcal{M}}(\mathsf{obs}(b_0) \alpha_1 \mathsf{obs}(b_1) \alpha_2 \cdots \alpha_m \mathsf{obs}(b_m))$.

The initial state of $\mathcal{B}(\mathcal{M})$ is the distribution that assigns 1 to the initial state of $\mathcal{M}$. Intuitively, on a given state $b \in \mathsf{Dist}(\mathcal{M})$ and an action α, there is at most one successor state $b^{\alpha,o}$ for each observation o. The probability of transitioning from b to $b^{\alpha,o}$ is the probability that o is observed given that the distribution on the states of $\mathcal{M}$ is b and action α is performed; $b^{\alpha,o}(z)$ is the conditional probability that the actual state of the POMDP is z. The formal definition follows.

Definition 1. *Let $\mathcal{M} = (Z, z_s, \mathsf{Act}, \Delta, \mathcal{O}, \mathsf{obs})$ be a POMDP. The belief MDP of $\mathcal{M}$, denoted $\mathcal{B}(\mathcal{M})$, is the tuple $(\mathsf{Dist}(Z), \delta_{z_s}, \mathsf{Act}, \Delta^{\mathcal{B}})$ where $\Delta^{\mathcal{B}}$ is defined as follows. For $b \in \mathsf{Dist}(Z)$, action $\alpha \in \mathsf{Act}$ and $o \in \mathcal{O}$, let*

$$p_{b,\alpha,o} = \sum_{z \in Z} b(z) \cdot \left(\sum_{z' \in Z \wedge \mathsf{obs}(z')=o} \Delta(z, \alpha)(z') \right).$$

$\Delta^{\mathcal{B}}(b, \alpha)$ is the unique distribution such that for each $o \in \mathcal{O}$, if $p_{b,\alpha,o} \neq 0$ then $\Delta^{\mathcal{B}}(b, \alpha)(b^{\alpha,o}) = p_{b,\alpha,o}$ where for all $z' \in Z$,

$$b^{\alpha,o}(z') = \begin{cases} \frac{\sum_{z \in Z} b(z) \cdot \Delta(z,\alpha)(z')}{p_{b,\alpha,o}} & \text{if } \mathsf{obs}(z') = o \\ 0 & \text{otherwise} \end{cases}.$$

Let $\mathcal{M}_i = (Z_i, z_s^i, \mathsf{Act}, \Delta_i, \mathcal{O}, \mathsf{obs}_i)$ for $i \in \{0, 1\}$ be POMDPs with the same set of actions and observations. In [14] the authors show that $\mathcal{M}_0$ and $\mathcal{M}_1$ are indistinguishable if and only if the beliefs $\delta_{z_s^0}$ and $\delta_{z_s^1}$ are *strongly belief bisimilar*. Strong belief bisimilarity coincides with the notion of bisimilarity of labeled MDPs: a pair of states $(b_0, b_1) \in \mathsf{Dist}(Z_0) \times \mathsf{Dist}(Z_1)$ is said to be strongly belief bisimilar if (i) $\mathsf{obs}(b_0) = \mathsf{obs}(b_1)$, (ii) for all $\alpha \in \mathsf{Act}, o \in \mathcal{O}$, $p_{b_0,\alpha,o} = p_{b_1,\alpha,o}$ and (iii) the pair $(b_0^{\alpha,o}, b_1^{\alpha,o})$ is strongly belief bisimilar if $p_{b_0,\alpha,o} = p_{b_1,\alpha,o} > 0$. Observe that, in general, belief MDPs are defined over an infinite state space. It is easy to see that, for a finite acyclic POMDP $\mathcal{M}$, $\mathcal{B}(\mathcal{M})$ is acyclic and has a finite number of reachable belief states. Let $\mathcal{M}_0$ and $\mathcal{M}_1$ be as above and assume further that $\mathcal{M}_0, \mathcal{M}_1$ are finite and acyclic with absorbing states $Z_{\mathsf{abs}} \subseteq Z_0 \cup Z_1$. As a consequence of the result from [14] and the observations above, we can determine if two states $(b_0, b_1) \in \mathsf{Dist}(Z_0) \times \mathsf{Dist}(Z_1)$ are strongly belief bisimilar using the on-the-fly procedure from Algorithm 1.

Algorithm 1. On-the-fly bisimulation for finite acyclic POMDPs

---

1: **function** BISIMILAR(beliefState b_0, beliefState b_1)
2:     **if** $\mathsf{obs}(b_0) \neq \mathsf{obs}(b_1)$ **then return** false
3:     **if** $\mathsf{support}(b_0) \cup \mathsf{support}(b_1) \subseteq Z_{\mathsf{abs}}$ **then return** true
4:     **for** $\alpha \in \mathsf{Act}$ **do**
5:         **for** $o \in \mathcal{O}$ **do**
6:             **if** $p_{b_0,\alpha,o} \neq p_{b_1,\alpha,o}$ **then return** false
7:             **if** $p_{b_0,\alpha,o} > 0$ and !BISIMILAR$(b_0^{\alpha,o}, b_1^{\alpha,o})$ **then return** false
8:     **return** true

---

4 Randomized Security Protocols

We now present our core process calculus for modeling security protocols with coin tosses. The calculus closely resembles the ones from [10,53]. First proposed in [39], it extends the applied π-calculus [5] by the inclusion of a new operator for probabilistic choice. As in the applied π-calculus, the calculus assumes that messages are terms in a first-order signature identified up-to an equational theory.

4.1 Terms, Equational Theories and Frames

A signature $\mathcal{F}$ contains a *finite* set of function symbols, each with an associated arity. We assume $\mathcal{F}$ contains two special disjoint sets, $\mathcal{N}_{\mathsf{pub}}$ and $\mathcal{N}_{\mathsf{priv}}$, of 0-ary symbols.[2] The elements of $\mathcal{N}_{\mathsf{pub}}$ are called *public names* and represent public nonces that can be used by the Dolev-Yao adversary. The elements of $\mathcal{N}_{\mathsf{priv}}$ are

---

[2] As we assume $\mathcal{F}$ is finite, we allow only a fixed number of public nonces are available to the adversary.

called *names* and represent secret nonces and secret keys. We also assume a set of variables that are partitioned into two disjoint sets $\mathcal{X}$ and $\mathcal{X}_w$. The variables in $\mathcal{X}$ are called *protocol variables* and are used as placeholders for messages input by protocol participants. The variables in $\mathcal{X}_w$ are called *frame variables* and are used to point to messages received by the Dolev-Yao adversary. Terms are built by the application of function symbols to variables and terms in the standard way. Given a signature $\mathcal{F}$ and $\mathcal{Y} \subseteq \mathcal{X} \cup \mathcal{X}_w$, we use $\mathcal{T}(\mathcal{F}, \mathcal{Y})$ to denote the set of terms built over $\mathcal{F}$ and $\mathcal{Y}$. The set of variables occurring in a term u is denoted by $\mathsf{vars}(u)$. A ground term is a term that contains no free variables.

A substitution σ is a partial function with a finite domain that maps variables to terms. $\mathsf{dom}(\sigma)$ will denote the domain and $\mathsf{ran}(\sigma)$ will denote the range. For a substitution σ with $\mathsf{dom}(\sigma) = \{x_1, \ldots, x_k\}$, we denote σ as $\{x_1 \mapsto \sigma(x_1), \ldots, x_k \mapsto \sigma(x_k)\}$. A substitution σ is said to be ground if every term in $\mathsf{ran}(\sigma)$ is ground and a substitution with an empty domain will be denoted as $\emptyset$. Substitutions can be applied to terms in the usual way and we write $u\sigma$ for the term obtained by applying the substitution σ to the term u.

Our process algebra is parameterized by an equational theory $(\mathcal{F}, E)$, where E is a set of $\mathcal{F}$-Equations. By an $\mathcal{F}$-Equation, we mean a pair $u = v$ where $u, v \in \mathcal{T}(\mathcal{F} \setminus \mathcal{N}_{\mathsf{priv}}, \mathcal{X})$ are terms that do not contain private names. We will assume that the equations of $(\mathcal{F}, E)$ can be oriented to produce a convergent rewrite system. Two terms u and v are said to be equal with respect to an equational theory $(\mathcal{F}, E)$, denoted $u =_E v$, if $E \vdash u = v$ in the first order theory of equality. We often identify an equational theory $(\mathcal{F}, E)$ by E when the signature is clear from the context.

In the calculus, all communication is mediated through an adversary: all outputs first go to an adversary and all inputs are provided by the adversary. Hence, processes are executed in an environment that consists of a frame $\varphi : \mathcal{X}_w \to \mathcal{T}(\mathcal{F}, \emptyset)$ and a ground substitution $\sigma : \mathcal{X} \to \mathcal{T}(\mathcal{F}, \emptyset)$. Intuitively, φ represents the sequence of messages an adversary has received from protocol participants and σ records the binding of the protocol variables to actual input messages. An adversary is limited to sending only those messages that it can deduce from the messages it has received thus far. Formally, a term $u \in \mathcal{T}(\mathcal{F}, \emptyset)$ is *deducible* from a frame φ with recipe $r \in \mathcal{T}(\mathcal{F} \setminus \mathcal{N}_{\mathsf{priv}}, \mathsf{dom}(\varphi))$ in equational theory E, denoted $\varphi \vdash^r_E u$, if $r\varphi =_E u$. We will often omit r and E and write $\varphi \vdash u$ if they are clear from the context.

We now recall an equivalence on frames, called *static equivalence* [5]. Intuitively, two frames are statically equivalent if the adversary cannot distinguish them by performing tests. The tests consists of checking whether two recipes deduce the same term. Formally, two frames φ_1 and φ_2 are said to be statically equivalent in equational theory E, denoted $\varphi_1 \equiv_E \varphi_2$, if $\mathsf{dom}(\varphi_1) - \mathsf{dom}(\varphi_2)$ and for all $r_1, r_2 \in \mathcal{T}(\mathcal{F} \setminus \mathcal{N}_{\mathsf{priv}}, \mathcal{X}_w)$ we have $r_1\varphi_1 =_E r_2\varphi_1$ iff $r_1\varphi_2 =_E r_2\varphi_2$.

4.2   Process Syntax

Processes in our calculus are the parallel composition of roles. Intuitively, a role models a single actor in a single session of the protocol. Syntactically, a role is derived from the grammar:

$$R ::= 0 \mid \mathsf{in}(x)^\ell \mid \mathsf{out}(u_0 \cdot R +_p u_1 \cdot R)^\ell \mid \mathsf{ite}([c_1 \wedge \ldots \wedge c_k], R, R)^\ell \mid (R \cdot R)$$

where p is a rational number in the unit interval $[0, 1]$, $\ell \in \mathbb{N}$, $x \in \mathcal{X}$, $u_0, u_1 \in \mathcal{T}(\mathcal{F}, \mathcal{X})$ and c_i is $u_i = v_i$ with $u_i, v_i \in \mathcal{T}(\mathcal{F}, \mathcal{X})$ for all $i \in \{1, \ldots, k\}$. The constructs $\mathsf{in}(x)^\ell$, $\mathsf{out}(u_0 \cdot R +_p u_1 \cdot R)^\ell$ and $\mathsf{ite}([c_1 \wedge \ldots \wedge c_k], R, R)^\ell$ are said to be labeled operations and $\ell \in \mathbb{N}$ is said to be their label. The role 0 does nothing. The role $\mathsf{in}(x)^\ell$ reads a term u from the public channel and binds it to x. The role $\mathsf{out}(u_0 \cdot R +_p u_1 \cdot R')^\ell$ outputs the term u_0 on the public channel and becomes R with probability p and it outputs the term u_1 and becomes R' with probability $1 - p$. A test $[c_1 \wedge \ldots \wedge c_k]$ is said to pass if for all $1 \leq i \leq k$, the equality c_i holds. The conditional role $\mathsf{ite}([c_1 \wedge \ldots \wedge c_k], R, R')^\ell$ becomes R if $[c_1 \wedge \ldots \wedge c_k]$ passes and otherwise it becomes R'. The role $R \cdot R'$ is the sequential composition of role R followed by role R'. The set of variables of a role R is the set of variables occurring in R. The construct $\mathsf{in}(x)^\ell \cdot R$ binds variable x in R. The set of free and bound variables in a role can be defined in the standard way. We will assume that the set of free variables and bound variables of a role are disjoint and that a bound variable is bound only once in a role. A role R is said to be *well-formed* if every labeled operation occurring in R has the same label ℓ; the label ℓ is said to be the label of the well-formed role R.

A process is the parallel composition of a finite set of roles $R_1, \ldots, R_n$, denoted $R_1 \mid \ldots \mid R_n$. We will use P and Q to denote processes. A process $R_1 \mid \ldots \mid R_n$ is said to be well-formed if each role is well-formed, the sets of variables of R_i and R_j are disjoint for $i \neq j$, and the labels of roles R_i and R_j are different for $i \neq j$. For the remainder of this paper, processes are assumed to be well-formed. The set of free (resp. bound) variables of P is the union of the sets of free (resp. bound) variables of its roles. P is said to be ground if the set of its free variables is empty. We shall omit labels when they are not relevant in a particular context.

Example 2. We model the electronic voting protocol from Example 1 in our formalism. The protocol is built over the equational theory with signature $\mathcal{F} = \{\mathsf{sk}/1, \mathsf{pk}/1, \mathsf{aenc}/3, \mathsf{adec}/2, \mathsf{pair}/2, \mathsf{fst}/1, \mathsf{snd}/1\}$ and the equations

$$E = \{\mathsf{adec}(\mathsf{aenc}(m, r, \mathsf{pk}(k)), \mathsf{sk}(k)) = m,$$
$$\mathsf{fst}(\mathsf{pair}(m_1, m_2)) = m_1, \ \mathsf{snd}(\mathsf{pair}(m_1, m_2)) = m_2\}.$$

The function sk (resp. pk) is used to generate a secret (resp. public) key from a nonce. For generation of their pubic key pairs, Alice, Bob and the election authority hold private names k_A, k_B and k_{EA}, respectively. The candidates will be modeled using public names c_0 and c_1 and the tokens will be modeled using private names t_A and t_B. Additionally, we will write y_i and r_i for $i \in \mathbb{N}$ to denote fresh input variables and private names, respectively. The roles of Alice, Bob and the election authority are as follows.

$$A(c_A) := \mathsf{in}(y_0) \cdot \mathsf{out}(\mathsf{aenc}(\mathsf{pair}(\mathsf{adec}(y_0, sk(k_A)), c_A), r_0, \mathsf{pk}(k_{EA})))$$

$$B(c_B) := \mathsf{in}(y_1) \cdot \mathsf{out}(\mathsf{aenc}(\mathsf{pair}(\mathsf{adec}(y_1, sk(k_B)), c_B), r_1, \mathsf{pk}(k_{EA})))$$

$$EA \quad := \mathsf{out}(\mathsf{aenc}(t_A, r_2, \mathsf{pk}(k_A))) \cdot \mathsf{out}(\mathsf{aenc}(t_B, r_3, \mathsf{pk}(k_B))) \cdot \mathsf{in}(y_3) \cdot \mathsf{in}(y_4) \cdot$$
$$\mathsf{ite}([\mathsf{fst}(\mathsf{adec}(y_3, sk(k_{EA}))) = t_A \wedge \mathsf{fst}(\mathsf{adec}(y_4, sk(k_{EA}))) = t_B],$$
$$\mathsf{out}(\mathsf{pair}(\mathsf{snd}(\mathsf{adec}(y_3, sk(k_{EA}))), \mathsf{snd}(\mathsf{adec}(y_4, sk(k_{EA})))) +_{\frac{1}{2}}$$
$$\mathsf{pair}(\mathsf{snd}(\mathsf{adec}(y_4, sk(k_{EA}))), \mathsf{snd}(\mathsf{adec}(y_3, sk(k_{EA}))))), 0)$$

In roles above, we write $\mathsf{out}(u_0)$ as shorthand for $\mathsf{out}(u_0 \cdot 0 +_1 u_0 \cdot 0)$. The entire protocol is $\mathsf{evote}(c_A, c_B) = A(c_A) \mid B(c_B) \mid EA$.

4.3 Process Semantics

An extended process is a 3-tuple (P, φ, σ) where P is a process, φ is a frame and σ is a ground substitution whose domain contains the free variables of P. We will write $\mathcal{E}$ to denote the set of all extended processes. Semantically, a ground process P with n roles is a POMDP $[\![P]\!] = (Z, z_s, \mathsf{Act}, \Delta, \mathcal{O}, \mathsf{obs})$, where $Z = \mathcal{E} \cup \{\mathsf{error}\}$, z_s is $(P, \emptyset, \emptyset)$, $\mathsf{Act} = (\mathcal{T}(\mathcal{F} \setminus \mathcal{N}_{\mathsf{priv}}, \mathcal{X}_w) \cup \{\tau, \} \times \{1, \ldots, n\})$, Δ is a function that maps an extended process and an action to a distribution on $\mathcal{E}$, $\mathcal{O}$ is the set of equivalence classes on frames over the static equivalence relation $\equiv_E$ and obs is as follows. Let $[\varphi]$ denote the equivalence class of φ with respect to $\equiv_E$. Define obs to be the function such that for any extended process $\eta = (P, \varphi, \sigma)$, $\mathsf{obs}(\eta) = [\varphi]$. We now give some additional notation needed for the definition of Δ. Given a measure μ on $\mathcal{E}$ and role R we define $\mu \cdot R$ to be the distribution μ_1 on $\mathcal{E}$ such that $\mu_1(P', \varphi, \sigma) = \mu(P, \varphi, \sigma)$ if $\mu(P, \varphi, \sigma) > 0$ and P' is $P \cdot R$ and 0 otherwise. Given a measure μ on $\mathcal{E}$ and a process Q, we define $\mu \mid Q$ to be the distribution μ_1 on $\mathcal{E}$ such that $\mu_1(P', \varphi, \sigma) = \mu(P, \varphi, \sigma)$ if $\mu(P, \varphi, \sigma) > 0$ and P' is $P \mid Q$ and 0 otherwise. The distribution $Q \mid \mu$ is defined analogously. For distributions μ_1, μ_2 over $\mathcal{E}$ and a rational number $p \in [0, 1]$, the convex combination $\mu_1 +_p^{\mathcal{E}} \mu_2$ is the distribution μ on $\mathcal{E}$ such that $\mu(\eta) = p \cdot \mu_1(\eta) + (1 - p) \cdot \mu_2(\eta)$ for all $\eta \in \mathcal{E}$. The definition of Δ is given in Fig. 1, where we write $(P, \varphi, \sigma) \xrightarrow{\alpha} \mu$ if $\Delta((P, \varphi, \sigma), \alpha) = \mu$. If $\Delta((P, \varphi, \sigma), \alpha)$ is undefined in Fig. 1 then $\Delta((P, \varphi, \sigma), \alpha) = \delta_{\mathsf{error}}$. Note that Δ is well-defined, as roles are deterministic.

4.4 Indistinguishability in Randomized Cryptographic Protocols

Protocols P and P' are said to indistinguishable if $[\![P]\!] \approx [\![P']\!]$. Many interesting properties of randomized security protocols can be specified using indistinguishability. For example, consider the simple electronic voting protocol from Example 2. We say that the protocol satisfies the vote privacy property if $\mathsf{evote}(c_0, c_1)$ and $\mathsf{evote}(c_1, c_0)$ are indistinguishable.

In the remainder of this section, we study the problem of deciding when two protocols are indistinguishable by a bounded Dolev-Yao adversary. We restrict our attention to indistinguishability of protocols over subterm convergent equational theories [4]. Before presenting our results, we give some relevant definitions. $(\mathcal{F}, E)$ is said to be *subterm convergent* if for every equation

$$\frac{r \in \mathcal{T}(\mathcal{F} \setminus \mathcal{N}_{\mathsf{priv}}, \mathcal{X}_w) \quad \varphi \vdash^r u \quad x \notin \mathsf{dom}(\sigma)}{(\mathsf{in}(x)^\ell, \varphi, \sigma) \xrightarrow{(r,\ell)} \delta_{(0, \varphi, \sigma \cup \{x \mapsto u\})}} \text{ IN}$$

$$\frac{i = |\mathsf{dom}(\varphi)| + 1 \quad \varphi_j = \varphi \cup \{w_{(i,\ell)} \mapsto u_j \sigma\} \text{ for } j \in \{0,1\}}{(\mathsf{out}(u_0 \cdot R_0 +_p u_1 \cdot R_1)^\ell, \varphi, \sigma) \xrightarrow{(\tau, \ell)} \delta_{(R_0, \varphi_0, \sigma)} +_p^{\mathcal{E}} \delta_{(R_1, \varphi_1, \sigma)}} \text{ OUT}$$

$$\frac{\forall i \in \{1, \ldots, k\}, \ c_i \text{ is } u_i = v_i \text{ and } u_i \sigma =_E v_i \sigma}{(\mathsf{ite}([c_1 \wedge \ldots \wedge c_k], R, R')^\ell, \varphi, \sigma) \xrightarrow{(\tau, \ell)} \delta_{(R, \varphi, \sigma)}} \text{ COND}_{\mathsf{IF}}$$

$$\frac{\exists i \in \{1, \ldots, k\}, \ c_i \text{ is } u_i = v_i \text{ and } u_i \sigma \neq_E v_i \sigma}{(\mathsf{ite}([c_1 \wedge \ldots \wedge c_k], R, R')^\ell, \varphi, \sigma) \xrightarrow{(\tau, \ell)} \delta_{(R', \varphi, \sigma)}} \text{ COND}_{\mathsf{ELSE}}$$

$$\frac{R \neq 0 \quad (R, \varphi, \sigma) \xrightarrow{\alpha} \mu}{(R \cdot R', \varphi, \sigma) \xrightarrow{\alpha} \mu \cdot R'} \text{ SEQ} \qquad \frac{(R, \varphi, \sigma) \xrightarrow{\alpha} \mu}{(0 \cdot R, \varphi, \sigma) \xrightarrow{\alpha} \mu} \text{ NULL}$$

$$\frac{(Q, \varphi, \sigma) \xrightarrow{\alpha} \mu}{(Q \mid Q', \varphi, \sigma) \xrightarrow{\alpha} \mu \mid Q'} \text{ PAR}_{\mathsf{L}} \qquad \frac{(Q', \varphi, \sigma) \xrightarrow{\alpha} \mu}{(Q \mid Q', \varphi, \sigma) \xrightarrow{\alpha} Q \mid \mu} \text{ PAR}_{\mathsf{R}}$$

Fig. 1. Process semantics

$u = v \in E$ oriented as a rewrite rule $u \rightarrow v$, either v is a proper subterm of u or v is a public name. A term u can be represented as a directed acyclic graph (dag), denoted $\mathsf{dag}(u)$ [4,51]. Every node in $\mathsf{dag}(u)$ is a function symbol, name or a variable. Nodes labeled by names and variables have out-degree 0. A node labeled with a function symbol f has out-degree equal to the arity of f where outgoing edges of the node are labeled from 1 to the arity of f. Every node of $\mathsf{dag}(u)$ represents a unique sub-term of u. The depth of a term u, denoted $\mathsf{depth}(u)$, is the length of the longest simple path from the root in $\mathsf{dag}(u)$. Given an action α, $\mathsf{depth}(\alpha) = 0$ if $\alpha = (\tau, j)$ and $\mathsf{depth}(\alpha) = m$ if $\alpha = (r, j)$ and $\mathsf{depth}(r) = m$.

Let P be a protocol such that $\llbracket P \rrbracket = (Z, z_s, \mathsf{Act}, \Delta, \mathcal{O}, \mathsf{obs})$. Define $\llbracket P \rrbracket_d$ to be the POMDP $(Z, z_s, \mathsf{Act}_d, \Delta, \mathcal{O}, \mathsf{obs})$ where $\mathsf{Act}_d \subseteq \mathsf{Act}$ is such that every $\alpha \in \mathsf{Act}$ has $\mathsf{depth}(\alpha) \leq d$. For a constant $d \in \mathbb{N}$, we define $\mathsf{InDist}(d)$ to be the decision problem that, given a subterm convergent theory $(\mathcal{F}, E)$ and protocols P and P' over $(\mathcal{F}, E)$, determines if $\llbracket P \rrbracket_d$ and $\llbracket P' \rrbracket_d$ are indistinguishable. We assume that the arity of the function symbols in $\mathcal{F}$ is given in unary. We have the following.

Theorem 1. *For any constant $d \in \mathbb{N}$, $\mathsf{InDist}(d)$ is in* **PSPACE**.

We now show $\mathsf{InDist}(d)$ is both **NP**-hard and **coNP**-hard by showing a reduction from $\#\mathsf{SAT}_\mathsf{D}$ to $\mathsf{InDist}(d)$. $\#\mathsf{SAT}_\mathsf{D}$ is the decision problem that, given a 3CNF formula ϕ and a constant $k \in \mathbb{N}$, checks if the number of satisfying assignments of ϕ is equal to k.

Theorem 2. *There is a $d_0 \in \mathbb{N}$ such that $\#SAT_D$ reduces to $\mathsf{InDist}(d)$ in logspace for every $d > d_0$. Thus, $\mathsf{InDist}(d)$ is **NP**-hard and **coNP**-hard for every $d > d_0$.*

5   Implementation and Evaluation

Using (the proof of) Proposition 1, we can solve the indistinguishability problem for randomized security protocols as follows. For protocols P, P', translate $\llbracket P \rrbracket, \llbracket P' \rrbracket$ into PFAs A, A' and determine if $\mathsf{A} \equiv \mathsf{A}'$ using the linear programming algorithm from [31]. We will henceforth refer to this approach as the PFA algorithm and the approach from Algorithm 1 as the OTF algorithm. We have implemented both the PFA and OTF algorithms as part of Stochastic Protocol ANalayzer (SPAN), which is a Java based tool for analyzing randomized security protocols. The tool is available for download at [1]. The main engine of SPAN translates a protocol into a POMDP, belief MDP or PFA by exploring all protocol executions and grouping equivalent states using an engine, KISS [4] or AKISS [16], for static equivalence. KISS is guaranteed to terminate for subterm convergent theories and AKISS provides support for XOR while considering a slightly larger class of equational theories called *optimally reducing*. Operations from rewriting logic are provided by queries to Maude [24] and support for arbitrary precision numbers is given by Apfloat [2]. Our experiments were conducted on an Intel core i7 dual quad core processor at 2.67 GHz with 12Gb of RAM. The host operating system was 64 bit Ubuntu 16.04.3 LTS.

Our comparison of the PFA and OTF algorithms began by examining how each approach scaled on a variety of examples (detailed at the end of this section). The results of the analysis are given in Fig. 2. For each example, we consider a fixed recipe depth and report the running times for 2 parties as well as the maximum number of parties for which one of the algorithms terminates within the timeout bound of 60 min. On small examples for which the protocols were indistinguishable, we found that the OTF and PFA algorithms were roughly equivalent. On large examples where the protocols were indistinguishable, such as the 3 ballot protocol, the PFA algorithm did not scale as well as the OTF algorithm. In particular, an out-of-memory exception often occurred during construction of the automata or the linear programming constraints. On examples for which the protocols were distinguishable, the OTF algorithm demonstrated a significant advantage. This was a result of the fact that the OTF approach analyzed the model as it was constructed. If at any point during model construction the bisimulation relation was determined not to hold, model construction was halted. By contrast, the PFA algorithm required the entire model to be constructed and stored before any analysis could take place.

In addition to stress-testing the tool, we also examined how each algorithm performed under various parameters of the mix-network example. The results are given in Fig. 3, where we examine how running times are affected by scaling the number of protocol participants and the recipe depth. Our results coincided with the observations from above. One interesting observation is that the number of beliefs explored on the 5 party example was identical for recipe depth 4 and recipe depth 10. The reason is that, for a given protocol input step, SPAN generates a

1	2	3	4	5	6	7	8	9	10
Protocol	Parties	Depth	Equiv	Time (s)				States	Beliefs
				PFA		OTF			
				Kiss	AKiSs	Kiss	Akiss		
DC-net	2	10	true	n/s	5.5	n/s	4	58	24
DC-net	3	10	true	n/s	OOM	n/s	3013	n/a	286
mix-net	2	10	false	TO	TO	.3	.4	n/a	7
mix-net	5	10	false	OOM	OOM	582	1586	n/a	79654
Evote	2	10	true	1	1	.5	1	34	33
Evote	8	10	true	105	105	131	124	94	93
3 Ballot	2	10	true	n/s	OOM	n/s	1444	n/a	408

Fig. 2. Experimental Results: Columns 1 and 2 describe the example being analyzed. Column 3 gives the maximum recipe depth and column 4 indicates when the example protocols were indistinguishable. Columns 5–8 give the running time (in seconds) for the respective algorithms and static equivalence engines. We report OOM for an out of memory exception and TO for a timeout - which occurs if no solution is generated in 60 min. Column 9 gives the number of states in the protocol's POMDP and Column 10 gives the number of belief states explored in the OTF algorithm. When information could not be determined due to a failure of the tool to terminate, we report n/a. For protocols using equational theories that were not subterm convergent, we write n/s (not supported) for the Kiss engine.

minimal set of recipes. This is in the sense that if recipes r_0, r_1 are generated at an input step with frame φ, then $r_0\varphi \neq_E r_1\varphi$. For the given number of public names available to the protocol, changing the recipe depth from 4 to 10 did not alter the number of unique terms that could be constructed by the attacker. We conclude this section by describing our benchmark examples, which are available at [3]. Evote is the simple electronic voting protocol derived from Example 2 and the DC-net, mix-net and 3 ballot protocols are described below.

Dinning Cryptographers Networks. In a simple DC-net protocol [38], two parties Alice and Bob want to anonymously publish two confidential bits m_A and m_B, respectively. To achieve this, Alice and Bob agree on three private random bits b_0, b_1 and b_2 and output a pair of messages according to the following scheme. In our modeling the protocol, the private bits are generated by a trusted third party who communicates them with Alice and Bob using symmetric encryption.

$$\text{If } b_0 = 0 \quad \text{Alice: } M_{A,0} = b_1 \oplus m_A, \ M_{A,1} = b_2$$
$$\text{Bob: } M_{B,0} = b_1, \ M_{B,1} = b_2 \oplus m_B$$
$$\text{If } b_0 = 1 \quad \text{Alice: } M_{A,0} = b_1, \ M_{A,1} = b_2 \oplus m_A$$
$$\text{Bob: } M_{B,0} = b_1 \oplus m_B, \ M_{B,1} = b_2$$

From the protocol output, the messages m_A and m_B can be retrieved as $M_{A,0} \oplus M_{B,0}$ and $M_{A,1} \oplus M_{B,1}$. The party to which the messages belong, however, remains unconditionally private, provided the exchanged secrets are not revealed.

1	2	3	4	5	6	7	8	9
PARTIES	DEPTH	EQUIV	TIME (S)				STATES	BELIEFS
			PFA		OTF			
			KISS	AKISS	KISS	AKISS		
2	1	true	.3	.3	.2	.3	15	12
3	1	true	1	1.2	.4	.9	81	50
4	1	true	47	47	2	6	2075	656
5	1	true	OOM	OOM	34	79	n/a	4032
5	2	false	OOM	OOM	13	33	n/a	1382
5	3	false	OOM	OOM	124	354	n/a	6934
5	4	false	OOM	OOM	580	1578	n/a	79654

Fig. 3. Detailed Experimental Results for Mix Networks: The columns have an identical meaning to the ones from Fig. 2. We report OOM for an out of memory exception and when information could not be determined due to a failure of the tool to terminate, we report n/a.

Mix Networks. A mix-network [21], is a routing protocol used to break the link between a message's sender and the message. This is achieved by routing messages through a series of proxy servers, called mixes. Each mix collects a batch of encrypted messages, privately decrypts each message and forwards the resulting messages in random order. More formally, consider a sender Alice (A) who wishes to send a message m to Bob (B) through Mix (M). Alice prepares a cipher-text of the form aenc(aenc(m, n_1, pk(B)), n_0, pk(M)) where aenc is asymmetric encryption, n_0, n_1 are nonces and pk(M), pk(B) are the public keys of the Mix and Bob, respectively. Upon receiving a batch of N such cipher-texts, the Mix unwraps the outer layer of encryption on each message using its secret key, randomly permutes and forwards the messages. A passive attacker, who observes all the traffic but does not otherwise modify the network, cannot (with high probability) correlate messages entering and exiting the Mix. Unfortunately, this simple design, known as a *threshold mix*, is vulnerable to a very simple active attack. To expose Alice as the sender of the message aenc(m, n_1, pk(B)), an attacker simply forwards Alice's message along with $N-1$ dummy messages to the Mix. In this way, the attacker can distinguish which of the Mix's N output messages is not a dummy message and hence must have originated from Alice.

3-Ballot Electronic Voting. We have modeled and analyzed the 3-ballot voting system from [54]. To simplify the presentation of this model, we first describe the major concepts behind 3-ballot voting schemes, as originally introduced by [50]. At the polling station, each voter is given 3 ballots at random. A ballot is comprised of a list of candidates and a ballot ID. When casting a vote, a voter begins by placing exactly one mark next to each candidate on one of the three ballots chosen a random. An additional mark is then placed next to the desired candidate on one of the ballots, again chosen at random. At the completion of the procedure, at least one mark should have been placed on each ballot and two ballots should have marks corresponding to the desired candidate. Once all of the votes have been cast, ballots are collected and released to a public bulletin board. Each voter retains a copy of one of the three ballots as a receipt, which can be used to verify his/her vote was counted.

In the full protocol, a registration agent is responsible for authenticating voters and receiving ballots and ballot ids generated by a vote manager. Once a voter marks his/her set of three ballots, they are returned to the vote manager who forwards them to one of three vote repositories. The vote repositories store the ballots they receive in a random position. After all votes have been collected in the repositories, they are released to a bulletin board by a vote collector. Communication between the registration agent, vote manager, vote repositories and vote collector is encrypted using asymmetric encryption and authenticated using digital signatures. In our modeling, we assume all parties behave honestly.

6   Conclusion

In this paper, we have considered the problem of model checking indistinguishability in randomized security protocols that are executed with respect to a Dolev-Yao adversary. We have presented two different algorithms for the indistinguishability problem assuming bounded recipe sizes. The algorithms have been implemented in the SPAN protocol analysis tool, which has been used to verify some well known randomized security protocols. We propose the following as part of future work: (i) extension of the current algorithms as well the tool to the case of unbounded recipe sizes; (ii) application of the tool for checking other randomized protocols; (iii) giving tight upper and lower bounds for the indistinguishability problem for the randomized protocols.

References

1. https://github.com/bauer-matthews/SPAN
2. http://www.apfloat.org/
3. https://github.com/bauer-matthews/SPAN/tree/master/src/test/resources/exam ples/indistinguishability
4. Abadi, M., Cortier, V.: Deciding knowledge in security protocols under equational theories. Theor. Comput. Sci. **367**(1–2), 2–32 (2006)
5. Abadi, M., Fournet, C.: Mobile values, new names, and secure communication. In: ACM SIGPLAN Notices, vol. 36, pp. 104–115. ACM (2001)
6. Adida, B.: Helios: web-based open-audit voting. In: USENIX Security Symposium, vol. 17, pp. 335–348 (2008)

7. Arapinis, M., Chothia, T., Ritter, E., Ryan, M.: Analysing unlinkability and anonymity using the applied pi calculus. In: Computer Security Foundations, pp. 107–121 (2010)
8. Armando, A., Compagna, L.: SAT-based model-checking for security protocols analysis. Int. J. Inf. Secur. **7**(1), 3–32 (2008)
9. Basin, D., Dreier, J., Sasse, R.: Automated symbolic proofs of observational equivalence. In: Computer and Communications Security, pp. 1144–1155 (2015)
10. Bauer, M.S., Chadha, R., Viswanathan, M.: Composing protocols with randomized actions. In: Piessens, F., Viganò, L. (eds.) POST 2016. LNCS, vol. 9635, pp. 189–210. Springer, Heidelberg (2016). https://doi.org/10.1007/978-3-662-49635-0_10
11. Ben-Or, M., Goldreich, O., Micali, S., Rivest, R.L.: A fair protocol for signing contracts. IEEE Trans. Inf. Theory **36**(1), 40–46 (1990)
12. Blanchet, B., Abadi, M., Fournet, C.: Automated verification of selected equivalences for security protocols. J. Log. Algebraic Program. **75**(1), 3–51 (2008)
13. Canetti, R., Cheung, L., Kaynar, D., Liskov, M., Lynch, N., Pereira, O., Segala, R.: Task-structured probabilistic I/O automata. In: Discrete Event Systems (2006)
14. Castro, P.S., Panangaden, P., Precup, D.: Equivalence relations in fully and partially observable Markov decision processes. In: International Joint Conference on Artificial Intelligence, vol. 9, pp. 1653–1658 (2009)
15. Chadha, R., Cheval, V., Ciobâcă, Ș., Kremer, S.: Automated verification of equivalence properties of cryptographic protocol. ACM Trans. Comput. Log. **17**(4), 23 (2016)
16. Chadha, R., Ciobâcă, Ș., Kremer, S.: Automated verification of equivalence properties of cryptographic protocols. In: Seidl, H. (ed.) ESOP 2012. LNCS, vol. 7211, pp. 108–127. Springer, Heidelberg (2012). https://doi.org/10.1007/978-3-642-28869-2_6
17. Chadha, R., Sistla, A.P., Viswanathan, M.: Model checking concurrent programs with nondeterminism and randomization. In: Foundations of Software Technology and Theoretical Computer Science, pp. 364–375 (2010)
18. Chadha, R., Sistla, A.P., Viswanathan, M.: Verification of randomized security protocols. In: Logic in Computer Science, pp. 1–12. IEEE (2017)
19. Chatzikokolakis, K., Palamidessi, C.: Making random choices invisible to the scheduler. In: Caires, L., Vasconcelos, V.T. (eds.) CONCUR 2007. LNCS, vol. 4703, pp. 42–58. Springer, Heidelberg (2007). https://doi.org/10.1007/978-3-540-74407-8_4
20. Chaum, D., Ryan, P.Y.A., Schneider, S.: A practical voter-verifiable election scheme. In: di Vimercati, S.C., Syverson, P., Gollmann, D. (eds.) ESORICS 2005. LNCS, vol. 3679, pp. 118–139. Springer, Heidelberg (2005). https://doi.org/10.1007/11555827_8
21. Chaum, D.L.: Untraceable electronic mail, return addresses, and digital pseudonyms. Commun. ACM **24**(2), 84–90 (1981)
22. Cheung, L.: Reconciling nondeterministic and probabilistic choices. Ph.D. thesis, Radboud University of Nijmegen (2006)
23. Cheval, V.: APTE: an algorithm for proving trace equivalence. In: Ábrahám, E., Havelund, K. (eds.) TACAS 2014. LNCS, vol. 8413, pp. 587–592. Springer, Heidelberg (2014). https://doi.org/10.1007/978-3-642-54862-8_50
24. Clavel, M., Durán, F., Eker, S., Lincoln, P., Martí-Oliet, N., Meseguer, J., Quesada, J.F.: Maude: specification and programming in rewriting logic. Theor. Comput. Sci. **285**(2), 187–243 (2002)
25. Cortier, V., Delaune, S.: A method for proving observational equivalence. In: Computer Security Foundations, pp. 266–276. IEEE (2009)

26. de Alfaro, L.: The verification of probabilistic systems under memoryless partial-information policies is hard. Technical report (1999)
27. Dehnert, C., Junges, S., Katoen, J.-P., Volk, M.: A storm is coming: a modern probabilistic model checker. In: Majumdar, R., Kunčak, V. (eds.) CAV 2017. LNCS, vol. 10427, pp. 592–600. Springer, Cham (2017). https://doi.org/10.1007/978-3-319-63390-9_31
28. Delaune, S., Kremer, S., Ryan, M.: Verifying privacy-type properties of electronic voting protocols. J. Comput. Secur. 17(4), 435–487 (2009)
29. Dingledine, R., Mathewson, N., Syverson, P.: Tor: the second-generation onion router. Technical report, DTIC Document (2004)
30. Dolev, D., Yao, A.: On the security of public key protocols. IEEE Trans. Inf. Theory 29(2), 198–208 (1983)
31. Doyen, L., Henzinger, T.A., Raskin, J.-F.: Equivalence of labeled Markov chains. Found. Comput. Sci. 19(03), 549–563 (2008)
32. Dreier, J., Duménil, C., Kremer, S., Sasse, R.: Beyond subterm-convergent equational theories in automated verification of stateful protocols. In: Maffei, M., Ryan, M. (eds.) POST 2017. LNCS, vol. 10204, pp. 117–140. Springer, Heidelberg (2017). https://doi.org/10.1007/978-3-662-54455-6_6
33. Durgin, N., Lincoln, P., Mitchell, J., Scedrov, A.: Multiset rewriting and the complexity of bounded security protocols. Comput. Secur. 12(2), 247–311 (2004)
34. Escobar, S., Meadows, C., Meseguer, J.: Maude-NPA: cryptographic protocol analysis modulo equational properties. In: Aldini, A., Barthe, G., Gorrieri, R. (eds.) FOSAD 2007-2009. LNCS, vol. 5705, pp. 1–50. Springer, Heidelberg (2009). https://doi.org/10.1007/978-3-642-03829-7_1
35. Even, S., Goldreich, O., Lempel, A.: A randomized protocol for signing contracts. Commun. ACM 28(6), 637–647 (1985)
36. Garcia, F.D., Van Rossum, P., Sokolova, A.: Probabilistic anonymity and admissible schedulers. arXiv preprint arXiv:0706.1019 (2007)
37. Goldschlag, D.M., Reed, M.G., Syverson, P.F.: Hiding routing information. In: Anderson, R. (ed.) IH 1996. LNCS, vol. 1174, pp. 137–150. Springer, Heidelberg (1996). https://doi.org/10.1007/3-540-61996-8_37
38. Golle, P., Juels, A.: Dining cryptographers revisited. In: Cachin, C., Camenisch, J.L. (eds.) EUROCRYPT 2004. LNCS, vol. 3027, pp. 456–473. Springer, Heidelberg (2004). https://doi.org/10.1007/978-3-540-24676-3_27
39. Goubault-Larrecq, J., Palamidessi, C., Troina, A.: A probabilistic applied pi-calculus. In: Shao, Z. (ed.) APLAS 2007. LNCS, vol. 4807, pp. 175–190. Springer, Heidelberg (2007). https://doi.org/10.1007/978-3-540-76637-7_12
40. Gunter, C.A., Khanna, S., Tan, K., Venkatesh, S.S.: DoS protection for reliably authenticated broadcast. In: Network and Distributed System Security (2004)
41. Hirschi, L., Baelde, D., Delaune, S.: A method for verifying privacy-type properties: the unbounded case. In: Security and Privacy, pp. 564–581 (2016)
42. Kiefer, S., Murawski, A.S., Ouaknine, J., Wachter, B., Worrell, J.: APEX: an analyzer for open probabilistic programs. In: Madhusudan, P., Seshia, S.A. (eds.) CAV 2012. LNCS, vol. 7358, pp. 693–698. Springer, Heidelberg (2012). https://doi.org/10.1007/978-3-642-31424-7_51
43. Kremer, S., Ryan, M.: Analysis of an electronic voting protocol in the applied pi calculus. In: Sagiv, M. (ed.) ESOP 2005. LNCS, vol. 3444, pp. 186–200. Springer, Heidelberg (2005). https://doi.org/10.1007/978-3-540-31987-0_14
44. Kwiatkowska, M., Norman, G., Parker, D.: PRISM 4.0: verification of probabilistic real-time systems. In: Gopalakrishnan, G., Qadeer, S. (eds.) CAV 2011. LNCS, vol. 6806, pp. 585–591. Springer, Heidelberg (2011). https://doi.org/10.1007/978-3-642-22110-1_47

45. Lenhardt, R.: Probabilistic automata with parameters. Master's thesis (2009)
46. Meadows, C.: Formal methods for cryptographic protocol analysis: emerging issues and trends. IEEE J. Sel. Areas Commun. **21**(1), 44–54 (2003)
47. Meadows, C.: Emerging issues and trends in formal methods in cryptographic protocol analysis: twelve years later. In: Martí-Oliet, N., Ölveczky, P.C., Talcott, C. (eds.) Logic, Rewriting, and Concurrency. LNCS, vol. 9200, pp. 475–492. Springer, Cham (2015). https://doi.org/10.1007/978-3-319-23165-5_22
48. Meier, S., Schmidt, B., Cremers, C., Basin, D.: The TAMARIN prover for the symbolic analysis of security protocols. In: Sharygina, N., Veith, H. (eds.) CAV 2013. LNCS, vol. 8044, pp. 696–701. Springer, Heidelberg (2013). https://doi.org/10.1007/978-3-642-39799-8_48
49. Reiter, M.K., Rubin, A.D.: Crowds: anonymity for web transactions. ACM Trans. Inf. Syst. Secur. **1**(1), 66–92 (1998)
50. Rivest, R.L.: The threeballot voting system (2006)
51. Rusinowitch, M., Turuani, M.: Protocol insecurity with finite number of sessions is NP-complete. Ph.D. thesis, INRIA (2001)
52. Ryan, P.Y.A., Bismark, D., Heather, J., Schneider, S., Xia, Z.: Prêt à voter: a voter-verifiable voting system. IEEE Trans. Inf. Forensics Secur. **4**(4), 662–673 (2009)
53. Bauer, M.S., Chadha, R., Viswanathan, M.: Modular verification of protocol equivalence in the presence of randomness. In: Foley, S.N., Gollmann, D., Snekkenes, E. (eds.) ESORICS 2017. LNCS, vol. 10492, pp. 187–205. Springer, Cham (2017). https://doi.org/10.1007/978-3-319-66402-6_12
54. Santin, A.O., Costa, R.G., Maziero, C.A.: A three-ballot-based secure electronic voting system. Secur. Priv. **6**(3), 14–21 (2008)
55. Schmidt, B., Meier, S., Cremers, C., Basin, D.: Automated analysis of Diffie-Hellman protocols and advanced security properties. In: Computer Security Foundations, pp. 78–94 (2012)
56. Shmatikov, V.: Probabilistic analysis of anonymity. In: Computer Security Foundations, pp. 119–128. IEEE (2002)
57. Tzeng, W.-G.: A polynomial-time algorithm for the equivalence of probabilistic automata. SIAM J. Comput. **21**(2), 216–227 (1992)

Lazy Self-composition for Security Verification

Weikun Yang[1], Yakir Vizel[1,3(✉)], Pramod Subramanyan[2], Aarti Gupta[1], and Sharad Malik[1]

[1] Princeton University, Princeton, USA
[2] University of California, Berkeley, Berkeley, USA
[3] The Technion, Haifa, Israel
yvizel@cs.technion.ac.il

Abstract. The secure information flow problem, which checks whether low-security outputs of a program are influenced by high-security inputs, has many applications in verifying security properties in programs. In this paper we present *lazy* self-composition, an approach for verifying secure information flow. It is based on self-composition, where two copies of a program are created on which a safety property is checked. However, rather than an eager duplication of the given program, it uses duplication lazily to reduce the cost of verification. This lazy self-composition is guided by an interplay between symbolic taint analysis on an abstract (single copy) model and safety verification on a refined (two copy) model. We propose two verification methods based on lazy self-composition. The first is a CEGAR-style procedure, where the abstract model associated with taint analysis is refined, on demand, by using a model generated by lazy self-composition. The second is a method based on bounded model checking, where taint queries are generated dynamically during program unrolling to guide lazy self-composition and to conclude an adequate bound for correctness. We have implemented these methods on top of the SEAHORN verification platform and our evaluations show the effectiveness of lazy self-composition.

1 Introduction

Many security properties can be cast as the problem of verifying secure information flow. A standard approach to verifying secure information flow is to reduce it to a safety verification problem on a "self-composition" of the program, i.e., two "copies" of the program are created [5] and analyzed. For example, to check for information leaks or non-interference [17], low-security (public) inputs are initialized to identical values in the two copies of the program, while high-security (confidential) inputs are unconstrained and can take different values. The safety check ensures that in all executions of the two-copy program, the values of the low-security (public) outputs are identical, i.e., there is no information leak from confidential inputs to public outputs. The self-composition approach is useful for

---

This work was supported in part by NSF Grant 1525936.

H. Chockler and G. Weissenbacher (Eds.): CAV 2018, LNCS 10982, pp. 136–156, 2018.
https://doi.org/10.1007/978-3-319-96142-2_11

checking general hyper-properties [11], and has been used in other applications, such as verifying constant-time code for security [1] and k-safety properties of functions like injectivity and monotonicity [32].

Although the self-composition reduction is sound and complete, it is challenging in practice to check safety properties on two copies of a program. There have been many efforts to reduce the cost of verification on self-composed programs, e.g., by use of type-based analysis [33], constructing product programs with aligned fragments [4], lockstep execution of loops [32], transforming Horn clause rules [14, 24], etc. The underlying theme in these efforts is to make it easier to derive *relational* invariants between the two copies, e.g., by keeping corresponding variables in the two copies near each other.

In this paper, we aim to improve the self-composition approach by making it *lazier* in contrast to eager duplication into two copies of a program. Specifically, we use symbolic taint analysis to track flow of information from high-security inputs to other program variables. (This is similar to dynamic taint analysis [30], but covers all possible inputs due to static verification.) This analysis works on an abstract model of a single copy of the program and employs standard model checking techniques for achieving precision and path sensitivity. When this abstraction shows a counterexample, we refine it using on-demand duplication of relevant parts of the program. Thus, our *lazy self-composition*[1] approach is guided by an interplay between symbolic taint analysis on an abstract (single copy) model and safety verification on a refined (two copy) model.

We describe two distinct verification methods based on lazy self-composition. The first is an iterative procedure for unbounded verification based on counterexample guided abstraction refinement (CEGAR) [9]. Here, the taint analysis provides a sound over-approximation for secure information flow, i.e., if a low-security output is proved to be untainted, then it is guaranteed to not leak any information. However, even a path-sensitive taint analysis can sometimes lead to "false alarms", i.e., a low-security output is tainted, but its value is unaffected by high-security inputs. For example, this can occur when a branch depends on a tainted variable, but the same (semantic, and not necessarily syntactic) value is assigned to a low-security output on both branches. Such false alarms for security due to taint analysis are then refined by lazily duplicating relevant parts of a program, and performing a safety check on the composed two-copy program. Furthermore, we use relational invariants derived on the latter to strengthen the abstraction within the iterative procedure.

Our second method also takes a similar abstraction-refinement view, but in the framework of bounded model checking (BMC) [6]. Here, we dynamically generate taint queries (in the abstract single copy model) during program unrolling, and use their result to simplify the duplication for self-composition (in the two copy model). Specifically, the second copy duplicates the statements (update logic) only if the taint query shows that the updated variable is possibly tainted. Furthermore, we propose a specialized early termination check for the BMC-

---

[1] This name is inspired by the *lazy abstraction* approach [20] for software model checking.

based method. In many secure programs, sensitive information is propagated in a localized context, but conditions exist that squash its propagation any further. We formulate the early termination check as a taint check on all live variables at the end of a loop body, i.e., if no live variable is tainted, then we can conclude that the program is secure without further loop unrolling. (This is under the standard assumption that inputs are tainted in the initial state. The early termination check can be suitably modified if tainted inputs are allowed to occur later.) Since our taint analysis is precise and path-sensitive, this approach can be beneficial in practice by unrolling the loops past the point where all taint has been squashed.

We have implemented these methods in the SEAHORN verification platform [18], which represents programs as CHC (Constrained Horn Clause) rules. Our prototype for taint analysis is flexible, with a fully symbolic encoding of the taint policy (i.e., rules for taint generation, propagation, and removal). It fully leverages SMT-based model checking techniques for precise taint analysis. Our prototypes allow rich security specifications in terms of annotations on low/high-security variables and locations in arrays, and predicates that allow information downgrading in specified contexts.

We present an experimental evaluation on benchmark examples. Our results clearly show the benefits of lazy self-composition vs. eager self-composition, where the former is much faster and allows verification to complete in larger examples. Our initial motivation in proposing the two verification methods was that we would find examples where one or the other method is better. We expect that easier proofs are likely to be found by the CEGAR-based method, and easier bugs by the BMC-based method. As it turns out, most of our benchmark examples are easy to handle by both methods so far. We believe that our general approach of lazy self-composition would be beneficial in other verification methods, and both our methods show its effectiveness in practice.

To summarize, this paper makes the following contributions.

- We present lazy self-composition, an approach to verifying secure information flow that reduces verification cost by exploiting the interplay between a path-sensitive symbolic taint analysis and safety checking on a self-composed program.
- We present IFC-CEGAR, a procedure for unbounded verification of secure information flow based on lazy self-composition using the CEGAR paradigm. IFC-CEGAR starts with a taint analysis abstraction of information flow and iteratively refines this abstraction using self-composition. It is tailored toward proving that programs have secure information flow.
- We present IFC-BMC, a procedure for bounded verification of secure information flow. As the program is being unrolled, IFC-BMC uses dynamic symbolic taint checks to determine which parts of the program need to be duplicated. This method is tailored toward bug-finding.
- We develop prototype implementations of IFC-CEGAR and IFC-BMC and present an experimental evaluation of these methods on a set of benchmarks/microbenchmarks. Our results demonstrate that IFC-CEGAR and IFC-

```
1   int steps = 0;
2   for (i = 0; i < N; i++) { zero[i] = product[i] = 0; }
3   for (i = 0; i < N*W; i++) {
4       int bi = bigint_extract_bit(a, i);
5       if (bi == 1) {
6           bigint_shiftleft(b, i, shifted_b, &steps);
7           bigint_add(product, shifted_b, product, &steps);
8       } else {
9           bigint_shiftleft(zero, i, shifted_zero, &steps);
10          bigint_add(product, shifted_zero, product, &steps);
11      }
12  }
```

Listing 1. "BigInt" Multiplication

BMC easily outperform an eager self-composition that uses the same backend verification engines.

2 Motivating Example

Listing 1 shows a snippet from a function that performs multiword multiplication. The code snippet is instrumented to count the number of iterations of the inner loop that are executed in `bigint_shiftleft` and `bigint_add` (not shown for brevity). These iterations are counted in the variable `steps`. The security requirement is that `steps` must not depend on the secret values in the array `a`; array `b` is assumed to be public.

Static analyses, including those based on security types, will conclude that the variable `steps` is "high-security." This is because `steps` is assigned in a conditional branch that depends on the high-security variable `bi`. However, this code is in fact safe because steps is incremented by the same value in both branches of the conditional statement.

Our lazy self-composition will handle this example by first using a symbolic taint analysis to conclude that the variable `steps` is tainted. It will then self-compose only those parts of the program related to computation of `steps`, and discover that it is set to identical values in both copies, thus proving the program is secure.

Now consider the case when the code in Listing 1 is used to multiply two "bigints" of differing widths, e.g., a 512b integer is multiplied with 2048b integer. If this occurs, the upper 1536 bits of a will all be zeros, and `bi` will not be a high-security variable for these iterations of the loop. Such a scenario can benefit from early-termination in our BMC-based method: our analysis will determine that no tainted value flows to the low security variable `steps` after iteration 512 and will immediately terminate the analysis.

3 Preliminaries

We consider First Order Logic modulo a theory $\mathcal{T}$ and denote it by $FOL(\mathcal{T})$. Given a program P, we define a *safety verification* problem w.r.t. P as a transition system $M = \langle X, Init(X), Tr(X, X'), Bad(X) \rangle$ where X denotes a set of (uninterpreted) constants, representing program variables; $Init$, Tr and Bad are (quantifier-free) formulas in $FOL(\mathcal{T})$ representing the initial states, transition relation and bad states, respectively. The states of a transition system correspond to structures over a signature $\Sigma = \Sigma_{\mathcal{T}} \cup X$. We write $Tr(X, X')$ to denote that Tr is defined over the signature $\Sigma_{\mathcal{T}} \cup X \cup X'$, where X is used to represent the pre-state of a transition, and $X' = \{a'|a \in X\}$ is used to represent the post-state.

A safety verification problem is to decide whether a transition system M is SAFE or UNSAFE. We say that M is UNSAFE iff there exists a number N such that the following formula is satisfiable:

$$Init(X_0) \wedge \left(\bigwedge_{i=0}^{N-1} Tr(X_i, X_{i+1}) \right) \wedge Bad(X_N) \tag{1}$$

where $X_i = \{a_i|a \in X\}$ is a copy of the program variables (uninterpreted constants) used to represent the state of the system after the execution of i steps.

When M is UNSAFE and $s_N \in Bad$ is reachable, the path from $s_0 \in Init$ to s_N is called a *counterexample* (CEX).

A transition system M is SAFE iff the transition system has no counterexample, of any length. Equivalently, M is SAFE iff there exists a formula Inv, called a *safe inductive invariant*, that satisfies: (i) $Init(X) \rightarrow Inv(X)$, (ii) $Inv(X) \wedge Tr(X, X') \rightarrow Inv(X')$, and (iii) $Inv(X) \rightarrow \neg Bad(X)$.

In SAT-based model checking (e.g., based on IC3 [7] or interpolants [23, 34]), the verification procedure maintains an *inductive trace* of formulas $[F_0(X), \ldots, F_N(X)]$ that satisfy: (i) $Init(X) \rightarrow F_0(X)$, (ii) $F_i(X) \wedge Tr(X, X') \rightarrow F_{i+1}(X')$ for every $0 \leq i < N$, and (iii) $F_i(X) \rightarrow \neg Bad(X)$ for every $0 \leq i \leq N$. A trace $[F_0, \ldots, F_N]$ is *closed* if $\exists 1 \leq i \leq N \cdot F_i \Rightarrow \left(\bigvee_{j=0}^{i-1} F_j \right)$. There is an obvious relationship between existence of closed traces and safety of a transition system: *A transition system T is SAFE iff it admits a safe closed trace.* Thus, safety verification is reduced to searching for a safe closed trace or finding a CEX.

4   Information Flow Analysis

Let P be a program over a set of program variables X. Recall that $Init(X)$ is a formula describing the initial states and $Tr(X, X')$ a transition relation. We assume a "stuttering" transition relation, namely, Tr is reflexive and therefore it can non-deterministically either move to the next state or stay in the same state. Let us assume that $H \subset X$ is a set of high-security variables and $L := X \backslash H$ is a set of low-security variables.

For each $x \in L$, let $Obs_x(X)$ be a predicate over program variables X that determines when variable x is adversary-observable. The precise definition of $Obs_x(X)$ depends on the threat model being considered. A simple model would be that for each low variable $x \in L$, $Obs_x(X)$ holds only at program completion – this corresponds to a threat model where the adversary can run a program that operates on some confidential data and observe its public (low-security) outputs after completion. A more sophisticated definition of $Obs_x(X)$ could consider, for example, a concurrently executing adversary. Appropriate definitions of $Obs_x(X)$ can also model declassification [29], by setting $Obs_x(X)$ to be false in program states where the declassification of x is allowed.

The *information flow* problem checks whether there exists an execution of P such that the value of variables in H affects a variable in $x \in L$ in some state where the predicate $Obs_x(X)$ holds. Intuitively, information flow analysis checks if low-security variables "leak" information about high-security variables.

We now describe our formulations of two standard techniques that have been used to perform information flow analysis. The first is based on taint analysis [30], but we use a symbolic (rather than a dynamic) analysis that tracks taint in a path-sensitive manner over the program. The second is based on self-composition [5], where two copies of the program are created and a safety property is checked over the composed program.

4.1   Symbolic Taint Analysis

When using taint analysis for checking information flow, we mark high-security variables with a "taint" and check if this taint can propagate to low-security variables. The propagation of taint through program variables of P is determined by both assignments and the control structure of P. In order to perform precise taint analysis, we formulate it as a safety verification problem. For this purpose, for each program variable $x \in X$, we introduce a new "taint" variable x_t. Let $X_t := \{x_t | x \in X\}$ be the set of taint variables where $x_t \in X_t$ is of sort Boolean. Let us define a transition system $M_t := \langle Y, Init_t, Tr_t, Bad_t \rangle$ where $Y := X \cup X_t$ and

$$Init_t(Y) := Init(X) \land \left(\bigwedge_{x \in H} x_t \right) \land \left(\bigwedge_{x \in L} \neg x_t \right) \tag{2}$$

$$Tr_t(Y, Y') := Tr(X, X') \land \hat{Tr}(Y, X_t') \tag{3}$$

$$Bad_t(Y) := \left(\bigvee_{x \in L} Obs_x(X) \land x_t \right) \tag{4}$$

Since taint analysis tracks information flow from high-security to low-security variables, variables in H_t are initialized to *true* while variables in L_t are initialized to *false*. W.l.o.g., let us denote the state update for a program variable $x \in X$ as: $x' = cond(X) ? \varphi_1(X) : \varphi_2(X)$. Let φ be a formula over Σ. We capture the taint of φ by:

$$\Theta(\varphi) = \begin{cases} false & \text{if } \varphi \cap X = \emptyset \\ \bigvee_{x \in \varphi} x_t & \text{otherwise} \end{cases}$$

Thus, $\hat{Tr}(X_t, X_t')$ is defined as: $\bigwedge_{x_t \in X_t} x_t' = \Theta(cond) \lor (cond ? \Theta(\varphi_1) : \Theta(\varphi_2))$

Intuitively, taint may propagate from x_1 to x_2 either when x_1 is assigned an expression that involves x_2 or when an assignment to x_1 is controlled by x_2. The bad states (Bad_t) are all states where a low-security variable is tainted and observable.

4.2 Self-composition

When using self-composition, information flow is tracked over an execution of two copies of the program, P and P_d. Let us denote $X_d := \{x_d | x \in X\}$ as the set of program variables of P_d. Similarly, let $Init_d(X_d)$ and $Tr_d(X_d, X_d')$ denote the initial states and transition relation of P_d. Note that $Init_d$ and Tr_d are computed from $Init$ and Tr by means of substitutions. Namely, substituting every occurrence of $x \in X$ or $x' \in X'$ with $x_d \in X_d$ and $x_d' \in X_d'$, respectively. Similarly to taint analysis, we formulate information flow over a self-composed program as a safety verification problem: $M_d := \langle Z, Init_d, Tr_d, Bad_d \rangle$ where $Z := X \cup X_d$ and

$$Init_d(Z) := Init(X) \wedge Init(X_d) \wedge \left(\bigwedge_{x \in L} x = x_d \right) \tag{5}$$

$$Tr_d(Z, Z') := Tr(X, X') \wedge Tr(X_d, X_d') \tag{6}$$

$$Bad_d(Z) := \left(\bigvee_{x \in L} Obs_x(X) \wedge Obs_x(X_d) \wedge \neg(x = x_d) \right) \tag{7}$$

In order to track information flow, variables in L_d are initialized to be equal to their counterpart in L, while variables in H_d remain unconstrained. A leak is captured by the bad states (i.e. Bad_d). More precisely, there exists a leak iff there exists an execution of M_d that results in a state where $Obs_x(X)$, $Obs_x(X_d)$ hold and $x \neq x_d$ for a low-security variable $x \in L$.

5   Lazy Self-composition for Information Flow Analysis

In this section, we introduce lazy self-composition for information flow analysis. It is based on an interplay between symbolic taint analysis on a single copy and safety verification on a self-composition, which were both described in the previous section.

Recall that taint analysis is imprecise for determining secure information flow in the sense that it may report spurious counterexamples, namely, spurious leaks. In contrast, self-composition is precise, but less efficient. The fact that self composition requires a duplication of the program often hinders its performance. The main motivation for lazy self-composition is to target both efficiency and precision.

Intuitively, the model for symbolic taint analysis M_t can be viewed as an abstraction of the self-composed model M_d, where the Boolean variables in M_t are predicates tracking the states where $x \neq x_d$ for some $x \in X$. This intuition is captured by the following statement: M_t over-approximates M_d.

Corollary 1. *If there exists a path in M_d from $Init_d$ to Bad_d then there exists a path in M_t from $Init_t$ to Bad_t.*

Corollary 2. *If there exists no path in M_t from $Init_t$ to Bad_t then there exists no path in M_d from $Init_d$ to Bad_d.*

This abstraction-based view relating symbolic taint analysis and self-composition can be exploited in different verification methods for checking secure information flow. In this paper, we focus on two – a CEGAR-based method (IFC-CEGAR) and a BMC-based method (IFC-BMC). These methods using lazy self-composition are now described in detail.

5.1 IFC-CEGAR

We make use of the fact that M_t can be viewed as an abstraction w.r.t. to M_d, and propose an abstraction-refinement paradigm for secure information flow analysis. In this setting, M_t is used to find a possible counterexample, i.e., a path that leaks information. Then, M_d is used to check if this counterexample is spurious or real. In case the counterexample is found to be spurious, IFC-CEGAR uses the proof that shows why the counterexample is not possible in M_d to refine M_t.

A sketch of IFC-CEGAR appears in Algorithm 1. Recall that we assume that solving a safety verification problem is done by maintaining an inductive trace. We denote the traces for M_t and M_d by $G = [G_0, \ldots, G_k]$ and $H = [H_0, \ldots, H_k]$, respectively. IFC-CEGAR starts by initializing M_t, M_d and their respective traces G and H (lines 1–4). The main loop of IFC-CEGAR (lines 5–18) starts by looking for a counterexample over M_t (line 6). In case no counterexample is found, IFC-CEGAR declares there are no leaks and returns SAFE.

If a counterexample π is found in M_t, IFC-CEGAR first updates the trace of M_d, i.e. H, by rewriting G (line 10). In order to check if π is spurious, IFC-CEGAR creates a new safety verification problem M_c, a version of M_d constrained by π (line 11) and solves it (line 12). If M_c has a counterexample, IFC-CEGAR returns UNSAFE. Otherwise, G is updated by H (line 16) and M_t is refined such that π is ruled out (line 17).

The above gives a high-level overview of how IFC-CEGAR operates. We now go into more detail. More specifically, we describe the functions ReWrite, Constraint and Refine. We note that these functions can be designed and implemented in several different ways. In what follows we describe some possible choices.

Proof-Based Abstraction. Let us assume that when solving M_t a counterexample π of length k is found and an inductive trace G is computed. Following a proof-based abstraction approach, Constraint() uses the length of π to bound the length of possible executions in M_d by k. Intuitively, this is similar to bounding the length of the computed inductive trace over M_d.

In case M_c has a counterexample, a real leak (of length k) is found. Otherwise, since M_c considers all possible executions of M_d of length k, IFC-CEGAR

Algorithm 1. Ifc-CEGAR (P,H)

Input: A program P and a set of high-security variables H
Output: SAFE, UNSAFE or UNKNOWN.

1 $M_t \leftarrow \texttt{ConstructTaintModel}(P,H)$
2 $M_d \leftarrow \texttt{ConstructSCModel}(P,H)$
3 $\mathbf{G} \leftarrow [G_0 = Init_t]$
4 $\mathbf{H} \leftarrow [H_0 = Init_d]$
5 **repeat**
6     $(\mathbf{G}, R_{taint}, \pi) \leftarrow \texttt{MC.Solve}(M_t, \mathbf{G})$
7   **if** $R_{taint} = SAFE$ **then**
8   **return** SAFE
9   **else**
10      $\mathbf{H} \leftarrow \texttt{ReWrite}(\mathbf{G}, \mathbf{H})$
11      $M_c \leftarrow \texttt{Constraint}(M_d, \pi)$
12      $(\mathbf{H}, R_s, \pi) \leftarrow \texttt{MC.Solve}(M_c, \mathbf{H})$
13   **if** $R_s = UNSAFE$ **then**
14   **return** UNSAFE
15   **else**
16        $\mathbf{G} \leftarrow \texttt{ReWrite}(\mathbf{H}, \mathbf{G})$
17        $M_t \leftarrow \texttt{Refine}(M_t, \mathbf{G})$
18 **until** ∞
19 **return** UNKNOWN

---

deduces that there are no counterexamples of length k. In particular, the counterexample π is ruled out. Ifc-CEGAR therefore uses this fact to refine M_t and $\mathbf{G}$.

Inductive Trace Rewriting. Consider the set of program variables X, taint variables X_t, and self compositions variables X_d. As noted above, M_t over-approximates M_d. Intuitively, it may mark a variable x as tainted when x does not leak information. Equivalently, if a variable x is found to be untainted in M_t then it is known to also not leak information in M_d. More formally, the following relation holds: $\neg x_t \rightarrow (x = x_d)$.

This gives us a procedure for rewriting a trace over M_t to a trace over M_d. Let $\mathbf{G} = [G_0, \ldots, G_k]$ be an inductive trace over M_t. Considering the definition of M_t, $\mathbf{G}$ can be decomposed and rewritten as: $G_i(Y) := \bar{G}_i(X) \wedge \bar{G}_i^t(X_t) \wedge \psi(X, X_t)$. Namely, $\bar{G}_i(X)$ and $\bar{G}_i^t(X_t)$ are sub-formulas of G_i over only X and X_t variables, respectively, and $\psi(X, X_t)$ is the part connecting X and X_t.

Since $\mathbf{G}$ is an inductive trace $G_i(Y) \wedge Tr_t(Y, Y') \rightarrow G_{i+1}(Y')$ holds. Following the definition of Tr_t and the above decomposition of G_i, the following holds:

$$\bar{G}_i(X) \wedge Tr(X, X') \rightarrow \bar{G}_{i+1}(X')$$

Let $H = [H_0, \ldots, H_k]$ be a trace w.r.t. M_d. We define the *update* of H by G as the trace $H^* = [H_0^*, \ldots, H_k^*]$, which is defined as follows:

$$H_0^* := Init_d \tag{8}$$

$$H_i^*(Z) := H_i(Z) \wedge \bar{G}_i(X) \wedge \bar{G}_i(X_d) \wedge \left(\bigwedge \{ x = x_d | G_i(Y) \rightarrow \neg x_t \} \right) \tag{9}$$

Intuitively, if a variable $x \in X$ is known to be untainted in M_t, using Corollary 2 we conclude that $x = x_d$ in M_d.

A similar update can be defined when updating a trace G w.r.t. M_t by a trace H w.r.t. M_d. In this case, we use the following relation: $\neg(x = x_d) \rightarrow x_t$. Let $H = [H_0(Z), \ldots, H_k(Z)]$ be the inductive trace w.r.t. M_d. H can be decomposed and written as $H_i(Z) := \bar{H}_i(X) \wedge \bar{H}_i^d(X_d) \wedge \phi(X, X_d)$.

Due to the definition of M_d and an inductive trace, the following holds:

$$\bar{H}_i(X) \wedge Tr(X, X') \rightarrow \bar{H}_i(X')$$

$$\bar{H}_i^d(X_d) \wedge Tr(X_d, X_d') \rightarrow \bar{H}_i^d(X_d')$$

We can therefore update a trace $G = [G_0, \ldots, G_k]$ w.r.t. M_t by defining the trace $G^* = [G_0^*, \ldots, G_k^*]$, where:

$$G_0^* := Init_d \tag{10}$$

$$G_i^*(Y) := G_i(Y) \wedge \bar{H}_i(X) \wedge \bar{H}_i^d(X) \wedge \left(\bigwedge \{ x_t | H_i(Z) \rightarrow \neg(x = x_d) \} \right) \tag{11}$$

Updating G by H, and vice-versa, as described above is based on the fact that M_t over-approximates M_d w.r.t. tainted variables (namely, Corollaries 1 and 2). It is therefore important to note that G^* in particular, does not "gain" more precision due to this process.

Lemma 1. *Let G be an inductive trace w.r.t. M_t and H an inductive trace w.r.t. M_d. Then, the updated H^* and G^* are inductive traces w.r.t. M_d and M_t, respectively.*

Refinement. Recall that in the current scenario, a counterexample was found in M_t, and was shown to be spurious in M_d. This fact can be used to refine both M_t and G.

As a first step, we observe that if $x = x_d$ in M_d, then $\neg x_t$ should hold in M_t. However, since M_t is an over-approximation it may allow x to be tainted, namely, allow x_t to be evaluated to *true*.

In order to refine M_t and G, we define a strengthening procedure for G, which resembles the updating procedure that appears in the previous section. Let $H = [H_0, \ldots, H_k]$ be a trace w.r.t. M_d and $G = [G_0, \ldots, G_k]$ be a trace w.r.t. M_t, then the strengthening of G is denoted as $G^r = [G_0^r, \ldots, G_k^r]$ such that:

$$G_0^r := Init_d \tag{12}$$

$$G_i^r(Y) := G_i(Y) \wedge \bar{H}_i(X) \wedge \bar{H}_i^s(X) \wedge \left(\bigwedge \{x_t | H_i(Z) \rightarrow \neg(x = x_d)\} \right) \wedge$$
$$\left(\bigwedge \{\neg x_t | H_i(Z) \rightarrow (x = x_d)\} \right) \tag{13}$$

The above gives us a procedure for strengthening G by using H. Note that since M_t is an over-approximation of M_d, it may allow a variable $x \in X$ to be tainted, while in M_d (and therefore in H), $x = x_d$. As a result, after strengthening G^r is not necessarily an inductive trace w.r.t. M_t, namely, $G_i^r \wedge Tr_t \rightarrow G_{i+1}^r{}'$ does not necessarily hold. In order to make G^r an inductive trace, M_t must be refined.

Let us assume that $G_i^r \wedge Tr_t \rightarrow G_{i+1}^r{}'$ does not hold. By that, $G_i^r \wedge Tr_t \wedge \neg G_{i+1}^r{}'$ is satisfiable. Considering the way G^r is strengthened, three exists $x \in X$ such that $G_i^r \wedge Tr_t \wedge x_t'$ is satisfiable and $G_{i+1}^r \Rightarrow \neg x_t$. The refinement step is defined by:

$$x_t' = G_i^r \ ? \ false \ : (\Theta(cond) \vee (cond \ ? \ \Theta(\varphi_1) \ : \ \Theta(\varphi_2)))$$

This refinement step changes the next state function of x_t such that whenever G_i holds, x_t is forced to be $false$ at the next time frame.

Lemma 2. *Let G^r be a strengthened trace, and let M_t^r be the result of refinement as defined above. Then, G^r is an inductive trace w.r.t M_t^r.*

Theorem 1. *Let $\mathfrak{A}$ be a sound and complete model checking algorithm w.r.t. $FOL(\mathcal{T})$ for some $\mathcal{T}$, such that $\mathfrak{A}$ maintains an inductive trace. Assuming IFC-CEGAR uses $\mathfrak{A}$, then IFC-CEGAR is both sound and complete.*

Proof (Sketch). Soundness follows directly from the soundness of taint analysis. For completeness, assume M_d is SAFE. Due to our assumption that $\mathfrak{A}$ is sound and complete, $\mathfrak{A}$ emits a closed inductive trace H. Intuitively, assuming H is of size k, then the next state function of every taint variable in M_t can be refined to be a constant $false$ after a specific number of steps. Then, H can be translated to a closed inductive trace G over M_t by following the above presented formalism. Using Lemma 2 we can show that a closed inductive trace exists for the refined taint model.

5.2   IFC-BMC

In this section we introduce a different method based on Bounded Model Checking (BMC) [6] that uses lazy self-composition for solving the information flow security problem. This approach is described in Algorithm 2. In addition to the program P, and the specification of high-security variables H, it uses an extra parameter BND that limits the maximum number of loop unrolls performed on the program P. (Alternatively, one can fall back to an unbounded verification method after BND is reached in BMC).

Algorithm 2. Ifc-BMC (P,H,BND)

Input: A program P, a set of high-security variables H, max unroll bound BND

Output: SAFE, UNSAFE or UNKNOWN.

1 $i \leftarrow 0$
2 **repeat**
3 | $M(i) \leftarrow$ LoopUnroll(P, i)
4 | $M_t(i) \leftarrow$ EncodeTaint$(M(i))$
5 | TR of $M_s(i) \leftarrow$ LazySC$(M(i), M_t(i))$
6 | Bad of $M_s(i) \leftarrow \bigvee_{y \in L} \neg(y = y')$
7 | $result \leftarrow$ SolveSMT$(M_s(i))$
8 | **if** $result = counterexample$ **then**
9 | | **return** UNSAFE
10 | $live\_taint \leftarrow$ CheckLiveTaint$(M_t(i))$
11 | **if** $live\_taint = false$ **then**
12 | | **return** SAFE
13 | $i \leftarrow i + 1$
14 **until** $i = BND$
15 **return** UNKNOWN

Algorithm 3. LazySC(M_t, M)

Input: A program model M and the corresponding taint program model M_t

Output: Transition relation of the self-composed program Tr_s

1 **for** each state update $x \leftarrow \varphi$ in transition relation of M **do**
2 | add state update $x \leftarrow \varphi$ to Tr_s
3 | $tainted \leftarrow$ SolveSMT(query on x_t in M_t)
4 | **if** $tainted = false$ **then**
5 | | add state update $x' \leftarrow x$ to Tr_s
6 | **else**
7 | | add state update $x' \leftarrow$ duplicate(φ) to Tr_s
8 **return** Tr_s

In each iteration of the algorithm (line 2), loops in the program P are unrolled (line 3) to produce a loop-free program, encoded as a transition system $M(i)$. A new transition system $M_t(i)$ is created (line 4) following the method described in Sect. 4.1, to capture precise taint propagation in the unrolled program $M(i)$. Then lazy self-composition is applied (line 5), as shown in detail in Algorithm 3, based on the interplay between the taint model $M_t(i)$ and the transition system $M(i)$. In detail, for each variable x updated in $M(i)$, where the state update is denoted $x := \varphi$, we use x_t in $M_t(i)$ to encode whether x is possibly tainted. We generate an SMT query to determine if x_t is satisfiable. If it is unsatisfiable, i.e., x_t evaluates to *False*, we can conclude that high security variables cannot affect the value of x. In this case, its duplicate variable x' in the self-composed program $M_s(i)$ is set equal to x, eliminating the need to duplicate the computation that will produce x'. Otherwise if x_t is satisfiable (or unknown), we duplicate φ and update x' accordingly.

The self-composed program $M_s(i)$ created by LazySC (Algorithm 3) is then checked by a bounded model checker, where a bad state is a state where any low-security output y ($y \in L$, where L denotes the set of low-security variables) has a different value than its duplicate variable y' (line 6). (For ease of exposition, a simple definition of bad states is shown here. This can be suitably modified to account for $Obs_x(X)$ predicates described in Sect. 4.) A counterexample produced by the solver indicates a leak in the original program P. We also use an early termination check for BMC encoded as an SMT-based query $CheckLiveTaint$, which essentially checks whether any live variable is tainted (line 10). If none of the live variables is tainted, i.e., any initial taint from high-security inputs has been squashed, then IFC-BMC can stop unrolling the program any further. If no conclusive result is obtained, IFC-BMC will return UNKNOWN.

6   Implementation and Experiments

We have implemented prototypes of IFC-CEGAR and IFC-BMC for information flow checking. Both are implemented on top of SEAHORN [18], a software verification platform that encodes programs as CHC (Constrained Horn Clause) rules. It has a frontend based on LLVM [22] and backends to Z3 [15] and other solvers. Our prototype has a few limitations. First, it does not support bit-precise reasoning and does not support complex data structures such as lists. Our implementation of symbolic taint analysis is flexible in supporting any given taint policy (i.e., rules for taint generation, propagation, and removal). It uses an encoding that fully leverages SMT-based model checking techniques for precise taint analysis. We believe this module can be independently used in other applications for security verification.

6.1   Implementation Details

IFC-CEGAR *Implementation.* As discussed in Sect. 5.1, the IFC-CEGAR implementation uses taint analysis and self-composition synergistically and is tailored toward proving that programs are secure. Both taint analysis and self-composition are implemented as LLVM-passes that instrument the program. Our prototype implementation executes these two passes interchangeably as the problem is being solved. The IFC-CEGAR implementation uses Z3's CHC solver engine called SPACER. SPACER, and therefore our IFC-CEGAR implementation, does not handle the bitvector theory, limiting the set of programs that can be verified using this prototype. Extending the prototype to support this theory will be the subject of future work.

IFC-BMC *Implementation.* In the IFC-BMC implementation, the loop unroller, taint analysis, and lazy self-composition are implemented as passes that work on CHC, to generate SMT queries that are passed to the backend Z3 solver. Since the IFC-BMC implementation uses Z3, and not SPACER, it can handle all the programs in our evaluation, unlike the IFC-CEGAR implementation.

Input Format. The input to our tools is a C-program with annotations indicating which variables are *secret* and the locations at which leaks should be checked. In addition, variables can be marked as *untainted* at specific locations.

6.2   Evaluation Benchmarks

For experiments we used a machine running Intel Core i7-4578U with 8GB of RAM. We tested our prototypes on several micro-benchmarks[2] in addition to benchmarks inspired by real-world programs. For comparison against eager self-composition, we used the SEAHORN backend solvers on a 2-copy version of the benchmark. fibonacci is a micro-benchmark that computes the N-th Fibonacci number. There are no secrets in the micro-benchmark, and this is a sanity check taken from [33]. list_4/8/16 are programs working with linked lists, the trailing number indicates the maximum number of nodes being used. Some linked list nodes contain secrets while others have public data, and the verification problem is to ensure that a particular function that operates on the linked list does not leak the secret data. modadd_safe is program that performs multi-word addition; modexp_safe/unsafe are variants of a program performing modular exponentiation; and pwdcheck_safe/unsafe are variants of program that compares an input string with a secret password. The verification problem in these examples is to ensure that an iterator in a loop does not leak secret information, which could allow a timing attack. Among these benchmarks, the list_4/8/16 use structs while modexp_safe/unsafe involve bitvector operations, both of which are not supported by SPACER, and thus not by our IFC-CEGAR prototype.

6.3   IFC-CEGAR Results

Table 1 shows the IFC-CEGAR results on benchmark examples with varying parameter values. The columns show the time taken by eager self-composition (Eager SC) and IFC-CEGAR, and the number of refinements in IFC-CEGAR. "TO" denotes a timeout of 300 s.

We note that all examples are secure and do not leak information. Since our path-sensitive symbolic taint analysis is more precise than a type-based taint analysis, there are few counterexamples and refinements. In particular, for our first example pwdcheck_safe, self-composition is not required as our path-sensitive taint analysis is able to prove that no taint propagates to the variables of interest. It is important to note that type-based taint analysis cannot prove that this example is secure. For our second example, pwdcheck2_safe, our path-sensitive taint analysis is not enough. Namely, it finds a counterexample, due to an implicit flow where a for-loop is conditioned on a tainted value, but there is no real leak because the loop executes a constant number of times.

---

[2] http://www.cs.princeton.edu/~aartig/benchmarks/ifc_bench.zip.

Table 1. Ifc-CEGAR results (time in seconds)

Benchmark	Parameter	Eager SC	Ifc-CEGAR	
		Time (s)	Time (s)	#Refinements
pwdcheck_safe	4	8.8	0.2	0
	8	TO	0.2	0
	16	TO	0.2	0
	32	TO	0.2	0
pwdcheck2_safe	$N > 8$	TO	61	1
modadd_safe	2048b	180	0.2	0
	4096b	TO	0.3	0

Our refinement-based approach can easily handle this case, where Ifc-CEGAR uses self-composition to find that the counterexample is spurious. It then refines the taint analysis model, and after one refinement step, it is able to prove that pwdcheck2_safe is secure. While these examples are fairly small, they clearly show that Ifc-CEGAR is superior to eager self-composition.

6.4 Ifc-BMC Results

The experimental results for Ifc-BMC are shown in Table 2, where we use some unsafe versions of benchmark examples as well. Results are shown for total time taken by eager self-composition (Eager SC) and the Ifc-BMC algorithm. (As before, "TO" denotes a timeout of 300 s.) Ifc-BMC is able to produce an answer significantly faster than eager self-composition for all examples. The last two columns show the time spent in taint checks in Ifc-BMC, and the number of taint checks performed.

Table 2. Ifc-BMC results (time in seconds)

Benchmark	Result	Eager SC	Ifc-BMC	Taint checks	#Taint checks
		Time (s)	Time (s)	Time (s)	
fibonacci	SAFE	0.55	0.1	0.07	85
list_4	SAFE	2.9	0.15	0.007	72
list_8	SAFE	3.1	0.6	0.02	144
list_16	SAFE	3.2	1.83	0.08	288
modexp_safe	SAFE	TO	0.05	0.01	342
modexp_unsafe	UNSAFE	TO	1.63	1.5	364
pwdcheck_safe	SAFE	TO	0.05	0.01	1222
pwdcheck_unsafe	UNSAFE	TO	1.63	1.5	809

To study the scalability of our prototype, we tested IFC-BMC on the modular exponentiation program with different values for the maximum size of the integer array in the program. These results are shown in Table 3. Although the IFC-BMC runtime grows exponentially, it is reasonably fast – less than 2 min for an array of size 64.

7 Related Work

A rich body of literature has studied the verification of secure information flow in programs. Initial work dates back to Denning and Denning [16], who introduced a program analysis to ensure that confidential data does not flow to non-confidential outputs. This notion of confidentiality relates closely to: (i) non-interference introduced by Goguen and Meseguer [17], and (ii) separability introduced by Rushby [27]. Each of these study a notion of secure information flow where confidential data is strictly not allowed to flow to any non-confidential output. These definitions are often too restrictive for practical programs, where secret data might sometimes be allowed to flow to some non-secret output (e.g., if the data is encrypted before output), i.e. they require declassification [29]. Our approach allows easy and fine-grained de-classification.

A large body of work has also studied the use of type systems that ensure secure information flow. Due to a lack of space, we review a few exemplars and refer the reader to Sabelfeld and Myers [28] for a detailed survey. Early work in this area dates back to Volpano et al. [35] who introduced a type system that maintains secure information based on the work of Denning and Denning [16]. Myers introduced the JFlow programming language (later known as Jif: Java information flow) [25] which extended Java with security types. Jif has been used to build clean slate, secure implementations of complex end-to-end systems, e.g. the Civitas [10] electronic voting system. More recently, Patrigiani et al. [26] introduced the Java Jr. language which extends Java with a security type system, automatically partitions the program into secure and non-secure parts and executes the secure parts inside so-called protected module architectures. In

Table 3. IFC-BMC results on modexp (time in seconds)

Benchmark	Parameter	Time (s)	#Taint checks
modexp	8	0.19	180
	16	1.6	364
	24	3.11	548
	32	8.35	732
	40	11.5	916
	48	21.6	1123
	56	35.6	1284
	64	85.44	1468

contrast to these approaches, our work can be applied to existing security-critical code in languages like C with the addition of only a few annotations.

A different approach to verifying secure information flow is the use of dynamic taint analysis (DTA) [3,12,13,21,30,31] which instruments a program with taint variables and taint tracking code. Advantages of DTA are that it is scalable to very large applications [21], can be accelerated using hardware support [13], and tracks information flow across processes, applications and even over the network [12]. However, taint analysis necessarily involves imprecision and in practice leads to both false positives and false negatives. False positives arise because taint analysis is an overapproximation. Somewhat surprisingly, false negatives are also introduced because tracking implicit flows using taint analysis leads to a deluge of false-positives [30], thus causing practical taint tracking systems to ignore implicit flows. Our approach does not have this imprecision.

Our formulation of secure information flow is based on the self-composition construction proposed by Barthe et al. [5]. A specific type of self-composition called product programs was considered by Barthe et al. [4], which does not allow control flow divergence between the two programs. In general this might miss certain bugs as it ignores implicit flows. However, it is useful in verifying crypto-graphic code which typically has very structured control flow. Almeida et al. [1] used the product construction to verify that certain functions in cryptographic libraries execute in constant-time.

Terauchi and Aiken [33] generalized self-composition to consider k-safety, which uses $k - 1$ compositions of a program with itself. Note that self-composition is a 2-safety property. An automated verifier for k-safety properties of Java programs based on Cartesian Hoare Logic was proposed by Sousa and Dillig [32]. A generalization of Cartesian Hoare Logic, called Quantitative Carte-sian Hoare Logic was introduced by Chen et al. [8]; the latter can also be used to reason about the execution time of cryptographic implementations. Among these efforts, our work is mostly closely related to that of Terauchi and Aiken [33], who used a type-based analysis as a preprocessing step to self-composition. We use a similar idea, but our taint analysis is more precise due to being path-sensitive, and it is used within an iterative CEGAR loop. Our path-sensitive taint analysis leads to fewer counterexamples and thereby cheaper self-composition, and our refinement approach can easily handle examples with benign branches. In con-trast to the other efforts, our work uses lazy instead of eager self-composition, and is thus more scalable, as demonstrated in our evaluation. A recent work [2] also employs trace-based refinement in security verification, but it does not use self-composition.

Our approach has some similarities to other problems related to tainting [19]. In particular, *Change-Impact Analysis* is the problem of determining what parts of a program are affected due to a change. Intuitively, it can be seen as a form of taint analysis, where the change is treated as taint. To solve this, Gyori et al. [19] propose a combination of an imprecise type-based approach with a pre-cise semantics-preserving approach. The latter considers the program before and after the change and finds relational equivalences between the two versions. These are then used to strengthen the type-based approach. While our work has some similarities, there are crucial differences as well. First, our taint analysis is not type-based, but is path-sensitive and preserves the correctness of the defined abstraction. Second, our lazy self-composition is a form of an abstraction-refinement framework, and allows a tighter integration between the imprecise (taint) and precise (self-composition) models.

8 Conclusions and Future Work

A well-known approach for verifying secure information flow is based on the notion of self-composition. In this paper, we have introduced a new approach for this verification problem based on *lazy self-composition*. Instead of eagerly duplicating the program, lazy self-composition uses a synergistic combination of symbolic taint analysis (on a single copy program) and self-composition by duplicating relevant parts of the program, depending on the result of the taint analysis. We presented two instances of lazy self-composition: the first uses taint analysis and self-composition in a CEGAR loop; the second uses bounded model checking to dynamically query taint checks and self-composition based on the results of these dynamic checks. Our algorithms have been implemented in the SEAHORN verification platform and results show that lazy self-composition is able to verify many instances not verified by eager self-composition.

In future work, we are interested in extending lazy self-composition to support learning of quantified relational invariants. These invariants are often required when reasoning about information flow in shared data structures of unbounded size (e.g., unbounded arrays, linked lists) that contain both high- and low-security data. We are also interested in generalizing lazy self-composition beyond information-flow to handle other k-safety properties like injectivity, associativity and monotonicity.

References

1. Almeida, J.B., Barbosa, M., Barthe, G., Dupressoir, F., Emmi, M.: Verifying constant-time implementations. In: 25th USENIX Security Symposium, USENIX Security, pp. 53–70 (2016)
2. Antonopoulos, T., Gazzillo, P., Hicks, M., Koskinen, E., Terauchi, T., Wei, S.: Decomposition instead of self-composition for proving the absence of timing channels. In: PLDI, pp. 362–375 (2017)
3. Babil, G.S., Mehani, O., Boreli, R., Kaafar, M.: On the effectiveness of dynamic taint analysis for protecting against private information leaks on Android-based devices. In: Proceedings of Security and Cryptography (2013)
4. Barthe, G., Crespo, J.M., Kunz, C.: Relational verification using product programs. In: Butler, M., Schulte, W. (eds.) FM 2011. LNCS, vol. 6664, pp. 200–214. Springer, Heidelberg (2011). https://doi.org/10.1007/978-3-642-21437-0_17
5. Barthe, G., D'Argenio, P.R., Rezk,T.: Secure information flow by self-composition. In: 17th IEEE Computer Security Foundations Workshop, CSFW-17, pp. 100–114 (2004)

6. Biere, A., Cimatti, A., Clarke, E., Zhu, Y.: Symbolic model checking without BDDs. In: Cleaveland, W.R. (ed.) TACAS 1999. LNCS, vol. 1579, pp. 193–207. Springer, Heidelberg (1999). https://doi.org/10.1007/3-540-49059-0_14
7. Bradley, A.R.: SAT-based model checking without unrolling. In: Jhala, R., Schmidt, D. (eds.) VMCAI 2011. LNCS, vol. 6538, pp. 70–87. Springer, Heidelberg (2011). https://doi.org/10.1007/978-3-642-18275-4_7
8. Chen, J., Feng, Y., Dillig, I.: Precise detection of side-channel vulnerabilities using quantitative Cartesian Hoare logic. In: Proceedings of the 2017 ACM SIGSAC Conference on Computer and Communications Security, CCS 2017, pp. 875–890. ACM, New York (2017)
9. Clarke, E., Grumberg, O., Jha, S., Lu, Y., Veith, H.: Counterexample-guided abstraction refinement. In: Emerson, E.A., Sistla, A.P. (eds.) CAV 2000. LNCS, vol. 1855, pp. 154–169. Springer, Heidelberg (2000). https://doi.org/10.1007/10722167_15
10. Clarkson, M.R., Chong, S., Myers, A.C.: Civitas: toward a secure voting system. In: Proceedings of the 2008 IEEE Symposium on Security and Privacy, SP 2008, pp. 354–368. IEEE Computer Society, Washington, DC (2008)
11. Clarkson, M.R., Schneider, F.B.: Hyperproperties. J. Comput. Secur. 18(6), 1157–1210 (2010)
12. Costa, M., Crowcroft, J., Castro, M., Rowstron, A., Zhou, L., Zhang, L., Barham, P.: Vigilante: end-to-end containment of Internet worms. In: Proceedings of the Symposium on Operating Systems Principles (2005)
13. Crandall, J.R., Chong, F.T.: Minos: control data attack prevention orthogonal to memory model. In: Proceedings of the 37th IEEE/ACM International Symposium on Microarchitecture (2004)
14. De Angelis, E., Fioravanti, F., Pettorossi, A., Proietti, M.: Relational verification through horn clause transformation. In: Rival, X. (ed.) SAS 2016. LNCS, vol. 9837, pp. 147–169. Springer, Heidelberg (2016). https://doi.org/10.1007/978-3-662-53413-7_8
15. de Moura, L., Bjørner, N.: Z3: an efficient SMT solver. In: Ramakrishnan, C.R., Rehof, J. (eds.) TACAS 2008. LNCS, vol. 4963, pp. 337–340. Springer, Heidelberg (2008). https://doi.org/10.1007/978-3-540-78800-3_24
16. Denning, D.E., Denning, P.J.: Certification of programs for secure information flow. Commun. ACM 20(7), 504–513 (1977)
17. Goguen, J.A., Meseguer, J.: Security policies and security models. In: 1982 IEEE Symposium on Security and Privacy, Oakland, CA, USA, 26–28 April 1982, pp. 11–20 (1982)
18. Gurfinkel, A., Kahsai, T., Komuravelli, A., Navas, J.A.: The SeaHorn verification framework. In: Kroening, D., Păsăreanu, C.S. (eds.) CAV 2015. LNCS, vol. 9206, pp. 343–361. Springer, Cham (2015). https://doi.org/10.1007/978-3-319-21690-4_20
19. Gyori, A., Lahiri, S.K., Partush, N.: Refining interprocedural change-impact analysis using equivalence relations. In: Proceedings of the 26th ACM SIGSOFT International Symposium on Software Testing and Analysis, Santa Barbara, CA, USA, 10–14 July 2017, pp. 318–328 (2017)
20. Henzinger, T.A., Jhala, R., Majumdar, R., Sutre, G.: Lazy abstraction. In: The SIGPLAN-SIGACT Symposium on Principles of Programming Languages, pp. 58–70 (2002)
21. Kang, M.G., McCamant, S., Poosankam, P., Song, D.: DTA++: dynamic taint analysis with targeted control-flow propagation. In: Proceedings of the Network and Distributed System Security Symposium (2011)

22. Lattner, C., Adve, V.S.: LLVM: a compilation framework for lifelong program analysis & transformation. In: 2nd IEEE/ACM International Symposium on Code Generation and Optimization, CGO, pp. 75–88 (2004)
23. McMillan, K.L.: Interpolation and SAT-based model checking. In: Hunt, W.A., Somenzi, F. (eds.) CAV 2003. LNCS, vol. 2725, pp. 1–13. Springer, Heidelberg (2003). https://doi.org/10.1007/978-3-540-45069-6_1
24. Mordvinov, D., Fedyukovich, G.: Synchronizing constrained horn clauses. In: EPiC Series in Computing, LPAR, vol. 46, pp. 338–355. EasyChair (2017)
25. Myers, A.C.: JFlow: practical mostly-static information flow control. In: Proceedings of the 26th Annual ACM SIGPLAN-SIGACT Symposium on Principles of Programming Languages. ACM (1999)
26. Patrignani, M., Agten, P., Strackx, R., Jacobs, B., Clarke, D., Piessens, F.: Secure compilation to protected module architectures. ACM Trans. Program. Lang. Syst. 37(2), 6:1–6:50 (2015)
27. Rushby, J.M.: Proof of separability a verification technique for a class of security kernels. In: Dezani-Ciancaglini, M., Montanari, U. (eds.) Programming 1982. LNCS, vol. 137, pp. 352–367. Springer, Heidelberg (1982). https://doi.org/10.1007/3-540-11494-7_23
28. Sabelfeld, A., Myers, A.C.: Language-based information-flow security. IEEE J. Sel. Areas Commun. 21(1), 5–19 (2006)
29. Sabelfeld, A., Sands, D.: Declassification: dimensions and principles. J. Comput. Secur. 17(5), 517–548 (2009)
30. Schwartz, E., Avgerinos, T., Brumley, D.: All you ever wanted to know about dynamic taint analysis and forward symbolic execution (but might have been afraid to ask). In: Proceedings of the 2010 IEEE Symposium on Security and Privacy (2010)
31. Song, D., et al.: BitBlaze: a new approach to computer security via binary analysis. In: Sekar, R., Pujari, A.K. (eds.) ICISS 2008. LNCS, vol. 5352, pp. 1–25. Springer, Heidelberg (2008). https://doi.org/10.1007/978-3-540-89862-7_1
32. Sousa, M., Dillig, I.: Cartesian hoare logic for verifying k-safety properties. In: Proceedings of the 37th ACM SIGPLAN Conference on Programming Language Design and Implementation, PLDI 2016, pp. 57–69. ACM, New York (2016)
33. Terauchi, T., Aiken, A.: Secure information flow as a safety problem. In: Hankin, C., Siveroni, I. (eds.) SAS 2005. LNCS, vol. 3672, pp. 352–367. Springer, Heidelberg (2005). https://doi.org/10.1007/11547662_24
34. Vizel, Y., Gurfinkel, A.: Interpolating property directed reachability. In: Biere, A., Bloem, R. (eds.) CAV 2014. LNCS, vol. 8559, pp. 260–276. Springer, Cham (2014). https://doi.org/10.1007/978-3-319-08867-9_17
35. Volpano, D., Irvine, C., Smith, G.: A sound type system for secure flow analysis. J. Comput. Secur. 4(2–3), 167–187 (1996)

SCInfer: Refinement-Based Verification
of Software Countermeasures Against
Side-Channel Attacks

Jun Zhang[1], Pengfei Gao[1], Fu Song[1(✉)],
and Chao Wang[2]

[1] ShanghaiTech University, Shanghai, China
songfu@shanghaitech.edu.cn
[2] University of Southern California,
Los Angeles, CA, USA

Abstract. Power side-channel attacks, capable of deducing secret using statistical analysis techniques, have become a serious threat to devices in cyber-physical systems and the Internet of things. Random masking is a widely used countermeasure for removing the statistical dependence between secret data and side-channel leaks. Although there are techniques for verifying whether software code has been perfectly masked, they are limited in accuracy and scalability. To bridge this gap, we propose a refinement-based method for verifying masking countermeasures. Our method is more accurate than prior syntactic type inference based approaches and more scalable than prior model-counting based approaches using SAT or SMT solvers. Indeed, it can be viewed as a gradual refinement of a set of semantic type inference rules for reasoning about distribution types. These rules are kept *abstract* initially to allow fast deduction, and then made *concrete* when the abstract version is not able to resolve the verification problem. We have implemented our method in a tool and evaluated it on cryptographic benchmarks including AES and MAC-Keccak. The results show that our method significantly outperforms state-of-the-art techniques in terms of both accuracy and scalability.

1 Introduction

Cryptographic algorithms are widely used in embedded computing devices, including SmartCards, to form the backbone of their security mechanisms. In general, security is established by assuming that the adversary has access to the input and output, but not internals, of the implementation. Unfortunately, in practice, attackers may recover cryptographic keys by analyzing physical information leaked through side channels. These so-called *side-channel attacks* exploit the statistical dependence between secret data and non-functional properties of a computing device such as the execution time [38], power consumption [39] and electromagnetic radiation [49]. Among them, *differential power analysis* (DPA) is an extremely popular and effective class of attacks [30,42].

This work was supported primarily by the National Natural Science Foundation of China (NSFC) grants 61532019 and 61761136011. Chao Wang was supported by the U.S. National Science Foundation (NSF) grant CNS-1617203.

H. Chockler and G. Weissenbacher (Eds.): CAV 2018, LNCS 10982, pp. 157–177, 2018.
https://doi.org/10.1007/978-3-319-96142-2_12

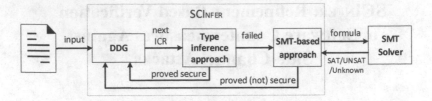

Fig. 1. Overview of SCINFER, where "ICR" denotes the intermediate computation result.

To thwart DPA attacks, *masking* has been proposed to break the statistical dependence between secret data and side-channel leaks through randomization. Although various masked implementations have been proposed, e.g., for AES or its non-linear components (S-boxes) [15,37,51,52], checking if they are correct is always tedious and error-prone. Indeed, there are published implementations [51,52] later shown to be incorrect [21,22]. Therefore, formally verifying these countermeasures is important.

Previously, there are two types of verification methods for masking countermeasures [54]: one is type inference based [10,44] and the other is model counting based [26,27]. Type inference based methods [10,44] are fast and sound, meaning they can quickly prove the computation is leakage free, e.g., if the result is syntactically independent of the secret data or has been masked by random variables not used elsewhere. However, syntactic type inference is *not* complete in that it may report *false positives*. In contrast, model counting based methods [26,27] are sound and complete: they check if the computation is statistically independent of the secret [15]. However, due to the inherent complexity of model counting, they can be extremely slow in practice.

The aforementioned gap, in terms of both accuracy and scalability, has not been bridged by more recent approaches [6,13,47]. For example, Barthe et al. [6] proposed some inference rules to prove masking countermeasures based on the observation that certain operators (e.g., XOR) are *invertible*: in the absence of such operators, purely algebraic laws can be used to normalize expressions of computation results to apply the rules of invertible functions. This normalization is applied to each expression once, as it is costly. Ouahma et al. [47] introduced a linear-time algorithm based on finer-grained syntactical inference rules. A similar idea was explored by Bisi et al. [13] for analyzing higher-order masking: like in [6,47], however, the method is not complete, and does not consider non-linear operators which are common in cryptographic software.

Our Contribution. We propose a refinement based approach, named SCINFER, to bridge the gap between prior techniques which are either fast but inaccurate or accurate but slow. Figure 1 depicts the overall flow, where the input consists of the program and a set of variables marked as *public*, *private*, or *random*. We first transform the program to an intermediate representation: the data dependency graph (DDG). Then, we traverse the DDG in a topological order to infer a *distribution type* for each intermediate computation result. Next, we check if all intermediate computation results are perfectly masked according to their types. If any of them cannot be resolved in this way, we invoke an SMT solver based refinement procedure, which leverages either satisfiability (SAT) solving or model counting (SAT#) to prove leakage freedom. In both cases, the result is fed back to improve the type system. Finally, based on the refined type inference rules, we continue to analyze other intermediate computation results.

Thus, SCInfer can be viewed as a synergistic integration of a semantic rule based approach for inferring *distribution types* and an SMT solver based approach for refining these inference rules. Our type inference rules (Sect. 3) are inspired by Barthe et al. [6] and Ouahma et al. [47] in that they are designed to infer distribution types of intermediate computation results. However, there is a crucial difference: their inference rules are syntactic with fixed accuracy, i.e., relying solely on structural information of the program, whereas ours are *semantic* and the accuracy can be gradually improved with the aid of our SMT solver based analysis. At a high level, our semantic type inference rules subsume their syntactic type inference rules.

The main advantage of using type inference is the ability to *quickly* obtain sound proofs: when there is no leak in the computation, often times, the type system can produce a proof quickly; furthermore, the result is always conclusive. However, if type inference fails to produce a proof, the verification problem remains unresolved. Thus, to be complete, we propose to leverage SMT solvers to resolve these *left-over* verification problems. Here, solvers are used to check either the satisfiability (SAT) of a logical formula or counting its satisfying solutions (SAT#), the later of which, although expensive, is powerful enough to completely decide if the computation is perfectly masked. Finally, by feeding solver results back to the type inference system, we can gradually improve its accuracy. Thus, overall, the method is both sound and complete.

We have implemented our method in a software tool named SCInfer and evaluated it on publicly available benchmarks [26, 27], which implement various cryptographic algorithms such as AES and MAC-Keccak. Our experiments show SCInfer is both effective in obtaining proofs quickly and scalable for handling realistic applications. Specifically, it can resolve most of the verification subproblems using type inference and, as a result, satisfiability (SAT) based analysis needs to be applied to few left-over cases. Only in rare cases, the most heavyweight analysis (SAT#) needs to be invoked.

To sum up, the main contributions of this work are as follows:

- We propose a new semantic type inference approach for verifying masking countermeasures. It is sound and efficient for obtaining proofs.
- We propose a method for gradually refining the type inference system using SMT solver based analysis, to ensure the overall method is complete.
- We implement the proposed techniques in a tool named SCInfer and demonstrate its efficiency and effectiveness on cryptographic benchmarks.

The remainder of this paper is organized as follows. After reviewing the basics in Sect. 2, we present our semantic type inference system in Sect. 3 and our refinement method in Sect. 4. Then, we present our experimental results in Sect. 5 and comparison with related work in Sect. 6. We give our conclusions in Sect. 7.

2 Preliminaries

In this section, we define the type of programs considered in this work and then review the basics of side-channel attacks and masking countermeasures.

2.1 Probabilistic Boolean Programs

Following the notation used in [15,26,27], we assume that the program P implements a cryptographic function, e.g., $c \leftarrow P(p, k)$ where p is the plaintext, k is the secret key and c is the ciphertext. Inside P, random variable r may be used to mask the secret key while maintaining the input-output behavior of P. Therefore, P may be viewed as a probabilistic program. Since loops, function calls, and branches may be removed via automated rewriting [26,27] and integer variables may be converted to bits, for verification purposes, we assume that P is a straight-line probabilistic Boolean program, where each instruction has a unique label and at most two operands.

Let k (resp. r) be the set of secret (resp. random) bits, p the public bits, and c the variables storing intermediate results. Thus, the set of variables is $V = k \cup r \cup p \cup c$. In addition, the program uses a set op of operators including negation ($\neg$), and ($\wedge$), or ($\vee$), and exclusive-or ($\oplus$). A *computation* of P is a sequence $c_1 \leftarrow i_1(p, k, r); \cdots ; c_n \leftarrow i_n(p, k, r)$

```
1  bool compute(bool r1,bool r2,
2                bool r3,bool k)
3  {
4     bool c1,c2,c3,c4,c5,c6;
5     c1 = k ⊕ r2;
6     c2 = r1 ⊕ r2;
7     c3 = c2 ⊕ c1;
8     c4 = c3 ⊕ c2;
9     c5 = c4 ⊕ r1;
10    c6 = c5 ∧ r3;
11    return c6;
12 }
```

Fig. 2. An example for masking countermeasure.

where, for each $1 \le i \le n$, the value of i_i is expressed in terms of p, k and r. Each random bit in r is uniformly distributed in $\{0, 1\}$; the sole purpose of using them in P is to ensure that $c_1, \cdots c_n$ are statistically independent of the secret k.

Data Dependency Graph (DDG). Our internal representation of P is a graph $\mathcal{G}_P = (N, E, \lambda)$, where N is the set of nodes, E is the set of edges, and λ is a labeling function.

- $N = L \uplus L_V$, where L is the set of instructions in P and L_V is the set of terminal nodes: $l_v \in L_V$ corresponds to a variable or constant $v \in k \cup r \cup p \cup \{0, 1\}$.
- $E \subseteq N \times N$ contains edge (l, l') if and only if $l : c = x \circ y$, where either x or y is defined by l'; or $l : c = \neg x$, where x is defined by l'.
- λ maps each $l \in N$ to a pair (val, op): $\lambda(l) = (c, \circ)$ for $l : c = x \circ y$; $\lambda(l) = (c, \neg)$ for $l : c = \neg x$; and $\lambda(l) = (v, \perp)$ for each terminal node l_v.

We may use $\lambda_1(l) = c$ and $\lambda_2(l) = \circ$ to denote the first and second elements of the pair $\lambda(l) = (c, \circ)$, respectively. We may also use $l.\text{lft}$ to denote the left child of l, and $l.\text{rgt}$ to denote the right child if it exists. A subtree rooted at node l corresponds to an intermediate computation result. When the context is clear, we may use the following terms exchangeably: a node l, the subtree T rooted at l, and the intermediate computation result $c = \lambda_1(l)$. Let $|P|$ denote the total number of nodes in the DDG.

Figure 2 shows an example where $k = \{k\}$, $r = \{r_1, r_2, r_3\}$, $c = \{c_1, c_2, c_3, c_4, c_5, c_6\}$ and $p = \emptyset$. On the left is a program written in a C-like language except that $\oplus$ denotes XOR and $\wedge$ denotes AND. On the right is the DDG, where

$$c_3 = c_2 \oplus c_1 = (r_1 \oplus r_2) \oplus (k \oplus r_2) = k \oplus r_1$$
$$c_4 = c_3 \oplus c_2 = ((r_1 \oplus r_2) \oplus (k \oplus r_2)) \oplus (r_1 \oplus r_2) = k \oplus r_2$$
$$c_5 = c_4 \oplus r_1 = (((r_1 \oplus r_2) \oplus (k \oplus r_2)) \oplus (r_1 \oplus r_2)) \oplus r_1 = k \oplus r_1 \oplus r_2$$
$$c_6 = c_5 \wedge r_3 = ((((r_1 \oplus r_2) \oplus (k \oplus r_2)) \oplus (r_1 \oplus r_2)) \oplus r_1) \wedge r_3 = (k \oplus r_1 \oplus r_2) \wedge r_3$$

Let $\mathsf{supp} : N \to k \cup r \cup p$ be a function mapping each node l to its support variables. That is, $\mathsf{supp}(l) = \emptyset$ if $\lambda_1(l) \in \{0, 1\}$; $\mathsf{supp}(l) = \{x\}$ if $\lambda_1(l) = x \in k \cup r \cup p$; and $\mathsf{supp}(l) = \mathsf{supp}(l.\mathtt{lft}) \cup \mathsf{supp}(l.\mathtt{rgt})$ otherwise. Thus, the function returns a set of variables that $\lambda_1(l)$ depends upon structurally.

Given a node l whose corresponding expression e is defined in terms of variables in V, we say that e is semantically dependent on a variable $r \in V$ if and only if there exist two assignments, π_1 and π_2, such that $\pi_1(r) \neq \pi_2(r)$ and $\pi_1(x) = \pi_2(x)$ for every $x \in V \setminus \{r\}$, and the values of e differ under π_1 and π_2.

Let $\mathsf{semd} : N \to r$ be a function such that $semd(l)$ denotes the set of *random variables* upon which the expression e of l semantically depends. Thus, $\mathsf{semd}(l) \subseteq \mathsf{supp}(l)$; and for each $r \in \mathsf{supp}(l) \setminus \mathsf{semd}(l)$, we know $\lambda_1(l)$ is semantically independent of r. More importantly, there is often a gap between $\mathsf{supp}(l) \cap r$ and $\mathsf{semd}(l)$, namely $\mathsf{semd}(l) \subseteq \mathsf{supp}(l) \cap r$, which is why our gradual refinement of semantic type inference rules can outperform methods based solely on syntactic type inference.

Consider the node l_{c_4} in Fig. 2: we have $\mathsf{supp}(l_{c_4}) = \{r_1, r_2, k\}$, $\mathsf{semd}(l_{c_4}) = \{r_2\}$, and $\mathsf{supp}(l_{c_4}) \cap r = \{r_1, r_2\}$. Furthermore, if the random bits are uniformly distributed in $\{0, 1\}$, then c_4 is both *uniformly distributed* and *secret independent* (Sect. 2.2).

2.2 Side-Channel Attacks and Masking

We assume the adversary has access to the public input p and output c, but not the secret k and random variable r, of the program $c \leftarrow P(p, k)$. However, the adversary may have access to side-channel leaks that reveal the joint distribution of at most d intermediate computation results $c_1, \cdots c_d$ (e.g., via differential power analysis [39]). Under these assumptions, the goal of the adversary is to deduce information of k. To model the leakage of each instruction, we consider a widely-used, value-based model, called the Hamming Weight (HW) model; other power leakage models such as the transition-based model [5] can be used similarly [6].

Let $[n]$ denote the set $\{1, \cdots, n\}$ of natural numbers where $n \geq 1$. We call a set with d elements a *d-set*. Given values (p, k) for (p, k) and a *d-set* $\{c_1, \cdots, c_d\}$ of intermediate computation results, we use $D_{p,k}(c_1, \cdots c_d)$ to denote their joint distribution induced by instantiating p and k with p and k, respectively. Formally, for each vector of values $v_1, \cdots, v_d$ in the probability space $\{0, 1\}^d$, we have $D_{p,k}(c_1, \cdots c_d)(v_1, \cdots, v_d) =$

$$\frac{|\{r \in \{0, 1\}^{|r|} \mid v_1 = i_1(p = p, k = k, r = r), \cdots, v_d = i_d(p = p, k = k, r = r)\}|}{2^{|r|}}.$$

Definition 1. *We say a d-set $\{c_1, \cdots, c_d\}$ of intermediate computation results is*

- *uniformly distributed if $D_{p,k}(c_1, \cdots, c_d)$ is a uniform distribution for any p and k.*
- *secret independent if $D_{p,k}(c_1, \cdots, c_d) = D_{p,k'}(c_1, \cdots, c_d)$ for any (p, k) and (p, k').*

Note that there is a difference between them: an uniformly distributed d-set is always secret independent, but a secret independent d-set is not always uniformly distributed.

Definition 2. *A program P is order-d perfectly masked if every k-set $\{c_1, \cdots, c_k\}$ of P such that $k \leq d$ is secret independent. When P is (order-1) perfectly masked, we may simply say it is perfectly masked.*

To decide if P is order-d perfectly masked, it suffices to check if there exist a d-set and two pairs (p, k) and (p, k') such that $D_{p,k}(c_1, \cdots, c_d) \neq D_{p,k'}(c_1, \cdots, c_d)$. In this context, the main challenge is computing $D_{p,k}(c_1, \cdots, c_d)$ which is essentially a *model-counting* (SAT#) problem. In the remainder of this paper, we focus on developing an efficient method for verifying (order-1) perfect masking, although our method can be extended to higher-order masking as well.

Gap in Current State of Knowledge. Existing methods for verifying masking countermeasures are either *fast but inaccurate*, e.g., when they rely solely on syntactic type inference (structural information provided by supp in Sect. 2.1) or *accurate but slow*, e.g., when they rely solely on model-counting. In contrast, our method gradually refines a set of semantic type-inference rules (i.e., using semd instead of supp as defined in Sect. 2.1) where constraint solvers (SAT and SAT#) are used on demand to resolve ambiguity and improve the accuracy of type inference. As a result, it can achieve the best of both worlds.

3   The Semantic Type Inference System

We first introduce our distribution types, which are inspired by prior work in [6, 13, 47], together with some auxiliary data structures; then, we present our inference rules.

3.1   The Type System

Let $T = \{\text{CST}, \text{RUD}, \text{SID}, \text{NPM}, \text{UKD}\}$ be the set of distribution types for intermediate computation results, where $[\![c]\!]$ denotes the type of $c \leftarrow \mathbf{i}(p, k, r)$. Specifically,

- $[\![c]\!] = \text{CST}$ means c is a constant, which implies that it is side-channel leak-free;
- $[\![c]\!] = \text{RUD}$ means c is randomized to uniform distribution, and hence leak-free;
- $[\![c]\!] = \text{SID}$ means c is secret independent, i.e., perfectly masked;
- $[\![c]\!] = \text{NPM}$ means c is not perfectly masked and thus has leaks; and
- $[\![c]\!] = \text{UKD}$ means c has an unknown distribution.

Definition 3. *Let* unq : $N \rightarrow \mathbf{r}$ *and* dom : $N \rightarrow \mathbf{r}$ *be two functions such that (i) for each terminal node $l \in L_V$, if $\lambda_1(l) \in \mathbf{r}$, then* unq$(l) = $ dom$(l) = \lambda_1(l)$; *otherwise* unq$(l) = $ dom$(l) = $ supp$(l) = \emptyset$; *and (ii) for each internal node $l \in L$, we have*

- unq$(l) = ($unq$(l.\mathtt{lft}) \cup $ unq$(l.\mathtt{rgt})) \setminus ($supp$(l.\mathtt{lft}) \cap $ supp$(l.\mathtt{rgt}))$;
- dom$(l) = ($dom$(l.\mathtt{lft}) \cup $ dom$(l.\mathtt{rgt})) \cap $ unq(l) *if $\lambda_2(l) = \oplus$; but* dom$(l) = \emptyset$ *otherwise.*

$$\text{Leaf}_1 \frac{\lambda_1(l) \in r}{[\![l]\!] = \text{RUD}} \qquad \text{Leaf}_2 \frac{\lambda_1(l) \in p \cup k}{[\![l]\!] = \text{UKD}} \qquad \text{Leaf}_3 \frac{\lambda_1(l) \in \{0, 1\}}{[\![l]\!] = \text{CST}}$$

$$\text{Xor-Rud}_1 \frac{\lambda_2(l) = \oplus \quad [\![l.\text{lft}]\!] = \text{RUD} \quad \text{dom}(l.\text{lft}) \setminus \text{semd}(l.\text{rgt}) \neq \emptyset}{[\![l]\!] = \text{RUD}} \qquad \text{Xor-Rud}_2 \frac{\lambda_2(l) = \oplus \quad [\![l.\text{rgt}]\!] = \text{RUD} \quad \text{dom}(l.\text{rgt}) \setminus \text{semd}(l.\text{lft}) \neq \emptyset}{[\![l]\!] = \text{RUD}}$$

$$\text{AO-Rud}_1 \frac{\lambda_2(l) \in \{\wedge, \vee\} \quad [\![l.\text{lft}]\!] = \text{RUD} \quad [\![l.\text{rgt}]\!] \notin \{\text{UKD}, \text{NPM}\} \quad \text{semd}(l.\text{lft}) \cap \text{semd}(l.\text{rgt}) = \emptyset}{[\![l]\!] = \text{SID}} \qquad \text{AO-Rud}_2 \frac{\lambda_2(l) \in \{\wedge, \vee\} \quad [\![l.\text{rgt}]\!] = \text{RUD} \quad [\![l.\text{lft}]\!] \notin \{\text{UKD}, \text{NPM}\} \quad \text{semd}(l.\text{rgt}) \cap \text{semd}(l.\text{lft}) = \emptyset}{[\![l]\!] = \text{SID}}$$

$$\text{AO-Rud}_3 \frac{\lambda_2(l) \in \{\wedge, \vee\} \quad [\![l.\text{lft}]\!] = [\![l.\text{rgt}]\!] = \text{RUD} \quad (\text{dom}(l.\text{lft}) \setminus \text{semd}(l.\text{rgt})) \cup (\text{dom}(l.\text{rgt}) \setminus \text{semd}(l.\text{lft})) \neq \emptyset}{[\![l]\!] = \text{SID}}$$

$$\text{Sid} \frac{\lambda_2(l) \in \{\oplus, \wedge, \vee\} \quad [\![l.\text{rgt}]\!] = [\![l.\text{lft}]\!] = \text{SID} \quad \text{semd}(l.\text{lft}) \cap \text{semd}(l.\text{rgt}) = \emptyset}{[\![l]\!] = \text{SID}}$$

$$\text{Not} \frac{\lambda_2(l) = \neg}{[\![l]\!] = [\![l.\text{lft}]\!]} \qquad \text{No-Key} \frac{\text{supp}(l) \cap k = \emptyset}{[\![l]\!] = \text{SID}} \qquad \text{Ukd} \frac{\text{no-rule is applicable at } l}{[\![l]\!] = \text{UKD}}$$

Fig. 3. Our semantic type-inference rules. The NPM type is not yet used here; its inference rules will be added in Fig. 4 since they rely on the SMT solver based analyses.

Both $\text{unq}(l)$ and $\text{dom}(l)$ are computable in time that is linear in $|P|$ [47]. Following the proofs in [6,47], it is easy to reach this observation: Given an intermediate computation result $c \leftarrow \mathbf{i}(p, k, r)$ labeled by l, the following statements hold:

1. if $|\text{dom}(l)| \neq \emptyset$, then $[\![c]\!] = \text{RUD}$;
2. if $[\![c]\!] = \text{RUD}$, then $[\![\neg c]\!] = \text{RUD}$; if $[\![c]\!] = \text{SID}$, then $[\![\neg c]\!] = \text{SID}$;
3. if $r \notin \text{semd}(l)$ for a random bit $r \in r$, then $[\![r \oplus c]\!] = \text{RUD}$;
4. for every $c' \leftarrow \mathbf{i}'(p, k, r)$ labeled by l', if $\text{semd}(l) \cap \text{semd}(l') = \emptyset$ and $[\![c]\!] = [\![c']\!] = \text{SID}$, then $[\![c \circ c']\!] = \text{SID}$.

Figure 3 shows our type inference rules that concretize these observations. When multiple rules could be applied to a node $l \in N$, we always choose the rules that can lead to $[\![l]\!] = \text{RUD}$. If no rule is applicable at l, we set $[\![l]\!] = \text{UKD}$. When the context is clear, we may use $[\![l]\!]$ and $[\![c]\!]$ exchangeably for $\lambda_1(l) = c$. The correctness of these inference rules is obvious by definition.

Theorem 1. *For every intermediate computation result $c \leftarrow \mathbf{i}(p, k, r)$ labeled by l,*

- *if $[\![c]\!] = \text{RUD}$, then c is uniformly distributed, and hence perfectly masked;*
- *if $[\![c]\!] = \text{SID}$, then c is guaranteed to be perfectly masked.*

To improve efficiency, our inference rules may be applied twice, first using the supp function, which extracts structural information from the program (cf. Sect. 2.1) and then using the semd function, which is slower to compute but also significantly more accurate. Since $\text{semd}(l) \subseteq \text{supp}(l)$ for all $l \in N$, this is always sound. Moreover, type inference is invoked for the second time only if, after the first time, $[\![l]\!]$ remains UKD.

Example 1. When using type inference with supp on the running example, we have

$$[\![r_1]\!] = [\![r_2]\!] = [\![r_3]\!] = [\![c_1]\!] = [\![c_2]\!] = [\![c_3]\!] = \text{RUD}, \quad [\![k]\!] = [\![c_4]\!] = [\![c_5]\!] = [\![c_6]\!] = \text{UKD}$$

When using type inference with semd (for the second time), we have

$$[\![r_1]\!] = [\![r_2]\!] = [\![r_3]\!] = [\![c_1]\!] = [\![c_2]\!] = [\![c_3]\!] = [\![c_4]\!] = [\![c_5]\!] = \text{RUD}, \quad [\![k]\!] = \text{UKD}, \quad [\![c_6]\!] = \text{SID}$$

3.2 Checking Semantic Independence

Unlike $\text{supp}(l)$, which only extracts structural information from the program and hence may be computed syntactically, $\text{semd}(l)$ is more expensive to compute. In this subsection, we present a method that leverages the SMT solver to check, for any intermediate computation result $c \leftarrow \mathbf{i}(p, k, r)$ and any random bit $r \in r$, whether c is semantically dependent of r. Specifically, we formulate it as a satisfiability (SAT) problem (formula Φ_s) defined as follows:

$$\Theta_s^{r=0}(c_0, p, k, r \setminus \{r\}) \wedge \Theta_s^{r=1}(c_1, p, k, r \setminus \{r\}) \wedge \Theta_s^{\neq}(c_0, c_1),$$

where $\Theta_s^{r=0}$ (resp. $\Theta_s^{r=1}$) encodes the relation $\mathbf{i}(p, k, r)$ with r replaced by 0 (resp. 1), c_0 and c_1 are copies of c and $\Theta_s^{\neq}$ asserts that the outputs differ even under the same inputs.

In logic synthesis and optimization, when $r \notin \text{semd}(l)$, r will be called the *don't care* variable [36]. Therefore, it is easy to see why the following theorem holds.

Theorem 2. *Φ_s is unsatisfiable iff the value of r does not affect the value of c, i.e., c is semantically independent of r. Moreover, the formula size of Φ_s is linear in $|P|$.*

$$\text{CP-RUD} \frac{[\![c_1, \cdots, c_k]\!] = \text{RUD} \quad [\![c_{k+1}]\!] = \text{RUD} \quad \text{semd}(c_1, \cdots, c_k) \cap \text{semd}(c_{k+1}) = \emptyset}{[\![c_1, \cdots, c_{k+1}]\!] = \text{RUD}}$$

$$\text{CP-SID}_1 \frac{[\![c_1, \cdots, c_k]\!], [\![c_{k+1}]\!] \in \{\text{SID}, \text{RUD}\} \quad [\![c_{k+1}]\!] \neq [\![c_1, \cdots, c_k]\!] \quad \text{semd}(c_1, \cdots, c_k) \cap \text{semd}(c_{k+1}) = \emptyset}{[\![c_1, \cdots, c_{k+1}]\!] = \text{SID}}$$

$$\text{CP-SID}_2 \frac{[\![c_1, \cdots, c_k]\!] = \text{RUD} \quad [\![c_{k+1}]\!] = \text{RUD} \quad (\text{dom}(c_1, \cdots, c_k) \setminus \text{semd}(c_{k+1})) \cap (\text{dom}(c_{k+1}) \setminus \text{semd}(c_1, \cdots, c_k)) \neq \emptyset}{[\![c_1, \cdots, c_{k+1}]\!] = \text{SID}}$$

$$\text{CP-UKD} \frac{\text{no-rule is appliable at } \{c_1, \cdots, c_{k+1}\}}{[\![c_1, \cdots, c_{k+1}]\!] = \text{UKD}}$$

Fig. 4. Our composition rules for handling *sets* of intermediate computation results.

3.3 Verifying Higher-Order Masking

The type system so far targets *first-order* masking. We now outline how it extends to verify higher-order masking. Generally speaking, we have to check, for any k-set $\{c_1, \cdots, c_k\}$ of intermediate computation results such that $k \leq d$, the joint distribution is either randomized to uniform distribution (RUD) or secret independent (SID).

To tackle this problem, we lift supp, semd, unq, and dom to *sets* of computation results as follows: for each k-set $\{c_1, \cdots, c_k\}$,

- $\text{supp}(c_1, \cdots, c_k) = \bigcup_{i \in [k]} \text{supp}(c_i)$;
- $\text{semd}(c_1, \cdots, c_k) = \bigcup_{i \in [k]} \text{semd}(c_i)$;
- $\text{unq}(c_1, \cdots, c_k) = (\bigcup_{i \in [k]} \text{unq}(c_i)) \setminus \bigcup_{i, j \in [k]} (\text{supp}(c_i) \cap \text{supp}(c_j))$; and
- $\text{dom}(c_1, \cdots, c_k) = (\bigcup_{i \in [k]} \text{dom}(c_i)) \cap \text{unq}(c_1, \cdots, c_k)$.

Our inference rules are extended by adding the composition rules shown in Fig. 4.

Theorem 3. *For every k-set* $\{c_1, \cdots, c_k\}$ *of intermediate computations results,*

- *if* $[\![c_1, \cdots, c_k]\!] = RUD$, *then* $\{c_1, \cdots, c_k\}$ *is guaranteed to be uniformly distributed, and hence perfectly masked;*
- *if* $[\![c_1, \cdots, c_k]\!] = SID$, *then* $\{c_1, \cdots, c_k\}$ *is guaranteed to be perfectly masked.*

We remark that the semd function in these composition rules could also be safely replaced by the supp function, just as before. Furthermore, to more efficiently verify that program P is perfect masked against order-d attacks, we can incrementally apply the type inference for each k-set, where $k = 1, 2, \ldots, d$.

4 The Gradual Refinement Approach

In this section, we present our method for gradually refining the type inference system by leveraging SMT solver based techniques. Adding solvers to the sound type system makes it complete as well, thus allowing it to detect side-channel leaks whenever they exist, in addition to proving the absence of such leaks.

4.1 SMT-Based Approach

For a given computation $c \leftarrow i(p, k, r)$, the verification of perfect masking (Definition 2) can be reduced to the *satisfiability* of the logical formula (Ψ) defined as follows:

$$\exists p. \exists k. \exists k'. \left(\sum_{v_r \in \{0,1\}^{|r|}} i(p, k, v_r) \neq \sum_{v_r \in \{0,1\}^{|r|}} i(p, k', v_r) \right).$$

Intuitively, given values (v_p, v_k) of (p, k), $count = \sum_{v_r \in \{0,1\}^{|r|}} i(v_p, v_k, v_r)$ denotes the number of assignments of the random variable r under which $i(v_p, v_k, r)$ is evaluated to logical 1. When random bits in r are uniformly distributed in the domain $\{0, 1\}$, $\frac{count}{2^{|r|}}$ is the probability of $i(v_p, v_k, r)$ being logical 1 for the given pair (v_p, v_k). Therefore, Ψ is unsatisfiable if and only if c is perfectly masked.

Following Eldib et al. [26,27], we encode the formula Ψ as a quantifier-free first-order logic formula to be solved by an off-the-shelf SMT solver (e.g., Z3):

$$\left(\bigwedge_{r=0}^{2^{|r|}-1} \Theta_k^r \right) \wedge \left(\bigwedge_{r=0}^{2^{|r|}-1} \Theta_{k'}^r \right) \wedge \Theta_{b2i} \wedge \Theta_{\neq}$$

- Θ_k^v (resp. $\Theta_{k'}^v$) for each $r \in \{0, \cdots, 2^{|r|-1}\}$: encodes a copy of the input-output relation of $i(p, k, r)$ (resp. $i(p, k', r)$) by replacing r with concrete values r. There are $2^{|r|}$ distinct copies, but share the same plaintext p.
- Θ_{b2i}: converts Boolean outputs of these copies to integers (true becomes 1 and false becomes 0) so that the number of assignments can be counted.
- $\Theta_{\neq}$: asserts the two summations, for k and k', differ.

Example 2. In the running example, for instance, verifying whether node c_4 is perfectly masked requires the SMT-based analysis. For brevity, we omit the detailed logical formula while pointing out that, by invoking the SMT solver six times, one can get the following result: $[\![c_1]\!] = [\![c_2]\!] = [\![c_3]\!] = [\![c_4]\!] = [\![c_5]\!] = [\![c_6]\!] = SID$.

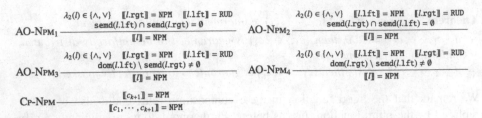

Fig. 5. Complementary rules used during refinement of the type inference (Fig. 3).

Although the SMT formula size is linear in $|P|$, the number of distinct copies is exponential of the number of random bits used in the computation. Thus, the approach cannot be applied to large programs. To overcome the problem, incremental algorithms [26,27] were proposed to reduce the formula size using partitioning and heuristic reduction.

Incremental SMT-Based Algorithm. Given a computation $c \leftarrow \mathbf{i}(p, k, r)$ that corresponds to a subtree T rooted at l in the DDG, we search for an internal node l_s in T (a *cut-point*) such that $\mathrm{dom}(l_s) \cap \mathrm{unq}(l) \neq \emptyset$. A cut-point is *maximal* if there is no other cut-point from l to l_s. Let $\widehat{T}$ be the *simplified tree* obtained from T by replacing every subtree rooted by a maximal cut-point with a random variable from $\mathrm{dom}(l_s) \cap \mathrm{unq}(l)$. Then, $\widehat{T}$ is SID iff T is SID.

The main observation is that: if l_s is a cut-point, there is a random variable $r \in \mathrm{dom}(l_s) \cap \mathrm{unq}(l)$, which implies $\lambda_1(l_s)$ is RUD. Here, $r \in \mathrm{unq}(l)$ implies $\lambda_1(l_s)$ can be seen as a *fresh* random variable when we evaluate l. Consider the node c_3 in our running example: it is easy to see $r_1 \in \mathrm{dom}(c_2) \cap \mathrm{unq}(c_3)$. Therefore, for the purpose of verifying c_3, the entire subtree rooted at c_2 can be replaced by the random variable r_1.

In addition to partitioning, heuristics rules [26,27] can be used to simplify SMT solving. (1) When constructing formula Φ of c, all random variables in $\mathrm{supp}(l) \backslash \mathrm{semd}(l)$, which are *don't cares*, can be replaced by constant 1 or 0. (2) The No-Key and Sid rules in Fig. 3 with the supp function are used to skip some checks by SMT.

Example 3. When applying incremental SMT-based approach to our running example, c_1 has to be decided by SMT, but c_2 is skipped due to No-Key rule.

As for c_3, since $r_1 \in \mathrm{dom}(c_2) \cap \mathrm{unq}(c_3)$, c_2 is a cut-point and the subtree rooted at c_2 can be replaced by r_1, leading to the simplified computation $r_1 \oplus (r_2 \oplus k)$ – subsequently it is skipped by the Sid rule with supp. Note that the above Sid rule is not applicable to the original subtree, because r_2 occurs in the support of both children of c_3.

There is no cut-point for c_4, so it is checked using the SMT solver. But since c_4 is semantically independent of r_1 (a *don't care* variable), to reduce the SMT formula size, we replace r_1 by 1 (or 0) when constructing the formula Φ.

4.2 Feeding SMT-Based Analysis Results Back to Type System

Consider a scenario where initially the type system (cf. Sect. 3) failed to resolve a node l, i.e., $[\![l]\!]$ = UKD, but the SMT-based approach resolved it as either NPM or SID. Such results should be *fed back* to improve the type system, which may lead to the following two favorable outcomes: (1) marking more nodes as perfectly masked (RUD or SID) and (2) marking more nodes as leaky (NPM), which means we can avoid expensive SMT calls for these nodes. More specifically, if SMT-based analysis shows that l is perfectly masked, the type of l can be refined to $[\![l]\!]$ = SID; feeding it back to the type system allows us to infer more types for nodes that structurally depend on l.

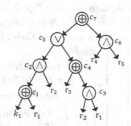

Fig. 6. Example for feeding back.

On the other hand, if SMT-based analysis shows l is not perfectly masked, the type of l can be refined to $[\![l]\!]$ = NPM; feeding it back allows the type system to infer that other nodes may be NPM as well. To achieve what is outlined in the second case above, we add the NPM-related type inference rules shown in Fig. 5. When they are added to the type system outlined in Fig. 3, more NPM type nodes will be deduced, which allows our method to skip the (more expensive) checking of NPM using SMT.

Example 4. Consider the example DDG in Fig. 6. By applying the original type inference approach with either supp or semd, we have

$$[\![c_1]\!] = [\![c_4]\!] = \text{RUD}, \quad [\![c_2]\!] = [\![c_3]\!] = [\![c_6]\!] = \text{SID}, \quad [\![c_5]\!] = [\![c_7]\!] = \text{UKD}.$$

In contrast, by applying SMT-based analysis to c_5, we can deduce $[\![c_5]\!]$ = SID. Feeding $[\![c_5]\!]$ = SID back to the original type system, and then applying the SID rule to c_7 = $c_5 \oplus c_6$, we are able to deduce $[\![c_7]\!]$ = SID. Without refinement, this was not possible.

4.3 The Overall Algorithm

Having presented all the components, we now present the overall procedure, which integrates the semantic type system and SMT-based method for gradual refinement. Algorithm 1 shows the pseudo code. Given the program P, the sets of public (p), secret (k), random (r) variables and an empty map π, it invokes SCInfer(P, p, k, r, π) to traverse the DDG in a topological order and annotate every node l with a distribution type from T. The subroutine TypeInfer implements the type inference rules outlined in Figs. 3 and 5, where the parameter f can be either supp or semd.

SCInfer first deduces the type of each node $l \in N$ by invoking TypeInfer with f = supp. Once a node l is annotated as UKD, a simplified subtree $\widehat{P}$ of the subtree rooted at l is constructed. Next, TypeInfer with f = semd is invoked to resolve the UKD node in $\widehat{P}$. If $\pi(l)$ becomes non-UKD afterward, TypeInfer with f = supp is invoked again to quickly deduce the types of the fan-out nodes in P. But if $\pi(l)$ remains UKD, SCInfer invokes the incremental SMT-based approach to decide whether l is either SID or NPM. This is sound and complete, unless the SMT solver runs out of time/memory, in which case UKD is assigned to l.

Algorithm 1. Function SCINFER(P, p, k, r, π)

```
1  Function SCINFER(P, p, k, r, π)
2      foreach l ∈ N in a topological order do
3          if l is a leaf then π(l) := ⟦l⟧;
4          else
5              TYPEINFER(l, P, p, k, r, π, supp);
6              if π(l) = UKD then
7                  let P̂ be the simplified tree of the subtree rooted by l in P;
8                  TYPEINFER(l, P̂, p, k, r, π, semd);
9                  if π(l) = UKD then
10                     res:=CheckBySMT(P̂, p, k, r);
11                     if res=Not-Perfectly-Masked then π(l) := NPM;
12                     else if res=Perfectly-Masked then π(l) := SID;
13                     else π(l) := UKD;
```

Theorem 4. *For every intermediate computation result $c \leftarrow i(p, k, r)$ labeled by l, our method in* SCINFER *guarantees to return sound and complete results:*

- *$\pi(l) = RUD$ iff c is uniformly distributed, and hence perfectly masked;*
- *$\pi(l) = SID$ iff c is secret independent, i.e., perfectly masked;*
- *$\pi(l) = NPM$ iff c is not perfectly masked (leaky);*

If timeout or memory out is used to bound the execution of the SMT solver, it is also possible that $\pi(l) = UKD$, meaning c has an unknown distribution (it may or may not be perfectly masked). It is interesting to note that, if we regard UKD as *potential leak* and at the same time. bound (or even disable) SMT-based analysis, Algorithm 1 degenerates to a *sound* type system that is both fast and potentially accurate.

5   Experiments

We have implemented our method in a verification tool named SCINFER, which uses Z3 [23] as the underlying SMT solver. We also implemented the syntactic type inference approach [47] and the incremental SMT-based approach [26,27] in the same tool for experimental comparison purposes. We conducted experiments on publicly available cryptographic software implementations, including fragments of AES and MAC-Keccak [26,27]. Our experiments were conducted on a machine with 64-bit Ubuntu 12.04 LTS, Intel Xeon(R) CPU E5-2603 v4, and 32 GB RAM.

Overall, results of our experiments show that (1) SCINFER is significantly more accurate than prior syntactic type inference method [47]; indeed, it solved tens of thousand of UKD cases reported by the prior technique; (2) SCINFER is at least twice faster than prior SMT-based verification method [26,27] on the large programs while maintaining the same accuracy; for example, SCINFER verified the benchmark named P12 in a few seconds whereas the prior SMT-based method took more than an hour.

Algorithm 2. Procedure TypeInfer(l, P, p, k, r, π, f)

1	**Procedure** TypeInfer(l, P, p, k, r, π, f)
2	$\quad$ **if** $\lambda_2(l) = \neg$ **then** $\pi(l) := \pi(l.\mathtt{lft})$;
3	$\quad$ **else if** $\lambda_2(l) = \oplus$ **then**
4	$\quad\quad$ **if** $\pi(l.\mathtt{lft}) = RUD \wedge dom(l.\mathtt{lft}) \setminus f(l.\mathtt{rgt}) \neq \emptyset$ **then** $\pi(l) := RUD$;
5	$\quad\quad$ **else if** $\pi(l.\mathtt{rgt}) = RUD \wedge dom(l.\mathtt{rgt}) \setminus f(l.\mathtt{lft}) \neq \emptyset$ **then** $\pi(l) := RUD$;
6	$\quad\quad$ **else if** $\pi(l.\mathtt{rgt}) = \pi(l.\mathtt{lft}) = SID \wedge f(l.\mathtt{lft}) \cap f(l.\mathtt{rgt}) \cap r = \emptyset$ **then**
7	$\quad\quad\quad$ $\pi(l) := SID$
8	$\quad\quad$ **else if** $supp(l) \cap k = \emptyset$ **then** $\pi(l) := SID$;
9	$\quad\quad$ **else** $\pi(l) := UKD$;
10	$\quad$ **else**
11	$\quad\quad$ **if** $\left(\begin{array}{l} ((\pi(l.\mathtt{lft}) = RUD \wedge \pi(l.\mathtt{rgt}) \notin \{UKD, NPM\}) \vee \\ (\pi(l.\mathtt{rgt}) = RUD \wedge \pi(l.\mathtt{lft}) \notin \{UKD, NPM\})) \\ \wedge f(l.\mathtt{lft}) \cap f(l.\mathtt{rgt}) \cap r = \emptyset \end{array} \right)$ **then** $\pi(l) := SID$;
12	$\quad\quad$ **else if** $\left(\begin{array}{l} (dom(l.\mathtt{rgt}) \setminus f(l.\mathtt{lft})) \cup (dom(l.\mathtt{lft}) \setminus f(l.\mathtt{rgt})) \neq \emptyset \\ \wedge \pi(l.\mathtt{lft}) = RUD \wedge \pi(l.\mathtt{rgt}) = RUD \end{array} \right)$ **then**
13	$\quad\quad\quad$ $\pi(l) := SID$
14	$\quad\quad$ **else if** $\left(\begin{array}{l} ((\pi(l.\mathtt{lft}) = RUD \wedge \pi(l.\mathtt{rgt}) = NPM) \vee \\ (\pi(l.\mathtt{rgt}) = RUD \wedge \pi(l.\mathtt{lft}) = NPM)) \\ \wedge f(l.\mathtt{lft}) \cap f(l.\mathtt{rgt}) \cap r = \emptyset \end{array} \right)$ **then** $\pi(l) := NPM$;
15	$\quad\quad$ **else if** $\left(\begin{array}{l} (\pi(l.\mathtt{lft}) = RUD \wedge \pi(l.\mathtt{rgt}) = NPM \wedge dom(l.\mathtt{lft}) \setminus f(l.\mathtt{rgt}) \neq \emptyset) \vee \\ (\pi(l.\mathtt{rgt}) = RUD \wedge \pi(l.\mathtt{lft}) = NPM \wedge dom(l.\mathtt{rgt}) \setminus f(l.\mathtt{lft}) \neq \emptyset) \end{array} \right)$ **then**
16	$\quad\quad\quad$ $\pi(l) := NPM$
17	$\quad\quad$ **else if** $(\pi(l.\mathtt{lft}) = \pi(l.\mathtt{rgt}) = SID) \wedge f(l.\mathtt{lft}) \cap f(l.\mathtt{rgt}) \cap r = \emptyset$ **then**
18	$\quad\quad\quad$ $\pi(l) := SID$
19	$\quad\quad$ **else if** $supp(l) \cap k = \emptyset$ **then** $\pi(l) := SID$;
20	$\quad\quad$ **else** $\pi(l) := UKD$;

5.1 Benchmarks

Table 1 shows the detailed statistics of the benchmarks, including seventeen examples (P1–P17), all of which have nonlinear operations. Columns 1 and 2 show the name of the program and a short description. Column 3 shows the number of instructions in the probabilistic Boolean program. Column 4 shows the number of DDG nodes denoting intermediate computation results. The remaining columns show the number of bits in the secret, public, and random variables, respectively. Remark that the number of random variables in each computation is far less than the one of the program. All these programs are transformed into Boolean programs where each instruction has at most two operands. Since the statistics were collected from the transformed code, they may have minor differences from statistics reported in prior work [26,27].

In particular, P1–P5 are masking examples originated from [10], P6–P7 are originated from [15], P8–P9 are the MAC-Keccak computation reordered examples originated from [11], P10–P11 are two experimental masking schemes for the Chi function in MAC-Keccak. Among the larger programs, P12–P17 are the regenerations of

Table 1. Benchmark statistics.

Name	Description	♯Loc	♯Nodes	|k|	|p|	|r|
P1	CHES13 Masked Key Whitening	79	32	16	16	16
P2	CHES13 De-mask and then Mask	67	38	8	0	16
P3	CHES13 AES Shift Rows	21	6	2	0	2
P4	CHES13 Messerges Boolean to Arithmetic (bit0)	23	6	2	0	2
P5	CHES13 Goubin Boolean to Arithmetic (bit0)	27	8	1	0	2
P6	Logic Design for AES S-Box (1st implementation)	32	9	2	0	2
P7	Logic Design for AES S-Box (2nd implementation)	40	11	2	0	3
P8	Masked Chi function MAC-Keccak (1st implementation)	59	18	3	0	4
P9	Masked Chi function MAC-Keccak (2nd implementation)	60	18	3	0	4
P10	Syn. Masked Chi func MAC-Keccak (1st implementation)	66	28	3	0	4
P11	Syn. Masked Chi func MAC-Keccak (2nd implementation)	66	28	3	0	4
P12	MAC-Keccak 512b Perfect masked	426k	197k	288	288	3205
P13	MAC-Keccak 512b De-mask and then mask (compiler error)	426k	197k	288	288	3205
P14	MAC-Keccak 512b Not-perfect Masking of Chi function (v1)	426k	197k	288	288	3205
P15	MAC-Keccak 512b Not-perfect Masking of Chi function (v2)	429k	198k	288	288	3205
P16	MAC-Keccak 512b Not-perfect Masking of Chi function (v3)	426k	197k	288	288	3205
P17	MAC-Keccak 512b Unmasking of Pi function	442k	205k	288	288	3205

MAC-Keccak reference code submitted to the SHA-3 competition held by NIST, where P13–P16 implement the masking of Chi functions using different masking schemes and P17 implements the de-masking of Pi function.

5.2   Experimental Results

We compared the performance of SCInfer, the purely syntactic type inference method (denoted Syn. Infer) and the incremental SMT-based method (denoted by SMT App). Table 2 shows the results. Column 1 shows the name of each benchmark. Column 2 shows whether it is perfectly masked (ground truth). Columns 3–4 show the results of the purely syntactic type inference method, including the number of nodes inferred as UKD type and the time in seconds. Columns 5–7 (resp. Columns 8–10) show the results of the incremental SMT-based method (resp. our method SCInfer), including the number of leaky nodes (NPM type), the number of nodes actually checked by SMT, and the time.

Compared with syntactic type inference method, our approach is significantly more accurate (e.g., see P4, P5 and P15). Furthermore, the time taken by both methods are comparable on small programs. On the large programs that are not perfectly masked (i.e., P13–P17), our method is slower since SCInfer has to resolve the UKD nodes reported by syntactic inference by SMT. However, it is interesting to note that, on the perfectly masked large program (P12), our method is faster.

Moreover, the UKD type nodes in P4, reported by the purely syntactic type inference method, are all proved to be perfectly masked by our semantic type inference system,

Table 2. Experimental results: comparison of three approaches.

Name	Masked	Syn. Infer [47]		SMT App [26,27]			SCInfer		
		UKD	Time	NPM	By SMT	Time	NPM	By SMT	Time
P1	No	16	≈0 s	16	16	0.39 s	16	16	0.39 s
P2	No	8	≈0 s	8	8	0.28 s	8	8	0.57 s
P3	Yes	0	≈0 s	0	0	≈0 s	0	0	≈0 s
P4	Yes	3	≈0 s	0	3	0.16 s	0	0	0.06 s
P5	Yes	3	≈0 s	0	3	0.15 s	0	2	0.25 s
P6	No	2	≈0 s	2	2	0.11 s	2	2	0.16 s
P7	No	2	0.01 s	1	2	0.11 s	1	1	0.26 s
P8	No	3	≈0 s	3	3	0.15 s	3	3	0.29 s
P9	No	2	≈0 s	2	2	0.11 s	2	2	0.23 s
P10	No	3	≈0 s	1	2	0.15 s	1	2	0.34 s
P11	No	4	≈0 s	1	3	0.2 s	1	3	0.5 s
P12	Yes	0	**1 min 5 s**	0	0	92 min 8 s	0	0	**3.8 s**
P13	No	4800	1 min 11 s	4800	4800	95 min 30 s	4800	4800	47 min 8 s
P14	No	3200	1 min 11 s	3200	3200	118 min 1 s	3200	3200	53 min 40 s
P15	No	**3200**	1 min 21 s	1600	3200	127 min 45 s	**1600**	**3200**	69 min 6 s
P16	No	4800	1 min 13 s	4800	4800	123 min 54 s	4800	4800	61 min 15 s
P17	No	17600	1 min 14 s	17600	16000	336 min 51 s	**17600**	**12800**	121 min 28 s

without calling the SMT solver at all. As for the three UKD type nodes in P5, our method proves them all by invoking the SMT solver only twice; it means that the feedback of the new SID types (discovered by SMT) allows our type system to improve its accuracy, which turns the third UKD node to SID.

Finally, compared with the original SMT-based approach, our method is at least twice faster on the large programs (e.g., P12–P17). Furthermore, the number of nodes actually checked by invoking the SMT solver is also lower than in the original SMT-based approach (e.g., P4–P5, and P17). In particular, there are 3200 UKD type nodes in P17, which are refined into NPM type by our new inference rules (cf. Fig. 5), and thus avoid the more expensive SMT calls.

To sum up, results of our experiments show that: SCInfer is fast in obtaining proofs in perfectly-masked programs, while retaining the ability to detect real leaks in not-perfectly-masked programs, and is scalable for handling realistic applications.

5.3 Detailed Statistics

Table 3 shows the more detailed statistics of our approach. Specifically, Columns 2–5 show the number of nodes in each distribution type deduced by our method. Column 6 shows the number of nodes actually checked by SMT, together with the time shown in Column 9. Column 7 shows the time spent on computing the semd function, which solves the SAT problem. Column 8 shows the time spent on computing the don't care variables. The last column shows the total time taken by SCInfer.

Table 3. Detailed statistics of our new method.

Name	SCInfer								
	Nodes					Time			
	RUD	SID	CST	NPM	SMT	semd	Don't care	SMT	Total
P1	16	0	0	16	16	≈0 s	≈0 s	0.39 s	0.39 s
P2	16	0	0	8	8	0.27 s	0.14 s	0.16 s	0.57 s
P3	6	0	0	0	0	≈0 s	≈0 s	≈0 s	≈0 s
P4	6	0	0	0	0	≈0 s	≈0 s	≈0 s	0.06 s
P5	6	2	0	0	2	0.08 s	0.05 s	0.05 s	0.25 s
P6	4	3	0	2	2	0.05 s	0.07 s	0.04 s	0.16 s
P7	5	5	0	1	1	0.14 s	0.09 s	0.03 s	0.26 s
P8	11	4	0	3	3	0.14 s	0.09 s	0.06 s	0.29 s
P9	12	4	0	2	2	0.13 s	0.07 s	0.03 s	0.23 s
P10	20	6	1	1	2	0.15 s	0.14 s	0.05 s	0.34 s
P11	19	7	1	1	3	0.23 s	0.2 s	0.07 s	0.5 s
P12	190400	6400	0	0	0	≈0 s	≈0 s	≈0 s	3.8 s
P13	185600	6400	0	4800	4800	29 min 33 s	16 min 5 s	1 min 25 s	47 min 8 s
P14	187200	6400	0	3200	3200	26 min 58 s	25 min 26 s	11 min 53 s	53 min 40 s
P15	188800	8000	0	1600	3200	33 min 30 s	33 min 55 s	1 min 35 s	69 min 6 s
P16	185600	6400	0	4800	4800	26 min 41 s	32 min 55 s	1 min 32 s	61 min 15 s
P17	185600	1600	0	17600	12800	33 min 25 s	83 min 59 s	3 min 57 s	121 min 28 s

Results in Table 3 indicate that most of the DDG nodes in these benchmark programs are either RUD or SID, and almost all of them can be quickly deduced by our type system. It explains why our new method is more efficient than the original SMT-based approach. Indeed, the original SMT-based approach spent a large amount of time on the static analysis part, which does code partitioning and applies the heuristic rules (cf. Sect. 4.1), whereas our method spent more time on computing the semd function.

Column 4 shows that, at least in these benchmark programs, Boolean constants are rare. Columns 5–6 show that, if our refined type system fails to prove perfect masking, it is usually not perfectly masked. Columns 7–9 show that, in our integrated method, most of the time is actually used to compute semd and don't care variables (SAT), while the time taken by the SMT solver to conduct model counting (SAT#) is relatively small.

6   Related Work

Many masking countermeasures [15,17,34,37,41,43,46,48,50–52] have been published over the years: although they differ in adversary models, cryptographic algorithms and compactness, a common problem is the lack of efficient tools to formally prove their correctness [21,22]. Our work aims to bridge the gap. It differs from simulation-based techniques [3,33,53] which aim to detect leaks only as opposed to prove their absence. It also differs from techniques designed for other types of side channels such as timing [2, 38], fault [12, 29] and cache [24, 35, 40], or computing security bounds for probabilistic countermeasures against remote attacks [45].

Although some verification tools have been developed for this application [6, 7, 10, 13, 14, 20, 26, 27, 47], they are either fast but inaccurate (e.g., type-inference techniques) or accurate but slow (e.g., model-counting techniques). For example, Bayrak et al. [10] developed a leak detector that checks if a computation result is *logically* dependent of the secret and, at the same time, *logically* independent of any random variable. It is fast but not accurate in that many leaky nodes could be incorrectly proved [26, 27]. In contrast, the model-counting based method proposed by Eldib et al. [26–28] is accurate, but also significantly less scalable because the size of logical formulas they need to build are exponential in the number of random variables. Moreover, for higher-order masking, their method is still not complete.

Our gradual refinement of a set of semantic type inference rules were inspired by recent work on proving probabilistic non-interference [6, 47], which exploit the unique characteristics of invertible operations. Similar ideas were explored in [7, 14, 20] as well. However, these prior techniques differ significantly from our method because their type-inference rules are syntactic and fixed, whereas ours are semantic and refined based on SMT solver based analysis (SAT and SAT#). In terms of accuracy, numerous unknowns occurred in the experimental results of [47] and two obviously perfect masking cases were not proved in [6]. Finally, although higher-order masking were addressed by prior techniques [13], they were limited to linear operations, whereas our method can handle both first-order and higher-order masking with non-linear operations.

An alternative way to address the model-counting problem [4, 18, 19, 32] is to use satisfiability modulo counting, which is a generalization of the satisfiability problem of SMT extended with counting constraints [31]. Toward this end, Fredrikson and Jha [31] have developed an efficient decision procedure for linear integer arithmetic (LIA) based on Barvinok's algorithm [8] and also applied their approach to differential privacy.

Another related line of research is automatically synthesizing countermeasures [1, 7, 9, 16, 25, 44, 54] as opposed to verifying them. While methods in [1, 7, 9, 44] rely on compiler-like pattern matching, the ones in [16, 25, 54] use inductive program synthesis based on the SMT approach. These emerging techniques, however, are orthogonal to our work reported in this paper. It would be interesting to investigate whether our approach could aid in the synthesis of masking countermeasures.

7 Conclusions and Future Work

We have presented a refinement based method for proving that a piece of cryptographic software code is free of power side-channel leaks. Our method relies on a set of semantic inference rules to reason about distribution types of intermediate computation results, coupled with an SMT solver based procedure for gradually refining these types to increase accuracy. We have implemented our method and demonstrated its efficiency and effectiveness on cryptographic benchmarks. Our results show that it outperforms state-of-the-art techniques in terms of both efficiency and accuracy.

For future work, we plan to evaluate our type inference systems for higher-order masking, extend it to handle integer programs as opposed to bit-blasting them to

Boolean programs, e.g., using satisfiability modulo counting [31], and investigate the synthesis of masking countermeasures based on our new verification method.

References

1. Agosta, G., Barenghi, A., Pelosi, G.: A code morphing methodology to automate power analysis countermeasures. In: ACM/IEEE Design Automation Conference, pp. 77–82 (2012)
2. Almeida, J.B., Barbosa, M., Barthe, G., Dupressoir, F., Emmi, M.: Verifying constant-time implementations. In: USENIX Security Symposium, pp. 53–70 (2016)
3. Arribas, V., Nikova, S., Rijmen, V.: VerMI: verification tool for masked implementations. IACR Cryptology ePrint Archive, p. 1227 (2017)
4. Aydin, A., Bang, L., Bultan, T.: Automata-based model counting for string constraints. In: Kroening, D., Păsăreanu, C.S. (eds.) CAV 2015. LNCS, vol. 9206, pp. 255–272. Springer, Cham (2015). https://doi.org/10.1007/978-3-319-21690-4_15
5. Balasch, J., Gierlichs, B., Grosso, V., Reparaz, O., Standaert, F.-X.: On the cost of lazy engineering for masked software implementations. In: Joye, M., Moradi, A. (eds.) CARDIS 2014. LNCS, vol. 8968, pp. 64–81. Springer, Cham (2015). https://doi.org/10.1007/978-3-319-16763-3_5
6. Barthe, G., et al.: Verified proofs of higher-order masking. In: Oswald, E., Fischlin, M. (eds.) EUROCRYPT 2015. LNCS, vol. 9056, pp. 457–485. Springer, Heidelberg (2015). https://doi.org/10.1007/978-3-662-46800-5_18
7. Barthe, G., Belaïd, S., Dupressoir, F., Fouque, P.-A., Grégoire, B., Strub, P.-Y., Zucchini, R.: Strong non-interference and type-directed higher-order masking. In: ACM Conference on Computer and Communications Security, pp. 116–129 (2016)
8. Barvinok, A.I.: A polynomial time algorithm for counting integral points in polyhedra when the dimension is fixed. Math. Oper. Res. 19(4), 769–779 (1994)
9. Bayrak, A.G., Regazzoni, F., Brisk, P., Standaert, F.-X., Ienne, P.: A first step towards automatic application of power analysis countermeasures. In: ACM/IEEE Design Automation Conference, pp. 230–235 (2011)
10. Bayrak, A.G., Regazzoni, F., Novo, D., Ienne, P.: Sleuth: automated verification of software power analysis countermeasures. In: Bertoni, G., Coron, J.-S. (eds.) CHES 2013. LNCS, vol. 8086, pp. 293–310. Springer, Heidelberg (2013). https://doi.org/10.1007/978-3-642-40349-1_17
11. Bertoni, G., Daemen, J., Peeters, M., Van Assche, G., Van Keer, R.: Keccak implementation overview (2013). https://keccak.team/files/Keccak-implementation-3.2.pdf
12. Biham, E., Shamir, A.: Differential fault analysis of secret key cryptosystems. In: Kaliski, B.S. (ed.) CRYPTO 1997. LNCS, vol. 1294, pp. 513–525. Springer, Heidelberg (1997). https://doi.org/10.1007/BFb0052259
13. Bisi, E., Melzani, F., Zaccaria, V.: Symbolic analysis of higher-order side channel countermeasures. IEEE Trans. Comput. 66(6), 1099–1105 (2017)
14. Bloem, R., Gross, H., Iusupov, R., Konighofer, B., Mangard, S., Winter, J.: Formal verification of masked hardware implementations in the presence of glitches. IACR Cryptology ePrint Archive, p. 897 (2017)
15. Blömer, J., Guajardo, J., Krummel, V.: Provably secure masking of AES. In: Handschuh, H., Hasan, M.A. (eds.) SAC 2004. LNCS, vol. 3357, pp. 69–83. Springer, Heidelberg (2004). https://doi.org/10.1007/978-3-540-30564-4_5
16. Blot, A., Yamamoto, M., Terauchi, T.: Compositional synthesis of leakage resilient programs. In: Maffei, M., Ryan, M. (eds.) POST 2017. LNCS, vol. 10204, pp. 277–297. Springer, Heidelberg (2017). https://doi.org/10.1007/978-3-662-54455-6_13

17. Canright, D., Batina, L.: A very compact "Perfectly Masked" S-box for AES. In: Bellovin, S.M., Gennaro, R., Keromytis, A., Yung, M. (eds.) ACNS 2008. LNCS, vol. 5037, pp. 446–459. Springer, Heidelberg (2008). https://doi.org/10.1007/978-3-540-68914-0_27
18. Chakraborty, S., Fremont, D.J., Meel, K.S., Seshia, S.A., Vardi, M.Y.: Distribution-aware sampling and weighted model counting for SAT. In: AAAI Conference on Artificial Intelligence, pp. 1722–1730 (2014)
19. Chakraborty, S., Meel, K.S., Vardi, M.Y.: A scalable approximate model counter. In: Schulte, C. (ed.) CP 2013. LNCS, vol. 8124, pp. 200–216. Springer, Heidelberg (2013). https://doi.org/10.1007/978-3-642-40627-0_18
20. Coron, J.-S.: Formal verification of side-channel countermeasures via elementary circuit transformations. IACR Cryptology ePrint Archive, p. 879 (2017)
21. Coron, J.-S., Prouff, E., Rivain, M.: Side channel cryptanalysis of a higher order masking scheme. In: Paillier, P., Verbauwhede, I. (eds.) CHES 2007. LNCS, vol. 4727, pp. 28–44. Springer, Heidelberg (2007). https://doi.org/10.1007/978-3-540-74735-2_3
22. Coron, J.-S., Prouff, E., Rivain, M., Roche, T.: Higher-order side channel security and mask refreshing. In: Moriai, S. (ed.) FSE 2013. LNCS, vol. 8424, pp. 410–424. Springer, Heidelberg (2014). https://doi.org/10.1007/978-3-662-43933-3_21
23. de Moura, L., Bjørner, N.: Z3: an efficient SMT solver. In: Ramakrishnan, C.R., Rehof, J. (eds.) TACAS 2008. LNCS, vol. 4963, pp. 337–340. Springer, Heidelberg (2008). https://doi.org/10.1007/978-3-540-78800-3_24
24. Doychev, G., Feld, D., Köpf, B., Mauborgne, L., Reineke, J.: CacheAudit: a tool for the static analysis of cache side channels. In: USENIX Security Symposium, pp. 431–446 (2013)
25. Eldib, H., Wang, C.: Synthesis of masking countermeasures against side channel attacks. In: Biere, A., Bloem, R. (eds.) CAV 2014. LNCS, vol. 8559, pp. 114–130. Springer, Cham (2014). https://doi.org/10.1007/978-3-319-08867-9_8
26. Eldib, H., Wang, C., Schaumont, P.: Formal verification of software countermeasures against side-channel attacks. ACM Trans. Softw. Eng. Methodol. 24(2), 11 (2014)
27. Eldib, H., Wang, C., Schaumont, P.: SMT-based verification of software countermeasures against side-channel attacks. In: Ábrahám, E., Havelund, K. (eds.) TACAS 2014. LNCS, vol. 8413, pp. 62–77. Springer, Heidelberg (2014). https://doi.org/10.1007/978-3-642-54862-8_5
28. Eldib, H., Wang, C., Taha, M., Schaumont, P.: QMS: evaluating the side-channel resistance of masked software from source code. In: ACM/IEEE Design Automation Conference, vol. 209, pp. 1–6 (2014)
29. Eldib, H., Wu, M., Wang, C.: Synthesis of fault-attack countermeasures for cryptographic circuits. In: Chaudhuri, S., Farzan, A. (eds.) CAV 2016. LNCS, vol. 9780, pp. 343–363. Springer, Cham (2016). https://doi.org/10.1007/978-3-319-41540-6_19
30. Clavier, C., et al.: Practical improvements of side-channel attacks on AES: feedback from the 2nd DPA contest. J. Cryptogr. Eng. 4(4), 259–274 (2014)
31. Fredrikson, M., Jha, S.: Satisfiability modulo counting: a new approach for analyzing privacy properties. In: ACM/IEEE Symposium on Logic in Computer Science, pp. 42:1–42:10 (2014)
32. Fremont, D.J., Rabe, M.N., Seshia, S.A.: Maximum model counting. In: AAAI Conference on Artificial Intelligence, pp. 3885–3892 (2017)
33. Goodwill, G., Jun, B., Jaffe, J., Rohatgi, P.: A testing methodology for side channel resistance validation. In: NIST Non-invasive Attack Testing Workshop (2011)
34. Goubin, L.: A sound method for switching between boolean and arithmetic masking. In: Koç, Ç.K., Naccache, D., Paar, C. (eds.) CHES 2001. LNCS, vol. 2162, pp. 3–15. Springer, Heidelberg (2001). https://doi.org/10.1007/3-540-44709-1_2

35. Grabher, P., Großschädl, J., Page, D.: Cryptographic side-channels from low-power cache memory. In: Galbraith, S.D. (ed.) Cryptography and Coding 2007. LNCS, vol. 4887, pp. 170–184. Springer, Heidelberg (2007). https://doi.org/10.1007/978-3-540-77272-9_11

36. Hachtel, G.D., Somenzi, F.: Logic Synthesis and Verification Algorithms. Kluwer (1996)

37. Ishai, Y., Sahai, A., Wagner, D.: Private circuits: securing hardware against probing attacks. In: Boneh, D. (ed.) CRYPTO 2003. LNCS, vol. 2729, pp. 463–481. Springer, Heidelberg (2003). https://doi.org/10.1007/978-3-540-45146-4_27

38. Kocher, P.C.: Timing attacks on implementations of Diffie-Hellman, RSA, DSS, and other systems. In: Koblitz, N. (ed.) CRYPTO 1996. LNCS, vol. 1109, pp. 104–113. Springer, Heidelberg (1996). https://doi.org/10.1007/3-540-68697-5_9

39. Kocher, P., Jaffe, J., Jun, B.: Differential power analysis. In: Wiener, M. (ed.) CRYPTO 1999. LNCS, vol. 1666, pp. 388–397. Springer, Heidelberg (1999). https://doi.org/10.1007/3-540-48405-1_25

40. Köpf, B., Mauborgne, L., Ochoa, M.: Automatic quantification of cache side-channels. In: Madhusudan, P., Seshia, S.A. (eds.) CAV 2012. LNCS, vol. 7358, pp. 564–580. Springer, Heidelberg (2012). https://doi.org/10.1007/978-3-642-31424-7_40

41. Messerges, T.S.: Securing the AES finalists against power analysis attacks. In: Goos, G., Hartmanis, J., van Leeuwen, J., Schneier, B. (eds.) FSE 2000. LNCS, vol. 1978, pp. 150–164. Springer, Heidelberg (2001). https://doi.org/10.1007/3-540-44706-7_11

42. Moradi, A., Barenghi, A., Kasper, T., Paar, C.: On the vulnerability of FPGA bitstream encryption against power analysis attacks: extracting keys from xilinx Virtex-II FPGAs. In: ACM Conference on Computer and Communications Security, pp. 111–124 (2011)

43. Moradi, A., Poschmann, A., Ling, S., Paar, C., Wang, H.: Pushing the limits: a very compact and a threshold implementation of AES. In: Paterson, K.G. (ed.) EUROCRYPT 2011. LNCS, vol. 6632, pp. 69–88. Springer, Heidelberg (2011). https://doi.org/10.1007/978-3-642-20465-4_6

44. Moss, A., Oswald, E., Page, D., Tunstall, M.: Compiler assisted masking. In: Prouff, E., Schaumont, P. (eds.) CHES 2012. LNCS, vol. 7428, pp. 58–75. Springer, Heidelberg (2012). https://doi.org/10.1007/978-3-642-33027-8_4

45. Ochoa, M., Banescu, S., Disenfeld, C., Barthe, G., Ganesh, V.: Reasoning about probabilistic defense mechanisms against remote attacks. In: IEEE European Symposium on Security and Privacy, EuroS&P, pp. 499–513 (2017)

46. Oswald, E., Mangard, S., Pramstaller, N., Rijmen, V.: A side-channel analysis resistant description of the AES S-Box. In: Gilbert, H., Handschuh, H. (eds.) FSE 2005. LNCS, vol. 3557, pp. 413–423. Springer, Heidelberg (2005). https://doi.org/10.1007/11502760_28

47. El Ouahma, I.B., Meunier, Q., Heydemann, K., Encrenaz, E.: Symbolic approach for side-channel resistance analysis of masked assembly codes. In: Security Proofs for Embedded Systems (2017)

48. Prouff, E., Rivain, M.: Masking against side-channel attacks: a formal security proof. In: Johansson, T., Nguyen, P.Q. (eds.) EUROCRYPT 2013. LNCS, vol. 7881, pp. 142–159. Springer, Heidelberg (2013). https://doi.org/10.1007/978-3-642-38348-9_9

49. Quisquater, J.-J., Samyde, D.: ElectroMagnetic analysis (EMA): measures and countermeasures for smart cards. In: Attali, I., Jensen, T. (eds.) E-smart 2001. LNCS, vol. 2140, pp. 200–210. Springer, Heidelberg (2001). https://doi.org/10.1007/3-540-45418-7_17

50. Reparaz, O., Bilgin, B., Nikova, S., Gierlichs, B., Verbauwhede, I.: Consolidating masking schemes. In: Gennaro, R., Robshaw, M. (eds.) CRYPTO 2015. LNCS, vol. 9215, pp. 764–783. Springer, Heidelberg (2015). https://doi.org/10.1007/978-3-662-47989-6_37

51. Rivain, M., Prouff, E.: Provably secure higher-order masking of AES. In: Mangard, S., Standaert, F.-X. (eds.) CHES 2010. LNCS, vol. 6225, pp. 413–427. Springer, Heidelberg (2010). https://doi.org/10.1007/978-3-642-15031-9_28

52. Schramm, K., Paar, C.: Higher order masking of the AES. In: Pointcheval, D. (ed.) CT-RSA 2006. LNCS, vol. 3860, pp. 208–225. Springer, Heidelberg (2006). https://doi.org/10.1007/11605805_14

53. Standaert, F.-X.: How (not) to use welch's t-test in side-channel security evaluations. IACR Cryptology ePrint Archive 2017:138 (2017)

54. Wang, C., Schaumont, P.: Security by compilation: an automated approach to comprehensive side-channel resistance. SIGLOG News 4(2), 76–89 (2017)

Symbolic Algorithms for Graphs and Markov Decision Processes with Fairness Objectives

Krishnendu Chatterjee[1]([✉]), Monika Henzinger[2], Veronika Loitzenbauer[3], Simin Oraee[4], and Viktor Toman[1]

[1] IST Austria, Klosterneuburg, Austria
krish.chat@gmail.com
[2] University of Vienna, Vienna, Austria
[3] Johannes Kepler University Linz, Linz, Austria
[4] Max Planck Institute for Software Systems, Kaiserslautern, Germany

Abstract. Given a model and a specification, the fundamental model-checking problem asks for algorithmic verification of whether the model satisfies the specification. We consider graphs and Markov decision processes (MDPs), which are fundamental models for reactive systems. One of the very basic specifications that arise in verification of reactive systems is the strong fairness (aka Streett) objective. Given different types of requests and corresponding grants, the objective requires that for each type, if the request event happens infinitely often, then the corresponding grant event must also happen infinitely often. All ω-regular objectives can be expressed as Streett objectives and hence they are canonical in verification. To handle the state-space explosion, symbolic algorithms are required that operate on a succinct implicit representation of the system rather than explicitly accessing the system. While explicit algorithms for graphs and MDPs with Streett objectives have been widely studied, there has been no improvement of the basic symbolic algorithms. The worst-case numbers of symbolic steps required for the basic symbolic algorithms are as follows: quadratic for graphs and cubic for MDPs. In this work we present the first sub-quadratic symbolic algorithm for graphs with Streett objectives, and our algorithm is sub-quadratic even for MDPs. Based on our algorithmic insights we present an implementation of the new symbolic approach and show that it improves the existing approach on several academic benchmark examples.

1 Introduction

In this work we present faster symbolic algorithms for graphs and Markov decision processes (MDPs) with strong fairness objectives. For the fundamental model-checking problem, the input consists of a *model* and a *specification*, and the algorithmic verification problem is to check whether the model *satisfies* the specification. We first describe the specific model-checking problem we consider and then our contributions.

H. Chockler and G. Weissenbacher (Eds.): CAV 2018, LNCS 10982, pp. 178–197, 2018.
https://doi.org/10.1007/978-3-319-96142-2_13

Models: Graphs and MDPs. Two standard models for reactive systems are graphs and Markov decision processes (MDPs). Vertices of a graph represent states of a reactive system, edges represent transitions of the system, and infinite paths of the graph represent non-terminating trajectories of the reactive system. MDPs extend graphs with probabilistic transitions that represent reactive systems with uncertainty. Thus graphs and MDPs are the de-facto model of reactive systems with nondeterminism, and nondeterminism with stochastic aspects, respectively [3,19].

Specification: Strong Fairness (aka Streett) Objectives. A basic and fundamental property in the analysis of reactive systems is the *strong fairness condition*, which informally requires that if events are enabled infinitely often, then they must be executed infinitely often. More precisely, the strong fairness conditions (aka Streett objectives) consist of k types of requests and corresponding grants, and the objective requires that for each type if the request happens infinitely often, then the corresponding grant must also happen infinitely often. After safety, reachability, and liveness, the strong fairness condition is one of the most standard properties that arise in the analysis of reactive systems, and chapters of standard textbooks in verification are devoted to it (e.g., [19, Chap. 3.3], [32, Chap. 3], [2, Chaps. 8, 10]). Moreover, all ω-regular objectives can be described by Streett objectives, e.g., LTL formulas and non-deterministic ω-automata can be translated to deterministic Streett automata [34] and efficient translation has been an active research area [16,23,28]. Thus Streett objectives are a canonical class of objectives that arise in verification.

Satisfaction. The basic notions of satisfaction for graphs and MDPs are as follows: For graphs the notion of satisfaction requires that there is a trajectory (infinite path) that belongs to the set of paths described by the Streett objective. For MDPs the satisfaction requires that there is a policy to resolve the nondeterminism such that the Streett objective is ensured almost-surely (with probability 1). Thus the algorithmic model-checking problem of graphs and MDPs with Streett objectives is a core problem in verification.

Explicit vs Symbolic Algorithms. The traditional algorithmic studies consider *explicit* algorithms that operate on the explicit representation of the system. In contrast, *implicit* or *symbolic* algorithms only use a set of predefined operations and do not explicitly access the system [20]. The significance of symbolic algorithms in verification is as follows: to combat the state-space explosion, large systems must be succinctly represented implicitly and then symbolic algorithms are scalable, whereas explicit algorithms do not scale as it is computationally too expensive to even explicitly construct the system.

Relevance. In this work we study symbolic algorithms for graphs and MDPs with Streett objectives. Symbolic algorithms for the analysis of graphs and MDPs are at the heart of many state-of-the-art tools such as SPIN, NuSMV for graphs [18,27] and PRISM, LiQuor, Storm for MDPs [17,22,29]. Our contributions are related to the algorithmic complexity of graphs and MDPs with Streett objectives for symbolic algorithms. We first present previous results and then our contributions.

Previous Results. The most basic algorithm for the problem for graphs is based on repeated SCC (strongly connected component) computation, and informally can be described as follows: for a given SCC, (a) if for every request type that is present in the SCC the corresponding grant type is also present in the SCC, then the SCC is identified as "good", (b) else vertices of each request type that has no corresponding grant type in the SCC are removed, and the algorithm recursively proceeds on the remaining graph. Finally, reachability to good SCCs is computed. The current best-known symbolic algorithm for SCC computation requires $O(n)$ symbolic steps, for graphs with n vertices [25], and moreover, the algorithm is optimal [15]. For MDPs, the SCC computation has to be replaced by MEC (maximal end-component) computation, and the current best-known symbolic algorithm for MEC computation requires $O(n^2)$ symbolic steps. While there have been several explicit algorithms for graphs with Streett objectives [12, 26], MEC computation [8–10], and MDPs with Streett objectives [7], as well as symbolic algorithms for MDPs with Büchi objectives [11], the current best-known bounds for symbolic algorithms with Streett objectives are obtained from the basic algorithms, which are $O(n \cdot \min(n, k))$ for graphs and $O(n^2 \cdot \min(n, k))$ for MDPs, where k is the number of types of request-grant pairs.

Our Contributions. In this work our main contributions are as follows:

- We present a symbolic algorithm that requires $O(n \cdot \sqrt{m \log n})$ symbolic steps, both for graphs and MDPs, where m is the number of edges. In the case $k = O(n)$, the previous worst-case bounds are quadratic ($O(n^2)$) for graphs and cubic ($O(n^3)$) for MDPs. In contrast, we present the first sub-quadratic symbolic algorithm both for graphs as well as MDPs. Moreover, in practice, since most graphs are sparse (with $m = O(n)$), the worst-case bounds of our symbolic algorithm in these cases are $O(n \cdot \sqrt{n \log n})$. Another interesting contribution of our work is that we also present an $O(n \cdot \sqrt{m})$ symbolic steps algorithm for MEC decomposition, which is relevant for our results as well as of independent interest, as MEC decomposition is used in many other algorithmic problems related to MDPs. Our results are summarized in Table 1.
- While our main contribution is theoretical, based on the algorithmic insights we also present a new symbolic algorithm implementation for graphs and MDPs with Streett objectives. We show that the new algorithm improves (by around 30%) the basic algorithm on several academic benchmark examples from the VLTS benchmark suite [21].

Technical Contributions. The two key technical contributions of our work are as follows:

- *Symbolic Lock Step Search:* We search for newly emerged SCCs by a local graph exploration around vertices that lost adjacent edges. In order to find small new SCCs first, all searches are conducted "in parallel", i.e., in lock-step, and the searches stop as soon as the first one finishes successfully. This approach has successfully been used to improve explicit algorithms [7,9,14,26]. Our contribution is a non-trivial symbolic variant (Sect. 3) which lies at the core of the theoretical improvements.

Table 1. Symbolic algorithms for Streett objectives and MEC decomposition.

Problem	Symbolic operations		
	Basic algorithm	Improved algorithm	Reference
Graphs with Streett	$O(n \cdot \min(n, k))$	$\mathbf{O(n\sqrt{m}\log n)}$	Theorem 2
MDPs with Streett	$O(n^2 \cdot \min(n, k))$	$\mathbf{O(n\sqrt{m}\log n)}$	Theorem 4
MEC decomposition	$O(n^2)$	$\mathbf{O(n\sqrt{m})}$	Theorem 3

– *Symbolic Interleaved MEC Computation:* For MDPs the identification of vertices that have to be removed can be interleaved with the computation of MECs such that in each iteration the computation of SCCs instead of MECs is sufficient to make progress [7]. We present a symbolic variant of this interleaved computation. This interleaved MEC computation is the basis for applying the lock-step search to MDPs.

2 Definitions

2.1 Basic Problem Definitions

Markov Decision Processes (MDPs) and Graphs. An MDP $P = ((V, E), (V_1, V_R), \delta)$ consists of a finite directed graph $G = (V, E)$ with a set of n vertices V and a set of m edges E, a partition of the vertices into *player 1 vertices* V_1 and *random vertices* V_R, and a probabilistic transition function δ. We call an edge (u, v) with $u \in V_1$ a *player 1 edge* and an edge (v, w) with $v \in V_R$ a *random edge*. For $v \in V$ we define $In(v) = \{w \in V \mid (w, v) \in E\}$ and $Out(v) = \{w \in V \mid (v, w) \in E\}$. The probabilistic transition function is a function from V_R to $\mathcal{D}(V)$, where $\mathcal{D}(V)$ is the set of probability distributions over V and a random edge $(v, w) \in E$ if and only if $\delta(v)[w] > 0$. Graphs are a special case of MDPs with $V_R = \emptyset$.

Plays and Strategies. A *play* or infinite path in P is an infinite sequence $\omega = \langle v_0, v_1, v_2, \ldots \rangle$ such that $(v_i, v_{i+1}) \in E$ for all $i \in \mathbb{N}$; we denote by Ω the set of all plays. A player 1 *strategy* $\sigma : V^* \cdot V_1 \to V$ is a function that assigns to every finite prefix $\omega \in V^* \cdot V_1$ of a play that ends in a player 1 vertex v a successor vertex $\sigma(\omega) \in V$ such that $(v, \sigma(\omega)) \in E$; we denote by Σ the set of all player 1 strategies. A strategy is *memoryless* if we have $\sigma(\omega) = \sigma(\omega')$ for any $\omega, \omega' \in V^* \cdot V_1$ that end in the same vertex $v \in V_1$.

Objectives. An *objective* ϕ is a subset of Ω said to be winning for player 1. We say that a play $\omega \in \Omega$ *satisfies the objective* if $\omega \in \phi$. For a vertex set $T \subseteq V$ the *reachability objective* is the set of infinite paths that contain a vertex of T, i.e., Reach$(T) = \{\langle v_0, v_1, v_2, \ldots \rangle \in \Omega \mid \exists j \geq 0 : v_j \in T\}$. Let $\text{Inf}(\omega)$ for $\omega \in \Omega$ denote the set of vertices that occur infinitely often in ω. Given a set TP of k pairs (L_i, U_i) of vertex sets $L_i, U_i \subseteq V$ with $1 \leq i \leq k$, the *Streett objective* is the set of infinite paths for which it holds *for each* $1 \leq i \leq k$ that whenever a vertex of L_i occurs infinitely often, then a vertex of U_i occurs infinitely often, i.e., Streett(TP) $= \{\omega \in \Omega \mid L_i \cap \text{Inf}(\omega) = \emptyset$ or $U_i \cap \text{Inf}(\omega) \neq \emptyset$ for all $1 \leq i \leq k\}$.

Almost-Sure Winning Sets. For any measurable set of plays $A \subseteq \Omega$ we denote by $\Pr_v^{\sigma}(A)$ the probability that a play starting at $v \in V$ belongs to A when player 1 plays strategy σ. A strategy σ is *almost-sure* (a.s.) *winning* from a vertex $v \in V$ for an objective ϕ if $\Pr_v^{\sigma}(\phi) = 1$. The *almost-sure winning set* $\langle\!\langle 1 \rangle\!\rangle_{as}(P, \phi)$ of player 1 is the set of vertices for which player 1 has an almost-sure winning strategy. In graphs the existence of an almost-sure winning strategy corresponds to the existence of a play in the objective, and the set of vertices for which player 1 has an (almost-sure) winning strategy is called the *winning set* $\langle\!\langle 1 \rangle\!\rangle(P, \phi)$ of player 1.

Symbolic Encoding of MDPs. Symbolic algorithms operate on sets of vertices, which are usually described by Binary Decision Diagrams (BDDs) [1,30]. In particular Ordered Binary Decision Diagrams [6] (OBDDs) provide a canonical symbolic representation of Boolean functions. For the computation of almost-sure winning sets of MDPs it is sufficient to encode MDPs with OBDDs and one additional bit that denotes whether a vertex is in V_1 or V_R.

Symbolic Steps. One symbolic step corresponds to one primitive operation as supported by standard symbolic packages like CuDD [35]. In this paper we only allow the same basic *set-based symbolic operations* as in [5,11,24,33], namely set operations and the following one-step symbolic operations for a set of vertices Z: (a) the one-step predecessor operator $\mathsf{Pre}(Z) = \{v \in V \mid Out(v) \cap Z \neq \emptyset\}$; (b) the one-step successor operator $\mathsf{Post}(Z) = \{v \in V \mid In(v) \cap Z \neq \emptyset\}$; and (c) the one-step *controllable* predecessor operator $\mathsf{CPre}_R(Z) = \{v \in V_1 \mid Out(v) \subseteq Z\} \cup \{v \in V_R \mid Out(v) \cap Z \neq \emptyset\}$; i.e., the CPre_R operator computes all vertices such that the successor belongs to Z with positive probability. This operator can be defined using the Pre operator and basic set operations as follows: $\mathsf{CPre}_R(Z) = \mathsf{Pre}(Z) \setminus (V_1 \cap \mathsf{Pre}(V \setminus Z))$. We additionally allow cardinality computation and picking an arbitrary vertex from a set as in [11].

Symbolic Model. Informally, a symbolic algorithm does not operate on explicit representation of the transition function of a graph, but instead accesses it through Pre and Post operations. For explicit algorithms, a $\mathsf{Pre}/\mathsf{Post}$ operation on a set of vertices (resp., a single vertex) requires $O(m)$ (resp., the order of indegree/outdegree of the vertex) time. In contrast, for symbolic algorithms $\mathsf{Pre}/\mathsf{Post}$ operations are considered unit-cost. Thus an interesting algorithmic question is whether better algorithmic bounds can be obtained considering $\mathsf{Pre}/\mathsf{Post}$ as unit operations. Moreover, the basic set operations are computationally less expensive (as they encode the relationship between the state variables) compared to the $\mathsf{Pre}/\mathsf{Post}$ symbolic operations (as they encode the transitions and thus the relationship between the present and the next-state variables). In all presented algorithms, the number of set operations is asymptotically at most the number of $\mathsf{Pre}/\mathsf{Post}$ operations. Hence in the sequel we focus on the number of $\mathsf{Pre}/\mathsf{Post}$ operations of algorithms.

Algorithmic Problem. Given an MDP P (resp. a graph G) and a set of Streett pairs TP, the problem we consider asks for a symbolic algorithm to compute the almost-sure winning set $\langle\!\langle 1 \rangle\!\rangle_{as}(P, \text{Streett(TP)})$ (resp. the winning set $\langle\!\langle 1 \rangle\!\rangle(G, \text{Streett(TP)})$), which is also called the *qualitative analysis* of MDPs (resp. graphs).

2.2   Basic Concepts Related to Algorithmic Solution

Reachability. For a graph $G = (V, E)$ and a set of vertices $S \subseteq V$ the set $\text{GRAPHREACH}(G, S)$ is the set of vertices of V that *can reach* a vertex of S within G, and it can be identified with at most $|\text{GRAPHREACH}(G, S)\backslash S| + 1$ many Pre operations.

Strongly Connected Components. For a set of vertices $S \subseteq V$ we denote by $G[S] = (S, E \cap (S \times S))$ the subgraph of the graph G induced by the vertices of S. An induced subgraph $G[S]$ is strongly connected if there exists a path in $G[S]$ between every pair of vertices of S. A *strongly connected component (SCC)* of G is a set of vertices $C \subseteq V$ such that the induced subgraph $G[C]$ is strongly connected and C is a maximal set in V with this property. We call an SCC *trivial* if it only contains a single vertex and no edges; and *non-trivial* otherwise. The SCCs of G partition its vertices and can be found in $O(n)$ symbolic steps [25]. A bottom SCC C in a directed graph G is an SCC with no edges from vertices of C to vertices of $V\backslash C$, i.e., an SCC without *outgoing* edges. Analogously, a top SCC C is an SCC with no *incoming* edges from $V\backslash C$. For more intuition for bottom and top SCCs, consider the graph in which each SCC is contracted into a single vertex (ignoring edges within an SCC). In the resulting directed acyclic graph the sinks represent the bottom SCCs and the sources represent the top SCCs. Note that every graph has at least one bottom and at least one top SCC. If the graph is not strongly connected, then there exist at least one top and at least one bottom SCC that are disjoint and thus one of them contains at most half of the vertices of G.

Random Attractors. In an MDP P the *random attractor* $Attr_R(P, W)$ of a set of vertices W is defined as $Attr_R(P, W) = \bigcup_{j \geq 0} Z_j$ where $Z_0 = W$ and $Z_{j+1} = Z_j \cup \text{CPre}_R(Z_j)$ for all $j > 0$. The attractor can be computed with at most $|Attr_R(P, W)\backslash W| + 1$ many CPre_R operations.

Maximal End-Components. Let X be a vertex set without outgoing random edges, i.e., with $Out(v) \subseteq X$ for all $v \in X \cap V_R$. A sub-MDP of an MDP P induced by a vertex set $X \subseteq V$ without outgoing random edges is defined as $P[X] = ((X, E \cap (X \times X)), (V_1 \cap X, V_R \cap X), \delta)$. Note that the requirement that X has no outgoing random edges is necessary in order to use the same probabilistic transition function δ. An *end-component* (EC) of an MDP P is a set of vertices $X \subseteq V$ such that (a) X has no outgoing random edges, i.e., $P[X]$ is a valid sub-MDP, (b) the induced sub-MDP $P[X]$ is strongly connected, and (c) $P[X]$ contains at least one edge. Intuitively, an end-component is a set of vertices for which player 1 can ensure that the play stays within the set and almost-surely reaches all the vertices in the set (infinitely often). An end-component is a *maximal end-component* (MEC) if it is maximal under set inclusion. An end-component is *trivial* if it consists of a single vertex (with a self-loop), otherwise it is *non-trivial*. The *MEC decomposition* of an MDP consists of all MECs of the MDP.

Good End-Components. All algorithms for MDPs with Streett objectives are based on finding good end-components, defined below. Given the union of all good end-components, the almost-sure winning set is obtained by computing the almost-sure winning set for the reachability objective with the union of all good end-components as the target set. The correctness of this approach is shown in [7,31] (see also [3, Chap. 10.6.3]). For Streett objectives a good end-component is defined as follows. In the special case of graphs they are called good components.

Definition 1 (Good end-component). *Given an MDP P and a set* TP $=$ $\{(L_j, U_j) \mid 1 \leq j \leq k\}$ *of target pairs, a* good end-component *is an end-component X of P such that for each* $1 \leq j \leq k$ *either* $L_j \cap X = \emptyset$ *or* $U_j \cap X \neq \emptyset$. *A* maximal good end-component *is a good end-component that is maximal with respect to set inclusion.*

Lemma 1 (Correctness of Computing Good End-Components [31, Corollary 2.6.5, Proposition 2.6.9]). *For an MDP P and a set* TP *of target pairs, let* $\mathcal{X}$ *be the set of all maximal good end-components. Then* $\langle\langle 1 \rangle\rangle_{as} \left(P, Reach(\bigcup_{X \in \mathcal{X}} X)\right)$ *is equal to* $\langle\langle 1 \rangle\rangle_{as} \left(P, Streett(\mathrm{TP})\right)$.

Iterative Vertex Removal. All the algorithms for Streett objectives maintain vertex sets that are candidates for good end-components. For such a vertex set S we (a) refine the maintained sets according to the SCC decomposition of $P[S]$ and (b) for a set of vertices W for which we know that it cannot be contained in a good end-component, we remove its random attractor from S. The following lemma shows the correctness of these operations.

Lemma 2 (Correctness of Vertex Removal [31, Lemma 2.6.10]). *Given an MDP* $P = ((V, E), (V_1, V_R), \delta)$, *let X be an end-component with* $X \subseteq S$ *for some* $S \subseteq V$. *Then*

(a) $X \subseteq C$ for one SCC C of $P[S]$ and
(b) $X \subseteq S \backslash Attr_R(P', W)$ for each $W \subseteq V \backslash X$ and each sub-MDP P' containing X.

Let X be a good end-component. Then X is an end-component and for each index j, $X \cap U_j = \emptyset$ implies $X \cap L_j = \emptyset$. Hence we obtain the following corollary.

Corollary 1 ([31, Corollary 4.2.2]). *Given an MDP P, let X be a good end-component with* $X \subseteq S$ *for some* $S \subseteq V$. *For each i with* $S \cap U_i = \emptyset$ *it holds that* $X \subseteq S \backslash Attr_R(P[S], L_i \cap S)$.

For an index j with $S \cap U_j = \emptyset$ we call the vertices of $S \cap L_j$ *bad vertices.* The set of all bad vertices $\mathrm{BAD}(S) = \bigcup_{1 \leq i \leq k}\{v \in L_i \cap S \mid U_i \cap S = \emptyset\}$ can be computed with $2k$ set operations.

3 Symbolic Divide-and-Conquer with Lock-Step Search

In this section we present a symbolic version of the lock-step search for strongly connected subgraphs [26]. This symbolic version is used in all subsequent results,

i.e., the sub-quadratic symbolic algorithms for graphs and MDPs with Streett
objectives, and for MEC decomposition.

Divide-and-Conquer. The common property of the algorithmic problems we consider in this work is that the goal is to identify subgraphs of the input graph
$G = (V, E)$ that are strongly connected and satisfy some additional properties. The difference between the problems lies in the required additional properties. We describe and analyze the Procedure LOCK-STEP-SEARCH that we use
in all our improved algorithms to efficiently implement a divide-and-conquer
approach based on the requirement of strong connectivity, that is, we divide
a subgraph $G[S]$, induced by a set of vertices S, into two parts that are not
strongly connected within $G[S]$ or detect that $G[S]$ is strongly connected.

Start Vertices of Searches. The input to Procedure LOCK-STEP-SEARCH is a
set of vertices $S \subseteq V$ and two subsets of S denoted by H_S and T_S. In the
algorithms that call the procedure as a subroutine, vertices contained in H_S
have lost incoming edges (i.e., they were a "head" of a lost edge) and vertices
contained in T_S have lost outgoing edges (i.e., they were a "tail" of a lost edge)
since the last time a superset of S was identified as being strongly connected. For
each vertex h of H_S the procedure conducts a backward search (i.e., a sequence
of Pre operations) within $G[S]$ to find the vertices of S that can reach h; and
analogously a forward search (i.e., a sequence of Post operations) from each
vertex t of T_S is conducted.

Intuition for the Choice of Start Vertices. If the subgraph $G[S]$ is not strongly
connected, then it contains at least one top SCC and at least one bottom SCC
that are disjoint. Further, if for a superset $S' \supset S$ the subgraph $G[S']$ was
strongly connected, then each top SCC of $G[S]$ contains a vertex that had an
additional incoming edge in $G[S']$ compared to $G[S]$, and analogously each bottom SCC of $G[S]$ contains a vertex that had an additional outgoing edge. Thus by
keeping track of the vertices that lost incoming or outgoing edges, the following
invariant will be maintained by all our improved algorithms.

Invariant 1 (Start Vertices Sufficient). *We have $H_S, T_S \subseteq S$. Either (a)
$H_S \cup T_S = \emptyset$ and $G[S]$ is strongly connected or (b) at least one vertex of each
top SCC of $G[S]$ is contained in H_S and at least one vertex of each bottom SCC
of $G[S]$ is contained in T_S.*

Lock-Step Search. The searches from the vertices of $H_S \cup T_S$ are performed in
lock-step, that is, (a) one step is performed in each of the searches before the
next step of any search is done and (b) all searches stop as soon as the first of
the searches finishes. This is implemented in Procedure LOCK-STEP-SEARCH as
follows. A step in the search from a vertex $t \in T_S$ (and analogously for $h \in H_S$)
corresponds to the execution of the iteration of the for-each loop for $t \in T_S$. In
an iteration of a for-each loop we might discover that we do not need to consider
this search further (see the paragraph on ensuring strong connectivity below)
and update the set T_S (via T_S') for future iterations accordingly. Otherwise the
set C_t is either strictly increasing in this step of the search or the search for t

Procedure. Lock-Step-Search(G, S, H_S, T_S)

```
/* Pre and Post defined w.r.t. to G                                      */
1  foreach v ∈ H_S ∪ T_S do  C_v ← {v}
2  while true do
3  │  H'_S ← H_S, T'_S ← T_S
4  │  foreach h ∈ H_S do /* search for top SCC                            */
5  │  │  C'_h ← (C_h ∪ Pre(C_h)) ∩ S
6  │  │  if |C'_h ∩ H'_S| > 1 then  H'_S ← H'_S\{h}
7  │  │  else
8  │  │  │  if C'_h = C_h then  return (C_h, H'_S, T'_S)
9  │  │  └  C_h ← C'_h
10 │  foreach t ∈ T_S do /* search for bottom SCC                         */
11 │  │  C'_t ← (C_t ∪ Post(C_t)) ∩ S
12 │  │  if |C'_t ∩ T'_S| > 1 then  T'_S ← T'_S\{t}
13 │  │  else
14 │  │  │  if C'_t = C_t then  return (C_t, H'_S, T'_S)
15 │  │  └  C_t ← C'_t
16 └  H_S ← H'_S, T_S ← T'_S
```

terminates and we return the set of vertices in $G[S]$ that are reachable from t. So the two for-each loops over the vertices of T_S and H_S that are executed in an iteration of the while-loop perform one step of each of the searches and the while-loop stops as soon as a search stops, i.e., a return statement is executed and hence this implements properties (a) and (b) of lock-step search. Note that the while-loop terminates, i.e., a return statement is executed eventually because for all $t \in T_S$ (and resp. for all $h \in H_S$) the sets C_t are monotonically increasing over the iterations of the while-loop, we have $C_t \subseteq S$, and if some set C_t does not increase in an iteration, then it is either removed from T_S and thus not considered further or a return statement is executed. Note that when a search from a vertex $t \in T_S$ stops, it has discovered a maximal set of vertices C that can be reached from t; and analogously for $h \in H_S$. Figure 1 shows a small intuitive example of a call to the procedure.

Comparison to Explicit Algorithm. In the *explicit* version of the algorithm [7,26] the search from vertex $t \in T_S$ performs a depth-first search that terminates exactly when every *edge* reachable from t is explored. Since any search that starts outside of a bottom SCC but reaches the bottom SCC has to explore more edges than the search started inside of the bottom SCC, the first search from a vertex of T_S that terminates has exactly explored (one of) the smallest (in the number of edges) bottom SCC(s) of $G[S]$. Thus on explicit graphs the explicit lock-step search from the vertices of $H_S \cup T_S$ finds (one of) the smallest (in the number of edges) top or bottom SCC(s) of $G[S]$ in time proportional to the number of searches times the number of edges in the identified SCC. In *symbolically* represented graphs it can happen (1) that a search started outside of a bottom (resp. top) SCC terminates earlier than the search started within

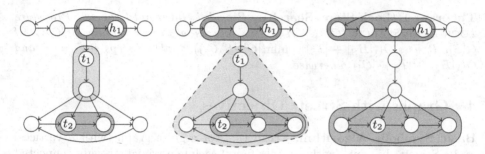

Fig. 1. An example of symbolic lock-step search showing the first three iterations of the main while-loop. Note that during the second iteration, the search started from t_1 is disregarded since it collides with t_2. In the subsequent fourth iteration, the search started from t_2 is returned by the procedure.

the bottom (resp. top) SCC and (2) that a search started in a larger (in the number of vertices) top or bottom SCC terminates before one in a smaller top or bottom SCC. We discuss next how we address these two challenges.

Ensuring Strong Connectivity. First, we would like the set returned by Procedure LOCK-STEP-SEARCH to indeed be a top or bottom SCC of $G[S]$. For this we use the following observation for bottom SCCs that can be applied to top SCCs analogously. If a search starting from a vertex of $t_1 \in T_S$ encounters another vertex $t_2 \in T_S$, $t_1 \neq t_2$, there are two possibilities: either (1) both vertices are in the same SSC or (2) t_1 can reach t_2 but not vice versa. In Case (1) the searches from both vertices can explore all vertices in the SCC and thus it is sufficient to only search from one of them. In Case (2) the SCC of t_1 has an outgoing edge and thus cannot be a bottom SCC. Hence in both cases we can remove the vertex t_1 from the set T_S while still maintaining Invariant 1. By Invariant 1 we further have that each search from a vertex of T_S that is not in a bottom SCC encounters another vertex of T_S in its search and therefore is removed from the set T_S during Procedure LOCK-STEP-SEARCH (if no top or bottom SCC is found earlier). This ensures that the returned set is either a top or a bottom SCC.[1]

Bound on Symbolic Steps. Second, observe that we can still bound the number of symbolic steps needed for the search that terminates first by the number of *vertices* in the smallest top or bottom SCC of $G[S]$, since this is an upper bound on the symbolic steps needed for the search started in this SCC. Thus provided Invariant 1, we can bound the number of symbolic steps in Procedure LOCK-STEP-SEARCH to identify a vertex set $C \subsetneq S$ such that C and $S \setminus C$ are not strongly connected in $G[S]$ by $O((|H_S| + |T_S|) \cdot \min(|C|, |S \setminus C|))$. In the algorithms that call Procedure LOCK-STEP-SEARCH we charge the number of symbolic steps in the procedure to the vertices in the smaller set of C and $S \setminus C$; this ensures that each vertex is charged at most $O(\log n)$ times over the whole algorithm. We obtain the following result (proof in [13, Appendix A]).

---

[1] To improve the practical performance, we return the updated sets H_S and T_S. By the above argument this preserves Invariant 1.

Theorem 1 (Lock-Step Search). *Provided Invariant 1 holds, Procedure* LOCK-STEP-SEARCH *(G, S, H_S, T_S) returns a top or bottom SCC C of $G[S]$. It uses $O((|H_S| + |T_S|) \cdot \min(|C|, |S \backslash C|))$ symbolic steps if $C \neq S$ and $O((|H_S| + |T_S|) \cdot |C|)$ otherwise.*

4 Graphs with Streett Objectives

Basic Symbolic Algorithm. Recall that for a given graph (with n vertices) and a Streett objective (with k target pairs) each non-trivial strongly connected subgraph without bad vertices is a good component. The basic symbolic algorithm for graphs with Streett objectives repeatedly removes bad vertices from each SCC and then recomputes the SCCs until all good components are found. The winning set then consists of the vertices that can reach a good component. We refer to this algorithm as STREETTGRAPHBASIC. For the pseudocode and more details see [13, Appendix B].

Proposition 1. *Algorithm* STREETTGRAPHBASIC *correctly computes the winning set in graphs with Streett objectives and requires $O(n \cdot \min(n, k))$ symbolic steps.*

Improved Symbolic Algorithm. In our improved symbolic algorithm we replace the recomputation of all SCCs with the search for a new top or bottom SCC with Procedure LOCK-STEP-SEARCH from vertices that have lost adjacent edges whenever there are not too many such vertices. We present the improved symbolic algorithm for graphs with Streett objectives in more detail as it also conveys important intuition for the MDP case. The pseudocode is given in Algorithm STREETTGRAPHIMPR.

Iterative Refinement of Candidate Sets. The improved algorithm maintains a set goodC of already identified good components that is initially empty and a set $\mathcal{X}$ of candidates for good components that is initialized with the SCCs of the input graph G. The difference to the basic algorithm lies in the properties of the vertex sets maintained in $\mathcal{X}$ and the way we identify sets that can be separated from each other without destroying a good component. In each iteration one vertex set S is removed from $\mathcal{X}$ and, after the removal of bad vertices from the set, either identified as a good component or split into several candidate sets. By Lemma 2 and Corollary 1 the following invariant is maintained throughout the algorithm for the sets in goodC and $\mathcal{X}$.

Invariant 2 (Maintained Sets). *The sets in $\mathcal{X} \cup$ goodC are pairwise disjoint and for every good component C of G there exists a set $Y \supseteq C$ such that either $Y \in \mathcal{X}$ or $Y \in$ goodC.*

Lost Adjacent Edges. In contrast to the basic algorithm, the subgraph induced by a set S contained in $\mathcal{X}$ is not necessarily strongly connected. Instead, we remember vertices of S that have lost adjacent edges since the last time a superset of S was determined to induce a strongly connected subgraph; vertices that lost

---

Algorithm. STREETTGRAPHIMPR. Improved Alg. for Graphs with Streett Obj.

Input : graph $G = (V, E)$ and Streett pairs $\text{TP} = \{(L_i, U_i) \mid 1 \leq i \leq k\}$
Output : $\langle\!\langle 1 \rangle\!\rangle (G, \text{Streett}(\text{TP}))$

1 $\mathcal{X} \leftarrow \text{ALLSCCs}(G)$; $\text{goodC} \leftarrow \emptyset$
2 **foreach** $C \in \mathcal{X}$ **do** $H_C \leftarrow \emptyset$; $T_C \leftarrow \emptyset$
3 **while** $\mathcal{X} \neq \emptyset$ **do**
4   remove some $S \in \mathcal{X}$ from $\mathcal{X}$
5      $B \leftarrow \bigcup_{1 \leq i \leq k: U_i \cap S = \emptyset}(L_i \cap S)$
6   **while** $B \neq \emptyset$ **do**
7          $S \leftarrow S \backslash B$
8          $H_S \leftarrow (H_S \cup \text{Post}(B)) \cap S$
9          $T_S \leftarrow (T_S \cup \text{Pre}(B)) \cap S$
10         $B \leftarrow \bigcup_{1 \leq i \leq k: U_i \cap S = \emptyset}(L_i \cap S)$
11   **if** $\text{Post}(S) \cap S \neq \emptyset$ **then** /* $G[S]$ contains at least one edge   */
12   **if** $|H_S| + |T_S| = 0$ **then** $\text{goodC} \leftarrow \text{goodC} \cup \{S\}$
13   **else if** $|H_S| + |T_S| \geq \sqrt{m / \log n}$ **then**
14   delete H_S and T_S
15             $\mathcal{C} \leftarrow \text{ALLSCCs}(G[S])$
16   **if** $|\mathcal{C}| = 1$ **then** $\text{goodC} \leftarrow \text{goodC} \cup \{S\}$
17   **else**
18   **foreach** $C \in \mathcal{C}$ **do** $H_C \leftarrow \emptyset$; $T_C \leftarrow \emptyset$
19                 $\mathcal{X} \leftarrow \mathcal{X} \cup \mathcal{C}$
20   **else**
21             $(C, H_S, T_S) \leftarrow \text{LOCK-STEP-SEARCH } (G, S, H_S, T_S)$
22   **if** $C = S$ **then** $\text{goodC} \leftarrow \text{goodC} \cup \{S\}$
23   **else** /* separate C and $S \backslash C$ */
24                 $S \leftarrow S \backslash C$
25                 $H_C \leftarrow \emptyset$; $T_C \leftarrow \emptyset$
26                 $H_S \leftarrow (H_S \cup \text{Post}(C)) \cap S$
27                 $T_S \leftarrow (T_S \cup \text{Pre}(C)) \cap S$
28                 $\mathcal{X} \leftarrow \mathcal{X} \cup \{S\} \cup \{C\}$

29 **return** $\text{GRAPHREACH}(G, \bigcup_{C \in \text{goodC}} C)$

---

incoming edges are contained in H_S and vertices that lost outgoing edges are contained in T_S. In this way we maintain Invariant 1 throughout the algorithm, which enables us to use Procedure LOCK-STEP-SEARCH with the running time guarantee provided by Theorem 1.

Identifying SCCs. Let S be the vertex set removed from $\mathcal{X}$ in a fixed iteration of Algorithm STREETTGRAPHIMPR after the removal of bad vertices in the inner while-loop. First note that if S is strongly connected and contains at least one edge, then it is a good component. If the set S was already identified as strongly connected in a previous iteration, i.e., H_S and T_S are empty, then S is identified as a good component in line 12. If many vertices of S have lost adjacent edges since the last time a super-set of S was identified as a strongly connected subgraph, then the SCCs of $G[S]$ are determined as in the basic algorithm. To achieve the optimal asymptotic upper bound, we say that many vertices of S have lost adjacent edges when we have $|H_S| + |T_S| \geq \sqrt{m/\log n}$, while lower thresholds are used in our experimental results. Otherwise, if not too many vertices of S lost adjacent edges, then we start a symbolic *lock-step search* for top SCCs from the vertices of H_S and for bottom SCCs from the vertices of T_S using Procedure LOCK-STEP-SEARCH. The set returned by the procedure is either a top or a bottom SCC C of $G[S]$ (Theorem 1). Therefore we can from now on consider C and $S \backslash C$ separately, maintaining Invariants 1 and 2.

Algorithm STREETTGRAPHIMPR. A succinct description of the pseudocode is as follows: Lines 1–2 initialize the set of candidates for good components with the SCCs of the input graph. In each iteration of the main while-loop one candidate is considered and the following operations are performed: (a) lines 5–10 iteratively remove all bad vertices; if afterwards the candidate is still strongly connected (and contains at least one edge), it is identified as a good component in the next step; otherwise it is partitioned into new candidates in one of the following ways: (b) if many vertices lost adjacent edges, lines 13–17 partition the candidate into its SCCs (this corresponds to an iteration of the basic algorithm); (c) otherwise, lines 20–28 use symbolic lock-step search to partition the candidate into one of its SCCs and the remaining vertices. The while-loop terminates when no candidates are left. Finally, vertices that can reach some good component are returned. We have the following result (proof in [13, Appendix B]).

Theorem 2 (Improved Algorithm for Graphs). *Algorithm* STREETT-GRAPH*IMPR correctly computes the winning set in graphs with Streett objectives and requires $O(n \cdot \sqrt{m \log n})$ symbolic steps.*

5 Symbolic MEC Decomposition

In this section we present a succinct description of the basic symbolic algorithm for MEC decomposition and then present the main ideas for the improved algorithm.

Basic symbolic algorithm for MEC decomposition. The basic symbolic algorithm for MEC decomposition maintains a set of identified MECs and a set of candidates for MECs, initialized with the SCCs of the MDP. Whenever a candidate is considered, either (a) it is identified as a MEC or (b) it contains vertices with outgoing random edges, which are then removed together with their random attractor from the candidate, and the SCCs of the remaining sub-MDP are added to the set of candidates. We refer to the algorithm as MECBASIC.

Proposition 2. *Algorithm* MECBASIC *correctly computes the MEC decomposition of MDPs and requires $O(n^2)$ symbolic steps.*

Improved Symbolic Algorithm for MEC Decomposition. The improved symbolic algorithm for MEC decomposition uses the ideas of symbolic lock-step search presented in Sect. 3. Informally, when considering a candidate that lost a few edges from the remaining graph, we use the symbolic lock-step search to identify some bottom SCC. We refer to the algorithm as MECIMPR. Since all the important conceptual ideas regarding the symbolic lock-step search are described in Sect. 3, we relegate the technical details to [13, Appendix C]. We summarize the main result (proof in [13, Appendix C]).

Theorem 3 (Improved Algorithm for MEC). *Algorithm* MECIMPR *correctly computes the MEC decomposition of MDPs and requires* $O(n \cdot \sqrt{m})$ *symbolic steps.*

6   MDPs with Streett Objectives

Basic Symbolic Algorithm. We refer to the basic symbolic algorithm for MDPs with Streett objectives as STREETTMDPBASIC, which is similar to the algorithm for graphs, with SCC computation replaced by MEC computation. The pseudocode of Algorithm STREETTMDPBASIC together with its detailed description is presented in [13, Appendix D].

Proposition 3. *Algorithm* STREETTMDPBASIC *correctly computes the almost-sure winning set in MDPs with Streett objectives and requires* $O(n^2 \cdot \min(n, k))$ *symbolic steps.*

Remark. The above bound uses the basic symbolic MEC decomposition algorithm. Using our improved symbolic MEC decomposition algorithm, the above bound could be improved to $O(n \cdot \sqrt{m} \cdot \min(n, k))$.

Improved Symbolic Algorithm. We refer to the improved symbolic algorithm for MDPs with Streett objectives as STREETTMDPIMPR. First we present the main ideas for the improved symbolic algorithm. Then we explain the key differences compared to the improved symbolic algorithm for graphs. A thorough description with the technical details and proofs is presented in [13, Appendix D].

– First, we improve the algorithm by interleaving the symbolic MEC computation with the detection of bad vertices [7,31]. This allows to replace the computation of MECs in each iteration of the while-loop with the computation of SCCs and an additional random attractor computation.
  • *Intuition of interleaved computation.* Consider a candidate for a good end-component S after a random attractor to some bad vertices is removed from it. After the removal of the random attractor, the set S does not have random vertices with outgoing edges. Consider that further BAD$(S) = \emptyset$ holds. If S is strongly connected and contains an edge, then it is a good end-component. If S is not strongly connected, then $P[S]$ contains at least two SCCs and some of them might have random vertices with outgoing edges. Since end-components are strongly connected and do not have

random vertices with outgoing edges, we have that (1) every good end-component is completely contained in one of the SCCs of $P[S]$ and (2) the random vertices of an SCC with outgoing edges and their random attractor do not intersect with any good end-component (see Lemma 2).

- *Modification from basic to improved algorithm.* We use these observations to modify the basic algorithm as follows: First, for the sets that are candidates for good end-components, we do not maintain the property that they are end-components, but only that they do not have random vertices with outgoing edges (it still holds that every maximal good end-component is either already identified or contained in one of the candidate sets). Second, for a candidate set S, we repeat the removal of bad vertices until $\text{BAD}(S) = \emptyset$ holds before we continue with the next step of the algorithm. This allows us to make progress after the removal of bad vertices by computing all SCCs (instead of MECs) of the remaining sub-MDP. If there is only one SCC, then this is a good end-component (if it contains at least one edge). Otherwise (a) we remove from each SCC the set of random vertices with outgoing edges and their random attractor and (b) add the remaining vertices of each SCC as a new candidate set.
- Second, as for the improved symbolic algorithm for graphs, we use the symbolic lock-step search to quickly identify a top or bottom SCC every time a candidate has lost a small number of edges since the last time its superset was identified as being strongly connected. The symbolic lock-step search is described in detail in Sect. 3.

Using interleaved MEC computation and lock-step search leads to a similar algorithmic structure for Algorithm STREETTMDPIMPR as for our improved symbolic algorithm for graphs (Algorithm STREETTGRAPHIMPR). The key differences are as follows: First, the set of candidates for good end-components is initialized with the MECs of the input graph instead of the SCCs. Second, whenever bad vertices are removed from a candidate, also their random attractor is removed. Further, whenever a candidate is partitioned into its SCCs, for each SCC, the random attractor of the vertices with outgoing random edges is removed. Finally, whenever a candidate S is separated into C and $S \backslash C$ via symbolic lock-step search, the random attractor of the vertices with outgoing random edges is removed from C, and the random attractor of C is removed from S.

Theorem 4 (Improved Algorithm for MDPs). *Algorithm* STREETT *MDP*IMPR *correctly computes the almost-sure winning set in MDPs with Streett objectives and requires* $O(n \cdot \sqrt{m \log n})$ *symbolic steps.*

7   Experiments

We present a basic prototype implementation of our algorithm and compare against the basic symbolic algorithm for graphs and MDPs with Streett objectives.

Models. We consider the academic benchmarks from the VLTS benchmark suite [21], which gives representative examples of systems with nondeterminism, and has been used in previous experimental evaluation (such as [4,11]).

Specifications. We consider random LTL formulae and use the tool Rabinizer [28] to obtain deterministic Rabin automata. Then the negations of the formulae give us Streett automata, which we consider as the specifications.

Graphs. For the models of the academic benchmarks, we first compute SCCs, as all algorithms for Streett objectives compute SCCs as a preprocessing step. For SCCs of the model benchmarks we consider products with the specification Streett automata, to obtain graphs with Streett objectives, which are the benchmark examples for our experimental evaluation. The number of transitions in the benchmarks ranges from 300K to 5Million.

MDPs. For MDPs, we consider the graphs obtained as above and consider a fraction of the vertices of the graph as random vertices, which is chosen uniformly at random. We consider 10%, 20%, and 50% of the vertices as random vertices for different experimental evaluation.

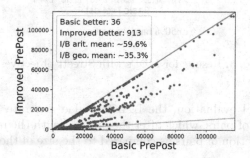

Fig. 2. Results for graphs with Streett objectives.

Experimental Evaluation. In the experimental evaluation we compare the number of symbolic steps (i.e., the number of Pre/Post operations[2]) executed by the algorithms, the comparison of running time yields similar results and is provided in [13, Appendix E]. As the initial preprocessing step is the same for all the algorithms (computing all SCCs for graphs and all MECs for MDPs), the comparison presents the number of symbolic steps executed after the preprocessing. The experimental results for graphs are shown in Fig. 2 and the experimental results for MDPs are shown in Fig. 3 (in each figure the two lines represent equality and an order-of-magnitude improvement, respectively).

Discussion. Note that the lock-step search is the key reason for theoretical improvement, however, the improvement relies on a large number of Streett pairs.

---

[2] Recall that the basic set operations are cheaper to compute, and asymptotically at most the number of Pre/Post operations in all the presented algorithms.

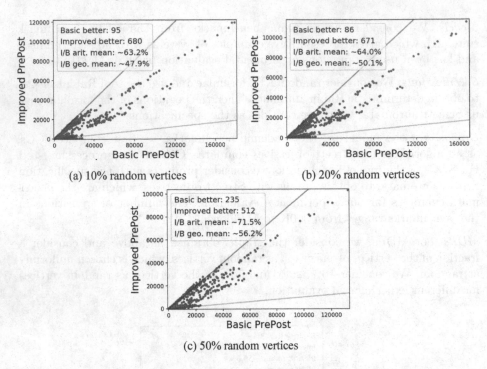

(a) 10% random vertices   (b) 20% random vertices

(c) 50% random vertices

Fig. 3. Results for MDPs with Streett objectives.

In the experimental evaluation, the LTL formulae generate Streett automata with small number of pairs, which after the product with the model accounts for an even smaller fraction of pairs as compared to the size of the state space. This has two effects:

- In the experiments the lock-step search is performed for a much smaller parameter value ($O(\log n)$ instead of the theoretically optimal bound of $\sqrt{m/\log n}$), and leads to a small improvement.
- For large graphs, since the number of pairs is small as compared to the number of states, the improvement over the basic algorithm is minimal.

In contrast to graphs, in MDPs even with small number of pairs as compared to the state-space, the interleaved MEC computation has a notable effect on practical performance, and we observe performance improvement even in large MDPs.

8   Conclusion

In this work we consider symbolic algorithms for graphs and MDPs with Streett objectives, as well as for MEC decomposition. Our algorithmic bounds match for both graphs and MDPs. In contrast, while SCCs can be computed in linearly many symbolic steps no such algorithm is known for MEC decomposition. An interesting direction of future work would be to explore further improved symbolic algorithms for MEC decomposition. Moreover, further improved symbolic algorithms for graphs and MDPs with Streett objectives is also an interesting direction of future work.

Acknowledgements. K. C. and M. H. are partially supported by the Vienna Science and Technology Fund (WWTF) grant ICT15-003. K. C. is partially supported by the Austrian Science Fund (FWF): S11407-N23 (RiSE/SHiNE), and an ERC Start Grant (279307: Graph Games). V. T. is partially supported by the European Union's Horizon 2020 research and innovation programme under the Marie Skłodowska-Curie Grant Agreement No. 665385. V. L. is partially supported by the Austrian Science Fund (FWF): S11408-N23 (RiSE/SHiNE), the ISF grant #1278/16, and an ERC Consolidator Grant (project MPM). For M. H. and V. L. the research leading to these results has received funding from the European Research Council under the European Union's Seventh Framework Programme (FP/2007-2013)/ERC Grant Agreement no. 340506.

References

1. Akers, S.B.: Binary decision diagrams. IEEE Trans. Comput. **C-27**(6), 509–516 (1978)
2. Alur, R., Henzinger, T.A.: Computer-aided verification (2004). http://www.cis.upenn.edu/group/cis673/
3. Baier, C., Katoen, J.P.: Principles of Model Checking. MIT Press, Cambridge (2008)
4. Barnat, J., Chaloupka, J., van de Pol, J.: Distributed algorithms for SCC decomposition. J. Log. Comput. **21**(1), 23–44 (2011)
5. Bloem, R., Gabow, H.N., Somenzi, F.: An algorithm for strongly connected component analysis in $n \log n$ symbolic steps. Form. Methods Syst. Des. **28**(1), 37–56 (2006)
6. Bryant, R.E.: Symbolic manipulation of Boolean functions using a graphical representation. In: Conference on Design Automation, DAC, pp. 688–694 (1985)
7. Chatterjee, K., Dvořák, W., Henzinger, M., Loitzenbauer, V.: Model and objective separation with conditional lower bounds: disjunction is harder than conjunction. In: LICS, pp. 197–206 (2016)
8. Chatterjee, K., Henzinger, M.: Faster and dynamic algorithms for maximal end-component decomposition and related graph problems in probabilistic verification. In: SODA, pp. 1318–1336 (2011)
9. Chatterjee, K., Henzinger, M.: An $O(n^2)$ time algorithm for alternating Büchi games. In: SODA, pp. 1386–1399 (2012)
10. Chatterjee, K., Henzinger, M.: Efficient and dynamic algorithms for alternating Büchi games and maximal end-component decomposition. J. ACM **61**(3), 15 (2014)
11. Chatterjee, K., Henzinger, M., Joglekar, M., Shah, N.: Symbolic algorithms for qualitative analysis of Markov decision processes with Büchi objectives. Form. Methods Syst. Des. **42**(3), 301–327 (2013)
12. Chatterjee, K., Henzinger, M., Loitzenbauer, V.: Improved algorithms for one-pair and k-pair Streett objectives. In: LICS, pp. 269–280 (2015)

13. Chatterjee, K., Henzinger, M., Loitzenbauer, V., Oraee, S., Toman, V.: Symbolic algorithms for graphs and Markov decision processes with fairness objectives. arXiv:1804.00206 (2018)
14. Chatterjee, K., Jurdziński, M., Henzinger, T.A.: Simple stochastic parity games. In: Baaz, M., Makowsky, J.A. (eds.) CSL 2003. LNCS, vol. 2803, pp. 100–113. Springer, Heidelberg (2003). https://doi.org/10.1007/978-3-540-45220-1_11
15. Chatterjee, K., Dvořák, W., Henzinger, M., Loitzenbauer, V.: Lower bounds for symbolic computation on graphs: strongly connected components, liveness, safety, and diameter. In: SODA, pp. 2341–2356 (2018)
16. Chatterjee, K., Gaiser, A., Křetínský, J.: Automata with generalized Rabin pairs for probabilistic model checking and LTL synthesis. In: Sharygina, N., Veith, H. (eds.) CAV 2013. LNCS, vol. 8044, pp. 559–575. Springer, Heidelberg (2013). https://doi.org/10.1007/978-3-642-39799-8_37
17. Ciesinski, F., Baier, C.: LiQuor: a tool for qualitative and quantitative linear time analysis of reactive systems. In: QEST, pp. 131–132 (2006)
18. Cimatti, A., Clarke, E., Giunchiglia, F., Roveri, M.: NUSMV: a new symbolic model checker. Int. J. Softw. Tools Technol. Transf. (STTT) 2(4), 410–425 (2000)
19. Clarke Jr., E.M., Grumberg, O., Peled, D.A.: Model Checking. MIT Press, Cambridge (1999)
20. Clarke, E., Grumberg, O., Peled, D.: Symbolic model checking. In: Model Checking. MIT Press (1999)
21. CWI/SEN2 and INRIA/VASY: The VLTS Benchmark Suite. http://cadp.inria.fr/resources/vlts
22. Dehnert, C., Junges, S., Katoen, J.-P., Volk, M.: A STORM is coming: a modern probabilistic model checker. In: Majumdar, R., Kunčak, V. (eds.) CAV 2017. LNCS, vol. 10427, pp. 592–600. Springer, Cham (2017). https://doi.org/10.1007/978-3-319-63390-9_31
23. Esparza, J., Křetínský, J.: From LTL to deterministic automata: a safraless compositional approach. In: Biere, A., Bloem, R. (eds.) CAV 2014. LNCS, vol. 8559, pp. 192–208. Springer, Cham (2014). https://doi.org/10.1007/978-3-319-08867-9_13
24. Gentilini, R., Piazza, C., Policriti, A.: Computing strongly connected components in a linear number of symbolic steps. In: SODA, pp. 573–582 (2003)
25. Gentilini, R., Piazza, C., Policriti, A.: Symbolic graphs: linear solutions to connectivity related problems. Algorithmica 50(1), 120–158 (2008)
26. Henzinger, M.R., Telle, J.A.: Faster algorithms for the nonemptiness of Streett automata and for communication protocol pruning. In: Karlsson, R., Lingas, A. (eds.) SWAT 1996. LNCS, vol. 1097, pp. 16–27. Springer, Heidelberg (1996). https://doi.org/10.1007/3-540-61422-2_117
27. Holzmann, G.J.: The model checker SPIN. IEEE Trans. Softw. Eng. 23(5), 279–295 (1997)
28. Komárková, Z., Křetínský, J.: Rabinizer 3: safraless translation of LTL to small deterministic automata. In: Cassez, F., Raskin, J.-F. (eds.) ATVA 2014. LNCS, vol. 8837, pp. 235–241. Springer, Cham (2014). https://doi.org/10.1007/978-3-319-11936-6_17
29. Kwiatkowska, M., Norman, G., Parker, D.: PRISM 4.0: verification of probabilistic real-time systems. In: Gopalakrishnan, G., Qadeer, S. (eds.) CAV 2011. LNCS, vol. 6806, pp. 585–591. Springer, Heidelberg (2011). https://doi.org/10.1007/978-3-642-22110-1_47
30. Lee, C.Y.: Representation of switching circuits by binary-decision programs. Bell Syst. Tech. J. 38(4), 985–999 (1959)

31. Loitzenbauer, V.: Improved algorithms and conditional lower bounds for problems in formal verification and reactive synthesis. Ph.D. thesis. University of Vienna (2016)
32. Manna, Z., Pnueli, A.: Temporal Verification of Reactive Systems: Progress (Draft) (1996)
33. Ravi, K., Bloem, R., Somenzi, F.: A comparative study of symbolic algorithms for the computation of fair cycles. In: Hunt, W.A., Johnson, S.D. (eds.) FMCAD 2000. LNCS, vol. 1954, pp. 162–179. Springer, Heidelberg (2000). https://doi.org/10.1007/3-540-40922-X_10
34. Safra, S.: On the complexity of ω-automata. In: FOCS, pp. 319–327 (1988)
35. Somenzi, F.: CUDD: CU decision diagram package release 3.0.0 (2015). http://vlsi.colorado.edu/~fabio/CUDD/

Attracting Tangles to Solve Parity Games

Tom van Dijk[(✉)]

Formal Models and Verification,
Johannes Kepler University, Linz, Austria
tom.vandijk@jku.at

Abstract. Parity games have important practical applications in formal verification and synthesis, especially to solve the model-checking problem of the modal mu-calculus. They are also interesting from the theory perspective, because they are widely believed to admit a polynomial solution, but so far no such algorithm is known.

We propose a new algorithm to solve parity games based on learning tangles, which are strongly connected subgraphs for which one player has a strategy to win all cycles in the subgraph. We argue that tangles play a fundamental role in the prominent parity game solving algorithms. We show that tangle learning is competitive in practice and the fastest solver for large random games.

1 Introduction

Parity games are turn-based games played on a finite graph. Two players *Odd* and *Even* play an infinite game by moving a token along the edges of the graph. Each vertex is labeled with a natural number *priority* and the winner of the game is determined by the parity of the highest priority that is encountered infinitely often. Player Odd wins if this parity is odd; otherwise, player Even wins.

Parity games are interesting both for their practical applications and for complexity theoretic reasons. Their study has been motivated by their relation to many problems in formal verification and synthesis that can be reduced to the problem of solving parity games, as parity games capture the expressive power of nested least and greatest fixpoint operators [11]. In particular, deciding the winner of a parity game is polynomial-time equivalent to checking non-emptiness of non-deterministic parity tree automata [21], and to the explicit model-checking problem of the modal μ-calculus [9,15,20].

Parity games are interesting in complexity theory, as the problem of determining the winner of a parity game is known to lie in UP ∩ co-UP [16], which is contained in NP ∩ co-NP [9]. This problem is therefore unlikely to be NP-complete and it is widely believed that a polynomial solution exists. Despite much effort, such an algorithm has not been found yet.

T. van Dijk—The author is supported by the FWF, NFN Grant S11408-N23 (RiSE).

H. Chockler and G. Weissenbacher (Eds.): CAV 2018, LNCS 10982, pp. 198–215, 2018.
https://doi.org/10.1007/978-3-319-96142-2_14

The main contribution of this paper is based on the notion of a *tangle*. A tangle is a strongly connected subgraph of a parity game for which one of the players has a strategy to win all cycles in the subgraph. We propose this notion and its relation to dominions and cycles in a parity game. Tangles are related to snares [10] and quasi-dominions [3], with the critical difference that tangles are strongly connected, whereas snares and quasi-dominions may be unconnected as well as contain vertices that are not in any cycles. We argue that tangles play a fundamental role in various parity game algorithms, in particular in priority promotion [3,5], Zielonka's recursive algorithm [25], strategy improvement [10,11,24], small progress measures [17], and in the recently proposed quasi-polynomial time progress measures [6,12].

The core insight of this paper is that tangles can be used to attract sets of vertices at once, since the losing player is forced to escape a tangle. This leads to a novel algorithm to solve parity games called *tangle learning*, which is based on searching for tangles along a top-down α-maximal decomposition of the parity game. New tangles are then attracted in the next decomposition. This naturally leads to learning nested tangles and, eventually, finding dominions. We prove that tangle learning solves parity games and present several extensions to the core algorithm, including *alternating* tangle learning, where the two players take turns maximally searching for tangles in their regions, and *on-the-fly* tangle learning, where newly learned tangles immediately refine the decomposition.

We relate the complexity of tangle learning to the number of learned tangles before finding a dominion, which is related to how often the solver is distracted by paths to higher winning priorities that are not suitable strategies.

We evaluate tangle learning in a comparison based on the parity game solver Oink [7], using the benchmarks of Keiren [19] as well as random parity games of various sizes. We compare tangle learning to priority promotion [3,5] and to Zielonka's recursive algorithm [25] as implemented in Oink.

2   Preliminaries

Parity games are two-player turn-based infinite-duration games over a finite directed graph $G = (V, E)$, where every vertex belongs to exactly one of two players called player *Even* and player *Odd*, and where every vertex is assigned a natural number called the *priority*. Starting from some initial vertex, a play of both players is an infinite path in G where the owner of each vertex determines the next move. The winner of such an infinite play is determined by the parity of the highest priority that occurs infinitely often along the play.

More formally, a parity game ∂ is a tuple $(V_\Diamond, V_\Box, E, \mathsf{pr})$ where $V = V_\Diamond \cup V_\Box$ is a set of vertices partitioned into the sets $V_\Diamond$ controlled by player *Even* and $V_\Box$ controlled by player *Odd*, and $E \subseteq V \times V$ is a left-total binary relation describing all moves, i.e., every vertex has at least one successor. We also write $E(u)$ for all successors of u and $u \to v$ for $v \in E(u)$. The function $\mathsf{pr}\colon V \to \{0, 1, \ldots, d\}$ assigns to each vertex a *priority*, where d is the highest priority in the game.

We write $\mathsf{pr}(v)$ for the priority of a vertex v and $\mathsf{pr}(V)$ for the highest priority of vertices V and $\mathsf{pr}(\partial)$ for the highest priority in the game ∂. Furthermore, we write $\mathrm{pr}^{-1}(i)$ for all vertices with the priority i. A *path* $\pi = v_0 v_1 \ldots$ is a sequence of vertices consistent with E, i.e., $v_i \to v_{i+1}$ for all successive vertices. A *play* is an infinite path. We denote with $\inf(\pi)$ the vertices in π that occur infinitely many times in π. Player Even wins a play π if $\mathrm{pr}(\inf(\pi))$ is even; player Odd wins if $\mathrm{pr}(\inf(\pi))$ is odd. We write $\mathrm{Plays}(v)$ to denote all plays starting at vertex v.

A *strategy* $\sigma \colon V \to V$ is a partial function that assigns to each vertex in its domain a single successor in E, i.e., $\sigma \subseteq E$. We refer to a strategy of player α to restrict the domain of σ to V_α. In the remainder, all strategies σ are of a player α. We write $\mathrm{Plays}(v, \sigma)$ for the set of plays from v consistent with σ, and $\mathrm{Plays}(V, \sigma)$ for $\{\pi \in \mathrm{Plays}(v, \sigma) \mid v \in V\}$.

A fundamental result for parity games is that they are memoryless determined [8], i.e., each vertex is either winning for player Even or for player Odd, and both players have a strategy for their winning vertices. Player α wins vertex v if they have a strategy σ such that all plays in $\mathrm{Plays}(v, \sigma)$ are winning for player α.

Several algorithms for solving parity games employ *attractor computation*. Given a set of vertices A, the attractor of A for a player α represents those vertices from which player α can force a play to visit A. We write $Attr_\alpha^\supseteq(A)$ to attract vertices in $\supseteq$ to A as player α, i.e.,

$$\mu Z \,.\, A \cup \{v \in V_\alpha \mid E(v) \cap Z \neq \emptyset\} \cup \{v \in V_{\overline{\alpha}} \mid E(v) \subseteq Z\}$$

Informally, we compute the α-attractor of A with a backward search from A, initially setting $Z := A$ and iteratively adding α-vertices with a successor in Z and $\overline{\alpha}$-vertices with no successors outside Z. We also obtain a strategy σ for player α, starting with an empty strategy, by selecting a successor in Z when we attract vertices of player α and when the backward search finds a successor in Z for the α-vertices in A. We call a set of vertices A α-maximal if $A = Attr_\alpha^\supseteq(A)$.

A *dominion* D is a set of vertices for which player α has a strategy σ such that all plays consistent with σ stay in D and are winning for player α. We also write a *p-dominion* for a dominion where p is the highest priority encountered infinitely often in plays consistent with σ, i.e., $p := \max\{\mathrm{pr}(\inf(\pi)) \mid \pi \in \mathrm{Plays}(D, \sigma)\}$.

3   Tangles

Definition 1. *A p-tangle is a nonempty set of vertices $U \subseteq V$ with $p = \mathrm{pr}(U)$, for which player $\alpha \equiv_2 p$ has a strategy $\sigma \colon U_\alpha \to U$, such that the graph (U, E'), with $E' := E \cap \left(\sigma \cup (U_{\overline{\alpha}} \times U)\right)$, is strongly connected and player α wins all cycles in (U, E').*

Informally, a tangle is a set of vertices for which player α has a strategy to win all cycles inside the tangle. Thus, player $\overline{\alpha}$ loses all plays that stay in U and is therefore forced to escape the tangle. The highest priority by which player α wins a play in (U, E') is p. We make several basic observations related to tangles.

1. A p-tangle from which player $\overline{\alpha}$ cannot leave is a p-dominion.
2. Every p-dominion contains one or more p-tangles.
3. Tangles may contain tangles of a lower priority.

Observation 1 follows by definition. Observation 2 follows from the fact that dominions won by player α with some strategy σ must contain strongly connected subgraphs where all cycles are won by player α and the highest winning priority is p. For observation 3, consider a p-tangle for which player $\overline{\alpha}$ has a strategy that avoids priority p while staying in the tangle. Then there is a p'-tangle with $p' < p$ in which player $\overline{\alpha}$ also loses.

We can in fact find a hierarchy of tangles in any dominion D with winning strategy σ by computing the set of winning priorities $\{\mathsf{pr}(\inf(\pi)) \mid \pi \in \mathrm{Plays}(D, \sigma)\}$. There is a p-tangle in D for every p in this set. Tangles are thus a natural substructure of dominions.

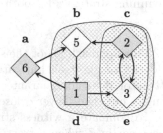

See for example Fig. 1. Player Odd wins this dominion with highest priority 5 and strategy $\{\mathbf{d} \rightarrow \mathbf{e}\}$. Player Even can also avoid priority 5 and then loses with priority 3. The 5-dominion $\{\mathbf{a}, \mathbf{b}, \mathbf{c}, \mathbf{d}, \mathbf{e}\}$ contains the 5-tangle $\{\mathbf{b}, \mathbf{c}, \mathbf{d}, \mathbf{e}\}$ and the 3-tangle $\{\mathbf{c}, \mathbf{e}\}$.

Fig. 1. A 5-dominion with a 5-tangle and a 3-tangle

4   Solving by Learning Tangles

Since player $\overline{\alpha}$ must escape tangles won by player α, we can treat a tangle as an abstract vertex controlled by player $\overline{\alpha}$ that can be attracted by player α, thus attracting all vertices of the tangle. This section proposes the *tangle learning* algorithm, which searches for tangles along a top-down α-maximal decomposition of the game. We extend the attractor to attract all vertices in a tangle when player $\overline{\alpha}$ is forced to play from the tangle to the attracting set. After extracting new tangles from regions in the decomposition, we iteratively repeat the procedure until a dominion is found. We show that tangle learning solves parity games.

4.1   Attracting Tangles

Given a tangle t, we denote its vertices simply by t and its witness strategy by $\sigma_T(t)$. We write $E_T(t)$ for the edges from $\overline{\alpha}$-vertices in the tangle to the rest of the game: $E_T(t) := \{v \mid u \rightarrow v \wedge u \in t \cap V_{\overline{\alpha}} \wedge v \in V \setminus t\}$. We write $T_{\square}$ for all tangles where $\mathsf{pr}(t)$ is odd (won by player Odd) and $T_{\lozenge}$ for all tangles where $\mathsf{pr}(t)$ is even. We write $TAttr_\alpha^{\supseteq, T}(A)$ to attract vertices in $\supseteq$ and vertices of tangles in T to A as player α, i.e.,

$$\mu Z \,.\, A \cup \{v \in V_\alpha \mid E(v) \cap Z \neq \emptyset\} \cup \{v \in V_{\overline{\alpha}} \mid E(v) \subseteq Z\}$$
$$\cup \{v \in t \mid t \in T_\alpha \wedge E_T(t) \neq \emptyset \wedge E_T(t) \subseteq Z\}$$

```
1  def solve(∂):
2      W◇ ← ∅, W□ ← ∅, σ◇ ← ∅, σ□ ← ∅, T ← ∅
3      while ∂ ≠ ∅ :
4          T, d ← search(∂, T)
5          α ← pr(d) mod 2
6          D, σ ← Attr_α^∂(d)
7          W_α ← W_α ∪ D, σ_α ← σ_α ∪ σ_T(d) ∪ σ
8          ∂ ← ∂ \ D, T ← T ∩ (∂ \ D)
9      return W◇, W□, σ◇, σ□
```

Algorithm 1. The `solve` algorithm which computes the winning regions and winning strategies for both players of a given parity game.

This approach is not the same as the subset construction. Indeed, we do not add the tangle itself but rather add all its vertices together. Notice that this attractor does not guarantee arrival in A, as player $\bar{\alpha}$ can stay in the added tangle, but then player $\bar{\alpha}$ loses.

To compute a witness strategy σ for player α, as with $Attr_\alpha^\partial$, we select a successor in Z when attracting single vertices of player α and when we find a successor in Z for the α-vertices in A. When we attract vertices of a tangle, we update σ for each tangle t sequentially, by updating σ with the strategy in $\sigma_T(t)$ of those α-vertices in the tangle for which we do not yet have a strategy in σ, i.e., $\{(u, v) \in \sigma_T(t) \mid u \notin \mathsf{dom}(\sigma)\}$. This is important since tangles can overlap.

In the following, we call a set of vertices A α-maximal if $A = TAttr_\alpha^{\partial,T}(A)$. Given a game ∂ and a set of vertices U, we write $\partial \cap U$ for the subgame ∂' where $V' := V \cap U$ and $E' := E \cap (V' \times V')$. Given a set of tangles T and a set of vertices U, we write $T \cap U$ for all tangles with all vertices in U, i.e., $\{t \in T \mid t \subseteq U\}$, and we extend this notation to $T \cap \partial'$ for the tangles in the game ∂', i.e., $T \cap V'$.

4.2   The `solve` Algorithm

We solve parity games by iteratively searching and removing a dominion of the game, as in [3,18,22]. See Algorithm 1. The `search` algorithm (described below) is given a game and a set of tangles and returns an updated set of tangles and a tangle d that is a dominion. Since the dominion d is a tangle, we derive the winner α from the highest priority (line 5) and use standard attractor computation to compute a dominion D (line 6). We add the dominion to the winning region of player α (line 7). We also update the winning strategy of player α using the witness strategy of the tangle d plus the strategy σ obtained during attractor computation. To solve the remainder, we remove all solved vertices from the game and we remove all tangles that contain solved vertices (line 8). When the entire game is solved, we return the winning regions and winning strategies of both players (lines 9). Reusing the (pruned) set of tangles for the next `search` call is optional; if `search` is always called with an empty set of tangles, the "forgotten" tangles would be found again.

```
1 def search(∂, T):
2     while true :
3         r ← ∅, Y ← ∅
4         while ∂ \ r ≠ ∅ :
5             ∂' ← ∂ \ r, T' ← T ∩ (∂ \ r)
6             p ← pr(∂'), α ← pr(∂') mod 2
7             Z, σ ← TAttr_α^{∂',T'} ({v ∈ ∂' | pr(v) = p})
8             A ← extract-tangles(Z, σ)
9             if ∃t ∈ A: E_T(t) = ∅ :  return T ∪ Y, t
10            r ← r ∪ (Z ↦ p), Y ← Y ∪ A
11        T ← T ∪ Y
```

Algorithm 2. The `search` algorithm which, given a game and a set of tangles, returns the updated set of tangles and a tangle that is a dominion.

4.3   The search Algorithm

The `search` algorithm is given in Algorithm 2. The algorithm iteratively computes a top-down decomposition of $∂$ into sets of vertices called *regions* such that each region is $α$-maximal for the player $α$ who wins the highest priority in the region. Each next region in the remaining subgame $∂'$ is obtained by taking all vertices with the highest priority p in $∂'$ and computing the tangle attractor set of these vertices for the player that wins that priority, i.e., player $α ≡_2 p$. As every next region has a lower priority, each region is associated with a unique priority p. We record the current region of each vertex in an auxiliary partial function $r: V → \{0, 1, \ldots, d\}$ called the region function. We record the new tangles found during each decomposition in the set Y.

In each iteration of the decomposition, we first obtain the current subgame $∂'$ (line 5) and the top priority p in $∂'$ (line 6). We compute the next region by attracting (with tangles) to the vertices of priority p in $∂'$ (line 7). We use the procedure `extract-tangles` (described below) to obtain new tangles from the computed region (line 8). For each new tangle, we check if the set of outgoing edges to the full game $E_T(t)$ is empty. If $E_T(t)$ is empty, then we have a dominion and we terminate the procedure (line 9). If no dominions are found, then we add the new tangles to Y and update r (line 10). After fully decomposing the game into regions, we add all new tangles to T (line 11) and restart the procedure.

4.4   Extracting Tangles from a Region

To search for tangles in a given region A of player $α$ with strategy $σ$, we first remove all vertices where player $\overline{α}$ can play to lower regions (in $∂'$) while player $α$ is constrained to $σ$, i.e.,

$$νZ . A ∩ (\{v ∈ V_{\overline{α}} \mid E'(v) ⊆ Z\} ∪ \{v ∈ V_α \mid σ(v) ∈ Z\})$$

This procedure can be implemented efficiently with a backward search, starting from all vertices of priority p that escape to lower regions. Since there can be multiple vertices of priority p, the reduced region may consist of multiple unconnected tangles. We compute all nontrivial bottom SCCs of the reduced region, restricted by the strategy σ. Every such SCC is a unique p-tangle.

4.5 Tangle Learning Solves Parity Games

We now prove properties of the proposed algorithm.

Lemma 1. *All regions recorded in r in Algorithm 2 are α-maximal in their subgame.*

Proof. This is vacuously true at the beginning of the search. Every region Z is α-maximal as Z is computed with *TAttr* (line 7). Therefore the lemma remains true when r is updated at line 10. New tangles are only added to T at line 11, after which r is reset to $\emptyset$. □

Lemma 2. *All plays consistent with σ that stay in a region are won by player α.*

Proof. Based on how the attractor computes the region, we show that all cycles (consistent with σ) in the region are won by player α. Initially, Z only contains vertices with priority p; therefore, any cycles in Z are won by player α. We consider two cases: (a) When attracting a single vertex v, any new cycles must involve vertices with priority p from the initial set A, since all other α-vertices in Z already have a strategy in Z and all other $\overline{\alpha}$-vertices in Z have only successors in Z, otherwise they would not be attracted to Z. Since p is the highest priority in the region, every new cycle is won by player α. (b) When attracting vertices of a tangle, we set the strategy for all attracted vertices of player α to the witness strategy of the tangle. Any new cycles either involve vertices with priority p (as above) or are cycles inside the tangle that are won by player α. □

Lemma 3. *Player $\overline{\alpha}$ can reach a vertex with the highest priority p from every vertex in the region, via a path in the region that is consistent with strategy σ.*

Proof. The proof is based on how the attractor computes the region. This property is trivially true for the initial set of vertices with priority p. We consider again two cases: (a) When attracting a single vertex v, v is either an α-vertex with a strategy to play to Z, or an $\overline{\alpha}$-vertex whose successors are all in Z. Therefore, the property holds for v. (b) Tangles are strongly connected w.r.t. their witness strategy. Therefore player $\overline{\alpha}$ can reach every vertex of the tangle and since the tangle is attracted to Z, at least one $\overline{\alpha}$-vertex can play to Z. Therefore, the property holds for all attracted vertices of a tangle. □

Lemma 4. *For each new tangle t, all successors of t are in higher α-regions.*

Proof. For every bottom SCC B (computed in `extract-tangles`), $E'(v) \subseteq B$ for all $\overline{\alpha}$-vertices $v \in B$, otherwise player $\overline{\alpha}$ could leave B and B would not be a bottom SCC. Recall that $E'(v)$ is restricted to edges in the subgame $\partial' = \partial \setminus$ r.

Therefore $E(v) \subseteq \mathsf{dom}(r) \cup B$ in the full game for all $\overline{\alpha}$-vertices $v \in B$. Recall that $E_T(t)$ for a tangle t refers to all successors for player $\overline{\alpha}$ that leave the tangle. Hence, $E_T(t) \subseteq \mathsf{dom}(r)$ for every tangle $t := B$. Due to Lemma 1, no $\overline{\alpha}$-vertex in B can escape to a higher $\overline{\alpha}$-region. Thus $E_T(t)$ only contains vertices from higher α-regions when the new tangle is found by `extract-tangles`. □

Lemma 5. *Every nontrivial bottom SCC B of the reduced region restricted by witness strategy σ is a unique p-tangle.*

Proof. All α-vertices v in B have a strategy $\sigma(v) \in B$, since B is a bottom SCC when restricted by σ. B is strongly connected by definition. Per Lemma 2, player α wins all plays consistent with σ in the region and therefore also in B. Thus, B is a tangle. Per Lemma 3, player $\overline{\alpha}$ can always reach a vertex of priority p, therefore any bottom SCC must include a vertex of priority p. Since p is the highest priority in the subgame, B is a p-tangle. Furthermore, the tangle must be unique. If the tangle was found before, then per Lemmas 1 and 4, it would have been attracted to a higher α-region. □

Lemma 6. *The lowest region in the decomposition always contains a tangle.*

Proof. The lowest region is always nonempty after reduction in `extract-tangles`, as there are no lower regions. Furthermore, this region contains non-trivial bottom SCCs, since every vertex must have a successor in the region due to Lemma 1. □

Lemma 7. *A tangle t is a dominion if and only if $E_T(t) = \emptyset$*

Proof. If the tangle is a dominion, then player $\overline{\alpha}$ cannot leave it, therefore $E_T(t) = \emptyset$. If $E_T(t) = \emptyset$, then player $\overline{\alpha}$ cannot leave the tangle and since all plays consistent with σ in the tangle are won by player α, the tangle is a dominion. □

Lemma 8. *$E_T(t) = \emptyset$ for every tangle t found in the highest region of player α.*

Proof. Per Lemma 4, $E_T(t) \subseteq \{v \in \mathsf{dom}(r) \mid r(v) \equiv_2 p\}$ when the tangle is found. There are no higher regions of player α, therefore $E_T(t) = \emptyset$. □

Lemma 9. *The `search` algorithm terminates by finding a dominion.*

Proof. There is always a highest region of one of the players that is not empty. If a tangle is found in this region, then it is a dominion (Lemmas 7 and 8) and Algorithm 2 terminates (line 9). If no tangle is found in this region, then the opponent can escape to a lower region. Thus, if no dominion is found in a highest region, then there is a lower region that contains a tangle (Lemma 6) that must be unique (Lemma 5). As there are only finitely many unique tangles, eventually a dominion must be found. □

Lemma 10. *The `solve` algorithm solves parity games.*

Proof. Every invocation of `search` returns a dominion of the game (Lemma 9). The α-attractor of a dominion won by player α is also a dominion of player α. Thus all vertices in D are won by player α. The winning strategy is derived as the witness strategy of d with the strategy obtained by the attractor at line 6. At the end of `solve` every vertex of the game is either in $W_\Diamond$ or $W_\Box$. $\Box$

4.6   Variations of Tangle Learning

We propose three different variations of tangle learning that can be combined.

The first variation is *alternating tangle learning*, where players take turns to maximally learn tangles, i.e., in a turn of player Even, we only search for tangles in regions of player Even, until no more tangles are found. Then we search only for tangles in regions of player Odd, until no more tangles are found. When changing players, the last decomposition can be reused.

The second variation is *on-the-fly tangle learning*, where new tangles immediately refine the decomposition. When new tangles are found, the decomposition procedure is reset to the highest region that attracts one of the new tangles, such that all regions in the top-down decomposition remain α-maximal. This is the region with priority $p := \max\{\min\{r(v) \mid v \in E_T(t)\} \mid t \in A\}$.

A third variation skips the reduction step in `extract-tangles` and only extracts tangles from regions where none of the vertices of priority p can escape to lower regions. This still terminates finding a dominion, as Lemma 6 still applies, i.e., we always extract tangles from the lowest region. Similar variations are also conceivable, such as only learning tangles from the lowest region.

5   Complexity

We establish a relation between the time complexity of tangle learning and the number of *learned* tangles.

Lemma 11. *Computing the top-down α-maximal decomposition of a parity game runs in time $O(dm + dn|T|)$ given a parity game with d priorities, n vertices and m edges, and a set of tangles T.*

Proof. The attractor $Attr_\alpha^\supset$ runs in time $O(n + m)$, if we record the number of remaining outgoing edges for each vertex [23]. The attractor $TAttr_\alpha^{\supset,T}$ runs in time $O(n + m + |T| + n|T|)$, if implemented in a similar style. As $m \geq n$, we simplify to $O(m + n|T|)$. Since the decomposition computes at most d regions, the decomposition runs in time $O(dm + dn|T|)$. $\Box$

Lemma 12. *Searching for tangles in the decomposition runs in time $O(dm)$.*

Proof. The `extract-tangles` procedure consists of a backward search, which runs in $O(n + m)$, and an SCC search based on Tarjan's algorithm, which also runs in $O(n+m)$. This procedure is performed at most d times (for each region). As $m \geq n$, we simplify to $O(dm)$. $\Box$

Lemma 13. *Tangle learning runs in time $O(dnm|T| + dn^2|T|^2)$ for a parity game with d priorities, n vertices, m edges, and $|T|$ learned tangles.*

Proof. Given Lemmas 11 and 12, each iteration in `search` runs in time $O(dm + dn|T|)$. The number of iterations is at most $|T|$, since we learn at least 1 tangle per iteration. Then `search` runs in time $O(dm|T| + dn|T|^2)$. Since each found dominion is then removed from the game, there are at most n calls to `search`. Thus tangle learning runs in time $O(dnm|T| + dn^2|T|^2)$.   □

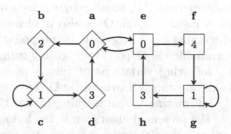

Fig. 2. A parity game that requires several turns to find a dominion.

The complexity of tangle learning follows from the number of tangles that are learned before each dominion is found. Often not all tangles in a game need to be learned to solve the game, only certain tangles. Whether this number can be exponential in the worst case is an open question. These tangles often serve to remove *distractions* that prevent the other player from finding better tangles. This concept is illustrated by the example in Fig. 2, which requires multiple turns before a dominion is found. The game contains 4 tangles: {c}, {g} (a dominion), {a, b, c, d} and {a, e}. The vertices {e, f, g, h} do not form a tangle, since the opponent wins the loop of vertex **g**. The tangle {a, b, c, d} is a dominion in the remaining game after $Attr_\square^\supset(\{g\})$ has been removed.

The tangle {g} is not found at first, as player Odd is distracted by **h**, i.e., prefers to play from **g** to **h**. Thus vertex **h** must first be attracted by the opponent. This occurs when player Even learns the tangle {a, e}, which is then attracted to **f**, which then attracts **h**. However, the tangle {a, e} is blocked, as player Even is distracted by **b**. Vertex **b** is attracted by player Odd when they learn the tangle {c}, which is attracted to **d**, which then attracts **b**. So player Odd must learn tangle {c} so player Even can learn tangle {a, e}, which player Even must learn so player Odd can learn tangle {g} and win the dominion {e, f, g, h}, after which player Odd also learns {a, b, c, d} and wins the entire game.

One can also understand the algorithm as the players learning that their opponent can now play from some vertex v via the learned tangle to a higher vertex w that is won by the opponent. In the example, we first learn that **b** actually leads to **d** via the learned tangle {c}. Now **b** is no longer safe for player

Even. However, player Even can now play from both **d** and **h** via the learned 0-tangle {**a**, **e**} to **f**, so **d** and **h** are no longer interesting for player Odd and vertex **b** is again safe for player Even.

6   Implementation

We implement four variations of tangle learning in the parity game solver Oink [7]. Oink is a modern implementation of parity game algorithms written in C++. Oink implements priority promotion [3], Zielonka's recursive algorithm [25], strategy improvement [11], small progress measures [17], and quasipolynomial time progress measures [12]. Oink also implements self-loop solving and winner-controlled winning cycle detection, as proposed in [23]. The implementation is publicly available via https://www.github.com/trolando/oink.

We implement the following variations of tangle learning: standard tangle learning (`tl`), alternating tangle learning (`atl`), on-the-fly tangle learning (`otftl`) and on-the-fly alternating tangle learning (`otfatl`). The implementation mainly differs from the presented algorithm in the following ways. We combine the `solve` and `search` algorithms in one loop. We remember the highest region that attracts a new tangle and reset the decomposition to that region instead of recomputing the full decomposition. In `extract-tangles`, we do not compute bottom SCCs for the highest region of a player, instead we return the entire reduced region as a single dominion (see also Lemma 8).

7   Empirical Evaluation

The goal of the empirical evaluation is to study tangle learning and its variations on real-world examples and random games. Due to space limitations, we do not report in detail on crafted benchmark families (generated by PGSolver [13]), except that none of these games is difficult in runtime or number of tangles.

We use the parity game benchmarks from model checking and equivalence checking proposed by Keiren [19] that are publicly available online. These are 313 model checking and 216 equivalence checking games. We also consider random games, in part because the literature on parity games tends to favor studying the behavior of algorithms on random games. We include two classes of self-loop-free random games generated by PGSolver [13] with a fixed number of vertices:

- fully random games (`randomgame N N 1 N x`)
  $N \in \{1000, 2000, 4000, 7000\}$
- large low out-degree random games (`randomgame N N 1 2 x`)
  $N \in \{10000, 20000, 40000, 70000, 100000, 200000, 400000, 700000, 1000000\}$

We generate 20 games for each parameter N, in total 80 fully random games and 180 low out-degree games. All random games have N vertices and up to N distinct priorities. We include low out-degree games, since algorithms may behave differently on games where all vertices have few available moves, as also suggested in [3]. In fact, as we see in the evaluation, fully random games appear trivial to solve, whereas games with few moves per vertex are more challenging. Furthermore, the fully random games have fewer vertices but require more disk space (40 MB per compressed file for $N = 7000$) than large low out-degree games (11 MB per compressed file for $N = 1000000$).

We compare four variations of tangle learning to the implementations of Zielonka's recursive algorithm (optimized version of Oink) and of priority promotion (implemented in Oink by the authors of [3]). The motivation for this choice is that [7] shows that these are the fastest parity game solving algorithms.

In the following, we also use *cactus plots* to compare the algorithms. Cactus plots show that an algorithm solved X input games within Y seconds individually.

Table 1. Runtimes in sec. and number of timeouts (20 min) of the solvers Zielonka (zlk), priority promotion (pp), and tangle learning (tl, atl, otftl, otfatl).

Solver	MC&EC	Random	Random (large)	
	Time	Time	Time	Timeouts
pp	503	21	12770	6
zlk	576	21	23119	13
otfatl	808	21	2281	0
atl	817	21	2404	0
otftl	825	21	2238	0
tl	825	21	2312	0

All experimental scripts and log files are available online via https://www.github.com/trolando/tl-experiments. The experiments were performed on a cluster of Dell PowerEdge M610 servers with two Xeon E5520 processors and 24 GB internal memory each. The tools were compiled with gcc 5.4.0.

7.1 Overall Results

Table 1 shows the cumulative runtimes of the six algorithms. For the runs that timed out, we simply used the timeout value of 1200 s, but this underestimates the actual runtime.

7.2 Model Checking and Equivalence Checking Games

See Fig. 3 for the cactus plot of the six solvers on model checking and equivalence checking games. This graph suggests that for most games, tangle learning is only slightly slower than the other algorithms. The tangle learning algorithms require at most 2× as much time for 12 of the 529 games. There is no significant difference between the four variations of tangle learning.

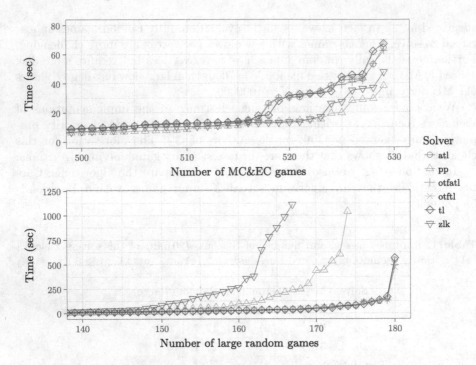

Fig. 3. Cactus plots of the solvers Zielonka (zlk), priority promotion (pp) and tangle learning (tl, atl, otftl, otfatl). The plot shows how many MC&EC games (top) or large random games (bottom) are (individually) solved within the given time.

The 529 games have on average 1.86 million vertices and 5.85 million edges, and at most 40.6 million vertices and 167.5 million edges. All equivalence checking games have 2 priorities, so every tangle is a dominion. The model checking games have 2 to 4 priorities. Tangle learning learns non-dominion tangles for only 30 games, and more than 1 tangle only for the 22 games that check the `infinitely_often_read_write` property. The most extreme case is 1,572,864 tangles for a game with 19,550,209 vertices. These are all 0-tangles that are then attracted to become part of 2-dominions.

That priority promotion and Zielonka's algorithm perform well is no surprise. See also Sect. 8.4. Solving these parity games requires few iterations for all algorithms, but tangle learning spends more time learning and attracting individual tangles, which the other algorithms do not do. Zielonka requires at most 27 iterations, priority promotion at most 28 queries and 9 promotions. Alternating tangle learning requires at most 2 turns. We conclude that these games are not complex and that their difficulty is related to their sheer size.

7.3 Random Games

Table 1 shows no differences between the algorithms for the fully random games. Tangle learning learns no tangles except dominions for any of these games. This agrees with the intuition that the vast number of edges in these games lets attractor-based algorithms quickly attract large portions of the game.

See Fig. 3 for a cactus plot of the solvers on the larger random games. Only 167 games were solved within 20 min each by Zielonka's algorithm and only 174 games by priority promotion. See Table 2 for details of the slowest 10 random games for alternating tangle learning. There is a clear correlation between the runtime, the number of tangles and the number of turns. One game is particularly interesting, as it requires significantly more time than the other games.

The presence of one game that is much more difficult is a feature of using random games. It is likely that if we generated a new set of random games, we would obtain different results. This could be ameliorated by experimenting on thousands of random games and even then it is still a game of chance whether some of these random games are significantly more difficult than the others.

Table 2. The 10 hardest random games for the `atl` algorithm, with time in seconds and size in number of vertices.

Time	543	148	121	118	110	83	81	73	68	52
Tangles	4,018	1,219	737	560	939	337	493	309	229	384
Turns	91	56	23	25	30	12	18	10	10	18
Size	1M	1M	700K	1M	700K	1M	1M	1M	1M	1M

8 Tangles in Other Algorithms

We argue that tangles play a fundamental role in various other parity game solving algorithms. We refer to [7] for descriptions of these algorithms.

8.1 Small Progress Measures

The small progress measures algorithm [17] iteratively performs local updates to vertices until a fixed point is reached. Each vertex is equipped with some measure that records a statistic of the best game either player knows that they can play from that vertex so far. By updating measures based on the successors, they essentially play the game backwards. When they can no longer perform updates, the final measures indicate the winning player of each vertex.

The measures in small progress measures record how often each even priority is encountered along the most optimal play (so far) until a higher priority is encountered. As argued in [7,14], player Even tries to visit vertices with even priorities as often as possible, while prioritizing plays with more higher even priorities. This often resets progress for lower priorities. Player Odd has the opposite goal, i.e., player Odd prefers to play to a lower even priority to avoid a higher even priority, even if the lower priority is visited infinitely often. When the measures record a play from some vertex that visits more vertices with some even priority than exist in the game, this indicates that player Even can force player Odd into a cycle, unless they concede and play to a higher even priority. A mechanism called cap-and-carryover [7] ensures via slowly rising measures that the opponent is forced to play to a higher even priority.

We argue that when small progress measures finds cycles of some priority p, this is due to the presence of a p-tangle, namely precisely those vertices whose measures increase beyond the number of vertices with priority p, since these measures can only increase so far in the presence of cycles out of which the opponent cannot escape except by playing to vertices with a higher even priority.

One can now understand small progress measures as follows. The algorithm indirectly searches for tangles of player Even, and then searches for the best escape for player Odd by playing to the lowest higher even priority. If no such escape exists for a tangle, then the measures eventually rise to $\top$, indicating that player Even has a dominion. Whereas tangle learning is affected by *distractions*, small progress measures is driven by the dual notion of *aversions*, i.e., high even vertices that player Odd initially tries to avoid. The small progress measures algorithm tends to find tangles repeatedly, especially when they are nested.

8.2   Quasi-polynomial Time Progress Measures

The quasi-polynomial time progress measures algorithm [12] is similar to small progress measures. This algorithm records the number of dominating even vertices along a play, i.e., such that every two such vertices are higher than all intermediate vertices. For example, in the path 1213142321563212, all vertices are dominated by each pair of underlined vertices of even priority. Higher even vertices are preferred, even if this (partially) resets progress on lower priorities.

Tangles play a similar role as with small progress measures. The presence of a tangle lets the value iteration procedure increase the measure up to the point where the other player "escapes" the tangle via a vertex outside of the tangle. This algorithm has a similar weakness to nested tangles, but it is less severe as progress on lower priorities is often retained. In fact, the lower bound game in [12], for which the quasi-polynomial time algorithm is slow, is precisely based on nested tangles and is easily solved by tangle learning.

8.3   Strategy Improvement

As argued by Fearnley [10], tangles play a fundamental role in the behavior of strategy improvement. Fearnley writes that instead of viewing strategy improvement as a process that tries to increase valuations, one can view it as a process that tries to force "consistency with snares" [10, Sect. 6], i.e., as a process that searches for escapes from tangles.

8.4   Priority Promotion

Priority promotion [3,5] computes a top-down α-maximal decomposition and identifies "closed α-regions", i.e., regions where the losing player cannot escape to lower regions. A closed α-region is essentially a collection of possibly unconnected tangles and vertices that are attracted to these tangles. Priority promotion then promotes the closed region to the lowest higher region that the losing player can play to, i.e., the lowest region that would attract one of the tangles in the region. Promoting is different from attracting, as tangles in a region can be promoted to a priority that they are not attracted to. Furthermore, priority promotion has no mechanism to remember tangles, so the same tangle can be discovered many times. This is somewhat ameliorated in extensions such as region recovery [2] and delayed promotion [1], which aim to decrease how often regions are recomputed.

Priority promotion has a good practical performance for games where computing and attracting individual tangles is not necessary, e.g., when tangles are only attracted once and all tangles in a closed region are attracted to the same higher region, as is the case with the benchmark games of [19].

8.5   Zielonka's Recursive Algorithm

Zielonka's recursive algorithm [25] also computes a top-down α-maximal decomposition, but instead of attracting from lower regions to higher regions, the algorithm attracts from higher regions to tangles in the subgame. Essentially, the algorithm starts with the tangles in the lowest region and attracts from higher regions to these tangles. When vertices from a higher α-region are attracted to tangles of player $\overline{\alpha}$, progress for player α is reset. Zielonka's algorithm also has no mechanism to store tangles and games that are exponential for Zielonka's algorithm, such as in [4], are trivially solved by tangle learning.

9   Conclusions

We introduced the notion of a tangle as a subgraph of the game where one player knows how to win all cycles. We showed how tangles and nested tangles play a fundamental role in various parity game algorithms. These algorithms are not explicitly aware of tangles and can thus repeatedly explore the same tangles. We proposed a novel algorithm called tangle learning, which identifies tangles in a parity game and then uses these tangles to attract sets of vertices at once. The key insight is that tangles can be used with the attractor to form bigger (nested) tangles and, eventually, dominions. We evaluated tangle learning in a comparison with priority promotion and Zielonka's recursive algorithm and showed that tangle learning is competitive for model checking and equivalence checking games, and outperforms other solvers for large random games.

We repeat Fearnley's assertion [10] that "a thorough and complete understanding of how snares arise in a game is a necessary condition for devising a polynomial time algorithm for these games". Fearnley also formulated the challenge to give a clear formulation of how the structure of tangles in a given game affects the difficulty of solving it. We propose that a difficult game for tangle learning must be one that causes alternating tangle learning to have many turns before a dominion is found.

214   T. van Dijk

Acknowledgements. We thank the anonymous referees for their helpful comments, Jaco van de Pol for the use of the computer cluster, and Armin Biere for generously supporting this research.

References

1. Benerecetti, M., Dell'Erba, D., Mogavero, F.: A delayed promotion policy for parity games. In: GandALF 2016, EPTCS, vol. 226, pp. 30–45 (2016)
2. Benerecetti, M., Dell'Erba, D., Mogavero, F.: Improving priority promotion for parity games. In: Bloem, R., Arbel, E. (eds.) HVC 2016. LNCS, vol. 10028, pp. 117–133. Springer, Cham (2016). https://doi.org/10.1007/978-3-319-49052-6_8
3. Benerecetti, M., Dell'Erba, D., Mogavero, F.: Solving parity games via priority promotion. In: Chaudhuri, S., Farzan, A. (eds.) CAV 2016. LNCS, vol. 9780, pp. 270–290. Springer, Cham (2016). https://doi.org/10.1007/978-3-319-41540-6_15
4. Benerecetti, M., Dell'Erba, D., Mogavero, F.: Robust exponential worst cases for divide-et-impera algorithms for parity games. In: GandALF, EPTCS, vol. 256, pp. 121–135 (2017)
5. Benerecetti, M., Dell'Erba, D., Mogavero, F.: Solving parity games via priority promotion. Formal Methods Syst. Des. **52**, 193–226 (2018)
6. Calude, C.S., Jain, S., Khoussainov, B., Li, W., Stephan, F.: Deciding parity games in quasipolynomial time. In: STOC, pp. 252–263. ACM (2017)
7. van Dijk, T.: Oink: an implementation and evaluation of modern parity game solvers. In: TACAS (2018). https://arxiv.org/pdf/1801.03859
8. Emerson, E.A., Jutla, C.S.: Tree automata, mu-calculus and determinacy (extended abstract). In: FOCS, pp. 368–377. IEEE Computer Society (1991)
9. Emerson, E.A., Jutla, C.S., Sistla, A.P.: On model checking for the mu-calculus and its fragments. Theor. Comput. Sci. **258**(1–2), 491–522 (2001)
10. Fearnley, J.: Non-oblivious strategy improvement. In: Clarke, E.M., Voronkov, A. (eds.) LPAR 2010. LNCS (LNAI), vol. 6355, pp. 212–230. Springer, Heidelberg (2010). https://doi.org/10.1007/978-3-642-17511-4_13
11. Fearnley, J.: Efficient parallel strategy improvement for parity games. In: Majumdar, R., Kunčak, V. (eds.) CAV 2017. LNCS, vol. 10427, pp. 137–154. Springer, Cham (2017). https://doi.org/10.1007/978-3-319-63390-9_8
12. Fearnley, J., Jain, S., Schewe, S., Stephan, F., Wojtczak, D.: An ordered approach to solving parity games in quasi polynomial time and quasi linear space. In: SPIN, pp. 112–121. ACM (2017)
13. Friedmann, O., Lange, M.: Solving parity games in practice. In: Liu, Z., Ravn, A.P. (eds.) ATVA 2009. LNCS, vol. 5799, pp. 182–196. Springer, Heidelberg (2009). https://doi.org/10.1007/978-3-642-04761-9_15
14. Gazda, M., Willemse, T.A.C.: Improvement in small progress measures. In: GandALF, EPTCS, vol. 193, pp. 158–171 (2015)
15. Mazala, R.: Infinite games. In: Grädel, E., Thomas, W., Wilke, T. (eds.) Automata Logics, and Infinite Games. LNCS, vol. 2500, pp. 23–38. Springer, Heidelberg (2002). https://doi.org/10.1007/3-540-36387-4_2
16. Jurdziński, M.: Deciding the winner in parity games is in UP ∩ co-UP. Inf. Process. Lett. **68**(3), 119–124 (1998)
17. Jurdziński, M.: Small progress measures for solving parity games. In: Reichel, H., Tison, S. (eds.) STACS 2000. LNCS, vol. 1770, pp. 290–301. Springer, Heidelberg (2000). https://doi.org/10.1007/3-540-46541-3_24

18. Jurdziński, M., Paterson, M., Zwick, U.: A deterministic subexponential algorithm for solving parity games. SIAM J. Comput. **38**(4), 1519–1532 (2008)
19. Keiren, J.J.A.: Benchmarks for parity games. In: Dastani, M., Sirjani, M. (eds.) FSEN 2015. LNCS, vol. 9392, pp. 127–142. Springer, Cham (2015). https://doi.org/10.1007/978-3-319-24644-4_9
20. Kozen, D.: Results on the propositional mu-calculus. Theor. Comput. Sci. **27**, 333–354 (1983)
21. Kupferman, O., Vardi, M.Y.: Weak alternating automata and tree automata emptiness. In: STOC, pp. 224–233. ACM (1998)
22. Schewe, S.: Solving parity games in big steps. J. Comput. Syst. Sci. **84**, 243–262 (2017)
23. Verver, M.: Practical improvements to parity game solving. Master's thesis, University of Twente (2013)
24. Vöge, J., Jurdziński, M.: A discrete strategy improvement algorithm for solving parity games. In: Emerson, E.A., Sistla, A.P. (eds.) CAV 2000. LNCS, vol. 1855, pp. 202–215. Springer, Heidelberg (2000). https://doi.org/10.1007/10722167_18
25. Zielonka, W.: Infinite games on finitely coloured graphs with applications to automata on infinite trees. Theor. Comput. Sci. **200**(1–2), 135–183 (1998)

SAT, SMT and Decision Procedures

Delta-Decision Procedures
for Exists-Forall Problems over the Reals

Soonho Kong[1]($\boxtimes$), Armando Solar-Lezama[2], and Sicun Gao[3]

[1] Toyota Research Institute, Cambridge, USA
soonho.kong@tri.global
[2] Massachusetts Institute of Technology,
Cambridge, USA
asolar@csail.mit.edu
[3] University of California, San Diego, USA
sicung@ucsd.edu

Abstract. We propose δ-complete decision procedures for solving satisfiability of nonlinear SMT problems over real numbers that contain universal quantification and a wide range of nonlinear functions. The methods combine interval constraint propagation, counterexample-guided synthesis, and numerical optimization. In particular, we show how to handle the interleaving of numerical and symbolic computation to ensure delta-completeness in quantified reasoning. We demonstrate that the proposed algorithms can handle various challenging global optimization and control synthesis problems that are beyond the reach of existing solvers.

1 Introduction

Much progress has been made in the framework of delta-decision procedures for solving nonlinear Satisfiability Modulo Theories (SMT) problems over real numbers [1,2]. Delta-decision procedures allow one-sided bounded numerical errors, which is a practically useful relaxation that significantly reduces the computational complexity of the problems. With such relaxation, SMT problems with hundreds of variables and highly nonlinear constraints (such as differential equations) have been solved in practical applications [3]. Existing work in this direction has focused on satisfiability of quantifier-free SMT problems. Going one level up, SMT problems with both free and universally quantified variables, which correspond to $\exists\forall$-formulas over the reals, are much more expressive. For instance, such formulas can encode the search for robust control laws in highly nonlinear dynamical systems, a central problem in robotics. Non-convex, multi-objective, and disjunctive optimization problems can all be encoded as $\exists\forall$-formulas, through the natural definition of "finding some x such that for all other x', x is better than x' with respect to certain constraints." Many other examples from various areas are listed in [4].

Counterexample-Guided Inductive Synthesis (CEGIS) [5] is a framework for program synthesis that can be applied to solve generic exists-forall problems. The

© The Author(s) 2018
H. Chockler and G. Weissenbacher (Eds.): CAV 2018, LNCS 10982, pp. 219–235, 2018.
https://doi.org/10.1007/978-3-319-96142-2_15

idea is to break the process of solving ∃∀-formulas into a loop between *synthesis* and *verification*. The synthesis procedure finds solutions to the existentially quantified variables and gives the solutions to the verifier to see if they can be validated, or falsified by *counterexamples*. The counterexamples are then used as learned constraints for the synthesis procedure to find new solutions. This method has been shown effective for many challenging problems, frequently generating more optimized programs than the best manual implementations [5].

A direct application of CEGIS to decision problems over real numbers, however, suffers from several problems. CEGIS is complete in finite domains because it can explicitly enumerate solutions, which can not be done in continuous domains. Also, CEGIS ensures progress by avoiding duplication of solutions, while due to numerical sensitivity, precise control over real numbers is difficult. In this paper we propose methods that bypass such difficulties.

We propose an integration of the CEGIS method in the branch-and-prune framework as a generic algorithm for solving nonlinear ∃∀-formulas over real numbers and prove that the algorithm is δ-complete. We achieve this goal by using CEGIS-based methods for turning universally-quantified constraints into pruning operators, which is then used in the branch-and-prune framework for the search for solutions on the existentially-quantified variables. In doing so, we take special care to ensure correct handling of numerical errors in the computation, so that δ-completeness can be established for the whole procedure.

The paper is organized as follows. We first review the background, and then present the details of the main algorithm in Sect. 3. We then give a rigorous proof of the δ-completeness of the procedure in Sect. 4. We demonstrated the effectiveness of the procedures on various global optimization and Lyapunov function synthesis problems in Sect. 5.

Related Work. Quantified formulas in real arithmetic can be solved using symbolic quantifier elimination (using cylindrical decomposition [6]), which is known to have impractically high complexity (double exponential [7]), and can not handle problems with transcendental functions. State-of-the-art SMT solvers such as CVC4 [8] and Z3 [9] provide quantifier support [10–13] but they are limited to decidable fragments of first-order logic. Optimization Modulo Theories (OMT) is a new field that focuses on solving a restricted form of quantified reasoning [14–16], focusing on linear formulas. Generic approaches to solving exists-forall problems such as [17] are generally based on CEGIS framework, and not intended to achieve completeness. Solving quantified constraints has been explored in the constraint solving community [18]. In general, existing work has not proposed algorithms that intend to achieve any notion of completeness for quantified problems in nonlinear theories over the reals.

2   Preliminaries

2.1   Delta-Decisions and CNF$^\forall$-Formulas

We consider first-order formulas over real numbers that can contain arbitrary nonlinear functions that can be numerically approximated, such as polynomials, exponential, and trignometric functions. Theoretically, such functions are called *Type-2 computable* functions [19]. We write this language as $\mathcal{L}_{\mathbb{R}_{\mathcal{F}}}$, formally defined as:

Definition 1 (The $\mathcal{L}_{\mathbb{R}_{\mathcal{F}}}$ Language). *Let $\mathcal{F}$ be the set of Type-2 computable functions. We define $\mathcal{L}_{\mathbb{R}_{\mathcal{F}}}$ to be the following first-order language:*

$$t := x \mid f(t), \text{ where } f \in \mathcal{F}, \text{ possibly 0-ary (constant)};$$
$$\varphi := t(\boldsymbol{x}) > 0 \mid t(\boldsymbol{x}) \geq 0 \mid \varphi \wedge \varphi \mid \varphi \vee \varphi \mid \exists x_i \varphi \mid \forall x_i \varphi.$$

Remark 1. Negations are not needed as part of the base syntax, as it can be defined through arithmetic: $\neg(t > 0)$ is simply $-t \geq 0$. Similarly, an equality $t = 0$ is just $t \geq 0 \wedge -t \geq 0$. In this way we can put the formulas in normal forms that are easy to manipulate.

We will focus on the $\exists\forall$-formulas in $\mathcal{L}_{\mathbb{R}_{\mathcal{F}}}$ in this paper. Decision problems for such formulas are equivalent to satisfiability of SMT with universally quantified variables, whose free variables are implicitly existentially quantified.

It is clear that, when the quantifier-free part of an $\exists\forall$ formula is in Conjunctive Normal Form (CNF), we can always push the universal quantifiers inside each conjunct, since universal quantification commute with conjunctions. Thus the decision problem for any $\exists\forall$-formula is equivalent to the satisfiability of formulas in the following normal form:

Definition 2 (CNF$^\forall$ Formulas in $\mathcal{L}_{\mathbb{R}_{\mathcal{F}}}$). *We say an $\mathcal{L}_{\mathbb{R}_{\mathcal{F}}}$-formula φ is in the CNF$^\forall$, if it is of the form*

$$. \varphi(\boldsymbol{x}) := \bigwedge_{i=0}^{m} \left(\forall \boldsymbol{y} (\bigvee_{j=0}^{k_i} c_{ij}(\boldsymbol{x}, \boldsymbol{y})) \right) \tag{1}$$

where c_{ij} are atomic constraints. Each universally quantified conjunct of the formula, i.e.,

$$\forall \boldsymbol{y} (\bigvee_{j=0}^{k_i} c_{ij}(\boldsymbol{x}, \boldsymbol{y}))$$

*is called as a $\forall$-**clause**. Note that $\forall$-clauses only contain disjunctions and no nested conjunctions. If all the $\forall$-clauses are vacuous, we say $\varphi(\boldsymbol{x})$ is a ground SMT formula.*

The algorithms described in this paper will assume that an input formula is in CNF$^\forall$ form. We can now define the δ-*satisfiability* problems for CNF$^\forall$-formulas.

Definition 3 (Delta-Weakening/Strengthening). *Let $\delta \in \mathbb{Q}^+$ be arbitrary. Consider an arbitrary CNF$^\forall$-formula of the form*

$$\varphi(\boldsymbol{x}) := \bigwedge_{i=0}^{m} \left(\forall \boldsymbol{y} (\bigvee_{j=0}^{k_i} f_{ij}(\boldsymbol{x}, \boldsymbol{y}) \circ 0) \right)$$

where $\circ \in \{>, \geq\}$. *We define the* δ-*weakening of* $\varphi(\boldsymbol{x})$ *to be:*

$$\varphi^{-\delta}(\boldsymbol{x}) := \bigwedge_{i=0}^{m} \left(\forall \boldsymbol{y} (\bigvee_{j=0}^{k_i} f_{ij}(\boldsymbol{x}, \boldsymbol{y}) \geq -\delta) \right).$$

Namely, we weaken the right-hand sides of all atomic formulas from 0 *to* $-\delta$. *Note how the difference between strict and nonstrict inequality becomes unimportant in the* δ-*weakening. We also define its dual, the* δ-*strengthening of* $\varphi(\boldsymbol{x})$:

$$\varphi^{+\delta}(\boldsymbol{x}) := \bigwedge_{i=0}^{m} \left(\forall \boldsymbol{y} (\bigvee_{j=0}^{k_i} f_{ij}(\boldsymbol{x}, \boldsymbol{y}) \geq +\delta) \right).$$

Since the formulas in the normal form no longer contain negations, the relaxation on the atomic formulas is implied by the original formula (and thus weaker), as was easily shown in [1].

Proposition 1. *For any* φ *and* $\delta \in \mathbb{Q}^+$, $\varphi^{-\delta}$ *is logically weaker, in the sense that* $\varphi \to \varphi^{-\delta}$ *is always true, but not vice versa.*

Example 1. Consider the formula

$$\forall y \, f(x, y) = 0.$$

It is equivalent to the $\mathrm{CNF}^\forall$-formula

$$(\forall y(-f(x, y) \geq 0) \wedge \forall y(f(x, y) \geq 0))$$

whose δ-weakening is of the form

$$(\forall y(-f(x, y) \geq -\delta) \wedge \forall y(f(x, y) \geq -\delta))$$

which is logically equivalent to

$$\forall y(\|f(x, y)\| \leq \delta).$$

We see that the weakening of $f(x, y) = 0$ by $\|f(x, y)\| \leq \delta$ defines a natural relaxation.

Definition 4 (Delta-Completeness). *Let* $\delta \in \mathbb{Q}^+$ *be arbitrary. We say an algorithm is* δ-*complete for* $\exists \forall$-*formulas in* $\mathcal{L}_{\mathbb{R}_{\mathcal{F}}}$, *if for any input* $\mathrm{CNF}^\forall$-*formula* φ, *it always terminates and returns one of the following answers correctly:*

- **unsat:** φ *is unsatisfiable.*
- δ-**sat:** $\varphi^{-\delta}$ *is satisfiable.*

When the two cases overlap, it can return either answer.

Algorithm 1. Branch-and-Prune

1: **function** SOLVE($f(x) = 0$, B_x, δ)
2:     $S \leftarrow \{B_x\}$
3:     **while** $S \neq \emptyset$ **do**
4:         $B \leftarrow S.\text{pop}()$
5:         $B' \leftarrow \text{FixedPoint}\Big(\lambda B.B \cap \text{Prune}(B, f(x) = 0), B\Big)$
6:         **if** $B' \neq \emptyset$ **then**
7:             **if** $\|f(B')\| > \delta$ **then**
8:                 $\{B_1, B_2\} \leftarrow \text{Branch}(B')$
9:                 $S.\text{push}(\{B_1, B_2\})$
10:             **else**
11:                 **return** δ-**sat**
12:             **end if**
13:         **end if**
14:     **end while**
15:     **return unsat**
16: **end function**

2.2   The Branch-and-Prune Framework

A practical algorithm that has been shown to be δ-complete for ground SMT formulas is the *branch-and-prune* method developed for interval constraint propagation [20]. A description of the algorithm in the simple case of an equality constraint is in Algorithm 1.

The procedure combines *pruning* and *branching* operations. Let $\mathcal{B}$ be the set of all boxes (each variable assigned to an interval), and $\mathcal{C}$ a set of constraints in the language. FixedPoint(g, B) is a procedure computing a fixedpoint of a function $g : \mathcal{B} \to \mathcal{B}$ with an initial input B. A pruning operation Prune : $\mathcal{B} \times \mathcal{C} \to \mathcal{B}$ takes a box $B \in \mathcal{B}$ and a constraint as input, and returns an ideally smaller box $B' \in \mathcal{B}$ (Line 5) that is guaranteed to still keep all solutions for all constraints if there is any. When such pruning operations do not make progress, the Branch procedure picks a variable, divides its interval by halves, and creates two sub-problems B_1 and B_2 (Line 8). The procedure terminates if either all boxes have been pruned to be empty (Line 15), or if a small box whose maximum width is smaller than a given threshold δ has been found (Line 11). In [2], it has been proved that Algorithm 1 is δ-complete iff the pruning operators satisfy certain conditions for being *well-defined* (Definition 5).

3   Algorithm

The core idea of our algorithm for solving $\text{CNF}^\forall$-formulas is as follows. We view the universally quantified constraints as a special type of pruning operators, which can be used to reduce possible values for the free variables based on their consistency with the universally-quantified variables. We then use these special $\forall$-pruning operators in an overall branch-and-prune framework to solve the full formula in a δ-complete way. A special technical difficulty for ensuring δ-completeness is to control numerical errors in the recursive search for counterexamples, which we solve using *double-sided error control*. We also improve quality of counterexamples using local-optimization algorithms in the $\forall$-pruning operations, which we call *locally-optimized counterexamples*.

In the following sections we describe these steps in detail. For notational simplicity we will omit vector symbols and assume all variable names can directly refer to vectors of variables.

3.1 $\forall$-Clauses as Pruning Operators

Consider an arbitrary CNF$^\forall$-formula[1]

$$\varphi(x) := \bigwedge_{i=0}^{m} \left(\forall y \left(\bigvee_{j=0}^{k_i} f_{ij}(x,y) \geq 0 \right) \right).$$

It is a conjunction of $\forall$-clauses as defined in Definition 2. Consequently, we only need to define pruning operators for $\forall$-clauses so that they can be used in a standard branch-and-prune framework. The full algorithm for such pruning operation is described in Algorithm 2.

Algorithm 2. $\forall$-Clause Pruning

1: **function** $\text{PRUNE}(B_x, B_y, \forall y \bigvee_{i=0}^{k} f_i(x,y) \geq 0, \delta', \varepsilon, \delta)$
2:     **repeat**
3:         $B_x^{\text{prev}} \leftarrow B_x$
4:         $\psi \leftarrow \bigwedge_i f_i(x,y) < 0$
5:         $\psi^{+\varepsilon} \leftarrow \text{Strengthen}(\psi, \varepsilon)$
6:         $b \leftarrow \text{Solve}(y, \psi^{+\varepsilon}, \delta')$ ▷ $0 < \delta' < \varepsilon < \delta$ should hold.
7:         **if** $b = \emptyset$ **then**
8:             **return** B_x ▷ No counterexample found, stop pruning.
9:         **end if**
10:        **for** $i \in \{0, ..., k\}$ **do**
11:            $B_i \leftarrow B_x \cap \text{Prune}\Big(B_x, f_i(x,b) \geq 0\Big)$
12:        **end for**
13:        $B_x \leftarrow \bigsqcup_{i=0}^{k} B_i$
14:    **until** $B_x \neq B_x^{\text{prev}}$
15:    **return** B_x
16: **end function**

In Algorithm 2, the basic idea is to use special y values that witness the *negation* of the original constraint to prune the box assignment on x. The two core steps are as follows.

---

[1] Note that without loss of generality we only use nonstrict inequality here, since in the context of δ-decisions the distinction between strict and nonstrict inequalities as not important, as explained in Definition 3.

1. Counterexample generation (Line 4 to 9). The query for a counterexample ψ is defined as the negation of the quantifier-free part of the constraint (Line 4). The method $\mathsf{Solve}(y, \psi, \delta)$ means to obtain a solution for the variables y δ-satisfying the logic formula ψ. When such a solution is found, we have a counterexample that can falsify the $\forall$-clause on some choice of x. Then we use this counterexample to prune on the domain of x, which is currently B_x. The strengthening operation on ψ (Line 5), as well as the choices of ε and δ', will be explained in the next subsection.
2. Pruning on x (Line 10 to 13). In the counterexample generation step, we have obtained a counterexample b. The pruning operation then uses this value to prune on the current box domain B_x. Here we need to be careful about the logical operations. For each constraint, we need to take the intersection of the pruned results on the counterexample point (Line 11). Then since the original clause contains the disjunction of all constraints, we need to take the box-hull ($\bigsqcup$) of the pruned results (Line 13).

We can now put the pruning operators defined for all $\forall$-clauses in the overall branch-and-prune framework shown in Algorithm 1.

The pruning algorithms are inspired by the CEGIS loop, but are different in multiple ways. First, we never explicitly compute any candidate solution for the free variables. Instead, we only prune on their domain boxes. This ensures that the size of domain box decreases (together with branching operations), and the algorithm terminates. Secondly, we do not explicitly maintain a collection of constraints. Each time the pruning operation works on previous box – i.e., the learning is done on the model level instead of constraint level. On the other hand, being unable to maintain arbitrary Boolean combinations of constraints requires us to be more sensitive to the type of Boolean operations needed in the pruning results, which is different from the CEGIS approach that treats solvers as black boxes.

3.2   Double-Sided Error Control

To ensure the correctness of Algorithm 2, it is necessary to avoid spurious counterexamples which do *not* satisfy the negation of the quantified part in a $\forall$-clause. We illustrate this condition by consider a *wrong* derivation of Algorithm 2 where we do not have the strengthening operation on Line 5 and try to find a counterexample by directly executing $b \leftarrow \mathsf{Solve}(y, \psi = \bigwedge_{i=0}^{k} f_i(x, y) < 0, \delta)$. Note that the counterexample query ψ can be highly nonlinear in general and not included in a decidable fragment. As a result, it must employ a delta-decision procedure (i.e. Solve with $\delta' \in \mathbb{Q}^+$) to find a counterexample. A consequence of relying on a delta-decision procedure in the counterexample generation step is that we may obtain a spurious counterexample b such that for some $x = a$:

$$\bigwedge_{i=0}^{k} f_i(a, b) \leq \delta \quad \text{instead of} \quad \bigwedge_{i=0}^{k} f_i(a, b) < 0.$$

Consequently the following pruning operations fail to reduce their input boxes because a spurious counterexample does not witness any inconsistencies between x and y. As a result, the fixedpoint loop in this $\forall$-Clause pruning algorithm will be terminated immediately after the first iteration. This makes the outermost branch-and-prune framework (Algorithm 1), which employs this pruning algorithm, solely rely on branching operations. It can claim that the problem is δ-satisfiable while providing an arbitrary box B as a model which is small enough ($\|B\| \leq \delta$) but does not include a δ-solution.

To avoid spurious counterexamples, we directly strengthen the counterexample query with $\varepsilon \in \mathbb{Q}^+$ to have

$$\psi^{+\varepsilon} := \bigwedge_{i=0}^{k} f_i(a, b) \leq -\varepsilon.$$

Then we choose a weakening parameter $\delta' \in \mathbb{Q}$ in solving the strengthened formula. By analyzing the two possible outcomes of this counterexample search, we show the constraints on δ', ε, and δ which guarantee the correctness of Algorithm 2:

- δ'-**sat case:** We have a and b such that $\bigwedge_{i=0}^{k} f_i(a, b) \leq -\varepsilon + \delta'$. For $y = b$ to be a valid counterexample, we need $-\varepsilon + \delta' < 0$. That is, we have

$$\delta' < \varepsilon. \tag{2}$$

  In other words, the strengthening factor ε should be greater than the weakening parameter δ' in the counterexample search step.
- **unsat case:** By checking the absence of counterexamples, it proved that $\forall y \bigvee_{i=0}^{k} f_i(x, y) \geq -\varepsilon$ for all $x \in B_x$. Recall that we want to show that $\forall y \bigvee_{i=0}^{k} f_i(x, y) \geq -\delta$ holds for some $x = a$ when Algorithm 1 uses this pruning algorithm and returns δ-sat. To ensure this property, we need the following constraint on ε and δ:

$$\varepsilon < \delta. \tag{3}$$

3.3 Locally-Optimized Counterexamples

The performance of the pruning algorithm for $CNF^{\forall}$-formulas depends on the quality of the counterexamples found during the search.

Figure 1a illustrates this point by visualizing a pruning process for an unconstrained minimization problem, $\exists x \in X_0 \forall y \in X_0 f(x) \leq f(y)$. As it finds a series of counterexamples CE_1, CE_2, CE_3, and CE_4, the pruning algorithms uses those counterexamples to contract the interval assignment on X from X_0 to X_1, X_2, X_3, and X_4 in sequence. In the search for a counterexample (Line 6 of Algorithm 2), it solves the strengthened query, $f(x) > f(y) + \delta$. Note that the query only requires a counterexample $y = b$ to be δ-away from a candidate x while it is clear that the further a counterexample is away from candidates, the more effective the pruning algorithm is.

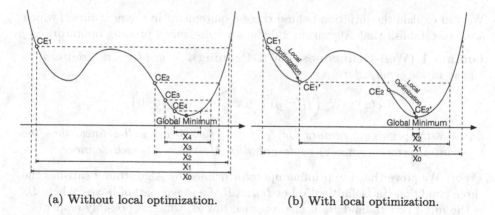

(a) Without local optimization.   (b) With local optimization.

Fig. 1. Illustrations of the pruning algorithm for CNF$^\forall$-formula with and without using local optimization.

Based on this observation, we present a way to improve the performance of the pruning algorithm for CNF$^\forall$-formulas. After we obtain a counterexample b, we locally-optimize it with the counterexample query ψ so that it "further violates" the constraints. Figure 1b illustrates this idea. The algorithm first finds a counterexample CE_1 then refines it to CE_1' by using a local-optimization algorithm (similarly, $CE_2 \to CE_2'$). Clearly, this refined counterexample gives a stronger pruning power than the original one. This refinement process can also help the performance of the algorithm by reducing the number of total iterations in the fixedpoint loop.

The suggested method is based on the assumption that local-optimization techniques are cheaper than finding a global counterexample using interval propagation techniques. In our experiments, we observed that this assumption holds practically. We will report the details in Sect. 5.

4 δ-Completeness

We now prove that the proposed algorithm is δ-complete for arbitrary CNF$^\forall$ formulas in $\mathcal{L}_{\mathbb{R}_\mathcal{F}}$. In the work of [2], δ-completeness has been proved for branch-and-prune for ground SMT problems, under the assumption that the pruning operators are *well-defined*. Thus, the key for our proof here is to show that the $\forall$-pruning operators satisfy the conditions of well-definedness.

The notion of a well-defined pruning operator is defined in [2] as follows.

Definition 5. *Let ϕ be a constraint, and $\mathcal{B}$ be the set of all boxes in $\mathbb{R}^n$. A pruning operator is a function $\mathsf{Prune} : \mathcal{B} \times \mathcal{C} \to \mathcal{B}$. We say such a pruning operator is well-defined, if for any $B \in \mathcal{B}$, the following conditions are true:*

1. $\mathsf{Prune}(B, \phi) \subseteq B$.
2. $B \cap \{a \in \mathbb{R}^n : \phi(a) \text{ is true.}\} \subseteq \mathsf{Prune}(B, \phi)$.
3. *Write $\mathsf{Prune}(B, \phi) = B'$. There exists a constant $c \in \mathbb{Q}^+$, such that, if $B' \neq \emptyset$ and $\|B'\| < \varepsilon$ for some $\varepsilon \in \mathbb{Q}^+$, then for all $a \in B'$, $\phi^{-c\varepsilon}(a)$ is true.*

We will explain the intuition behind these requirements in the next proof, which aims to establish that Algorithm 2 defines a well-defined pruning operator.

Lemma 1 (Well-Definedness of ∀-Pruning). *Consider an arbitrary ∀-clause in the generic form*

$$c(x) := \forall y \Big(f_1(x, y) \geq 0 \vee \ldots \vee f_k(x, y) \geq 0 \Big).$$

Suppose the pruning operators for $f_1 \geq 0, \ldots, f_k \geq 0$ are well-defined, then the ∀-pruning operation for $c(x)$ as described in Algorithm 2 is well-defined.

Proof. We prove that the pruning operator defined by Algorithm 2 satisfies the three conditions in Definition 5. Let $B_0, \ldots, B_k$ be a sequence of boxes, where B_0 is the input box B_x and B_k is the returned box B, which is possibly empty.

The first condition requires that the pruning operation for $c(x)$ is reductive. That is, we want to show that $B_x \subseteq B_x^{\mathrm{prev}}$ holds in Algorithm 2. If it does not find a counterexample (Line 8), we have $B_x = B_x^{\mathrm{prev}}$. So the condition holds trivially. Consider the case where it finds a counterexample b. The pruned box B_x is obtained through box-hull of all the B_i boxes (Line 13), which are results of pruning on B_x^{prev} using ordinary constraints of the form $f_i(x, b) \geq 0$ (Line 11), for a counterexample b. Following the assumption that the pruning operators are well-defined for each ordinary constraint f_i used in the algorithm, we know that $B_i \subseteq B_x^{\mathrm{prev}}$ holds as a loop invariant for the loop from Line 10 to Line 12. Thus, taking the box-hull of all the B_i, we obtain B_x that is still a subset of B_x^{prev}.

The second condition requires that the pruning operation does not eliminate real solutions. Again, by the assumption that the pruning operation on Line 11 does not lose any valid assignment on x that makes the ∀-clause true. In fact, since y is universally quantified, any choice of assignment $y = b$ will preserve solution on x as long as the ordinary pruning operator is well-defined. Thus, this condition is easily satisfied.

The third condition is the most nontrivial to establish. It ensures that when the pruning operator does not prune a box to the empty set, then the box should not be "way off", and in fact, should contain points that satisfy an appropriate relaxation of the constraint. We can say this is a notion of "faithfulness" of the pruning operator. For constraints defined by simple continuous functions, this can be typically guaranteed by the modulus of continuity of the function (Lipschitz constants as a special case). Now, in the case of ∀-clause pruning, we need to prove that the faithfulness of the ordinary pruning operators that are used translates to the faithfulness of the ∀-clause pruning results. First of all, this condition would not hold, if we do not have the strengthening operation when searching for counterexamples (Line 5). As is shown in Example 1, because of the weakening that δ-decisions introduce when searching for a counterexample, we may obtain a *spurious counterexample* that does not have pruning power. In other words, if we keep using a wrong counterexample that already satisfies the condition, then we are not able to rule out wrong assignments on x. Now, since we have introduced ε-strengthening at the counterexample search, we know that b obtained on Line 6 is a true counterexample. Thus, for some $x = a$, $f_i(a, b) < 0$

for every i. By assumption, the ordinary pruning operation using b on Line 11 guarantees faithfulness. That is, suppose the pruned result B_i is not empty and $\|B_i\| \leq \varepsilon$, then there exists constant c_i such that $f_i(x, b) \geq -c_i\varepsilon$ is true. Thus, we can take the $c = \min_i c_i$ as the constant for the pruning operator defined by the full clause, and conclude that the disjunction $\bigvee_{i=0}^{k} f_i(x, y) < -c\varepsilon$ holds for $\|B_x\| \leq \varepsilon$.

Using the lemma, we follow the results in [2], and conclude that the branch-and-prune method in Algorithm 1 is delta-complete:

Theorem 1 (δ-Completeness). *For any $\delta \in \mathbb{Q}^+$, using the proposed $\forall$-pruning operators defined in Algorithm 2 in the branch-and-prune framework described in Algorithm 1 is δ-complete for the class of $CNF^\forall$-formulas in $\mathcal{L}_{\mathbb{R}_\mathcal{F}}$, assuming that the pruning operators for all the base functions are well-defined.*

Proof. Following Theorem 4.2 (δ-Completeness of ICP_ε) in [2], a branch-and-prune algorithm is δ-complete iff the pruning operators in the algorithm are all well-defined. Following Lemma 1, Algorithm 2 always defines well-defined pruning operators, assuming the pruning operators for the base functions are well-defined. Consequently, Algorithms 2 and 1 together define a delta-complete decision procedure for $CNF^\forall$-problems in $\mathcal{L}_{\mathbb{R}_\mathcal{F}}$.

5   Evaluation

Implementation. We implemented the algorithms on top of dReal [21], an open-source delta-SMT framework. We used IBEX-lib [22] for interval constraints pruning and CLP [23] for linear programming. For local optimization, we used NLopt [24]. In particular, we used SLSQP (Sequential Least-Squares Quadratic Programming) local-optimization algorithm [25] for differentiable constraints and COBYLA (Constrained Optimization BY Linear Approximations) local-optimization algorithm [26] for non-differentiable constraints. The prototype solver is able to handle $\exists\forall$-formulas that involve most standard elementary functions, including power, exp, log, $\sqrt{\cdot}$, trigonometric functions (sin, cos, tan), inverse trigonometric functions (arcsin, arccos, arctan), hyperbolic functions (sinh, cosh, tanh), etc.

Experiment environment. All experiments were ran on a 2017 Macbook Pro with 2.9 GHz Intel Core i7 and 16 GB RAM running MacOS 10.13.4. All code and benchmarks are available at https://github.com/dreal/CAV18.

Parameters. In the experiments, we chose the strengthening parameter $\epsilon = 0.99\delta$ and the weakening parameter in the counterexample search $\delta' = 0.98\delta$. In each call to NLopt, we used 1e–6 for both of absolute and relative tolerances on function value, 1e–3 s for a timeout, and 100 for the maximum number of evaluations. These values are used as stopping criteria in NLopt.

Table 1. Experimental results for nonlinear global optimization problems: The first 19 problems (Ackley 2D – Zettl) are unconstrained optimization problems and the last five problems (Rosenbrock Cubic – Simionescu) are constrained optimization problems. We ran our prototype solver over those instances with and without local-optimization option ("L-Opt." and "No L-Opt." columns) and compared the results. We chose $\delta = 0.0001$ for all instances.

Name	Solution			Time (sec)		
	Global	No L-Opt.	L-Opt.	No L-Opt.	L-Opt.	Speed up
Ackley 2D	0.00000	0.00000	0.00000	0.0579	0.0047	12.32
Ackley 4D	0.00000	0.00005	0.00000	8.2256	0.1930	42.62
Aluffi Pentini	−0.35230	−0.35231	−0.35239	0.0321	0.1868	0.17
Beale	0.00000	0.00003	0.00000	0.0317	0.0615	0.52
Bohachevsky1	0.00000	0.00006	0.00000	0.0094	0.0020	4.70
Booth	0.00000	0.00006	0.00000	0.5035	0.0020	251.75
Brent	0.00000	0.00006	0.00000	0.0095	0.0017	5.59
Bukin6	0.00000	0.00003	0.00003	0.0093	0.0083	1.12
Cross in tray	−2.06261	−2.06254	−2.06260	0.5669	0.1623	3.49
Easom	−1.00000	−1.00000	−1.00000	0.0061	0.0030	2.03
EggHolder	−959.64070	−959.64030	−959.64031	0.0446	0.0211	2.11
Holder Table 2	−19.20850	−19.20846	−19.20845	52.9152	41.7004	1.27
Levi N13	0.00000	0.00000	0.00000	0.1383	0.0034	40.68
Ripple 1	−2.20000	−2.20000	−2.20000	0.0059	0.0065	0.91
Schaffer F6	0.00000	0.00004	0.00000	0.0531	0.0056	9.48
Testtube holder	−10.87230	−10.87227	−10.87230	0.0636	0.0035	18.17
Trefethen	−3.30687	−3.30681	−3.30685	3.0689	1.4916	2.06
W Wavy	0.00000	0.00000	0.00000	0.1234	0.0138	8.94
Zettl	−0.00379	−0.00375	−0.00379	0.0070	0.0069	1.01
Rosenbrock Cubic	0.00000	0.00005	0.00002	0.0045	0.0036	1.25
Rosenbrock Disk	0.00000	0.00002	0.00000	0.0036	0.0028	1.29
Mishra Bird	−106.76454	−106.76449	−106.76451	1.8496	0.9122	2.03
Townsend	−2.02399	−2.02385	−2.02390	2.6216	0.5817	4.51
Simionescu	−0.07262	−0.07199	−0.07200	0.0064	0.0048	1.33

5.1 Nonlinear Global Optimization

We encoded a range of highly nonlinear $\exists\forall$-problems from constrained and unconstrained optimization literature [27, 28]. Note that the standard optimization problem

$$\min f(x) \text{ s.t. } \varphi(x), \quad x \in \mathbb{R}^n,$$

can be encoded as the logic formula:

$$\varphi(x) \wedge \forall y \Big(\varphi(y) \rightarrow f(x) \leq f(y) \Big).$$

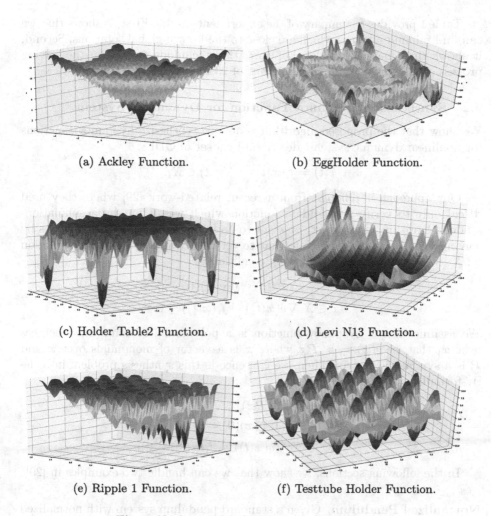

(a) Ackley Function.

(b) EggHolder Function.

(c) Holder Table2 Function.

(d) Levi N13 Function.

(e) Ripple 1 Function.

(f) Testtube Holder Function.

Fig. 2. Nonlinear global optimization examples.

As plotted in Fig. 2, these optimization problems are non-trivial: they are highly non-convex problems that are designed to test global optimization or genetic programming algorithms. Many such functions have a large number of local minima. For example, Ripple 1 Function [27].

$$f(x_1, x_2) = \sum_{i=1}^{2} -e^{-2(\log 2)\left(\frac{x_1 - 0.1}{0.8}\right)^2} (\sin^6(5\pi x_i) + 0.1\cos^2(500\pi x_i))$$

defined in $x_i \in [0, 1]$ has 252004 local minima with the global minima $f(0.1, 0.1) = -2.2$. As a result, local-optimization algorithms such as gradient-descent would not work for these problems for itself. By encoding them as $\exists\forall$-problems, we can perform guaranteed global optimization on these problems.

Table 1 provides a summary of the experiment results. First, it shows that we can find minimum values which are close to the known global solutions. Second, it shows that enabling the local-optimization technique speeds up the solving process significantly for 20 instances out of 23 instances.

5.2 Synthesizing Lyapunov Function for Dynamical System

We show that the proposed algorithm is able to synthesize Lyapunov functions for nonlinear dynamic systems described by a set of ODEs:

$$\dot{x}(t) = f_i(x(t)), \quad \forall x(t) \in X_i.$$

Our approach is different from a recent related-work [29] where they used dReal only to verify a candidate function which was found by a simulation-guided algorithm. In contrast, we want to do both of search and verify steps by solving a single $\exists\forall$-formula. Note that to verify a Lyapunov candidate function $v : X \to \mathbb{R}^+$, v satisfies the following conditions:

$$\forall x \in X \setminus 0 \ v(x)(0) = 0$$
$$\forall x \in X \ \nabla v(x(t))^T \cdot f_i(x(t)) \leq 0.$$

We assume that a Lyapunov function is a polynomial of some fixed degrees over x, that is, $v(x) = z^T P z$ where z is a vector of monomials over x and P is a symmetric matrix. Then, we can encode this synthesis problem into the $\exists\forall$-formula:

$$\exists P \ [(v(x) = (z^T P z)) \wedge$$
$$(\forall x \in X \setminus 0 \ v(x)(0) = 0) \wedge$$
$$(\forall x \in X \ \nabla v(x(t))^T \cdot f_i(x(t)) \leq 0)]$$

In the following sections, we show that we can handle two examples in [29].

Normalized Pendulum. Given a standard pendulum system with normalized parameters

$$\begin{bmatrix} \dot{x}_1 \\ \dot{x}_2 \end{bmatrix} = \begin{bmatrix} x_2 \\ -\sin(x_1) - x_2 \end{bmatrix}$$

and a quadratic template for a Lyapunov function $v(x) = x^T P x = c_1 x_1 x_2 + c_2 x_1^2 + c_3 x_2^2$, we can encode this synthesis problem into the following $\exists\forall$-formula:

$$\exists c_1 c_2 c_3 \ \forall x_1 x_2 \ [((50 c_3 x_1 x_2 + 50 x_1^2 c_1 + 50 x_2^2 c_2 > 0.5) \wedge$$
$$(100 c_1 x_1 x_2 + 50 x_2 c_3 + (-x_2 - \sin(x_1)(50 x_1 c_3 + 100 x_2 c_2)) < -0.5)) \vee$$
$$\neg((0.01 \leq x_1^2 + x_2^2) \wedge (x_1^2 + x_2^2 \leq 1))]$$

Our prototype solver takes 44.184 s to synthesize the following function as a solution to the problem for the bound $\|x\| \in [0.1, 1.0]$ and $c_i \in [0.1, 100]$ using $\delta = 0.05$:

$$v = 40.6843 x_1 x_2 + 35.6870 x_1^2 + 84.3906 x_2^2.$$

Damped Mathieu System. Mathieu dynamics are time-varying and defined by the following ODEs:

$$\begin{bmatrix} \dot{x}_1 \\ \dot{x}_2 \end{bmatrix} = \begin{bmatrix} x_2 \\ -x_2 - (2 + \sin(t))x_1 \end{bmatrix}.$$

Using a quadratic template for a Lyapunov function $v(x) = x^T P x = c_1 x_1 x_2 + c_2 x_1^2 + c_3 x_2^2$, we can encode this synthesis problem into the following $\exists\forall$-formula:

$$\exists c_1 c_2 c_3 \, \forall x_1 x_2 t \, [(50 x_1 x_2 c_2 + 50 x_1^2 c_1 + 50 x_2^2 c_3 > 0) \wedge$$
$$(100 c_1 x_1 x_2 + 50 x_2 c_2 + (-x_2 - x_1(2 + \sin(t)))(50 x_1 c_2 + 100 x_2 c_3) < 0)$$
$$\vee \neg((0.01 \le x_1^2 + x_2^2) \wedge (0.1 \le t) \wedge (t \le 1) \wedge (x_1^2 + x_2^2 \le 1))]$$

Our prototype solver takes $26.533\,\mathrm{s}$ to synthesize the following function as a solution to the problem for the bound $\|x\| \in [0.1, 1.0]$, $t \in [0.1, 1.0]$, and $c_i \in [45, 98]$ using $\delta = 0.05$:

$$V = 54.6950 x_1 x_2 + 90.2849 x_1^2 + 50.5376 x_2^2.$$

6   Conclusion

We have described delta-decision procedures for solving exists-forall formulas in the first-order theory over the reals with computable real functions. These formulas can encode a wide range of hard practical problems such as general constrained optimization and nonlinear control synthesis. We use a branch-and-prune framework, and design special pruning operators for universally-quantified constraints such that the procedures can be proved to be delta-complete, where suitable control of numerical errors is crucial. We demonstrated the effectiveness of the procedures on various global optimization and Lyapunov function synthesis problems.

References

1. Gao, S., Avigad, J., Clarke, E.M.: Delta-decidability over the reals. In: LICS, pp. 305–314 (2012)
2. Gao, S., Avigad, J., Clarke, E.M.: δ-complete decision procedures for satisfiability over the reals. In: Gramlich, B., Miller, D., Sattler, U. (eds.) IJCAR 2012. LNCS (LNAI), vol. 7364, pp. 286–300. Springer, Heidelberg (2012). https://doi.org/10.1007/978-3-642-31365-3_23
3. Kong, S., Gao, S., Chen, W., Clarke, E.: dReach: δ-reachability analysis for hybrid systems. In: Baier, C., Tinelli, C. (eds.) TACAS 2015. LNCS, vol. 9035, pp. 200–205. Springer, Heidelberg (2015). https://doi.org/10.1007/978-3-662-46681-0_15
4. Ratschan, S.: Applications of quantified constraint solving over the reals-bibliography. arXiv preprint arXiv:1205.5571 (2012)

5. Solar-Lezama, A.: Program Synthesis by Sketching. University of California, Berkeley (2008)
6. Collins, G.E.: Hauptvortrag: quantifier elimination for real closed fields by cylindrical algebraic decomposition. In: Automata Theory and Formal Languages, pp. 134–183 (1975)
7. Brown, C.W., Davenport, J.H.: The complexity of quantifier elimination and cylindrical algebraic decomposition. In: ISSAC-2007 (2007)
8. Barrett, C., et al.: CVC4. In: Gopalakrishnan, G., Qadeer, S. (eds.) CAV 2011. LNCS, vol. 6806, pp. 171–177. Springer, Heidelberg (2011). https://doi.org/10.1007/978-3-642-22110-1_14
9. de Moura, L., Bjørner, N.: Z3: an efficient SMT solver. In: Ramakrishnan, C.R., Rehof, J. (eds.) TACAS 2008. LNCS, vol. 4963, pp. 337–340. Springer, Heidelberg (2008). https://doi.org/10.1007/978-3-540-78800-3_24
10. de Moura, L., Bjørner, N.: Efficient e-matching for SMT solvers. In: Pfenning, F. (ed.) CADE 2007. LNCS (LNAI), vol. 4603, pp. 183–198. Springer, Heidelberg (2007). https://doi.org/10.1007/978-3-540-73595-3_13
11. Bjørner, N., Phan, A.-D., Fleckenstein, L.: νZ - an optimizing SMT solver. In: Baier, C., Tinelli, C. (eds.) TACAS 2015. LNCS, vol. 9035, pp. 194–199. Springer, Heidelberg (2015). https://doi.org/10.1007/978-3-662-46681-0_14
12. Ge, Y., Barrett, C., Tinelli, C.: Solving quantified verification conditions using satisfiability modulo theories. In: Pfenning, F. (ed.) CADE 2007. LNCS (LNAI), vol. 4603, pp. 167–182. Springer, Heidelberg (2007). https://doi.org/10.1007/978-3-540-73595-3_12
13. Reynolds, A., Deters, M., Kuncak, V., Tinelli, C., Barrett, C.: Counterexample-guided quantifier instantiation for synthesis in SMT. In: Kroening, D., Păsăreanu, C.S. (eds.) CAV 2015. LNCS, vol. 9207, pp. 198–216. Springer, Cham (2015). https://doi.org/10.1007/978-3-319-21668-3_12
14. Nieuwenhuis, R., Oliveras, A.: On SAT modulo theories and optimization problems. In: Biere, A., Gomes, C.P. (eds.) SAT 2006. LNCS, vol. 4121, pp. 156–169. Springer, Heidelberg (2006). https://doi.org/10.1007/11814948_18
15. Cimatti, A., Franzén, A., Griggio, A., Sebastiani, R., Stenico, C.: Satisfiability modulo the theory of costs: foundations and applications. In: Esparza, J., Majumdar, R. (eds.) TACAS 2010. LNCS, vol. 6015, pp. 99–113. Springer, Heidelberg (2010). https://doi.org/10.1007/978-3-642-12002-2_8
16. Sebastiani, R., Tomasi, S.: Optimization in SMT with $\mathcal{LA}(Q)$ Cost Functions. In: Gramlich, B., Miller, D., Sattler, U. (eds.) IJCAR 2012. LNCS (LNAI), vol. 7364, pp. 484–498. Springer, Heidelberg (2012). https://doi.org/10.1007/978-3-642-31365-3_38
17. Dutertre, B.: Solving exists/forall problems with yices. In: Workshop on Satisfiability Modulo Theories (2015)
18. Nightingale, P.: Consistency for quantified constraint satisfaction problems. In: van Beek, P. (ed.) CP 2005. LNCS, vol. 3709, pp. 792–796. Springer, Heidelberg (2005). https://doi.org/10.1007/11564751_66
19. Weihrauch, K.: Computable Analysis: An Introduction. Springer, New York (2000). https://doi.org/10.1007/978-3-642-56999-9
20. Benhamou, F., Granvilliers, L.: Continuous and interval constraints. In: Rossi, F., van Beek, P., Walsh, T. (eds.) Handbook of Constraint Programming. Elsevier (2006)
21. Gao, S., Kong, S., Clarke, E.M.: dReal: an SMT solver for nonlinear theories over the reals. In: CADE, pp. 208–214 (2013)

22. Trombettoni, G., Araya, I., Neveu, B., Chabert, G.: Inner regions and interval linearizations for global optimization. In: Burgard, W., Roth, D. (eds.) Proceedings of the Twenty-Fifth AAAI Conference on Artificial Intelligence, AAAI 2011, San Francisco, California, USA, 7–11 August 2011. AAAI Press (2011)
23. Lougee-Heimer, R.: The common optimization interface for operations research: promoting open-source software in the operations research community. IBM J. Res. Dev. **47**(1), 57–66 (2003)
24. Johnson, S.G.: The NLopt nonlinear-optimization package (2011)
25. Kraft, D.: Algorithm 733: Tomp-Fortran modules for optimal control calculations. ACM Trans. Math. Softw. **20**(3), 262–281 (1994)
26. Powell, M.: Direct search algorithms for optimization calculations. Acta Numerica **7**, 287–336 (1998)
27. Jamil, M., Yang, X.S.: A literature survey of benchmark functions for global optimisation problems. Int. J. Math. Model. Numer. Optimisation **4**(2), 150–194 (2013)
28. Wikipedia contributors: Test functions for optimization – Wikipedia. The Free Encyclopedia (2017)
29. Kapinski, J., Deshmukh, J.V., Sankaranarayanan, S., Arechiga, N.: Simulation-guided lyapunov analysis for hybrid dynamical systems. In: HSCC 2014, Berlin, Germany, 15–17 April 2014, pp. 133–142 (2014)

Solving Quantified Bit-Vectors Using Invertibility Conditions

Aina Niemetz[1]([⊠]) [iD], Mathias Preiner[1] [iD],
Andrew Reynolds[2] [iD], Clark Barrett[1] [iD],
and Cesare Tinelli[2] [iD]

[1] Stanford University, Stanford, USA
niemetz@cs.stanford.edu
[2] The University of Iowa, Iowa City, USA

Abstract. We present a novel approach for solving quantified bit-vector formulas in Satisfiability Modulo Theories (SMT) based on computing symbolic inverses of bit-vector operators. We derive conditions that precisely characterize when bit-vector constraints are invertible for a representative set of bit-vector operators commonly supported by SMT solvers. We utilize syntax-guided synthesis techniques to aid in establishing these conditions and verify them independently by using several SMT solvers. We show that invertibility conditions can be embedded into quantifier instantiations using Hilbert choice expressions, and give experimental evidence that a counterexample-guided approach for quantifier instantiation utilizing these techniques leads to performance improvements with respect to state-of-the-art solvers for quantified bit-vector constraints.

1 Introduction

Many applications in hardware and software verification rely on Satisfiability Modulo Theories (SMT) solvers for bit-precise reasoning. In recent years, the quantifier-free fragment of the theory of fixed-size bit-vectors has received a lot of interest, as witnessed by the number of applications that generate problems in that fragment and by the high, and increasing, number of solvers that participate in the corresponding division of the annual SMT competition. Modeling properties of programs and circuits, e.g., universal safety properties and program invariants, however, often requires the use of *quantified* bit-vector formulas. Despite a multitude of applications, reasoning efficiently about such formulas is still a challenge in the automated reasoning community.

The majority of solvers that support quantified bit-vector logics employ instantiation-based techniques [8,21,22,25], which aim to find conflicting ground instances of quantified formulas. For that, it is crucial to select good instantiations for the universal variables, or else the solver may be overwhelmed by the

This work was partially supported by DARPA under award No. FA8750-15-C-0113 and the National Science Foundation under award No. 1656926.

H. Chockler and G. Weissenbacher (Eds.): CAV 2018, LNCS 10982, pp. 236–255, 2018.
https://doi.org/10.1007/978-3-319-96142-2_16

number of ground instances generated. For example, consider a quantified formula $\psi = \forall x.\,(x + s \not\approx t)$ where x, s and t denote bit-vectors of size 32. To prove that ψ is unsatisfiable we can instantiate x with all 2^{32} possible bit-vector values. However, ideally, we would like to find a proof that requires much fewer instantiations. In this example, if we instantiate x with the symbolic term $t - s$ (the inverse of $x + s \approx t$ when solved for x), we can immediately conclude that ψ is unsatisfiable since $(t - s) + s \not\approx t$ simplifies to false.

Operators in the theory of bit-vectors are not always invertible. However, we observe it is possible to identify quantifier-free conditions that precisely *characterize* when they are. We do that for a representative set of operators in the standard theory of bit-vectors supported by SMT solvers. For example, we have proven that the constraint $x \cdot s \approx t$ is solvable for x if and only if $(-s \mid s)\ \&\ t \approx t$ is satisfiable. Using this observation, we develop a novel approach for solving quantified bit-vector formulas that utilizes invertibility conditions to generate symbolic instantiations. We show that invertibility conditions can be embedded into quantifier instantiations using Hilbert choice functions in a sound manner. This approach has compelling advantages with respect to previous approaches, which we demonstrate in our experiments.

More specifically, this paper makes the following *contributions*.

- We derive and present invertibility conditions for a representative set of bit-vector operators that allow us to model all bit-vector constraints in SMT-LIB [3].
- We provide details on how invertibility conditions can be automatically synthesized using syntax-guided synthesis (SyGuS) [1] techniques, and make public 162 available challenge problems for SyGuS solvers that are encodings of this task.
- We prove that our approach can efficiently reduce a class of quantified formulas, which we call *unit linear invertible*, to quantifier-free constraints.
- Leveraging invertibility conditions, we implement a novel quantifier instantiation scheme as an extension of the SMT solver CVC4 [2], which shows improvements with respect to state-of-the-art solvers for quantified bit-vector constraints.

Related Work. Quantified bit-vector logics are currently supported by the SMT solvers Boolector [16], CVC4 [2], Yices [7], and Z3 [6] and a Binary Decision Diagram (BDD)-based tool called Q3B [14]. Out of these, only CVC4 and Z3 provide support for combining quantified bit-vectors with other theories, e.g., the theories of arrays or real arithmetic. Arbitrarily nested quantifiers are handled by all but Yices, which only supports bit-vector formulas of the form $\exists \boldsymbol{x} \forall \boldsymbol{y}.\,Q[\boldsymbol{x}, \boldsymbol{y}]$ [8]. For quantified bit-vectors, CVC4 employs counterexample guided quantifier instantiation (CEGQI) [22], where concrete models of a set of ground instances and the negation of the input formula (the counterexamples) serve as instantiations for the universal variables. In Z3, model-based quantifier instantiation (MBQI) [10] is combined with a template-based model finding procedure [25]. In contrast to CVC4, Z3 not only relies on concrete counterexamples as candidates for quantifier instantiation but generalizes these counterexamples to generate symbolic instantiations by selecting ground terms with the same model value. Boolector employs a syntax-guided synthesis approach to synthesize interpretations for Skolem functions based on a set of ground instances of the formula, and uses a counterexample refinement loop similar to MBQI [21]. Other counterexample-guided approaches for quantified formulas in SMT solvers have been considered by Bjørner and Janota [4] and by Reynolds et al. [23], but they have mostly targeted quantified linear arithmetic and do not specifically address bit-vectors. Quantifier elimination for a fragment of bit-vectors that covers modular linear arithmetic has been recently addressed by John and Chakraborty [13], although we do not explore that direction in this paper.

2   Preliminaries

We assume the usual notions and terminology of many-sorted first-order logic with equality (denoted by $\approx$). Let S be a set of *sort symbols*, and for every sort $\sigma \in S$ let X_σ be an infinite set of *variables of sort* σ. We assume that sets X_σ are pairwise disjoint and define X as the union of sets X_σ. Let Σ be a *signature* consisting of a set $\Sigma^s \subseteq S$ of sort symbols and a set Σ^f of interpreted (and sorted) function symbols $f^{\sigma_1 \cdots \sigma_n \sigma}$ with arity $n \geq 0$ and $\sigma_1, ..., \sigma_n, \sigma \in \Sigma^s$. We assume that a signature Σ includes a Boolean sort Bool and the Boolean constants $\top$ (true) and $\bot$ (false). Let $\mathcal{I}$ be a Σ -*interpretation* that maps: each $\sigma \in \Sigma^s$ to a non-empty set $\sigma^\mathcal{I}$ (the *domain* of $\mathcal{I}$), with $\mathsf{Bool}^\mathcal{I} = \{\top, \bot\}$; each $x \in X_\sigma$ to an element $x^\mathcal{I} \in \sigma^\mathcal{I}$; and each $f^{\sigma_1 \cdots \sigma_n \sigma} \in \Sigma^f$ to a total function $f^\mathcal{I} \colon \sigma_1^\mathcal{I} \times ... \times \sigma_n^\mathcal{I} \to \sigma^\mathcal{I}$ if $n > 0$, and to an element in $\sigma^\mathcal{I}$ if $n = 0$. If $x \in X_\sigma$ and $v \in \sigma^\mathcal{I}$, we denote by $\mathcal{I}[x \mapsto v]$ the interpretation that maps x to v and is otherwise identical to $\mathcal{I}$. We use the usual inductive definition of a satisfiability relation $\models$ between Σ-interpretations and Σ-formulas.

We assume the usual definition of well-sorted terms, literals, and formulas as Bool terms with variables in X and symbols in Σ, and refer to them as Σ-terms, Σ-atoms, and so on. A *ground* term/formula is a Σ-term/formula without variables. We define $\boldsymbol{x} = (x_1, ..., x_n)$ as a tuple of variables and write $Q\boldsymbol{x}\varphi$ with $Q \in \{\forall, \exists\}$ for a *quantified* formula $Qx_1 \cdots Qx_n\varphi$. We use $\mathrm{Lit}(\varphi)$ to denote the set of Σ-literals of Σ-formula φ. For a Σ-term or Σ-formula e, we denote the *free variables* of e (defined as usual) as $FV(e)$ and use $e[\boldsymbol{x}]$ to denote that the variables in $\boldsymbol{x}$ occur free in e. For a tuple of Σ-terms $\boldsymbol{t} = (t_1, ..., t_n)$, we write $e[\boldsymbol{t}]$ for the term or formula obtained from e by simultaneously replacing each occurrence of x_i in e by t_i. Given a Σ-formula $\varphi[x]$ with $x \in X_\sigma$, we use Hilbert's *choice* operator ε [12] to describe *properties* of x. We define a *choice function* $\varepsilon x. \varphi[x]$ as a term where x is bound by ε. In every interpretation $\mathcal{I}$, $\varepsilon x. \varphi[x]$ denotes some value $v \in \sigma^\mathcal{I}$ such that $\mathcal{I}[x \mapsto v]$ satisfies $\varphi[x]$ if such values exist, and denotes an arbitrary element of $\sigma^\mathcal{I}$ otherwise. This means that the formula $\exists x. \varphi[x] \Leftrightarrow \varphi[\varepsilon x. \varphi[x]]$ is satisfied by every interpretation.

A *theory* T is a pair (Σ, I), where Σ is a signature and I is a non-empty class of Σ-interpretations (the *models* of T) that is closed under variable reassignment, i.e., every Σ-interpretation that only differs from an $\mathcal{I} \in I$ in how it interprets

Table 1. Set of considered bit-vector operators with corresponding SMT-LIB 2 syntax.

Symbol	SMT-LIB syntax	Sort
$\approx, <_u, >_u, <_s, >_s$	=, bvult, bvugt, bvslt, bvsgt	$\sigma_{[n]} \times \sigma_{[n]} \to$ Bool
$\sim, -$	bvnot, bvneg	$\sigma_{[n]} \to \sigma_{[n]}$
$\&, \|, \ll, \gg, \gg_a$	bvand, bvor, bvshl, bvlshr, bvashr	$\sigma_{[n]} \times \sigma_{[n]} \to \sigma_{[n]}$
$+, \cdot, \bmod, \div$	bvadd, bvmul, bvurem, bvudiv	$\sigma_{[n]} \times \sigma_{[n]} \to \sigma_{[n]}$
$\circ$	concat	$\sigma_{[n]} \times \sigma_{[m]} \to \sigma_{[n+m]}$
$[u:l]$	extract	$\sigma_{[n]} \to \sigma_{[u-l+1]}, 0 \le l \le u < n$

variables is also in I. A Σ-formula φ is T-*satisfiable* (resp. T-*unsatisfiable*) if it is satisfied by some (resp. no) interpretation in I; it is T-*valid* if it is satisfied by all interpretations in I. A choice function $\varepsilon x. \varphi[x]$ is *(T-)valid* if $\exists x. \varphi[x]$ is *(T-)* valid. We refer to a term t as ε -*(T-)valid* if all occurrences of choice functions in t are (T-)valid. We will sometimes omit T when the theory is understood from context.

We will focus on the theory $T_{BV} = (\Sigma_{BV}, I_{BV})$ of fixed-size bit-vectors as defined by the SMT-LIB 2 standard [3]. The signature Σ_{BV} includes a unique sort for each positive bit-vector width n, denoted here as $\sigma_{[n]}$. Similarly, $X_{[n]}$ is the set of *bit-vector variables* of sort $\sigma_{[n]}$, and X_{BV} is the union of all sets $X_{[n]}$. We assume that Σ_{BV} includes all *bit-vector constants* of sort $\sigma_{[n]}$ for each n, represented as bit-strings. However, to simplify the notation we will sometimes denote them by the corresponding natural number in $\{0, \ldots, 2^{n-1}\}$. All interpretations $\mathcal{I} \in I_{BV}$ are identical except for the value they assign to variables. They interpret sort and function symbols as specified in SMT-LIB 2. All function symbols in Σ_{BV}^f are overloaded for every $\sigma_{[n]} \in \Sigma_{BV}^s$. We denote a Σ_{BV}-term (or *bit-vector term*) t of width n as $t_{[n]}$ when we want to specify its bit-width explicitly. We use $\max_{s[n]}$ or $\min_{s[n]}$ for the *maximum* or *minimum signed value* of width n, e.g., $\max_{s[4]} = 0111$ and $\min_{s[4]} = 1000$. The width of a bit-vector sort or term is given by the function κ, e.g., $\kappa(\sigma_{[n]}) = n$ and $\kappa(t_{[n]}) = n$.

Without loss of generality, we consider a restricted set of bit-vector function symbols (or *bit-vector operators*) Σ_{BV}^f as listed in Table 1. The selection of operators in this set is arbitrary but complete in the sense that it suffices to express all bit-vector operators defined in SMT-LIB 2.

3   Invertibility Conditions for Bit-Vector Constraints

This section formally introduces the concept of an invertibility condition and shows that such conditions can be used to construct symbolic solutions for a class of quantifier-free bit-vector constraints that have a linear shape.

Consider a bit-vector literal $x + s \approx t$ and assume that we want to solve for x. If the literal is *linear* in x, that is, has only one occurrence of x, a general solution for x is given by the inverse of bit-vector addition over equality: $x = t - s$. Computing the inverse of a bit-vector operation, however, is not always possible.

For example, for $x \cdot s \approx t$, an inverse always exists only if s always evaluates to an odd bit-vector. Otherwise, there are values for s and t where no such inverse exists, e.g., $x \cdot 2 \approx 3$. However, even if there is no unconditional inverse for the general case, we can identify the condition under which a bit-vector operation is invertible. For the bit-vector multiplication constraint $x \cdot s \approx t$ with $x \notin FV(s) \cup FV(t)$, the *invertibility condition* for x can be expressed by the formula $(-s \mid s) \,\&\, t \approx t$.

Definition 1 *(Invertibility Condition).* *Let $\ell[x]$ be a Σ_{BV}-literal. A quantifier-free Σ_{BV}-formula ϕ_c is an* invertibility condition *for x in $\ell[x]$ if $x \notin FV(\phi_c)$ and $\phi_c \Leftrightarrow \exists x.\,\ell[x]$ is T_{BV}-valid.*

An invertibility condition for a literal $\ell[x]$ provides the *exact conditions* under which $\ell[x]$ is solvable for x. We call it an "invertibility" condition because we can use Hilbert choice functions to express *all* such conditional solutions with a *single* symbolic term, that is, a term whose possible values are exactly the solutions for x in $\ell[x]$. Recall that a choice function $\varepsilon y.\,\varphi[y]$ represents a solution for a formula $\varphi[x]$ if there exists one, and represents an arbitrary value otherwise. We may use a choice function to describe inverse solutions for a literal $\ell[x]$ with invertibility condition ϕ_c as $\varepsilon y.\,(\phi_c \Rightarrow \ell[y])$. For example, for the general case of bit-vector multiplication over equality the choice function is defined as $\varepsilon y.\,((-s \mid s) \,\&\, t \approx t \;\Rightarrow\; y \cdot s \approx t)$.

Lemma 2. *If ϕ_c is an invertibility condition for an ε-valid Σ_{BV}-literal $\ell[x]$ and r is the term $\varepsilon y.\,(\phi_c \Rightarrow \ell[y])$, then r is ε-valid and $\ell[r] \Leftrightarrow \exists x.\,\ell[x]$ is T_{BV}-valid.*[1]

Intuitively, the lemma states that when $\ell[x]$ is satisfiable (under condition ϕ_c), any value returned by the choice function $\varepsilon y.\,(\phi_c \Rightarrow \ell[y])$ is a solution of $\ell[x]$ (and thus $\exists x.\,\ell[x]$ holds). Conversely, if there exists a value v for x that makes $\ell[x]$ true, then there is a model of T_{BV} that interprets $\varepsilon y.\,(\phi_c \Rightarrow \ell[y])$ as v.

Now, suppose that Σ_{BV}-literal ℓ is again linear in x but that x occurs arbitrarily deep in ℓ. Consider, for example, a literal $s_1 \cdot (s_2 + x) \approx t$ where x does not occur in s_1, s_2 or t. We can solve this literal for x by recursively computing the (possibly conditional) inverses of all bit-vector operations that involve x. That is, first we solve $s_1 \cdot x' \approx t$ for x', where x' is a fresh variable abstracting $s_2 + x$, which yields the choice function $x' = \varepsilon y.\,((-s_1 \mid s_1) \,\&\, t \approx t \;\Rightarrow\; s_1 \cdot y \approx t)$. Then, we solve $s_2 + x \approx x'$ for x, which yields the solution $x = x' - s_2 = \varepsilon y.\,((-s_1 \mid s_1) \,\&\, t \approx t \;\Rightarrow\; s_1 \cdot y \approx t) - s_2$.

Figure 1 describes in pseudo code the procedure to solve for x in an arbitrary literal $\ell[x] = e[x] \bowtie t$ that is linear in x. We assume that $e[x]$ is built over the set of bit-vector operators listed in Table 1. Function solve recursively constructs a symbolic solution by computing (conditional) inverses as follows. Let function getInverse$(x, \ell[x])$ return a term t' that is the inverse of x in $\ell[x]$, i.e., such that $\ell[x] \Leftrightarrow x \approx t'$. Furthermore, let function getIC$(x, \ell[x])$ return the invertibility condition ϕ_c for x in $\ell[x]$. If $e[x]$ has the form $\diamond(e_1, \ldots, e_n)$ with $n > 0$, x must

---

[1] All proofs can be found in an extended version of this paper [19].

$\mathsf{solve}(x, e[x] \bowtie t):$

  If $e = x$

    If $\bowtie \in \{\approx\}$ then return t

    else return $\varepsilon y. (\mathsf{getIC}(x, x \bowtie t) \Rightarrow y \bowtie t)$.

  else $e = \diamond(e_1, \ldots, e_i[x], \ldots, e_n)$ with $n > 0$ and $x \notin FV(e_j)$ for all $j \neq i$.

    Let $d[x'] = \diamond(e_1, \ldots, e_{i-1}, x', e_{i+1}, \ldots, e_n)$ where x' is a fresh variable.

    If $\bowtie \in \{\approx, \not\approx\}$ and $\diamond \in \{\sim, -, +\}$

    then let $t' = \mathsf{getInverse}(x', d[x'] \approx t)$ and return $\mathsf{solve}(x, e_i \bowtie t')$

    else let $\phi_c = \mathsf{getIC}(x', d[x'] \bowtie t)$ and return $\mathsf{solve}(x, e_i \approx \varepsilon y. (\phi_c \Rightarrow d[y] \bowtie t))$.

Fig. 1. Function solve for constructing a symbolic solution for x given a linear literal $e[x] \bowtie t$.

occur in exactly one of the subterms $e_1, \ldots, e_n$ given that e is linear in x. Let d be the term obtained from e by replacing e_i (the subterm containing x) with a fresh variable x'. We solve for subterm $e_i[x]$ (treating it as a variable x') and compute an inverse $\mathsf{getInverse}(x', d[x'] \approx t)$, if it exists. Note that for a disequality $e[x] \not\approx t$, it suffices to compute the inverse over equality and propagate the disequality down. (For example, for $e_i[x] + s \not\approx t$, we compute the inverse $t' = \mathsf{getInverse}(x', x' + s \approx t) = t - s$ and recurse on $e_i[x] \not\approx t'$.) If no inverse for $e[x] \bowtie t$ exists, we first determine the invertibility condition ϕ_c for $d[x']$ via $\mathsf{getIC}(x', d[x'] \bowtie t)$, construct the choice function $\varepsilon y. (\phi_c \Rightarrow d[y] \bowtie t)$, and set it equal to $e_i[x]$, before recursively solving for x. If $e[x] = x$ and the given literal is an equality, we have reached the base case and return t as the solution for x. Note that in Fig. 1, for simplicity we omitted one case for which an inverse can be determined, namely $x \cdot c \approx t$ where c is an odd constant.

Theorem 3. *Let $\ell[x]$ be an ε-valid Σ_{BV}-literal linear in x, and let $r = \mathsf{solve}(x, \ell[x])$. Then r is ε-valid, $FV(r) \subseteq FV(\ell) \setminus \{x\}$ and $\ell[r] \Leftrightarrow \exists x. \ell[x]$ is T_{BV}-valid.*

Tables 2 and 3 list the invertibility conditions for bit-vector operators $\{\cdot, \bmod, \div, \&, |, \gg, \gg_a, \ll, \circ\}$ over relations $\{\approx, \not\approx, <_u, >_u\}$. Due to space restrictions we omit the conditions for signed inequalities since they can be expressed in terms of unsigned inequality. We omit the invertibility conditions over $\{\leq_u, \geq_u\}$ since they can generally be constructed by combining the corresponding conditions for equality and inequality—although there might be more succinct equivalent conditions. Finally, we omit the invertibility conditions for operators $\{\sim, -, +\}$ and literals $x \bowtie t$ over inequality since they are basic bounds checks, e.g., for $x <_s t$ we have $t \not\approx \min$. The invertibility condition for $x \not\approx t$ and for the extract operator is $\top$.[2]

---

[2] All the omitted invertibility conditions can be found in the extended version of this paper [19].

The idea of computing the inverse of bit-vector operators has been used successfully in a recent local search approach for solving quantifier-free bit-vector constraints by Niemetz et al. [17]. There, target values are propagated via inverse value computation. In contrast, our approach does not determine single inverse values based on concrete assignments but aims at finding symbolic solutions through the generation of conditional inverses. In an extended version of that work [18], the same authors present rules for inverse value computation over equality but they provide no proof of correctness for them. We define invertibility conditions not only over equality but also disequality and (un)signed inequality, and verify their correctness up to a certain bit-width.

3.1   Synthesizing Invertibility Conditions

We have defined invertibility conditions for all bit-vector operators in Σ_{BV} where no general inverse exists (162 in total). A noteworthy aspect of this work is that we were able to leverage syntax-guided synthesis (SyGuS) technology [1] to help identify these conditions. The problem of finding invertibility conditions for a literal of the form $x \diamond s \bowtie t$ (or, dually, $s \diamond x \bowtie t$) linear in x can be recast as a SyGuS problem by asking whether there exists a binary Boolean function C such that the (second-order) formula $\exists C \forall s \forall t. ((\exists x. x \diamond s \bowtie t) \Leftrightarrow C(s,t))$ is satisfiable. If a SyGuS solver is able to synthesize the function C, then C can be used as the invertibility condition for $x \diamond s \bowtie t$. To simplify the SyGuS problem we chose a bit-width of 4 for x, s, and t and eliminated the quantification over x in the formula above by expanding it to

$$\exists C \forall s \forall t. \left(\bigvee_{i=0}^{15} i \diamond s \bowtie t \right) \Leftrightarrow C(s,t)$$

Since the search space for SyGuS solvers heavily depends on the input grammar (which defines the solution space for C), we decided to use two grammars with the same set of Boolean connectives but different sets of bit-vector operators:

$$O_r = \{\neg, \wedge, \approx, <_u, <_s, 0, \min_s, \max_s, s, t, \sim, -, \&, |\}$$
$$O_g = \{\neg, \wedge, \vee, \approx, <_u, <_s, \geq_u, \geq_s, 0, \min_s, \max_s, s, t, \sim, +, -, \&, |, \gg, \ll\}$$

The selection of constants in the grammar turned out to be crucial for finding solutions, e.g., by adding $\min_s$ and $\max_s$ we were able to synthesize substantially more invertibility conditions for signed inequalities. For each of the two sets of operators, we generated 140 SyGuS problems[3], one for each combination of bit-vector operator $\diamond \in \{\cdot, \bmod, \div, \&, |, \gg, \gg_a, \ll\}$ over relation $\bowtie \in \{\approx, \not\approx, <_u, \leq_u, >_u, \geq_u, <_s, \leq_s, >_s, \geq_s\}$, and used the SyGuS extension of the CVC4 solver [22] to solve these problems.

Using operators O_r (O_g) we were able to synthesize 98 (116) out of 140 invertibility conditions, with 118 unique solutions overall. When we found more

---

[3] Available at https://cvc4.cs.stanford.edu/papers/CAV2018-QBV/.

Table 2. Conditions for the invertibility of bit-vector operators over (dis)equality. Those for $\cdot$, $\&$ and $\mid$ are given modulo commutativity of those operators.

$\ell[x]$	$\approx$	$\not\approx$
$x \cdot s \bowtie t$	$(-s \mid s) \,\&\, t \approx t$	$s \not\approx 0 \vee t \not\approx 0$
$x \bmod s \bowtie t$	$\sim(-s) \geq_u t$	$s \not\approx 1 \vee t \not\approx 0$
$s \bmod x \bowtie t$	$(t + t - s) \,\&\, s \geq_u t$	$s \not\approx 0 \vee t \not\approx 0$
$x \div s \bowtie t$	$(s \cdot t) \div s \approx t$	$s \not\approx 0 \vee t \not\approx {\sim}0$
$s \div x \bowtie t$	$s \div (s \div t) \approx t$	$\begin{cases} s \,\&\, t \approx 0 & \text{for } \kappa(s) = 1 \\ \top & \text{otherwise} \end{cases}$
$x \,\&\, s \bowtie t$	$t \,\&\, s \approx t$	$s \not\approx 0 \vee t \not\approx 0$
$x \mid s \bowtie t$	$t \mid s \approx t$	$s \not\approx {\sim}0 \vee t \not\approx {\sim}0$
$x \gg s \bowtie t$	$(t \ll s) \gg s \approx t$	$t \not\approx 0 \vee s <_u \kappa(s)$
$s \gg x \bowtie t$	$\bigvee_{i=0}^{\kappa(s)} s \gg i \approx t$	$s \not\approx 0 \vee t \not\approx 0$
$x \gg_a s \bowtie t$	$(s <_u \kappa(s) \Rightarrow (t \ll s) \gg_a s \approx t) \wedge (s \geq_u \kappa(s) \Rightarrow (t \approx {\sim}0 \vee t \approx 0))$	$\top$
$s \gg_a x \bowtie t$	$\bigvee_{i=0}^{\kappa(s)} s \gg_a i \approx t$	$(t \not\approx 0 \vee s \not\approx 0) \wedge (t \not\approx {\sim}0 \vee s \not\approx {\sim}0)$
$x \ll s \bowtie t$	$(t \gg s) \ll s \approx t$	$t \not\approx 0 \vee s <_u \kappa(s)$
$s \ll x \bowtie t$	$\bigvee_{i=0}^{\kappa(s)} s \ll i \approx t$	$s \not\approx 0 \vee t \not\approx 0$
$x \circ s \bowtie t$	$s \approx t[\kappa(s) - 1 : 0]$	$\top$
$s \circ x \bowtie t$	$s \approx t[\kappa(t) - 1 : \kappa(t) - \kappa(s)]$	$\top$

than one solution for a condition (either with operators O_r and O_g, or manually) we chose the one that involved the smallest number of bit-vector operators. Thus, we ended up using 79 out of 118 synthesized conditions and 83 manually crafted conditions.

In some cases, the SyGuS approach was able to synthesize invertibility conditions that were smaller than those we had manually crafted. For example, we manually defined the invertibility condition for $x \cdot s \approx t$ as $(t \approx 0) \vee ((t \,\& \, -t) \geq_u (s \,\&\, -s) \wedge (s \not\approx 0))$. With SyGuS we obtained $((-s \mid s) \,\&\, t) \approx t$. For some other cases, however, the synthesized solution involved more bit-vector operators than needed. For example, for $x \bmod s \not\approx t$ we manually defined the invertibility condition $(s \not\approx 1) \vee (t \not\approx 0)$, whereas SyGuS produced the solution $\sim(-s) \mid t \not\approx 0$. For the majority of invertibility conditions, finding a solution did not require more than one hour of CPU time on an Intel Xeon E5-2637 with 3.5 GHz. Interestingly, the most time-consuming synthesis task (over 107 h of CPU time) was finding condition $((t + t) - s) \,\&\, s \geq_u t$ for $s \bmod x \approx t$. A small number of synthesized solutions were only correct for a bit-width of 4, e.g., solution $(\sim s \ll s) \ll s <_s t$ for $x \div s <_s t$. In total, we found 6 width-dependent synthesized solutions, all of them for bit-vector operators $\div$ and mod. For those, we used the manually crafted invertibility conditions instead.

Table 3. Conditions for the invertibility of bit-vector operators over unsigned inequality. Those for $\cdot$, $\&$ and $|$ are given modulo commutativity of those operators.

$\ell[x]$	$<_u$	$>_u$
$x \cdot s \bowtie t$	$t \not\approx 0$	$t <_u -s \mid s$
$x \bmod s \bowtie t$	$t \not\approx 0$	$t <_u \sim(-s)$
$s \bmod x \bowtie t$	$t \not\approx 0$	$t <_u s$
$x \div s \bowtie t$	$0 <_u s \wedge 0 <_u t$	$\sim 0 \div s >_u t$
$s \div x \bowtie t$	$0 <_u \sim(-t \& s) \wedge 0 <_u t$	$t <_u \sim 0$
$x \& s \bowtie t$	$t \not\approx 0$	$t <_u s$
$x \mid s \bowtie t$	$s <_u t$	$t <_u \sim 0$
$x \gg s \bowtie t$	$t \not\approx 0$	$t <_u \sim s \gg s$
$s \gg x \bowtie t$	$t \not\approx 0$	$t <_u s$
$x \gg_a s \bowtie t$	$t \not\approx 0$	$t <_u \sim 0$
$s \gg_a x \bowtie t$	$(s <_u t \vee s \geq_s 0) \wedge t \not\approx 0$	$s <_s (s \gg \sim t) \vee t <_u s$
$x \ll s \bowtie t$	$t \not\approx 0$	$t <_u \sim 0 \ll s$
$s \ll x \bowtie t$	$t \not\approx 0$	$\bigvee\limits_{i=0}^{\kappa(s)} (s \ll i) >_u t$
$x \circ s \bowtie t$	$t_x \approx 0 \Rightarrow s <_u t_s$	$t_x \approx \sim 0 \Rightarrow s >_u t_s$
	where $t_x = t[\kappa(t)-1 : \kappa(t) - \kappa(x)]$, $t_s = t[\kappa(s)-1:0]$	
$s \circ x \bowtie t$	$s \leq_u t_s \wedge (s \approx t_s \Rightarrow t_x \not\approx 0)$	$s \geq_u t_s \wedge s \approx t_s \Rightarrow t_x \not\approx \sim 0$
	where $t_x = t[\kappa(x)-1:0]$, $t_s = t[\kappa(t)-1 : \kappa(t) - \kappa(s)]$	

3.2   Verifying Invertibility Conditions

We verified the correctness of all 162 invertibility conditions for bit-widths from 1 to 65 by checking for each bit-width the T_{BV}-unsatisfiability of the formula $\neg(\phi_c \Leftrightarrow \exists x. \, \ell[x])$ where ℓ ranges over the literals in Tables 2 and 3 with s and t replaced by fresh constants, and ϕ_c is the corresponding invertibility condition.

In total, we generated 12,980 verification problems and used all participating solvers of the quantified bit-vector division of SMT-competition 2017 to verify them. For each solver/benchmark pair we used a CPU time limit of one hour and a memory limit of 8 GB on the same machines as those mentioned in the previous section. We consider an invertibility condition to be verified for a certain bit-width if at least one of the solvers was able to report unsatisfiable for the corresponding formula within the given time limit. Out of the 12,980 instances, we were able to verify 12,277 (94.6%).

Overall, all verification tasks (including timeouts) required a total of 275 days of CPU time. The success rate of each individual solver was 91.4% for Boolector, 85.0% for CVC4, 50.8% for Q3B, and 92% for Z3. We observed that on 30.6% of the problems, Q3B exited with a Python exception without returning any result. For bit-vector operators $\{\sim, -, +, \&, |, \gg, \gg_a, \ll, \circ\}$, over all relations, and for operators $\{\cdot, \div, \bmod\}$ over relations $\{\not\approx, \leq_u, \leq_s\}$, we were able to verify all invertibility conditions for all bit-widths in the range 1–65. Interestingly, no solver was able to verify the invertibility conditions for $x \bmod s <_s t$ with a bit-width of 54 and $s \bmod x <_u t$ with bit-widths 35–37 within the allotted time. We attribute this to the underlying heuristics used by the SAT solvers in these systems. All other conditions for $<_s$ and $<_u$ were verified for all bit-vector operators up to bit-width 65. The remaining conditions for operators $\{\cdot,$ $\div, \bmod\}$ over relations $\{\approx, >_u, \geq_u, >_s, \geq_s\}$ were verified up to at least a bit-width of 14. We discovered 3 conditions for $s \div x \bowtie t$ with $\bowtie \in \{\not\approx, >_s, \geq_s\}$ that were not correct for a bit-width of 1. For each of these cases, we added an additional invertibility condition that correctly handles that case.

We leave to future work the task of formally proving that our invertibility conditions are correct for all bit-widths. Since this will most likely require the development of an interactive proof, we could leverage some recent work by Ekici et al. [9] that includes a formalization in the Coq proof assistant of the SMT-LIB theory of bit-vectors.

4   Counterexample-Guided Instantiation for Bit-Vectors

In this section, we leverage techniques from the previous section for constructing symbolic solutions to bit-vector constraints to define a novel instantiation-based technique for quantified bit-vector formulas. We first briefly present the overall theory-independent procedure we use for quantifier instantiation and then show how it can be specialized to quantified bit-vectors using invertibility conditions.

We use a counterexample-guided approach for quantifier instantiation, as given by procedure $\mathsf{CEGQI}_{\mathcal{S}}$ in Fig. 2. To simplify the exposition here, we focus on input problems expressed as a single formula in prenex normal form and with up to one quantifier alternation. We stress, though, that the approach applies in general to arbitrary sets of quantified formulas in some Σ-theory T with a decidable quantifier-free fragment. The procedure checks via instantiation the T-satisfiability of a quantified input formula φ of the form $\exists y \forall x. \, \psi[x, y]$ where ψ is quantifier-free and x and y are possibly empty sequences of variables. It maintains an evolving set Γ, initially empty, of quantifier-free instances of the input formula. During each iteration of the procedure's loop, there are three possible cases: (1) if Γ is T-unsatisfiable, the input formula φ is also T-unsatisfiable and "unsat" is returned; (2) if Γ is T-satisfiable but not together with $\neg\psi[y, x]$, the negated body of φ, then Γ entails φ in T, hence φ is T-satisfiable and "sat" is returned. (3) If neither of previous cases holds, the procedure adds to Γ an instance of ψ obtained by replacing the variables x with some terms t, and continues. The procedure CEGQI is parametrized by a *selection function* $\mathcal{S}$ that generates the terms t.

Definition 4 *(Selection Function). A selection function takes as input a tuple of variables x, a model $\mathcal{I}$ of T, a quantifier-free Σ-formula $\psi[x]$, and a set Γ of Σ-formulas such that $x \notin FV(\Gamma)$ and $\mathcal{I} \models \Gamma \cup \{\neg\psi\}$. It returns a tuple of ε-valid terms t of the same type as x such that $FV(t) \subseteq FV(\psi) \setminus x$.*

CEGQI$_S(\exists \boldsymbol{y} \forall \boldsymbol{x}. \psi[\boldsymbol{y}, \boldsymbol{x}])$
$\Gamma := \emptyset$
Repeat:
   1. If Γ is T-unsatisfiable, then return "unsat".
   2. Otherwise, if $\Gamma' = \Gamma \cup \{\neg\psi[\boldsymbol{y}, \boldsymbol{x}]\}$ is T-unsatisfiable, then return "sat".
   3. Otherwise, let $\mathcal{I}$ be a model of T and Γ' and $\boldsymbol{t} = \mathcal{S}(\boldsymbol{x}, \psi, \mathcal{I}, \Gamma)$. $\Gamma := \Gamma \cup \{\psi[\boldsymbol{y}, \boldsymbol{t}]\}$.

Fig. 2. A counterexample-guided quantifier instantiation procedure CEGQI$_S$, parameterized by a selection function $\mathcal{S}$, for determining the T-satisfiability of $\exists \boldsymbol{y} \forall \boldsymbol{x}. \psi[\boldsymbol{y}, \boldsymbol{x}]$ with ψ quantifier-free and $FV(\psi) = \boldsymbol{y} \cup \boldsymbol{x}$.

Definition 5. *Let $\psi[\boldsymbol{x}]$ be a quantifier-free Σ-formula. A selection function is:*

1. *Finite for $\boldsymbol{x}$ and ψ if there is a finite set $\mathcal{S}^*$ such that $\mathcal{S}(\boldsymbol{x}, \psi, \mathcal{I}, \Gamma) \in \mathcal{S}^*$ for all legal inputs $\mathcal{I}$ and Γ.*
2. *Monotonic for $\boldsymbol{x}$ and ψ if for all legal inputs $\mathcal{I}$ and Γ, $\mathcal{S}(\boldsymbol{x}, \psi, \mathcal{I}, \Gamma) = \boldsymbol{t}$ only if $\psi[\boldsymbol{t}] \notin \Gamma$.*

Procedure CEGQI$_S$ is refutation-sound and model-sound for any selection function $\mathcal{S}$, and terminating for selection functions that are finite and monotonic.

Theorem 6 (Correctness of CEGQI$_S$). *Let $\mathcal{S}$ be a selection function and let $\varphi = \exists \boldsymbol{y} \forall \boldsymbol{x}. \psi[\boldsymbol{y}, \boldsymbol{x}]$ be a legal input for CEGQI$_S$. Then the following hold.*

1. *If CEGQI$_S(\varphi)$ returns "unsat", then φ is T-unsatisfiable.*
2. *If CEGQI$_S(\varphi)$ returns "sat" for some final Γ, then φ is T-equivalent to $\exists \boldsymbol{y}. \bigwedge_{\gamma \in \Gamma} \gamma$.*
3. *If $\mathcal{S}$ is finite and monotonic for $\boldsymbol{x}$ and ψ, then CEGQI$_S(\varphi)$ terminates.*

Thanks to this theorem, to define a T-satisfiability procedure for quantified Σ-formulas, it suffices to define a selection function satisfying the criteria of Definition 4. We do that in the following section for T_{BV}.

4.1 Selection Functions for Bit-Vectors

In Fig. 3, we define a (class of) selection functions $\mathcal{S}_c^{BV}$ for quantifier-free bit-vector formulas, which is parameterized by a *configuration* c, a value of the enumeration type $\{\mathbf{m}, \mathbf{k}, \mathbf{s}, \mathbf{b}\}$. The selection function collects in the set M all the literals occurring in Γ' that are satisfied by $\mathcal{I}$. Then, it collects in the set N a *projected form* of each literal in M. This form is computed by the function project$_c$ parameterized by configuration c. That function transforms its input literal into a form suitable for function solve from Fig. 1. We discuss the intuition for projection operations in more detail below.

After constructing set N, the selection function computes a term t_i for each variable x_i in tuple $\boldsymbol{x}$, which we call the *solved form* of x_i. To do that, it first

$\mathcal{S}_c^{BV}(\boldsymbol{x}, \psi, \mathcal{I}, \Gamma)$ where $c \in \{\mathbf{m}, \mathbf{k}, \mathbf{s}, \mathbf{b}\}$

Let $M = \{\ell \mid \mathcal{I} \models \ell, \ell \in \mathrm{Lit}(\psi)\}$, $N = \{\mathrm{project}_c(\mathcal{I}, \ell) \mid \ell \in M\}$.
For $i = 1, \ldots, n$ where $\boldsymbol{x} = (x_1, \ldots, x_n)$:
   Let $N_i = \bigcup_{\ell[x_1, \ldots, x_{i-1}] \in N} \mathrm{linearize}(x_i, \mathcal{I}, \ell[t_1, \ldots, t_{i-1}])$.

$$\text{Let } t_i = \begin{cases} \mathrm{solve}(x_i, \mathrm{choose}(N_i)) & \text{if } N_i \text{ is non-empty} \\ x_i^{\mathcal{I}} & \text{otherwise} \end{cases}$$

   $t_j := t_j \{x_i \mapsto t_i\}$ for each $j < i$.
Return $(t_1, \ldots, t_n)$.

$\mathrm{project}_{\mathbf{m}}(\mathcal{I}, s \bowtie t)$: return $\top$ $\mathrm{project}_{\mathbf{s}}(\mathcal{I}, s \bowtie t)$: return $s \approx t + (s - t)^{\mathcal{I}}$

$\mathrm{project}_{\mathbf{k}}(\mathcal{I}, s \bowtie t)$: return $s \bowtie t$ $\mathrm{project}_{\mathbf{b}}(\mathcal{I}, s \bowtie t)$: return $\begin{cases} s \approx t & \text{if } s^{\mathcal{I}} = t^{\mathcal{I}} \\ s \approx t + 1 & \text{if } s^{\mathcal{I}} > t^{\mathcal{I}} \\ s \approx t - 1 & \text{if } s^{\mathcal{I}} < t^{\mathcal{I}} \end{cases}$

Fig. 3. Selection functions $\mathcal{S}_c^{BV}$ for quantifier-free bit-vector formulas. The procedure is parameterized by a configuration c, one of either $\mathbf{m}$ (model value), $\mathbf{k}$ (keep), $\mathbf{s}$ (slack), or $\mathbf{b}$ (boundary).

constructs a set of literals N_i all linear in x_i. It considers literals ℓ from N and replaces all previously solved variables $x_1, \ldots, x_{i-1}$ by their respective solved forms to obtain the literal $\ell' = \ell[t_1, \ldots, t_{i-1}]$. It then calls function linearize on literal ℓ' which returns a *set* of literals, each obtained by replacing all but one occurrence of x_i in ℓ with the value of x_i in $\mathcal{I}$.[4]

Example 7. Consider an interpretation $\mathcal{I}$ where $x^{\mathcal{I}} = 1$, and Σ_{BV}-terms a and b with $x \notin FV(a) \cup FV(b)$. We have that $\mathrm{linearize}(x, \mathcal{I}, x \cdot (x + a) \approx b)$ returns the set $\{1 \cdot (x + a) \approx b, x \cdot (1 + a) \approx b\}$; $\mathrm{linearize}(x, \mathcal{I}, x \geq_u a)$ returns the singleton set $\{x \geq_u a\}$; $\mathrm{linearize}(x, \mathcal{I}, a \not\approx b)$ returns the empty set. $\triangle$

If the set N_i is non-empty, the selection function heuristically chooses a literal from N_i (indicated in Fig. 3 with $\mathrm{choose}(N_i)$). It then computes a solved form t_i for x_i by solving the chosen literal for x_i with the function solve described in the previous section. If N_i is empty, we let t_i is simply the value of x_i in the given model $\mathcal{I}$. After that, x_i is eliminated from all the previous terms $t_1, \ldots, t_{i-1}$ by replacing it with t_i. After processing all n variables of $\boldsymbol{x}$, the tuple $(t_1, \ldots, t_n)$ is returned.

The configurations of selection function $\mathcal{S}_c^{BV}$ determine how literals in M are modified by the $\mathrm{project}_c$ function prior to computing solved forms, based on the current model $\mathcal{I}$. With the *model value* configuration $\mathbf{m}$, the selection function effective ignores the structure of all literals in M and (because the set N_i is empty) ends up choosing the value $x_i^{\mathcal{I}}$ as the solved form variable

---

[4] This is a simple heuristic to generate literals that can be solved for x_i. More elaborate heuristics could be used in practice.

x_i, for each i. On the other end of the spectrum, the configuration **k** *keeps* all literals in M unchanged. The remaining two configurations have an effect on how disequalities and inequalities are handled by $\mathsf{project}_c$. With configuration **s** $\mathsf{project}_c$ normalizes any kind of literal (equality, inequality or disequality) $s \bowtie t$ to an equality by adding the *slack* value $(s - t)^{\mathcal{I}}$ to t. With configuration **b** it maps equalities to themselves and inequalities and disequalities to an equality corresponding to a *boundary point* of the relation between s and t based on the current model. Specifically, it adds one to t if s is greater than t in $\mathcal{I}$, it subtracts one if s is smaller than t, and returns $s \approx t$ if their value is the same. These two configurations are inspired by quantifier elimination techniques for linear arithmetic [5,15]. In the following, we provide an end-to-end example of our technique for quantifier instantiation that makes use of selection function $\mathcal{S}_c^{BV}$.

Example 8. Consider formula $\varphi = \exists \boldsymbol{y}. \forall x_1. (x_1 \cdot a \leq_u b)$ where a and b are terms with no free occurrences of x_1. To determine the satisfiability of φ, we invoke $\mathsf{CEGQI}_{\mathcal{S}^{BV}}$ on φ for some configuration c. Say that in the first iteration of the loop, we find that $\Gamma' = \Gamma \cup \{x_1 \cdot a >_u b\}$ is satisfied by some model $\mathcal{I}$ of T_{BV} such that $x_1^{\mathcal{I}} = 1$, $a^{\mathcal{I}} = 1$, and $b^{\mathcal{I}} = 0$. We invoke $\mathcal{S}_c^{BV}((x_1), \mathcal{I}, \Gamma')$ and first compute $M = \{x_1 \cdot a >_u b\}$, the set of literals of Γ' that are satisfied by $\mathcal{I}$. The table below summarizes the values of the internal variables of $\mathcal{S}_c^{BV}$ for the various configurations:

Config	N_1	t_1
m	$\emptyset$	1
k	$\{x_1 \cdot a >_u b\}$	$\varepsilon z. (a <_u -b \mid b) \Rightarrow z \cdot a >_u b$
s, b	$\{x_1 \cdot a \approx b+1\}$	$\varepsilon z. ((-a \mid a) \mathrel{\&} b+1 \approx b+1) \Rightarrow z \cdot a \approx b+1$

In each case, $\mathcal{S}_c^{BV}$ returns the tuple (t_1), and we add the instance $t_1 \cdot a \leq_u b$ to Γ. Consider configuration **k** where t_1 is the choice expression $\varepsilon z. ((a <_u -b \mid b) \Rightarrow z \cdot a >_u b)$. Since t_1 is ε-valid, due to the semantics of ε, this instance is equivalent to:

$$((a <_u -b \mid b) \Rightarrow k \cdot a >_u b) \wedge k \cdot a \leq_u b \tag{1}$$

for fresh variable k. This formula is T_{BV}-satisfiable if and only if $\neg(a <_u -b \mid b)$ is T_{BV}-satisfiable. In the second iteration of the loop in $\mathsf{CEGQI}_{\mathcal{S}_c^{BV}}$, set Γ contains formula (1) above. We have two possible outcomes:

(i) $\neg(a <_u -b \mid b)$ is T_{BV}-unsatisfiable. Then (1) and hence Γ are T_{BV}-unsatisfiable, and the procedure terminates with "unsat".

(ii) $\neg(a <_u -b \mid b)$ is satisfied by some model $\mathcal{J}$ of T_{BV}. Then $\exists z. z \cdot a \leq_u b$ is false in $\mathcal{J}$ since the invertibility condition of $z \cdot a \leq_u b$ is false in $\mathcal{J}$. Hence, $\Gamma' = \Gamma \cup \{x_1 \cdot a >_u b\}$ is unsatisfiable, and the algorithm terminates with "sat".

In fact, we argue later that quantified bit-vector formulas like φ above, which contain only one occurrence of a universal variable, require at most one instantiation before $\mathsf{CEGQI}_{\mathcal{S}_k^{BV}}$ terminates. The same guarantee does not hold with the other configurations. In particular, configuration **m** generates the instantiation where t_1 is 1, which simplifies to $a \leq_u b$. This may not be sufficient to show that Γ or Γ' is unsatisfiable in the second iteration of the loop and the algorithm may resort to *enumerating* a repeating pattern of instantiations, such as $x_1 \mapsto 1, 2, 3, \ldots$ and so on. This obviously does not scale for problems with large bit-widths. $\triangle$

More generally, we note that $\mathsf{CEGQI}_{\mathcal{S}_k^{BV}}$ terminates with at most one instance for input formulas whose body has just one literal and a single occurrence of each universal variable. The same guarantee does not hold for instance for quantified formulas whose body has multiple disjuncts. For some intuition, consider extending the second conjunct of (1) with an additional disjunct, i.e. $(k \cdot a \leq_u b \vee \ell[k])$. A model can be found for this formula in which the invertibility condition $(a <_u -b \mid b)$ is still satisfied, and hence we are not guaranteed to terminate on the second iteration of the loop. Similarly, if the literals of the input formula have multiple occurrences of x_1, then multiple instances may be returned by the selection function since the literals returned by linearize in Fig. 3 depend on the model value of x_1, and hence more than one possible instance may be considered in loop in Fig. 2.

The following theorem summarizes the properties of our selection functions. In the following, we say a quantified formula is *unit linear invertible* if it is of the form $\forall x.\ell[x]$ where ℓ is linear in x and has an invertibility condition for x. We say a selection function is *n-finite* for a quantified formula ψ if the number of possible instantiations it returns is at most n for some positive integer n.

Theorem 9. *Let $\psi[x]$ be a quantifier-free formula in the signature of T_{BV}.*

1. $\mathcal{S}_c^{BV}$ *is a finite selection function for x and ψ for all $c \in \{\mathbf{m}, \mathbf{k}, \mathbf{s}, \mathbf{b}\}$.*
2. $\mathcal{S}_\mathbf{m}^{BV}$ *is monotonic.*
3. $\mathcal{S}_\mathbf{k}^{BV}$ *is 1-finite if ψ is unit linear invertible.*
4. $\mathcal{S}_\mathbf{k}^{BV}$ *is monotonic if ψ is unit linear invertible.*

This theorem implies that counterexample-guided instantiation using configuration $\mathcal{S}_\mathbf{m}^{BV}$ is a decision procedure for quantified bit-vectors. However, in practice the worst-case number of instances considered by this configuration for a variable $x_{[n]}$ is proportional to the number of its possible values (2^n), which is practically infeasible for sufficiently large n. More interestingly, counterexample-guided instantiation using $\mathcal{S}_\mathbf{k}^{BV}$ is a decision procedure for quantified formulas that are unit linear invertible, and moreover has the guarantee that at most one instantiation is returned by this selection function. Hence, formulas in this fragment can be effectively reduced to quantifier-free bit-vector constraints in at most two iterations of the loop of procedure $\mathsf{CEGQI}_{\mathcal{S}}$ in Fig. 2.

4.2   Implementation

We implemented the new instantiation techniques described in this section as an extension of CVC4, which is a DPLL(T)-based SMT solver [20] that supports quantifier-free bit-vector constraints, (arbitrarily nested) quantified formulas, and support for choice expressions. For the latter, all choice expressions $\varepsilon x.\,\varphi[x]$ are eliminated from assertions by replacing them with a fresh variable k of the same type and adding $\varphi[k]$ as a new assertion, which notice is sound since all choice expressions we consider are ε-valid. In the remainder of the paper, we will refer to our extension of the solver as **cegqi**. In the following, we discuss important implementation details of the extension.

Handling Duplicate Instantiations. The selection functions $\mathcal{S}_{\mathsf{s}}^{BV}$ and $\mathcal{S}_{\mathsf{b}}^{BV}$ are not guaranteed to be monotonic, neither is $\mathcal{S}_{\mathsf{k}}^{BV}$ for quantified formulas that contain more than one occurrence of universal variables. Hence, when applying these strategies to arbitrary quantified formulas, we use a two-tiered strategy that invokes $\mathcal{S}_{\mathsf{m}}^{BV}$ as a second resort if the instance for the terms returned by a selection function already exists in Γ.

Linearizing Rewrites. Our selection function in Fig. 3 uses the function linearize to compute literals that are linear in the variable x_i to solve for. The way we presently implement linearize makes those literals dependent on the value of x_i in the current model $\mathcal{I}$, with the risk of overfitting to that model. To address this limitation, we use a set of equivalence-preserving rewrite rules whose goal is to reduce the number of occurrences of x_i to one when possible, by applying basic algebraic manipulations. As a trivial example, a literal like $x_i + x_i \approx a$ is rewritten first to $2 \cdot x_i \approx a$ which is linear in x_i if a does not contain x_i. In that case, this literal, and so the original one, has an invertibility condition as discussed in Sect. 3.

Variable Elimination. We use procedure solve from Sect. 3 not only for selecting quantifier instantiations, but also for eliminating variables from quantified formulas. In particular, for a quantified formula of the form $\forall x \boldsymbol{y}.\,\ell \Rightarrow \varphi[x, \boldsymbol{y}]$, if ℓ is linear in x and $\mathsf{solve}(x, \ell)$ returns a term s containing no ε-expressions, we can replace this formula by $\forall \boldsymbol{y}.\,\varphi[s, \boldsymbol{y}]$. When ℓ is an equality, this is sometimes called destructive equality resolution (DER) and is an important implementation-level optimization in state-of-the-art bit-vector solvers [25]. As shown in Fig. 1, we use the getInverse function to increase the likelihood that solve returns a term that contains no ε-expressions.

Handling Extract. Consider formula $\forall x_{[32]}.\,(x[31:16] \not\approx a_{[16]} \vee x[15:0] \not\approx b_{[16]})$. Since all invertibility conditions for the extract operator are $\top$, rather than producing choice expressions we have found it more effective to eliminate extracts via rewriting. As a consequence, we independently solve constraints for *regions* of quantified variables when they appear underneath applications of extract operations. In this example, we let the solved form of x be $y_{[16]} \circ z_{[16]}$ where y and z are fresh variables, and subsequently solve for these variables in $y \approx a$ and $z \approx b$. Hence, we may instantiate x with $a \circ b$, a term that we would not have found by considering the two literals independently in the negated body of the formula above.

5   Evaluation

We implemented our techniques in the solver **cegqi** and considered four configurations **cegqi**$_c$, where **c** is one of $\{m, k, s, b\}$, corresponding to the four selection function configurations described in Sect. 4. Out of these four configurations, **cegqi**$_m$ is the only one that does not employ our new techniques but uses only model values for instantiation. It can thus be considered our base configuration. All configurations enable the optimizations described in Sect. 4.2 when applicable. We compared them against all entrants of the quantified bit-vector division of the 2017 SMT competition SMT-COMP: Boolector [16], CVC4 [2], Q3B [14] and Z3 [6]. With the exception of Q3B, all solvers are related to our approach since they are instantiation-based. However, none of these solvers utilizes invertibility conditions when constructing instantiations. We ran all experiments on the StarExec logic solving service [24] with a 300 s CPU and wall clock time limit and 100 GB memory limit.

We evaluated our approach on all 5,151 benchmarks from the quantified bit-vector logic (BV) of SMT-LIB [3]. The results are summarized in Table 4. Configuration **cegqi**$_b$ solves the highest number of unsatisfiable benchmarks (4, 399), which is 30 more than the next best configuration **cegqi**$_s$ and 37 more than

Table 4. Results on satisfiable and unsatisfiable benchmarks with a 300 s timeout.

unsat	Boolector	CVC4	Q3B	Z3	cegqi$_m$	cegqi$_k$	cegqi$_s$	cegqi$_b$
h-uauto	14	12	93	24	10	103	105	**106**
keymaera	3917	3790	3781	**3923**	3803	3798	3888	3918
psyco	**62**	**62**	49	**62**	**62**	39	**62**	61
scholl	57	36	13	**67**	36	27	36	35
tptp	55	52	**56**	**56**	**56**	**56**	**56**	**56**
uauto	**137**	72	131	**137**	72	72	135	**137**
ws-fixpoint	74	71	**75**	74	**75**	74	**75**	**75**
ws-ranking	16	8	18	**19**	15	11	12	11
Total unsat	4332	4103	4216	4362	4129	4180	4369	**4399**
sat	Boolector	CVC4	Q3B	Z3	cegqi$_m$	cegqi$_k$	cegqi$_s$	cegqi$_b$
h-uauto	15	10	**17**	13	16	**17**	16	**17**
keymaera	**108**	21	24	**108**	20	13	36	75
psyco	131	**132**	50	131	**132**	60	**132**	129
scholl	**232**	160	201	204	203	188	208	211
tptp	**17**	**17**	**17**	**17**	**17**	**17**	**17**	**17**
uauto	14	14	15	**16**	14	14	14	14
ws-fixpoint	45	49	**54**	36	45	51	49	50
ws-ranking	19	15	**37**	33	33	31	31	32
Total sat	**581**	418	415	558	480	391	503	545
Total (5151)	4913	4521	4631	4920	4609	4571	4872	**4944**

the next best external solver, Z3. Compared to the instantiation-based solvers Boolector, CVC4 and Z3, the performance of **cegqi$_b$** is particularly strong on the h-uauto family, which are verification conditions from the Ultimate Automizer tool [11]. For satisfiable benchmarks, Boolector solves the most (581), which is 36 more than our best configuration **cegqi$_b$**.

Overall, our best configuration **cegqi$_b$** solved 335 more benchmarks than our base configuration **cegqi$_m$**. A more detailed runtime comparison between the two is provided by the scatter plot in Fig. 4. Moreover, **cegqi$_b$** solved 24 more benchmarks than the best external solver, Z3. In terms of uniquely solved instances, **cegqi$_b$** was able to solve 139 benchmarks that were not solved by Z3, whereas Z3 solved 115 benchmarks that **cegqi$_b$** did not. Overall, **cegqi$_b$** was able to solve 21 of the 79 benchmarks (26.6%) not solved by any of the other solvers. For 18 of these 21 benchmarks, it terminated after considering no more than 4 instantiations. These cases indicate that using symbolic terms for instantiation solves problems for which other techniques, such as those that enumerate instantiations based on model values, do not scale.

Interestingly, configuration **cegqi$_k$**, despite having the strong guarantees given by Theorem 9, performed relatively poorly on this set (with 4, 571 solved instances overall). We attribute this to the fact that most of the quantified formulas in this set are not unit linear invertible. In total, we found that only 25.6% of the formulas considered during solving were unit linear invertible. However, only a handful of benchmarks were such that *all* quantified formulas in the problem were unit linear invertible. This might explain the superior performance of **cegqi$_s$** and **cegqi$_b$** which use invertibility conditions but in a less monolithic way.

For some intuition on this, consider the problem $\forall x.\,(x > a \vee x < b)$ where a and b are such that $a > b$ is T_{BV}-valid. Intuitively, to show that this formula is unsatisfiable requires the solver to find an x between b and a. This is apparent when considering the dual problem $\exists x.\,(x \leq a \wedge x \geq b)$. Configuration **cegqi$_b$** is capable of finding such an x, for instance, by considering the instantiation $x \mapsto a$ when solving for the boundary point of the first disjunct. Configuration **cegqi$_k$**, on the other hand, would instead consider the instantiation of x for two terms that witness ε-expressions: some k_1 that is

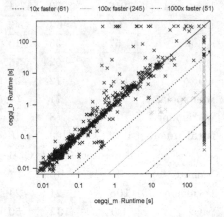

Fig. 4. Configuration **cegqi$_m$** vs. **cegqi$_b$**.

never smaller than a, and some k_2 that is never greater that b. Neither of these terms necessarily resides in between a and b since the solver may subsequently consider models where $k_1 > b$ and $k_2 < a$. This points to a potential use for invertibility conditions that solve multiple literals simultaneously, something we are currently investigating.

6   Conclusion

We have presented a new class of strategies for solving quantified bit-vector formulas based on invertibility conditions. We have derived invertibility conditions for the majority of operators in a standard theory of fixed-width bit-vectors. An implementation based on this approach solves over 25% of previously unsolved verification benchmarks from SMT LIB, and outperforms all other state-of-the-art bit-vector solvers overall.

In future work, we plan to develop a framework in which the correctness of invertibility conditions can be formally established independently of bit-width. We are working on deriving invertibility conditions that are optimal for linear constraints, in the sense of admitting the simplest propositional encoding. We also are investigating conditions that cover additional bit-vector operators, some cases of non-linear literals, as well as those that cover multiple constraints. While this is a challenging task, we believe efficient syntax-guided synthesis solvers can continue to help push progress in this direction. Finally, we plan to investigate the use of invertibility conditions for performing quantifier elimination on bit-vector constraints. This will require a procedure for deriving concrete witnesses from choice expressions.

References

1. Alur, R., Bodík, R., Juniwal, G., Martin, M.M.K., Raghothaman, M., Seshia, S.A., Singh, R., Solar-Lezama, A., Torlak, E., Udupa, A.: Syntax-guided synthesis. In: Formal Methods in Computer-Aided Design, FMCAD 2013, Portland, OR, USA, 20–23 October 2013, pp. 1–8 (2013)
2. Barrett, C., et al.: CVC4. In: Gopalakrishnan, G., Qadeer, S. (eds.) CAV 2011. LNCS, vol. 6806, pp. 171–177. Springer, Heidelberg (2011). https://doi.org/10.1007/978-3-642-22110-1_14. http://dl.acm.org/citation.cfm?id=2032305.2032319
3. Barrett, C., Stump, A., Tinelli, C.: The SMT-LIB standard: version 2.0. In: Gupta, A., Kroening, D. (eds.) Proceedings of the 8th International Workshop on Satisfiability Modulo Theories, Edinburgh, UK (2010)
4. Bjørner, N., Janota, M.: Playing with quantified satisfaction. In: 20th International Conferences on Logic for Programming, Artificial Intelligence and Reasoning - Short Presentations, LPAR 2015, Suva, Fiji, 24–28 November 2015, pp. 15–27 (2015)
5. Cooper, D.C.: Theorem proving in arithmetic without multiplication. In: Meltzer, B., Michie, D. (eds.) Machine Intelligence, vol. 7, pp. 91–100. Edinburgh University Press (1972)
6. de Moura, L., Bjørner, N.: Z3: an efficient SMT solver. In: Ramakrishnan, C.R., Rehof, J. (eds.) TACAS 2008. LNCS, vol. 4963, pp. 337–340. Springer, Heidelberg (2008). https://doi.org/10.1007/978-3-540-78800-3_24. http://dl.acm.org/citation.cfm?id=1792734.1792766
7. Dutertre, B.: Yices 2.2. In: Biere, A., Bloem, R. (eds.) CAV 2014. LNCS, vol. 8559, pp. 737–744. Springer, Cham (2014). https://doi.org/10.1007/978-3-319-08867-9_49

8. Dutertre, B.: Solving exists/forall problems in yices. In: Workshop on Satisfiability Modulo Theories (2015)
9. Ekici, B., et al.: SMTCoq: a plug-in for integrating SMT solvers into Coq. In: Majumdar, R., Kunčak, V. (eds.) CAV 2017. LNCS, vol. 10427, pp. 126–133. Springer, Cham (2017). https://doi.org/10.1007/978-3-319-63390-9_7
10. Ge, Y., de Moura, L.: Complete instantiation for quantified formulas in satisfiabiliby modulo theories. In: Bouajjani, A., Maler, O. (eds.) CAV 2009. LNCS, vol. 5643, pp. 306–320. Springer, Heidelberg (2009). https://doi.org/10.1007/978-3-642-02658-4_25
11. Heizmann, M., et al.: Ultimate automizer with an on-demand construction of Floyd-Hoare automata. In: Legay, A., Margaria, T. (eds.) TACAS 2017. LNCS, vol. 10206, pp. 394–398. Springer, Heidelberg (2017). https://doi.org/10.1007/978-3-662-54580-5_30
12. Hilbert, D., Bernays, P.: Grundlagen der Mathematik. Die Grundlehren der mathematischen Wissenschaften. Verlag von Julius Springer, Berlin (1934)
13. John, A.K., Chakraborty, S.: A layered algorithm for quantifier elimination from linear modular constraints. Formal Methods Syst. Des. **49**(3), 272–323 (2016). https://doi.org/10.1007/s10703-016-0260-9
14. Jonáš, M., Strejček, J.: Solving quantified bit-vector formulas using binary decision diagrams. In: Creignou, N., Le Berre, D. (eds.) SAT 2016. LNCS, vol. 9710, pp. 267–283. Springer, Cham (2016). https://doi.org/10.1007/978-3-319-40970-2_17
15. Loos, R., Weispfenning, V.: Applying linear quantifier elimination (1993)
16. Niemetz, A., Preiner, M., Biere, A.: Boolector 2.0 system description. J. Satisfiability Boolean Model. Comput. **9**, 53–58 (2014). (published 2015)
17. Niemetz, A., Preiner, M., Biere, A.: Precise and complete propagation based local search for satisfiability modulo theories. In: Chaudhuri, S., Farzan, A. (eds.) CAV 2016. LNCS, vol. 9779, pp. 199–217. Springer, Cham (2016). https://doi.org/10.1007/978-3-319-41528-4_11
18. Niemetz, A., Preiner, M., Biere, A.: Propagation based local search for bit-precise reasoning. Formal Methods Syst. Des. **51**(3), 608–636 (2017). https://doi.org/10.1007/s10703-017-0295-6
19. Niemetz, A., Preiner, M., Reynolds, A., Barrett, C., Tinelli, C.: On solving quantified bit-vectors using invertibility conditions. eprint arXiv:cs.LO/1804.05025 (2018)
20. Nieuwenhuis, R., Oliveras, A., Tinelli, C.: Solving SAT and SAT modulo theories: from an abstract Davis-Putnam-Logemann-Loveland Procedure to DPLL(T). J. ACM **53**(6), 937–977 (2006)
21. Preiner, M., Niemetz, A., Biere, A.: Counterexample-guided model synthesis. In: Tools and Algorithms for the Construction and Analysis of Systems - 23rd International Conference, TACAS 2017, Held as Part of the European Joint Conferences on Theory and Practice of Software, ETAPS 2017, Uppsala, Sweden, 22–29 April 2017, Proceedings, Part I, pp. 264–280 (2017)
22. Reynolds, A., Deters, M., Kuncak, V., Tinelli, C., Barrett, C.: Counterexample-guided quantifier instantiation for synthesis in SMT. In: Kroening, D., Păsăreanu, C.S. (eds.) CAV 2015. LNCS, vol. 9207, pp. 198–216. Springer, Cham (2015). https://doi.org/10.1007/978-3-319-21668-3_12
23. Reynolds, A., King, T., Kuncak, V.: Solving quantified linear arithmetic by counterexample-guided instantiation. Formal Methods Syst. Des. **51**(3), 500–532 (2017). https://doi.org/10.1007/s10703-017-0290-y

24. Stump, A., Sutcliffe, G., Tinelli, C.: StarExec: a cross-community infrastructure for logic solving. In: Demri, S., Kapur, D., Weidenbach, C. (eds.) IJCAR 2014. LNCS (LNAI), vol. 8562, pp. 367–373. Springer, Cham (2014). https://doi.org/10.1007/978-3-319-08587-6_28
25. Wintersteiger, C.M., Hamadi, Y., de Moura, L.M.: Efficiently solving quantified bit-vector formulas. Formal Methods Syst. Des. **42**(1), 3–23 (2013)

Understanding and Extending Incremental Determinization for 2QBF

Markus N. Rabe[1]([⊠]), Leander Tentrup[2], Cameron Rasmussen[1], and Sanjit A. Seshia[1]

[1] University of California, Berkeley,
Berkeley, USA
rabe@berkeley.edu
[2] Saarland University, Saarbrücken, Germany

Abstract. Incremental determinization is a recently proposed algorithm for solving quantified Boolean formulas with one quantifier alternation. In this paper, we formalize incremental determinization as a set of inference rules to help understand the design space of similar algorithms. We then present additional inference rules that extend incremental determinization in two ways. The first extension integrates the popular CEGAR principle and the second extension allows us to analyze different cases in isolation. The experimental evaluation demonstrates that the extensions significantly improve the performance.

1 Introduction

Solving quantified Boolean formulas (QBFs) is one of the core challenges in automated reasoning and is particularly important for applications in verification and synthesis. For example, program synthesis with syntax guidance [1,2] and the synthesis of reactive controllers from LTL specifications has been encoded in QBF [3,4]. Many of these problems require only formulas with one quantifier alternation (2QBF), which are the focus of this paper.

Algorithms for QBF and program synthesis largely rely on the counterexample-guided inductive synthesis principle (CEGIS) [5], originating in abstraction refinement (CEGAR) [6,7]. For example, for program synthesis, CEGIS-style algorithms alternate between generating candidate programs and checking them for counter-examples, which allows us to lift arbitrary verification approaches to synthesis algorithms. Unfortunately, this approach often degenerates into a plain guess-and-check loop when counter-examples cannot be generalized effectively. This carries over to the simpler setting of 2QBF. For example, even for a simple formula such as $\forall x.\exists y.\ x = y$, where x and y are 32-bit numbers, most QBF algorithms simply enumerate all 2^{32} pairs of assignments. In fact, even the modern QBF solvers diverge on this formula when preprocessing is deactivated.

Recently, Incremental Determinization (ID) has been suggested to overcome this problem [8]. ID represents a departure from the CEGIS approach in that it

© The Author(s) 2018
H. Chockler and G. Weissenbacher (Eds.): CAV 2018, LNCS 10982, pp. 256–274, 2018.
https://doi.org/10.1007/978-3-319-96142-2_17

is structured around identifying which variables have unique Skolem functions. (To prove the truth of a 2QBF $\forall x. \exists y.\ \varphi$ we have to find Skolem functions f mapping x to y such that $\varphi[f/y]$ is valid.) After assigning Skolem functions to a few of the existential variables, the propagation procedure determines Skolem functions for other variables that are uniquely implied by that assignment. When the assignment of Skolem functions turns out to be incorrect, ID analyzes the conflict, derives a conflict clause, and backtracks some of the assignments. In other words, ID lifts CDCL to the space of Skolem functions.

ID can solve the simple example given above and shows good performance on various application benchmarks. Yet, the QBF competitions have shown that the relative performance of ID and CEGIS still varies a lot between benchmarks [9]. A third family of QBF solvers, based on the *expansion* of universal variables [10–12], shows yet again different performance characteristics and outperforms both ID and CEGIS on some (few) benchmarks. This variety of performance characteristics of different approaches indicates that current QBF solvers could be significantly improved by integrating the different reasoning principles.

In this paper, we first formalize and generalize ID [8] (Sect. 3). This helps us to disentangle the working principles of the algorithm from implementation-level design choices. Thereby our analysis of ID enables a systematic and principled search for better algorithms for quantified reasoning. To demonstrate the value and flexibility of the formalization, we present two extensions of ID that integrate CEGIS-style inductive reasoning (Sect. 4) and expansion (Sect. 5). In the experimental evaluation we demonstrate that both extensions significantly improve the performance compared to plain ID (Sect. 6).

Related Work. This work is written in the tradition of works such as the Model Evolution Calculus [13], AbstractDPLL [14], MCSAT [15], and recent calculi for QBF [16], which present search algorithms as inference rules to enable the study and extension of these algorithms. ID and the inference rules presented in this paper can be seen as an instantiation of the more general frameworks, such as MCSAT [15] or Abstract Conflict Driven Learning [17].

Like ID, quantified conflict-driven clause learning (QCDCL) lifts CDCL to QBF [18,19]. The approaches differ in that QCDCL does not reason about functions, but only about values of variables. Fazekas et al. have formalized QCDCL as inference rules [16].

2QBF solvers based on CEGAR/CEGIS search for universal assignments and matching existential assignments using two SAT solvers [5,20,21]. There are several generalizations of this approach to QBF with more than one quantifier alternation [22–26].

2   Preliminaries

Quantified Boolean formulas over a finite set of variables $x \in X$ with domain $\mathbb{B} = \{0, 1\}$ are generated by the following grammar:

$$\varphi := 0 \mid 1 \mid x \mid \neg\varphi \mid (\varphi) \mid \varphi \vee \varphi \mid \varphi \wedge \varphi \mid \exists x.\ \varphi \mid \forall x.\ \varphi$$

We consider all other logical operations, including implication, XOR, and equality as syntactic sugar with the usual definitions. We abbreviate multiple quantifications $Qx_1.Qx_2.\ldots Qx_n.\varphi$ using the same quantifier $Q \in \{\forall, \exists\}$ by the quantification over the set of variables $X = \{x_1, \ldots, x_n\}$, denoted as $QX.\varphi$.

An *assignment* $\boldsymbol{x}$ to a set of variables X is a function $\boldsymbol{x} : X \to \mathbb{B}$ that maps each variable $x \in X$ to either $\mathbf{1}$ or $\mathbf{0}$. Given a propositional formula φ over variables X and an assignment $\boldsymbol{x}'$ to $X' \subseteq X$, we define $\varphi(\boldsymbol{x}')$ to be the formula obtained by replacing the variables X' by their truth value in $\boldsymbol{x}'$. By $\varphi(\boldsymbol{x}', \boldsymbol{x}'')$ we denote the replacement by multiple assignments for disjoint sets $X', X'' \subseteq X$.

A quantifier $Q\,x.\,\varphi$ for $Q \in \{\exists, \forall\}$ *binds* the variable x in its subformula φ and we assume w.l.o.g. that every variable is bound at most once in any formula. A *closed* QBF is a formula in which all variables are bound. We define the dependency set of an existentially quantified variable y in a formula φ as the set $dep(y)$ of universally quantified variables x such that φ's subformula $\exists y.\,\psi$ is a subformula of φ's subformula $\forall x.\psi'$. A *Skolem function* f_y maps assignments to $dep(y)$ to a truth value. We define the truth of a QBF φ as the existence of Skolem functions $f_Y = \{f_{y_1}, \ldots, f_{y_n}\}$ for the existentially quantified variables $Y = \{y_1, \ldots, y_n\}$, such that $\varphi(\boldsymbol{x}, f_Y(\boldsymbol{x}))$ holds for every $\boldsymbol{x}$, where $f_Y(\boldsymbol{x})$ is the assignment to Y that the Skolem functions f_Y provide for $\boldsymbol{x}$.

A formula is in *prenex normal form*, if the formula is closed and starts with a sequence of quantifiers followed by a propositional subformula. A formula φ is in the kQBF fragment for $k \in \mathbb{N}^+$ if it is closed, in prenex normal form, and has exactly $k-1$ alternations between $\exists$ and $\forall$ quantifiers.

A *literal* l is either a variable $x \in X$, or its negation $\neg x$. Given a set of literals $\{l_1, \ldots, l_n\}$, their disjunction $(l_1 \vee \ldots \vee l_n)$ is called a *clause* and their conjunction $(l_1 \wedge \ldots \wedge l_n)$ is called a *cube*. We use $\bar{l}$ to denote the literal that is the logical negation of l. We denote the variable of a literal by $var(l)$ and lift the notion to clauses $var(l_1 \vee \cdots \vee l_n) = \{var(l_1), \ldots, var(l_n)\}$.

A propositional formula is in conjunctive normal form (CNF), if it is a conjunction of clauses. A prenex QBF is in prenex conjunctive normal form (PCNF) if its propositional subformula is in CNF. Every QBF φ can be transformed into an equivalent PCNF with size $O(|\varphi|)$ [27].

Resolution is a well-known proof rule that allows us to merge two clauses as follows. Given two clauses $C_1 \vee v$ and $C_2 \vee \neg v$, we call $C_1 \otimes_v C_2 = C_1 \vee C_2$ their *resolvent* with pivot v. The resolution rule states that $C_1 \vee v$ and $C_2 \vee \neg v$ imply their resolvent. Resolution is refutationally complete for propositional Boolean formulas, i.e. for every propositional Boolean formula that is equivalent to false we can derive the empty clause.

For *quantified* Boolean formulas, however, we need additional proof rules. The two most prominent ways to make resolution complete for QBF are to add either *universal reduction* or *universal expansion*, leading to the proof systems Q-resolution [28] and $\forall$Exp-Res [10,29], respectively.

Universal expansion eliminates a single universal variable by creating two copies of the subformulas of its quantifier. Let $Q_1.\forall x.Q_2.\ \varphi$ be a QBF in PCNF, where

Q_1 and Q_2 each are a sequence of quantifiers, and let Q_2 quantify over variables X. Universal expansion yields the *equivalent* formula $Q_1.Q_2.Q_2'.\ \varphi[1/x, X'/X] \wedge \varphi[0/x]$, where Q_2' is a copy of Q_2 but quantifying over a fresh set of variables X' instead of X. The term $\varphi[1/x,\ X'/X]$ denotes the φ where x is replaced by 1 and the variables X are replaced by their counterparts in X'.

Universal reduction allows us to drop universal variables from clauses when none of the existential variables in that clause may depend on them. Let C a clause of a QBF and let l be a literal of a universally quantified variable in C. Let us further assume that $\bar{l}$ does not occur in C. If all existential variables v in C we have $var(l) \notin dep(v)$, universal reduction allows us to remove l from C. The resulting formula is equivalent to the original formula.

Stack. For convenience, we use a stack data structure to describe the algorithm. Formally, a stack is a finite sequence. Given a stack S, we use $S(i)$ to denote the i-th element of the stack, starting with index 0, and we use $S.S'$ to denote concatenation. We use $S[0, i]$ to denote the prefix up to element i of S. All stacks we consider are stacks of sets. In a slight abuse of notation, we also use stacks as the union of their elements when it is clear from the context. We also introduce an operation specific to stacks of sets S: We define $add(S, i, x)$ to be the stack that results from extending the set on level i by element x.

2.1   Unique Skolem Functions

Incremental determinization builds on the notion of unique Skolem functions. Let $\forall X.\exists Y.\ \varphi$ be a 2QBF in PCNF and let χ be a formula over X characterizing the *domain* of the Skolem functions we are currently interested in. We say that a variable $v \in Y$ has a *unique Skolem function* for domain χ, if for each assignment $\boldsymbol{x}$ with $\chi(\boldsymbol{x})$ there is a *unique* assignment $\boldsymbol{v}$ to v such that $\varphi(\boldsymbol{x}, \boldsymbol{v})$ is satisfiable. In particular, a unique Skolem function is a Skolem function:

Lemma 1. *If all existential variables have a unique Skolem function for the full domain $\chi = 1$, the formula is true.*

The semantic characterization of unique Skolem functions above does not help us with the computation of Skolem functions directly. We now introduce a local approximation of unique Skolem functions and show how it can be used as a propagation procedure.

We consider a set of variables $D \subseteq X \cup Y$ with $D \supseteq X$ and focus on the subset $\varphi|_D$ of clauses that only contain variables in D. We further assume that the existential variables in D already have unique Skolem functions for χ in the formula $\varphi|_D$. We now define how to extend D by an existential variable $v \notin D$. To define a Skolem function for v we only consider the clauses with *unique consequence* v, denoted $\mathcal{U}_v$, that contain a literal of v and otherwise only literals of variables in D. (Note that $\varphi|_D \cup \mathcal{U}_v = \varphi|_{D \cup \{v\}}$.) We define that variable v has a *unique Skolem function relative to D* for χ, if for all assignments to D satisfying χ and φ there is a unique assignment to v satisfying $\mathcal{U}_v$.

In order to determine unique Skolem functions relative to a set D in practice, we split the definition into the two statements deterministic and unconflicted. Each statement can be checked by a SAT solver and together they imply that variable v has a unique Skolem function relative to D.

Given a clause C with unique consequence v, let us call $\neg(C \setminus \{v, \neg v\})$ the *antecedent* of C. Further, let $\mathcal{A}_l = \bigvee_{C \in \mathcal{U}_v, l \in C} \neg(C \setminus \{v, \neg v\})$ be the disjunction of antecedents for the unique consequences containing the literal l of v. It is clear that whenever $\mathcal{A}_v$ is satisfied, v needs to be true, and whenever $\mathcal{A}_{\neg v}$ is satisfied, v need to be false. We define:

$$\text{deterministic}(v, \varphi, \chi, D) := \forall D. \; \varphi|_D \wedge \chi \implies \mathcal{A}_v \vee \mathcal{A}_{\neg v}$$
$$\text{unconflicted}(v, \varphi, \chi, D) := \forall D. \; \varphi|_D \wedge \chi \implies \neg(\mathcal{A}_v \wedge \mathcal{A}_{\neg v})$$

deterministic states that v needs to be assigned either true or false for every assignment to D in the domain χ that is consistent with the existing Skolem function definitions $\varphi|_D$. Accordingly, unconflicted states that v does not have to be true and false at the same time (which would indicate a conflict) for any such assignment. Unique Skolem functions relative to a set D approximate unique Skolem functions as follows:

Lemma 2. *Let the existential variables in D have unique Skolem functions for domain χ and let $v \in Y$ have a unique Skolem function relative to D for domain χ. Then v has a unique Skolem function for domain χ.*

3   Inference Rules for Incremental Determinization

In this section, we develop a nondeterministic algorithm that formalizes and generalizes ID. We describe the algorithm in terms of inference rules that specify how the state of the algorithm can be developed. The state of the algorithm consists of the following elements:

- The solver status $S \in \{\text{Ready}, \text{Conflict}(L, \boldsymbol{x}), \text{SAT}, \text{UNSAT}\}$. The conflict status has two parameters: a clause L that is used to compute the learnt clause and the assignment $\boldsymbol{x}$ to the universals witnessing the conflict.
- A stack C of sets of clauses. $C(0)$ contains the original and the learnt clauses. $C(i)$ for $i > 0$ contain temporary clauses introduced by decisions.
- A stack D of sets of variables. The union of all levels in the stack represent the set of variables that currently have unique Skolem functions and the clauses in $C|_D$ represent these Skolem functions. $D(0)$ contains the universals and the existentials whose Skolem functions do not depend on decisions.
- A formula χ over $D(0)$ characterizing the set of assignments to the universals for which we still need to find a Skolem function.
- A formula α over variables $D(0)$ representing a *temporary* restriction on the domain of the Skolem functions.

We assume that we are given a 2QBF in PCNF $\forall X.\exists Y. \; \varphi$ and that all clauses in φ contain an existential variable. (If φ contains a non-tautological clause

$$\text{PROPAGATE} \quad \frac{(\text{Ready}, C, D, \chi, \alpha) \quad v \notin D \quad \text{deterministic}(v, C, \chi \wedge \alpha, D) \quad \text{unconflicted}(v, C, \chi \wedge \alpha, D)}{(\text{Ready}, C, add(D, |D| - 1, v), \chi, \alpha)}$$

$$\text{DECIDE} \quad \frac{(\text{Ready}, C, D, \chi, \alpha) \quad v \notin D \quad \text{all } c \in \delta \text{ have unique consequence } v}{(\text{Ready}, C.\delta, D.\emptyset, \chi, \alpha)}$$

$$\text{SAT} \quad \frac{(\text{Ready}, C, D, \chi, 1) \quad D = X \cup Y}{(\text{SAT}, C, D, \chi, 1)}$$

Fig. 1. Inference rules needed to prove true QBF

without existential variables, the formula is trivially false by universal reduction.) We define $(\text{Ready}, \varphi, X, 1, 1)$ to be the initial state of the algorithm. That is, the clause stack C initially has height 1 and contains the clauses of the formula φ. We initialize D as the stack of height 1 containing the universals.

Before we dive into the inference rules, we want to point out that some of the rules in this calculus are not computable in polynomial time. The judgements deterministic and unconflicted require us to solve a SAT problem and are, in general, NP-complete. This is still easier than the 2QBF problem itself (unless NP includes Π_2^P) and in practice they can be discharged quickly by SAT solvers.

3.1 True QBF

We continue with describing the basic version of ID, consisting of the rules in Figs. 1 and 2, and first focus on the rules in Fig. 1, which suffice to prove true 2QBFs. PROPAGATE allows us to add a variable to D, if it has a unique Skolem function relative to D. (The notation $add(D, |D| - 1, v)$ means that we add v to the last level of the stack.) The judgements deterministic and unconflicted involve the current set of clauses C (i.e. the union of all sets of clauses in the sequence C). These checks are restricted to the domain $\chi \wedge \alpha$. Both χ and α are true throughout this section; we discuss their use in Sects. 4 and 5.

Invariant 1. All existential variables in D have a unique Skolem function for the domain $\chi \wedge \alpha$ in the formula $\forall X. \exists Y. C|_D$, where $C|_D$ are the clauses in C that contain only variables in D.

If PROPAGATE identifies all variables to have unique Skolem functions relative to the growing set D, we know that they also have unique Skolem functions (Lemma 2). We can then apply SAT to reach the SAT state, representing that the formula has been proven true (Lemma 1).

Lemma 3. *ID cannot reach the SAT state for false QBF.*

Proof. Let us assume we reached the SAT state for a false 2QBF and prove the statement by way of contradiction. The SAT state can only be reached by the rule SAT and requires $D = X \cup Y$. By Invariant 1 all variables have a Skolem function in $\forall X.\exists Y.\ C$. Since C includes φ, this Skolem function does not violate any clause in φ, which means it is indeed a proof. □

When PROPAGATE is unable to determine the existence of a unique Skolem function (i.e. for variables where the judgement deterministic does not hold) we can use the rule DECIDE to introduce additional clauses such that deterministic holds and propagation can continue. Note that additional clauses make it easier to satisfy deterministic and adding the clause v (i.e. a unit clause) even *ensures* that deterministic holds for v.

Assuming we consider a true 2QBF, we can pick a Skolem function f_y for each existential variable y and encode it using DECIDE. We can simply consider the truth table of f_y in terms of the universal variables and define δ to be the set of clauses $\{\neg \boldsymbol{x} \vee v \mid f_y(\boldsymbol{x})\} \cup \{\neg \boldsymbol{x} \vee \neg v \mid \neg f_y(\boldsymbol{x})\}$. (Here we interpret the assignment $\boldsymbol{x}$ as a conjunction of literals.) These clauses have unique consequence v and they guarantee that v is deterministic. Further, they guarantee that v is unconflicted, as otherwise f_y would not be a Skolem function, so we can apply PROPAGATE to add v to D. Repeating this process for every variable let us reach the point where $Y \subseteq D$ and we can apply SAT to reach the SAT state.

Lemma 4. *ID can reach the SAT state for true QBF.*

Note that proving the truth of a QBF in this way requires guessing correct Skolem functions for all existentials. In Subsect. 3.4 we discuss how termination is guaranteed with a simpler type of decisions.

$$\text{CONFLICT} \quad \frac{(\mathsf{Ready}, C, D, \chi, \alpha) \qquad \boldsymbol{x} \text{ refutes } \mathsf{unconflicted}(v, C, \chi \wedge \alpha, D)}{(\mathsf{Conflict}(\{v, \neg v\}, \boldsymbol{x}), C, D, \chi, \alpha)}$$

$$\text{ANALYZE} \quad \frac{(\mathsf{Conflict}(L, \boldsymbol{x}), C, D, \chi, \alpha) \qquad c \in C(0) \qquad l \in L \qquad \bar{l} \in c}{(\mathsf{Conflict}(L \otimes_{var(l)} c, \boldsymbol{x}), C, D, \chi, \alpha)}$$

$$\text{LEARN} \quad \frac{(\mathsf{Conflict}(L, \boldsymbol{x}), C, D, \chi, \alpha) \qquad var(L) \not\subseteq D}{(\mathsf{Ready}, add(C, 0, L), D, \chi, \alpha)}$$

$$\text{UNSAT} \quad \frac{(\mathsf{Conflict}(L, \boldsymbol{x}), C, D, \chi, \alpha) \qquad var(L) \subseteq D(0) \qquad \boldsymbol{x} \not\models L}{(\mathsf{UNSAT}, C, D, \chi, \alpha)}$$

$$\text{BACKTRACK} \quad \frac{(S, C, D, \chi, \alpha) \qquad 0 < dlvl \leq |C|}{(S, C[0, dlvl], D[0, dlvl], \chi, \alpha)}$$

Fig. 2. Additional inference rules needed to disprove false QBF

3.2 False QBF

To disprove false 2QBFs, i.e. formulas that do not have a Skolem function, we need the rules in Fig. 2 in addition to PROPAGATE and DECIDE from Fig. 1. The conflict state can only be reached via the rule CONFLICT, which requires that a variable v is conflicted, i.e. unconflicted fails. The CONFLICT rule stores the assignment x to D that proves the conflict and it creates the nucleus of the learnt clause $\{v, \neg v\}$. Via ANALYZE we can then resolve that nucleus with clauses in $C(0)$, which consists of the original clauses and the clauses learnt so far. We are allowed to add the learnt clause back to $C(0)$ by applying LEARN.

Invariant 2. $C(0)$ is equivalent to φ.

Note that $C(0)$ and φ are propositional formulas over $X \cup Y$. Their equivalence means that they have the same set of satisfying assignments. We prove Invariant 2 together with the next invariant.

Invariant 3. Clause L in conflict state $\mathsf{Conflict}(L, x)$ is implied by φ.

Proof. $C(0)$ contains φ initially and is only ever changed by adding clauses through the LEARN rule, so $C(0) \Rightarrow \varphi$ holds throughout the computation.

We prove the other direction of Invariants 2 and 3 by mutual induction. Initially, $C(0)$ consists exactly of the clauses φ, satisfying Invariant 2. The nucleus of the learnt clause $v \vee \neg v$ is trivially true, so it is implied by any formula, which gives us the base case of Invariant 3. ANALYZE is the only rule modifying L, and hence soundness of resolution together with Invariant 2 already gives us the induction step for Invariant 3 [30]. Since LEARN is the only rule changing $C(0)$, Invariant 3 implies the induction step of Invariant 2. □

When adding the learnt clause to $C(0)$ we have to make sure that Invariant 1 is preserved. LEARN hence requires that we have backtracked far enough with BACKTRACK, such that at least one of the variables in L is not in D anymore. In this way, L may become part of future Skolem function definitions, but will first have to be checked for causing conflicts by PROPAGATE.

If all variables in L are in $D(0)$ and the assignment x from the conflict violates L, we can conclude the formula to be false using UNSAT. The soundness of this step follows from the fact that x includes an assignment satisfying $C(0)|_{D(0)}$ (i.e. the clauses defining the Skolem functions for $D(0)$), Invariants 1 and 3.

Lemma 5. *ID cannot reach the UNSAT state for true QBF.*

We will now show that we can disprove any false QBF. The main difficulty in this proof is to show that from any Ready state we can learn a *new* clause, i.e. a clause that is semantically different to any clause in $C(0)$, and then return to the Ready state. Since there are only finitely many semantically different clauses over variables $X \cup Y$, and we cannot terminate in any other way (Lemma 5), we eventually have to find a clause L with $var(L) \subseteq D(0)$, which enables us to go to the UNSAT state.

From the Ready state, we can always add more variables to D with DECIDE and PROPAGATE, until we reach a conflict. (Otherwise we would reach a state where $D = Y$ we were able to prove SAT, contradicting Lemma 5.) We only enter a Conflict state for a variable v, if there are two clauses $(c_1 \vee v)$ and $(c_2 \vee \neg v)$ with unique consequence v such that $x \models \neg c_1 \wedge \neg c_2$ (see definition of unconflicted).

In order to apply ANALYZE, we need to make sure that $(c_1 \vee v)$ and $(c_2 \vee \neg v)$ are in $C(0)$. We can guarantee this by restricting DECIDE as follows: We say a decision for a variable v' is *consistent with the unique consequences* in state (Ready, C, D, χ, α), if unconflicted($v, C.\delta, \chi \wedge \alpha, D$). We can construct such a decision easily by applying DECIDE only on variables that are not conflicted already (i.e. unconflicted($v, C, \chi \wedge \alpha, D$)) and by defining δ to be the CNF representation of $\neg \mathcal{A}_v \Rightarrow \neg v$ (i.e. require v to be false, unless a unique consequence containing literal v applies). It is clear that for this δ no new conflict for v is introduced and hence unconflicted($v, C.\delta, \chi \wedge \alpha, D$).

Assuming that all decisions are taken consistent with the unique consequences, we know that when we encounter a conflict for variable v, we did not apply DECIDE for v, and hence the clauses $(c_1 \vee v)$ and $(c_2 \vee \neg v)$ causing the conflict must be in $C(0)$. We can hence apply ANALYZE twice with clauses $(c_1 \vee v)$ and $(c_2 \vee \neg v)$ and obtain the learnt clause $L = c_1 \vee c_2$. Since $x \models \neg c_1 \wedge \neg c_2$, the learnt clause is violated by x. As x refutes unconflicted($v, C, \chi \wedge \alpha, D$) by construction, it must satisfy the clauses $C|_D$ and learnt clause L hence cannot be in $C|_D$. Further, L only contains variables that are in D, as $(c_1 \vee v)$ and $(c_2 \vee \neg v)$ were clauses with unique consequence v. So, L would have been in $C|_D$, if it existed in C already, and hence L is new. We can either add the new clause to $C(0)$ after backtracking, or we can conclude UNSAT.

Lemma 6. *ID can reach the UNSAT state for false QBF.*

The clause learning process considered here only applies one actual resolution step per conflict ($L_1 \otimes_v L_2$). In practice, we probably want to apply multiple resolution steps before applying LEARN. It is possible to use the conflicting assignment x to (implicitly) construct an implication graph and mimic the clause learning of SAT solvers [8, 31].

3.3   Example

We now discuss the application of the inference rules along the following formula:

$$
\begin{aligned}
\forall x_1, x_2.\ \exists y_1, \dots, y_4.\ & (x_1 \vee \neg y_1) \wedge (x_2 \vee \neg y_1) \wedge (\neg x_1 \vee \neg x_2 \vee y_1) \wedge && (1)\\
& (\neg x_2 \vee y_2) \wedge (\neg y_1 \vee y_2) \wedge (x_2 \vee y_1 \vee \neg y_2) \wedge && (2)\\
& (y_1 \vee \neg y_3) \wedge (y_2 \vee \neg y_3) \wedge && (3)\\
& (\neg y_1 \vee y_4) \wedge (\neg y_3 \vee \neg y_4) && (4)
\end{aligned}
$$

Initially, the state of the algorithm is the tuple (Ready, $\varphi, X, 1, 1$). The rule PROPAGATE can be applied to y_1 in the initial state, as we are in the Ready state, $y_1 \notin X$, and because y_1 satisfies the checks deterministic and unconflicted:

The antecedents of y_1 are $\mathcal{A}_{y_1} = x_1 \wedge x_2$ and $\mathcal{A}_{\neg y_1} = \neg x_1 \vee \neg x_2$ (see clauses in line (1)). It is easy to check that both $\mathcal{A}_{y_1} \vee \mathcal{A}_{\neg y_1}$ nor $\neg(\mathcal{A}_{y_1} \wedge \mathcal{A}_{\neg y_1})$ hold for all assignments to x_1 and x_2. The state resulting from the application of PROPAGATE is (Ready, φ, $X \cup \{y_1\}$, $\mathbf{1}$, $\mathbf{1}$). (Alternatively, we could apply DECIDE in the initial state, but deriving unique Skolem functions is generally preferable.)

While PROPAGATE was not applicable to y_2 before, it now is, as the increased set D made y_2 deterministic (see clauses in line (2)). We can thus derive the state (Ready, φ, $X \cup \{y_1, y_2\}$, $\mathbf{1}$, $\mathbf{1}$).

Now, we ran out of variables to propagate and the only applicable rule is DECIDE. We arbitrarily choose y_3 as our decision variable and arbitrarily introduce a single clause $\delta = \{(\neg y_1 \vee \neg y_2 \vee y_3)\}$, arriving in the state (Ready, $\varphi.\delta$, $X \cup \{y_1, y_2\}$, $\mathbf{1}$, $\mathbf{1}$). In this step we can immediately apply PROPAGATE (consider δ and the clauses in line (3)) to add the decision variable to the set D and arrive at (Ready, $\varphi.\delta$, $X \cup \{y_1, y_2, y_3\}$, $\mathbf{1}$, $\mathbf{1}$).

We can now apply BACKTRACK to undo the last decision, but this would not be productive. Instead identify y_4 to be conflicted and we enter a conflict state with CONFLICT: (Conflict($\{y_4, \neg y_4\}$, $x_1 \wedge x_2$), $\varphi.\delta$, $X \cup \{y_1, y_2, y_3\}$, $\mathbf{1}$, $\mathbf{1}$). To resolve the conflict we apply ANALYZE twice - once with each of the clauses in line (4) - bringing us into state (Conflict($\{\neg y_1, \neg y_3\}$, $x_1 \wedge x_2$), $\varphi.\delta$, $X \cup \{y_1, y_2, y_3\}$, $\mathbf{1}$, $\mathbf{1}$). We can backtrack one level such that $D = X \cup \{y_1, y_2\}$ and then apply LEARN to enter state (Ready, $\varphi \cup \{(\neg y_1 \vee \neg y_3)\}$, $X \cup \{y_1, y_2\}$, $\mathbf{1}$, $\mathbf{1}$).

The rest is simple: we apply PROPAGATE on y_3 and take a decision for y_4. As no other variable can depend on y_4 we can take an arbitrary decision for y_4 that makes y_4 deterministic, as long as this does not make y_4 conflicted. Finally, we can propagate y_4 and then apply SAT to conclude that we have found Skolem functions for all existential variables.

3.4   Termination

So far, we have described sound and nondeterministic algorithms that allow us to prove or disprove any 2QBF. We can easily turn the algorithm in the proof of Lemma 6 into a *deterministic* algorithm that terminates for both true and false QBF by introducing an arbitrary ordering of variables and assignments: Whenever there is nondeterminism in the application of one of the rules as described in Lemma 6, pick the smallest variable for which one of the rules is applicable. When multiple rules are applicable for that variable, pick them in the order they appear in the figures. When the inference rule allows multiple assignments, pick the smallest. In particular, this guarantees that the existential variables are added to D in the arbitrarily picked order, as for any existential not in D we can either apply PROPAGATE, DECIDE, or CONFLICT.

Restricting DECIDE to decisions that are consistent with the unique consequences may be unintuitive for true QBF, where we try to find a Skolem function. However, whenever we make the 2QBF false by introducing clauses with DECIDE, we will eventually go to a conflict state and learn a new clause. Deriving the learnt clause for conflicted variable v from two clauses with unique consequence v (as described for Lemma 6) means that we push the constraints

	SAT $\exists Y.\ \varphi$	2QBF $\forall X.\ \exists Y.\ \varphi$
State	Partial assignment of values	Partial assignment of functions
Propagation	unit propagation	unique Skolem function w.r.t. D
Decision	unit clause	clause with unique consequence
Conflict	unit clauses y and $\neg y$	$\exists X$ that implies y and $\neg y$
Learning	clause	clause

Fig. 3. Concepts in ID and their counterparts in CDCL

towards *smaller* variables in the variable ordering. The learnt clause will thus improve the Skolem function for a smaller variable or cause another conflict for a smaller variable. In the extreme case, we will eventually learn clauses that look like function table entries, as used in Lemma 4, i.e. clauses containing exactly one existential variable. At some point, even with our restriction for DECIDE, we cannot make a "wrong" decision: The cases for which a variable does not have a clause with unique consequence are either irrelevant for the satisfaction of the 2QBF or our restricted decisions happen to make the right assignment.

In cases where no static ordering of variables is used - as it will be the case in any practical approach - the termination for true QBF is less obvious but follows the same argument: Given enough learnt clauses, the relationships between the variables are dense enough such that even naive decisions suffice.

3.5 Pure Literals

The original paper on ID introduces the notion of *pure literals* for QBF that allows us to propagate a variable v even if it is not deterministic, if for a literal l of v, all clauses c that l occurs in are either satisfied or l is the unique consequence of c. The formalization presented in this section allows us to conclude that pure literals are a special case of DECIDE: We can introduce clauses defining v to be of polarity $\bar{l}$ whenever all clauses containing l are satisfied by another literal.

That is, we can precisely characterize the minimal set of cases in which v has to be of polarity l and the decision is guaranteed to never introduce unnecessary conflicts. The same definition cannot be made when l occurs in clauses where it is not a unique consequence, as then the clause contains another variable that is not deterministic yet.

3.6 Relation of ID and CDCL

There are some obvious similarities between ID and conflict-driven clause learning (CDCL) for SAT. Both algorithms modify their partial assignments by propagation, decisions, clause learning, and backtracking. The main difference between the algorithms is that, while CDCL solvers maintain a partial assignment of Boolean values to variables, ID maintains a partial assignment of functions to variables (which is represented by the clauses $C|_D$). We summarized our observations in Fig. 3.

$$\text{INDUCTIVEREFINEMENT}\ \frac{(\text{Conflict}(L, \boldsymbol{x}), C, D, \chi, \alpha)\qquad \varphi(\boldsymbol{x}|x, \boldsymbol{y})}{(\text{Conflict}(L, \boldsymbol{x}), C, D, \chi \wedge \neg\varphi(\boldsymbol{y}), \alpha)}$$

$$\text{FAILED}\ \frac{(\text{Conflict}(L, \boldsymbol{x}), C, D, \chi, \alpha)\qquad \varphi(\boldsymbol{x}|x)\ \text{is unsatisfiable}}{(\text{UNSAT}, C, D, \chi, \alpha)}$$

Fig. 4. Inference rules adding inductive reasoning to ID

4 Inductive Reasoning

The CEGIS approach to solving a 2QBF $\forall X.\, \exists Y.\, \varphi$ is to iterate over X assignments $\boldsymbol{x}$ and check if there is an assignment $\boldsymbol{y}$ such that $\varphi(\boldsymbol{x}, \boldsymbol{y})$ is valid. Upon every successful iteration we exclude all assignments to X for which $\boldsymbol{y}$ is a matching assignment. If the space of X assignments is exhausted we conclude the formula is true, and if we find an assignment to X for which there is no matching Y assignment, the formula is false [21].

While this approach shows poor performance on some problems, as discussed in the introduction, it is widely popular and has been successfully applied in many cases. In this section we present a way how it can be integrated in ID in an elegant way. The simplicity of the CEGIS approach carries over to our extension of ID - we only need the two additional inference rules in Fig. 4.

We exploit the fact that ID already generates assignments $\boldsymbol{x}$ to X in its conflict check. Whenever ID is in a conflict state, the rules in Fig. 4 allow us to check if there is an assignment $\boldsymbol{y}$ to Y that together with $|_X$, which is the part of $\boldsymbol{x}$ defining variables in X, satisfies φ. If there is such an assignment $\boldsymbol{y}$, we can let the Skolem functions output $\boldsymbol{y}$ for the input $\boldsymbol{x}$. But the output $\boldsymbol{y}$ may work for other assignments to X, too. The set of all assignments to X for which $\boldsymbol{y}$ works as an output, is easily characterized by $\varphi(\boldsymbol{y})$.[1] INDUCTIVEREFINEMENT allows us to exclude the assignments $\varphi(0)$ from χ, which represents the domain (i.e. assignments to X) for which we still need to find a Skolem function.

This gives rise to a new invariant, stating that $\neg\chi$ only includes assignments to X for which we know that there is an assignment to Y satisfying φ. With this invariant it is clear that Lemma 3 also holds for arbitrary χ.

Invariant 4. $\forall X.\exists Y.\ \neg\chi \Rightarrow \varphi$

It is easy to check that PROPAGATE preserves Invariant 1 also if χ and α are not 1. Invariants 2 and 3 are unaffected by the rules in this section. To make sure that Lemma 5 is preserved as well, we thus only have to inspect FAILED, which is trivially sound.

---

[1] We can actually exploit the Skolem functions that do not depend on decisions and exclude $C(0)(\boldsymbol{y}_{\overline{D(0)}})$ from χ instead, i.e. the set of assignments to $D(0)$ to which the part of $\boldsymbol{y}$ that is not in $D(0)$ is a solution.

$$\text{ASSUME} \; \frac{(\text{Ready}, C, D, \chi, \alpha) \qquad var(l) \in D(0)}{(\text{Ready}, C, D, \chi, \alpha \wedge l)}$$

$$\text{CLOSE} \; \frac{(\text{Ready}, C, D, \chi, \alpha) \qquad D = X \cup Y}{(\text{Ready}, C(0), D(0), \chi \wedge \neg \alpha, \mathbf{1})}$$

Fig. 5. Inference rules adding case distinctions to ID

A Portfolio Approach? In principle, we could generate assignments x independently from the conflict check of ID. The result would be a portfolio approach that simply executes ID and CEGIS in parallel and takes the result from whichever method terminates first. The idea behind our extension is that conflict assignments are more selective and may thus increase the probability that we hit a refuting assignment to X. Also ID may profit from excluding groups of assignments for which frequently cause conflicts. We revisit this question in Sect. 6.

Example. We extend the example from Subsect. 3.3 from the point where we entered the conflict state $(\text{Conflict}(\{y_4, \neg y_4\}, x_1 \wedge x_2), \varphi.\delta, X \cup \{y_1, y_2, y_3\}, \mathbf{1}, \mathbf{1})$. We can apply INDUCTIVEREFINEMENT, checking that there is indeed a solution to φ for the assignment x_1, x_2 to the universals (e.g. $y_1, y_2, \neg y_3, y_4$). Instead of doing the standard conflict analysis as in our previous example, we can apply LEARN to add the (useless) clause $y_4 \vee \neg y_4$ to $C(0)$ without any backtracking. That is, we effectively ignore the conflict and go to state $(\text{Ready}, \varphi \cup \{(y_4 \vee \neg y_4)\}.\delta, X \cup \{y_1, y_2, y_3\}, \neg x_1 \vee \neg x_2, \mathbf{1})$.

There is no assignment to X that provokes a conflict for y_4, other than the one we excluded through INDUCTIVEREFINEMENT. We can thus take an arbitrary decision for y_4 that is consistent with the unique consequences (see Subsect. 3.2), PROPAGATE y_4, and then conclude the formula to be true.

5 Expansion

Universal expansion (defined in Sect. 2) is another fundamental proof rule that deals with universal variables. It has been used in early QBF solvers [10] and has later been integrated in CEGAR-style QBF solvers [26,32].

One way to look at the expansion of a universal variable x is that it introduces a case distinction over the possible values of x in the Skolem functions. However, instead of creating a copy of the formula explicitly, which often caused a blowup in required memory, we can reason about the two cases sequentially. The rules in Fig. 5 extend ID by universal expansion in this spirit.

Using ASSUME we can, at any point, assume that a variable v in $D(0)$, i.e. a variable that has a unique Skolem function without any decisions, has a particular value. This is represented by extending α by the corresponding literal of v, which restricts the domain of the Skolem function that we try to construct for subsequent deterministic and unconflicted checks. Invariant 1 and Lemma 5 already accommodate the case that α is not **1**.

When we reach a point where D contains all variables, we cannot apply SAT, as that requires α to be true. In this case, Invariant 1 only guarantees us that the function we constructed is correct on the domain $\chi \wedge \alpha$. We can hence restrict the domain for which we still need to find a Skolem function and strengthen χ by $\neg\alpha$. In particular, CLOSE maintains Invariant 4. When χ ends up being equivalent to **0**, Invariant 4 guarantees that the original formula is true. (In this case we can reach the SAT state easily, as we know that from now on every application of PROPAGATE must succeed.[2])

Note that ASSUME does not restrict us to assumptions on single variables. Together with DECIDE and PROPAGATE it is possible to introduce variables with arbitrary definitions, add them to $D(0)$, and then assume an outcome with the rule ASSUME.

Example. Again, we consider the formula from Subsect. 3.3. Instead of the reasoning steps described in Subsect. 3.3, we start using ASSUME with literal x_2. Whenever checking deterministic or unconflicted in the following, we will thus restrict ourselves to universal assignments that set x_2 to true. It is easy to check that this allows us to propagate not only y_1 and y_2, but also y_3. A decision (e.g. $\delta' = \{(y_4)\}$) for y_4 allows us to also propagate y_4 (this time without potential for conflicts), arriving in state (Ready, $\varphi.\delta', X \cup \{y_1, y_2, y_3, y_4\}, \mathbf{1}, x_2$).

We can CLOSE this case concluding that under the assumption x_2 we have found a Skolem function. We enter the state (Ready, $\varphi, X, \neg x_2, \mathbf{1}$) which indicates that in the future we only have to consider universal assignments with $\neg x_2$. Also for the case $\neg x_2$, we cannot encounter conflicts for this formula. Expansion hence allows us to prove this formula without any conflicts.

6 Experimental Evaluation

We extended the QBF solver CADET [8] by the extensions described in Sects. 4 and 5. We use the CADET-IR and CADET-E to denote the extensions of CADET by inductive reasoning (Sect. 4) and universal expansion (Sect. 5), respectively. We also combined both extensions and refer to this version as CADET-IR-E. The experiments in this section evaluate these extensions against the basic version of CADET and against other successful QBF solvers of the recent years, in particular GhostQ [33], RAReQS [32], Qesto [23], DepQBF [19] in version 6, and CAQE [24,26]. For every solver except CADET and GhostQ, we use Bloqqer [34] in version 031 as preprocessor. For our experiments, we used a machine with a 3.6 GHz quad-core Intel Xeon processor and 32 GB of memory. The timeout and memout were set to 600 s and 8 GB. We evaluated the

---

[2] Technically, we could replace SAT by a rule that allows us to enter the SAT state whenever χ is **0**, which arguably would be more elegant. But that would require us to introduce the CLOSE rule already for the basic ID inference system.

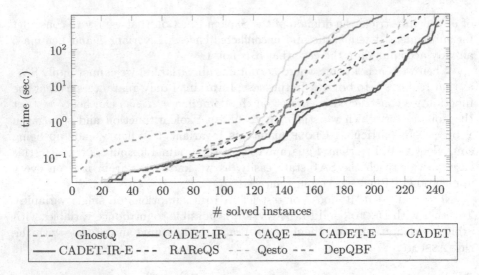

Fig. 6. Cactus plot comparing solvers on the QBFEval-2017 2QBF benchmark.

solvers on the benchmark sets of the last competitive evaluation of QBF solvers, QBFEval-2017 [9].

How Does Inductive Reasoning Affect the Performance? In Fig. 6 we see that CADET-IR clearly dominates plain CADET. It also dominates all solvers that relied on clause-level CEGAR and Bloqqer (CAQE, Qesto, RAReQS).

Only GhostQ beats CADET-IR and solves 5 more formulas (of 384). A closer look revealed that there are many formulas for which CADET-IR and GhostQ show widely different runtimes hinting at potential for future improvement.

GhostQ is based on the CEGAR principle, but reconstructs a circuit representation from the clauses instead of operating on the clauses directly [33]. This makes GhostQ a representative of QBF solvers working with so called "structured" formulas (i.e. not CNF). CADET, on the other hand, refrains from identifying logic gates in CNF formulas and directly operates with the "unstructured" CNF representation. In the ongoing debate in the QBF community on the best representation of formulas for solving quantified formulas, our experimental findings can thus be interpreted as a tie between the two philosophies.

Is the Inductive Reasoning Extension Just a Portfolio-Approach? To settle this question, we created a version of CADET-IR, called IR-only, that exclusively applies inductive reasoning by generating assignments to the universals and applying INDUCTIVEREASONING. This version of CADET does not learn any clauses, but otherwise uses the same code as CADET-IR. On the QBFEval-2017 benchmark, IR-only and CADET together solved 235 problems within the time limit, while CADET-IR solved 243 problems. That is, even though the combined runtime of CADET and IR-only was twice the runtime of CADET-IR,

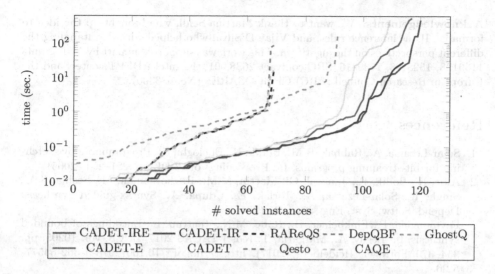

Fig. 7. Cactus plot comparing solver performance on the Hardware Fixpoint formulas. Some but not all of these formulas are part of QBFEval-2017. The formulas encode diameter problems that are known to be hard for classical QBF search algorithms [35].

they solved fewer problems. CADET-IR also uniquely solved 22 problems. This indicates that CADET-IR improves over the portfolio approach.

How Does Universal Expansion Affect the Performance? CADET-E clearly dominates plain CADET on QBFEval-2017, but compared to CADET-IR and some of the other QBF solvers, CADET-E shows mediocre performance overall. However, for some subsets of formulas, such as the Hardware Fixpoint formulas shown in Fig. 7, CADET-E dominated CADET, CADET-IR, and all other solvers. We also combined the two extensions of CADET to obtain CADET-IR-E. While this helped to improve the performance on the Hardware Fixpoint formulas even further, it did not change the overall picture on QBFEval-2017.

7 Conclusion

Reasoning in quantified logics is one of the major challenges in computer-aided verification. Incremental Determinization (ID) introduced a new algorithmic principle for reasoning in 2QBF and delivered first promising results [8]. In this work, we formalized and generalized ID to improve the understanding of the algorithm and to enable future research on the topic. The presentation of the algorithm as a set of inference rules has allowed us to disentangle the design choices from the principles of the algorithm (Sect. 3). Additionally, we have explored two extensions of ID that both significantly improve the performance: The first one integrates the popular CEGAR-style algorithms and Incremental Determinization (Sect. 4). The second extension integrates a different type of reasoning termed universal expansion (Sect. 5).

Acknowledgements. We want to thank Martina Seidl, who brought up the idea to formalize ID as inference rules, and Vijay D'Silva, who helped with disentangling the different perspectives on the algorithm. This work was supported in part by NSF grants 1139138, 1528108, 1739816, SRC contract 2638.001, the Intel ADEPT center, and the European Research Council (ERC) Grant OSARES (No. 683300).

References

1. Solar-Lezama, A., Rabbah, R.M., Bodík, R., Ebcioglu, K.: Programming by sketching for bit-streaming programs. In: Proceedings of PLDI, pp. 281–294 (2005)
2. Alur, R., Bodik, R., Juniwal, G., Martin, M.M., Raghothaman, M., Seshia, S.A., Singh, R., Solar-Lezama, A., Torlak, E., Udupa, A.: Syntax-guided synthesis. Depend. Softw. Syst. Eng. **40**, 1–25 (2015)
3. Faymonville, P., Finkbeiner, B., Rabe, M.N., Tentrup, L.: Encodings of bounded synthesis. In: Legay, A., Margaria, T. (eds.) TACAS 2017. LNCS, vol. 10205, pp. 354–370. Springer, Heidelberg (2017). https://doi.org/10.1007/978-3-662-54577-5_20
4. Bloem, R., Könighofer, R., Seidl, M.: SAT-based synthesis methods for safety specs. In: McMillan, K.L., Rival, X. (eds.) VMCAI 2014. LNCS, vol. 8318, pp. 1–20. Springer, Heidelberg (2014). https://doi.org/10.1007/978-3-642-54013-4_1
5. Solar-Lezama, A., Tancau, L., Bodík, R., Seshia, S.A., Saraswat, V.A.: Combinatorial sketching for finite programs. In: Proceedings of the 12th International Conference on Architectural Support for Programming Languages and Operating Systems (ASPLOS), pp. 404–415. ACM Press, October 2006
6. Clarke, E., Grumberg, O., Jha, S., Lu, Y., Veith, H.: Counterexample-guided abstraction refinement. In: Emerson, E.A., Sistla, A.P. (eds.) CAV 2000. LNCS, vol. 1855, pp. 154–169. Springer, Heidelberg (2000). https://doi.org/10.1007/10722167_15
7. Jha, S., Seshia, S.A.: A theory of formal synthesis via inductive learning. Acta Inf. **54**(7), 693–726 (2017)
8. Rabe, M.N., Seshia, S.A.: Incremental determinization. In: Creignou, N., Le Berre, D. (eds.) SAT 2016. LNCS, vol. 9710, pp. 375–392. Springer, Cham (2016). https://doi.org/10.1007/978-3-319-40970-2_23
9. Pulina, L.: The ninth QBF solvers evaluation - preliminary report. In: Proceedings of QBF@SAT. CEUR Workshop Proceedings, vol. 1719, pp. 1–13. CEUR-WS.org (2016)
10. Biere, A.: Resolve and expand. In: Hoos, H.H., Mitchell, D.G. (eds.) SAT 2004. LNCS, vol. 3542, pp. 59–70. Springer, Heidelberg (2005). https://doi.org/10.1007/11527695_5
11. Pigorsch, F., Scholl, C.: An AIG-based QBF-solver using SAT for preprocessing. In: Proceedings of DAC, pp. 170–175. IEEE (2010)
12. Charwat, G., Woltran, S.: Dynamic programming-based QBF solving. In: Lonsing, F., Seidl, M. (eds.) Proceedings of Quantified Boolean Formulas. CEUR Workshop Proceedings, vol. 1719, pp. 27–40 (2016)
13. Baumgartner, P., Tinelli, C.: The model evolution calculus. In: Baader, F. (ed.) CADE 2003. LNCS (LNAI), vol. 2741, pp. 350–364. Springer, Heidelberg (2003). https://doi.org/10.1007/978-3-540-45085-6_32
14. Nieuwenhuis, R., Oliveras, A., Tinelli, C.: Abstract DPLL and abstract DPLL modulo theories. In: Baader, F., Voronkov, A. (eds.) LPAR 2005. LNCS (LNAI), vol. 3452, pp. 36–50. Springer, Heidelberg (2005). https://doi.org/10.1007/978-3-540-32275-7_3

15. de Moura, L., Jovanović, D.: A model-constructing satisfiability calculus. In: Giacobazzi, R., Berdine, J., Mastroeni, I. (eds.) VMCAI 2013. LNCS, vol. 7737, pp. 1–12. Springer, Heidelberg (2013). https://doi.org/10.1007/978-3-642-35873-9_1
16. Fazekas, K., Seidl, M., Biere, A.: A duality-aware calculus for quantified Boolean formulas. In: Proceedings of SYNASC, pp. 181–186. IEEE Computer Society (2016)
17. D'Silva, V., Haller, L., Kroening, D.: Abstract conflict driven learning. In: Proceedings POPL, pp. 143–154. ACM (2013)
18. Giunchiglia, E., Narizzano, M., Tacchella, A.: QuBE: a system for deciding quantified Boolean formulas satisfiability. In: Goré, R., Leitsch, A., Nipkow, T. (eds.) IJCAR 2001. LNCS, vol. 2083, pp. 364–369. Springer, Heidelberg (2001). https://doi.org/10.1007/3-540-45744-5_27
19. Lonsing, F., Biere, A.: DepQBF: a dependency-aware QBF solver. JSAT **7**(2–3), 71–76 (2010)
20. Ranjan, D., Tang, D., Malik, S.: A comparative study of 2QBF algorithms. In: Proceedings of SAT. ACM (2004)
21. Janota, M., Marques-Silva, J.: Abstraction-based algorithm for 2QBF. In: Sakallah, K.A., Simon, L. (eds.) SAT 2011. LNCS, vol. 6695, pp. 230–244. Springer, Heidelberg (2011). https://doi.org/10.1007/978-3-642-21581-0_19
22. Janota, M., Klieber, W., Marques-Silva, J., Clarke, E.: Solving QBF with counterexample guided refinement. In: Cimatti, A., Sebastiani, R. (eds.) SAT 2012. LNCS, vol. 7317, pp. 114–128. Springer, Heidelberg (2012). https://doi.org/10.1007/978-3-642-31612-8_10
23. Janota, M., Marques-Silva, J.: Solving QBF by clause selection. In: Proceedings of IJCAI, pp. 325–331. AAAI Press (2015)
24. Rabe, M.N., Tentrup, L.: CAQE: a certifying QBF solver. In: Proceedings of FMCAD, pp. 136–143 (2015)
25. Bloem, R., Braud-Santoni, N., Hadzic, V.: QBF solving by counterexample-guided expansion. CoRR, vol. abs/1611.01553 (2016.). http://arxiv.org/abs/1611.01553
26. Tentrup, L.: On expansion and resolution in CEGAR based QBF solving. In: Majumdar, R., Kunčak, V. (eds.) CAV 2017. LNCS, vol. 10427, pp. 475–494. Springer, Cham (2017). https://doi.org/10.1007/978-3-319-63390-9_25
27. Tseitin, G.S.: On the complexity of derivation in propositional calculus. In: Studies in Constructive Mathematics and Mathematical Logic, Reprinted in [36], vol. 2, no. 115–125, pp. 10–13 (1968)
28. Buning, H., Karpinski, M., Flogel, A.: Resolution for quantified Boolean formulas. Inf. Comput. **117**(1), 12–18 (1995)
29. Janota, M., Marques-Silva, J.: Expansion-based QBF solving versus Q-resolution. Theoret. Comput. Sci. **577**, 25–42 (2015)
30. Robinson, J.A.: A machine-oriented logic based on the resolution principle. J. ACM **12**(1), 23–41 (1965)
31. Marques-Silva, J.P., Sakallah, K.A.: GRASP - a new search algorithm for satisfiability. In: Proceedings of CAD, pp. 220–227. IEEE (1997)
32. Janota, M., Klieber, W., Marques-Silva, J., Clarke, E.M.: Solving QBF with counterexample guided refinement. Artif. Intell. **234**, 1–25 (2016)
33. Klieber, W., Sapra, S., Gao, S., Clarke, E.: A non-prenex, non-clausal QBF solver with game-state learning. In: Strichman, O., Szeider, S. (eds.) SAT 2010. LNCS, vol. 6175, pp. 128–142. Springer, Heidelberg (2010). https://doi.org/10.1007/978-3-642-14186-7_12

34. Biere, A., Lonsing, F., Seidl, M.: Blocked clause elimination for QBF. In: Bjørner, N., Sofronie-Stokkermans, V. (eds.) CADE 2011. LNCS (LNAI), vol. 6803, pp. 101–115. Springer, Heidelberg (2011). https://doi.org/10.1007/978-3-642-22438-6_10
35. Tang, D., Yu, Y., Ranjan, D., Malik, S.: Analysis of search based algorithms for satisfiability of propositional and quantified Boolean formulas arising from circuit state space diameter problems. In: Hoos, H.H., Mitchell, D.G. (eds.) SAT 2004. LNCS, vol. 3542, pp. 292–305. Springer, Heidelberg (2005). https://doi.org/10.1007/11527695_23
36. Siekmann, J., Wrightson, G.: Automation of Reasoning: 2: Classical Papers on Computational Logic 1967–1970. Springer, Heidelberg (1983)

The Proof Complexity of SMT Solvers

Robert Robere[1]([✉]), Antonina Kolokolova[2], and Vijay Ganesh[3]

[1] University of Toronto, Toronto, Canada
robere@cs.toronto.edu
[2] Memorial University of Newfoundland, St. John's, Canada
kol@mun.ca
[3] University of Waterloo, Waterloo, Canada
vijay.ganesh@uwaterloo.ca

Abstract. The resolution proof system has been enormously helpful in deepening our understanding of conflict-driven clause-learning (CDCL) SAT solvers. In the interest of providing a similar proof complexity-theoretic analysis of satisfiability modulo theories (SMT) solvers, we introduce a generalization of resolution called Res(T). We show that many of the known results comparing resolution and CDCL solvers lift to the SMT setting, such as the result of Pipatsrisawat and Darwiche showing that CDCL solvers with "perfect" non-deterministic branching and an asserting clause-learning scheme can polynomially simulate general resolution. We also describe a stronger version of Res(T), Res*(T), capturing SMT solvers allowing introduction of new literals. We analyze the theory EUF of equality with uninterpreted functions, and show that the Res*(EUF) system is able to simulate an earlier calculus introduced by Bjørner and de Moura for the purpose of analyzing DPLL(EUF). Further, we show that Res*(EUF) (and thus SMT algorithms with clause learning over EUF, new literal introduction rules and perfect branching) can simulate the Frege proof system, which is well-known to be far more powerful than resolution. Finally, we prove under the Exponential Time Hypothesis (ETH) that *any* reduction from EUF to SAT (such as the Ackermann reduction) must, in the worst case, produce an instance of size $\Omega(n \log n)$ from an instance of size n.

1 Introduction

It is common practice in formal verification literature to view SAT/SMT solver algorithms as proof systems and study their properties, such as soundness, completeness and termination, using proof-theoretic tools [GHN+04, ORC09, Tin12]. However, much work remains in applying the powerful lens of proof complexity theory in understanding the relative power of these solvers. All too often, the power of SAT and SMT (satisfiability modulo theories) solving algorithms is determined by how they perform at the annual SAT or SMTCOMP competitions [BHJ17, smt]. While such competitions are an extremely useful practical test of the power of solving methods, they do not address fundamental questions

© The Author(s) 2018
H. Chockler and G. Weissenbacher (Eds.): CAV 2018, LNCS 10982, pp. 275–293, 2018.
https://doi.org/10.1007/978-3-319-96142-2_18

such as which heuristics are truly responsible for the power of these solvers or what are the lower bounds for these methods when viewed as proof systems.

Solvers, by their very nature, are a tangled jumble of heuristics that interact with each other in complicated ways. Many SMT solvers run into hundreds of thousands of lines of code, making them very hard to analyze. It is often difficult to discern which sets of heuristics are universally useful, which sets are tailored to a class of instances, and how their interactions actually help solver performance. A purely empirical approach, while necessary, is far from sufficient in deepening our understanding of solver algorithms. What is needed is an appropriate combination of empirical and theoretical approaches to understanding the power of solvers. Fortunately, proof complexity theory provides a powerful lens through which to mathematically analyze solver algorithms as proof systems and to understand their relative power via lower bounds. The value of using proof complexity theory to better understand solving algorithms as proof systems is three-fold: first, it allows us to identify key ingredients of a solving algorithm and prove lower bounds to non-deterministic combinations of such ingredients. That is, we can analyze the countably many variants of a solving algorithm in a unified manner via a single analysis, rather than analyzing different configurations of the same set of proof-theoretic ingredients; second, proof complexity-theoretic tools allow us to recognize the relative power of two proof systems, via appropriate lower bounds, even if both have worst-case exponential time complexity; finally, proof complexity theory brings with it a rich literature and connections to other sub-fields of complexity theory (e.g., circuit complexity) that we may be able to leverage in analyzing solver algorithms. Many proof complexity theorists and logicians have long recognized this, and there is rich literature on the analysis of SAT solving algorithms such as DPLL and conflict-driven clause-learning (CDCL) solvers [PD11,BKS04,BBJ14,AFT11]. In this paper, we lift some of these results to the setting of SMT solvers, following the work of Bjørner and de Moura [BM14].

Our focus is primarily the proof complexity-theoretic analysis of the "DPLL(T) method"[1], the prime engine behind many modern SMT solvers [GHN+04,Tin12]. (While other approaches to solving first-order formulas have been studied, DPLL(T) remains a fundamental and dominant approach.) A DPLL(T)-based SMT solver takes as input a Boolean combination of first-order theory T atoms or their negation (aka, theory literals), and decides whether such an input is satisfiable. Informally, a typical DPLL(T)-based SMT solver S

---

[1] Prior to mid 2000's, SAT researchers and complexity theorists confusingly used the term DPLL to refer to both the original algorithm proposed by Davis, Putnam, Loveland, and Loeggemann in 1960, as well as the newer algorithm by Joao Marques-Silva and Karem Sakallah that added clause learning to DPLL (proposed in 1996), even though they are vastly different in power as proof systems. We will follow the literature and use DPLL(T) to indicate a "modern" SMT solver with clause learning and restarts, but, we urge SMT solver researchers to use the more appropriate term CDCL(T) rather than DPLL(T) to refer to the lazy approach to SMT.

is essentially a CDCL Boolean SAT solver that calls out a theory solver T_s during its search to perform *theory propagations* and *theory conflict-clause learning*. The typical theory solver T_s is designed to accept only quantifier-free conjunction of theory T literals (the T in the term DPLL(T)), while the SAT solver "handles" the Boolean structure of input formulas. Roughly speaking, the SMT solver S works as follows: First, it constructs a Boolean abstraction B_F of the input formula F, by replacing theory literals by Boolean variables. If B_F is UNSAT, S returns UNSAT. Otherwise, satisfying assignments to the Boolean abstraction B_F are found, which in turn correspond to conjunctions of theory literals. Such conjunctions are then input to the theory solver T_s, which may deduce new implied formulas (via theory propagation and conflict clause learning) that are then used to help prune the search space of assignments to F. The solver S returns SAT upon finding a satisfying theory assignment to the input F, and UNSAT otherwise. (For further details, we refer the reader to the excellent exposition on this topic by Tinelli [Tin12].)

A Brief Description of the Res(T) Proof System: To abstractly model a DPLL(T)-based SMT solver S, we define a proof system Res(T) below for a given first-order theory T. The Res in Res(T) refers to the general resolution proof system for Boolean logic. Without loss of generality, we assume that Res(T) accepts theory formulas in conjunctive normal form (CNF). Let $\mathcal{F}$ denote a CNF with propositional variables representing atoms from an underlying theory T, and for any clause C in FF let vars(F) denote the set of propositional atoms occurring in F. The proof rules of Res(T) augment the resolution proof rule as follows: A proof in Res(T) is a general resolution refutation of $\mathcal{F}$, where at any step the theory T-solver can add to the set of clauses an arbitrary clause C such that $T \vDash C$ and every propositional atom in vars(C) occurs in the original formula. That is, each line of a Res(T) proof is deduced by one of the following rules:

Resolution. $C \vee \ell, D \vee \bar{\ell} \vdash C \vee D$, for previously derived clauses C and D.

Theory Derivation. $\vdash C$ for any clause C such that $T \vDash C$ and for which every theory literal in C occurs in the input formula.

For example, a theory of linear arithmetic may introduce a clause $(x \geq 5 \vee y \geq 7 \vee x + y < 12)$, which can then be used in the subsequent steps of a resolution proof, provided each of those literals occurred in the original CNF formula $\mathcal{F}$. The filter on the theory rule of Res(T) models the fact that in many modern SMT solvers, the "theory solver" is only allowed to reason about literals which already occur in the formula. Recent solvers such as Z3, Yices [Z3,Yic] break this rule and allow the theory solver to introduce new propositional atoms; to model this we introduce the stronger variant Res$^*(T)$ with a strengthened theory rule:

Strong Theory Derivation: $\vdash C$ for any clause C such that $T \vDash C$.

1.1 Our Contributions

We prove the following results about the two systems $\mathsf{Res}(T)$, $\mathsf{Res}^*(T)$ and the complexity of SMT solving.

1. We show that $\mathsf{DPLL}(T)$ with an arbitrary asserting clause learning scheme and non-deterministic branching and theory propagation is equivalent (as a proof system) to $\mathsf{Res}(T)$ for *any* theory T. More precisely: if the theory solver in $\mathsf{DPLL}(T)$ can only reason about literals in the input, then it is equivalent to $\mathsf{Res}(T)$; if it can reason about arbitrary literals then it is equivalent to $\mathsf{Res}^*(T)$. (See Sect. 3)
2. When the theory T is E, the theory of pure equalities, $\mathsf{Res}^*(E)$ is equivalent to the $SP(E)$ system of Bjørner et al. [BDdM08], which seems to have no efficient proofs of the PHP. (See Sect. 5.1)
3. When the theory T is EUF (equality with uninterpreted function symbols), the proof system $\mathsf{Res}^*(\mathsf{EUF})$ can simulate E-Res, a different generalization of resolution introduced by Bjorner and de Moura [BM14] for the purpose of simulating standard implementations of $\mathsf{DPLL}(\mathsf{EUF})$. Furthermore, $\mathsf{Res}^*(\mathsf{EUF})$ can simulate the powerful Frege proof system. (See Sect. 5.2)
4. When T is LA, a theory of linear arithmetic over a set of numbers containing integers, $\mathsf{Res}(\mathsf{LA})$ can polynomially simulate the system $\mathsf{R}(\mathsf{lin})$ of Raz and Tzameret [RT08], and thus has polynomial size proofs of several hard tautologies such as the pigeonhole principle and Tseitin tautologies. (See Sect. 5.3)
5. Finally, we prove under the Exponential Time Hypothesis (ETH) that *any* reduction from EUF to SAT (such as the Ackermann reduction) must, in the worst case, produce an instance of size $\Omega(n \log n)$ from an instance of size n. (See Sect. 6)

These results seem to suggest that our generalization is the "right" proof system corresponding to $\mathsf{DPLL}(T)$, as it characterizes proofs produced by $\mathsf{DPLL}(T)$ and it can simulate other proof systems introduced in the literature to capture $\mathsf{DPLL}(T)$ for particular theories T.

1.2 Previous Work

Among the previous proof systems combining resolution with non-propositional reasoning are $\mathsf{R}(\mathsf{CP})$ proof system of [Kra98], where propositional variables are replaced with linear inequalities, and $\mathsf{R}(\mathsf{lin})$ introduced by Raz and Tzameret [RT08], which reasons with linear equalities, modifying the resolution rule. $\mathsf{R}(\mathsf{lin})$ polynomially simulates $\mathsf{R}(\mathsf{CP})$ when all coefficients in an $\mathsf{R}(\mathsf{CP})$ proof are polynomially bounded. In the SMT community, Bjørner et al. [BDdM08, BM14] introduced calculi capturing the power of resolution over the theory of equality and equality with uninterpreted functions. They show that these systems capture the power of resolution over the corresponding theories, extended with rules for introducing new atoms. Our results supersede previous work since our simulations hold for any first-order theory T.

2   Preliminaries

2.1   Propositional Proof Systems

In this paper, all proof systems are defined by a set of "allowed lines" equipped with a list of deduction rules that allow us to deduce new lines from old ones. We first recall the *resolution* system, which is a refutation system for propositional formulas in CNF (product of sums) form. The lines of a resolution proof are disjunctions of boolean literals called *clauses*, and these lines are equipped with a single deduction rule called the *resolution rule*: given two clauses of the form $C \vee \ell$, $D \vee \overline{\ell}$ we deduce the clause $C \vee D$. If $\phi = C_1 \wedge C_2 \wedge \cdots \wedge C_m$ is an unsatisfiable CNF formula then a resolution refutation of ϕ is a sequence of clauses $C_1, C_2, \ldots, C_m, C_{m+1}, \ldots, C_t$ where C_t is the empty clause and all clauses C_i with $i > m$ are deduced from earlier clauses by applying the resolution rule.

Observe that clauses satisfy a *subsumption principle*: if C, D are clauses such that $C \subseteq D$ then every assignment satisfying C also satisfies D. This implies that we can safely add a *weakening rule* to resolution which, from a clause C, derives the clause $C \vee x$ for any literal x not already occurring in C. The subsumption principle implies that this weakening rule does not change the power of resolution, as any use of a clause $D \supseteq C$ can be eliminated or replaced with C.

We also consider the *Frege* proof system, which captures standard "textbook-style" proofs. The lines of a Frege system are given by arbitrary boolean formulas, and from two boolean formulas we can deduce any new boolean formula which follows under typical boolean reasoning (e.g. deducing the conjunction of two formulas, the disjunction of their negation, and so on). Crucially, Frege proofs allow applying a generalized "resolution rule" to arbitrary polynomial-size formulas.

The power of different propositional proof systems are compared using the notion of an *polynomial simulation (p-simulation)*. Proof system A *polynomially simulates* (or p-simulates) proof system B if, for every unsatisfiable formula $\mathcal{F}$, the shortest refutation proof of $\mathcal{F}$ in A is at most polynomially longer than the shortest refutation proof of a formula $\mathcal{F}$ in B. For example, the Frege proof system p-simulates the Resolution proof system, but the converse is widely conjectured not to hold.

2.2   First-Order Theories

In this paper we study proof systems for first-order theories. For the sake of completeness we recall some relevant definitions from first-order logic, but remark that this is essentially standard fare.

Let $\mathcal{L}$ be a first-order signature (a list of constant symbols, function symbols, and predicate symbols). Given a set of $\mathcal{L}$-sentences $\mathcal{A}$ and an $\mathcal{L}$-sentence B we write $\mathcal{A} \models B$ if every model of $\mathcal{A}$ is also a model of B. A *first order theory* (or simply a *theory*) is a set of $\mathcal{L}$-sentences that is consistent (that is, it has a model) and is closed under $\models$. The *decision problem* for a theory T is the following: given a set S of literals over $\mathcal{L}$, decide if there is a model $\mathcal{M}$ of T such that $\mathcal{M} \models S$.

The *satisfiability problem* for T, also denoted T-SAT, is the following: given a quantifier-free formula $\mathcal{F}$ in T in conjunctive normal form (CNF), decide if there is a model $\mathcal{M}$ of T such that $\mathcal{M} \vDash \mathcal{F}$.

A simple example of a theory is E, the conjunctive theory of equality. The signature of E contains a single predicate symbol $=$ and an infinite list of constant symbols. It is axiomatized by the standard axioms of equality (reflexivity, symmetry, and transitivity), and a sample sentence in E would be the formula $a \neq b \vee b \neq c \vee a = c$, which encodes the transitivity of equality between the constant symbols a, b, and c. Following the SMT literature, we will call terms from the theory (such as a and b) *theory variables*, and the atoms derived from these terms (such as $a \neq b$ or $a = c$) will be called *theory literals* or just *literals*. We note that the decision problem for E can be decided very efficiently [DST80]; in contrast, the satisfiability problem for E is easily seen to be NP-complete.

3   Res(T): Resolution Modulo Theories

We now define a generalization of resolution which captures the type of reasoning modulo a first-order theory that is common in SMT solvers. We give two variants: the first, denoted Res(T), allows the deduction of any clause C of theory literals such that $T \vDash C$ and for which every literal in C already occurs in the input formula. This is intended to model "standard" lazy SMT solvers [NOT06] which only reason about literals in the input formula.

The second, more powerful variant is denoted Res*(T), and allows the deduction of any clause of literals C such that $T \vDash C$, *even if* the new clause contains literals which do not occur in the input formula. We introduce this to explore the power of lazy SMT solvers that are allowed to introduce new literals from the theory, and note that there are well-known examples in the SMT literature which show that introducing new literals can drastically decrease the length of refutations (e.g. the *diamond equalities* [BDdM08]). Indeed, in Sect. 5.2 we show that this power can drastically increase the proof theoretic strength of SMT solvers.

Definition 1 (Res(T), Res*(T)). *Let T be a theory and let $\mathcal{F}$ be an quantifier-free CNF formula over T. The lines of a* Res(T) *(*Res*(T)*) proof are quantifier-free clauses of theory literals deduced from $\mathcal{F}$ and T by the following derivation rules.*

Resolution. $C \vee \ell, D \vee \bar{\ell} \vdash C \vee D$.

Weakening. $C \vdash C \vee \ell$ *for any theory literal ℓ occurring in the input formula.*

Theory Derivation (Res(T)). $\vdash C$ *for any clause C satisfying $T \vDash C$ and for which every literal in C occurs in the input formula.*

Strong Theory Derivation (Res*(T)). $\vdash C$ *for any clause C satisfying $T \vDash C$. A refutation of $\mathcal{F}$ is a proof in which the final line is the empty clause.*

It is easy to see that both $\mathsf{Res}(T)$ and $\mathsf{Res}^*(T)$ are sound since all rules are sound, and completeness follows from a straightforward modification of the usual proof of resolution completeness (see, e.g. Jukna [Juk12]).

Technically speaking, $\mathsf{Res}(T)$ is *not* a (formal) propositional proof system as defined by Cook and Reckhow [CR79] since the proofs may not be efficiently verifiable if deductions from the theory T are computationally difficult to verify. However, all theories considered in this paper (cf. Sect. 5) are very efficiently decidable, and thus the corresponding $\mathsf{Res}(T)$ proofs are efficiently verifiable.

Note that the clauses introduced by the theory derivations are arbitrary theorems of T; this means there is no direct information exchange between the resolution proof and the theory. It is enough to derive clauses in the theory derivation rules rather than arbitrary formulas since every axiom can be written in CNF form, and introduced as a sequence of clauses. The strong theory derivation rule can introduce new theory literals which might not have been present in the initial formula—we emphasize that the new theory literals can even contain theory *variables* (i.e. first-order terms) that did not occur in the original formula. We will see that this ability to introduce new literals seems to give $\mathsf{Res}^*(T)$ extra power over general resolution.

4   Lazy SMT Solvers and $\mathsf{Res}(T)$

In this section we show that lazy SMT solvers and resolution modulo theories are polynomially-equivalent as proof systems, provided that the SMT solvers are given a set of branching and restart decisions *a priori*.

We model SMT solvers by the algorithm schema[2] $\mathsf{DPLL}(T)$, which is given in Algorithm 1. Using this schema we prove two results: first, if the theory solver in $\mathsf{DPLL}(T)$ can only reason about literals occurring in its input formula, then $\mathsf{DPLL}(T)$ is polynomially equivalent to $\mathsf{Res}(T)$. Second, if the theory solver is strengthened so that it is allowed to introduce new literals then the resulting solver can polynomially simulate $\mathsf{Res}^*(T)$. The proofs of these results use techniques developed for comparing Boolean CDCL solvers and resolution by Pipatsrisawat and Darwiche [PD11].

---

[2] In the literature, SMT solvers are typically defined as abstract state-transition systems (see, for instance, [GHN+04,BM14]); we have chosen to define it instead as an algorithm schema (cf. Algorithm 1) inspired by the abstract definition of a CDCL solver by Pipatsrisawat and Darwiche [PD11].

Algorithm 1. DPLL(T)

Input: CNF formula $\mathcal{F}$ over T-literals;
Output: SAT or UNSAT
Let $\sigma = \emptyset$ be an initially empty partial assignment of T-literals;
Let Γ be an initially empty collection of learned clauses;
while *true* **do**

> **if** $\mathcal{F} \wedge \Gamma \wedge \sigma \vdash_1 \emptyset$ **then**
>> **if** $\sigma = \emptyset$ **then**
>>> **return** UNSAT;
>>
>> Apply the **clause learning scheme** to learn a conflict clause C, add it to Γ;
>> Backjump σ to the second highest decision level in C;
>
> **else if** $\sigma \vDash^T \emptyset$ **then**
>> Apply the **T-conflict scheme** to learn a conflict clause C, add it to Γ;
>> Backjump σ to the second highest decision level in C;
>
> **else**
>> **if** σ *satisfies* $\mathcal{F}$ **then**
>>> **return** SAT;
>>
>> Apply the **restart scheme** to decide whether or not to restart;
>> **if** *restart* **then**
>>> Set $\sigma = \emptyset$;
>>> Restart loop;
>>
>> Apply the **T-propagate scheme**;
>> Unit propagate literals to completion and update σ accordingly;
>> Apply the **branching scheme** to choose a decision literal ℓ, set $\sigma = \sigma \cup \{\ell\}$;

If T is a theory and A, B are formulas over T then we write $A \vDash^T B$ as a shorthand for $T \cup \{A\} \vDash B$ (i.e. every model of the theory T that satisfies A also satisfies B). We also define *unit resolution*, which describes the action of the *unit propagator*.

Definition 2 (Unit Resolution). *Let $\mathcal{F}$ be a collection of clauses over an arbitrary theory T. A clause C is derivable from $\mathcal{F}$ by* unit resolution *if there exists a resolution proof from $\mathcal{F}$ of C such that in each application of the resolution rule, one of the clauses is a unit clause. If C is derivable from $\mathcal{F}$ by unit resolution then we write $\mathcal{F} \vdash_1 C$. If $\mathcal{F} \vdash_1 \emptyset$ then we say $\mathcal{F}$ is* unit refutable, *otherwise it is* unit consistent.

A DPLL(T) algorithm is defined by specifying algorithms for each of the bolded "schemes" in Algorithm 1:

Clause Learning Scheme. When a clause in the database is falsified by the current partial assignment, the **Clause Learning Scheme** is applied to learn a new clause C which is added to the database of stored clauses.

Restart Scheme. The solver applies the **Restart Scheme** to decide whether or not to restart its search, discarding the current partial assignment σ and saving the list of learned clauses.

Branching Scheme. The **Branching Scheme** is applied to choose an unassigned variable from the formula $\mathcal{F}$ or from the learned clauses Γ and assign the variable a Boolean value.

T-Propagate Scheme. During search, the $\mathsf{DPLL}(T)$ solver can hand the theory solver the current partial assignment σ and ask whether or not it should unit-propagate a literal; if a unit propagation is possible the theory solver will return a clause C from the theory witnessing this unit propagation.

T-Conflict Scheme. When the theory solver detects that the current partial assignment σ contradicts the theory, the T-**Conflict Scheme** is applied to learn a new clause of literals C, $\neg C \subseteq \sigma$, which is added to the clause database.

We pay particular interest to the specification of the T-propagate scheme. The next definition describes two types of propagation schemes: a *weak* propagation scheme is only allowed to return clauses which propagate literals in the formula, while the more powerful *strong* propagation scheme returns a clause of literals from the theory that may contain new literals.

Definition 3. *A weak T-propagate scheme is an algorithm which takes as input a conjunction of theory literals σ over T and returns (if possible) a clause $C = \neg\sigma \vee \ell$ where $T \vDash C$ and the literal ℓ occurs in the input formula of the $\mathsf{DPLL}(T)$ algorithm.*

A strong T-propagate scheme is an algorithm which takes as input a conjunction of literals σ over T, and if possible returns a clause C of literals from T such that $T \vDash C$ and $\neg\sigma \subseteq C$. An algorithm equipped with a strong T-propagate scheme will be called a $\mathsf{DPLL}^*(T)$ solver.

A $\mathsf{DPLL}(T)$ algorithm equipped with a weak T-propagation scheme is equivalent to the basic theory propagation rules found in SMT solvers (see, for example, [BM14, NOT06]). For technical convenience we assume that the weak T-propagate scheme adds a clause to the database "certifying" the unit propagation, while in actual implementations the clause would likely not be added and the literal would simply be propagated. Recent SMT solvers [Yic, Z3] have strengthened the interaction between the SAT solver and the theory solver, allowing the theory solver to return constraints over new variables; this is modelled very generally by strong T-propagate schemes.

4.1 DPLL(T) and Res(T)

We now prove the main result of this section, after introducing some preliminaries from [PD11] that are suitably modified for our setting. Fix a theory T. An *assignment trail* is a sequence of pairs $\sigma = \{(\ell_i, d_i)\}_{i=1}^{t}$ where each literal ℓ_i is a literal from the theory and each $d_i \in \{\mathsf{d}, \mathsf{p}\}$, indicating that the literal was set by a decision or a unit propagation. The *decision level* of a literal ℓ_i in σ

is the number of decision literals occurring in σ up to and including ℓ_i. Given an assignment trail σ and a clause C we say that C is *asserting* if it contains exactly one literal occurring in σ at the highest decision level. A clause learning scheme is *asserting* if all conflict clauses produced by the scheme are asserting with respect to the assignment trail at the time of conflict.

An *extended branching sequence* is an ordered sequence $B = \{\beta_1, \beta_2, \ldots, \beta_t\}$ where each β_i is either (1) a literal from the theory, (2) a symbol $x \in \{\mathsf{R}, \mathsf{NR}\}$, to denote a restart or no-restart, respectively, or (3) a clause C such that $T \vDash C$. Intuitively, extended branching sequences are used to provide a DPLL(T) solver with a list of instructions for how to proceed in its execution. For instance, whenever the solver calls the Branching Scheme, we consume the next β_i from the sequence, and if it is a literal from the theory then the solver assigns that literal. Similarly, when the DPLL(T) solver calls the Restart Scheme it uses the branching sequence to dictate whether or not to restart, and when the solver calls the T-propagate scheme it uses the sequence to dictate which clause to learn. If the symbol does not correctly match the current scheme being called then the solver halts in error, and if the branching sequence is empty, then the algorithm proceeds using the heuristics defined by the algorithm.

We now introduce *absorbed* clauses (and their duals, *empowering* clauses), which were originally defined by Pipatsrisawat and Darwiche [PD11] and independently by Atserias et al. [AFT11]. One should think of the absorbed clauses as being learned "implicitly"—they may not necessarily appear in $\mathcal{F}$, but, if we assign all but one of the literals in the clause to false then unit propagation in DPLL(T) will set the final literal to true.

Definition 4 (Empowering Clauses). *Let $\mathcal{F}$ be a collection of clauses over an arbitrary theory T and let A be a DPLL(T) solver. Let α be a conjunction of literals, and let $C = (\neg\alpha \Rightarrow \ell)$ be a clause. We say that C is* empowering *with respect to $\mathcal{F}$ at ℓ if the following holds: (1) $\mathcal{F} \cup T \vDash C$, (2) $\mathcal{F} \wedge \alpha$ is unit consistent, and (3) any execution of A on $\mathcal{F}$ that satisfies α without setting ℓ does not unit-propagate ℓ. The literal ℓ is said to be* empowering. *If item (1), (2) are satisfied but (3) is false then we say that the solver A and $\mathcal{F}$ absorbs C at ℓ; if A and $\mathcal{F}$ absorbs C at at every literal then the clause is simply* absorbed.

For an example, consider the set of clauses $(x \vee y \vee z), (\neg z \vee a), (\neg a \vee b)$. The clause $(x \vee y \vee b)$ is absorbed by this set of clauses as, for instance, if we falsify x and y then the unit-propagator will force b to be set to true. Thus in the DPLL(T) algorithm the unit propagator will behave as though this clause is learned even though it is not (if we remove the final clause $\neg a \vee b$, then $(x \vee y \vee b)$ is empowering but not absorbed).

The next lemma shows that for any theory clause C, there is an extended branching sequence which can be applied to absorb that clause.

Lemma 5. *Let $\mathcal{F}$ be an unsatisfiable CNF over a theory T and let Π be any* Res(T) *proof from $\mathcal{F}$. Let $\Pi_T \subseteq \Pi$ be the set of clauses in Π derived using the theory rule. For any DPLL(T) algorithm A there is an extended branching sequence B such that after applying B to the solver A every clause in Π_T will be absorbed.*

Proof. Order Π_T arbitrarily as $C_1, C_2, \ldots, C_t$ and remove any clause that is absorbed or already in $\mathcal{F}$, as these are clearly already absorbed. We construct B directly: add the negations of literals in C_1 to B until one literal remains, and then add the clause C_1 to the extended branching sequence. By definition the weak T-propagator will be called and will return C_1, adding it to the clause database. Restart and continue to the next theory clause in order.

Our proof of mutual simulations between $\mathsf{Res}(T)$ and $\mathsf{DPLL}(T)$ crucially relies on the following technical lemma (which is a modified version of a lemma from [PD11]).

Lemma 6. *Let $\mathcal{F}$ be an unsatisfiable, unit-consistent CNF over literals from a theory T and let Π be any $\mathsf{Res}(T)$ proof from $\mathcal{F}$. Let Π_T be the set of clauses in Π derived using the theory rule. Then there exists a clause C in Π that is both empowering and unit-refutable with respect to $\mathcal{F} \cup \Pi_T$.*

Proof. Let Π denote a $\mathsf{Res}(T)$-refutation of $\mathcal{F}$ and assume without loss of generality (by applying Lemma 5) that the first derived clauses in Π are in Π_T. If every clause in Π is unit-refutable from $\mathcal{F}$, then the empty clause is unit-refutable and thus $\mathcal{F}$ is not unit-consistent, which is a contradiction. So, assume that there exists a clause C_i which is the first clause in Π by this ordering such that it is not unit-refutable. Since Π is a $\mathsf{Res}(T)$-proof, C_i is one of three types: either it is a clause in $\mathcal{F}$, it is a clause derived from the theory rule, or C_i was derived by applying the resolution rule to two clauses C_j, C_k. If $C_i \in \mathcal{F}$ then it is clearly unit-refutable, which is a contradiction. If C_i was derived from the theory rule then it is unit-refutable with respect to Π_T, which is again a contradiction. Finally, suppose that C_i was derived by applying the resolution rule to clauses C_j and C_k, and write $C_j = (\alpha \Rightarrow \ell)$, $C_k = (\beta \Rightarrow \bar{\ell})$ where ℓ is the resolved literal and $j, k < i$ in the ordering of clauses in Π. Since C_j and C_k are both unit-refutable, assume by way of contradiction that neither C_j nor C_k are empowering. It follows by definition that both clauses are absorbed at every literal. Thus, if we consider $\mathcal{F} \wedge \alpha \wedge \beta$, it follows by the absorption property that $\mathcal{F} \wedge \alpha \wedge \beta \vdash_1 \ell, \mathcal{F} \wedge \alpha \wedge \beta \vdash_1 \neg\ell$ which implies that $\mathcal{F} \wedge \alpha \wedge \beta \vdash_1^T \emptyset$. However, $\overline{C_i} = \alpha \wedge \beta$, and thus we have concluded C_i is unit-refutable, which is a contradiction! Thus at least one of C_j or C_k is both empowering and unit-refutable.

The gist of the Lemma 6 is simple: if clauses $C \vee \ell$ and $D \vee \bar{\ell}$ are both absorbed by a collection of clauses $\mathcal{C}$, then asserting $\overline{C} \wedge \overline{D}$ in the DPLL solver will hit a conflict since it will unit-imply both ℓ and $\bar{\ell}$. In the main theorem, proved next, we show that empowering and unit-refutable clauses will be absorbed by the solver after sufficiently many restarts.

Theorem 7. *The $\mathsf{DPLL}(T)$ system with an asserting clause learning scheme, non-deterministic branching and T-propagation polynomially simulates $\mathsf{Res}(T)$. Equivalently: for any unsatisfiable CNF $\mathcal{F}$ over a theory T, and any $\mathsf{Res}(T)$ refutation Π of $\mathcal{F}$ there exists an extended branching sequence B such that running a $\mathsf{DPLL}(T)$ algorithm on input $\mathcal{F}$ using B will refute $\mathcal{F}$ in time polynomial in the length of $|\Pi|$.*

Proof. Let $\mathcal{F}$ be an unsatisfiable CNF over the theory T, and let Π be a $\mathsf{Res}(T)$ refutation of $\mathcal{F}$. Let $\Pi_T \subseteq \Pi$ be the set of clauses in Π derived using the theory rule, and write $\Pi = C_1, C_2, \ldots, C_m$. As a first step, apply Lemma 5 and construct an extended branching sequence B' which leads to the absorbtion of all clauses in Π_T. We prove the following claim, from which the theorem directly follows.

Claim. Let C be any unit-refutable and empowering clause with respect to $\mathcal{F}$. Then there exists an extended branching sequence B of polynomial size such that after applying B the clause C will be absorbed.

Let ℓ be any empowering literal of C, and write $C = (\alpha \Rightarrow \ell)$. Let B be any extended branching sequence in which all literals in α are assigned. Since C is empowering, it follows that $\mathcal{F} \wedge \alpha$ is unit-consistent. Extending B with the decision literal $\neg\ell$ will therefore cause a conflict since C is unit-refutable. Let C' be the asserting clause obtained by applying the clause learning scheme to $B \cup \{\neg\ell\}$. If $\mathcal{F} \wedge C'$ absorbs C at ℓ, then we are done and we continue to the next empowering literal. Otherwise, we resolve whatever conflicts the solver needs to resolve (possibly adding more learned clauses along the way) until the branching sequence is unit-consistent.

Observe that after this process we must have that $\mathcal{F} \wedge C' \vdash_1 \ell'$ where ℓ' is some literal at the same decision level as ℓ, since the clause learning scheme is asserting. Thus the number of literals at the maximum decision level has reduced by one. At this point, we restart and do exactly the same sequence of branchings—each time, as argued above, we reduce the number of literals at the maximum decision level by 1. Since ℓ is a literal at the maximum decision level, it implies that after at most $O(n)$ restarts (and $O(n^2)$ learned clauses) we will have absorbed the clause C at ℓ. Repeating this process at most n times for each empowering literal in C we can absorb C, and it is clear that the number of learned clauses is polynomial from the analysis.

We are now ready to finish the proof. Apply the claim repeatedly to the first empowering and unit-refutable clause in Π to absorb that clause—by Lemma 6, such a clause will exist as long as the CNF $\mathcal{F}$ is not unit-refutable; a $\mathsf{DPLL}(T)$ solver can obtain an arbitrary theory clause by setting relevant literals in the branching sequence and using theory propagation. Since the length of the proof Π is finite (length m), it follows that this process must terminate after at most m iterations. At this point, there can not be such an empowering and unit-refutable clause, and so by Lemma 6 it follows that $\mathcal{F}$ (with its learned clauses) is now unit-refutable, and so the $\mathsf{DPLL}(T)$ algorithm halts and outputs UNSAT.

The reverse direction of the theorem is straightforward, and thus we have the following corollary:

Corollary 8. *The* $\mathsf{DPLL}(T)$ *system with an asserting clause learning scheme, non-deterministic branching and T-propagation is polynomially equivalent to* $\mathsf{Res}(T)$.

A key point of the above simulation is that it does not depend on whether or not the T-propagation scheme is weak or strong—since the clauses learned by the scheme are specified in advance by the extended branching sequence the same proof will apply if we began with a $\mathsf{Res}^*(T)$ proof instead. Of course, if we begin with a $\mathsf{Res}^*(T)$ proof instead of a $\mathsf{Res}(T)$ proof we may use the full power of the theory derivation rule, requiring that we use a $\mathsf{DPLL}^*(T)$ algorithm with a strong T-propagation scheme instead. We record this observation as a second theorem.

Theorem 9. *The* $\mathsf{DPLL}^*(T)$ *system with an asserting clause learning scheme, non-deterministic branching and T-propagation is polynomially equivalent to* $\mathsf{Res}^*(T)$.

5   Case Studies: Resolution Modulo Common Theories

In this section, we study the power of $\mathsf{Res}(T)$ over theories that are common in the SMT context—namely, we focus on the theory of equality E, the theory of uninterpreted function symbols EUF, and the theory of linear arithmetic LA.

5.1   Resolution over E: A Theory of Equality

We first consider E, the theory of equality. Bjørner et al. [BDdM08] introduced a proof-theoretic calculus called $\mathsf{SP}(E)$ for reasoning over the theory of equality—in a prototype of our main result, they showed that proofs in $\mathsf{SP}(E)$ exactly characterized proofs produced by a simple model SMT solver. In this section we show that the theory $\mathsf{Res}^*(E)$ is polynomially-equivalent to $\mathsf{SP}(E)$, which is evidence that our general framework is the correct way of capturing the power of SMT solvers.

Let us first reproduce the rules of $\mathsf{SP}(E)$ from [BDdM08]: **Cut.** $C \vee \ell,\ D \vee \neg \ell \vdash C \vee D$, **E-Dis.** $C \vee a \neq a \vdash C$, **E-Eqs.** $C \vee a = b \vee a = c \vdash C \vee a = b \vee b \neq c$, **Sup.** $C \vee a = b,\ D[a] \vdash C \vee D[b]$. Observe that the Sup rule allows replacing some occurrences of a term a in atoms of a clause D with b (not necessarily for all occurrences of a). Both the Sup rule and the E-Eqs rule can introduce literals that did not occur in the initial formula.

Proposition 10. $\mathsf{Res}^*(E)$ *and* $\mathsf{SP}(E)$ *are polynomially equivalent.*

Proof (Sketch). Bjørner et al. show that $\mathsf{SP}(E)$ exactly characterizes the proofs produced by a simple theoretical model of an SMT solver, which we will denote by $\mathsf{DPLL}(e + \Delta)$ [BDdM08, Theorem 4.1]. Examining the solver $\mathsf{DPLL}(e + \Delta)$ from [BDdM08], it is not hard to see it is equivalent to the algorithm $\mathsf{DPLL}^*(E)$ (that is, $\mathsf{DPLL}(T)$ with a strong T propagation rule). The equivalence between $\mathsf{Res}^*(E)$ and $\mathsf{DPLL}^*(E)$ follows by the Corollary of Theorem 9.

In the conclusion of [BDdM08] it is stated that there are no short $\mathsf{SP}(E)$ proofs of the following encoding of the pigeonhole principle (PHP): there are clauses of the form $(d_i = r_1 \vee \ldots d_i = r_n)$, for $i \in [1, n+1]$, enforcing that the ith pigeon must travel to some hole, and clauses of the form $(d_i \neq d_j)$ for

$i, j \in [1, n+1]$ which, when combined with the first family of clauses and the transitivity axioms of E, imply that no two pigeons can travel to the same hole. Since their $\mathsf{SP}(\mathrm{E})$ system is equivalent to $\mathsf{Res}^*(\mathrm{E})$ it follows that the lower bounds on $\mathsf{SP}(\mathrm{E})$ carry over:

Corollary 11. *If* $\mathsf{SP}(\mathrm{E})$ *does not have polynomial-size refutations of the pigeonhole principle, then neither does* $\mathsf{Res}^*(\mathrm{E})$.

5.2   Resolution over EUF: Equality with Uninterpreted Functions

Next, we study the theory EUF, which is an extension of the theory of equality to contain uninterpreted function symbols. The signature of EUF consists of an unlimited set of uninterpreted function symbols and constant symbols; a term in the theory is thus inductively defined as either a constant symbol or an application of a function symbol to a sequence of terms: $f(t_1, \ldots, t_k)$. There is one relational symbol = interpreted as equality between terms, so theory literals of EUF are of the form $t = t'$ for terms t, t'.

The axioms of EUF state that = is an equivalence relation, together with a family of *congruence axioms* for the function symbols stating, for any k-ary function symbol f and any sequences of terms $t_1, t_2, \ldots, t_k$, $t'_1, t'_2, \ldots, t'_k$, if $t_1 = t'_1, \ldots, t_k = t'_k$, then $f(t_1, \ldots, t_k) = f(t'_1, \ldots, t'_k)$. The decision problem for EUF can be decided in time $O(n \log n)$ by the Downey-Sethi-Tarjan congruence closure algorithm [DST80].

Using EUF as a central example, Bjorner and de Moura [BM14] observed that $\mathsf{DPLL}(T)$ suffers some serious limitations in terms of access to the underlying theory. To resolve this, they modified $\mathsf{DPLL}(\mathrm{EUF})$ with a set of non-deterministic rules that allowed it to dynamically introduce clauses corresponding to the congruence and transitivity axioms. To characterize the strength of this new algorithm, they introduced a variant of resolution called E-Res, extending $\mathsf{SP}(\mathrm{E})$ from [BDdM08] to reasoning over uninterpreted functions. We show that the $\mathsf{Res}^*(\mathrm{EUF})$ proof system can polynomially-simulate the E-Res system, which again suggests that we have the "correct" proof system for capturing SMT reasoning. Due to space considerations, we leave the proof to the full version of the paper.

Theorem 12. *The system* E-Res *is polynomially simulated by* $\mathsf{Res}^*(\mathrm{EUF})$.

However, unlike the case of $\mathsf{SP}(\mathrm{E})$ the converse direction is not so clear. The theory rule in $\mathsf{Res}^*(\mathrm{EUF})$ is fundamentally *semantic*: it allows one to derive *any* clause which follows from the theory EUF semantically; this is in contrast to the E-Res system which is fundamentally syntactic. Thus, to show that E-Res polynomially simulates EUF, one would need to show that any use of the theory rule in a $\mathsf{Res}^*(\mathrm{EUF})$ proof could be somehow replaced with a short proof in E-Res. We leave this as an open problem.

Next, we show that $\mathsf{Res}^*(\mathrm{EUF})$ and E-Res can efficiently simulate the Frege proof system, which is a very powerful propositional proof system studied in proof complexity. We note that the simulation crucially relies on the introduction of new theory literals; this suggests that an SMT solver which can intelligently introduce new theory literals has the potential to be extremely powerful.

Theorem 13. Res*(EUF) *(and, in fact,* E-Res*) can efficiently simulate the Frege proof system.*

Proof Sketch. We show the stronger statement that E-Res simulates Frege. The idea of the proof is to introduce constants $e_0 \neq e_1$ corresponding to FALSE and TRUE; every positive literal x in the original formula is replaced by $x = e_1$, and negative literal $\neg x$ by $x = e_0$. Then introduce uninterpreted function symbols N, O, A, together with constraints that make N, O, A behave as NOT, OR and AND, respectively (such as $N(e_0) = e_1 \wedge N(e_1) = e_0$). So formulas in the Frege refutation are iteratively transformed into expressions of the form $t_F = e_0$ or $t_F = e_1$, where t_F is a term obtained by replacing Boolean connectives in a formula F by N, O, A. As the Frege proof ends with an empty sequent, the corresponding E-Res proof ends with an empty clause. See the full version for details.

5.3 Resolution over LA: A Theory of Linear Arithmetic

Finally, we study the theory of linear arithmetic LA. A formula in the theory LA over a domain D is a conjunction of expressions of the form $\Sigma_{i=1}^n a_i x_i \circ b$, where $\circ \in \{=, \leq, <, \neq, \geq, >\}$, and $a_i, x_i \in D$ — usually, D is integers or reals[3]. We show that Res(LA) polynomially simulates the proof system R(lin) introduced by Raz and Tzameret [RT08]. This is interesting, as R(lin) has polynomial-size proofs of several difficult tautologies considered in proof complexity, such as the pigeonhole principle, Tseitin tautologies and the clique-colouring principle.

In the proof system R(lin) propositional variables are linear equations over integers. The input formula is a CNF over such equations, together with $\bigwedge_{i=1}^n (x_i = 0 \vee x_i = 1)$ clauses ensuring 0/1 assignment. The rules of inference consist of a modified resolution rule, together with two structural rules, weakening and simplification:

R(lin)-**cut.** Let $(A \vee L_1)$, $(B \vee L_2)$ be two clauses containing linear equalities L_1 and L_2, respectively. From these two clauses, derive a clause $(A \vee B \vee (L_1 - L_2))$.
Weakening. From a (possibly empty) clause A derive $(A \vee L)$ for any equation L.
Simplification. From $(A \vee k = 0)$, where $k \neq 0$ is a constant, derive A.

Proposition 14. Res(LA) *polynomially simulates* R(lin).

---

[3] Some definitions of linear arithmetic do not include disequalities; however, as disequalities and strict inequalities occur naturally in SMT context, SMT-oriented linear arithmetic solvers do incorporate mechanisms for dealing with them.

Proof. We show how to simulate rules of R(lin) in Res(LA). We can assume, without loss of generality, that Res(LA) has a weakening rule which simulates weakening of R(lin) directly. For the simplification rule, note that LA $\vDash k \neq 0$ for any $k \neq 0$; one application of the resolution rule on $(k \neq 0)$ and $(A \vee k = 0)$ results in A.

Finally, let L_1 be $\Sigma_{i=1}^n a_i x_i = b$ and L_2 be $\Sigma_{i=1}^n c_i x_i = d$. From $(A \vee L_1)$, $(B \vee L_2)$ we want to derive $(A \vee B \vee L_1 - L2)$. First derive in LA a clause $C = (\Sigma_{i=1}^n a_i x_i \neq b \vee \Sigma_{i=1}^n c_i x_i \neq d \vee \Sigma_{i=1}^n (a_i - c_i) x_i = b - d)$. Resolving $(A \vee L_1)$ with C, and then resolving the resulting clause with $(B \vee L_2)$ gives the desired $(A \vee B \vee (L_1 - L_2))$.

Note that we didn't need to specify whether LA is over the integers, rationals or reals, and hence the proof works for any of them. Also, in order to establish our simulations it is sufficient to consider a fragment of LA with only equalities and inequalities, and produce only unit clauses and width-3 clauses of a fixed form.

Corollary 15. Res(LA) *has polynomial-size proofs of the pigeonhole principle, Tseitin tautologies and a clique-colouring principle for $k = \sqrt{(n)}$ size clique and $k' = (\log n)^2 / 8 \log \log n$ size colouring.*

6 Lazy vs. Eager Reductions and the Exponential Time Hypothesis

Throughout this paper we have primarily discussed the *Lazy* approach to SMT. In this section, we consider the *Eager* approach, in which an input formula $\mathcal{F}$ over a theory T is reduced to an equisatisfiable propositional formula $\mathcal{G}$, which is then solved using a suitable (Boolean) solver.

The Eager approach is still used in several modern SMT solvers such as the STP solver for bit-vectors and arrays [GD07]. A common eager reduction used when solving equations over the theory of equality, E (or its generalization to uninterpreted function symbols EUF), is the *Ackermann reduction*. Let us first describe a simple version of the Ackermann reduction over the theory E.

Let $\mathcal{F}$ denote a CNF over literals from the theory E—so, each literal is of the form $a = b$ for constant terms a, b—which we will ultimately transform into a Boolean SAT instance. Let n denote the number of constant terms occurring in $\mathcal{F}$, let m denote the number of distinct literals occurring in $\mathcal{F}$, and consider the literal $a = b$ and the literal $b = a$ to be the same. For each literal $a = b$ introduce a Boolean variable $x_{a=b}$, and for each clause of literals $\bigvee_i a_i = b_i$ create a clause $\bigvee_i x_{a_i=b_i}$. To encode the transitivity of equality, for each triple of terms (a, b, c) occurring in the initial CNF $\mathcal{F}$ introduce a clause of the form $\neg x_{a=b} \vee \neg x_{b=c} \vee x_{a=c}$. Note that the final formula will have $O(n^2)$ Boolean variables corresponding to each possible term $a = b$—a potential quadratic blow-up—which is unavoidable using this encoding due to the transitivity axioms. Observe that this blow-up only occurs in the eager approach—in the lazy approach to solving we only need to consider the literals $a = b$ which occur in the original formula $\mathcal{F}$. It is therefore natural to wonder if this blow-up in the number of input variables can somehow be avoided.

In fact, one can construct a more clever Eager reduction from E-SAT to SAT which only introduces $O(n \log n)$ boolean variables; however, this more clever encoding does not represent the literals $a = b$ as Boolean variables $x_{a=b}$ and instead uses a more complicated pointer construction. This improved reduction turns out to be the best possible under the well-known (and widely believed) *Exponential Time Hypothesis*, which is a strengthening of P $\neq$ NP.

Exponential Time Hypothesis (ETH). There is no deterministic or randomized algorithm for SAT running in time $2^{o(n)}$, where n is the number of input variables.

Theorem 16. *Let $\mathcal{F}$ be an instance of E-SAT with n distinct terms. For any polynomial-time reduction R from E-SAT to SAT, the boolean formula $R(\mathcal{F})$ must have $\Omega(n \log n)$ variables unless ETH fails.*

Proof. By way of contradiction, suppose that ETH holds and let R be a reduction from E-SAT to SAT which introduces $o(n \log n)$ variables. Let 2-CSP denote a constraint satisfaction problem with two variables per constraint. The theorem follows almost immediately from the following result of Traxler [Tra08].

Theorem 17 (Theorem 1 in [Tra08], Rephrased). *Consider any 2-CSP $C_1 \wedge C_2 \wedge \cdots \wedge C_m$ over an alphabet Σ of size d, where each constraint is of the form $x \neq a \vee y \neq b$ for variables x, y and constants $a, b \in \Sigma$. Unless ETH fails, every algorithm for this problem requires time d^{cn} for some universal constant $c > 0$.*

There is a simple reduction from the restriction of 2-CSP described in the above theorem to E-SAT. Introduce terms $e_1, e_2, \ldots, e_d$, each intended to represent a symbol from the universe Σ, and also terms $x_1, x_2, \ldots, x_n$ for each variable x occurring in the original CSP instance. Now, for each $i \neq j$ introduce unit clauses $e_i \neq e_j$, and similarly for each $i \in [n]$ add a clause of the form $x_i = e_1 \vee x_i = e_2 \vee \cdots \vee x_i = e_d$. Finally, for each constraint in the 2-CSP of the form $x_i \neq a \vee x_j \neq b$ introduce a clause $x_i \neq e_a \vee x_j \neq e_b$, where e_a, e_b are the terms corresponding to the symbols a, b. Let $\mathcal{F}'$ denote the final E-SAT instance, and it is clear that $\mathcal{F}'$ is satisfiable if and only if the original 2-CSP is satisfiable, and also that $\mathcal{F}'$ has $n + d$ constant terms.

Now, apply the Ackermann reduction R to $\mathcal{F}'$, obtaining a SAT instance $R(\mathcal{F}')$. By assumption the final SAT instance has $o((n+d) \log(n+d))$ variables; running the standard brute-force algorithm for SAT gives an algorithm running in $2^{o((n+d) \log(n+d))}$ time for the 2-CSP variant described above. However, by the above theorem, every algorithm for this 2-CSP variant requires time at least $d^{cn} = 2^{cn \log d}$, which violates ETH if $d \approx n$.

7   Conclusion

In this paper, we studied SMT solvers through the lens of proof complexity, introducing a generalization of the resolution proof system and arguing that it correctly models the "lazy" SMT framework DPLL(T) [NOT06]. We further presented and analyzed a stronger version Res*(T) that allows for the introduction of new literals, and showed that it models DPLL*(T), which is a modification of an SMT solver that can introduce new theory literals; this captures the new literal introduction in solvers such as Yices and Z3 [Z3,Yic].

There are many natural directions to pursue. First, although we have not considered it here, it is natural to introduce an *intermediate* proof system between Res(T) and Res*(T) which is allowed to introduce new theory *literals* but *not* new theory *variables*. For instance, if we have the formula $a = f(b) \land a = c$ in EUF, then this intermediate proof system could introduce the theory literal $c = f(b)$ but *not* the theory literal $f(c) = f(a)$, whereas both are allowed to be introduced by Res*(T). It is not clear to us if this intermediate system can simulate Frege, and we suggest studying it in its own right.

A second direction that we believe is quite interesting is extending our results on EUF to capture the *extended Frege* system, which is the most powerful proof system typically studied in proposition proof complexity. Intuitively, it seems that EUF by itself is not strong enough to capture extended Frege; we consider finding a new theory T which can capture it an interesting open problem.

References

[AFT11] Atserias, A., Fichte, J.K., Thurley, M.: Clause-learning algorithms with many restarts and bounded-width resolution. J. Artif. Intell. Res. **40**, 353–373 (2011)

[BBJ14] Bonet, M.L., Buss, S., Johannsen, J.: Improved separations of regular resolution from clause learning proof systems. J. Artif. Intell. Res. **49**, 669–703 (2014)

[BDdM08] Bjørner, N., Dutertre, B., de Moura, L.: Accelerating lemma learning using joins - DPLL(Join). In: 15th International Conference on Logic for Programming Artificial Intelligence and Reasoning, LPAR 2008 (2008)

[BHJ17] Balyo, T., Heule, M.J.H., Järvisalo, M.: SAT competition 2016: recent developments. In: Singh, S.P., Markovitch, S. (eds.) Proceedings of the Thirty-First AAAI Conference on Artificial Intelligence, 4–9 February 2017, San Francisco, California, USA, pp. 5061–5063. AAAI Press (2017)

[BKS04] Beame, P., Kautz, H.A., Sabharwal, A.: Towards understanding and harnessing the potential of clause learning. J. Artif. Intell. Res. **22**, 319–351 (2004)

[BM14] Bjørner, N., de Moura, L.: Tractability and modern SMT solvers. In: Bordeaux, L., Hamadi, Y., Kohli, P. (eds.) Tractability: Practical Approaches to Hard Problems, pp. 350–377. Cambridge University Press (2014)

[CR79] Cook, S.A., Reckhow, R.A.: The relative efficiency of propositional proof systems. J. Symb. Log. **44**(1), 36–50 (1979)

[DST80] Downey, P.J., Sethi, R., Tarjan, R.E.: Variations on the common subexpression problem. J. ACM (JACM) **27**(4), 758–771 (1980)

[GD07] Ganesh, V., Dill, D.L.: A Decision procedure for bit-vectors and arrays. In: Damm, W., Hermanns, H. (eds.) CAV 2007. LNCS, vol. 4590, pp. 519–531. Springer, Heidelberg (2007). https://doi.org/10.1007/978-3-540-73368-3_52

[GHN+04] Ganzinger, H., Hagen, G., Nieuwenhuis, R., Oliveras, A., Tinelli, C.: DPLL(T): fast decision procedures. In: Alur, R., Peled, D.A. (eds.) CAV 2004. LNCS, vol. 3114, pp. 175–188. Springer, Heidelberg (2004). https://doi.org/10.1007/978-3-540-27813-9_14

[Juk12] Jukna, S.: Boolean Function Complexity: Advances and Frontiers. Springer, Heidelberg (2012). https://doi.org/10.1007/978-3-642-24508-4

[Kra98] Krajíček, J.: Discretely ordered modules as a first-order extension of the cutting planes proof system. J. Symb. Log. **63**(04), 1582–1596 (1998)

[NOT06] Nieuwenhuis, R., Oliveras, A., Tinelli, C.: Solving SAT and SAT modulo theories. J. ACM **53**(6), 937–977 (2006)

[ORC09] Oliveras, A., Rodr1guez-Carbonell, E.: Combining decision procedures: the Nelson-Oppen approach. Techniques (2009)

[PD11] Pipatsrisawat, K., Darwiche, A.: On the power of clause-learning SAT solvers as resolution engines. Artif. Intell. **175**(2), 512–525 (2011)

[RT08] Raz, R., Tzameret, I.: Resolution over linear equations and multilinear proofs. Annals Pure Appl. Log. **155**(3), 194–224 (2008)

[smt] The Annual SMTCOMP Competition Website. http://www.smtcomp.org

[Tin12] Tinelli, C.: Foundations of Lazy SMT and DPLL(T) (2012)

[Tra08] Traxler, P.: The time complexity of constraint satisfaction. In: Grohe, M., Niedermeier, R. (eds.) IWPEC 2008. LNCS, vol. 5018, pp. 190–201. Springer, Heidelberg (2008). https://doi.org/10.1007/978-3-540-79723-4_18

[Yic] The Yices SMT Solver. http://yices.csl.sri.com/

[Z3] The Z3 Theorem Prover. https://github.com/Z3Prover

Model Generation for Quantified Formulas: A Taint-Based Approach

Benjamin Farinier[1,2(✉)], Sébastien Bardin[1], Richard Bonichon[1],
and Marie-Laure Potet[2]

[1] CEA, LIST, Software Safety and Security Lab,
Université Paris-Saclay, Gif-sur-Yvette, France
{benjamin.farinier,sebastien.bardin,
richard.bonichon}@cea.fr
[2] Univ. Grenoble Alpes, Verimag,
Grenoble, France
{benjamin.farinier,
marie-laure.potet}@univ-grenoble-alpes.fr

Abstract. We focus in this paper on generating models of quantified first-order formulas over built-in theories, which is paramount in software verification and bug finding. While standard methods are either geared toward proving the absence of a solution or targeted to specific theories, we propose a generic and radically new approach based on a reduction to the quantifier-free case. Our technique thus allows to reuse all the efficient machinery developed for that context. Experiments show a substantial improvement over state-of-the-art methods.

1 Introduction

Context. Software verification methods have come to rely increasingly on reasoning over logical formulas modulo theory. In particular, the ability to generate models (i.e., find solutions) of a formula is of utmost importance, typically in the context of bug finding or intensive testing—symbolic execution [21] or bounded model checking [7]. Since *quantifier-free first-order formulas* on well-suited theories are sufficient to represent many reachability properties of interest, the Satisfiability Modulo Theory (SMT) [6,25] community has primarily dedicated itself to designing solvers able to efficiently handle such problems.

Yet, universal quantifiers are sometimes needed, typically when considering preconditions or code abstraction. Unfortunately, most theories handled by SMT-solvers are undecidable in the presence of universal quantifiers. There exist dedicated methods for a few decidable quantified theories, such as Presburger arithmetic [9] or the array property fragment [8], but there is no general and effective enough approach for the model generation problem over universally quantified formulas. Indeed, generic solutions for quantified formulas involving

© The Author(s) 2018
H. Chockler and G. Weissenbacher (Eds.): CAV 2018, LNCS 10982, pp. 294–313, 2018.
https://doi.org/10.1007/978-3-319-96142-2_19

heuristic instantiation and refutation are best geared to proving the unsatisfiability of a formula (i.e., absence of solution) [13,20], while recent proposals such as local theory extensions [2], finite instantiation [31,32] or model-based instantiation [20,29] either are too narrow in scope, or handle quantifiers on free sorts only, or restrict themselves to finite models, or may get stuck in infinite refinement loops.

Goal and Challenge. Our goal is to propose a generic and efficient approach to the model generation problem over arbitrary quantified formulas with support for theories commonly found in software verification. Due to the huge effort made by the community to produce state-of-the-art solvers for quantifier-free theories (QF-*solvers*), it is highly desirable for this solution to be compatible with current leading decision procedures, namely SMT approaches.

Proposal. Our approach turns a quantified formula into a quantifier-free formula with the guarantee that any model of the latter contains a model of the former. The benefits are threefold: the transformed formula is easier to solve, it can be sent to standard QF-solvers, and a model for the initial formula is deducible from a model of the transformed one. The idea is to ignore quantifiers but strengthen the quantifier-free part of the formula with an *independence condition* constraining models to be independent from the (initially) quantified variables.

Contributions. This paper makes the following contributions:

We propose a novel and generic framework for model generation of quantified formula (Sect. 5, Algorithm 1) relying on the inference of *sufficient independence condition* (Sect. 4). We prove its *correctness* (Theorem 1, mechanized in Coq) and its *efficiency* under reasonable assumptions (Propositions 4 and 5). Especially our approach implies only a linear overhead in the formula size. We also briefly study its *completeness*, related to the notion of *weakest independence condition*.

We define a taint-based procedure for the inference of independence conditions (Sect. 5.2), composed of a theory-independent core (Algorithm 2) together with theory-dependent refinements. We propose such refinements for a large class of operators (Sect. 6.2), encompassing notably arrays and bitvectors.

Finally, we present a concrete implementation of our method specialized on arrays and bitvectors (Sect. 7). Experiments on SMT-LIB benchmarks and software verification problems notably demonstrate that we are able not only to very effectively lift quantifier-free decision procedures to the quantified case, but also to supplement recent advances, such as finite or model-based quantifier instantiation [20,29,31,32]. Indeed, we concretely supply SMT solvers with the ability to efficiently address an extended set of software verification questions.

Discussions. Our approach supplements state-of-the-art model generation on quantified formulas by providing a more generic handling of satisfiable problems.

We can deal with quantifiers on any sort and we are not restricted to finite models. Moreover, this is a lightweight preprocessing approach requiring a single call to the underlying quantifier-free solver. The method also extends to *partial* elimination of universal quantifiers, or reduction to *quantified-but-decidable* formulas (Sect. 5.4).

While techniques *a la* E-matching allow to lift quantifier-free solvers to the unsatisfiability checking of quantified formulas, this works provides a mechanism to lift them to the satisfiability checking and model generation of quantified formulas, yielding a more symmetric handling of quantified formulas in SMT. This new approach paves the way to future developments such as the definition of more precise inference mechanisms of independence conditions, the identification of interesting subclasses for which inferring weakest independence conditions is feasible, and the combination with other quantifier instantiation techniques.

2 Motivation

Let us take the code sample in Fig. 1 and suppose we want to reach function `analyze_me`. For this purpose, we need a model (a.k.a., solution) of the reachability condition $\phi \triangleq ax + b > 0$, where a, b and x are symbolic variables associated to the program variables a, b and x. However, while the values of a and b are user-controlled, the value of x is not. Therefore if we want to reach `analyze_me` in a reproducible manner, we actually need a model of $\phi_\forall \triangleq \forall x.ax + b > 0$, which *involves universal quantification*. While this specific formula is simple, model generation for quantified formulas is notoriously difficult: PSPACE-complete for booleans, undecidable for uninterpreted functions or arrays.

```
int main () {
  int a = input ();
  int b = input ();

  int x = rand ();

  if (a * x + b > 0) {
    analyze_me ();
  }
  else {
    ...;
  }
}
```

Quantified reachability condition

(1) $\forall x.ax + b > 0$

Taint variable constraint

(2) $a^\bullet \wedge b^\bullet \wedge \neg(x^\bullet)$ $(a^\bullet, b^\bullet, x^\bullet : \text{fresh boolean})$

Independence condition

(3) $((a^\bullet \wedge x^\bullet) \vee (a^\bullet \wedge a = 0) \vee (x^\bullet \wedge x = 0)) \wedge b^\bullet$

(4) $((\top \wedge \bot) \vee (\top \wedge a = 0) \vee (\bot \wedge x = 0)) \wedge \top$

(5) $a = 0$

Quantifier-free approximation of (1)

(6) $(ax + b > 0) \wedge (a = 0)$

Fig. 1. Motivating example

Reduction to the Quantifier-Free Case Through Independence. We propose to ignore the universal quantification over x, but *restrict models to those* *which do not depend on* x. For example, model $\{a = 1, x = 1, b = 0\}$ does depend on x, as taking $x = 0$ invalidates the formula, while model $\{a = 0, x = 1, b = 1\}$ is *independent of* x. We call constraint $\psi \triangleq (a = 0)$ an *independence condition*: any interpretation of ϕ satisfying ψ will be independent of x, and therefore a model of $\phi \wedge \psi$ will give us a model of $\phi_\forall$.

Inference of Independence Conditions Through Tainting. Figure 1 details in its right part a way to infer such independence conditions. Given a quantified reachability condition (1), we first associate to every variable v a (boolean) *taint variable* $v^\bullet$ indicating whether the solution may depend on v (value $\top$) or not (value $\bot$). Here, $x^\bullet$ is set to $\bot$, $a^\bullet$ and $b^\bullet$ are set to $\top$ (2). An independence condition (3)—a formula modulo theory—is then constructed using both initial and taint variables. We extend taint constraints to terms, $t^\bullet$ indicating here whether t may depend on x or not, and we require the top-level term (i.e., the formula) to be tainted to $\top$ (i.e., to be indep. from x). Condition (3) reads as follows: in order to enforce that $(ax + b > 0)^\bullet$ holds, we enforce that $(ax)^\bullet$ and $b^\bullet$ hold, and for $(ax)^\bullet$ we require that either $a^\bullet$ and $x^\bullet$ hold, or $a^\bullet$ holds and $a = 0$ (absorbing the value of x), or the symmetric case. We see that $\cdot^\bullet$ is defined recursively and combines a *systematic part* (if $t^\bullet$ holds then $f(t)^\bullet$ holds, for any f) with a *theory-dependent part* (here, based on $\times$). After simplifications (4), we obtain $a = 0$ as an independence condition (5) which is adjoined to the reachability condition freed of its universal quantification (6). A QF-solver provides a model of (6) (e.g., $\{a = 0, b = 1, x = 5\}$), lifted into a model of (1) by discarding the valuation of x (e.g., $\{a = 0, b = 1\}$).

In this specific example the inferred independence condition (5) is the most generic one and (1) and (6) are equisatisfiable. Yet, in general it may be an under-approximation, constraining the variables more than needed and yielding a correct but incomplete decision method: a model of (6) can still be turned into a model of (1), but (6) might not have a model while (1) has.

3   Notations

We consider the framework of many-sorted first-order logic with equality, and we assume standard definitions of sorts, signatures and terms. Given a tuple of variables $\boldsymbol{x} \triangleq (x_1, \ldots, x_n)$ and a quantifier $\mathcal{Q}$ ($\forall$ or $\exists$), we shorten $\mathcal{Q}x_1 \ldots \mathcal{Q}x_n.\Phi$ as $\mathcal{Q}\boldsymbol{x}.\Phi$. A formula is in *prenex normal form* if it is written as $\mathcal{Q}_1\boldsymbol{x}_1 \ldots \mathcal{Q}_n\boldsymbol{x}_n.\Phi$ with Φ a quantifier-free formula. A formula is in *Skolem normal form* if it is in prenex normal form with only universal quantifiers. We write $\Phi(\boldsymbol{x})$ to denote that the free variables of Φ are in $\boldsymbol{x}$. Let $\boldsymbol{t} \triangleq (t_1, \ldots, t_n)$ be a term tuple, we write $\Phi(\boldsymbol{t})$ for the formula obtained from Φ by replacing each occurrence of x_i in Φ by t_i. An *interpretation* $\mathcal{I}$ associates a domain to each sort of a signature and a value to each symbol of a formula, and $[\![\Delta]\!]_\mathcal{I}$ denotes the evaluation of term Δ over $\mathcal{I}$. A *satisfiability relation* $\models$ between interpretations and formulas is defined inductively as usual. A *model* of Φ is an interpretation $\mathcal{I}$ satisfying $\mathcal{I} \models \Phi$. We sometimes refer to models as "solutions". Formula Ψ *entails* formula Φ, written $\Psi \models \Phi$, if every interpretation satisfying Ψ satisfies Φ as well. Two formulas are equivalent, denoted $\Psi \equiv \Phi$, if they have the same models. A *theory* $\mathcal{T} \triangleq (\Sigma, \mathcal{I})$ restricts symbols in Σ to be interpreted in $\mathcal{I}$. The quantifier-free fragment of $\mathcal{T}$ is denoted QF-$\mathcal{T}$.

Convention. Letters $a, b, c \ldots$ denote uninterpreted symbols and variables. Letters $x, y, z \ldots$ denote quantified variables. $\boldsymbol{a}, \boldsymbol{b}, \boldsymbol{c}$ denote sets of uninterpreted symbols. $\boldsymbol{x}, \boldsymbol{y}, \boldsymbol{z} \ldots$ denote sets of quantified variables. Finally, $\mathsf{a}, \mathsf{b}, \mathsf{c} \ldots$ denote valuations of associated (sets of) symbols.

In the rest of this paper, we assume w.l.o.g. that all formulas are in Skolem normal form. Recall that any formula ϕ in classical logic can be normalized into a formula ψ in Skolem normal form such that any model of ϕ can be lifted into a model of ψ, and vice versa. This strong relation, much closer to formula equivalence than to formula equisatisfiability, ensures that our correctness and completeness results all along the paper hold for arbitrarily quantified formula.

Companion Technical Report. *Additional technical details (proofs, experiments, etc.) are available online at* http://benjamin.farinier.org/cav2018/.

4   Musing with Independence

4.1   Independent Interpretations, Terms and Formulas

A solution (x, a) of Φ does not depend on $\boldsymbol{x}$ if $\Phi(\boldsymbol{x}, \boldsymbol{a})$ is always true or always false, for all possible valuations of $\boldsymbol{x}$ as long as $\boldsymbol{a}$ is set to a. More formally, we define the independence of an interpretation of Φ w.r.t. $\boldsymbol{x}$ as follows:

Definition 1 (Independent interpretation)

- *Let $\Phi(\boldsymbol{x}, \boldsymbol{a})$ a formula with free variables $\boldsymbol{x}$ and $\boldsymbol{a}$. Then an interpretation $\mathcal{I}$ of $\Phi(\boldsymbol{x}, \boldsymbol{a})$ is independent of $\boldsymbol{x}$ if for all interpretations $\mathcal{J}$ equal to $\mathcal{I}$ except on $\boldsymbol{x}$, $\mathcal{I} \models \Phi$ if and only if $\mathcal{J} \models \Phi$.*
- *Let $\Delta(\boldsymbol{x}, \boldsymbol{a})$ a term with free variables $\boldsymbol{x}$ and $\boldsymbol{a}$. Then an interpretation $\mathcal{I}$ of $\Delta(\boldsymbol{x}, \boldsymbol{a})$ is independent of $\boldsymbol{x}$ if for all interpretations $\mathcal{J}$ equal to $\mathcal{I}$ except on $\boldsymbol{x}$, $[\![\Delta(\boldsymbol{x}, \boldsymbol{a})]\!]_{\mathcal{I}} = [\![\Delta(\boldsymbol{x}, \boldsymbol{a})]\!]_{\mathcal{J}}$.*

Regarding formula $ax + b > 0$ from Fig. 1, $\{a = 0, b = 1, x = 1\}$ is independent of x while $\{a = 1, b = 0, x = 1\}$ is not. Considering term $(t[a \leftarrow b])[c]$, with t an array written at index a then read at index c, $\{a = 0, b = 42, c = 0, t = [\ldots]\}$ is independent of t (evaluates to 42) while $\{a = 0, b = 1, c = 2, t = [\ldots]\}$ is not (evaluates to $t[2]$). We now define independence for formulas and terms.

Definition 2 (Independent formula and term)

- *Let $\Phi(\boldsymbol{x}, \boldsymbol{a})$ a formula with free variables $\boldsymbol{x}$ and $\boldsymbol{a}$. Then $\Phi(\boldsymbol{x}, \boldsymbol{a})$ is independent of $\boldsymbol{x}$ if $\forall \boldsymbol{x}.\forall \boldsymbol{y}.(\Phi(\boldsymbol{x}, \boldsymbol{a}) \Leftrightarrow \Phi(\boldsymbol{y}, \boldsymbol{a}))$ is true for any value of $\boldsymbol{a}$.*
- *Let $\Delta(\boldsymbol{x}, \boldsymbol{a})$ a term with free variables $\boldsymbol{x}$ and $\boldsymbol{a}$. Then $\Delta(\boldsymbol{x}, \boldsymbol{a})$ is independent of $\boldsymbol{x}$ if $\forall \boldsymbol{x}.\forall \boldsymbol{y}.(\Delta(\boldsymbol{x}, \boldsymbol{a}) = \Delta(\boldsymbol{y}, \boldsymbol{a}))$ is true for any value of $\boldsymbol{a}$.*

Definition 2 of formula and term independence is far stronger than Definition 1 of interpretation independence. Indeed, it can easily be checked that if a formula Φ (resp. a term Δ) is independent of x, then any interpretation of Φ (resp. Δ) is independent of x. However, the converse is false as formula $ax+b > 0$ is not independent of x, but has an interpretation $\{a = 0, b = 1, x = 1\}$ which is.

4.2 Independence Conditions

Since it is rarely the case that a formula (resp. term) is independent from a set of variables x, we are interested in *Sufficient Independence Conditions*. These conditions are additional constraints that can be added to a formula (resp. term) in such a way that they make the formula (resp. term) independent of x.

Definition 3 (Sufficient Independence Condition (SIC))

- *A Sufficient Independence Condition for a formula $\Phi(x, a)$ with regard to x is a formula $\Psi(a)$ such that $\Psi(a) \models (\forall x.\forall y.\Phi(x, a) \Leftrightarrow \Phi(y, a))$.*
- *A Sufficient Independence Condition for a term $\Delta(x, a)$ with regard to x, is a formula $\Psi(a)$ such that $\Psi(a) \models (\forall x.\forall y.\Delta(x, a) = \Delta(y, a))$.*

We denote by $\text{SIC}_{\Phi,x}$ (resp. $\text{SIC}_{\Delta,x}$) a Sufficient Independence Condition for a formula $\Phi(x, a)$ (resp. for a term $\Delta(x, a)$) with regard to x. For example, $a = 0$ is a $\text{SIC}_{\Phi,x}$ for formula $\Phi \triangleq ax + b > 0$, and $a = c$ is a $\text{SIC}_{\Delta,t}$ for term $\Delta \triangleq (t[a \leftarrow b])[c]$. Note that $\bot$ is always a SIC, and that SIC are closed under $\wedge$ and $\vee$. Proposition 1 clarifies the interest of SIC for model generation.

Proposition 1 (Model generalization). *Let $\Phi(x, a)$ a formula and Ψ a $\text{SIC}_{\Phi,x}$. If there exists an interpretation $\{x, a\}$ such that $\{x, a\} \models \Psi(a) \wedge \Phi(x, a)$, then $\{a\} \models \forall x.\Phi(x, a)$.*

Proof (sketch of). Appendix C.1 of the companion technical report.

For the sake of completeness, we introduce now the notion of *Weakest Independence Condition* for a formula $\Phi(x, a)$ with regard to x (resp. a term $\Delta(x, a)$). We will denote such conditions $\text{WIC}_{\Phi,x}$ (resp. $\text{WIC}_{\Delta,x}$).

Definition 4 (Weakest Independence Condition (WIC))

- *A Weakest Independence Condition for a formula $\Phi(x, a)$ with regard to x is a $\text{SIC}_{\Phi,x}$ Π such that, for any other $\text{SIC}_{\Phi,x}$ Ψ, $\Psi \models \Pi$.*
- *A Weakest Independence Condition for a term $\Delta(x, a)$ with regard to x is a $\text{SIC}_{\Delta,x}$ Π such that, for any other $\text{SIC}_{\Delta,x}$ Ψ, $\Psi \models \Pi$.*

Note that $\Omega \triangleq \forall x.\forall y.(\Phi(x, a) \Leftrightarrow \Phi(y, a))$ is always a $\text{WIC}_{\Phi,x}$, and any formula Π is a $\text{WIC}_{\Phi,x}$ if and only if $\Pi \equiv \Omega$. Therefore all syntactically different WIC have the same semantics. As an example, both SIC $a = 0$ and $a = c$ presented earlier are WIC. Proposition 2 emphasizes the interest of WIC for model generation.

Proposition 2 (Model specialization). *Let $\Phi(x, a)$ a formula and $\Pi(a)$ a* WIC$_{\Phi,x}$. *If there exists an interpretation* {a} *such that* {a} $\models \forall x.\Phi(x, a)$, *then* {x, a} $\models \Pi(a) \wedge \Phi(x, a)$ *for any valuation* x *of* x.

Proof (sketch of). Appendix C.2 of the companion technical report.

From now on, our goal is to infer from a formula $\forall x.\Phi(x, a)$ a SIC$_{\Phi,x}$ $\Psi(a)$, find a model for $\Psi(a) \wedge \Phi(x, a)$ and generalize it. This SIC$_{\Phi,x}$ should be as weak—in the sense "less coercive"—as possible, as otherwise $\bot$ could always be used, which would not be very interesting for our overall purpose.

For the sake of simplicity, previous definitions omit to mention the theory to which the SIC belongs. If the theory $\mathcal{T}$ of the quantified formula is decidable we can always choose $\forall x.\forall y.(\Phi(x, a) \Leftrightarrow \Phi(y, a))$ as a SIC, but it is simpler to directly use a $\mathcal{T}$-solver. *The challenge is, for formulas in an undecidable theory $\mathcal{T}$, to find a non-trivial* SIC *in its quantifier-free fragment* QF-$\mathcal{T}$.

Under this constraint, we cannot expect a systematic construction of WIC, as it would allow to decide the satisfiability of any quantified theory with a decidable quantifier-free fragment. Yet informally, the closer a SIC is to be a WIC, the closer our approach is to completeness. Therefore this notion might be seen as a fair gauge of the quality of a SIC. *Having said that, we leave a deeper study on the inference of* WIC *as future work.*

5   Generic Framework for SIC-Based Model Generation

We describe now our overall approach. Algorithm 1 presents our SIC-based generic framework for model generation (Sect. 5.1). Then, Algorithm 2 proposes a taint-based approach for SIC inference (Sect. 5.2). Finally, we discuss complexity and efficiency issues (Sect. 5.3) and detail extensions (Sect. 5.4), such as partial elimination.

From now on, we do not distinguish anymore between terms and formulas, their treatment being symmetric, and we call targeted variables the variables we want to be independent of.

5.1   SIC-Based Model Generation

Our model generation technique is described in Algorithm 1. Function solveQ takes as input a formula $\forall x.\Phi(x, a)$ over a theory $\mathcal{T}$. It first calculates a SIC$_{\Phi,x}$ $\Psi(a)$ in QF-$\mathcal{T}$. Then it solves $\Phi(x, a) \wedge \Psi(a)$. Finally, depending on the result and whether $\Psi(a)$ is a WIC$_{\Phi,x}$ or not, it answers SAT, UNSAT or UNKNOWN. solveQ is parametrized by two functions solveQF and inferSIC:

solveQF is a decision procedure (typically a SMT solver) for QF-$\mathcal{T}$. solveQF is said to be *correct* if each time it answers SAT (resp. UNSAT) the formula is satisfiable (resp. unsatisfiable); it is said to be *complete* if it always answers SAT or UNSAT, never UNKNOWN.

Algorithm 1. SIC-based model generation for quantified formulas

---

Parameter: solveQF
> **Input:** $\Phi(v)$ a formula in QF-$\mathcal{T}$
> **Output:** SAT (v) with $\mathbf{v} \models \Phi$, UNSAT or UNKNOWN

Parameter: inferSIC
> **Input:** Φ a formula in QF-$\mathcal{T}$, and $\boldsymbol{x}$ a set of targeted variables
> **Output:** Ψ a SIC$_{\Phi,\boldsymbol{x}}$ in QF-$\mathcal{T}$

Function solveQ:
> **Input:** $\forall \boldsymbol{x}.\Phi(\boldsymbol{x}, \boldsymbol{a})$ a universally quantified formula over theory $\mathcal{T}$
> **Output:** SAT (a) with $\mathbf{a} \models \forall \boldsymbol{x}.\Phi(\boldsymbol{x}, \boldsymbol{a})$, UNSAT or UNKNOWN
> Let $\Psi(\boldsymbol{a}) \triangleq \mathtt{inferSIC}(\Phi(\boldsymbol{x}, \boldsymbol{a}), \boldsymbol{x})$
> **match** solveQF $(\Phi(\boldsymbol{x}, \boldsymbol{a}) \wedge \Psi(\boldsymbol{a}))$
>> **with** SAT (x, a) **return** SAT (a)
>> **with** UNSAT
>>> **if** Ψ *is a* WIC$_{\Phi,\boldsymbol{x}}$ **then return** UNSAT
>>> **else return** UNKNOWN
>>
>> **with** UNKNOWN **return** UNKNOWN

`inferSIC` takes as input a formula Φ in QF-$\mathcal{T}$ and a set of targeted variables $\boldsymbol{x}$, and produces a SIC$_{\Phi,\boldsymbol{x}}$ in QF-$\mathcal{T}$. It is said to be *correct* if it always returns a SIC, and *complete* if all the SIC it returns are WIC. A possible implementation of `inferSIC` is described in Algorithm 2 (Sect. 5.2).

Function `solveQ` enjoys the two following properties, where correctness and completeness are defined as for `solveQF`.

Theorem 1 (Correctness and completeness)

– *If* `solveQF` *and* `inferSIC` *are correct, then* `solveQ` *is correct.*
– *If* `solveQF` *and* `inferSIC` *are complete, then* `solveQ` *is complete.*

Proof (sketch of). Follow directly from Propositions 1 and 2 (Sect. 4.2).

5.2 Taint-Based SIC Inference

Algorithm 2 presents a taint-based implementation of function `inferSIC`. It consists of a (syntactic) core calculus described here, refined by a (semantic) theory-dependent calculus `theorySIC` described in Sect. 6. From formula $\Phi(\boldsymbol{x}, \boldsymbol{a})$ and targeted variables $\boldsymbol{x}$, `inferSIC` is defined recursively as follow.

If Φ is a constant it returns $\top$ as constants are independent of any variable. If Φ is a variable v, it returns $\top$ if we may depend on v (i.e., $v \notin \boldsymbol{x}$), $\bot$ otherwise. If Φ is a function $f(\phi_1, \ldots, \phi_n)$, it first recursively computes for every sub-term ϕ_i a SIC$_{\phi_i,\boldsymbol{x}}$ ψ_i. Then these results are sent with Φ to `theorySIC` which computes a SIC$_{\Phi,\boldsymbol{x}}$ Ψ. The procedure returns the disjunction between Ψ and the conjunction of the ψ_i's. Note that `theorySIC` default value $\bot$ is absorbed by the disjunction.

Algorithm 2. Taint-based SIC inference

Parameter: theorySIC
> **Input:** f a function symbol, its parameters ϕ_i, $\boldsymbol{x}$ a set of targeted variables
> and ψ_i their associated $\text{SIC}_{\phi_i,\boldsymbol{x}}$
> **Output:** Ψ a $\text{SIC}_{f(\phi_i),\boldsymbol{x}}$
> **Default:** Return $\bot$

Function inferSIC($\Phi,\boldsymbol{x}$):
> **Input:** Φ a formula and $\boldsymbol{x}$ a set of targeted variables
> **Output:** Ψ a $\text{SIC}_{\Phi,\boldsymbol{x}}$
>
> **either** Φ *is a constant* **return** $\top$
> **either** Φ *is a variable* v **return** $v \notin \boldsymbol{x}$
> **either** Φ *is a function* $f(\phi_1,..,\phi_n)$
> > Let $\psi_i \triangleq \text{inferSIC}(\phi_i,\boldsymbol{x})$ for all $i \in \{1,..,n\}$
> > Let $\Psi \triangleq \text{theorySIC}(f,(\phi_1,..,\phi_n),(\psi_1,..,\psi_n),\boldsymbol{x})$
> > **return** $\Psi \vee \bigwedge_i \psi_i$

The intuition is that if the ϕ_i's are independent of $\boldsymbol{x}$, then $f(\phi_1,\ldots,\phi_n)$ is. Therefore Algorithm 2 is said to be *taint-based* as, when theorySIC is left to its default value, it acts as a form of taint tracking [15,27] inside the formula.

Proposition 3 (Correctness). *Given a formula $\Phi(\boldsymbol{x},\boldsymbol{a})$ and assuming that theorySIC is correct, then inferSIC($\Phi,\boldsymbol{x}$) indeed computes a $\text{SIC}_{\Phi,\boldsymbol{x}}$.*

Proof (sketch of). This proof has been mechanized in Coq[1].

Note that on the other hand, completeness does not hold: in general inferSIC does not compute a WIC, cf. discussion in Sect. 5.4.

5.3   Complexity and Efficiency

We now evaluate the overhead induced by Algorithm 1 in terms of formula size and complexity of the resolution—the running time of Algorithm 1 itself being expected to be negligible (preprocessing).

Definition 5. *The size of a term is inductively defined as $size(x) \triangleq 1$ for x a variable, and $size(f(t_1,\ldots,t_n)) \triangleq 1 + \Sigma_i\, size(t_i)$ otherwise. We say that theorySIC is bounded in size if there exists K such that, for all terms Δ, $size(theorySIC(\Delta,\cdot)) \leq K$.*

Proposition 4 (Size bound). *Let N be the maximal arity of symbols defined by theory $\mathcal{T}$. If theorySIC is bounded in size by K, then for all formula Φ in $\mathcal{T}$, $size(inferSIC(\Phi,\cdot)) \leq (K+N) \cdot size(\Phi)$.*

---

[1] http://benjamin.farinier.org/cav2018/.

Proposition 5 (Complexity bound). *Let us suppose* theorySIC *bounded in size, and let Φ be a formula belonging to a theory $\mathcal{T}$ with polynomial-time checkable solutions. If Ψ is a* SIC$_{\Phi,}$ *produced by* inferSIC, *then a solution for $\Phi \wedge \Psi$ is checkable in time polynomial in size of Φ.*

Proof (sketch of). Appendices C.3 and C.4 of the companion technical report.

These propositions demonstrate that, for formula landing in complex enough theories, our method lifts QF-solvers to the quantified case (in an approximated way) without any significant overhead, as long as theorySIC is bounded in size. This latter constraint can be achieved by systematically binding sub-terms to (constant-size) fresh names and having theorySIC manipulates these binders.

5.4 Discussions

Extension. Let us remark that our framework encompasses partial quantifier elimination as long as the remaining quantifiers are handled by solveQF. For example, we may want to remove quantifications over arrays but keep those on bitvectors. In this setting, inferSIC can also allow some level of quantification, providing that solveQF handles them.

About WIC. As already stated, inferSIC does not propagate WIC in general. For example, considering formulas $t_1 \triangleq (x < 0)$ and $t_2 \triangleq (x \geq 0)$, then WIC$_{t_1,x} = \bot$ and WIC$_{t_2,x} = \bot$. Hence inferSIC returns $\bot$ as SIC for $t_1 \vee t_2$, while actually WIC$_{t_1 \vee t_2,x} = \top$.

Nevertheless, we can already highlight a few cases where WIC can be computed. (1) inferSIC does propagate WIC on one-to-one uninterpreted functions. (2) If no variable of x appears in any sub-term of $f(t,t')$, then the associated WIC is $\top$. While a priori naive, this case becomes interesting when combined with simplifications (Sect. 7.1) that may eliminate x. (3) If a sub-term falls in a sub-theory admitting quantifier elimination, then the associated WIC is computed by eliminating quantifiers in $(\forall.x.y.\Phi(x,a) \Leftrightarrow \Phi(y,a))$. (4) We may also think of dedicated patterns: regarding bitvectors, the WIC for $x \leq a \Rightarrow x \leq x+k$ is $a \leq \mathtt{Max} - k$. *Identifying under which condition* WIC *propagation holds is a strong direction for future work.*

6 Theory-Dependent SIC Refinements

We now present theory-dependent SIC refinements for theories relevant to program analysis: booleans, fixed-size bitvectors and arrays — recall that uninterpreted functions are already handled by Algorithm 2. We then propose a generalization of these refinements together with a correctness proof for a larger class of operators.

6.1 Refinement on Theories

We recall `theorySIC` takes four parameters: a function symbol f, its arguments $(t_1, \ldots, t_n)$, their associated SIC $(t_1^\bullet, \ldots, t_n^\bullet)$, and targeted variables x. `theorySIC` pattern-matches the function symbol and returns the associated SIC according to rules in Fig. 2. If a function symbol is not supported, we return the default value $\bot$. Constants and variables are handled by `inferSIC`. For the sake of simplicity, rules in Fig. 2 are defined recursively, but can easily fit the interface required for `theorySIC` in Algorithm 2 by turning recursive calls into parameters.

Booleans and Ite. Rules for the boolean theory (Fig. 2a) handles $\Rightarrow$, $\wedge$, $\vee$ and ite (if-then-else). For binary operators, the SIC is the conjunction of the SIC associated to one of the two sub-terms and a constraint on this sub-term that forces the result of the operator to be constant—e.g., to be equal to $\bot$ (resp. $\top$) for the antecedent (resp. consequent) of an implication. These equality constraints are based on absorbing elements of operators.

Inference for the ite operator is more subtle. Intuitively, if its condition is independent of some x, we use it to select the SIC_x of the sub-term that will be selected by the ite operator. If the condition is dependent of x, then we cannot use it anymore to select a SIC_x. In this case, we return the conjunction of the SIC_x of both sub-terms and the constraint that the two sub-terms are equal.

$$(a \Rightarrow b)^\bullet \triangleq (a^\bullet \wedge a = \bot) \vee (b^\bullet \wedge b = \top)$$
$$(a \wedge b)^\bullet \triangleq (a^\bullet \wedge a = \bot) \vee (b^\bullet \wedge b = \bot)$$
$$(a \vee b)^\bullet \triangleq (a^\bullet \wedge a = \top) \vee (b^\bullet \wedge b = \top)$$
$$(\text{ite } c\, a\, b)^\bullet \triangleq (c^\bullet \wedge \text{ite } c\, a^\bullet\, b^\bullet) \vee (a^\bullet \wedge b^\bullet \wedge a = b)$$

$$(a_n \wedge b_n)^\bullet \triangleq (a_n^\bullet \wedge a_n = 0_n) \vee (b_n^\bullet \wedge b_n = 0_n)$$
$$(a_n \vee b_n)^\bullet \triangleq (a_n^\bullet \wedge a_n = 1_n) \vee (b_n^\bullet \wedge b_n = 1_n)$$
$$(a_n \times b_n)^\bullet \triangleq (a_n^\bullet \wedge a_n = 0_n) \vee (b_n^\bullet \wedge b_n = 0_n)$$
$$(a_n \ll b_n)^\bullet \triangleq (b_n^\bullet \wedge b_n \geq n)$$

(a) Booleans and ite   (b) Fixed-size bitvectors

$$(\text{select } (\text{store } a\, i\, e)\, j)^\bullet \triangleq (\text{ite } (i = j)\, e\, (\text{select } a\, j))^\bullet$$
$$\triangleq ((i = j)^\bullet \wedge (\text{ite } (i = j)\, e^\bullet\, (\text{select } a\, j)^\bullet)) \vee (e^\bullet \wedge (\text{select } a\, j)^\bullet \wedge (e = \text{select } a\, j))$$
$$\triangleq (i^\bullet \wedge j^\bullet \wedge (\text{ite } (i = j)\, e^\bullet\, (\text{select } a\, j)^\bullet)) \vee (e^\bullet \wedge (\text{select } a\, j)^\bullet \wedge (e = \text{select } a\, j))$$

(c) Arrays

Fig. 2. Examples of refinements for `theorySIC`

Bitvectors and Arrays. Rules for bitvectors (Fig. 2b) follow similar ideas, with constant $\top$ (resp. $\bot$) substituted by 1_n (resp. 0_n), the bitvector of size n full of ones (resp. zeros). Rules for arrays (Fig. 2c) are derived from the theory axioms. The definition is recursive: rules need be applied until reaching either a store at the position where the select occurs, or the initial array variable.

As a rule of thumb, good SIC can be derived from function axioms in the form of rewriting rules, as done for arrays. Similar constructions can be obtained for example for stacks or queues.

6.2 $\mathcal{R}$-Absorbing Functions

We propose a generalization of the previous theory-dependent SIC refinements to a larger class of functions, and prove its correctness.

Intuitively, if a function has an absorbing element, constraining one of its operands to be equal to this element will ensure that the result of the function is independent of the other operands. However, it is not enough when a relation between some elements is needed, such as with $(t[a \leftarrow b])\,[c]$ where constraint $a = c$ ensures the independence with regards to t. We thus generalize the notion of absorption to $\mathcal{R}$-absorption, where $\mathcal{R}$ is a relation between function arguments.

Definition 6. *Let $f : \tau_1 \times \cdots \times \tau_n \to \tau$ a function. f is $\mathcal{R}$-absorbing if there exists $\mathcal{I}_\mathcal{R} \subset \{1, \cdots, n\}$ and $\mathcal{R}$ a relation between $\alpha_i : \tau_i$, $i \in \mathcal{I}_\mathcal{R}$ such that, for all $b \triangleq (b_1, \ldots, b_n)$ and $c \triangleq (c_1, \ldots, c_n) \in \tau_1 \times \cdots \times \tau_n$, if $\mathcal{R}(b|_{\mathcal{I}_\mathcal{R}})$ and $b|_{\mathcal{I}_\mathcal{R}} = c|_{\mathcal{I}_\mathcal{R}}$ where $\cdot|_{\mathcal{I}_\mathcal{R}}$ is the projection on $\mathcal{I}_\mathcal{R}$, then $f(b) = f(c)$.*
$\mathcal{I}_\mathcal{R}$ is called the support of the relation of absorption $\mathcal{R}$.

For example, $(a, b) \mapsto a \lor b$ has two pairs $\langle \mathcal{R}, \mathcal{I}_\mathcal{R} \rangle$ coinciding with the usual notion of absorption, $\langle a{=}\top, \{1_a\} \rangle$ and $\langle b{=}\top, \{2_b\} \rangle$. Function $(x, y, z) \mapsto xy + z$ has among others the pair $\langle x{=}0, \{1_x, 3_z\} \rangle$, while $(a, b, c, t) \mapsto (t[a \leftarrow b])\,[c]$ has the pair $\langle a{=}c, \{1_a, 3_c\} \rangle$. We can now state the following proposition:

Proposition 6. *Let $f(t_1, \ldots, t_n)$ be a $\mathcal{R}$-absorbing function of support $\mathcal{I}_\mathcal{R}$, and let $t_i^\bullet$ be a $\mathrm{SIC}_{t_i, x}$ for some x. Then $\mathcal{R}(t_{i \in \mathcal{I}_\mathcal{R}}) \bigwedge_{i \in \mathcal{I}_\mathcal{R}} t_i^\bullet$ is a $\mathrm{SIC}_{f, x}$.*

Proof (sketch of). Appendix C.5 of the companion technical report.

Previous examples (Sect. 6.1) can be recast in term of $\mathcal{R}$-absorbing function, proving their correctness (cf. companion technical report). Note that regarding our end-goal, we should only accept $\mathcal{R}$-absorbing functions in QF-$\mathcal{T}$.

7   Experimental Evaluation

This section describes the implementation of our method (Sect. 7.1) for bitvectors and arrays (ABV), together with experimental evaluation (Sect. 7.2).

7.1   Implementation

Our prototype TFML (*Taint engine for ForMuLa*)[2] comprises 7 klocs of OCaml. Given an input formula in the SMT-LIB format [5] (ABV theory), TFML performs several normalizations before adding taint information following Algorithm 1. The process ends with simplifications as taint usually introduces many constant values, and a new SMT-LIB formula is output.

Sharing with Let-Binding. This stage is crucial as it allows to avoid term duplication in theorySIC (Algorithm 2, Sect. 5.3, and Proposition 4). We introduce new names for relevant sub-terms in order to easily share them.

Simplifications. We perform constant propagation and rewriting (standard rules, e.g. $x - x \mapsto 0$ or $x \times 1 \mapsto x$) on both initial and transformed formulas – equality is soundly approximated by syntactic equality.

---

[2] http://benjamin.farinier.org/cav2018/.

Shadow Arrays. We encode taint constraints over arrays through *shadow arrays*. For each array declared in the formula, we declare a (taint) shadow array. The default value for all cells of the shadow array is the taint of the original array, and for each value stored (resp. read) in the original array, we store (resp. read) the taint of the value in the shadow array. As logical arrays are infinite, we cannot constrain all the values contained in the initial shadow array. Instead, we rely on a common trick in array theory: we constrain only cells corresponding to a relevant read index in the formula.

Iterative Skolemization. While we have supposed along the paper to work on skolemized formulas, we have to be more careful in practice. Indeed, skolemization introduce dependencies between a skolemized variable and all its preceding universally quantified variables, blurring our analysis and likely resulting in considering the whole formula as dependent. Instead, we follow an iterative process: 1. Skolemize the first block of existentially quantified variables; 2. Compute the independence condition for any targeted variable in the first block of universal quantifiers and remove these quantifiers; 3. Repeat. This results in full Skolemization together with the construction of an independence condition, while avoiding many unnecessary dependencies.

7.2 Evaluation

Objective. We experimentally evaluate the following research questions: *RQ1* How does our approach perform with regard to state-of-the-art approaches for model generation of quantified formulas? *RQ2* How effective is it at lifting quantifier-free solvers into (SAT-only) quantified solvers? *RQ3* How efficient is it in terms of preprocessing time and formula size overhead? We evaluate our method on a set of formulas combining arrays and bitvectors (paramount in software verification), against state-of-the-art solvers for these theories.

Protocol. The experimental setup below runs on an Intel(R) Xeon(R) E5-2660 v3 @ 2.60 GHz, 4 GB RAM per process, and a TIMEOUT of 1000 s per formula.

Table 1. Answers and resolution time (in seconds, include TIMEOUT)

			Boolector•	CVC4	CVC4•	CVC4$_E$	CVC4$_E$•	Z3	Z3•	Z3$_E$	Z3$_E$•
SMT-LIB	#	SAT	**399**	84	242	84	242	261	366	87	366
		UNSAT	N/A	0	N/A	0	N/A	165	N/A	0	N/A
		UNKNOWN	870	1185	1027	1185	1027	843	903	1182	903
	Total time		**349**	165	194 667	165	196 934	270 150	36 480	192	41 935
BINSEC	#	SAT	**1042**	951	954	951	954	953	**1042**	953	**1042**
		UNSAT	N/A	62	N/A	62	N/A	319	N/A	62	N/A
		UNKNOWN	379	408	467	408	467	149	379	406	379
	Total time		**1152**	64 761	76 811	64 772	77 009	30 235	11 415	135	11 604

Solver•: solver enhanced with our method. Z3$_E$, CVC4$_E$: essentially E-matching

Metrics. For *RQ1* we compare the number of SAT and UNKNOWN answers between solvers supporting quantification, with and without our approach. For *RQ2*, we compare the number of SAT and UNKNOWN answers between quantifier-free solvers enhanced by our approach and solvers supporting quantification. For *RQ3*, we measure preprocessing time and formulas size overhead.

Benchmarks. We consider two sets of ABV formulas. First, a set of 1421 formulas from (a modified version of) the symbolic execution tool BINSEC [12] representing quantified reachability queries (cf. Sect. 2) over BINSEC benchmark programs (security challenges, e.g. `crackme` or vulnerability finding). The initial (array) memory is quantified so that models depend only on user input. Second, a set of 1269 ABV formulas generated from formulas of the QF-ABV category of SMT-LIB [5] – sub-categories `brummayerbiere`, `dwp formulas` and `klee selected`. The generation process consists in universally quantifying some of the initial array variables, mimicking quantified reachability problems.

Competitors. For *RQ1*, we compete against the two state-of-the-art SMT solvers for quantified formulas CVC4 [4] (finite model instantiation [31]) and Z3 [14] (model-based instantiation [20]). We also consider degraded versions $CVC4_E$ and $Z3_E$ that roughly represent standard E-matching [16]. For *RQ2* we use Boolector [10], one of the very best QF-ABV solvers.

Table 2. Complementarity of our approach with existing solvers (SAT instances)

		CVC4•			Z3•			Boolector•		
SMT-LIB	CVC4	−10	+168	[252]				−10	+325	[409]
	Z3				−119	+224	[485]	−86	+224	[485]
BINSEC	CVC4	−25	+28	[979]				−25	+116	[1067]
	Z3				−25	+114	[1067]	−25	+114	[1067]

Results. Tables 1 and 2 and Fig. 3 sum up our experimental results, which have all been cross-checked for consistency. Table 1 reports the number of successes (SAT or UNSAT) and failures (UNKNOWN), plus total solving times. The • sign indicates formulas preprocessed with our approach. In that case it is impossible to correctly answer UNSAT (no WIC checking), the UNSAT line is thus N/A. Since Boolector does not support quantified ABV formulas, we only give results with our approach enabled. Table 1 reads as follow: of the 1269 SMT-LIB formulas, standalone Z3 solves 426 formulas (261 SAT, 165 UNSAT), and 366 (all SAT) if preprocessed. Interestingly, our approach always improves the underlying solver in terms of solved (SAT) instances, either in a significant way (SMT-LIB) or in a modest way (BINSEC). Yet, recall that in a software verification setting every win matters (possibly new bug found or new assertion proved). For Z3•, it also strongly reduces computation time. Last but not least, Boolector• (a pure QF-solver) turns out to have the best performance on SAT-instances, beating state-of-the-art approaches both in terms of solved instances and computation time.

Table 2 substantiates the complementarity of the different methods,
and reads as follow: for SMT-LIB,
Boolector• solves 224 (SAT) formulas missed by Z3, while Z3 solves 86
(SAT) formulas missed by Boolector•,
and 485 (SAT) formulas are solved by
either one of them.

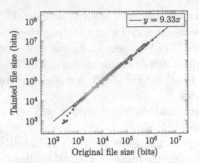

Maximal size ratio 12.48
Minimal size ratio 2.81
Average size ratio 8.73
Standard deviation 0.78

Figure 3 shows formula size aver-
aging a 9-fold increase (min 3, max
12): yet they are easier to solve
because they are more constrained.
Regarding performance and overhead
of the tainting process, *taint time is
almost always less than 1s* in our
experiments (not shown here), 4 min
for worst case, clearly dominated by
resolution time. The worst case is due

Fig. 3. Overhead in formula size

to a pass of linearithmic complexity which can be optimized to be logarithmic.

Pearls. We show hereafter two particular applications of our method. Table 3
reports results of another symbolic execution experiment, on the grub example.

On this example, Boolector• completely outperforms existing approaches. As a second
application, while the main drawback of our
method is that it precludes proving UNSAT,
this is easily mitigated by complementing
the approach with another one geared (or
able) to proving UNSAT, yielding efficient
solvers for quantified formulas, as shown in
Table 4.

Table 3. GRUB example

		Boolector•	Z3
#	SAT	**540**	1
	UNSAT	N/A	42
	UNKNOWN	355	852
Total time		**16 732**	159 765

Conclusion. Experiments demonstrate the
relevance of our taint-based technique for
model generation. (*RQ1*) Results in Table 1
shows that our approach greatly facilitates
the resolution process. *On these examples,
our method performs better than state-of-
the-art solvers but also strongly complements
them (Table 2).* (*RQ2*) Moreover, Table 1
demonstrates that our technique is highly
effective at lifting quantifier-free solvers to
quantified formulas, in both number of SAT
answers and computation time. *Indeed, once*

Table 4. Best approaches

		Former	New	
		Z3	B•	B• ▷ Z3
SMT-LIB	SAT	261	399	485
	UNSAT	165	N/A	165
	UNKNOWN	843	870	619
	Time	270 150	350	94 610
BINSEC	SAT	953	1042	1067
	UNSAT	319	N/A	319
	UNKNOWN	149	379	35
	Time	64 761	1 152	1 169

*lifted, Boolector performs better (for SAT-only) than Z3 or CVC4 with full quan-
tifier support.* Finally (*RQ3*) our tainting method itself is very efficient both in
time and space, making it perfect either for a preprocessing step or for a deeper

integration into a solver. In our current prototype implementation, we consider the cost to be low. *The companion technical report contains a few additional experiments on bitvectors and integer arithmetic, including the example from Fig. 1.*

8   Related Work

Traditional approaches to solving quantified formulas essentially involve either generic methods geared to proving unsatisfiability and validity [16], or complete but dedicated approaches for particular theories [8,36]. Besides, some recent methods [20,22,31] aim to be correct and complete for larger classes of theories.

Generic Method for Unsatisfiability. Broadly speaking, these methods iteratively instantiate axioms until a contradiction is found. They are generic w.r.t. the underlying theory and allow to reuse standard theory solvers, but termination is not guaranteed. Also, they are more suited to prove unsatisfiability than to find models. In this family, E-matching [13,16] shows reasonable cost when combined with conflict-based instantiation [30] or semantic triggers [17,18]. In pure first-order logic (without theories), quantifiers are mainly handled through resolution and superposition [1,26] as done in Vampire [24,33] and E [34].

Complete Methods for Specific Theories. Much work has been done on designing complete decision procedures for quantified theories of interest, notably array properties [8], quantified theory of bitvectors [23,36], Presburger arithmetic or Real Linear Arithmetic [9,19]. Yet, they usually come at a high cost.

Generic Methods for Model Generation. Some recent works detail attempts at more general approaches to model generation.

Local theory extensions [2,22] provide means to extend some decidable theories with free symbols and quantifications, retaining decidability. The approach identifies specific forms of formulas and quantifications (bounded), such that these theory extensions can be solved using finite instantiation of quantifiers together with a decision procedure for the original theory. The main drawback is that the formula size can increase a lot.

Model-based quantifier instantiation is an active area of research notably developed in Z3 and CVC4. The basic line is to consider the partial model under construction in order to find the right quantifier instantiations, typically in a try-and-refine manner. Depending on the variants, these methods favors either satisfiability or unsatisfiability. They build on the underlying quantifier-free solver and can be mixed with E-matching techniques, yet each refinement yields a solver call and the refinement process may not terminate. Ge and de Moura [20] study decidable fragments of first-order logic modulo theories for which model-based quantifier instantiation yields soundness and refutational completeness. Reynolds *et al.* [30], Barbosa [3] and Preiner *et al.* [28] use models to guide the instantiation process towards instances refuting the current model. *Finite model quantifier instantiation* [31,32] reduces the search to finite models, and is indeed

geared toward model generation rather than unsatisfiability. Similar techniques
have been used in program synthesis [29].

We drop support for the unsatisfiable case but get more flexibility: we deal
with quantifiers on any sort, the approach terminates and is lightweight, in the
sense that it requires a single call to the underlying quantifier-free solver.

Other. Our method can be seen as taking inspiration from program taint analysis [15,27] developed for checking the non-interference [35] of public and secrete
input in security-sensitive programs. As far as the analogy goes, our approach
should not be seen as checking non-interference, but rather as inferring preconditions of non-interference. Moreover, our formula-tainting technique is closer
to dynamic program-tainting than to static program-tainting, in the sense that
precise dependency conditions are statically inserted at preprocess-time, then
precisely explored at solving-time.

Finally, Darvas *et al.* [11] presents a bottom-up formula strengthening
method. Their goal differ from ours, as they are interested in formula well-definedness (rather than independence) and validity (rather than model generation).

9 Conclusion

This paper addresses the problem of generating models of quantified first-order
formulas over built-in theories. We propose a correct and generic approach based
on a reduction to the quantifier-free case through the inference of independence
conditions. The technique is applicable to any theory with a decidable quantifier-free case and allows to reuse all the work done on quantifier-free solvers. The
method significantly enhances the performances of state-of-the-art SMT solvers
for the quantified case, and supplements the latest advances in the field.

Future developments aim to tackle the definition of more precise inference
mechanisms of independence conditions, the identification of interesting sub-classes for which inferring weakest independence conditions is feasible, and the
combination with other quantifier instantiation techniques.

References

1. Bachmair, L., Ganzinger, H.: Rewrite-based equational theorem proving with selection and simplification. J. Log. Comput. **4**(3), 217–247 (1994)
2. Bansal, K., Reynolds, A., King, T., Barrett, C.W., Wies, T.: Deciding local theory extensions via e-matching. In: Kroening, D., Păsăreanu, C.S. (eds.) CAV 2015. LNCS, vol. 9207, pp. 87–105. Springer, Cham (2015). https://doi.org/10.1007/978-3-319-21668-3_6
3. Barbosa, H.: Efficient instantiation techniques in SMT (work in progress). In: Proceedings of the 5th Workshop on Practical Aspects of Automated Reasoning, Co-located with International Joint Conference on Automated Reasoning (IJCAR 2016), Coimbra, Portugal, 2 July 2016, pp. 1–10 (2016)

4. Barrett, C., et al.: CVC4. In: Gopalakrishnan, G., Qadeer, S. (eds.) CAV 2011. LNCS, vol. 6806, pp. 171–177. Springer, Heidelberg (2011). https://doi.org/10.1007/978-3-642-22110-1_14
5. Barrett, C., Stump, A., Tinelli, C.: The SMT-LIB standard: version 2.0. In: Gupta, A., Kroening, D. (eds.) Proceedings of the 8th International Workshop on Satisfiability Modulo Theories (Edinburgh, UK) (2010)
6. Barrett, C.W., Sebastiani, R., Seshia, S.A., Tinelli, C.: Satisfiability modulo theories. In: Handbook of Satisfiability, pp. 825–885 (2009)
7. Biere, A.: Bounded model checking. In: Handbook of Satisfiability, pp. 457–481 (2009)
8. Bradley, A.R., Manna, Z., Sipma, H.B.: What's decidable about arrays? In: Emerson, E.A., Namjoshi, K.S. (eds.) VMCAI 2006. LNCS, vol. 3855, pp. 427–442. Springer, Heidelberg (2005). https://doi.org/10.1007/11609773_28
9. Brillout, A., Kroening, D., Rümmer, P., Wahl, T.: Beyond quantifier-free interpolation in extensions of presburger arithmetic. In: Jhala, R., Schmidt, D. (eds.) VMCAI 2011. LNCS, vol. 6538, pp. 88–102. Springer, Heidelberg (2011). https://doi.org/10.1007/978-3-642-18275-4_8
10. Brummayer, R., Biere, A.: Boolector: an efficient smt solver for bit-vectors and arrays. In: Kowalewski, S., Philippou, A. (eds.) TACAS 2009. LNCS, vol. 5505, pp. 174–177. Springer, Heidelberg (2009). https://doi.org/10.1007/978-3-642-00768-2_16
11. Darvas, Á., Mehta, F., Rudich, A.: Efficient well-definedness checking. In: Armando, A., Baumgartner, P., Dowek, G. (eds.) IJCAR 2008. LNCS (LNAI), vol. 5195, pp. 100–115. Springer, Heidelberg (2008). https://doi.org/10.1007/978-3-540-71070-7_8
12. David, R., Bardin, S., Ta, T.D., Mounier, L., Feist, J., Potet, M., Marion, J.: BINSEC/SE: a dynamic symbolic execution toolkit for binary-level analysis. In: IEEE 23rd International Conference on Software Analysis, Evolution, and Reengineering, SANER 2016, Osaka, Japan, 14–18 March 2016, vol. 1, pp. 653–656 (2016)
13. de Moura, L.M., Bjørner, N.: Efficient e-matching for SMT solvers. In: Pfenning, F. (ed.) CADE 2007. LNCS (LNAI), vol. 4603, pp. 183–198. Springer, Heidelberg (2007). https://doi.org/10.1007/978-3-540-73595-3_13
14. de Moura, L.M., Bjørner, N.: Z3: an efficient SMT solver. In: Ramakrishnan, C.R., Rehof, J. (eds.) TACAS 2008. LNCS, vol. 4963, pp. 337–340. Springer, Heidelberg (2008). https://doi.org/10.1007/978-3-540-78800-3_24
15. Denning, D.E., Denning, P.J.: Certification of programs for secure information flow. Commun. ACM 20(7), 504–513 (1977)
16. Detlefs, D., Nelson, G., Saxe, J.B.: Simplify: a theorem prover for program checking. J. ACM 52(3), 365–473 (2005)
17. Dross, C., Conchon, S., Kanig, J., Paskevich, A.: Reasoning with triggers. In: 10th International Workshop on Satisfiability Modulo Theories, SMT 2012, Manchester, UK, 30 June–1 July 2012, pp. 22–31 (2012)
18. Dross, C., Conchon, S., Kanig, J., Paskevich, A.: Adding decision procedures to SMT solvers using axioms with triggers. J. Autom. Reason 56(4), 387–457 (2016)
19. Farzan, A., Kincaid, Z.: Linear arithmetic satisfiability via strategy improvement. In: Proceedings of the Twenty-Fifth International Joint Conference on Artificial Intelligence, IJCAI 2016, New York, NY, USA, 9–15 July 2016, pp. 735–743 (2016)
20. Ge, Y., de Moura, L.M.: Complete instantiation for quantified formulas in satisfiabiliby modulo theories. In: Bouajjani, A., Maler, O. (eds.) CAV 2009. LNCS, vol. 5643, pp. 306–320. Springer, Heidelberg (2009). https://doi.org/10.1007/978-3-642-02658-4_25

21. Godefroid, P., Levin, M.Y., Molnar, D.A.: SAGE: whitebox fuzzing for security testing. ACM Queue **10**(1), 20 (2012)
22. Ihlemann, C., Jacobs, S., Sofronie-Stokkermans, V.: On local reasoning in verification. In: Ramakrishnan, C.R., Rehof, J. (eds.) TACAS 2008. LNCS, vol. 4963, pp. 265–281. Springer, Heidelberg (2008). https://doi.org/10.1007/978-3-540-78800-3_19
23. Jonáš, M., Strejček, J.: Solving quantified bit-vector formulas using binary decision diagrams. In: Creignou, N., Le Berre, D. (eds.) SAT 2016. LNCS, vol. 9710, pp. 267–283. Springer, Cham (2016). https://doi.org/10.1007/978-3-319-40970-2_17
24. Kovács, L., Voronkov, A.: First-order theorem proving and VAMPIRE. In: Sharygina, N., Veith, H. (eds.) CAV 2013. LNCS, vol. 8044, pp. 1–35. Springer, Heidelberg (2013). https://doi.org/10.1007/978-3-642-39799-8_1
25. Kroening, D., Strichman, O.: Decision Procedures - An Algorithmic Point of View. Texts in Theoretical Computer Science. An EATCS Series. Springer, Heidelberg (2008). https://doi.org/10.1007/978-3-662-50497-0
26. Nieuwenhuis, R., Rubio, A.: Paramodulation-based theorem proving. In: Handbook of Automated Reasoning, vol. 2, pp. 371–443 (2001)
27. Ørbæk, P.: Can you trust your data? In: Mosses, P.D., Nielsen, M., Schwartzbach, M.I. (eds.) CAAP 1995. LNCS, vol. 915, pp. 575–589. Springer, Heidelberg (1995). https://doi.org/10.1007/3-540-59293-8_221
28. Preiner, M., Niemetz, A., Biere, A.: Counterexample-guided model synthesis. In: Legay, A., Margaria, T. (eds.) TACAS 2017. LNCS, vol. 10205, pp. 264–280. Springer, Heidelberg (2017). https://doi.org/10.1007/978-3-662-54577-5_15
29. Reynolds, A., Deters, M., Kuncak, V., Tinelli, C., Barrett, C.: Counterexample-guided quantifier instantiation for synthesis in SMT. In: Kroening, D., Păsăreanu, C.S. (eds.) CAV 2015. LNCS, vol. 9207, pp. 198–216. Springer, Cham (2015). https://doi.org/10.1007/978-3-319-21668-3_12
30. Reynolds, A., Tinelli, C., de Moura, L.M.: Finding conflicting instances of quantified formulas in SMT. In: Formal Methods in Computer-Aided Design, FMCAD 2014, Lausanne, Switzerland, 21–24 October 2014, pp. 195–202 (2014)
31. Reynolds, A., Tinelli, C., Goel, A., Krstić, S.: Finite model finding in SMT. In: Sharygina, N., Veith, H. (eds.) CAV 2013. LNCS, vol. 8044, pp. 640–655. Springer, Heidelberg (2013). https://doi.org/10.1007/978-3-642-39799-8_42
32. Reynolds, A., et al.: Quantifier instantiation techniques for finite model finding in SMT. In: Bonacina, M.P. (ed.) CADE 2013. LNCS (LNAI), vol. 7898, pp. 377–391. Springer, Heidelberg (2013). https://doi.org/10.1007/978-3-642-38574-2_26
33. Riazanov, A., Voronkov, A.: The design and implementation of VAMPIRE. AI Commun. **15**(2–3), 91–110 (2002)
34. Schulz, S.: E - a brainiac theorem prover. AI Commun. **15**(2–3), 111–126 (2002)
35. Smith, G.: Principles of secure information flow analysis. In: Christodorescu, M., Jha, S., Maughan, D., Song, D., Wang, C. (eds.) Malware Detection. ADIS, vol. 27, pp. 291–307. Springer, Boston (2007). https://doi.org/10.1007/978-0-387-44599-1_13
36. Wintersteiger, C.M., Hamadi, Y., de Moura, L.M.: Efficiently solving quantified bit-vector formulas. In: Proceedings of 10th International Conference on Formal Methods in Computer-Aided Design, FMCAD 2010, Lugano, Switzerland, 20–23 October, pp. 239–246 (2010)

Concurrency

Partial Order Aware Concurrency Sampling

Xinhao Yuan[✉], Junfeng Yang[✉], and Ronghui Gu

Columbia University, New York, USA
{xinhaoyuan,junfeng,rgu}@cs.columbia.edu

Abstract. We present POS, a concurrency testing approach that samples the partial order of concurrent programs. POS uses a novel priority-based scheduling algorithm that dynamically reassigns priorities regarding the partial order information and formally ensures that each partial order will be explored with significant probability. POS is simple to implement and provides a probabilistic guarantee of error detection better than state-of-the-art sampling approaches. Evaluations show that POS is effective in covering the partial-order space of micro-benchmarks and finding concurrency bugs in real-world programs, such as Firefox's JavaScript engine SpiderMonkey.

1 Introduction

Concurrent programs are notoriously difficult to test. Executions of different threads can interleave arbitrarily, and any such interleaving may trigger unexpected errors and lead to serious production failures [13]. Traditional testing over concurrent programs relies on the system scheduler to interleave executions (or events) and is limited to detect bugs because some interleavings are repeatedly tested while missing many others.

Systematic testing [9,16,18,28–30], instead of relying on the system scheduler, utilizes formal methods to systematically schedule concurrent events and attempt to cover all possible interleavings. However, the interleaving space of concurrent programs is exponential to the execution length and often far exceeds the testing budget, leading to the so-called *state-space explosion* problem. Techniques such as partial order reduction (POR) [1,2,8,10] and dynamic interface reduction [11] have been introduced to reduce the interleaving space. But, in most cases, the reduced space of a complex concurrent program is still too large to test exhaustively. Moreover, systematic testing often uses a deterministic search algorithm (e.g., the depth-first search) that only slightly adjusts the interleaving at each iteration, e.g., flip the order of two events. Such a search may very well get stuck in a homogeneous interleaving subspace and waste the testing budget by exploring mostly equivalent interleavings.

To mitigate the state-space explosion problem, randomized scheduling algorithms are proposed to *sample*, rather than enumerating, the interleaving space

© The Author(s) 2018
H. Chockler and G. Weissenbacher (Eds.): CAV 2018, LNCS 10982, pp. 317–335, 2018.
https://doi.org/10.1007/978-3-319-96142-2_20

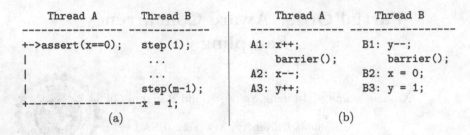

```
    Thread A          Thread B              Thread A          Thread B
----------------   --------------        ----------------   ----------------
+->assert(x==0);   step(1);              A1: x++;           B1: y--;
|                     ...                    barrier();         barrier();
|                     ...                 A2: x--;           B2: x = 0;
|                  step(m-1);             A3: y++;           B3: y = 1;
+-------------------x = 1;
           (a)                                        (b)
```

Fig. 1. (a) An example illustrating random walk's weakness in probabilistic guarantee of error detection, where variable x is initially 0; (b) An example illustrating PCT's redundancy in exploring the partial order.

while still keeping the diversity of the interleavings explored [28]. The most straightforward sampling algorithm is *random walk*: at each step, randomly pick an *enabled* event to execute. Previous work showed that even such a sampling outperformed the exhaustive search at finding errors in real-world concurrent programs [24]. This can be explained by applying the *small-scope hypothesis* [12, Sect. 5.1.3] to the domain of concurrency error detection [17]: errors in real-world concurrent programs are non-adversarial and can often be triggered if a small number of events happen in the right order, which sampling has a good probability to achieve.

Random walk, however, has a unsurprisingly poor probabilistic guarantee of error detection. Consider the program in Fig. 1a. The assertion of thread A fails if, and only if, the statement "x = 1" of thread B is executed before this assertion. Without knowing which order (between the assertion and "x = 1") triggers this failure as a priori, we should sample both orders uniformly because the probabilistic guarantee of detecting this error is the *minimum* sampling probability of these two orders. Unfortunately, random walk may yield extremely non-uniform sampling probabilities for different orders when only a small number of events matter. In this example, to trigger the failure, the assertion of thread A has to be delayed (or not picked) by m times in random walk, making its probabilistic guarantee as low as $1/2^m$.

To sample different orders more uniformly, *Probabilistic Concurrency Testing* (PCT) [4] depends on a user-provided parameter d, the number of events to delay, to randomly pick d events within the execution, and inserts a preemption before each of the d events. Since the events are picked randomly by PCT, the corresponding interleaving space is sampled more uniformly, resulting in a much stronger probabilistic guarantee than random walk. Consider the program in Fig. 1a again. To trigger the failure, there is no event needed to be delayed, other than having the right thread (i.e. thread B) to run first. Thus, the probability trigger (or avoid) the failure is $1/2$, which is much higher than $1/2^m$.

However, PCT does not consider the partial order of events entailed by a concurrent program, such that the explored interleavings are still quite redundant. Consider the example in Fig. 1b. Both A1 and B1 are executed before the barrier and do not race with any statement. Statements A2 and B2 form a race, and so do statements A3 and B3. Depending on how each race is resolved, the program events have total four different partial orders. However, without considering the effects of barriers, PCT will attempt to delay A1 or B1 in vain. Furthermore, without considering the race condition, PCT may first test an interleaving A2 → A3 → B2 → B3 (by delaying A3 and B2), and then test a partial-order equivalent and thus completely redundant interleaving A2 → B2 → A3 → B3 (by delaying A3 and B3). Such redundancies in PCT waste testing resources and weaken the probabilistic guarantee.

Towards addressing the above challenges, this paper makes three main contributions. First, we present a concurrency testing approach, named *partial order sampling* (POS), that samples the concurrent program execution based on the partial orders and provides strong probabilistic guarantees of error detection. In contrast to the sophisticated algorithms and heavy bookkeeping used in prior POR work, the core algorithm of POS is much more straightforward. In POS, each event is assigned with a random priority and, at each step, the event with the highest priority is executed. After each execution, all events that race with the executed event will be reassigned with a fresh random priority. Since each event has its own priority, POS (1) samples the orders of a group of dependent events uniformly and (2) uses one execution to sample independent event groups in parallel, both benefiting its probabilistic guarantee. The priority reassignment is also critical. Consider racing events e_1 and e_2, and an initial priority assignment that runs e_1 first. Without the priority reassignment, e_2 may very well be delayed again when a new racing event e_3 occurs because e_2's priority is more likely to be small (the reason that e_2 is delayed after e_1 at the first place). Such priority reassignments ensure that POS samples the two orders of e_2 and e_3 uniformly.

Secondly, the probabilistic guarantee of POS has been formally analyzed and shown to be exponentially stronger than random walk and PCT for general programs. The probability for POS to execute any partial order can be calculated by modeling the ordering constraints as a bipartite graph and computing the probability that these constraints can be satisfied by a random priority assignment. Although prior POR work typically have soundness proofs of the space reduction [1,8], those proofs depend on an exhaustive searching strategy and it is unclear how they can be adapted to randomized algorithms. Some randomized algorithms leverage POR to heuristically avoid redundant exploration, but no formal analysis of their probabilistic guarantee is given [22,28]. To the best of our knowledge, POS is the first work to sample partial orders with formal probabilistic guarantee of error detection.

Lastly, POS has been implemented and evaluated using both randomly generated programs and real world concurrent software such as Firefox's JavaScript engine SpiderMonkey in SCTBench [24]. Our POS implementation supports shared-memory multithreaded programs using Pthreads. The evaluation results show that POS provided 134.1× stronger overall guarantees than random walk and PCT on randomly generated programs, and the error detection is 2.6× faster than random walk and PCT on SCTBench. POS managed to find the six most difficult bugs in SCTBench with the highest probability among all algorithms evaluated and performed the best among 20 of the total 32 non-trivial bugs in our evaluation.

Related Work. There is a rich literature of concurrency testing. Systematic testing [9,14,18,28] exhaustively enumerates all possible schedules of a program, which suffers from the state-space explosion problem. Partial order reduction techniques [1,2,8,10] alleviate this problem by avoiding exploring schedules that are redundant under partial order equivalence but rely on bookkeeping the massive exploration history to identify redundancy and it is unclear how they can be applied to the sampling methods.

PCT [4] explores schedules containing orderings of small sets of events and guarantees probabilistic coverage of finding bugs involving rare orders of a small number of events. PCT, however, does not take partial orders into account and becomes ineffective when dealing with a large number of ordering events. Also, the need of user-provided parameters diminishes the coverage guarantee, as the parameters are often provided imprecisely. Chistikov et al. [5] introduced hitting families to cover all admissible total orders of a set of events. However, this approach may cover redundant total orders that correspond to the same partial order. RAPOS [22] leverages the ideas from the partial order reduction, resembling our work in its goal, but does not provide a formal proof for its probabilistic guarantee. Our micro-benchmarks show that POS has a 5.0× overall advantage over RAPOS (see Sect. 6.1).

Coverage-driven concurrency testing [26,32] leverages relaxed coverage metrics to discover rarely explored interleavings. Directed testing [21,23] focuses on exploring specific types of interleavings, such as data races and atomicity violations, to reveal bugs. There is a large body of other work showing how to detect concurrency bugs using static analysis [19,25] or dynamic analysis [7,15,20]. But none of them can be effectively applied to real-world software systems, while still have formal probabilistic guarantees.

2   Running Example

Figure 2 shows the running example of this paper. In this example, we assume that memory accesses are sequentially consistent and all shared variables (e.g., x, w, etc.) are initialized to be 0. The program consists of two threads, i.e., A and B. Thread B will be blocked at B4 by wait(w) until $w > 0$. Thread A will set w to be 1 at A3 via signal(w) and unblock thread B. The assertion at A4 will fail if, and only if, the program is executed in the following total order:

$$B1 \rightarrow A1 \rightarrow B2 \rightarrow B3 \rightarrow A2 \rightarrow A3 \rightarrow B4 \rightarrow B5 \rightarrow B6 \rightarrow A4$$

To detect this bug, random walk has to make the correct choice at every step. Among all ten steps, three of them only have a single option: A2 and A3 must be executed first to enable B4, and A4 is the only statement left at the last step. Thus, the probability of reaching the bug is $1/2^7 = 1/128$. As for PCT, we have

```
global int x = y = z = w = 0;

        Thread A                    Thread B
--------------------        --------------------
                            local int a = b = 0;
A1: x++;                    B1: x = 1;
A2: y++;                    B2: a = x;
A3: signal(w);             B3: y = a;
A4: assert(z < 5);         B4: wait(w);
                            B5: b = y;
                            B6: z = a + b;
```

Fig. 2. The running example involving two threads.

to insert two preemption points just before statements B2 and A2 among ten statements, thus the probability for PCT is $1/10 \times 1/10 \times 1/2 = 1/200$, where this $1/2$ comes from the requirement that thread B has to be executed first.

In POS, this bug can be detected with a substantial probability of $1/48$, much higher than other approaches. Indeed, our formal guarantees ensure that any behavior of this program can be covered with a probability of at least $1/60$.

3   Preliminary

Concurrent Machine Model. Our concurrent abstract machine models a *finite* set of processes and a set of shared objects. The machine state is denoted as s, which consists of the local state of each process and the state of shared objects. The abstract machine assumes the sequential consistency and allows the arbitrary interleaving among all processes. At each step, starting from s, any running process can be randomly selected to make a move to update the state to s' and generate an event e, denoted as $s \xrightarrow{e} s'$.

An event e is a tuple $e := (\text{pid}, \text{intr}, \text{obj}, \text{ind})$, where pid is the process ID, intr is the statement (or instruction) pointer, obj is the shared object accessed by this step (we assume each statement only access at most a single shared object), and ind indicates how many times this intr has been executed and is used to distinguish different runs of the same instruction. For example, the execution of the statement "A2: y++" in Fig. 2 will generate the event $(A, A2, y, 0)$. Such an event captures the information of the corresponding step and can be used to replay the execution. In other words, given the starting state s and the event e, the resulting state s' of a step "$\xrightarrow{e}$" is determined.

A trace t is a list of events generated by a sequence of program transitions (or steps) starting from the initial machine state (denoted as s_0). For example, the following program execution:

$$s_0 \xrightarrow{e_0} s_1 \xrightarrow{e_1} \cdots \xrightarrow{e_n} s_{n+1}$$

generates the trace $t := e_0 \bullet e_1 \bullet \cdots \bullet e_n$, where the symbol "$\bullet$" means "cons-ing" an event to the trace. Trace events can be accessed by index (e.g., $t[1] = e_1$).

A trace can be used to replay a sequence of executions. In other words, given the initial machine state s_0 and the trace t, the resulting state of running t (denoted as "$\texttt{State}(t)$") is determined.

We write $\texttt{En}(s) := \{e \mid \exists s', s \xrightarrow{e} s'\}$ as the set of events *enabled* (or allowed to be executed) at state s. Take the program in Fig. 2 as an example. Initially, both A1 and B1 can be executed, and the corresponding two events form the enabled set $\texttt{En}(s_0)$. The blocking wait at B4, however, can be enabled only after being signaled at A3. A state s is called a *terminating* state if, and only if, $\texttt{En}(s) = \emptyset$. We assume that any disabled event will eventually become enabled and every process must end with either a terminating state or an error state. This indicates that all traces are finite. For readability, we often abbreviate $\texttt{En}(\texttt{State}(t))$, i.e., the enabled event set after executing trace t, as $\texttt{En}(t)$.

Partial Order of Traces. Two events e_0 and e_1 are called *independent* events (denoted as $e_0 \perp e_1$) if, and only if, they neither belong to the same process nor access the same object:

$$e_0 \perp e_1 := (e_0.\texttt{pid} \neq e_1.\texttt{pid}) \wedge (e_0.\texttt{obj} \neq e_1.\texttt{obj})$$

The execution order of independent events does not affect the resulting state. If a trace t can be generated by swapping adjacent and independent events of another trace t', then these two traces t and t' are *partial order equivalent*. Intuitively, partial order equivalent traces are guaranteed to lead the program to the same state. The *partial order* of a trace is characterized by the orders between all *dependent* events plus their *transitive closure*. Given a trace t, its partial order relation "$\sqsubset_t$" is defined as the *minimal* relation over its events that satisfies:

(1) $\forall i\ j,\ i < j \wedge t[i] \not\perp t[j] \implies t[i] \sqsubset_t t[j]$
(2) $\forall i\ j\ k,\ t[i] \sqsubset_t t[j] \wedge t[j] \sqsubset_t t[k] \implies t[i] \sqsubset_t t[k]$

Two traces with the same partial order relation and the same event set must be partial order equivalent.

Given an event order $\mathcal{E}$ and its order relation $\sqsubset_\mathcal{E}$, we say a trace t follows $\mathcal{E}$ and write "$t \simeq \mathcal{E}$" if, and only if,

$$\forall e_0\ e_1,\ e_0 \sqsubset_t e_1 \implies e_0 \sqsubset_\mathcal{E} e_1$$

We write "$t \models \mathcal{E}$" to denote that $\mathcal{E}$ is exactly the partial order of trace t:

$$t \models \mathcal{E} := \quad \forall e_0\ e_1,\ e_0 \sqsubset_t e_1 \iff e_0 \sqsubset_\mathcal{E} e_1$$

Probabilistic Error-Detection Guarantees. Each partial order of a concurrent program may lead to a different and potentially incorrect outcome. Therefore, any possible partial order has to be explored. The *minimum* probability of these explorations are called the probabilistic error-detection guarantee of a randomized scheduler.

Algorithm 1 presents a framework to formally reason about this guarantee. A sampling procedure Sample samples a terminating trace t of a program. It starts

---

Algorithm 1. Sample a trace using scheduler Sch and random variable R

```
1: procedure Sample(Sch, R)
2:     t ← [ ]
3:     while En(t) ≠ ∅ do
4:         e ← Sch(En(t), R)
5:         t ← t • e
6:     end while
7:     return t
8: end procedure
```

---

with the empty trace and repeatedly invokes a randomized scheduler (denoted as Sch) to append an event to the trace until the program terminates. The randomized scheduler Sch selects an enabled event from $En(t)$ and the randomness comes from the random variable parameter, i.e., R.

A naive scheduler can be purely random without any strategy. A sophisticated scheduler may utilize additional information, such as the properties of the current trace and the enabled event set.

Given the randomized scheduler Sch on R and any partial order $\mathcal{E}$ of a program, we write "$P(\text{Sample}(\text{Sch}, \text{R}) \models \mathcal{E})$" to denote the probability of covering $\mathcal{E}$, i.e., generating a trace whose partial order is exactly $\mathcal{E}$ using Algorithm 1. The *probabilistic error-detection guarantee* of the scheduler Sch on R is then defined as the minimum probability of covering the partial order $\mathcal{E}$ of any terminating trace of the program:

$$\min_{\mathcal{E}} P(\text{Sample}(\text{Sch}, \text{R}) \models \mathcal{E})$$

4 POS - Algorithm and Analysis

In this section, we first present BasicPOS, a priority-based scheduler and analyze its probability of covering a given partial order (see Sect. 4.1). Based on the analysis of BasicPOS, we then show that such a priority-based algorithm can be dramatically improved by introducing the *priority reassignment*, resulting in our POS algorithm (see Sect. 4.2). Finally, we present how to calculate the *probabilistic error-detection guarantee* of POS on general programs (see Sect. 4.3).

4.1 BasicPOS

In BasicPOS, each event is associated with a random and immutable priority, and, at each step, the enabled event with the highest priority will be picked to execute. We use Pri to denote the map from events to priorities and describe BasicPOS in Algorithm 2, which instantiates the random variable R in Algorithm 1 with Pri. The priority $Pri(e)$ of every event e is independent with each other and follows the uniform distribution $\mathcal{U}(0, 1)$.

We now consider in what condition would BasicPOS sample a trace that follows a given partial order $\mathcal{E}$ of a program. It means that the generated trace t,

---

Algorithm 2. Sample a trace with BasicPOS under the priority map Pri

```
1: procedure Sample_BasicPOS(Pri)                              ▷ Pri ~ U(0, 1)
2:     t ← [ ]
3:     while En(t) ≠ ∅ do
4:         e* ← arg max_{e∈En(t)} Pri(e)
5:         t ← t • e*
6:     end while
7:     return t
8: end procedure
```

---

at the end of each loop iteration (line 5 in Algorithm 2), must satisfy the invariant "$t \simeq \mathcal{E}$". Thus, the event priorities have to be properly ordered such that, given a trace t satisfies "$t \simeq \mathcal{E}$", the enabled event e^* with the highest priority must satisfies "$t \bullet e^* \simeq \mathcal{E}$". In other words, given "$t \simeq \mathcal{E}$", for any $e \in En(t)$ and "$t \bullet e \not\simeq \mathcal{E}$", there must be some $e' \in En(t)$ satisfying "$t \bullet e' \simeq \mathcal{E}$" and a proper priority map where e' has a higher priority, i.e., $Pri(e') > Pri(e)$. Thus, e will not be selected as the event e^* at line 4 in Algorithm 2. The following Lemma 1 indicates that such an event e' always exists:

Lemma 1

$$\forall t\, e,\; t \simeq \mathcal{E} \,\wedge\, e \in En(t) \,\wedge\, t \bullet e \not\simeq \mathcal{E}$$
$$\implies \exists e',\; e' \in En(t) \,\wedge\, t \bullet e' \simeq \mathcal{E} \,\wedge\, e' \sqsubset_\mathcal{E} e$$

Proof. We can prove it by contradiction. Since traces are finite, we assume that some traces are counterexamples to the lemma and t is the longest such trace. In other words, we have $t \simeq \mathcal{E}$ and there exists $e \in En(t) \wedge t \bullet e \not\simeq \mathcal{E}$ such that:

$$\forall e',\; e' \in En(t) \,\wedge\, t \bullet e' \simeq \mathcal{E} \implies \neg(e' \sqsubset_\mathcal{E} e) \tag{1}$$

Since $\mathcal{E}$ is the partial order of a terminating trace and the traces t has not terminated yet, we know that there must exist an event $e' \in En(t)$ such that $t \bullet e' \simeq \mathcal{E}$. Let $t' := t \bullet e'$, by (1), we have that $\neg(e' \sqsubset_\mathcal{E} e)$ and

$$e \in En(t')$$
$$\wedge\; t' \bullet e \not\simeq \mathcal{E}$$
$$\wedge\; \forall e'',\; e'' \in En(t') \,\wedge\, t' \bullet e'' \simeq \mathcal{E} \implies \neg(e'' \sqsubset_\mathcal{E} e)$$

First two statements are intuitive. The third one also holds, otherwise, $e' \sqsubset_\mathcal{E} e$ can be implied by the transitivity of partial orders using e''. Thus, t' is a counterexample that is longer than t, contradicting to our assumption.   □

Thanks to Lemma 1, we then only need to construct a priority map such that this e' has a higher priority. Let "$e \bowtie_\mathcal{E} e' := \exists t,\; t \simeq \mathcal{E} \wedge \{e, e'\} \subseteq En(t)$" denote that e and e' can be *simultaneously enabled* under $\mathcal{E}$. We write

$$PS_\mathcal{E}(e) := \{e' \mid e' \sqsubset_\mathcal{E} e \,\wedge\, e \bowtie_\mathcal{E} e'\}$$

as the set of events that can be simultaneously enabled with but have to be selected prior to e in order to follow $\mathcal{E}$. We have that any e' specified by Lemma 1 must belong to $\mathrm{PS}_{\mathcal{E}}(e)$. Let $V_{\mathcal{E}}$ be the event set ordered by $\mathcal{E}$. The priority map Pri can be constructed as below:

$$\bigwedge_{e \in V_{\mathcal{E}},\ e' \in \mathrm{PS}_{\mathcal{E}}(e)} \mathrm{Pri}(e) < \mathrm{Pri}(e') \qquad \text{(Cond-BasicPOS)}$$

The traces sampled by BasicPOS using this Pri will always follow $\mathcal{E}$.

Although (Cond-BasicPOS) is not the necessary condition to sample a trace following a desired partial order, from our observation, it gives a good estimation for the worst cases. This leads us to locate the major weakness of BasicPOS: the *constraint propagation* of priorities. An event e with a large $\mathrm{PS}_{\mathcal{E}}(e)$ set may have a relatively low priority since its priority has to be lower than all the events in $\mathrm{PS}_{\mathcal{E}}(e)$. Thus, for any simultaneously enabled event e' that has to be delayed after e, $\mathrm{Pri}(e')$ must be even smaller than $\mathrm{Pri}(e)$, which is unnecessarily hard to satisfy for a random $\mathrm{Pri}(e')$. Due to this constraints propagation, the probability that a priority map Pri satisfies (Cond-BasicPOS) can be as low as $1/|V_{\mathcal{E}}|!$.

Here, we explain how BasicPOS samples the following trace that triggers the bug described in Sect. 2:

$$t_{bug} := (B, B1, x, 0) \bullet (A, A1, x, 0) \bullet (B, B2, x, 0) \bullet (B, B3, y, 0) \bullet (A, A2, y, 0)$$
$$\bullet (A, A3, w, 0) \bullet (B, B4, w, 0) \bullet (B, B5, y, 0) \bullet (B, B6, z, 0) \bullet (A, A4, z, 0)$$

To sample trace t_{bug}, according to (Cond-BasicPOS), the priority map has to satisfy the following constraints:

$$\mathrm{Pri}(t_{bug}[0] = (B, B1, x, 0)) > \mathrm{Pri}(t_{bug}[1] = (A, A1, x, 0))$$
$$\mathrm{Pri}(t_{bug}[1]) > \mathrm{Pri}(t_{bug}[2] = (B, B2, x, 0))$$
$$\mathrm{Pri}(t_{bug}[2]) > \mathrm{Pri}(t_{bug}[4] = (A, A2, y, 0))$$
$$\mathrm{Pri}(t_{bug}[3] = (B, B3, y, 0)) > \mathrm{Pri}(t_{bug}[4])$$
$$\mathrm{Pri}(t_{bug}[6] = (B, B4, w, 0)) > \mathrm{Pri}(t_{bug}[9] = (A, A4, z, 0))$$
$$\mathrm{Pri}(t_{bug}[7] = (B, B5, y, 0)) > \mathrm{Pri}(t_{bug}[9])$$
$$\mathrm{Pri}(t_{bug}[8] = (B, B6, z, 0)) > \mathrm{Pri}(t_{bug}[9])$$

Note that these are also the necessary constraints for BasicPOS to follow the partial order of t_{bug}. The probability that a random Pri satisfies the constraints is $1/120$. The propagation of the constraints can be illustrated by the first three steps:

$$\mathrm{Pri}(t_{bug}[0]) > \mathrm{Pri}(t_{bug}[1]) > \mathrm{Pri}(t_{bug}[2]) > \mathrm{Pri}(t_{bug}[4])$$

that happens in the probability of $1/24$. However, on the other hand, random walk can sample these three steps in the probability of $1/8$.

4.2 POS

We will now show how to improve BasicPOS by eliminating the propagation of priority constraints. Consider the situation when an event e (delayed at some trace t) becomes eligible to schedule right after scheduling some e', i.e.,

$$t \simeq \mathcal{E} \ \wedge \ \{e, e'\} \subseteq \text{En}(t) \ \wedge \ t \bullet e \not\simeq \mathcal{E} \ \wedge \ t \bullet e' \bullet e \simeq \mathcal{E}$$

If we reset the priority of e right after scheduling e', all the constraints causing the delay of e will not be propagated to the event e'' such that $e \in \text{PS}_{\mathcal{E}}(e'')$. However, there is no way for us to know which e should be reset after e' during the sampling, since $\mathcal{E}$ is unknown and not provided. Notice that

$$t \simeq \mathcal{E} \ \wedge \ \{e, e'\} \subseteq \text{En}(t) \ \wedge \ t \bullet e \not\simeq \mathcal{E} \ \wedge \ t \bullet e' \bullet e \simeq \mathcal{E} \implies e.\text{obj} = e'.\text{obj}$$

If we reset the priority of all the events that access the same object with e', the propagation of priority constraints will also be eliminated.

To analyze how POS works to follow $\mathcal{E}$ under the reassignment scheme, we have to model how many priorities need to be reset at each step. Note that blindly reassigning priorities of all delayed events at each step would be suboptimal, which degenerates the algorithm to random walk. To give a formal and more precise analysis, we introduce the object index functions for trace t and partial order $\mathcal{E}$:

$$\text{I}(t, e) := \ |\{e' \mid e' \in t \ \wedge \ e.\text{obj} = e'.\text{obj}\}|$$
$$\text{I}_{\mathcal{E}}(e) := \ |\{e' \mid e' \sqsubset_{\mathcal{E}} e \ \wedge \ e.\text{obj} = e'.\text{obj}\}|$$

Intuitively, when $e \in \text{En}(t)$, scheduling e on t will operate $e.\text{obj}$ after $\text{I}(t, e)$ previous events. A trace t follows $\mathcal{E}$ if every step (indicated by $t[i]$) operates the object $t[i].\text{obj}$ after $\text{I}_{\mathcal{E}}(t[i])$ previous events in the trace.

We then index (or version) the priority of event e using the index function as $\text{Pri}(e, \text{I}(t, e))$ and introduce POS shown in Algorithm 3. By proving that

$$\forall e', \ \text{I}(t, e) \leq \text{I}(t \bullet e', e) \ \wedge \ (\text{I}(t, e) = \text{I}(t \bullet e', e) \iff e.\text{obj} \neq e'.\text{obj})$$

we have that scheduling an event e will *increase* the priority version of all the events accessing $e.\text{obj}$, resulting in the priority reassignment.

We can then prove that the following statements hold:

$$\forall t \ e, \ t \simeq \mathcal{E} \wedge e \in \text{En}(t) \implies (t \bullet e \simeq \mathcal{E} \iff \text{I}(t, e) = \text{I}_{\mathcal{E}}(e))$$
$$\forall t \ e, \ t \simeq \mathcal{E} \wedge e \in \text{En}(t) \wedge t \bullet e \not\simeq \mathcal{E} \implies \text{I}(t, e) < \text{I}_{\mathcal{E}}(e)$$

To ensure that the selection of e^* on trace t follows $\mathcal{E}$ at the line 4 of Algorithm 3, any e satisfying $\text{I}(t, e) < \text{I}_{\mathcal{E}}(e)$ has to have a smaller priority than some e' satisfying $\text{I}(t, e') = \text{I}_{\mathcal{E}}(e)$ and such e' must exist by Lemma 1. In this way, the priority constraints for POS to sample $\mathcal{E}$ are as below:

$$\bigwedge \text{Pri}(e, i) < \text{Pri}(e', \text{I}_{\mathcal{E}}(e')) \text{ for some } i < \text{I}_{\mathcal{E}}(e')$$

which is bipartite and the propagation of priority constraints is eliminated. The effectiveness of POS is guaranteed by Theorem 1.

Algorithm 3. Sample a trace with POS under versioned priority map `Pri`

```
1: procedure SamplePOS(Pri)                                    ▷ Pri ~ U(0,1)
2:     t ← []
3:     while En(t) ≠ ∅ do
4:         e* ← arg maxe∈En(t) Pri(e, I(t,e))
5:         t ← t.e*
6:     end while
7:     return t
8: end procedure
```

Theorem 1. *Given any partial order $\mathcal{E}$ of a program with $\mathcal{P} > 1$ processes. Let*

$$D_{\mathcal{E}} := |\{(e,e') \mid e \sqsubset_{\mathcal{E}} e' \wedge e \not\lessdot e' \wedge e \bowtie_{\mathcal{E}} e'\}|$$

be the number of races in $\mathcal{E}$, we have that

1. $D_{\mathcal{E}} \leq |V_{\mathcal{E}}| \times (\mathcal{P} - 1)$, *and*
2. *POS has at least the following probability to sample a trace $t \simeq \mathcal{E}$:*

$$\left(\frac{1}{\mathcal{P}}\right)^{|V_{\mathcal{E}}|} R^{U}$$

where $R = \mathcal{P} \times |V_{\mathcal{E}}|/(|V_{\mathcal{E}}| + D_{\mathcal{E}}) \geq 1$ and $U = (|V_{\mathcal{E}}| - \lceil D_{\mathcal{E}}/(\mathcal{P} - 1)\rceil)/2 \geq 0$

Please refer to the technical report [33] for the detailed proof and the construction of priority constraints.

Here, we show how POS improves BasicPOS over the example in Sect. 2. The priority constraints for POS to sample the partial order of t_{bug} are as below:

$$\mathrm{Pri}(t_{bug}[0],0) > \mathrm{Pri}(t_{bug}[1],0)$$
$$\mathrm{Pri}(t_{bug}[1],1) > \mathrm{Pri}(t_{bug}[2],1)$$
$$\mathrm{Pri}(t_{bug}[2],2) > \mathrm{Pri}(t_{bug}[4],0)$$
$$\mathrm{Pri}(t_{bug}[3],0) > \mathrm{Pri}(t_{bug}[4],0)$$
$$\mathrm{Pri}(t_{bug}[6],1) > \mathrm{Pri}(t_{bug}[9],0)$$
$$\mathrm{Pri}(t_{bug}[7],2) > \mathrm{Pri}(t_{bug}[9],0)$$
$$\mathrm{Pri}(t_{bug}[8],0) > \mathrm{Pri}(t_{bug}[9],0)$$

Since each $\mathrm{Pri}(e,i)$ is independently random following $\mathcal{U}(0,1)$, the probability of `Pri` satisfying the constraints is $1/2 \times 1/2 \times 1/3 \times 1/4 = 1/48$.

4.3   Probability Guarantee of POS on General Programs

We now analyze how POS performs on general programs compared to random walk and PCT. Consider a program with $\mathcal{P}$ processes and $\mathcal{N}$ total events. It is generally common for a program have substantial non-racing events, for example, accessing shared variables protected by locks, semaphores, and condition

328   X. Yuan et al.

variables, etc. We assume that there exists a ratio $0 \le \alpha \le 1$ such that in any partial order there are at least $\alpha\mathcal{N}$ non-racing events.

Under this assumption, for random walk, we can construct an adversary program with the worst case probability as $1/\mathcal{P}^{\mathcal{N}}$ for almost any α [33]. For PCT, since only the order of the $(1 - \alpha)\mathcal{N}$ events may affect the partial order, the number of preemptions needed for a partial order in the worst case becomes $(1 - \alpha)\mathcal{N}$, and thus the worst case probability bound is $1/\mathcal{N}^{(1-\alpha)\mathcal{N}}$. For POS, the number of races $D_{\mathcal{E}}$ is reduced to $(1-\alpha)\mathcal{N} \times (\mathcal{P} - 1)$ in the worst case, Theorem 1 guarantees the probability lower bound as

$$\frac{1}{\mathcal{P}^{\mathcal{N}}} \left(\frac{1}{1 - (1 - 1/P)\alpha} \right)^{\alpha\mathcal{N}/2}$$

Thus, POS advantages random walk when $\alpha > 0$ and degenerates to random walk when $\alpha = 0$. Also, POS advantages PCT if $\mathcal{N} > \mathcal{P}$ (when $\alpha = 0$) or $\mathcal{N}^{1/\alpha-1} > \mathcal{P}^{1/\alpha}\sqrt{1 + \alpha/\mathcal{P} - \alpha}$ (when $0 < \alpha < 1$). For example, when $\mathcal{P} = 2$ and $\alpha = 1/2$, POS advantages PCT if $\mathcal{N} > 2\sqrt{3}$. In other words, in this case, POS is better than PCT if there are at least four total events.

5   Implementation

The algorithm of POS requires a pre-determined priority map, while the implementation could decide the event priority on demand when new events appear. The implementation of POS is shown in Algorithm 4, where lines 14–18 are for the priority reassignment. Variable s represents the current program state with the following interfaces:

- s.Enabled() returns the current set of enabled events.
- s.Execute(e) returns the resulting state after executing e in the state of s.
- s.IsRacing(e, e') returns if there is a race between e and e'.

In the algorithm, if a race is detected during the scheduling, the priority of the delayed event in the race will be removed and then be reassigned at lines 6–9.

Relaxation for Read-Only Events. The abstract interface s.IsRacing(...) allows us to relax our model for read-only events. When both e and e' are read-only events, s.IsRacing(e, e') returns false even if they are accessing the same object. Our evaluations show that this relaxation improves the execution time of POS.

Fairness Workaround. POS is probabilistically fair. For an enabled event e with priority $p > 0$, the cumulative probability for e to delay by $k \to \infty$ steps without racing is at most $(1-p^{\mathcal{P}})^k \to 0$. However, it is possible that POS delays events for prolonged time, slowing down the test. To alleviate this, the current implementation resets all event priorities for every 10^3 voluntary context switch events, e.g., `sched_yield()` calls. This is only useful for speeding up few benchmark programs that have busy loops (`sched_yield()` calls were added by SCTBench creators) and has minimal impact on the probability of hitting bugs.

Algorithm 4. Testing a program with POS

```
 1: procedure POS(s)                              ▷ s: the initial state of the program
 2:     pri ← [ε ↦ −∞]  ▷ Initially, no priority is assigned except the special symbol ε
 3:     while s.Enabled() ≠ ∅ do
 4:         e* ← ε                                        ▷ Assume ε ∉ s.Enabled()
 5:         for each e ∈ s.Enabled() do
 6:             if e ∉ pri then
 7:                 newPriority ← U(0, 1)
 8:                 pri ← pri[e ↦ newPriority]
 9:             end if
10:             if pri(e*) < pri(e) then
11:                 e* ← e
12:             end if
13:         end for
14:         for each e ∈ s.Enabled() do                          ▷ Update priorities
15:             if e ≠ e* ∧ s.IsRacing(e, e*) then
16:                 pri ← pri \ {e}    ▷ The priority will be reassigned in the next step
17:             end if
18:         end for
19:         s ← s.Execute(e*)
20:     end while
21:     return s
22: end procedure
```

---

6 Evaluation

To understand the performance of POS and compare with other sampling methods, we conducted experiments on both micro benchmarks (automatically generated) and macro benchmarks (including real-world programs).

6.1 Micro Benchmark

We generated programs with a small number of static events as the micro benchmarks. We assumed multi-threaded programs with t threads and each thread executes m events accessing o objects. To make the program space tractable, we chose $t = m = o = 4$, resulting 16 total events. To simulate different object access patterns in real programs, we chose to randomly distribute events accessing different objects with the following configurations:

- Each object has respectively {4,4,4,4} accessing events. (Uniform)
- Each object has respectively {2,2,6,6} accessing events. (Skewed)

The results are shown in Table 1. The benchmark columns show the characteristics of each generated program, including (1) the configuration used for generating the program; (2) the number of distinct partial orders in the program; (3) the maximum number of preemptions needed for covering all partial orders; and (4) the maximum number of races in any partial order. We measured the

Table 1. Coverage on the micro benchmark programs. Columns under "benchmark" are program characteristics explained in Sect. 6.1. "0(x)" represents incomplete coverage.

	Benchmark			Coverage				
Conf.	PO. count	Max prempt.	Max races	RW	PCT	RAPOS	BasicPOS	POS
Uniform	4478	6	19	2.65e−08	0(4390)	1.84e−06	0(4475)	7.94e−06
	7413	6	20	3.97e−08	0(7257)	3.00e−07	2.00e−08	5.62e−06
	1554	5	19	8.37e−08	0(1540)	1.78e−06	4.00e−08	8.54e−06
	6289	6	20	1.99e−08	0(6077)	1.34e−06	0(6288)	6.62e−06
	1416	6	21	1.88e−07	0(1364)	1.99e−05	1.80e−07	4.21e−05
Skewed	39078	7	27	5.89e−09	0(33074)	0(39044)	0(38857)	1.20e−07
	19706	7	24	4.97e−09	0(18570)	0(19703)	0(19634)	5.00e−07
	19512	6	27	2.35e−08	0(16749)	1.00e−07	0(19502)	1.36e−06
	8820	6	23	6.62e−09	0(8208)	1.00e−07	0(8816)	1.20e−06
	7548	7	25	1.32e−08	0(7438)	1.30e−06	2.00e−08	3.68e−06
Geo-mean*				2.14e−08	2.00e−08	4.11e−07	2.67e−08	2.87e−06

Table 2. Coverage on the micro benchmark programs - 50% read

	Benchmark			Coverage					
Conf.	PO. count	Max prempt.	Max races	RW	PCT	RAPOS	BasicPOS	POS	POS*
Uniform	896	6	16	7.06e−08	0(883)	9.42e−06	2.00e−08	9.32e−06	1.41e−05
	1215	6	18	3.53e−08	0(1204)	8.70e−06	6.00e−08	1.22e−05	1.51e−05
	1571	7	17	8.83e−09	0(1523)	4.22e−06	0(1566)	7.66e−06	1.09e−05
	3079	6	15	1.99e−08	0(3064)	8.20e−07	1.20e−07	7.08e−06	7.68e−06
	1041	4	18	2.51e−07	0(1032)	3.05e−05	2.20e−06	3.32e−05	4.85e−05
Skewed	3867	6	19	6.62e−09	0(3733)	1.24e−06	8.00e−08	4.04e−06	4.24e−06
	1057	6	20	2.12e−07	0(1055)	4.68e−06	2.08e−06	2.79e−05	2.80e−05
	1919	6	20	2.09e−07	0(1917)	2.02e−06	3.80e−07	1.48e−05	1.48e−05
	11148	7	21	4.71e−08	0(10748)	4.00e−08	0(11128)	1.58e−06	3.02e−06
	4800	7	19	3.97e−08	0(4421)	5.00e−07	0(4778)	1.58e−06	4.80e−06
Geo-mean*				4.77e−08	2.00e−08	2.14e−06	1.05e−07	7.82e−06	1.08e−05

coverage of each sampling method on each program by the minimum hit ratio on any partial order of the program. On every program, we ran each sampling methods for 5×10^7 times (except for random walk, for which we calculated the exact probabilities). If a program was not fully covered by an algorithm within the sample limit, the coverage is denoted as "0(x)", where x is the number of covered partial orders. We let PCT sample the exact number of the preemptions needed for each case. We tweaked PCT to improve its coverage by adding a dummy event at the beginning of each thread, as otherwise PCT cannot preempt the actual first event of each thread. The results show that POS performed the best among all algorithms. For each algorithm, we calculated the overall performance as the geometric mean of the coverage.[1] POS overall performed $\sim$7.0$\times$ better compared to other algorithms ($\sim$134.1$\times$ excluding RAPOS and BasicPOS).

To understand our relaxation of read-only events, we generated another set of programs with the same configurations, but with half of the events read-only. The results are shown in Table 2, where the relaxed algorithm is denoted as POS*. Overall, POS* performed roughly $\sim$1.4$\times$ as good as POS and $\sim$5.0$\times$ better compared to other algorithms ($\sim$226.4$\times$ excluding RAPOS and BasicPOS).

6.2   Macro Benchmark

We used SCTBench [24], a collection of concurrency bugs on multi-threaded programs, to evaluate POS on practical programs. SCTBench collected 49 concurrency bugs from previous parallel workloads [3,27] and concurrency testing/verification work [4,6,18,21,31]. SCTBench comes with a concurrency testing tool, Maple [32], which intercepts `pthread` primitives and shared memory accesses, as well as controls their interleaving. When a bug is triggered, it will be caught by Maple and reported back. We implemented POS with the relaxation of read-only events in Maple. Each sampling method was evaluated in SCTBench by the ratio of tries and hits of the bug in each case. For each case, we ran each sampling method on it until the number of tries reaches 10^4. We recorded the bug hit count h and the total runs count t, and calculated the ratio as h/t.

Two cases in SCTBench are not adopted: `parsec-2.0-streamcluster2` and `radbench-bug1`. Because neither of the algorithms can hit their bugs once, which conflicts with previous results. We strengthened the case `safestack-bug1` by internally repeating the case for 10^4 times (and shrunk the run limit to 500). This amortizes the per-run overhead of Maple, which could take up to a few seconds. We modified PCT to reset for every internal loop. We evaluated variants of PCT algorithms of PCT-d, representing PCT with $d-1$ preemption points, to reduce the disadvantage of a sub-optimal d. The results are shown in Table 3. We ignore cases in which all algorithms can hit the bugs with more than half of their tries. The cases are sorted based on the minimum hit ratio across algorithms. The performance of each algorithm is aggregated by calculating the geometric mean of hit ratios[2] on every case. The best hit ratio for each case is marked as blue.

The results of macro benchmark experiments can be highlighted as below:

- Overall, POS performed the best in hitting bugs in SCTBench. The geometric mean of POS is $\sim$2.6$\times$ better than PCT and $\sim$4.7$\times$ better than random walk. Because the buggy interleavings in each case are not necessarily the most

---

[1] For each case that an algorithm does not have the full coverage, we conservatively account the coverage as $\frac{1}{5 \times 10^7}$ into the geometric mean.

[2] For each case that an algorithm cannot hit once within the limit, we conservatively account the hit ratio as $1/t$ in the calculation of the geometric mean.

difficult ones to sample, POS may not perform overwhelmingly better than others, as in micro benchmarks.
- Among all 32 cases shown in the table, POS performed the best among all algorithms in 20 cases, while PCT variants were the best in 10 cases and random walk was the best in three cases.
- POS is able to hit all bugs in SCTBench, while all PCT variants missed one case within the limit (and one case with hit ratio of 0.0002), and random walk missed three cases (and one case with hit ratio of 0.0003).

Table 3. Bug hit ratios on macro benchmark programs

Case	RW	PCT-2	PCT-3	PCT-4	PCT-5	PCT-20	POS
01 stringbuffer-jdk1.4	0.0638	0.0000	0.0193	0.0420	0.0600	0.0332	0.0833
02 reorder_10_bad	0.0000	0.0007	0.0014	0.0017	0.0021	0.0000	0.0308
03 reorder_20_bad	0.0000	0.0015	0.0027	0.0040	0.0043	0.0021	0.1709
04 twostage_100_bad	0.0000	0.0000	0.0000	0.0002	0.0002	0.0000	0.0047
05 radbench-bug2	0.0003	0.0000	0.0010	0.0030	0.0045	0.0000	0.0418
06 safestack-bug1$\times 10^4$	0.0480	0.0000	0.0000	0.0000	0.0000	0.0000	0.2440
07 WSQ	0.0002	0.0484	0.0813	0.1054	0.1190	0.1444	0.0497
08 WSQ-State	0.0092	0.0003	0.0015	0.0017	0.0019	0.0146	0.0926
09 IWSQ-State	0.0643	0.0006	0.0040	0.0073	0.0121	0.0618	0.1380
10 IWSQ	0.0010	0.0461	0.0775	0.0984	0.1183	0.1205	0.0500
11 reorder_5_bad	0.0018	0.0061	0.0110	0.0122	0.0126	0.0089	0.0668
12 queue_bad	0.9999	0.0068	0.1415	0.2621	0.3511	0.6176	0.9999
13 reorder_4_bad	0.0074	0.0118	0.0206	0.0263	0.0294	0.0294	0.0795
14 qsort_mt	0.0097	0.0117	0.0239	0.0328	0.0398	0.0937	0.0958
15 reorder_3_bad	0.0246	0.0255	0.0457	0.0580	0.0660	0.0920	0.0997
16 wronglock_bad	0.3272	0.0351	0.0630	0.0942	0.1142	0.2508	0.4227
17 bluetooth_driver_bad	0.0628	0.0390	0.0597	0.0778	0.0791	0.1334	0.0847
18 radbench-bug6	0.3026	0.0461	0.0748	0.1011	0.1220	0.1435	0.2305
19 wronglock_3_bad	0.3095	0.0683	0.1137	0.1454	0.1741	0.2689	0.3625
20 twostage_bad	0.0806	0.1213	0.1959	0.2448	0.2804	0.2579	0.1212
21 deadlock01_bad	0.3668	0.0904	0.1714	0.2468	0.3160	0.8363	0.3315
22 account_bad	0.1173	0.2140	0.1929	0.1748	0.1628	0.1189	0.3367
23 token_ring_bad	0.1245	0.1367	0.1717	0.1923	0.2021	0.2171	0.1724
24 circular_buffer_bad	0.9159	0.1301	0.2888	0.4226	0.5180	0.7114	0.9369
25 carter01_bad	0.4706	0.1591	0.2974	0.4043	0.5007	0.9583	0.4999
26 ctrace-test	0.2380	0.2755	0.3342	0.3459	0.3453	0.2099	0.4680
27 pbzip2-0.9.4	0.3768	0.2321	0.2736	0.3048	0.3245	0.3609	0.6268
28 stack_bad	0.6051	0.2800	0.4060	0.4811	0.5365	0.7352	0.6210
29 lazy01_bad	0.6089	0.5386	0.5645	0.5906	0.6112	0.6887	0.3313
30 streamcluster3	0.3523	0.4970	0.5020	0.4979	0.5009	0.4849	0.4421
31 aget-bug2	0.4961	0.3993	0.4691	0.5036	0.5285	0.6117	0.9395
32 barnes	0.5180	0.5050	0.5049	0.5048	0.5052	0.5043	0.4846
Geo-mean*	0.0380	0.0213	0.0459	0.0604	0.0692	0.0694	0.1795

7 Conclusion

We have presented POS, a concurrency testing approach to sample the partial order of concurrent programs. POS's core algorithm is simple and lightweight: (1) assign a random priority to each event in a program; (2) repeatedly execute the event with the highest priority; and (3) after executing an event, reassign its racing events with random priorities. We have formally shown that POS has an exponentially stronger probabilistic error-detection guarantee than existing randomized scheduling algorithms. Evaluations have shown that POS is effective in covering the partial-order space of micro-benchmarks and finding concurrency bugs in real-world programs such as Firefox's JavaScript engine SpiderMonkey.

Acknowledgements. We thank the anonymous reviewers for their helpful feedbacks that greatly improved this paper. We thank Madan Musuvathi for insightful discussions. This research was supported in part by NSF CNS-1564055, ONR N00014-16-1-2263, and ONR N00014-17-1-2788 grants.

References

1. Abdulla, P., Aronis, S., Jonsson, B., Sagonas, K.: Optimal dynamic partial order reduction. In: Proceedings of the 41st ACM SIGPLAN-SIGACT Symposium on Principles of Programming Languages, POPL 2014, pp. 373–384. ACM, San Diego (2014)
2. Albert, E., Arenas, P., de la Banda, M.G., Gómez-Zamalloa, M., Stuckey, P.J.: Context-sensitive dynamic partial order reduction. In: Majumdar, R., Kunčak, V. (eds.) CAV 2017. LNCS, vol. 10426, pp. 526–543. Springer, Cham (2017). https://doi.org/10.1007/978-3-319-63387-9_26
3. Bienia, C.: Benchmarking Modern Multiprocessors. Princeton University, Princeton (2011)
4. Burckhardt, S., Kothari, P., Musuvathi, M., Nagarakatte, S.: A randomized scheduler with probabilistic guarantees of finding bugs. In: Proceedings of the Fifteenth Edition of ASPLOS on Architectural Support for Programming Languages and Operating Systems, ASPLOS XV, pp. 167–178. ACM, Pittsburgh (2010)
5. Chistikov, D., Majumdar, R., Niksic, F.: Hitting families of schedules for asynchronous programs. In: Chaudhuri, S., Farzan, A. (eds.) CAV 2016. LNCS, vol. 9780, pp. 157–176. Springer, Cham (2016). https://doi.org/10.1007/978-3-319-41540-6_9
6. Cordeiro, L., Fischer, B.: Verifying multi-threaded software using SMT-based context-bounded model checking. In: Proceedings of the 33rd International Conference on Software Engineering, ICSE 2011, pp. 331–340. ACM, Waikiki (2011)
7. Flanagan, C., Freund, S.N.: FastTrack: efficient and precise dynamic race detection. In: Proceedings of the 30th ACM SIGPLAN Conference on Programming Language Design and Implementation, PLDI 2009, pp. 121–133. ACM, Dublin (2009)
8. Flanagan, C., Godefroid, P.: Dynamic partial-order reduction for model checking software. In: Proceedings of the 32nd ACM SIGPLAN-SIGACT Symposium on Principles of Programming Languages, POPL 2005, pp. 110–121. ACM, Long Beach (2005)

9. Godefroid, P.: Model checking for programming languages using VeriSoft. In: Proceedings of the 24th ACM SIGPLAN-SIGACT Symposium on Principles of Programming Languages, POPL 1997, pp. 174–186. ACM, Paris (1997)

10. Godefroid, P.: Partial-Order Methods for the Verification of Concurrent Systems: An Approach to the State-Explosion Problem. Springer, New York (1996). https://doi.org/10.1007/3-540-60761-7

11. Guo, H., Wu, M., Zhou, L., Hu, G., Yang, J., Zhang, L.: Practical software model checking via dynamic interface reduction. In: Proceedings of the Twenty-Third ACM Symposium on Operating Systems Principles, SOSP 2011, pp. 265–278. ACM, Cascais (2011)

12. Jackson, D.: Software Abstractions: Logic, Language, and Analysis. The MIT Press, Cambridge (2006)

13. Jackson, J.: Nasdaq's Facebook Glitch Came From Race Conditions. http://www.cio.com/article/706796/

14. Leesatapornwongsa, T., Hao, M., Joshi, P., Lukman, J.F., Gunawi, H.S.: SAMC: semantic-aware model checking for fast discovery of deep bugs in cloud systems. In: Proceedings of the 11th USENIX Conference on Operating Systems Design and Implementation, OSDI 2014, pp. 399–414. USENIX Association, Broomfield (2014)

15. Lu, S., Tucek, J., Qin, F., Zhou, Y.: AVIO: detecting atomicity violations via access interleaving invariants. In: Proceedings of the 12th International Conference on Architectural Support for Programming Languages and Operating Systems, ASPLOS XII, pp. 37–48. ACM, San Jose (2006)

16. Musuvathi, M., Park, D.Y.W., Chou, A., Engler, D.R., Dill, D.L.: CMC: a pragmatic approach to model checking real code. In: Proceedings of the 5th Symposium on Operating Systems Design and implementation, OSDI 2002, pp. 75–88. USENIX Association, Boston (2002)

17. Musuvathi, M., Qadeer, S.: Iterative context bounding for systematic testing of multithreaded programs. In: Proceedings of the 28th ACM SIGPLAN Conference on Programming Language Design and Implementation, PLDI 2007, pp. 446–455. ACM, San Diego (2007)

18. Musuvathi, M., Qadeer, S., Ball, T., Basler, G., Nainar, P.A., Neamtiu, I.: Finding and reproducing Heisenbugs in concurrent programs. In: Proceedings of the 8th USENIX Conference on Operating Systems Design and Implementation, OSDI 2008, pp. 267–280. USENIX Association, San Diego (2008)

19. Naik, M., Aiken, A., Whaley, J.: Effective static race detection for Java. In: Proceedings of the 27th ACM SIGPLAN Conference on Programming Language Design and Implementation, PLDI 2006, pp. 308–319. ACM, Ottawa (2006)

20. O'Callahan, R., Choi, J.-D.: Hybrid dynamic data race detection. In: Proceedings of the Ninth ACM SIGPLAN Symposium on Principles and Practice of Parallel Programming, PPoPP 2003, pp. 167–178. ACM, San Diego (2003)

21. Park, S., Lu, S., Zhou, Y.: CTrigger: exposing atomicity violation bugs from their hiding places. In: Proceedings of the 14th International Conference on Architectural Support for Programming Languages and Operating Systems, ASPLOS XIV, pp. 25–36. ACM, Washington, D.C. (2009)

22. Sen, K.: Effective random testing of concurrent programs. In: Proceedings of the Twenty-Second IEEE/ACM International Conference on Automated Software Engineering, ASE 2007, pp. 323–332. ACM, Atlanta (2007)

23. Sen, K.: Race directed random testing of concurrent programs. In: Proceedings of the 29th ACM SIGPLAN Conference on Programming Language Design and Implementation, PLDI 2008, pp. 11–21. ACM, Tucson (2008)

24. Thomson, P., Donaldson, A.F., Betts, A.: Concurrency testing using controlled schedulers: an empirical study. ACM Trans. Parallel Comput. 2(4), 23:1–23:37 (2016)
25. Voung, J.W., Jhala, R., Lerner, S.: RELAY: static race detection on millions of lines of code. In: Proceedings of the the 6th Joint Meeting of the European Software Engineering Conference and the ACM SIGSOFT Symposium on the Foundations of Software Engineering, ESEC-FSE 2007, pp. 205–214. ACM, Dubrovnik (2007)
26. Wang, C., Said, M., Gupta, A.: Coverage guided systematic concurrency testing. In: Proceedings of the 33rd International Conference on Software Engineering, ICSE 2011, pp. 221–230. ACM, Waikiki (2011)
27. Woo, S.C., Ohara, M., Torrie, E., Singh, J.P., Gupta, A.: The SPLASH-2 programs: characterization and methodological considerations. In: Proceedings of the 22nd Annual International Symposium on Computer Architecture, ISCA 1995, pp. 24–36. ACM, S. Margherita Ligure (1995)
28. Yang, J., Chen, T., Wu, M., Xu, Z., Liu, X., Lin, H., Yang, M., Long, F., Zhang, L., Zhou, L.: MODIST: transparent model checking of unmodified distributed systems. In: Proceedings of the 6th USENIX Symposium on Networked Systems Design and Implementation, NSDI 2009, pp. 213–228. USENIX Association, Boston (2009)
29. Yang, J., Sar, C., Engler, D.: EXPLODE: a lightweight, general system for finding serious storage system errors. In: Proceedings of the 7th USENIX Symposium on Operating Systems Design and Implementation - Volume 7, OSDI 2006, p. 10. USENIX Association, Seattle (2006)
30. Yang, J., Twohey, P., Engler, D., Musuvathi, M.: Using model checking to find serious file system errors. In: Proceedings of the 6th Conference on Symposium on Operating Systems Design & Implementation - Volume 6, OSDI 2004, p. 19. USENIX Association, San Francisco (2004)
31. Yang, Y., Chen, X., Gopalakrishnan, G.: Inspect: a runtime model checker for multithreaded C programs. Technical report UUCS-08-004, University of Utah, Salt Lake City, UT, USA (2008)
32. Yu, J., Narayanasamy, S., Pereira, C., Pokam, G.: Maple: a coverage-driven testing tool for multithreaded programs. In: Proceedings of the ACM International Conference on Object Oriented Programming Systems Languages and Applications, OOPSLA 2012, pp. 485–502. ACM, Tucson (2012)
33. Yuan, X., Yang, J., Gu, R.: Partial order aware concurrency sampling (extended version). Technical report, Columbia University, New York, NY, USA (2018)

Reasoning About TSO Programs Using Reduction and Abstraction

Ahmed Bouajjani[1], Constantin Enea[1], Suha Orhun Mutluergil[2(✉)], and Serdar Tasiran[3]

[1] IRIF, University Paris Diderot and CNRS, Paris, France
{abou,cenea}@irif.fr
[2] Koc University, Istanbul, Turkey
smutluergil@ku.edu.tr
[3] Amazon Web Services, New York, USA
tasirans@amazon.com

Abstract. We present a method for proving that a program running under the Total Store Ordering (TSO) memory model is robust, i.e., all its TSO computations are equivalent to computations under the Sequential Consistency (SC) semantics. This method is inspired by Lipton's reduction theory for proving atomicity of concurrent programs. For programs which are not robust, we introduce an abstraction mechanism that allows to construct robust programs over-approximating their TSO semantics. This enables the use of proof methods designed for the SC semantics in proving invariants that hold on the TSO semantics of a non-robust program. These techniques have been evaluated on a large set of benchmarks using the infrastructure provided by CIVL, a generic tool for reasoning about concurrent programs under the SC semantics.

1 Introduction

A classical memory model for shared-memory concurrency is Sequential Consistency (SC) [16], where the actions of different threads are interleaved while the program order between actions of each thread is preserved. For performance reasons, modern multiprocessors implement weaker memory models, e.g., Total Store Ordering (TSO) [19] in x86 machines, which relax the program order. For instance, the main feature of TSO is the write-to-read relaxation, which allows reads to overtake writes. This relaxation reflects the fact that writes are buffered before being flushed non-deterministically to the main memory.

Nevertheless, most programmers usually assume that memory accesses happen instantaneously and atomically like in the SC memory model. This assumption is safe for data-race free programs [3]. However, many programs employing lock-free synchronization are not data-race free, e.g., programs implementing synchronization operations and libraries implementing concurrent objects. In

This work is supported in part by the European Research Council (ERC) under the European Union's Horizon 2020 research and innovation programme (grant agreement No. 678177).

H. Chockler and G. Weissenbacher (Eds.): CAV 2018, LNCS 10982, pp. 336–353, 2018.
https://doi.org/10.1007/978-3-319-96142-2_21

most cases, these programs are designed to be robust against relaxations, i.e., they admit the same behaviors as if they were run under SC. Memory fences must be included appropriately in programs in order to prevent non-SC behaviors. Getting such programs right is a notoriously difficult and error-prone task. Robustness can also be used as a proof method, that allows to reuse the existing SC verification technology. Invariants of a robust program running under SC are also valid for the TSO executions. Therefore, the problem of checking robustness of a program against relaxations of a memory model is important.

In this paper, we address the problem of checking robustness in the case of TSO. We present a methodology for proving robustness which uses the concepts of left/right mover in Lipton's reduction theory [17]. Intuitively, a program statement is a left (resp., right) mover if it commutes to the left (resp., right) with respect to the statements in the other threads. These concepts have been used by Lipton [17] to define a program rewriting technique which enlarges the atomic blocks in a given program while preserving the same set of behaviors. In essence, robustness can also be seen as an atomicity problem: every write statement corresponds to two events, inserting the write into the buffer and flushing the write from the buffer to the main memory, which must be proved to happen atomically, one after the other. However, differently from Lipton's reduction theory, the events that must be proved atomic do not correspond syntactically to different statements in the program. This leads to different uses of these concepts which cannot be seen as a direct instantiation of this theory.

In case programs are not robust, or they cannot be proven robust using our method, we define a program abstraction technique that roughly, makes reads non-deterministic (this follows the idea of combining reduction and abstraction introduced in [12]). The non-determinism added by this abstraction can lead to programs which can be proven robust using our method. Then, any invariant (safety property) of the abstraction, which is valid under the SC semantics, is also valid for the TSO semantics of the original program. As shown in our experiments, this abstraction leads in some cases to programs which reach exactly the same set of configurations as the original program (but these configurations can be reached in different orders), which implies no loss of precision.

We tested the applicability of the proposed reduction and abstraction based techniques on an exhaustive benchmark suite containing 34 challenging programs (from [2,7]). These techniques were precise enough for proving robustness of 32 of these programs. One program (presented in Fig. 3) is not robust, and required abstraction in order to derive a robust over-approximation. There is only one program which cannot be proved robust using our techniques (although it is robust). We believe however that an extension of our abstraction mechanism to atomic read-write instructions will be able to deal with this case. We leave this question for future work.

An extended version of this paper with missing proofs can be found at [8].

2   Overview

The TSO memory model allows strictly more behaviors than the classic SC memory model: writes are first stored in a thread-local buffer and

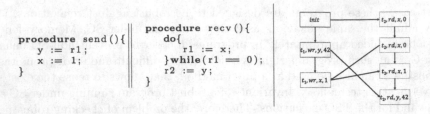

```
procedure send(){          procedure recv(){
    y := r1;                   do{
    x := 1;                        r1 := x;
}                              }while(r1 == 0);
                               r2 := y;
                           }
```

Fig. 1. An example message passing program and a sample trace. Edges of the trace shows the happens before order of global accesses and they are simplified by applying transitive reduction.

non-deterministically flushed into the shared memory at a later time (also, the write buffers are accessed first when reading a shared variable). However, in practice, many programs are *robust*, i.e., they have exactly the same behaviors under TSO and SC. Robustness implies for instance, that any invariant proved under the SC semantics is also an invariant under the TSO semantics. We describe in the following a sound methodology for checking that a program is *robust*, which avoids modeling and verifying TSO behaviors. Moreover, for non-robust programs, we show an abstraction mechanism that allows to obtain robust programs over-approximating the behaviors of the original program.

As a first example, consider the simple "message passing" program in Fig. 1. The **send** method sets the value of the "communication" variable y to some predefined value from register $r1$. Then, it raises a flag by setting the variable x to 1. Another thread executes the method **recv** which waits until the flag is set and then, it reads y (and stores the value to register $r2$). This program is robust, TSO doesn't enable new behaviors although the writes may be delayed. For instance, consider the following TSO execution (we assume that $r1 = 42$):

$$(t_1, isu) \qquad\qquad (t_1, isu)(t_1, com, y, 42) \qquad\qquad (t_1, com, x, 1)$$
$$\quad (t_2, rd, x, 0) \qquad\qquad\qquad (t_2, rd, x, 0) \qquad\qquad\qquad (t_2, rd, x, 1)(t_2, rd, y, 42)$$

The actions of each thread (t_1 or t_2) are aligned horizontally, they are either *issue* actions (isu) for writes being inserted into the local buffer (e.g., the first (t_1, isu) represents the write of y being inserted to the buffer), *commit* actions (com) for writes being flushed to the main memory (e.g., $(t_1, com, y, 42)$ represents the write $y := 42$ being flushed and executed on the shared memory), and *read* actions for reading values of shared variables. Every assignment generates two actions, an issue and a commit. The issue action is "local", it doesn't enable or disable actions of other threads.

The above execution can be "mimicked" by an SC execution. If we had not performed the isu actions of t_1 that early but delayed them until just before their corresponding com actions, we would obtain a valid SC execution of the same program with no need to use store buffers:

$$(t_1, wr, y, 42) \qquad\qquad (t_1, wr, x, 1)$$
$$(t_2, rd, x, 0) \qquad\qquad (t_2, rd, x, 0) \qquad\qquad (t_2, rd, x, 1)(t_2, rd, y, 42)$$

Above, consecutive *isu* and *com* actions are combined into a single *write* action (*wr*). This intuition corresponds to an equivalence relation between TSO executions and SC executions: if both executions contain the same actions on the shared variables (performing the same accesses on the same variables with the same values) and the order of actions on the same variable are the same for both executions, we say that these executions have the same *trace* [20], or that they are *trace-equivalent*. For instance, both the SC and TSO executions given above have the same trace given in Fig. 1. The notion of trace is used to formalize robustness for programs running under TSO [7]: a program is called *robust* when every TSO execution has the same trace as an SC execution.

Our method for showing robustness is based on proving that every TSO execution can be permuted to a trace-equivalent SC execution (where issue actions are immediately followed by the corresponding commit actions). We say that an action α moves right until another action β in an execution if we can swap α with every later action until β while preserving the feasibility of the execution (e.g., not invalidating reads and keeping the actions enabled). We observe that if α moves right until β then the execution obtained by moving α just before β has the same trace with the initial execution. We also have the dual notion of moves-left with a similar property. As a corollary, if every issue action moves right until the corresponding commit action or every commit action moves left until the corresponding issue action, we can find an equivalent SC execution. For our execution above, the issue actions of the first thread move right until their corresponding *com* actions. Note that there is a commit action which doesn't move left: moving $(t_1, com, x, 1)$ to the left of $(t_2, rd, x, 0)$ is not possible since it would disable this read.

In general, issue actions and other thread local actions (e.g. statements using local registers only) move right of other threads' actions. Moreover, issue actions (t, isu) move right of commit actions of the same thread that correspond to writes issued before (t, isu). For the message passing program, the issue actions move right until their corresponding commits in all TSO executions since commits cannot be delayed beyond actions of the same thread (for instance reads). Hence, we can safely deduce that the message passing program is robust. However, this reasoning may fail when an assignment is followed by a read of a shared variable in the same thread.

```
procedure foo(){
    x := 1;
    r1 := z;
    fence
    r2 := y;
}
```
```
procedure bar(){
    y := 1;
    fence
    r3:= x;
}
```

Fig. 2. An example store buffering program.

Consider the "store-buffering" like program in Fig. 2. This program is also robust. However, the issue action generated by x := 1 might not always move right until the corresponding commit. Consider the following execution (we assume that initially, $z = 5$):

$$(t_1, isu) \qquad\qquad (t_1, rd, z, 5) \qquad\qquad\qquad\qquad\qquad (t_1, com, x, 1) \ldots$$
$$\qquad (t_2, isu) \qquad\qquad\qquad (t_2, com, y, 1)(t_2, \tau)(t_2, rd, x, 0) \qquad\qquad \ldots$$

Here, we assumed that t_1 executes foo and t_2 executes bar. The fence instruction generates an action τ. The first issue action of t_1 cannot be moved to the right until the corresponding commit action since this would violate the program order. Moreover, the corresponding commit action does not move left due to the read action of t_2 on x (which would become infeasible).

The key point here is that a later read action by the same thread, $(t_1, rd, z, 5)$, doesn't allow to move the issue action to the right (until the commit). However, this read action moves to the right of other threads actions. So, we can construct an equivalent SC execution by first moving the read action right after the commit $(t_1, com, x, 1)$ and then move the issue action right until the commit action.

In general, we say that an issue (t, isu) of a thread t moves right until the corresponding commit if each read action of t after (t, isu) can move right until the next action of t that follows both the read and the commit. Actually, this property is not required for all such reads. The read actions that follow a fence cannot happen between the issue and the corresponding commit actions. For instance, the last read action of foo cannot happen between the first issue of foo and its corresponding commit action. Such reads that follow a fence are not required to move right. In addition, we can omit the right-moves check for read actions that read from the thread local buffer (see Sect. 3 for more details).

In brief, our method for checking robustness does the following for every write instruction (assignment to a shared variable): either the commit action of this write moves left or the actions of later read instructions that come before a fence move right in all executions. This semantic condition can be checked using the concept of movers [17] as follows: every write instruction is either a left-mover or all the read instructions that come before a fence and can be executed later than the write (in an SC execution) are right-movers. Note that this requires no modeling and verification of TSO executions.

For non-robust programs that might reach different configurations under TSO than under SC, we define an abstraction mechanism that replaces read instructions with "non-deterministic" reads that can read more values than the original instructions. The abstracted program has more behaviors than the original one (under both SC and TSO), but it may turn to be robust. When it is robust, we get that any property of its SC semantics holds also for the TSO semantics of the original program.

Consider the work stealing queue implementation in Fig. 3. A queue is represented with an array items. Its head and tail indices are stored in the shared variables H and T, respectively. There are three procedures that can operate on this queue: any number of threads may execute the steal method and remove an element from the head of the queue, and a single unique thread may execute put or take methods nondeterministically. The put method inserts an element at the tail index and the take method removes an element from the tail index.

```
                                    procedure put(var elt){
                                       local t;
                                       t := T;
                                       items[t] := elt;
                                       T := t+1;
                                    }
      var H,T,items;

      procedure steal(){            procedure take(){
         local h,t,res;                local h,t,res;
      L1:h := H;                     L1:t := T;
         t := T;                        T := t-1;
         if(h ≥ t)                      h := H;     //havoc(h, h ≤ H);
            return -1;                  if( t < h ){
         res := items[h];                  T := h;
         if( cas(H,h,h+1) )               return -1;
            return res;                 }
         else                           res := items[t];
            goto L1;                    if( t > h )
      }                                    return res;
                                       T := h+1;
                                       if( cas(H,h,h+1) )
                                          return task;
                                       else
                                          goto L1;
                                    }
```

Fig. 3. Work stealing queue.

This program is not robust. If there is a single element in the queue and the take method takes it by delaying its writes after some concurrent steals, one of the concurrent steals might also remove this last element. Popping the same element twice is not possible under SC, but it is possible under TSO semantics. However, we can still prove some properties of this program under TSO. Our robustness check fails on this program because the writes of the worker thread (executing the put and take methods) are not left movers and the read from the variable H in the take method is not a right mover. This read is not a right mover w.r.t. successful CAS actions of the steal procedure that increment H.

We apply an abstraction on the instruction of the take method that reads from H such that instead of reading the exact value of H, it can read any value less than or equal to the value of H. We write this instruction as havoc(h, h ≤ H) (it assigns to h a nondeterministic value satisfying the constraint h ≤ H). Note that this abstraction is sound in the sense that it reaches more states under SC/TSO than the original program.

The resulting program is robust. The statement havoc(h, h ≤ H) is a right mover w.r.t. successful CAS actions of the stealer threads. Hence, for all the write instructions, the reachable read instructions become right movers and our check succeeds. The abstract program satisfies the specification of an idempotent work stealing queue (elements can be dequeued multiple times) which implies that the original program satisfies this specification as well.

3   TSO Robustness

We present the syntax and the semantics of a simple programming language used to state our results. We define both the TSO and the SC semantics, an

$$\langle prog \rangle ::= \text{program } \langle pid \rangle \text{ vars } \langle var \rangle^* \ \langle thread \rangle^*$$

$$\langle thread \rangle ::= \text{thread } \langle tid \rangle \text{ regs } \langle reg \rangle^* \text{ init } \langle label \rangle \text{ begin } \langle linst \rangle^* \text{ end}$$

$$\langle linst \rangle ::= \langle label \rangle : \langle inst \rangle ; \text{ goto } \langle label \rangle ;$$

$$\langle inst \rangle ::= \langle var \rangle := \langle expr \rangle$$
$$\mid \ \langle reg \rangle := \langle expr \rangle$$
$$\mid \ \langle reg \rangle := \langle var \rangle$$
$$\mid \ \text{fence}$$
$$\mid \ \langle reg \rangle := \text{cas}(\langle var \rangle, \langle expr \rangle, \langle expr \rangle)$$
$$\mid \ \text{skip}$$
$$\mid \ \text{assume } \langle bexpr \rangle$$

Fig. 4. Syntax of the programs. The star (*) indicates zero or more occurrences of the preceding element. $\langle pid \rangle$, $\langle tid \rangle$, $\langle var \rangle$, $\langle reg \rangle$ and $\langle label \rangle$ are elements of their given domains representing the program identifiers, thread identifiers, shared variables, registers and instruction labels, respectively. $\langle expr \rangle$ is an arithmetic expression over $\langle reg \rangle^*$. Similarly, $\langle bexpr \rangle$ is a boolean expression over $\langle reg \rangle^*$.

abstraction of executions called *trace* [20] that intuitively, captures the happens-before relation between actions in an execution, and the notion of robustness.

Syntax. We consider a simple programming language which is defined in Fig. 4. Each program $\mathcal{P}$ has a finite number of shared variables $\overrightarrow{x}$ and a finite number of threads $(\overrightarrow{t})$. Also, each thread t_i has a finite set of local registers $(\overrightarrow{r_i})$ and a start label l_i^0. Bodies of the threads are defined as finite sequences of labelled instructions. Each instruction is followed by a goto statement which defines the evolution of the program counter. Note that multiple instructions can be assigned to the same label which allows us to write non-deterministic programs and multiple goto statements can direct the control to the same label which allows us to mimic imperative constructs like loops and conditionals. An assignment to a shared variable $\langle var \rangle := \langle expr \rangle$ is called a *write instruction*. Also, an instruction of the form $\langle reg \rangle := \langle var \rangle$ is called a *read instruction*.

Instructions can read from or write to shared variables or registers. Each instruction accesses at most one shared variable. We assume that the program $\mathcal{P}$ comes with a domain $\mathcal{D}$ of values that are stored in variables and registers, and a set of functions $\mathcal{F}$ used to calculate arithmetic and boolean expressions.

The fence statement empties the buffer of the executing thread. The cas (compare-and-swap) instruction checks whether the value of its input variable is equal to its second argument. If so, it writes sets third argument as the value of the variable and returns *true*. Otherwise, it returns *false*. In either case, cas empties the buffer immediately after it executes. The assume statement allows us to check conditions. If the boolean expression it contains holds at that state, it behaves like a skip. Otherwise, the execution blocks. Formal description of the instructions are given in Fig. 5.

$$\frac{x := ae(\overrightarrow{r_t}) \in ins(pc(t)) \quad v = eval(ae(\overrightarrow{r_t})) \quad x \in \overrightarrow{x}}{(pc, mem, buf) \xrightarrow{(t,isu)}_{TSO} (pc', mem, buf[t \to buf(t) \circ \langle (x,v) \rangle)])}$$

$$\frac{buf(t) = \langle (x,v) \rangle \circ buf' \quad x \in \overrightarrow{x}}{(pc, mem, buf) \xrightarrow{(t,com,x,v)}_{TSO} (pc, mem, buf[t \to buf'])}$$

$$\frac{r := ae(\overrightarrow{r_t}) \in ins(pc(t)) \quad v = eval(ae(\overrightarrow{r_t})) \quad r \in \overrightarrow{r_t}}{(pc, mem, buf) \xrightarrow{(t,\tau)}_{TSO} (pc', mem[r \to v], buf)}$$

$$\frac{r := x \in ins(pc(t)) \quad x \in \overrightarrow{x} \quad v = mem(x) \quad x \notin varsOfBuf(buf(t)) \quad r \in \overrightarrow{r_t}}{(pc, mem, buf) \xrightarrow{(t,rd,x,v)}_{TSO} (pc', mem[r \to v], buf)}$$

$$\frac{r := x \in ins(pc(t)) \quad x \in \overrightarrow{x} \quad buf = \alpha \circ \langle (x,v) \rangle \circ \beta \quad x \notin varsOfBuf(\beta) \quad r \in \overrightarrow{r_t}}{(pc, mem, buf) \xrightarrow{(t,rd,x,v)}_{TSO} (pc', mem[r \to v], buf)}$$

$$\frac{\mathbf{fence} \in ins(pc(t)) \quad buf(t) = \epsilon}{(pc, mem, buf) \xrightarrow{(t,\tau)}_{TSO} (pc', mem, buf)}$$

$$\frac{r := cas(x, ae_1(\overrightarrow{r_t}), ae_2(\overrightarrow{r_t})) \in ins(pc(t)) \quad mem(x) = eval(ae_1(\overrightarrow{r_t})) \quad buf(t) = \epsilon \quad v = eval(ae_2(\overrightarrow{r_t}))}{(pc, mem, buf) \xrightarrow{(t,isu)(t,com,x,v)}_{TSO} (pc', mem[r \to 1][x \to v], buf)}$$

$$\frac{r := cas(x, ae_1(\overrightarrow{r_t}), ae_2(\overrightarrow{r_t})) \in ins(pc(t)) \quad mem(x) \neq eval(ae_1(\overrightarrow{r_t})) \quad buf(t) = \epsilon \quad v = mem(x)}{(pc, mem, buf) \xrightarrow{(t,rd,x,v)}_{TSO} (pc', mem[r \to 0], buf)}$$

$$\frac{\mathbf{assume}\ be(\overrightarrow{r_t}) \in ins(pc(t)) \quad eval(be(\overrightarrow{r_t})) = \top}{(pc, mem, buf) \xrightarrow{(t,\tau)}_{TSO} (pc', mem, buf)}$$

Fig. 5. The TSO transition relation. The function ins takes a label l and returns the set of instructions labelled by l. We always assume that $x \in \overrightarrow{x}$, $r \in \overrightarrow{r_t}$ and $pc' = pc[t \to l']$ where $pc(t) : inst\ goto\ l'$; is a labelled instruction of t and $inst$ is the instruction described at the beginning of the rule. The evaluation function $eval$ calculates the value of an arithmetic or boolean expression based on mem (ae stands for arithmetic expression). Sequence concatenation is denoted by $\circ$. The function $varsOfBuf$ takes a sequence of pairs and returns the set consisting of the first fields of these pairs.

TSO Semantics. Under the TSO memory model, each thread maintains a local queue to buffer write instructions. A state s of the program is a triple of the form (pc, mem, buf). Let $\mathcal{L}$ be the set of available labels in the program $\mathcal{P}$. Then, $pc : \overrightarrow{t} \to \mathcal{L}$ shows the next instruction to be executed for each thread, $mem : \bigcup_{t_i \in \overrightarrow{t}} \overrightarrow{r_i} \cup \overrightarrow{x} \to \mathcal{D}$ represents the current values in shared variables and registers and $buf : \overrightarrow{t} \to (\overrightarrow{x} \times \mathcal{D})^*$ represents the contents of the buffers.

There is a special initial state $s_0 = (pc_0, mem_0, buf_0)$. At the beginning, each thread t_i points to its initial label l_i^0 i.e., $pc_0(t_i) = l_i^0$. We assume that there is a special default value $0 \in \mathcal{D}$. All the shared variables and registers are initiated as 0 i.e., $mem_0(x) = 0$ for all $x \in \bigcup_{t_i \in \overrightarrow{t}} \overrightarrow{r_i} \cup \overrightarrow{x}$. Lastly, all the buffers are initially empty i.e., $buf_0(t_i) = \epsilon$ for all $t_i \in \overrightarrow{t}$.

The transition relation $\rightarrow_{TSO}$ between program states is defined in Fig. 5. Transitions are labelled by actions. Each action is an element from $\overrightarrow{t} \times (\{\tau, isu\} \cup (\{com, rd\} \times \overrightarrow{x} \times \mathcal{D}))$. Actions keep the information about the thread performing the transition and the actual parameters of the reads and the writes to shared variables. We are only interested in accesses to shared variables, therefore, other transitions are labelled with τ as thread local actions.

A TSO execution of a program $\mathcal{P}$ is a sequence of actions $\pi = \pi_1, \pi_2, \ldots, \pi_n$ such that there exists a sequence of states $\sigma = \sigma_0, \sigma_1, \ldots, \sigma_n$, $\sigma_0 = s_0$ is the initial state of $\mathcal{P}$ and $\sigma_{i-1} \xrightarrow{\pi_i} \sigma_i$ is a valid transition for any $i \in \{1, \ldots, n\}$. We assume that buffers are empty at the end of the execution.

SC Semantics. Under SC, a program state is a pair of the form (pc, mem) where pc and mem are defined as above. Shared variables are read directly from the memory mem and every write updates directly the memory mem. To make the relationship between SC and TSO executions more obvious, every write instruction generates isu and com actions which follow one another in the execution (each isu is immediately followed by the corresponding com). Since there are no write buffers, fence instructions have no effect under SC.

Traces and TSO Robustness. Consider a (TSO or SC) execution π of $\mathcal{P}$. The trace of π is a graph, denoted by $Tr(\pi)$: Nodes of $Tr(\pi)$ are actions of π except the τ actions. In addition, isu and com actions are unified in a single node. The isu action that puts an element into the buffer and the corresponding com action that drains that element from the buffer correspond to the same node in the trace. Edges of $Tr(\pi)$ represent the happens before order (hb) between these actions. The hb is union of four relations. The program order po keeps the order of actions performed by the same thread excluding the com actions. The store order so keeps the order of com actions on the same variable that write different values[1]. The read-from relation, denoted by rf, relates a com action to a rd action that reads its value. Lastly, the from-reads relation fr relates a rd action to a com action that overwrites the value read by rd; it is defined as the composition of rf and so.

We say that the program $\mathcal{P}$ is TSO robust if for any TSO execution π of $\mathcal{P}$, there exists an SC execution π' such that $Tr(\pi) = Tr(\pi')$. It has been proven that robustness implies that the program reaches the same valuations of the shared memory under both TSO and SC [7].

4   A Reduction Theory for Checking Robustness

We present a methodology for checking robustness which builds on concepts introduced in Lipton's reduction theory [17]. This theory allows to rewrite a

---

[1] Our definition of store order deviates slightly from the standard definition which relates any two writes writing on the same variable, independently of values. The notion of TSO trace robustness induced by this change is slightly weaker than the original definition, but still implies preservation of any safety property from the SC semantics to the TSO semantics. The results concerning TSO robustness used in this paper (Lemma 1) are also not affected by this change. See [8] for more details.

given concurrent program (running under SC) into an equivalent one that has larger atomic blocks. Proving robustness is similar in spirit in the sense that one has to prove that issue and commit actions can happen together atomically. However, differently from the original theory, these actions do not correspond to different statements in the program (they are generated by the same write instruction). Nevertheless, we show that the concepts of left/right movers can be also used to prove robustness.

Movers. Let $\pi = \pi_1, \ldots, \pi_n$ be an SC execution. We say that the action π_i *moves right (resp., left)* in π if the sequence $\pi_1, \ldots, \pi_{i-1}, \pi_{i+1}, \pi_i, \pi_{i+2}, \ldots, \pi_n$ (resp., $\pi_1, \ldots, \pi_{i-2}, \pi_i, \pi_{i-1}, \pi_{i+1} \ldots, \pi_n$) is also a valid execution of $\mathcal{P}$, the thread of π_i is different than the thread of π_{i+1} (resp., π_{i-1}), and both executions reach to the same end state σ_n. Since every issue action is followed immediately by the corresponding commit action, an issue action moves right, resp., left, when the commit action also moves right, resp., left, and vice-versa.

Let instOf_π be a function, depending on an execution π, which given an action $\pi_i \in \pi$, gives the labelled instruction that generated π_i. Then, a labelled instruction ℓ is a *right (resp., left) mover* if for all SC executions π of $\mathcal{P}$ and for all actions π_i of π such that $\mathsf{instOf}(\pi_i) = \ell$, π_i moves right (resp., left) in π.

A labelled instruction is a *non-mover* if it is neither left nor right mover, and it is a *both mover* if it is both left and right mover.

Reachability Between Instructions. An instruction ℓ' is *reachable from* the instruction ℓ if ℓ and ℓ' both belong to the same thread and there exists an SC execution π and indices $1 \leq i < j \leq |\pi|$ such that $\mathsf{instOf}_\pi(\pi_i) = \ell$ and $\mathsf{instOf}_\pi(\pi_j) = \ell'$. We say that ℓ' is reachable from ℓ *before a fence* if π_k is not an action generated by a `fence` instruction in the same thread as ℓ, for all $i < k < j$. When ℓ is a write instruction and ℓ' a read instruction, we say that ℓ' is *buffer-free* reachable from ℓ if π_k is not an action generated by a `fence` instruction in the same thread as ℓ or a write action on the same variable that ℓ' reads-from, for all $i < k < j$.

Definition 1. *We say that a write instruction ℓ_w is atomic if it is a left mover or every read instruction ℓ_r buffer-free reachable from ℓ_w is a right mover. We say that $\mathcal{P}$ is write atomic if every write instruction ℓ_w in $\mathcal{P}$ is atomic.*

Note that all of the notions used to define write atomicity (movers and instruction reachability) are based on SC executions of the programs. The following result shows that write atomicity implies robustness.

Theorem 1 (Soundness). *If $\mathcal{P}$ is write atomic, then it is robust.*

We will prove the contrapositive of the statement. For the proof, we need the notion of minimal violation defined in [7]. A minimal violation is a TSO execution in which the sum of the number of same thread actions between isu and corresponding com actions for all writes is minimal. A minimal violation is of the form $\pi = \pi_1, (t, isu), \pi_2, (t, rd, y, *), \pi_3, (t, com, x, *), \pi_4$ such that π_1 is an SC execution, only t can delay com actions, the first delayed action is the $(t, com, x, *)$ action after π_3 and it corresponds to (t, isu) after π_1, π_2 does not contain any com or $fence$ actions by t (writes of t are delayed until after $(t, rd, y, *))$, $(t, rd, y, *) \rightarrow_{hb+} act$ for all $act \in \pi_3 \circ \{(t, com, x, *)\}$ (isu and com actions of other threads are counted as one action for this case), π_3 doesn't contain any action of t, π_4 contains only and all of the com actions of t that are delayed in $(t, isu) \circ \pi_2$ and no com action in $(t, com, x, *) \circ \pi_4$ touches y.

Minimal violations are important for us because of the following property:

Lemma 1 (Completeness of Minimal Violations [7]). *The program $\mathcal{P}$ is robust iff it does not have a minimal violation.*

Before going into the proof of Theorem 1, we define some notations. Let π be a sequence representing an execution or a fragment of it. Let Q be a set of thread identifiers. Then, $\pi|_Q$ is the projection of π on actions from the threads in Q. Similarly, $\pi|_n$ is the projection of π on first n elements for some number n. $sz(\pi)$ gives the length of the sequence π. We also define a product operator $\otimes$. Let π and ρ be some execution fragments. Then, $\pi \otimes \rho$ is same as π except that if the ith isu action of π is not immediately followed by a com action by the same thread, then i^{th} com action of ρ is inserted after this isu. The product operator helps us to fill unfinished writes in one execution fragment by inserting commit actions from another fragment immediately after the issue actions.

Proof (Theorem 1). Assume $\mathcal{P}$ is not robust. Then, there exists a minimal violation $\pi = \pi_1, \alpha, \pi_2, \theta, \pi_3, \beta, \pi_4$ satisfying the conditions described before, where $\alpha = (t, isu)$, $\theta = (t, rd, y, *)$ and $\beta = (t, com, x, *)$. Below, we show that the write instruction $w = \mathsf{instOf}(\alpha)$ is not atomic.

1. w is not a left mover.
   1.1. $\rho = \pi_1, \pi_2|_{\overrightarrow{t} \setminus \{t\}}, \pi_3|_{\overrightarrow{t} \setminus \{t\}}|_{sz(\pi_3|_{\overrightarrow{t} \setminus \{t\}})-1}, \gamma, (\alpha, \beta)$ is an SC execution of $\mathcal{P}$ where γ is the last action of π_3. γ is a read or write action on x performed by a thread t' other than t and value of γ is different from what is written by β.
      1.1.1. ρ is an SC execution because t never changes value of a shared variable in π_2 and π_3. So, even we remove actions of t in those parts, actions of other threads are still enabled. Since other threads perform only SC operations in π, $\pi_1, \pi_2|_{\overrightarrow{t} \setminus \{t\}}, \pi_3|_{\overrightarrow{t} \setminus \{t\}}$ is an SC execution. From π, we also know that the first enabled action of t is α if we delay the actions of t in π_2 and π_3.
      1.1.2. The last action of π_3 is γ. By definition of a minimal violation, we know that $\theta \rightarrow_{hb+} \alpha$ and π_3 does not contain any action of t. So, there must exist an action $\gamma \in \pi_3$ such that either γ reads from x and $\gamma \rightarrow_{fr} \beta$ in π or γ writes to x and $\gamma \rightarrow_{st} \beta$ in π. Moreover, γ is the last action of π_3 because if there are other actions after γ, we can delete them and can obtain another minimal violation which is shorter than π and hence contradict the minimality of π.
   1.2. $\rho' = \pi_1, \pi_2|_{\overrightarrow{t} \setminus \{t\}}, \pi_3|_{\overrightarrow{t} \setminus \{t\}}|_{sz(\pi_3|_{\overrightarrow{t} \setminus \{t\}})-1}, (\alpha, \beta), \gamma$ is an SC execution with a different end state than ρ defined in 1.1 has or it is not an SC execution, where $\mathsf{instOf}(\gamma') = \mathsf{instOf}(\gamma)$.

1.2.1. In the last state of ρ, x has the value written by β. If γ is a write action on x, then x has a different value at the end of ρ' due to the definition of a minimal violation. If γ is a read action on x, then it does not read the value written by β in ρ. However, γ reads this value in ρ'. Hence, ρ' is not a valid SC execution.

2. There exists a read instruction r buffer-free reachable from w such that r is not a right mover. We will consider two cases: Either there exists a rd action of t on variable z in π_2 such that there is a later write action by another thread t' on z in π_2 that writes a different value or not. Moreover, z is not a variable that is touched by the delayed commits in π_4 i.e., it does not read its value from the buffer.

  2.1. We first evaluate the negation of above condition. Assume that for all actions γ and γ' such that γ occurs before γ' in π_2, either $\gamma \neq (t, rd, z, v_z)$ or $\gamma' \neq (t', isu)(t', com, z, v_z')$. Then, $r = \mathsf{instOf}(\theta)$ is not a right mover and it is buffer-free reachable from w.

    2.1.1. $\rho = \pi_1, \pi_2|_{\overrightarrow{t}\setminus\{t\}}, \pi_2|_{\{t\}} \otimes \pi_4, \theta, \theta'$ is a valid SC execution of $\mathcal{P}$ where $\theta' = (t', isu)(t', com, y, *)$ for some $t \neq t'$.

      2.1.1.1. ρ is an SC execution. $\pi_1, \pi_2|_{\overrightarrow{t}\setminus\{t\}}$ is a valid SC execution since t does not update value of a shared variable in π_2. Moreover, all of the actions of t become enabled after this sequence since t never reads value of a variable updated by another thread in π_2. Lastly, the first action of π_3 is enabled after this sequence.

      2.1.1.2. The first action of π_3 is $\theta' = (t', isu)(t', com, y, *)$. Let θ' be the first action of π_3. Since $\theta \rightarrow_{hb} \theta'$ in π and θ' is not an action of t by definition of minimal violation, the only case we have is $\theta \rightarrow_{fr} \theta'$. Hence, θ' is a write action on y that writes a different value than θ reads.

      2.1.1.3. r is buffer-free reachable from w. ρ is a SC execution, first action of ρ after $\pi_1, \pi_2|_{\overrightarrow{t}\setminus\{t\}}$ is α, β; $w = \mathsf{instOf}((\alpha, \beta))$, $r = \mathsf{instOf}(\theta)$ and actions of t in ρ between α, β and θ are not instances of a fence instruction or write to y.

    2.1.2. $\rho' = \pi_1, \pi_2|_{\overrightarrow{t}\setminus\{t\}}, \pi_2|_{\{t\}} \otimes \pi_4, \theta', \theta$ is not a valid SC execution.

      2.1.2.1. In the last state of ρ, the value of y seen by t is the value read in θ. It is different than the value written by θ'. However, at the last state of ρ', the value of y t sees must be the value θ' writes. Hence, ρ' is not a valid SC execution.

  2.2. Assume that there exists $\gamma = (t, rd, z, v_z)$ and $\gamma' = (t', isu)(t', com, z, v_z')$ in π_2. Then, $r = \mathsf{instOf}(\gamma)$ is not a right mover and r is buffer-free reachable from w.

    2.2.1. Let $\imath$ be the index of γ and j be the index of γ' in π_2. Then, define $\rho = \pi_1, \pi_2|_{j-1}|_{\overrightarrow{t}\setminus\{t\}}, \pi_2|_i|_{\{t\}} \otimes \pi_4, \gamma'$. ρ is an SC execution of $\mathcal{P}$.

      2.2.1.1. ρ is an SC execution. $\pi_1, \pi_2|_{j-1}|_{\overrightarrow{t}\setminus\{t\}}$ prefix is a valid SC execution because t does not update any shared variable in π_2. Moreover, all of the actions of t in $\pi_2|_i|_{\{t\}} \otimes \pi_4$ become enabled after this sequence since t never reads a value of a variable updated by another thread in π_2 and γ' is the next enabled in π_2 after this sequence since it is a write action.

2.2.2. Let i and j be indices of γ and γ' in π_2 respectively. Define $\rho' = \pi_1, \pi_2|_{j-1}|_{\overrightarrow{t}\backslash\{t\}}, \pi_2|_{i-1}|_{\{t\}} \otimes \pi_4, \gamma', \gamma$. Then, ρ' is not a valid SC execution.

   2.2.2.1. In the last state of ρ, value of z seen by t is v_z. It is different than the v'_z, value written by γ'. However, in the last state of ρ', the value of z t sees must be v'_z. Hence, ρ' is not a valid SC execution.

2.2.3. r is buffer-free reachable from w because ρ defined in 2.2.1 is an SC execution, first action after $\pi_1, \pi_2|_{j-1}|_{\overrightarrow{t}\backslash\{t\}}$ is α, β, $w = \mathsf{instOf}((\alpha, \beta))$, $r = \mathsf{instOf}(\gamma)$ and actions of t in ρ between α, β and θ are not instances of a fence instruction or a write to z by t.

5   Abstractions and Verifying Non-robust Programs

In this section, we introduce program abstractions which are useful for verifying non-robust TSO programs (or even robust programs – see an example at the end of this section). In general, a program $\mathcal{P}'$ abstracts another program $\mathcal{P}$ for some semantic model $\mathbb{M} \in \{\mathrm{SC}, \mathrm{TSO}\}$ if every shared variable valuation σ reachable from the initial state in an $\mathbb{M}$ execution of $\mathcal{P}$ is also reachable in an $\mathbb{M}$ execution of $\mathcal{P}'$. We denote this abstraction relation as $\mathcal{P} \preceq_{\mathbb{M}} \mathcal{P}'$.

In particular, we are interested in *read instruction abstractions*, which replace instructions that read from a shared variable with more "liberal" read instructions that can read more values (this way, the program may reach more shared variable valuations). We extend the program syntax in Sect. 3 with havoc instructions of the form $\mathtt{havoc}(\langle reg \rangle, \langle varbexpr \rangle)$, where $\langle varbexpr \rangle$ is a boolean expression over a set of registers and a single shared variable $\langle var \rangle$. The meaning of this instruction is that the register reg is assigned with any value that satisfies $varbexpr$ (where the other registers and the variable var are interpreted with their current values). The program abstraction we consider will replace read instructions of the form $\langle reg \rangle := \langle var \rangle$ with havoc instructions $\mathtt{havoc}(\langle reg \rangle, \langle varbexpr \rangle)$.

While replacing read instructions with havoc instructions, we must guarantee that the new program reaches at least the same set of shared variable valuations after executing the havoc as the original program after the read. Hence, we allow such a rewriting only when the boolean expression $varbexpr$ is weaker (in a logical sense) than the equality $reg = var$ (hence, there exists an execution of the havoc instruction where $reg = var$).

Lemma 2. *Let $\mathcal{P}$ be a program and $\mathcal{P}'$ be obtained from $\mathcal{P}$ by replacing an instruction $l_1 : x := r; \textbf{goto } l_2$ of a thread t with $l_1 : \boldsymbol{havoc}(r, \phi(x, \overrightarrow{r})); \textbf{goto } l_2$ such that $\forall x, r.\ x = r \implies \phi(x, \overrightarrow{r})$ is valid. Then, $\mathcal{P} \preceq_{SC} \mathcal{P}'$ and $\mathcal{P} \preceq_{TSO} \mathcal{P}'$.*

The notion of trace extends to programs that contain havoc instructions as follows. Assume that $(t, hvc, x, \phi(x))$ is the action generated by an instruction $\mathtt{havoc}(r, \phi(x, \overrightarrow{r}))$, where x is a shared variable and $\overrightarrow{r}$ a set of registers (the

```
                                      procedure bar(){
                                        do{
        procedure foo(){                   r1 = x;
          x := 1;                          //havoc(r1,(x ≠ 0)?r1 = x ∨ r1 = 0 : r1 = 0)
          r2 := y;                       }while(r1 == 0);
        }                                y := 1;

                                      }
```

Fig. 6. An example program that needs a read abstraction to pass our robustness checks. The **havoc** statement in comments reads as follows: if value of x is not 0 then $r1$ gets either the value of x or 0. Otherwise, it is 0.

action stores the constraint ϕ where the values of the registers are instantiated with their current values – the shared variable x is the only free variable in $\phi(x)$). Roughly, the hvc actions are special cases of rd actions. Consider an execution π where an action $\alpha = (t, hvc, x, \phi(x))$ is generated by reading the value of a write action $\beta = (com, x, v)$ (i.e., the value v was the current value of x when the havoc instruction was executed). Then, the trace of π contains a read-from edge $\beta \rightarrow_{rf} \alpha$ as for regular read actions. However, fr edges are created differently. If α was a rd action we would say that we have $\alpha \rightarrow_{fr} \gamma$ if $\beta \rightarrow_{rf} \alpha$ and $\beta \rightarrow_{st} \gamma$. For the havoc case, the situation is a little bit different. Let $\gamma = (com, x, v')$ be an action. We have $\alpha \rightarrow_{fr} \gamma$ if and only if either $\beta \rightarrow_{rf} \alpha$, $\beta \rightarrow_{st} \gamma$ and $\phi(v')$ is false or $\alpha \rightarrow_{fr} \gamma'$ and $\gamma' \rightarrow_{st} \gamma$ where γ' is an action. Intuitively, there is a from-read dependency from an havoc action to a commit action, only when the commit action invalidates the constraint $\phi(x)$ of the havoc (or if it follows such a commit in store order).

The notion of write-atomicity (Definition 1) extends to programs with havoc instructions by interpreting havoc instructions $\mathtt{havoc}(r, \phi(x, \overrightarrow{r}))$ as regular read instructions $r := x$. Theorem 1 which states that write-atomicity implies robustness can also be easily extended to this case.

Read abstractions are useful in two ways. First, they allow us to prove properties of non-robust program as the work stealing queue example in Fig. 3. We can apply appropriate read abstractions to relax the original program so that it becomes robust in the end. Then, we can use SC reasoning tools on the robust program to prove invariants of the program.

Second, read abstractions could be helpful for proving robustness directly. The method based on write-atomicity we propose for verifying robustness is sound but not complete. Some incompleteness scenarios can be avoided using read abstractions. If we can abstract read instructions such that the new program reaches exactly the same states (in terms of shared variables) as the original one, it may help to avoid executions that violate mover checks.

Consider the program in Fig. 6. The write statement x := 1 in procedure foo is not atomic. It is not a left mover due to the read of x in the do-while loop of bar. Moreover, the later read from y is buffer-free reachable from this write and it is not a right mover because of the write to y in bar. To make it atomic, we apply read abstraction to the read instruction of bar that reads from x. In the new relaxed read, $r1$ can read 0 along with the value of x when x is not zero as shown in the comments below the instruction. With this abstraction, the write to x becomes a left mover because reads from x after the write can now read the old value which was 0. Thus, the program becomes write-atomic. If we think of TSO traces of the abstract program and replace hvc nodes with rd nodes, we get exactly the TSO traces of the original program. However, the abstraction adds more SC traces to the program and the program becomes robust.

6   Experimental Evaluation

To test the practical value of our method, we have considered the benchmark for checking TSO robustness described in [2], which consists of 34 programs. This benchmark is quite exhaustive, it includes examples introduced in previous works on this subject. Many of the programs in this benchmark are easy to prove being write-atomic. Every write is followed by no buffer-free read instruction which makes them trivially atomic (like the message passing program in Fig. 1). This holds for 20 out of the 34 programs. Out of the remaining programs, 13 required mover checks and 4 required read abstractions to show robustness (our method didn't succeed on one of the programs in the benchmark, explained at the end of this section). Except Chase-Lev, the initial versions of all the 12 examples are trace robust[2]. Besides Chase-Lev, read-abstractions are equivalent to the original programs in terms of reachable shared variable configurations. Detailed information for these examples can be found in Table 1.

To check whether writes/reads are left/right movers and the soundness of abstractions, we have used the tool CIVL [13]. This tool allows to prove assertions about concurrent programs (Owicki-Gries annotations) and also to check whether an instruction is a left/right mover. The buffer-free read instructions reachable from a write before a fence were obtained using a trivial analysis of the control-flow graph (CFG) of the program. This method is a sound approximation of the definition in Sect. 4 but it was sufficient for all the examples.

Our method was not precise enough to prove robustness for only one example, named as nbw-w-lr-rl in [7]. This program contains a method with explicit calls to the lock and unlock methods of a spinlock. The instruction that writes to the lock variable inside the unlock method is not atomic, because of the reads from the lock variable and the calls to the getAndSet primitive inside the lock method. Abstracting the reads from the lock variable is not sufficient in this case due to the conflicts with getAndSet actions. However, we believe that read abstractions could be extended to getAndSet instructions (which both read and write to a shared variable atomically) in order to deal with this example.

---

[2] If we consider the standard notion of *so* (that relates any two writes on the same variable independent of their values), all examples except MCSLock and dc-locking become non trace robust.

Table 1. Benchmark results. The second column (RB) stands for the robustness status of the original program according to our extended *hb* definition. RA column shows the number of read abstractions performed. RM column represents the number of read instructions that are checked to be right movers and the LM column represents the write instructions that are shown to be left movers. PO shows the total number of proof obligations generated and VT stands for the total verification time in seconds.

Name	RB	RA	RM	LM	PO	VT
Chase-Lev	−	1	2	-	149	0.332
FIFO-iWSQ	+	-	2	-	124	0.323
LIFO-iWSQ	+	-	1	-	109	0.305
Anchor-iWSQ	+	-	1	-	109	0.309
MCSLock	+	2	2	-	233	0.499
r+detour	+	-	1	-	53	0.266
r+detours	+	-	1	-	64	0.273
sb+detours+coh	+	-	2	-	108	0.322
sb+detours	+	-	1	1	125	0.316
write+r+coh	+	-	1	-	78	0.289
write+r	+	-	1	-	48	0.261
dc-locking	+	1	4	1	52	0.284
inline_pgsql	+	2	2	-	90	0.286

7 Related Work

The weakest correctness criterion that enables SC reasoning for proving invariants of programs running under TSO is *state-robustness* i.e., the reachable set of states is the same under both SC and TSO. However, this problem has high complexity (non-primitive recursive for programs with a finite number of threads and a finite data domain [6]). Therefore, it is difficult to come up with an efficient and precise solution. A symbolic decision procedure is presented in [1] and over-approximate analyses are proposed in [14,15].

Due to the high complexity of state-robustness, stronger correctness criteria with lower complexity have been proposed. Trace-robustness (that we call simply robustness in our paper) is one of the most studied criteria in the literature. Bouajjani et al. [9] have proved that deciding trace-robustness is PSPACE-complete, resp., EXPSPACE-complete, for a finite, resp., unbounded, number of threads and a finite data domain.

There are various tools for checking trace-robustness. TRENCHER [7] applies to bounded-thread programs with finite data. In theory, the approach in Trencher can be applied to infinite-state programs, but implementing it is not obvious because it requires solving non-trivial reachability queries in such programs. In comparison, our approach (and our implementation based on CIVL) applies to infinite state programs. All our examples consider infinite data domains, while

Chase-Lev, FIFO-iWSQ, LIFO-iWSQ, Anchor-iWSQ, MCSLock, dc-locking and inline_pgsql have an unbounded number of threads. MUSKETEER [4] provides an approximate solution by checking existence of critical cycles on the control-flow graph. While Musketeer can deal with infinite data (since data is abstracted away), it is restricted to bounded-thread programs. Thus, it cannot deal with the unbounded thread examples mentioned above. Furthermore, Musketeer cannot prove robust even some examples with finitely many threads, e.g., nbw_w_wr, write+r, r+detours, sb+detours+coh. Other tools for approximate robustness checking, to which we compare in similar ways, have been proposed in [5,10,11].

Besides trace-robustness, there are other correctness criteria like triangular race freedom (TRF) and persistence that are stronger than state-robustness. Persistence [2] is incomparable to trace-robustness, and TRF [18] is stronger than both trace-robustness and persistence. Our method can verify examples that are state-robust but neither persistent nor TRF.

Reduction and abstraction techniques were used for reasoning on SC programs. QED [12] is a tool that supports statement transformations as a way of abstracting programs combined with a mover analysis. Also, CIVL [13] allows proving location assertions in the context of the Owicki-Gries logic which is enhanced with Lipton's reduction theory [17]. Our work enables the use of such tools for reasoning about the TSO semantics of a program.

References

1. Abdulla, P.A., Atig, M.F., Chen, Y.-F., Leonardsson, C., Rezine, A.: Counter-example guided fence insertion under TSO. In: Flanagan, C., König, B. (eds.) TACAS 2012. LNCS, vol. 7214, pp. 204–219. Springer, Heidelberg (2012). https://doi.org/10.1007/978-3-642-28756-5_15
2. Abdulla, P.A., Atig, M.F., Ngo, T.-P.: The best of both worlds: trading efficiency and optimality in fence insertion for TSO. In: Vitek, J. (ed.) ESOP 2015. LNCS, vol. 9032, pp. 308–332. Springer, Heidelberg (2015). https://doi.org/10.1007/978-3-662-46669-8_13
3. Adve, S.V., Hill, M.D.: A unified formalization of four shared-memory models. IEEE Trans. Parallel Distrib. Syst. 4(6), 613–624 (1993)
4. Alglave, J., Kroening, D., Nimal, V., Poetzl, D.: Don't sit on the fence. In: Biere, A., Bloem, R. (eds.) CAV 2014. LNCS, vol. 8559, pp. 508–524. Springer, Cham (2014). https://doi.org/10.1007/978-3-319-08867-9_33
5. Alglave, J., Maranget, L.: Stability in weak memory models. In: Gopalakrishnan, G., Qadeer, S. (eds.) CAV 2011. LNCS, vol. 6806, pp. 50–66. Springer, Heidelberg (2011). https://doi.org/10.1007/978-3-642-22110-1_6
6. Atig, M.F., Bouajjani, A., Burckhardt, S., Musuvathi, M.: On the verification problem for weak memory models. ACM Sigplan Not. 45(1), 7–18 (2010)
7. Bouajjani, A., Derevenetc, E., Meyer, R.: Checking and enforcing robustness against TSO. In: Felleisen, M., Gardner, P. (eds.) ESOP 2013. LNCS, vol. 7792, pp. 533–553. Springer, Heidelberg (2013). https://doi.org/10.1007/978-3-642-37036-6_29
8. Bouajjani, A., Enea, C., Mutluergil, S.O., Tasiran, S.: Reasoning about TSO programs using reduction and abstraction. CoRR, abs/1804.05196 (2018)

9. Bouajjani, A., Meyer, R., Möhlmann, E.: Deciding robustness against total store ordering. In: Aceto, L., Henzinger, M., Sgall, J. (eds.) ICALP 2011. LNCS, vol. 6756, pp. 428–440. Springer, Heidelberg (2011). https://doi.org/10.1007/978-3-642-22012-8_34
10. Burckhardt, S., Musuvathi, M.: Effective program verification for relaxed memory models. In: Gupta, A., Malik, S. (eds.) CAV 2008. LNCS, vol. 5123, pp. 107–120. Springer, Heidelberg (2008). https://doi.org/10.1007/978-3-540-70545-1_12
11. Burnim, J., Sen, K., Stergiou, C.: Sound and complete monitoring of sequential consistency for relaxed memory models. In: Abdulla, P.A., Leino, K.R.M. (eds.) TACAS 2011. LNCS, vol. 6605, pp. 11–25. Springer, Heidelberg (2011). https://doi.org/10.1007/978-3-642-19835-9_3
12. Elmas, T., Qadeer, S., Tasiran, S.: A calculus of atomic actions. In: ACM Symposium on Principles of Programming Languages, p. 14. Association for Computing Machinery Inc., January 2009
13. Hawblitzel, C., Qadeer, S., Tasiran, S.: Automated and modular refinement reasoning for concurrent programs. In: Computer Aided Verification (2015)
14. Kuperstein, M., Vechev, M., Yahav, E.: Partial-coherence abstractions for relaxed memory models. In: ACM SIGPLAN Notices, vol. 46, pp. 187–198. ACM (2011)
15. Kuperstein, M., Vechev, M., Yahav, E.: Automatic inference of memory fences. ACM SIGACT News 43(2), 108–123 (2012)
16. Lamport, L.: How to make a multiprocessor computer that correctly executes multiprocess programs. IEEE Trans. Comput. 100(9), 690–691 (1979)
17. Lipton, R.J.: Reduction: a method of proving properties of parallel programs. Commun. ACM 18(12), 717–721 (1975)
18. Owens, S.: Reasoning about the implementation of concurrency abstractions on x86-TSO. In: D'Hondt, T. (ed.) ECOOP 2010. LNCS, vol. 6183, pp. 478–503. Springer, Heidelberg (2010). https://doi.org/10.1007/978-3-642-14107-2_23
19. Sewell, P., Sarkar, S., Owens, S., Nardelli, F.Z., Myreen, M.O.: x86-TSO: a rigorous and usable programmer's model for x86 multiprocessors. Commun. ACM 53(7), 89–97 (2010)
20. Shasha, D., Snir, M.: Efficient and correct execution of parallel programs that share memory. ACM Trans. Program. Lang. Syst. (TOPLAS) 10(2), 282–312 (1988)

Quasi-Optimal Partial Order Reduction

Huyen T. T. Nguyen[1] , César Rodríguez[1,3], Marcelo Sousa[2], Camille Coti[1] ,
and Laure Petrucci[1(✉)]

[1] LIPN, CNRS UMR 7030, Université Paris 13,
Sorbonne Paris Cité, Villetaneuse, France
{tnguyen,cesar.rodriguez}@lipn.fr,
{camille.coti,laure.petrucci}@lipn.univ-paris13.fr
[2] University of Oxford, Oxford, UK
marcelo.sousa@cs.ox.ac.uk
[3] Diffblue Ltd., Oxford, UK

Abstract. A dynamic partial order reduction (DPOR) algorithm
is optimal when it always explores at most one representative per
Mazurkiewicz trace. Existing literature suggests that the reduction
obtained by the non-optimal, state-of-the-art Source-DPOR (SDPOR)
algorithm is comparable to optimal DPOR. We show the first program
with $\mathcal{O}(n)$ Mazurkiewicz traces where SDPOR explores $\mathcal{O}(2^n)$ redundant
schedules (as this paper was under review, we were made aware of the
recent publication of another paper [3] which contains an independently-
discovered example program with the same characteristics). We furthermore identify the cause of this blow-up as an NP-hard problem. Our
main contribution is a new approach, called Quasi-Optimal POR, that
can arbitrarily approximate an optimal exploration using a provided constant k. We present an implementation of our method in a new tool
called DPU using specialised data structures. Experiments with DPU,
including Debian packages, show that optimality is achieved with low
values of k, outperforming state-of-the-art tools.

1 Introduction

Dynamic partial-order reduction (DPOR) [1,10,19] is a mature approach to
mitigate the state explosion problem in stateless model checking of multi-
threaded programs. DPORs are based on Mazurkiewicz trace theory [13], a true-
concurrency semantics where the set of executions of the program is partitioned
into equivalence classes known as Mazurkiewicz traces (M-traces). In a DPOR,
this partitioning is defined by an independence relation over concurrent actions
that is computed dynamically and the method explores executions which are rep-
resentatives of M-traces. The exploration is *sound* when it explores all M-traces,
and it is considered *optimal* [1] when it explores each M-trace only once.

Since two independent actions might have to be explored from the same
state in order to explore all M-traces, a DPOR algorithm uses independence to
compute a provably-sufficient subset of the enabled transitions to explore for each
state encountered. Typically this involves the combination of forward reasoning

© The Author(s) 2018
H. Chockler and G. Weissenbacher (Eds.): CAV 2018, LNCS 10982, pp. 354–371, 2018.
https://doi.org/10.1007/978-3-319-96142-2_22

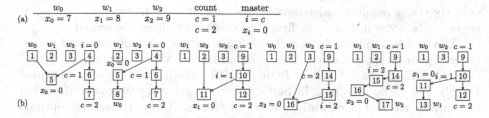

Fig. 1. (a) Programs; (b) partially-ordered executions;

(persistent sets [11] or source sets [1,4]) with backward reasoning (sleep sets [11]) to obtain a more efficient exploration. However, in order to obtain optimality, a DPOR needs to compute sequences of transitions (as opposed to sets of enabled transitions) that avoid visiting a previously visited M-trace. These sequences are stored in a data structure called *wakeup trees* in [1] and known as *alternatives* in [19]. Computing these sequences thus amounts to deciding whether the DPOR needs to visit yet another M-trace (or all have already been seen).

In this paper, we prove that computing alternatives in an optimal DPOR is an NP-complete problem. To the best our knowledge this is the first formal complexity result on this important subproblem that optimal and non-optimal DPORs need to solve. The program shown in Fig. 1(a) illustrates a practical consequence of this result: the non-optimal, state-of-the-art SDPOR algorithm [1] can explore here $\mathcal{O}(2^n)$ interleavings but the program has only $\mathcal{O}(n)$ M-traces.

The program contains $n := 3$ *writer* threads w_0, w_1, w_2, each writing to a different variable. The thread *count* increments $n - 1$ times a zero-initialized counter c. Thread *master* reads c into variable i and writes to x_i.

The statements $x_0 = 7$ and $x_1 = 8$ are independent because they produce the same state regardless of their execution order. Statements $i = c$ and any statement in the *count* thread are dependent or *interfering*: their execution orders result in different states. Similarly, $x_i = 0$ interferes with exactly one *writer* thread, depending on the value of i.

Using this independence relation, the set of executions of this program can be partitioned into six M-traces, corresponding to the six partial orders shown in Fig. 1(b). Thus, an optimal DPOR explores six executions ($2n$-executions for n writers). We now show why SDPOR explores $\mathcal{O}(2^n)$ in the general case. Conceptually, SDPOR is a loop that (1) runs the program, (2) identifies two dependent statements that can be swapped, and (3) reverses them and re-executes the program. It terminates when no more dependent statements can be swapped.

Consider the interference on the counter variable c between the *master* and the *count* thread. Their execution order determines which *writer* thread interferes with the *master* statement $x_i = 0$. If $c = 1$ is executed just before $i = c$, then $x_i = 0$ interferes with w_1. However, if $i = c$ is executed before, then $x_i = 0$ interferes with w_0. Since SDPOR does not track relations between dependent statements, it will naively try to reverse the race between $x_i = 0$ and *all writer threads*, which results in exploring $\mathcal{O}(2^n)$ executions. In this program, exploring only six traces requires understanding the entanglement between both interferences as the order in which the first is reversed determines the second.

As a trade-off solution between solving this NP-complete problem and potentially explore an exponential number of redundant schedules, we propose a hybrid approach called Quasi-Optimal POR (QPOR) which can turn a non-optimal DPOR into an optimal one. In particular, we provide a polynomial algorithm to compute alternative executions that can arbitrarily approximate the optimal solution based on a user specified constant k. The key concept is a new notion of k-*partial alternative*, which can intuitively be seen as a "good enough" alternative: they revert two interfering statements while remembering the resolution of the last $k - 1$ interferences.

The major differences between QPOR and the DPORs of [1] are that: (1) QPOR is based on prime event structures [17], a partial-order semantics that has been recently applied to programs [19,21], instead of a sequential view to thread interleaving, and (2) it computes k-partial alternatives with an $\mathcal{O}(n^k)$ algorithm while optimal DPOR corresponds to computing ∞-partial alternatives with an $\mathcal{O}(2^n)$ algorithm. For the program shown in Fig. 1(a), QPOR achieves optimality with $k = 2$ because races are coupled with (at most) another race. As expected, the cost of computing k-partial alternatives and the reductions obtained by the method increase with higher values of k.

Finding k-partial alternatives requires decision procedures for traversing the causality and conflict relations in event structures. Our main algorithmic contribution is to represent these relations as a set of trees where events are encoded as one or two nodes in two different trees. We show that checking causality/conflict between events amounts to an efficient traversal in one of these trees.

In summary, our main contributions are:

- Proof that computing alternatives for optimal DPOR is NP-complete (Sect. 4).
- Efficient data structures and algorithms for (1) computing k-partial alternatives in polynomial time, and (2) represent and traverse partial orders (Sect. 5).
- Implementation of QPOR in a new tool called DPU and experimental evaluations against SDPOR in NIDHUGG and the testing tool MAPLE (Sect. 6).
- Benchmarks with $\mathcal{O}(n)$ M-traces where SDPOR explores $\mathcal{O}(2^n)$ executions (Sect. 6).

Furthermore, in Sect. 6 we show that: (1) low values of k often achieve optimality; (2) even with non-optimal explorations DPU greatly outperforms NIDHUGG; (3) DPU copes with production code in Debian packages and achieves much higher state space coverage and efficiency than MAPLE.

Proofs for all our formal results are available in the unabridged version [15].

2   Preliminaries

In this section we provide the formal background used throughout the paper.

Concurrent Programs. We consider deterministic concurrent programs composed of a fixed number of threads that communicate via shared memory and synchronize using mutexes (Fig. 1(a) can be trivially modified to satisfy this). We also assume that local statements can only modify shared memory within a mutex block. Therefore, it suffices to only consider races of mutex accesses.

Formally, a *concurrent program* is a structure $P := \langle \mathcal{M}, \mathcal{L}, T, m_0, l_0 \rangle$, where $\mathcal{M}$ is the set of *memory states* (valuations of program variables, including instruction pointers), $\mathcal{L}$ is the set of *mutexes*, m_0 is the *initial memory state*, l_0 is the *initial mutexes state* and T is the set of *thread statements*. A thread statement $t := \langle i, f \rangle$ is a pair where $i \in \mathbb{N}$ is the *thread identifier* associated with the statement and $f \colon \mathcal{M} \to (\mathcal{M} \times \Lambda)$ is a *partial* function that models the transformation of the memory as well as the *effect* $\Lambda := \{\texttt{loc}\} \cup (\{\texttt{acq}, \texttt{rel}\} \times \mathcal{L})$ of the statement with respect to thread synchronization. Statements of $\texttt{loc}$ effect model local thread code. Statements associated with $\langle \texttt{acq}, x \rangle$ or $\langle \texttt{rel}, x \rangle$ model lock and unlock operations on a mutex x. Finally, we assume that (1) functions f are PTIME-decidable; (2) $\texttt{acq}/\texttt{rel}$ statements do not modify the memory; and (3) $\texttt{loc}$ statements modify thread-shared memory only within lock/unlock blocks. When (3) is violated, then P has a *datarace* (undefined behavior in almost all languages), and our technique can be used to find such statements, see Sect. 6.

We use *labelled transition systems* (*LTS*) semantics for our programs. We associate a program P with the *LTS* $M_P := \langle \mathcal{S}, \to, A, s_0 \rangle$. The set $\mathcal{S} := \mathcal{M} \times (\mathcal{L} \to \{0,1\})$ are the *states* of M_P, i.e., pairs of the form $\langle m, v \rangle$ where m is the state of the memory and v indicates when a mutex is locked (1) or unlocked (0). The *actions* in $A \subseteq \mathbb{N} \times \Lambda$ are pairs $\langle i, b \rangle$ where i is the identifier of the thread that executes some statement and b is the effect of the statement. We use the function $p \colon A \to \mathbb{N}$ to retrieve the thread identifier. The *transition relation* $\to \subseteq \mathcal{S} \times A \times \mathcal{S}$ contains a triple $\langle m, v \rangle \xrightarrow{\langle i,b \rangle} \langle m', v' \rangle$ exactly when there is some thread statement $\langle i, f \rangle \in T$ such that $f(m) = \langle m', b \rangle$ and either (1) $b = \texttt{loc}$ and $v' = v$, or (2) $b = \langle \texttt{acq}, x \rangle$ and $v(x) = 0$ and $v' = v_{|x \mapsto 1}$, or (3) $b = \langle \texttt{rel}, x \rangle$ and $v' = v_{|x \mapsto 0}$. Notation $f_{x \mapsto y}$ denotes a function that behaves like f for all inputs except for x, where $f(x) = y$. The *initial state* is $s_0 := \langle m_0, l_0 \rangle$.

Furthermore, if $s \xrightarrow{a} s'$ is a transition, the action a is *enabled* at s. Let *enabl*(s) denote the set of actions enabled at s. A sequence $\sigma := a_1 \ldots a_n \in A^*$ is a *run* when there are states $s_1, \ldots, s_n$ satisfying $s_0 \xrightarrow{a_1} s_1 \ldots \xrightarrow{a_n} s_n$. We define *state*$(\sigma) := s_n$. We let *runs*$(M_P)$ denote the set of all runs and *reach*$(M_P) := \{state(\sigma) \in \mathcal{S} \colon \sigma \in runs(M_P)\}$ the set of all *reachable states*.

Independence. Dynamic partial-order reduction methods use a notion called independence to avoid exploring concurrent interleavings that lead to the same state. We recall the standard notion of independence for actions in [11]. Two actions $a, a' \in A$ *commute* at a state $s \in \mathcal{S}$ iff

- if $a \in enabl(s)$ and $s \xrightarrow{a} s'$, then $a' \in enabl(s)$ iff $a' \in enabl(s')$; and
- if $a, a' \in enabl(s)$, then there is a state s' such that $s \xrightarrow{a.a'} s'$ and $s \xrightarrow{a'.a} s'$.

Independence between actions is an under-approximation of commutativity. A binary relation $\Diamond \subseteq A \times A$ is an *independence* on M_P if it is symmetric, irreflexive, and every pair $\langle a, a' \rangle$ in $\Diamond$ commutes at every state in $reach(M_P)$.

In general M_P has multiple independence relations, clearly $\emptyset$ is always one of them. We define relation $\Diamond_P \subseteq A \times A$ as the smallest irreflexive, symmetric relation where $\langle i, b \rangle \, \Diamond_P \, \langle i', b' \rangle$ holds if $i \neq i'$ and either $b = \texttt{loc}$ or $b = \texttt{acq } x$ and $b' \notin \{\texttt{acq } x, \texttt{rel } x\}$. By construction $\Diamond_P$ is always an independence.

Labelled Prime Event Structures. *Prime event structures* (PES) are well-known non-interleaving, partial-order semantics [7,8,16]. Let X be a set of actions. A PES *over* X is a structure $\mathcal{E} := \langle E, <, \#, h \rangle$ where E is a set of *events*, $< \subseteq E \times E$ is a strict partial order called *causality relation*, $\# \subseteq E \times E$ is a symmetric, irreflexive *conflict relation*, and $h \colon E \to X$ is a labelling function. Causality represents the happens-before relation between events, and conflict between two events expresses that any execution includes at most one of them. Figure 2(b) shows a PES over $\mathbb{N} \times \Lambda$ where causality is depicted by arrows, conflicts by dotted lines, and the labelling h is shown next to the events, e.g., $1 < 5$, $8 < 12$, $2 \# 8$, and $h(1) = \langle 0, \texttt{loc} \rangle$. The *history* of an event e, $\lceil e \rceil := \{ e' \in E \colon e' < e \}$, is the least set of events that need to happen before e.

The notion of concurrent execution in a PES is captured by the concept of *configuration*. A configuration is a (partially ordered) execution of the system, i.e., a set $C \subseteq E$ of events that is *causally closed* (if $e \in C$, then $\lceil e \rceil \subseteq C$) and *conflict-free* (if $e, e' \in C$, then $\neg(e \# e')$). In Fig. 2(b), the set $\{8, 9, 15\}$ is a configuration, but $\{3\}$ or $\{1, 2, 8\}$ are not. We let $conf(\mathcal{E})$ denote the set of all configurations of $\mathcal{E}$, and $[e] := \lceil e \rceil \cup \{e\}$ the *local configuration* of e. In Fig. 2(b), $[11] = \{1, 8, 9, 10, 11\}$. A configuration represents a set of *interleavings* over X. An interleaving is a sequence in X^* that labels any topological sorting of the events in C. In Fig. 2(b), $inter(\{1, 8\}) = \{ab, ba\}$ with $a := \langle 0, \texttt{loc} \rangle$ and $b := \langle 1, \texttt{acq } m \rangle$.

The *extensions* of C are the events not in C whose histories are included in C: $ex(C) := \{ e \in E \colon e \notin C \wedge \lceil e \rceil \subseteq C \}$. The *enabled* events of C are the extensions that can form a larger configuration: $en(C) := \{ e \in ex(C) \colon C \cup \{e\} \in conf(\mathcal{E}) \}$. Finally, the *conflicting extensions* of C are the extensions that are not enabled: $cex(C) := ex(C) \setminus en(C)$. In Fig. 2(b), $ex(\{1, 8\}) = \{2, 9, 15\}$, $en(\{1, 8\}) = \{9, 15\}$, and $cex(\{1, 8\}) = \{2\}$. See [20] for more information on PES concepts.

Parametric Unfolding Semantics. We recall the program PES semantics of [19,20] (modulo notation differences). For a program P and any independence $\Diamond$ on M_P we define a PES $\mathcal{U}_{P,\Diamond}$ that represents the behavior of P, i.e., such that the interleavings of its set of configurations equals $runs(M_P)$.

Each event in $\mathcal{U}_{P,\Diamond}$ is defined by a canonical name of the form $e := \langle a, H \rangle$, where $a \in A$ is an action of M_P and H is a configuration of $\mathcal{U}_{P,\Diamond}$. Intuitively, e represents the action a after the *history* (or the causes) H. Figure 2(b) shows an example. Event 11 is $\langle \langle 0, \texttt{acq } m \rangle, \{1, 8, 9, 10\} \rangle$ and event 1 is $\langle \langle 0, \texttt{loc} \rangle, \emptyset \rangle$. Note the inductive nature of the name, and how it allows to uniquely identify each event. We define the *state of a configuration* as the state reached by *any* of its interleavings. Formally, for $C \in conf(\mathcal{U}_{P,\Diamond})$ we define $state(C)$ as s_0 if $C = \emptyset$

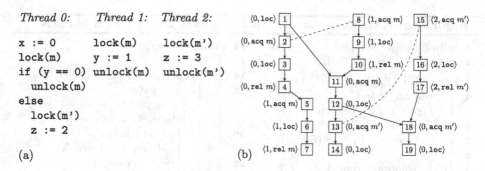

Fig. 2. (a) A program P; (b) its unfolding semantics $\mathcal{U}_{P,\diamond_P}$.

and as $state(\sigma)$ for some $\sigma \in inter(C)$ if $C \neq \emptyset$. Despite its appearance $state(C)$ is well-defined because *all* sequences in $inter(C)$ reach the *same* state, see [20] for a proof.

Definition 1 (Unfolding). *Given a program P and some independence relation $\diamond$ on $M_P := \langle \mathcal{S}, \rightarrow, A, s_0 \rangle$, the unfolding of P under $\diamond$, denoted $\mathcal{U}_{P,\diamond}$, is the* PES *over A constructed by the following fixpoint rules:*

1. *Start with a* PES *$\mathcal{E} := \langle E, <, \#, h \rangle$ equal to $\langle \emptyset, \emptyset, \emptyset, \emptyset \rangle$.*
2. *Add a new event $e := \langle a, C \rangle$ to E for any configuration $C \in conf(\mathcal{E})$ and any action $a \in A$ if a is enabled at $state(C)$ and $\neg(a \diamond h(e'))$ holds for every $<$-maximal event e' in C.*
3. *For any new e in E, update $<$, $\#$, and h as follows: for every $e' \in C$, set $e' < e$; for any $e' \in E \setminus C$, set $e' \# e$ if $e \neq e'$ and $\neg(a \diamond h(e'))$; set $h(e) := a$.*
4. *Repeat steps 2 and 3 until no new event can be added to E; return $\mathcal{E}$.*

Step 1 creates an empty PES with only one (empty) configuration. Step 2 inserts a new event $\langle a, C \rangle$ by finding a configuration C that enables an action a which is dependent with all causality-maximal events in C. In Fig. 2, this initially creates events 1, 8, and 15. For event $1 := \langle \langle 0, \texttt{loc} \rangle, \emptyset \rangle$, this is because action $\langle 0, \texttt{loc} \rangle$ is enabled at $state(\emptyset) = s_0$ and there is no $<$-maximal event in $\emptyset$ to consider. Similarly, the state of $C_1 := \{1, 8, 9, 10\}$ enables action $a_1 := \langle 0, \texttt{acq } m \rangle$, and both $h(1)$ and $h(10)$ are dependent with a_1 in $\diamond_P$. As a result $\langle a_1, C_1 \rangle$ is an event (number 11). Furthermore, while $a_2 := \langle 0, \texttt{loc} \rangle$ is enabled at $state(C_2)$, with $C_2 := \{8, 9, 10\}$, a_2 is independent of $h(10)$ and $\langle a_2, C_2 \rangle$ is not an event.

After inserting an event $e := \langle a, C \rangle$, Definition 1 declares all events in C causal predecessors of e. For any event e' in E but not in $[e]$ such that $h(e')$ is dependent with a, the order of execution of e and e' yields different states. We thus set them in conflict. In Fig. 2, we set $2 \# 8$ because $h(2)$ is dependent with $h(8)$ and $2 \notin [8]$ and $8 \notin [2]$.

3 Unfolding-Based DPOR

This section presents an algorithm that exhaustively explores all deadlock states of a given program (a *deadlock* is a state where no thread is enabled).

Algorithm 1. Unfolding-based POR exploration. See text for definitions.

1 Initially, set $U := \emptyset$,	14 **Function** cexp(C)
2 and call Explore($\emptyset, \emptyset, \emptyset$).	15 $R := \emptyset$
	16 **foreach** *event* $e \in C$ *of type* acq
3 **Procedure** Explore(C, D, A)	17 $e_t := $ pt(e)
4 Add $ex(C)$ to U	18 $e_m := $ pm(e)
5 if $en(C) \subseteq D$ **return**	19 **while** $\neg(e_m \leq e_t)$ **do**
6 if $A = \emptyset$	20 $e_m := $ pm(e_m)
7 | Choose e from $en(C) \setminus D$	21 if $(e_m < e_t)$ **break**
8 else	22 $e_m := $ pm(e_m)
9 | Choose e from $A \cap en(C)$	23 $\hat{e} := \langle h(e), [e_t] \cup [e_m] \rangle$
10 Explore($C \cup \{e\}, D, A \setminus \{e\}$)	24 Add $\hat{e}$ to R
11 if $\exists J \in$ Alt($C, D \cup \{e\}$)	25 **return** R
12 | Explore($C, D \cup \{e\}, J \setminus C$)	
13 $U := U \cap Q_{C,D}$	

For the rest of the paper, unless otherwise stated, we let P be a *terminating* program (i.e., $runs(M_P)$ is a finite set of finite sequences) and $\Diamond$ an independence on M_P. Consequently, $\mathcal{U}_{P,\Diamond}$ has finitely many events and configurations.

Our POR algorithm (Algorithm 1) analyzes P by exploring the configurations of $\mathcal{U}_{P,\Diamond}$. It visits all $\subseteq$-maximal configurations of $\mathcal{U}_{P,\Diamond}$, which correspond to the deadlock states in $reach(M_P)$, and organizes the exploration as a binary tree.

Explore(C,D,A) has a global set U that stores all events of $\mathcal{U}_{P,\Diamond}$ discovered so far. The three arguments are: C, the configuration to be explored; D (for *disabled*), a set of events that shall never be visited (included in C) again; and A (for *add*), used to direct the exploration towards a configuration that conflicts with D. A call to Explore(C,D,A) visits all maximal configurations of $\mathcal{U}_{P,\Diamond}$ which contain C and do not contain D, and the first one explored contains $C \cup A$.

The algorithm first adds $ex(C)$ to U. If C is a maximal configuration (i.e., there is no enabled event) then line 5 returns. If C is not maximal but $en(C) \subseteq D$, then all possible events that could be added to C have already been explored and this call was redundant work. In this case the algorithm also returns and we say that it has explored a *sleep-set blocked* (SSB) execution [1]. Algorithm 1 next selects an event enabled at C, if possible from A (line 7 and 9) and makes a recursive call (left subtree) that explores *all* configurations that contain all events in $C \cup \{e\}$ and no event from D. Since that call visits all maximal configurations containing C and e, it remains to visit those containing C but not e. At line 11 we determine if any such configuration exists. Function Alt returns a set of configurations, so-called *clues*. A clue is a witness that a $\subseteq$-maximal configuration exists in $\mathcal{U}_{P,\Diamond}$ which contains C and not $D \cup \{e\}$.

Definition 2 (Clue). *Let D and U be sets of events, and C a configuration such that $C \cap D = \emptyset$. A clue to D after C in U is a configuration $J \subseteq U$ such that $C \cup J$ is a configuration and $D \cap J = \emptyset$.*

Definition 3 (Alt function). *Function* Alt *denotes* any *function such that* Alt(B,F) *returns a set of clues to F after B in U, and the set is non-empty if $\mathcal{U}_{P,\diamond}$ has at least one maximal configuration C where $B \subseteq C$ and $C \cap F = \emptyset$.*

When Alt returns a clue J, the clue is passed in the second recursive call (line 12) to "mark the way" (using set A) in the subsequent recursive calls at line 10, and guide the exploration towards the maximal configuration that J witnesses. Definition 3 does not identify a concrete implementation of Alt. It rather indicates how to implement Alt so that Algorithm 1 terminates and is complete (see below). Different PORs in the literature can be reframed in terms of Algorithm 1. SDPOR [1] uses clues that mark the way with only one event ahead ($|J \setminus C| = 1$) and can hit SSBs. Optimal DPORs [1,19] use size-varying clues that guide the exploration provably guaranteeing that any SSB will be avoided.

Algorithm 1 is *optimal* when it does not explore a SSB. To make Algorithm 1 optimal Alt needs to return clues that are *alternatives* [19], which satisfy stronger constraints. When that happens, Algorithm 1 is equivalent to the DPOR in [19] and becomes optimal (see [20] for a proof).

Definition 4 (Alternative [19]). *Let D and U be sets of events and C a configuration such that $C \cap D = \emptyset$. An* alternative *to D after C in U is a clue J to D after C in U such that $\forall e \in D : \exists e' \in J, e \# e'$.*

Line 13 removes from U events that will not be necessary for Alt to find clues in the future. The events preserved, $Q_{C,D} := C \cup D \cup \#(C \cup D)$, include all events in $C \cup D$ as well as every event in U that is in conflict with some event in $C \cup D$. The preserved events will suffice to compute alternatives [19], but other non-optimal implementations of Alt could allow for more aggressive pruning.

The $\subseteq$-maximal configurations of Fig. 2(b) are $[7] \cup [17]$, $[14]$, and $[19]$. Our algorithm starts at configuration $C = \emptyset$. After 10 recursive calls it visits $C = [7] \cup [17]$. Then it backtracks to $C = \{1\}$, calls Alt$(\{1\}, \{2\})$, which provides, e.g., $J = \{1,8\}$, and visits $C = \{1,8\}$ with $D = \{2\}$. After 6 more recursive calls it visits $C = [14]$, backtracks to $C = [12]$, calls Alt$([12], \{2,13\}])$, which provides, e.g., $J = \{15\}$, and after two more recursive calls it visits $C = [12] \cup \{15\}$ with $D = \{2,13\}$. Finally, after 4 more recursive calls it visits $C = [19]$.

Finally, we focus on the correctness of Algorithm 1, and prove termination and soundness of the algorithm:

Theorem 1 (Termination). *Regardless of its input, Algorithm 1 always stops.*

Theorem 2 (Completeness). *Let $\hat{C}$ be a $\subseteq$ maximal configuration of $\mathcal{U}_{P,\diamond}$. Then Algorithm 1 calls* Explore(C,D,A) *at least once with $C = \hat{C}$.*

4 Complexity

This section presents complexity results about the only non-trivial steps in Algorithm 1: computing $ex(C)$ and the call to Alt$(\cdot,\cdot)$. An implementation of

$\mathtt{Alt}(B,F)$ that systematically returns B would satisfy Definition 3, but would also render Algorithm 1 unusable (equivalent to a DFS in M_P). On the other hand the algorithm becomes optimal when $\mathtt{Alt}$ returns alternatives. Optimality comes at a cost:

Theorem 3. *Given a finite* PES $\mathcal{E}$, *some configuration* $C \in conf(\mathcal{E})$, *and a set* $D \subseteq ex(C)$, *deciding if an alternative to* D *after* C *exists in* $\mathcal{E}$ *is NP-complete.*

Theorem 3 assumes that $\mathcal{E}$ is an arbitrary PES. Assuming that $\mathcal{E}$ is the unfolding of a program P under $\Diamond_P$ does not reduce this complexity:

Theorem 4. *Let* P *be a program and* U *a causally-closed set of events from* $\mathcal{U}_{P,\Diamond_P}$. *For any configuration* $C \subseteq U$ *and any* $D \subseteq ex(C)$, *deciding if an alternative to* D *after* C *exists in* U *is NP-complete.*

These complexity results lead us to consider (in next section) new approaches that avoid the NP-hardness of computing alternatives while still retaining their capacity to prune the search.

Finally, we focus on the complexity of computing $ex(C)$, which essentially reduces to computing $cex(C)$, as computing $en(C)$ is trivial. Assuming that $\mathcal{E}$ is given, computing $cex(C)$ for some $C \in conf(\mathcal{E})$ is a linear problem. However, for any realistic implementation of Algorithm 1, $\mathcal{E}$ is not available (the very goal of Algorithm 1 is to find all of its events). So a useful complexity result about $cex(C)$ necessarily refers to the orignal system under analysis. When $\mathcal{E}$ is the unfolding of a Petri net [14], computing $cex(C)$ is NP-complete:

Theorem 5. *Let* N *be a Petri net,* t *a transition of* N, $\mathcal{E}$ *the unfolding of* N *and* C *a configuration of* $\mathcal{E}$. *Deciding if* $h^{-1}(t) \cap cex(C) = \emptyset$ *is NP-complete.*

Fortunately, computing $cex(C)$ for programs is a much simpler task. Function $\mathtt{cexp}(C)$, shown in Algorithm 1, computes and returns $cex(C)$ when $\mathcal{E}$ is the unfolding of some program. We explain $\mathtt{cexp}(C)$ in detail in Sect. 5.3. But assuming that functions $\mathtt{pt}$ and $\mathtt{pm}$ can be computed in constant time, and relation $<$ decided in $\mathcal{O}(\log|C|)$, as we will show, clearly $\mathtt{cexp}$ works in time $\mathcal{O}(n^2 \log n)$, where $n := |C|$, as both loops are bounded by the size of C.

5   New Algorithm for Computing Alternatives

This section introduces a new class of clues, called k-partial alternatives. These can arbitrarily reduce the number of redundant explorations (SSBs) performed by Algorithm 1 and can be computed in polynomial time. Specialized data structures and algorithms for k-partial alternatives are also presented.

Definition 5 (k-partial alternative). *Let* U *be a set of events,* $C \subseteq U$ *a configuration,* $D \subseteq U$ *a set of events, and* $k \in \mathbb{N}$ *a number. A configuration* J *is a* k-partial alternative to D after C *if there is some* $\hat{D} \subseteq D$ *such that* $|\hat{D}| = k$ *and* J *is an alternative to* $\hat{D}$ *after* C.

A k-partial alternative needs to conflict with only k (instead of all) events in D. An alternative is thus an ∞-partial alternative. If we reframe SDPOR in terms of Algorithm 1, it becomes an algorithm using *singleton 1-partial* alternatives. While k-partial alternatives are a very simple concept, most of their simplicity stems from the fact that they are expressed within the elegant framework of PES semantics. Defining the same concept on top of sequential semantics (often used in the POR literature [1,2,9–11,23]), would have required much more complex device.

We compute k-partial alternatives using a *comb* data structure:

Definition 6 (Comb). *Let A be a set. An A-comb c of size $n \in \mathbb{N}$ is an ordered collection of spikes $\langle s_1, \ldots, s_n \rangle$, where each spike $s_i \in A^*$ is a sequence of elements over A. Furthermore, a combination over c is any tuple $\langle a_1, \ldots, a_n \rangle$ where $a_i \in s_i$ is an element of the spike.*

It is possible to compute k-partial alternatives (and by extension optimal alternatives) to D after C in U using a comb, as follows:

1. Select k (or $|D|$, whichever is smaller) arbitrary events $e_1, \ldots, e_k$ from D.
2. Build a U-comb $\langle s_1, \ldots, s_k \rangle$ of size k, where spike s_i contains all events in U in conflict with e_i.
3. Remove from s_i any event $\hat{e}$ such that either $[\hat{e}] \cup C$ is not a configuration or $[\hat{e}] \cap D \neq \emptyset$.
4. Find combinations $\langle e'_1, \ldots, e'_k \rangle$ in the comb satisfying $\neg(e'_i \# e'_j)$ for $i \neq j$.
5. For any such combination the set $J := [e'_1] \cup \ldots \cup [e'_k]$ is a k-partial alternative.

Step 3 guarantees that J is a clue. Steps 1 and 2 guarantee that it will conflict with at least k events from D. It is straightforward to prove that the procedure will find a k-partial alternative to D after C in U when an ∞-partial alternative to D after C exists in U. It can thus be used to implement Definition 3.

Steps 2, 3, and 4 require to decide whether a given pair of events is in conflict. Similarly, step 3 requires to decide if two events are causally related. Efficiently computing k-partial alternatives thus reduces to efficiently computing causality and conflict between events.

5.1 Computing Causality and Conflict for PES Events

In this section we introduce an efficient data structure for deciding whether two events in the unfolding of a program are causally related or in conflict.

As in Sect. 3, let P be a program, M_P its LTS semantics, and $\Diamond_P$ its independence relation (defined in Sect. 2). Additionally, let $\mathcal{E}$ denote the PES $\mathcal{U}_{P,\Diamond_P}$ of P extended with a new event $\bot$ that causally precedes every event in $\mathcal{U}_{P,\Diamond_P}$.

The unfolding $\mathcal{E}$ represents the dependency of actions in M_P through the causality and conflict relations between events. By definition of $\Diamond_P$ we know that for any two events $e, e' \in \mathcal{E}$:

- If e and e' are events from the same thread, then they are either causally related or in conflict.

– If e and e' are lock/unlock operations on the same variable, then similarly they are either causally related or in conflict.

This means that the causality/conflict relations between all events of one thread can be tracked using a tree. For every thread of the program we define and maintain a so-called *thread tree*. Each event of the thread has a corresponding node in the tree. A tree node n is the parent of another tree node n' iff the event associated with n is the immediate causal predecessor of the event associated with n'. That is, the ancestor relation of the tree encodes the causality relations of events in the thread, and the branching of the tree represents conflict. Given two events e, e' of the same thread we have that $e < e'$ iff $\neg(e \# e')$ iff the tree node of e is an ancestor of the tree node of e'.

We apply the same idea to track causality/conflict between $\texttt{acq}$ and $\texttt{rel}$ events. For every lock $l \in \mathcal{L}$ we maintain a separate *lock tree*, containing a node for each event labelled by either $\langle \texttt{acq}, l \rangle$ or $\langle \texttt{rel}, l \rangle$. As before, the ancestor relation in a lock tree encodes the causality relations of all events represented in that tree. Events of type $\texttt{acq}/\texttt{rel}$ have tree nodes in both their lock and thread trees. Events for $\texttt{loc}$ actions are associated to only one node in the thread tree.

This idea gives a procedure to decide a causality/conflict query for two events when they belong to the same thread or modify the same lock. But we still need to decide causality and conflict for other events, e.g., $\texttt{loc}$ events of different threads. Again by construction of $\Diamond_P$, the only source of conflict/causality for events are the causality/conflict relations between the causal predecessors of the two. These relations can be summarized by keeping two mappings for each event:

Definition 7. *Let $e \in E$ be an event of $\mathcal{E}$. We define the* thread mapping *$tmax \colon E \times \mathbb{N} \to E$ as the only function that maps every pair $\langle e, i \rangle$ to the unique $<$-maximal event from thread i in $[e]$, or $\bot$ if $[e]$ contains no event from thread i. Similarly, the* lock mapping *$lmax \colon E \times \mathcal{L} \to E$ maps every pair $\langle e, l \rangle$ to the unique $<$-maximal event $e' \in [e]$ such that $h(e')$ is an action of the form $\langle \texttt{acq}, l \rangle$ or $\langle \texttt{rel}, l \rangle$, or $\bot$ if no such event exists in $[e]$.*

The information stored by the thread and lock mappings enables us to decide causality and conflict queries for arbitrary pairs of events:

Theorem 6. *Let $e, e' \in \mathcal{E}$ be two arbitrary events from resp. threads i and i', with $i \neq i'$. Then $e < e'$ holds iff $e \leqslant tmax(e', i)$. And $e \# e'$ holds iff there is some $l \in \mathcal{L}$ such that $lmax(e, l) \# lmax(e', l)$.*

As a consequence of Theorem 6, deciding whether two events are related by causality or conflict reduces to deciding whether two nodes from the *same* lock or thread tree are ancestors.

5.2   Computing Causality and Conflict for Tree Nodes

This section presents an efficient algorithm to decide if two nodes of a tree are ancestors. The algorithm is similar to a search in a skip list [18].

Let $\langle N, \prec, r \rangle$ denote a tree, where N is a set of *nodes*, $\prec \subseteq N \times N$ is the *parent relation*, and $r \in N$ is the root. Let $d(n)$ be the depth of each node in the tree, with $d(r) = 0$. A node n is an *ancestor* of n' if it belongs to the only path from r to n'. Finally, for a node $n \in N$ and some integer $g \in \mathbb{N}$ such that $g \leq d(n)$ let $q(n, g)$ denote the unique ancestor n' of n such that $d(n') = g$.

Given two *distinct* nodes $n, n' \in N$, we need to efficiently decide whether n is an ancestor of n'. The key idea is that if $d(n) = d(n')$, then the answer is clearly negative; and if the depths are different and w.l.o.g. $d(n) < d(n')$, then we have that n is an ancestor of n' iff nodes n and $n'' := q(n', d(n))$ are the same node.

To find n'' from n', a linear traversal of the branch starting from n' would be expensive for deep trees. Instead, we propose to use a data structure similar to a skip list. Each node stores a pointer to the parent node *and* also a number of pointers to ancestor nodes at distances $s^1, s^2, s^3, \ldots$, where $s \in \mathbb{N}$ is a user-defined *step*. The number of pointers stored at a node n is equal to the number of trailing zeros in the s-ary representation of $d(n)$. For instance, for $s := 2$ a node at depth 4 stores 2 pointers (apart from the pointer to the parent) pointing to the nodes at depth $4 - s^1 = 2$ and depth $4 - s^2 = 0$. Similarly a node at depth 12 stores a pointer to the ancestor (at depth 11) and pointers to the ancestors at depths 10 and 8. With this algorithm computing $q(n, g)$ requires traversing $\log(d(n) - g)$ nodes of the tree.

5.3   Computing Conflicting Extensions

We now explain how function cexp(C) in Algorithm 1 works. A call to cexp(C) constructs and returns all events in $cex(C)$. The function works only when the PES being explored is the unfolding of a program P under the independence $\Diamond_P$.

Owing to the properties of $\mathcal{U}_{P,\Diamond_P}$, all events in $cex(C)$ are labelled by acq actions. Broadly speaking, this is because only the actions from different threads that are co-enabled *and* are dependent create conflicts in $\mathcal{U}_{P,\Diamond_P}$. And this is only possible for acq statements. For the same reason, an event labelled by $a := \langle i, \langle acq, l \rangle \rangle$ exists in $cex(C)$ iff there is some event $e \in C$ such that $h(e) = a$.

Function cexp exploits these facts and the lock tree introduced in Sect. 5.1 to compute $cex(C)$. Intuitively, it finds every event e labelled by an $\langle acq, l \rangle$ statement and tries to "execute" it before the $\langle rel, l \rangle$ that happened before e (if there is one). If it can, it creates a new event $\hat{e}$ with the same label as e.

Function pt(e) returns the only immediate causal predecessor of event e in its own thread. For an acq/rel event e, function pm(e) returns the parent node of event e in its lock tree (or $\bot$ if e is the root). So for an acq event it returns a rel event, and for a rel event it returns an acq event.

6   Experimental Evaluation

We implemented QPOR in a new tool called DPU (*Dynamic Program Unfolder*, available at https://github.com/cesaro/dpu/releases/tag/v0.5.2). DPU is a stateless model checker for C programs with POSIX threading. It uses the

LLVM infrastructure to parse, instrument, and JIT-compile the program, which is assumed to be data-deterministic. It implements k-partial alternatives (k is an input), optimal POR, and context-switch bounding [6].

DPU does not use data-races as a source of thread interference for POR. It will not explore two execution orders for the two instructions that exhibit a data-race. However, it can be instructed to detect and report data races found during the POR exploration. When requested, this detection happens for a user-provided percentage of the executions explored by POR.

6.1   Comparison to SDPOR

In this section we investigate the following experimental questions: (a) How does QPOR compare against SDPOR? (b) For which values of k do k-partial alternatives yield optimal exploration?

We use realistic programs that expose complex thread synchronization patterns including a job dispatcher, a multiple-producer multiple-consumer scheme, parallel computation of π, and a thread pool. Complex synchronizations patterns are frequent in these examples, including nested and intertwined critical sections or conditional interactions between threads based on the processed data, and provide means to highlight the differences between POR approaches and drive improvement. Each program contains between 2 and 8 assertions, often ensuring invariants of the used data structures. All programs are safe and have between 90 and 200 lines of code. We also considered the SV-COMP'17 benchmarks, but almost all of them contain very simple synchronization patterns, not representative of more complex concurrent algorithms. On these benchmarks QPOR and SDPOR perform an almost identical exploration, both timeout on exactly the same instances, and both find exactly the same bugs.

In Table 1, we present a comparison between DPU and NIDHUGG [2], an efficient implementation of SDPOR for multithreaded C programs. We run k-partial alternatives with $k \in \{1, 2, 3\}$ and optimal alternatives. The number of SSB executions dramatically decreases as k increases. With $k = 3$ almost no instance produces SSBs (except MPC(4,5)) and optimality is achieved with $k = 4$. Programs with simple synchronization patterns, e.g., the PI benchmark, are explored optimally both with $k = 1$ and by SDPOR, while more complex synchronization patterns require $k > 1$.

Overall, if the benchmark exhibits many SSBs, the run time reduces as k increases, and optimal exploration is the fastest option. However, when the benchmark contains few SSBs (cf., MPAT, PI, POKE), k-partial alternatives can be slightly faster than optimal POR, an observation inline with previous literature [1]. Code profiling revealed that when the comb is large and contains many solutions, both optimal and non-optimal POR will easily find them, but optimal POR spends additional time constructing a larger comb. This suggests that optimal POR would profit from a lazy comb construction algorithm.

DPU is faster than NIDHUGG in the majority of the benchmarks because it can greatly reduce the number of SSBs. In the cases where both tools explore the

Table 1. Comparing QPOR and SDPOR. Machine: Linux, Intel Xeon 2.4 GHz. TO: timeout after 8 min. Columns are: Th: nr. of threads; Confs: maximal configurations; Time in seconds, Memory in MB; SSB: Sleep-set blocked executions. N/A: analysis with lower k yielded 0 SSBs.

Benchmark			DPU (k=1)		DPU (k=2)		DPU (k=3)		DPU (optimal)		NIDHUGG		
Name	Th	Confs	Time	SSB	Time	SSB	Time	SSB	Time	Mem	Time	Mem	SSB
DISP(5,2)	8	137	0.8	1K	0.4	43	0.4	0	**0.4**	37	1.2	33	2K
DISP(5,3)	9	2K	5.4	11K	1.3	595	1.0	1	**1.0**	37	10.8	33	13K
DISP(5,4)	10	15K	58.5	105K	16.4	6K	10.3	213	**10.3**	87	109	33	115K
DISP(5,5)	11	151K	TO	–	476	53K	280	2K	**257**	729	TO	33	–
DISP(5,6)	12	?	TO	–	TO	–	TO	–	TO	1131	TO	33	–
MPAT(4)	9	384	0.5	0	N/A		N/A		**0.5**	37	0.6	33	0
MPAT(5)	11	4K	2.4	0	N/A		N/A		2.7	37	**1.8**	33	0
MPAT(6)	13	46K	50.6	0	N/A		N/A		73.2	214	**21.5**	33	0
MPAT(7)	15	645K	TO	–	TO	–	TO	–	TO	660	**359**	33	0
MPAT(8)	17	?	TO	–	TO	–	TO	–	TO	689	TO	33	–
MPC(2,5)	8	60	0.6	560	0.4	0			**0.4**	38	2.0	34	3K
MPC(3,5)	9	3K	26.5	50K	3.0	3K	1.7	0	**1.7**	38	70.7	34	90K
MPC(4,5)	10	314K	TO	–	TO	–	391	30K	**296**	239	TO	33	–
MPC(5,5)	11	?	TO	–	TO	–	TO	–	TO	834	TO	34	–
PI(5)	6	120	**0.4**	0	N/A		N/A		0.5	39	19.6	35	0
PI(6)	7	720	**0.7**	0	N/A		N/A		0.7	39	123	35	0
PI(7)	8	5K	**3.5**	0	N/A		N/A		4.0	45	TO	34	–
PI(8)	9	40K	48.1	0	N/A		N/A		**42.9**	246	TO	34	–
POL(7,3)	14	3K	48.5	72K	2.9	1K	**1.9**	6	1.9	39	74.1	33	90K
POL(8,3)	15	4K	153	214K	5.5	3K	**3.0**	10	3.0	52	251	33	274K
POL(9,3)	16	5K	464	592K	9.5	5K	**4.8**	15	4.8	73	TO	33	–
POL(10,3)	17	7K	TO	–	17.2	9K	**6.8**	21	7.1	99	TO	33	–
POL(11,3)	18	10K	TO	–	27.2	12K	**9.7**	28	10.6	138	TO	33	–
POL(12,3)	19	12K	TO	–	46.3	20K	**13.5**	36	16.4	184	TO	33	–

same set of executions, DPU is in general faster than NIDHUGG because it JIT-compiles the program, while NIDHUGG interprets it. All the benchmark in Table 1 are data-race free, but NIDHUGG cannot be instructed to ignore data-races and will attempt to revert them. DPU was run with data-race detection disabled. Enabling it will incur in approximatively 10% overhead. In contrast with previous observations [1,2], the results in Table 1 show that SSBs can dramatically slow down the execution of SDPOR.

6.2 Evaluation of the Tree-Based Algorithms

We now evaluate the efficiency of our tree-based algorithms from Sect. 5 answering: (a) What are the average/maximal depths of the thread/lock sequential trees? (b) What is the average depth difference on causality/conflict queries? (c) What is the best step for branch skip lists? We do not compare our algorithms against others because to the best of our knowledge none is available (other than a naive implementation of the mathematical definition of causality/conflict).

We run DPU with an optimal exploration over 15 selected programs from Table 1, with 380 to 204K maximal configurations in the unfolding. In total, the 15 unfoldings contain 246 trees (150 thread trees and 96 lock trees) with 5.2M nodes. Figure 3 shows the average depth of the nodes in each tree (subfigure a) and the maximum depth of the trees (subfigure b), for each of the 246 trees.

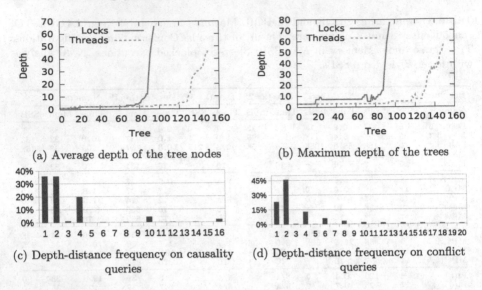

(a) Average depth of the tree nodes

(b) Maximum depth of the trees

(c) Depth-distance frequency on causality queries

(d) Depth-distance frequency on conflict queries

Fig. 3. (a), (b) Depths of trees; (c), (d) frequency of depth distances

While the average depth of a node is 22.7, as much as 80% of the trees have a maximum depth of less than 8 nodes, and 90% of them less than 16 nodes. The average of 22.7 is however larger because deeper trees contain proportionally more nodes. The depth of the deepest node of every tree was between 3 and 77.

We next evaluate depth differences in the causality and conflict queries over these trees. Figure 3(a) and (b) respectively show the frequency of various depth distances associated to causality and conflict queries made by optimal POR.

Surprisingly, depth differences are very small for both causality and conflict queries. When deciding causality between events, as much as 92% of the queries were for tree nodes separated by a distance between 1 and 4, and 70% had a difference of 1 or 2 nodes. This means that optimal POR, and specifically the procedure that adds $ex(C)$ to the unfolding (which is the main source of causality queries), systematically performs causality queries which are trivial with the proposed data structures. The situation is similar for checking conflicts: 82% of the queries are about tree nodes whose depth difference is between 1 and 4.

These experiments show that most queries on the causality trees require very short walks, which strongly drives to use the data structure proposed in Sect. 5. Finally, we chose a (rather arbitrary) skip step of 4. We observed that other values do not significantly impact the run time/memory consumption for most benchmarks, since the depth difference on causality/conflict requests is very low.

6.3   Evaluation Against the State-of-the-Art on System Code

We now evaluate the scalability and applicability of DPU on five multithreaded programs in two Debian packages: *blktrace* [5], a block layer I/O tracing mechanism, and *mafft* [12], a tool for multiple alignment of amino acid or nucleotide sequences. The code size of these utilities ranges from 2K to 40K LOC, and *mafft* is parametric in the number of threads.

We compared DPU against MAPLE [24], a state-of-the-art testing tool for multithreaded programs, as the top ranked verification tools from SV-COMP'17 are still unable to cope with such large and complex multi-threaded code. Unfortunately we could not compare against NID-HUGG because it cannot deal with the (abundant) C-library calls in these programs.

Table 2 presents our experimental results. We use DPU with optimal exploration and the modified version of MAPLE used in [22]. To test the effectiveness of both approaches in state space coverage and bug finding, we introduce bugs in 4 of the benchmarks (ADD, DND, MDL, PLA). For the safe benchmark BLK, we perform exhaustive state-space exploration using MAPLE's DFS

Table 2. Comparing DPU with Maple (same machine). LOC: lines of code; Execs: nr. of executions; R: safe or unsafe. Other columns as before. Timeout: 8 min.

Benchmark			DPU			MAPLE		
Name	LOC	Th	Time	Ex	R	Time	Ex	R
ADD(2)	40K	3	24.3	2	U	2.7	2	S
ADD(4)	40K	5	25.5	24	U	34.5	24	U
ADD(6)	40K	7	48.1	720	U	TO	316	U
ADD(8)	40K	9	TO	14K	U	TO	329	U
ADD(10)	40K	11	TO	14K	U	TO	295	U
BLK(5)	2K	2	0.9	1	S	4.6	1	S
BLK(15)	2K	2	0.9	5	S	23.3	5	S
BLK(18)	2K	2	1.0	180	S	TO	105	S
BLK(20)	2K	2	1.5	1147	S	TO	106	S
BLK(22)	2K	2	2.6	5424	S	TO	108	S
BLK(24)	2K	2	10.0	20K	S	TO	105	S
DND(2,4)	16K	3	11.1	80	U	122	80	U
DND(4,2)	16K	5	11.8	96	S	151	96	S
DND(4,4)	16K	5	TO	13K	U	TO	360	U
DND(6,2)	16K	7	149.3	4320	S	TO	388	S
MDL(1,4)	38K	7	26.1	1	U	1.4	1	U
MDL(2,2)	38K	5	29.2	9	U	13.3	9	U
MDL(2,3)	38K	5	46.2	576	U	TO	304	U
MDL(3,2)	38K	7	31.1	256	U	402	256	U
MDL(4,3)	38K	9	TO	14K	U	TO	329	U
PLA(1,5)	41K	2	22.8	1	U	1.7	1	U
PLA(2,4)	41K	3	37.2	80	U	142.4	80	U
PLA(4,3)	41K	5	160.5	1368	U	TO	266	U
PLA(6,3)	41K	7	TO	4580	U	TO	269	U

mode. On this benchmark, DPU outperfors MAPLE by several orders of magnitude: DPU explores up to 20K executions covering the entire state space in 10 s, while MAPLE only explores up to 108 executions in 8 min.

For the remaining benchmarks, we use the random scheduler of MAPLE, considered to be the best baseline for bug finding [22]. First, we run DPU to retrieve a bound on the number of random executions to answer whether both tools are able to find the bug within the same number of executions. MAPLE found bugs in all buggy programs (except for one variant in ADD) even though DPU greatly outperforms and is able to achieve much more state space coverage.

6.4 Profiling a Stateless POR

In order to understand the cost of each component of the algorithm, we profile DPU on a selection of 7 programs from Table 1. DPU spends between 30% and 90% of the run time executing the program (65% in average). The remaining time is spent computing alternatives, distributed as follows: adding events to the event structure (15% to 30%), building the spikes of a new comb (1% to 50%), searching for solutions in the comb (less than 5%), and computing conflicting extensions (less than 5%). Counterintuitively, building the *comb* is more expensive than exploring it, even in the optimal case. Filling the spikes seems to be more memory-intensive than exploring the comb, which exploits data locality.

7   Conclusion

We have shown that computing alternatives in an optimal DPOR exploration is NP-complete. To mitigate this problem, we introduced a new approach to compute alternatives in polynomial time, approximating the optimal exploration with a user-defined constant. Experiments conducted on benchmarks including Debian packages show that our implementation outperforms current verification tools and uses appropriate data structures. Our profiling results show that running the program is often more expensive than computing alternatives. Hence, efforts in reducing the number of redundant executions, even if significantly costly, are likely to reduce the overall execution time.

References

1. Abdulla, P., Aronis, S., Jonsson, B., Sagonas, K.: Optimal dynamic partial order reduction. In: The 41st Annual ACM SIGPLAN-SIGACT Symposium on Principles of Programming Languages (POPL 2014). ACM (2014)
2. Abdulla, P.A., et al.: Stateless model checking for TSO and PSO. In: Baier, C., Tinelli, C. (eds.) TACAS 2015. LNCS, vol. 9035, pp. 353–367. Springer, Heidelberg (2015). https://doi.org/10.1007/978-3-662-46681-0_28
3. Abdulla, P.A., Aronis, S., Jonsson, B., Sagonas, K.: Source sets: a foundation for optimal dynamic partial order reduction. J. ACM **64**(4), 25:1–25:49 (2017). https://doi.org/10.1145/3073408
4. Abdulla, P., Aronis, S., Jonsson, B., Sagonas, K.: Comparing source sets and persistent sets for partial order reduction. In: Aceto, L., et al. (eds.) Models, Algorithms, Logics and Tools. LNCS, vol. 10460, pp. 516–536. Springer, Cham (2017). https://doi.org/10.1007/978-3-319-63121-9_26
5. blktrace. http://brick.kernel.dk/snaps/
6. Coons, K.E., Musuvathi, M., McKinley, K.S.: Bounded partial-order reduction. In: OOPSLA, pp. 833–848 (2013)
7. Esparza, J.: A false history of true concurrency: from Petri to tools. In: van de Pol, J., Weber, M. (eds.) SPIN 2010. LNCS, vol. 6349, pp. 180–186. Springer, Heidelberg (2010). https://doi.org/10.1007/978-3-642-16164-3_13
8. Esparza, J., Heljanko, K.: Unfoldings – A Partial-Order Approach to Model Checking. EATCS Monographs in Theoretical Computer Science. Springer, Heidelberg (2008). https://doi.org/10.1007/978-3-540-77426-6
9. Farzan, A., Holzer, A., Razavi, N., Veith, H.: Con2colic testing. In: Proceedings of the 2013 9th Joint Meeting on Foundations of Software Engineering, ESEC/FSE 2013, pp. 37–47. ACM, New York (2013)
10. Flanagan, C., Godefroid, P.: Dynamic partial-order reduction for model checking software. In: Principles of Programming Languages (POPL), pp. 110–121. ACM (2005). https://doi.org/10.1145/1040305.1040315
11. Godefroid, P. (ed.): Partial-Order Methods for the Verification of Concurrent Systems - An Approach to the State-Explosion Problem. LNCS, vol. 1032. Springer, Heidelberg (1996). https://doi.org/10.1007/3-540-60761-7
12. MAFFT. http://mafft.cbrc.jp/alignment/software/
13. Mazurkiewicz, A.: Trace theory. In: Brauer, W., Reisig, W., Rozenberg, G. (eds.) ACPN 1986. LNCS, vol. 255, pp. 278–324. Springer, Heidelberg (1987). https://doi.org/10.1007/3-540-17906-2_30

14. McMillan, K.L.: Using unfoldings to avoid the state explosion problem in the veri-fication of asynchronous circuits. In: von Bochmann, G., Probst, D.K. (eds.) CAV 1992. LNCS, vol. 663, pp. 164–177. Springer, Heidelberg (1993). https://doi.org/10.1007/3-540-56496-9_14

15. Nguyen, H.T.T., Rodríguez, C., Sousa, M., Coti, C., Petrucci, L.: Quasi-optimal partial order reduction. CoRR abs/1802.03950 (2018). http://arxiv.org/abs/1802.03950

16. Nielsen, M., Plotkin, G., Winskel, G.: Petri nets, event structures and domains, part I. Theor. Comput. Sci. **13**(1), 85–108 (1981)

17. Nielsen, M., Plotkin, G., Winskel, G.: Petri nets, event structures and domains. In: Kahn, G. (ed.) Semantics of Concurrent Computation. LNCS, vol. 70, pp. 266–284. Springer, Heidelberg (1979). https://doi.org/10.1007/BFb0022474

18. Pugh, W.: Skip lists: a probabilistic alternative to balanced trees. In: Dehne, F., Sack, J.-R., Santoro, N. (eds.) WADS 1989. LNCS, vol. 382, pp. 437–449. Springer, Heidelberg (1989). https://doi.org/10.1007/3-540-51542-9_36

19. Rodríguez, C., Sousa, M., Sharma, S., Kroening, D.: Unfolding-based partial order reduction. In: Proceedings of the CONCUR, pp. 456–469 (2015)

20. Rodríguez, C., Sousa, M., Sharma, S., Kroening, D.: Unfolding-based partial order reduction. CoRR abs/1507.00980 (2015). http://arxiv.org/abs/1507.00980

21. Sousa, M., Rodríguez, C., D'Silva, V., Kroening, D.: Abstract interpretation with unfoldings. CoRR abs/1705.00595 (2017). https://arxiv.org/abs/1705.00595

22. Thomson, P., Donaldson, A.F., Betts, A.: Concurrency testing using controlled schedulers: an empirical study. TOPC **2**(4), 23:1–23:37 (2016)

23. Yang, Y., Chen, X., Gopalakrishnan, G., Kirby, R.M.: Efficient stateful dynamic partial order reduction. In: Havelund, K., Majumdar, R., Palsberg, J. (eds.) SPIN 2008. LNCS, vol. 5156, pp. 288–305. Springer, Heidelberg (2008). https://doi.org/10.1007/978-3-540-85114-1_20

24. Yu, J., Narayanasamy, S., Pereira, C., Pokam, G.: Maple: a coverage-driven testing tool for multithreaded programs. In: OOPSLA, pp. 485–502 (2012)

On the Completeness of Verifying Message Passing Programs Under Bounded Asynchrony

Ahmed Bouajjani[1], Constantin Enea[1(✉)], Kailiang Ji[1], and Shaz Qadeer[2]

[1] IRIF, University Paris Diderot and CNRS, Paris, France
{abou,cenea,jkl}@irif.fr
[2] Microsoft Research, Redmond, USA
qadeer@microsoft.com

Abstract. We address the problem of verifying message passing programs, defined as a set of processes communicating through unbounded FIFO buffers. We introduce a bounded analysis that explores a special type of computations, called k-synchronous. These computations can be viewed as (unbounded) sequences of interaction phases, each phase allowing at most k send actions (by different processes), followed by a sequence of receives corresponding to sends in the same phase. We give a procedure for deciding *k-synchronizability* of a program, i.e., whether every computation is equivalent (has the same happens-before relation) to one of its k-synchronous computations. We show that reachability over k-synchronous computations and checking k-synchronizability are both PSPACE-complete.

1 Introduction

Communication with asynchronous message passing is widely used in concurrent and distributed programs implementing various types of systems such as cache coherence protocols, communication protocols, protocols for distributed agreement, device drivers, etc. An asynchronous message passing program is built as a collection of processes running in parallel, communicating asynchronously by sending messages to each other via channels or message buffers. Messages sent to a given process are stored in its entry buffer, waiting for the moment they will be received by the process. Sending messages is not blocking for the sender process, which means that the message buffers are supposed to be of unbounded size.

Such programs are hard to get right. Asynchrony introduces a tremendous amount of new possible interleavings between actions of parallel processes, and makes it very hard to apprehend the effect of all of their computations. Due

---

This work is supported in part by the European Research Council (ERC) under the European Union's Horizon 2020 research and innovation programme (grant agreement No. 678177).

H. Chockler and G. Weissenbacher (Eds.): CAV 2018, LNCS 10982, pp. 372–391, 2018.
https://doi.org/10.1007/978-3-319-96142-2_23

to this complexity, verifying properties (invariants) of such systems is hard. In particular, when buffers are ordered (FIFO buffers), the verification of invariants (or dually of reachability queries) is undecidable even when each process is finite-state [10].

Therefore, an important issue is the design of verification approaches that avoid considering the full set of computations to draw useful conclusions about the correctness of the considered programs. Several such approaches have been proposed including partial-order techniques, bounded analysis techniques, etc., e.g., [4,6,13,16,23]. Due to the hardness of the problem and its undecidability, these techniques have different limitations: either applicable only when buffers are bounded (e.g., partial-order techniques), or limited in scope, or do not provide any guarantees of termination or insight about the completeness of the analysis.

In this paper, we propose a new approach for the analysis and verification of asynchronous message-passing programs with unbounded FIFO buffers, which provides a decision procedure for checking state reachability for a wide class of programs, and which is also applicable for bounded-analysis in the general case.

We first define a bounding concept for prioritizing the enumeration of program behaviors. This concept is guided by our conviction that the behaviors of well designed programs can be seen as successions of *bounded interaction phases*, each of them being a sequence of send actions (by different processes), followed by a sequence of receive actions (again by different processes) corresponding to send actions belonging to the same interaction phase. For instance, interaction phases corresponding to *rendezvous communications* are formed of a single send action followed immediately by its corresponding receive. More complex interactions are the result of exchanges of messages between processes. For instance two processes can send messages to each other, and therefore their interaction starts with two send actions (in any order), followed by the two corresponding receive actions (again in any order). This exchange schema can be generalized to any number of processes. We say that an interaction phase is k-*bounded*, for a given $k > 0$, if its number of send actions is less than or equal to k. For instance rendezvous interactions are precisely 1-bounded phases. In general, we call k-*exchange* any k-bounded interaction phase. Given $k > 0$, we consider that a computation is k-*synchronous* if it is a succession of k-exchanges. It can be seen that, in k-synchronous computations the sum of the sizes of all messages buffers is bounded by k. However, as it will be explained later, boundedness of the messages buffers does not guarantee that there is a k such that all computations are k-synchronous.

Then, we introduce a new bounded analysis which for a given k, considers only computations that are *equivalent* to k-synchronous computations. The equivalence relation on computations is based on a notion of *trace* corresponding to a *happens-before* relation capturing the program order (the order of actions in the code of a process) and the precedence order between sends and their corresponding receives. Two computations are equivalent if they have the same trace, i.e., they differ only in the order of causally independent actions. We show that this analysis is PSPACE-complete when processes have a finite number of states.

An important feature of our bounding concept is that it is possible to decide its completeness for systems composed of finite-state processes, but with unbounded message buffers: For any given k, it is possible to decide whether every computation of the program (under the asynchronous semantics) is equivalent to (i.e., has the same trace as) a k-synchronous computation of that program. When this holds, we say that the program is k-synchronizable[1]. Knowing that a program is k-synchronizable allows to conclude that an invariant holds for all computations of the program if no invariant violations have been found by its k-bounded exchange analysis. Notice that k-synchronizability of a program *does not* imply that all its behaviours use bounded buffers. Consider for instance a program with two processes, a producer that consists of a loop of sends, and a consumer that consists of a loop of receives. Although there are computations where the entry buffer of the consumer is arbitrarily large, the program is 1-synchronizable because all its computations are equivalent to computations where each message sent by the producer is immediately received by the consumer.

Importantly, we show that checking k-synchronizability of a program, with possibly infinite-state processes, can be reduced in linear time to checking state reachability under the k-synchronous semantics (i.e., without considering all the program computations). Therefore, for finite-state processes, checking k-synchronizability is PSPACE and it is possible to decide invariant properties without dealing with unbounded message buffers when the programs are k-synchronizable (the overall complexity being PSPACE).

Then, a method for verifying asynchronous message passing programs can be defined, based on iterating k-bounded analyses with increasing value of k, starting from $k = 1$. If for some k, a violation (i.e., reachability of an error state) is detected, then the iteration stops and the conclusion is that the program is not correct. On the other hand, if for some k, the program is shown to be k-synchronizable and no violations have been found, then again the iteration terminates and the conclusion is that the program is correct.

However, it is possible that the program is *not* k-synchronizable for any k. In this case, if the program is correct then the iteration above will not terminate. Thus, an important issue is to determine whether a program is *synchronizable*, i.e., *there exists a k such that the program is k-synchronizable*. This problem is hard, and we believe that it is undecidable, but we do not have a formal proof.

We have applied our theory to a set of nontrivial examples, two of them being presented in Sect. 2. All the examples are synchronizable, which confirms our conviction that non-synchronizability should correspond to an ill-designed system (and therefore it should be reported as an anomaly).

An extended version of this paper with missing proofs can be found at [9].

---

[1] A different notion of synchronizability has been defined in [4] (see Sect. 8).

2 Motivating Examples

We provide in this section examples illustrating the relevance and the applicability of our approach. Figure 1 shows a *commit protocol* allowing a client to update a memory that is replicated in two processes, called *nodes*. The access to the nodes is controlled by a manager. Figure 2 shows an execution of this protocol. This system is 1-synchronizable, i.e., every execution is equivalent to one where only rendezvous communication is used. Intuitively, this holds because mutually interacting components are never in the situation where messages sent from one to the other are crossing messages sent in the other direction (i.e., the components are "talking" to each other at the same time). For instance, the execution in Fig. 2 is 1-synchronizable because its *conflict graph* (shown in the same figure) is acyclic. Nodes in the conflict graph are matching send-receive pairs (numbered from 1 to 6 in the figure), and edges correspond to the program order between actions in these pairs. The label of an edge records whether the actions related by program order are sends or receives, e.g., the edge from 1 to 2 labeled by RS represents the fact that the receive of the send-receive pair 1

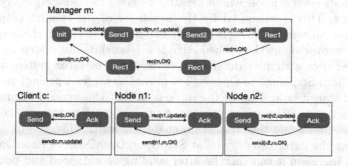

Fig. 1. A distributed commit protocol. Each process is defined as a labeled transition system. Transitions are labeled by send and receive actions, e.g., send(c, m, update) is a send from the client c to the manager m with payload update. Similarly, rec(c, OK) denotes process c receiving a message OK.

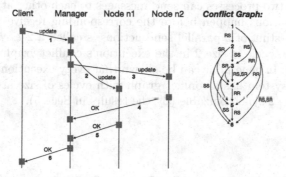

Fig. 2. An execution of the distributed commit protocol and its conflict graph.

is before the send of the send-receive pair 2, in program order. For the moment, these labels should be ignored, their relevance will be discussed in Sect. 5. The conflict graph being acyclic means that matching pairs of send-receive actions are "serializable", which implies that this execution is equivalent to one where every send is immediately followed by the matching receive (as in rendezvous communication).

Although the message buffers are bounded in all the computations of the commit protocol, this is not true for every 1-synchronizable system. There are asynchronous computations where buffers have an arbitrarily big size, which are equivalent to synchronous computations. This is illustrated by a (family of) computations shown in Fig. 4a of the system modeling an elevator described in Fig. 3 (a simplified version of the system described in [14]). This system consists of three processes: User models the user of the elevator, Elevator models the elevator's controller, and Door models the elevator's door which reacts to commands received from the controller. The execution in Fig. 4a models an interaction where the user sends an unbounded number of requests for closing the door, which generates an unbounded number of messages in the entry buffer of Elevator. These computations are 1-synchronizable since they are equivalent to a 1-synchronous computation where Elevator receives immediately every message sent by User. This is witnessed by the acyclicity of the conflict graph of this computation (shown on the right of the same figure). It can be checked that the elevator system without the dashed edge is a 1-synchronous system.

Consider now a slightly different version of the elevator system where the transition from Stopping2 to Opening2 is moved to target Opening1 instead (see the dashed transition in Fig. 3). It can be seen that this version reaches exactly the same set of configurations (tuples of process local states) as the previous one. Indeed, modifying that transition enables Elevator to send a message open to Door, but the latter can only be at StopDoor, OpenDoor, or ResetDoor at this point, and therefore it can (maybe after sending doorStopped and doorOpened) receive at state ResetDoor the message open. However, receiving this message doesn't change Door's state, and the set of reachable configurations of the system remains the same. This version of the system is not 1-synchronizable as it is shown in Fig. 4b: once the doorStopped message sent by Door is received by Elevator[2], these two processes can send messages to each other at the same time (the two send actions happen before the corresponding receives). This mutual interaction consisting of 2 parallel send actions is called a 2-*exchange* and it is witnessed by the cycle of size 2 in the execution's conflict graph (shown on the right of Fig. 4b). In general, it can be shown that every execution of this version of the elevator system has a conflict graph with cycles of size at most 2, which implies that it is 2-synchronizable (by the results in Sect. 5).

---

[2] Door sends the message from state StopDoor, and Elevator is at state Stopping2 before receiving the message.

3   Message Passing Systems

We define a message passing system as the composition of a set of processes that exchange messages, which can be stored in FIFO buffers before being received (we assume one buffer per process, storing incoming messages from all the other processes). Each process is described as a state machine that evolves by executing send or receive actions. An execution of such a system can be represented abstractly using a partially-ordered set of events, called a *trace*. The partial order in a trace represents the causal relation between events. We show that these systems satisfy *causal delivery*, i.e., the order in which messages are received by a process is consistent with the causal relation between the corresponding sendings.

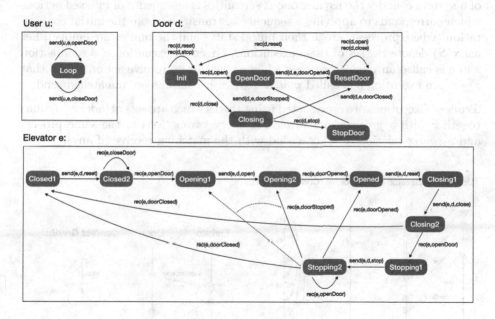

Fig. 3. A system modeling an elevator.

We fix sets $\mathbb{P}$ and $\mathbb{V}$ of process ids and message payloads, and sets $S = \{\text{send}(p, q, v) : p, q \in \mathbb{P}, v \in \mathbb{V}\}$ and $R = \{\text{rec}(q, v) : q \in \mathbb{P}, v \in \mathbb{V}\}$ of *send actions* and *receive actions*. Each send $\text{send}(p, q, v)$ combines two process ids p, q denoting the sender and the receiver of the message, respectively, and a message payload v. Receive actions specify the process q receiving the message, and the message payload v. The process executing an action $a \in S \cup R$ is denoted $\text{proc}(a)$, i.e., $\text{proc}(a) = p$ for all $a = \text{send}(p, q, v)$ or $a = \text{rec}(p, v)$, and the destination q of a send $s = \text{send}(p, q, v) \in S$ is denoted $\text{dest}(s)$. The set of send, resp., receive, actions a of process p, i.e., with $\text{proc}(a) = p$, is denoted S_p, resp., R_p.

A *message passing system* is a tuple $\mathcal{S} = ((L_p, \delta_p, l_p^0) \mid p \in \mathbb{P})$ where L_p is the set of local states of process p, $\delta_p \subseteq L \times (S_p \cup R_p) \times L$ is a transition relation describing the evolution of process p, and l_p^0 is the initial state of process p. Examples of message passing systems can be found in Figs. 1 and 3.

We fix a set $\mathbb{M}$ of message identifiers, and the sets $S_{id} = \{s_i : s \in S, i \in \mathbb{M}\}$ and $R_{id} = \{r_i : r \in R, i \in \mathbb{M}\}$ of indexed actions. Message identifiers are used to pair send and receive actions. We denote the message id of an indexed send/receive action a by $\mathsf{msg}(a)$. Indexed send and receive actions $s \in S_{id}$ and $r \in R_{id}$ are *matching*, written $s \mapsto r$, when $\mathsf{msg}(s) = \mathsf{msg}(r)$.

A configuration $c = \langle l, b \rangle$ is a vector l of local states along with a vector b of message buffers (sequences of message payloads tagged with message identifiers). The transition relation $\xrightarrow{a}$ (with label $a \in S_{id} \cup R_{id}$) between configurations is defined as expected. Every send action enqueues the message into the destination's buffer, and every receive dequeues a message from the buffer. An execution of a system S under the asynchronous semantics is a sequence of indexed actions which corresponds to applying a sequence of transitions from the initial configuration (where processes are in their initial states and the buffers are empty). Let $\mathsf{asEx}(S)$ denote the set of these executions. Given an execution e, a send action s in e is called an *unmatched send* when e contains no receive action r such that $s \mapsto r$. An execution e is called *matched* when it contains no unmatched send.

Traces. Executions are represented using traces which are sets of indexed actions together with a *program order* relating every two actions of the same process and a *source* relation relating a send with the matching receive (if any).

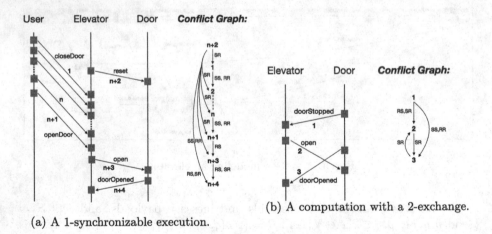

(a) A 1-synchronizable execution.

(b) A computation with a 2-exchange.

Fig. 4. Executions of the elevator.

Formally, a *trace* is a tuple $t = (A, po, src)$ where $A \subseteq S_{id} \cup R_{id}$, $po \subseteq A^2$ defines a total order between actions of the same process, and $src \subseteq S_{id} \times R_{id}$ is a relation s.t. $src(a, a')$ iff $a \mapsto a'$. The *trace* $tr(e)$ of an execution e is (A, po, src) where A is the set of all actions in e, $po(a, a')$ iff $\mathsf{proc}(a) = \mathsf{proc}(a')$ and a occurs before a' in e, and $src(a, a')$ iff $a \mapsto a'$. Examples of traces can be found in Figs. 2

and 4. The union of po and src is acyclic. Let $\mathrm{asTr}(\mathcal{S}) = \{tr(e) : e \in \mathrm{asEx}(\mathcal{S})\}$ be the set of traces of $\mathcal{S}$ under the asynchronous semantics.

Traces abstract away the order of non-causally related actions, e.g., two sends of different processes that could be executed in any order. Two executions have the same trace when they only differ in the order between such actions. Formally, given an execution $e = e_1 \cdot a \cdot a' \cdot e_2$ with $tr(e) = (A, po, src)$, where $e_1, e_2 \in (S_{id} \cup R_{id})^*$ and $a, a' \in S_{id} \cup R_{id}$, we say that $e' = e_1 \cdot a' \cdot a \cdot e_2$ is derived from e by a *valid swap* iff $(a, a') \notin po \cup src$. A permutation e' of an execution e is *conflict-preserving* when e' can be derived from e through a sequence of valid swaps. For simplicity, whenever we use the term permutation we mean conflict-preserving permutation. For instance, a permutation of $\mathrm{send}_1(p_1, q, \_)$ $\mathrm{send}_2(p_2, q, \_)$ $\mathrm{rec}_1(q, \_)$ $\mathrm{rec}_2(q, \_)$ is $\mathrm{send}_1(p_1, q, \_)$ $\mathrm{rec}_1(q, \_)$ $\mathrm{send}_2(p_2, q, \_)$ $\mathrm{rec}_2(q, \_)$ and a permutation of the execution $\mathrm{send}_1(p_1, q_1, \_)$ $\mathrm{send}_2(p_2, q_2, \_)$ $\mathrm{rec}_2(q_2, \_)$ $\mathrm{rec}_1(q_1, \_)$ is $\mathrm{send}_1(p_1, q_1, \_)$ $\mathrm{rec}_1(q_1, \_)$ $\mathrm{send}_2(p_2, q_2, \_)$ $\mathrm{rec}_2(q_2, \_)$.

Note that the set of executions having the same trace are permutations of one another. Also, a system $\mathcal{S}$ cannot distinguish between permutations of executions or equivalently, executions having the same trace.

Causal Delivery. The asynchronous semantics ensures a property known as *causal delivery*, which intuitively, says that the order in which messages are received by a process q is consistent with the "causal" relation between them. Two messages are causally related if for instance, they were sent by the same process p or one of the messages was sent by a process p after the other one was received by the same process p. This property is ensured by the fact that the message buffers have a FIFO semantics and a sent message is instantaneously enqueued in the destination's buffer. For instance, the trace (execution) on the left of Fig. 5 satisfies causal delivery. In particular, the messages $v1$ and $v3$ are causally related, and they are received in the same order by $q2$. On the right of Fig. 5, we give a trace where the messages v_1 and v_3 are causally related, but received in a different order by $q2$, thus violating causal delivery. This trace is not valid because the message $v1$ would be enqueued in the buffer of $q2$ before $\mathrm{send}(p, q1, v2)$ is executed and thus, before $\mathrm{send}(q1, q2, v3)$ as well.

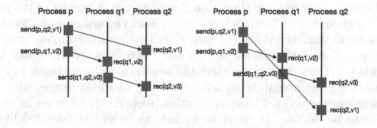

Fig. 5. A trace satisfying causal delivery (on the left) and a trace violating causal delivery (on the right).

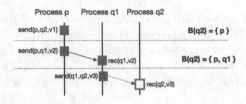

Fig. 6. An execution of the 1-synchronous semantics.

Formally, for a trace $t = (A, po, src)$, the transitive closure of $po \cup src$, denoted by $\leadsto_t$, is called the *causal relation* of t. For instance, for the trace t on the left of Fig. 5, we have that $send(p, q2, v1) \leadsto_t send(q1, q2, v3)$. A trace t satisfies *causal delivery* if for every two send actions s_1 and s_2 in A,

$$(s_1 \leadsto_t s_2 \land \mathsf{dest}(s_1) = \mathsf{dest}(s_2)) \implies (\nexists r_2 \in A. \; s_2 \vdash r_2) \lor$$
$$(\exists r_1, r_2 \in A. \; s_1 \vdash r_1 \land s_2 \vdash r_2 \land (r_2, r_1) \notin po)$$

It can be easily proved that every trace $t \in \mathrm{asTr}(\mathcal{S})$ satisfies causal delivery.

4 Synchronizability

We define a property of message passing systems called *k-synchronizability* as the equality between the set of traces generated by the asynchronous semantics and the set of traces generated by a particular semantics called *k-synchronous*.

The *k*-synchronous semantics uses an extended version of the standard rendez-vous primitive where more than one process is allowed to send a message and a process can send multiple messages, but all these messages must be received before being allowed to send more messages. This primitive is called *k-exchange* if the number of sent messages is at most k. For instance, the execution $send_1(p_1, p_2, \_) \; send_2(p_2, p_1, \_) \; rec_1(p_2, \_) \; rec_2(p_1, \_)$ is an instance of a 2-exchange. To ensure that the *k*-synchronous semantics is prefix-closed (if it admits an execution, then it admits all its prefixes), we allow messages to be dropped during a *k*-exchange transition. For instance, the prefix of the previous execution without the last receive $(rec_2(p_1, \_))$ is also an instance of a 2-exchange. The presence of unmatched send actions must be constrained in order to ensure that the set of executions admitted by the *k*-synchronous semantics satisfies causal delivery. Consider for instance, the sequence of 1-exchanges in Fig. 6, a 1-exchange with one unmatched send, followed by two 1-exchanges with matching pairs of send/receives. The receive action $(rec(q2, v3))$ pictured as an empty box needs to be disabled in order to exclude violations of causal delivery. To this, the semantics tracks for each process p a set of processes $B(p)$ from which it is forbidden to receive messages. For the sequence of 1-exchanges in Fig. 6, the unmatched $send(p, q2, v1)$ disables any receive by $q2$ of a message sent by p (otherwise, it will be even a violation of the FIFO semantics of $q2$'s buffer). Therefore, the first 1-exchange results in $B(q2) = \{p\}$. The second 1-exchange stinguishable faithfully

(the message from p to $q1$) forbids $q2$ to receive any message from $q1$. Otherwise, this message will be necessarily causally related to $v1$, and receiving it will lead to a violation of causal delivery. Therefore, when reaching $send(q1, q2, v_3)$ the receive $rec(q_2, v_3)$ is disabled because $q1 \in B(q2)$.

k-EXCHANGE

$$\frac{\begin{array}{c} e \in S_{id}^* \cdot R_{id}^* \qquad |e| \le 2 \cdot k \\ (l, \epsilon) \xrightarrow{e} (l', b), \text{ for some } b \qquad \forall s, r \in e.\ s \mapsto r \implies \mathsf{proc}(s) \notin B(\mathsf{dest}(s)) \\ B'(q) = B(q) \cup \{p : \exists s \in e \cap S_{id}.\ ((\nexists r \in e.\ s \mapsto r) \wedge p = \mathsf{proc}(s) \wedge q = \mathsf{dest}(s)) \\ \vee (\mathsf{proc}(s) \in B(q) \wedge \mathsf{dest}(s) = p)\} \end{array}}{(l, B) \xrightarrow{e}_k (l', B')}$$

Fig. 7. The synchronous semantics. Above, ϵ is a vector where all the components are ϵ, and $\xrightarrow{e}$ is the transition relation of the asynchronous semantics.

Formally, a configuration $c' = (l, B)$ in the synchronous semantics is a vector l of local states together with a function $B : \mathbb{P} \to 2^{\mathbb{P}}$. The transition relation $\Rightarrow_k$ is defined in Fig. 7. A k-EXCHANGE transition corresponds to a sequence of transitions of the asynchronous semantics starting from a configuration with empty buffers. The sequence of transitions is constrained to be a sequence of at most k sends followed by a sequence of receives. The receives are enabled depending on previous unmatched sends as explained above, using the function B. The semantics defined by $\Rightarrow_k$ is called the k-synchronous semantics.

Executions and traces are defined as in the case of the asynchronous semantics, using $\Rightarrow_k$ for some fixed k instead of $\to$. The set of executions, resp., traces, of S under the k-synchronous semantics is denoted by $\mathrm{sEx}_k(S)$, resp., $\mathrm{sTr}_k(S)$. The executions in $\mathrm{sEx}_k(S)$ and the traces in $\mathrm{sTr}_k(S)$ are called k-synchronous.

An execution e such that $tr(e)$ is k-synchronous is called k-synchronizable. We omit k when it is not important. The set of executions generated by a system S under the k-synchronous semantics is prefix-closed. Therefore, the set of its k-synchronizable executions is prefix-closed as well. Also, k-synchronizable and k-synchronous executions are undistinguishable up to permutations.

Definition 1. *A message passing system S is called* k-synchronizable *when* $\mathrm{asTr}(S) = \mathrm{sTr}_k(S)$.

It can be easily proved that k-synchronizable systems reach exactly the same set of local state vectors under the asynchronous and the k-synchronous semantics. Therefore, any assertion checking or invariant checking problem for a k-synchronizable system S can be solved by considering the k-synchronous semantics instead of the asynchronous one. This holds even for the problem of detecting deadlocks. Therefore, all these problems become decidable for finite-state k-synchronizable systems, whereas they are undecidable in the general case (because of the FIFO message buffers).

5   Characterizing Synchronous Traces

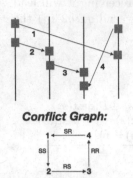

Conflict Graph:

Fig. 8. A trace and its conflict graph.

We give a characterization of the traces generated by the k-synchronous semantics that uses a notion of *conflict-graph* similar to the one used in conflict serializability [27]. The nodes of the conflict graph correspond to pairs of matching actions (a send and a receive) or to unmatched sends, and the edges represent the program order relation between the actions represented by these nodes.

For instance, an execution with an acyclic conflict graph, e.g., the execution in Fig. 2, is "equivalent" to an execution where every receive immediately follows the matching send. Therefore, it is an execution of the 1-synchronous semantics. For arbitrary values of k, the conflict graph may contain cycles, but of a particular form. For instance, traces of the 2-synchronous semantics may contain a cycle of size 2 like the one in Fig. 4(b). More generally, we show that the conflict graph of a k-synchronous trace cannot contain cycles of size strictly bigger than k. However, this class of cycles is not sufficient to precisely characterize the k-synchronous traces. Consider for instance the trace on top of Fig. 8. Its conflict-graph contains a cycle of size 4 (shown on the bottom), but the trace is not 4-synchronous. The reason is that the messages tagged by 1 and 4 must be sent during the same exchange transition, but receiving message 4 needs that the message 3 is sent after 2 is received. Therefore, it is not possible to schedule all the send actions before all the receives. Such scenarios correspond to cycles in the conflict graph where at least one receive is before a send in the program order (witnessed by the edge labeled by *RS*). We show that excluding such cycles, in addition to cycles of size strictly bigger than k, is a precise characterization of k-synchronous traces.

The *conflict-graph* of a trace $t = (A, po, src)$ is the labeled directed graph $CG_t = \langle V, E, \ell_E \rangle$ where: (1) the set of nodes V includes one node for each pair of matching send and receive actions, and each unmatched send action in t, and (2) the set of edges E is defined by: $(v, v') \in E'$ iff there exist actions $a \in \text{act}(v)$ and $a' \in \text{act}(v')$ such that $(a, a') \in po$ (where $\text{act}(v)$ is the set of actions of trace t corresponding to the graph node v). The label of the edge (v, v') records whether a and a' are send or receive actions, i.e., for all $X, Y \in \{S, R\}$, $XY \in \ell(v, v')$ iff $a \in X_{id}$ and $a' \in Y_{id}$.

A direct consequence of previous results on conflict serializability [27] is that a trace is 1-synchronous whenever its conflict-graph is acyclic. A cycle of a conflict graph CG_t is called *bad* when it contains an edge labeled by *RS*. Otherwise, it is called *good*. The following result is a characterization of k-synchronous traces.

Theorem 1. *A trace t satisfying causal delivery is k-synchronous iff every cycle in its conflict-graph is good and of size at most k.*

Theorem 1 can be used to define a runtime monitoring algorithm for k-synchronizability checking. The monitor records the conflict-graph of the trace produced by the system and checks whether it contains some bad cycle, or a cycle of size bigger than k. While this approach requires dealing with unbounded message buffers, the next section shows that this is not necessary. Synchronizability violations, if any, can be exposed by executing the system under the *synchronous* semantics.

6   Checking Synchronizability

We show that checking k-synchronizability can be reduced to a reachability problem under the *k-synchronous* semantics (where message buffers are bounded). This reduction holds for arbitrary, possibly infinite-state, systems. More precisely, since the set of (asynchronous) executions of a system is prefix-closed, if a system S admits a synchronizability violation, then it also admits a *borderline* violation, for which every strict prefix is synchronizable. We show that every *borderline* violation can be "simulated"[3] by the synchronous semantics of an instrumentation of S where the receipt of exactly one message is delayed (during every execution). We describe a monitor that observes executions of the instrumentation (under the synchronous semantics) and identifies synchronizability violations (there exists a run of this monitor that goes to an error state whenever such a violation exists).

6.1   Borderline Synchronizability Violations

For a system S, a violation e to k-synchronizability is called *borderline* when every strict prefix of e is k-synchronizable. Figure 9(a) gives an example of a borderline violation to 1-synchronizability (it is the same execution as in Fig. 4(b)).

We show that every borderline violation e ends with a receive action and this action is included in every cycle of $CG_{tr(e)}$ that is bad or exceeds the bound k. Given a cycle $c = v, v_1, \ldots, v_n, v$ of a conflict graph CG_t, the node v is called a *critical* node of c when (v, v_1) is an SX edge with $X \in \{S, R\}$ and (v_n, v) is an YR edge with $Y \in \{S, R\}$.

Lemma 1. *Let e be a borderline violation to k-synchronizability of a system S. Then, $e = e' \cdot r$ for some $e' \in (S_{id} \cup R_{id})^*$ and $r \in R_{id}$. Moreover, the node v of $CG_{tr(e)}$ representing r (and the corresponding send) is a critical node of every cycle of $CG_{tr(e)}$ which is bad or of size bigger than k.*

6.2   Simulating Borderline Violations on the Synchronous Semantics

Let S' be a system obtained from S by "delaying" the reception of exactly one nondeterministically chosen message: S' contains an additional process π and exactly one message sent by a process in S is non-deterministically redirected

---

[3] We refer to the standard notion of (stuttering) simulation where one system mimics the transitions of the other system.

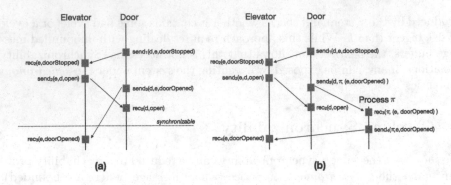

Fig. 9. A borderline violation to 1-synchronizability.

to π^4, which sends it to the original destination at a later time[5]. We show that the synchronous semantics of $\mathcal{S}'$ "simulates" a permutation of every borderline violation of $\mathcal{S}$. Figure 9(b) shows the synchronous execution of $\mathcal{S}'$ that corresponds to the borderline violation in Fig. 9(a). It is essentially the same except for delaying the reception of doorOpened by sending it to π who relays it to the elevator at a later time.

The following result shows that the k-synchronous semantics of $\mathcal{S}'$ "simulates" all the borderline violations of $\mathcal{S}$, modulo permutations.

Lemma 2. *Let* $e = e_1 \cdot \mathrm{send}_i(p, q, v) \cdot e_2 \cdot \mathrm{rec}_i(q, v)$ *be a borderline violation to k-synchronizability of $\mathcal{S}$. Then, $\mathrm{sEx}_k(\mathcal{S}')$ contains an execution e' of the form:*

$$e' = e'_1 \cdot \mathrm{send}_i(p, \pi, (q, v)) \cdot \mathrm{rec}_i(\pi, (q, v)) \cdot e'_2 \cdot \mathrm{send}_j(\pi, q, v) \cdot \mathrm{rec}_j(q, v)$$

such that $e'_1 \cdot \mathrm{send}_i(p, q, v) \cdot e'_2$ *is a permutation of* $e_1 \cdot \mathrm{send}_i(p, q, v) \cdot e_2$.

Checking k-synchronizability for $\mathcal{S}$ on the system $\mathcal{S}'$ would require that every (synchronous) execution of $\mathcal{S}'$ can be transformed to an execution of $\mathcal{S}$ by applying an homomorphism σ where the send/receive pair with destination π is replaced with the original send action and the send/receive pair initiated by π is replaced with the original receive action (all the other actions are left unchanged). However, this is not true in general. For instance, $\mathcal{S}'$ may admit an execution $\mathrm{send}_i(p, \pi, (q, v)) \cdot \mathrm{rec}_i(\pi, (q, v)) \cdot \mathrm{send}_j(p, q, v') \cdot \mathrm{rec}_j(q, v') \cdot \mathrm{send}_{i'}(\pi, q, v) \cdot \mathrm{rec}_{i'}(q, v)$ where a message sent after the one redirected to π is received earlier, and the two messages were sent by the same process p. This execution is possible under the 1-synchronous semantics of $\mathcal{S}'$. Applying the homomorphism σ, we get the execution $\mathrm{send}_i(p, q, v) \cdot \mathrm{send}_j(p, q, v') \cdot \mathrm{rec}_j(q, v') \cdot \mathrm{rec}_i(q, v)$ which violates causal delivery and therefore, it is not admitted by the asynchronous semantics

---

[4] Meaning that every transition labeled by a send action $\mathrm{send}(p, q, v)$ is doubled by a transition labeled by $\mathrm{send}(p, \pi, (q, v))$, and such a send to π is enabled only once throughout the entire execution.

[5] The process π stores the message (q, v) it receives in its state and has one transition where it can send v to the original destination q.

of $\mathcal{S}$. Our solution to this problem is to define a monitor $\mathcal{M}_{causal}$, i.e., a process which reads every transition label in the execution and advances its local state, which excludes such executions of $\mathcal{S}'$ when run under the synchronous semantics, i.e., it blocks the system $\mathcal{S}'$ whenever applying some transition would lead to an execution which, modulo the homomorphism σ, is a violation of causal delivery. This monitor is based on the same principles that we used to exclude violations of causal delivery in the synchronous semantics in the presence of unmatched sends (the component B from a synchronous configuration).

6.3   Detecting Synchronizability Violations

We complete the reduction of checking k-synchronizability to a reachability problem under the k-synchronous semantics by describing a monitor $\mathcal{M}_{viol}(k)$, which observes executions in the k-synchronous semantics of $\mathcal{S}' \parallel \mathcal{M}_{causal}$ and checks whether they represent violations to k-synchronizability; $\mathcal{M}_{viol}(k)$ goes to an error state whenever such a violation exists.

Essentially, $\mathcal{M}_{viol}(k)$ observes the sequence of k-exchanges in an execution and tracks a conflict graph cycle, if any, interpreting $send_i(p, \pi, (q, v)) \cdot rec_i(\pi, (q, v))$ as in the original system $\mathcal{S}$, i.e., as $send_i(p, q, v)$, and $send_i(\pi, q, v) \cdot rec_i(q, v)$ as $rec_i(q, v)$. By Lemma 2, every cycle that is a witness for *non* k-synchronizability includes the node representing the pair $send_i(p, q, v)$, $rec_i(q, v)$. Moreover, the successor of this node in the cycle represents an action that is executed by p and the predecessor an action executed by q. Therefore, the monitor searches for a conflict-graph path from a node representing an action of p to a node representing an action of q. Whenever it finds such a path it goes to an error state.

Figure 10 lists the definition of $\mathcal{M}_{viol}(k)$ as an abstract state machine. By the construction of $\mathcal{S}'$, we assume w.l.o.g., that both the send to π and the send from π are executed in isolation as an instance of 1-exchange. When observing the send to π, the monitor updates the variable `conflict`, which in general stores the process executing the last action in the cycle, to p. Also, a variable `count`, which becomes 0 when the cycle has strictly more than k nodes, is initialized to k. Then, for every k-exchange transition in the execution, $\mathcal{M}_{viol}(k)$ non-deterministically picks pairs of matching send/receive or unmatched sends to continue the conflict-graph path, knowing that the last node represents an action of the process stored in `conflict`. The rules for choosing pairs of matching send/receive to advance the conflict-graph path are pictured on the right of Fig. 10 (advancing the conflict-graph path with an unmatched send doesn't modify the value of `conflict`, it just decrements the value of `count`). There are two cases depending on whether the last node in the path conflicts with the send or the receive of the considered pair. One of the two processes involved in this pair of send/receive equals the current value of `conflict`. Therefore, `conflict` can either remain unchanged or change to the value of the other process. The variable `lastIsRec` records whether the current conflict-graph path ends in a conflict due to a receive action. If it is the case, and the next conflict is between

386   A. Bouajjani et al.

```
function conflict: ℙ ∪ {⊥}
function lastIsRec: 𝔹
function sawRS: 𝔹
function count: ℕ

rule send_i(p, π, (q, v)) · rec_i(π, (q, v)):
  conflict := p
  count := k
//for every i, dest(s_i) ≠ π and proc(s_i) ≠ π
rule s_1 · ... · s_n · r_1 · ... · r_m:
  for i = 1 to n
    if ( * ∧ ∃j. s_i ↦ r_j ∧ conflict ∈ {proc(s_i), dest(s_i)})
      if ( * )
        conflict := proc(s_i)
        if (lastIsRec) sawRS := true
        lastIsRec := false
      else
        conflict := dest(s_i)
        lastIsRec := true
      count--
    if ( * ∧ proc(s_i) = conflict ∧ ∀j. ¬s_i ↦ r_j )
      count--
      lastIsRec := false
rule send_i(π, q, v) · rec_i(q, v):
  assert conflict = q ⟹ (count > 0 ∧ ¬sawRS)
```

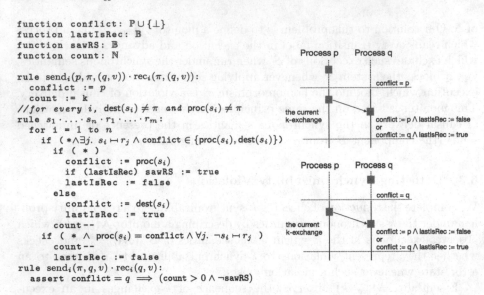

Fig. 10. The monitor $\mathcal{M}_{viol}(k)$. $\mathbb{B}$ is the set of Booleans and $\mathbb{N}$ is the set of natural numbers. Initially, conflict is $\bot$, while lastIsRec and sawRS are false.

this receive and a send, then sawRS is set to true to record the fact that the path contains an RS labeled edge (leading to a potential bad cycle).

When π sends its message to q, the monitor checks whether the conflict-graph path it discovered ends in a node representing an action of q. If this is the case, this path together with the node representing the delayed send forms a cycle. Then, if sawRS is true, then the cycle is bad and if count reached the value 0, then the cycle contains more than k nodes. In both cases, the current execution is a violation to k-synchronizability.

The set of executions in the k-synchronous semantics of $\mathcal{S}'$ composed with $\mathcal{M}_{causal}$ and $\mathcal{M}_{viol}(k)$, in which the latter goes to an error state, is denoted by $\mathcal{S}'_k \| \mathcal{M}_{causal} \| \neg \mathcal{M}_{viol}(k)$.

Theorem 2. *For a given k, a system $\mathcal{S}$ is k-synchronizable iff the set of executions $\mathcal{S}'_k \| \mathcal{M}_{causal} \| \neg \mathcal{M}_{viol}(k)$ is empty.*

Given a system $\mathcal{S}$, an integer k, and a local state l, *the reachability problem under the k-synchronous semantics* asks whether there exists a k-synchronous execution of $\mathcal{S}$ reaching a configuration (l, B) with $l = l_p$ for some $p \in \mathbb{P}$. Theorem 2 shows that checking k-synchronizability can be reduced to a reachability problem under the k-synchronous semantics. This reduction holds for arbitrary (infinite-state) systems, which implies that k-synchronizability can be checked using the existing assertion checking technology. Moreover, for finite-state systems, where each process has a finite number of local states (message buffers can still be unbounded), it implies that checking this property is PSPACE-complete.

Theorem 3. *For a finite-state system S, the reachability problem under the k-synchronous semantics and the problem of checking k-synchronizability of S are decidable and PSPACE-complete.*

7 Experimental Evaluation

Name	Proc	Loc	k	Time
Elevator	3	90	2	64.3s
OSR	4	63	1	1.28s
German	5	335	2	38m
Two-phase commit	4	57	1	1.43s
Replication storage	6	100	4	92.8s

Fig. 11. Experimental results.

As a proof of concept, we have applied our procedure for checking k-synchronizability to a set of examples extracted from the distribution of the P language[6]. Two-phase commit and Elevator are presented in Sect. 2, German is a model of the cache-coherence protocol with the same name, OSR is a model of a device driver, and Replication Storage is a model of a protocol ensuring eventual consistency of a replicated register. These examples cover common message communication patterns that occur in different domains: distributed systems (Two-phase commit, Replication storage), device drivers (Elevator, OSR), cache-coherence protocols (German). We have rewritten these examples in the Promela language and used the Spin model checker[7] for discharging the reachability queries. For a given program, its k-synchronous semantics and the monitors defined in Sect. 6 are implemented as ghost code. Finding a conflict-graph cycle which witnesses non k-synchronizability corresponds to violating an assertion.

The experimental data is listed in Fig. 11: Proc, resp., Loc, is the number of processes, resp., the number of lines of code (loc) of the original program, k is the *minimal* integer for which the program is k-synchronizable, and Time gives the number of minutes needed for this check. The ghost code required to check k-synchronizability takes 250 lines of code in average.

8 Related Work

Automatic verification of asynchronous message passing systems is undecidable in general [10]. A number of decidable subclasses has been proposed. The class of systems, called *synchronizable* as well, in [4], requires that a system generates the same sequence of send actions when executed under the asynchronous semantics as when executed under a synchronous semantics based on rendezvous communication. These systems are all 1-synchronizable, but the inclusion is strict (the 1-synchronous semantics allows unmatched sends). The techniques proposed in [4] to check that a system is synchronizable according to their definition cannot be extended to k-synchronizable systems. Other classes of systems that are 1-synchronizable have been proposed in the context of session types,

---

[6] Available at https://github.com/p-org.
[7] Available at http://spinroot.com.

e.g., [12,20,21,26]. A sound but incomplete proof method for distributed algorithms that is based on a similar idea of avoiding reasoning about all program computations is introduced in [3]. Our class of synchronizable systems differs also from classes of communicating systems that restrict the type of communication, e.g., lossy-communication [2], half-duplex communication [11], or the topology of the interaction, e.g., tree-based communication in concurrent pushdowns [19,23].

The question of deciding if all computations of a communicating system are equivalent (in the language theoretic sense) to computations with bounded buffers has been studied in, e.g., [17], where this problem is proved to be undecidable. The link between that problem and our synchronizability problem is not (yet) clear, mainly because non synchronizable computations may use bounded buffers.

Our work proposes a solution to the question of defining adequate (in terms of coverage and complexity) parametrized bounded analyses for message passing programs, providing the analogous of concepts such as context-bounding or delay-bounding defined for shared-memory concurrent programs. Bounded analyses for concurrent systems was initiated by the work on bounded-context switch analysis [25,28,29]. For shared-memory programs, this work has been extended to unbounded threads or larger classes of behaviors, e.g., [8,15,22,24]. Few bounded analyses incomparable to ours have been proposed for message passing systems, e.g., [6,23]. Contrary to our work, these works on bounded analyses in general do not propose decision procedures for checking if the analysis is complete (covers all reachable states). The only exception is [24], which concerns shared-memory.

Partial-order reduction techniques, e.g., [1,16], allow to define equivalence classes on behaviors, based on notions of action independence and explore (ideally) only one representative of each class. This has lead to efficient algorithmic techniques for enhanced model-checking of concurrent shared-memory programs that consider only a subset of relevant action interleavings. In the worst case, these techniques will still need to explore all of the interleavings. Moreover, these techniques are not guaranteed to terminate when the buffers are unbounded.

The work in [13] defines a particular class of schedulers, that roughly, prioritize receive actions over send actions, which is complete in the sense that it allows to construct the whole set of reachable states. Defining an analysis based on this class of schedulers has the same drawback as partial-order reductions, in the worst case, it needs to explore all interleavings, and termination is not guaranteed.

The approach in this work is related to robustness checking [5,7]. The general paradigm is to decide that a program has the same behaviors under two semantics, one being weaker than the other, by showing a polynomial reduction to a state reachability problem under the stronger semantics. For instance, in our case, the class of message passing programs with unbounded FIFO channels is Turing powerful, but still, surprisingly, k-synchronizability of these programs is decidable and PSPACE-complete. The results in [5,7] cannot be applied in our context: the class of programs and their semantics are different, and the corresponding robustness checking algorithms are based on distinct concepts and techniques.

References

1. Abdulla, P.A., Aronis, S., Jonsson, B., Sagonas, K.F.: Optimal dynamic partial order reduction. In: Jagannathan, S., Sewell, P. (eds.) The 41st Annual ACM SIGPLAN-SIGACT Symposium on Principles of Programming Languages, POPL 2014, San Diego, CA, USA, 20-21 January 2014, pp. 373–384. ACM (2014). https://doi.org/10.1145/2535838.2535845
2. Abdulla, P.A., Jonsson, B.: Verifying programs with unreliable channels. Inf. Comput. **127**(2), 91–101 (1996). https://doi.org/10.1006/inco.1996.0053
3. Bakst, A., von Gleissenthall, K., Kici, R.G., Jhala, R.: Verifying distributed programs via canonical sequentialization. PACMPL **1**(OOPSLA), 110:1–110:27 (2017). https://doi.org/10.1145/3133934
4. Basu, S., Bultan, T.: On deciding synchronizability for asynchronously communicating systems. Theor. Comput. Sci. **656**, 60–75 (2016). https://doi.org/10.1016/j.tcs.2016.09.023
5. Bouajjani, A., Derevenetc, E., Meyer, R.: Robustness against relaxed memory models. In: Hasselbring, W., Ehmke, N.C. (eds.) Software Engineering 2014, Kiel, Deutschland. LNI, vol. 227, pp. 85–86. GI (2014). http://eprints.uni-kiel.de/23752/
6. Bouajjani, A., Emmi, M.: Bounded phase analysis of message-passing programs. In: Flanagan, C., König, B. (eds.) TACAS 2012. LNCS, vol. 7214, pp. 451–465. Springer, Heidelberg (2012). https://doi.org/10.1007/978-3-642-28756-5_31
7. Bouajjani, A., Emmi, M., Enea, C., Ozkan, B.K., Tasiran, S.: Verifying robustness of event-driven asynchronous programs against concurrency. In: Yang, H. (ed.) ESOP 2017. LNCS, vol. 10201, pp. 170–200. Springer, Heidelberg (2017). https://doi.org/10.1007/978-3-662-54434-1_7
8. Bouajjani, A., Emmi, M., Parlato, G.: On sequentializing concurrent programs. In: Yahav, E. (ed.) SAS 2011. LNCS, vol. 6887, pp. 129–145. Springer, Heidelberg (2011). https://doi.org/10.1007/978-3-642-23702-7_13
9. Bouajjani, A., Enea, C., Ji, K., Qadeer, S.: On the completeness of verifying message passing programs under bounded asynchrony. arXiv:1804.06612 [cs.PL]
10. Brand, D., Zafiropulo, P.: On communicating finite-state machines. J. ACM **30**(2), 323–342 (1983). https://doi.org/10.1145/322374.322380
11. Cécé, G., Finkel, A.: Verification of programs with half-duplex communication. Inf. Comput. **202**(2), 166–190 (2005). https://doi.org/10.1016/j.ic.2005.05.006
12. Deniélou, P.-M., Yoshida, N.: Multiparty session types meet communicating automata. In: Seidl, H. (ed.) ESOP 2012. LNCS, vol. 7211, pp. 194–213. Springer, Heidelberg (2012). https://doi.org/10.1007/978-3-642-28869-2_10
13. Desai, A., Garg, P., Madhusudan, P.: Natural proofs for asynchronous programs using almost-synchronous reductions. In: Black, A.P., Millstein, T.D. (eds.) Proceedings of the 2014 ACM International Conference on Object Oriented Programming Systems Languages & Applications, OOPSLA 2014, part of SPLASH 2014, Portland, OR, USA, 20–24 October 2014, pp. 709–725. ACM (2014). https://doi.org/10.1145/2660193.2660211

14. Desai, A., Gupta, V., Jackson, E.K., Qadeer, S., Rajamani, S.K., Zufferey, D.: P: safe asynchronous event-driven programming. In: Boehm, H., Flanagan, C. (eds.) ACM SIGPLAN Conference on Programming Language Design and Implementation, PLDI 2013, Seattle, WA, USA, 16–19 June 2013, pp. 321–332. ACM (2013). https://doi.org/10.1145/2462156.2462184

15. Emmi, M., Qadeer, S., Rakamaric, Z.: Delay-bounded scheduling. In: Ball, T., Sagiv, M. (eds.) Proceedings of the 38th ACM SIGPLAN-SIGACT Symposium on Principles of Programming Languages, POPL 2011, Austin, TX, USA, 26–28 January 2011, pp. 411–422. ACM (2011). https://doi.org/10.1145/1926385.1926432

16. Flanagan, C., Godefroid, P.: Dynamic partial-order reduction for model checking software. In: Palsberg, J., Abadi, M. (eds.) Proceedings of the 32nd ACM SIGPLAN-SIGACT Symposium on Principles of Programming Languages, POPL 2005, Long Beach, California, USA, 12–14 January 2005, pp. 110–121. ACM (2005). https://doi.org/10.1145/1040305.1040315

17. Genest, B., Kuske, D., Muscholl, A.: On communicating automata with bounded channels. Fundam. Inform. 80(1–3), 147–167 (2007). http://content.iospress.com/articles/fundamenta-informaticae/fi80-1-3-09

18. Gupta, A., Malik, S. (eds.): CAV 2008. LNCS, vol. 5123. Springer, Heidelberg (2008). https://doi.org/10.1007/978-3-540-70545-1

19. Heußner, A., Leroux, J., Muscholl, A., Sutre, G.: Reachability analysis of communicating pushdown systems. Logical Methods Comput. Sci. 8(3) (2012). https://doi.org/10.2168/LMCS-8(3:23)2012

20. Honda, K., Vasconcelos, V.T., Kubo, M.: Language primitives and type discipline for structured communication-based programming. In: Hankin, C. (ed.) ESOP 1998. LNCS, vol. 1381, pp. 122–138. Springer, Heidelberg (1998). https://doi.org/10.1007/BFb0053567

21. Honda, K., Yoshida, N., Carbone, M.: Multiparty asynchronous session types. J. ACM 63(1), 9:1–9:67 (2016). https://doi.org/10.1145/2827695

22. Kidd, N., Jagannathan, S., Vitek, J.: One stack to run them all. In: van de Pol, J., Weber, M. (eds.) SPIN 2010. LNCS, vol. 6349, pp. 245–261. Springer, Heidelberg (2010). https://doi.org/10.1007/978-3-642-16164-3_18

23. La Torre, S., Madhusudan, P., Parlato, G.: Context-bounded analysis of concurrent queue systems. In: Ramakrishnan, C.R., Rehof, J. (eds.) TACAS 2008. LNCS, vol. 4963, pp. 299–314. Springer, Heidelberg (2008). https://doi.org/10.1007/978-3-540-78800-3_21

24. La Torre, S., Madhusudan, P., Parlato, G.: Model-checking parameterized concurrent programs using linear interfaces. In: Touili, T., Cook, B., Jackson, P. (eds.) CAV 2010. LNCS, vol. 6174, pp. 629–644. Springer, Heidelberg (2010). https://doi.org/10.1007/978-3-642-14295-6_54

25. Lal, A., Reps, T.W.: Reducing concurrent analysis under a context bound to sequential analysis. In: Gupta and Malik [18], pp. 37–51. https://doi.org/10.1007/978-3-540-70545-1_7

26. Lange, J., Tuosto, E., Yoshida, N.: From communicating machines to graphical choreographies. In: Rajamani, S.K., Walker, D. (eds.) Proceedings of the 42nd Annual ACM SIGPLAN-SIGACT Symposium on Principles of Programming Languages, POPL 2015, Mumbai, India, 15–17 January 2015, pp. 221–232. ACM (2015). https://doi.org/10.1145/2676726.2676964

27. Papadimitriou, C.H.: The serializability of concurrent database updates. J. ACM 26(4), 631–653 (1979).

28. Qadeer, S., Rehof, J.: Context-bounded model checking of concurrent software. In: Halbwachs, N., Zuck, L.D. (eds.) TACAS 2005. LNCS, vol. 3440, pp. 93–107. Springer, Heidelberg (2005). https://doi.org/10.1007/978-3-540-31980-1_7
29. Qadeer, S., Wu, D.: KISS: keep it simple and sequential. In: Pugh, W., Chambers, C. (eds.) Proceedings of the ACM SIGPLAN 2004 Conference on Programming Language Design and Implementation 2004, Washington, DC, USA, 9–11 June 2004, pp. 14–24. ACM (2004). https://doi.org/10.1145/996841.996845

Constrained Dynamic Partial Order Reduction

Elvira Albert[1] , Miguel Gómez-Zamalloa[1](✉) , Miguel Isabel[1] ,
and Albert Rubio[2]

[1] Complutense University of Madrid,
Madrid, Spain
mzamalloa@fdi.ucm.es
[2] Universitat Politècnica de Catalunya,
Barcelona, Spain

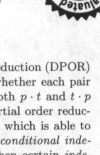

Abstract. The cornerstone of dynamic partial order reduction (DPOR) is the notion of *independence* that is used to decide whether each pair of concurrent events p and t are in a race and thus both $p \cdot t$ and $t \cdot p$ must be explored. We present *constrained* dynamic partial order reduction (CDPOR), an extension of the DPOR framework which is able to avoid redundant explorations based on the notion of *conditional independence*—the execution of p and t commutes only when certain *independence constraints* (ICs) are satisfied. ICs can be declared by the programmer, but importantly, we present a novel SMT-based approach to automatically synthesize ICs in a static pre-analysis. A unique feature of our approach is that we have succeeded to exploit ICs within the state-of-the-art DPOR algorithm, achieving *exponential* reductions over existing implementations.

1 Introduction

Partial Order Reduction (POR) is based on the idea that two interleavings can be considered equivalent if one can be obtained from the other by swapping adjacent, non-conflicting *independent* execution steps. Such equivalence class is called a Mazurkiewicz trace, and POR guarantees that it is sufficient to explore one interleaving per equivalence class. Early POR algorithms [8,10,20] relied on static over-approximations to detect possible *future* conflicts. The Dynamic-POR (DPOR) algorithm, introduced by Godefroid [9] in 2005, was a breakthrough in the area because it does not need to look at the future. It keeps track of the independence races witnessed along its execution and uses them to decide the required exploration dynamically, without the need of static approximation. DPOR is nowadays considered one of the most scalable techniques for

---

This work was funded partially by the Spanish MECD Salvador de Madariaga Mobility Grants PRX17/00297 and PRX17/00303, the Spanish MINECO projects TIN2015-69175-C4-2-R and TIN2015-69175-C4-3-R, and by the CM project S2013/ICE-3006.

H. Chockler and G. Weissenbacher (Eds.): CAV 2018, LNCS 10982, pp. 392–410, 2018.
https://doi.org/10.1007/978-3-319-96142-2_24

software verification. The key of DPOR algorithms is in the dynamic construction of two types of sets at each scheduling point: the *sleep set* that contains processes whose exploration has been proved to be redundant (and hence should not be selected), and the *backtrack set* that contains the processes that have not been proved independent with previously explored steps (and hence need to be explored). Source-DPOR (SDPOR) [1,2] improves the precision to compute backtrack sets (named *source* sets), proving optimality of the resulting algorithm for *any* number of processes w.r.t. an *unconditional independence* relation.

Challenge. When considering (S)DPOR with unconditional independence, if a pair of events is not independent in all possible executions, they are treated as potentially dependent and their interleavings explored. Unnecessary exploration can be avoided using conditional independence. E.g., two processes executing respectively the atomic instructions $if(z \geq 0)$ $z = x$; and $x = x + 1$; would be considered dependent even if $z \leq -1$—this is indeed an *independence constraint* (IC) for these two instructions. Conditional independence was early introduced in the context of POR [11,15]. The first algorithm that has used notions of conditional independence within the state-of-the-art DPOR algorithm is Context-Sensitive DPOR (CSDPOR) [3]. However, CSDPOR does not use ICs (it rather checks state equivalence dynamically during the exploration) and exploits conditional (context-sensitive) independence only *partially* to extend the sleep sets. Our challenge is twofold: (i) extend the DPOR framework to exploit ICs during the exploration in order to both reduce the backtrack sets and expand the sleep sets as much as possible, (ii) statically synthesize ICs in an automatic pre-analysis.

Contributions. The main contributions of this work can be summarized as:

1. We introduce sufficient conditions –that can be checked dynamically– to soundly exploit ICs within the DPOR framework.
2. We extend the state-of-the-art DPOR algorithm with new forms of pruning (by means of expanding sleep sets and reducing backtrack sets).
3. We present an SMT-based approach to automatically synthesize ICs for *atomic blocks*, whose applicability goes beyond the DPOR context.
4. We experimentally show the exponential gains achieved by CDPOR on some typical concurrency benchmarks used in the DPOR literature before.

2   Background

In this section we introduce some notations, the basic notions on the POR theory and the state-of-the-art DPOR algorithm that we will extend in Sect. 3.

Our work is formalized for a general model of concurrent systems, in which a program is composed of *atomic blocks* of code. An atomic block can contain just one (global) statement that affects the global state, a sequence of local statements (that only read and write the local state of the process) followed by a global statement, or a block of code with possibly several global statements but whose execution cannot interleave with other processes because it has been implemented as atomic (e.g., using locks, semaphores, etc.). Each atomic block in the program is given a unique block identifier. We use $spawn(P[ini])$ to create a new process. Depending on the programming language, P can be the name of a method and $[ini]$ initial values for the parameters, or P can be the identifier of the initial block to execute and $[ini]$ the initialization instructions, etc., in every case with mechanisms to continue the execution from one block to the following one. Notice that the use of atomic blocks in our formalization generalizes the particular case of considering atomicity at the level of single instructions.

As previous work on DPOR [1–3], we assume the state space does not contain cycles, executions have finite unbounded length and processes are deterministic (i.e., at a given time there is at most one event a process can execute). Let Σ be the set of states of the system. There is a unique initial state $s_0 \in \Sigma$. The execution of a process p is represented as a partial function $execute_p : \Sigma \mapsto \Sigma$ that moves the system from one state to a subsequent state. Each application of the function $execute_p$ represents the execution of an *atomic block* of the code that p is running, denoted as *event* (or execution step) of process p. An *execution sequence* E (also called *derivation*) of a system is a finite sequence of events of its processes starting from s_0, and it is uniquely characterized by the sequence of processes that perform steps of E. For instance, $p \cdot q \cdot q$ denotes the execution sequence that first performs one step in p, followed by two steps in q. We use ϵ to denote the empty sequence. The state of the system after E is denoted by $s_{[E]}$. The set of processes enabled in state s (i.e., that can perform an execution step from s) is denoted by $enabled(s)$.

2.1   Basics of Partial Order Reduction

An *event* e of the form (p, i) denotes the i-th occurrence of process p in an execution sequence, and $\hat{e}$ denotes the process p of event e, which is extended to sequences of events in the natural way. We write $\bar{e}$ to refer to the identifier of the atomic block of code the event e is executing. The set of events in execution sequence E is denoted by $dom(E)$. We use $e <_E e'$ to denote that event e occurs before event e' in E, s.t. $<_E$ establishes a total order between events in E, and $E \leq E'$ to denote that sequence E is a prefix of sequence E'. Let $dom_{[E]}(w)$ denote the set of events in execution sequence $E.w$ that are in sequence w, i.e., $dom(E.w) \backslash dom(E)$. If w is a single process p, we use $next_{[E]}(p)$ to denote the single event in $dom_{[E]}(p)$. If P is a set of processes, $next_{[E]}(P)$ denotes the set of $next_{[E]}(p)$ for all $p \in P$. The core concept in POR is that of the *happens-before* partial order among the events in execution sequence E, denoted by $\rightarrow_E$. This relation defines a subset of the $<_E$ total order, such that any two sequences with the same happens-before order are equivalent. Any linearization E' of $\rightarrow_E$ on $dom(E)$ is an execution sequence with exactly the same happens-before relation $\rightarrow_{E'}$ as $\rightarrow_E$. Thus, $\rightarrow_E$ induces a set of equivalent execution sequences, all with the same happens-before relation. We use $E \simeq E'$ to denote that E and E' are linearizations of the same happens-before relation. The happens-before partial order has traditionally been defined in terms of a *dependency* relation between

Algorithm 1. (Source+Context-sensitive)+Constrained DPOR algorithm

```
1: procedure EXPLORE(E)
2:    if (∃p ∈ (enabled(s_[E])\sleep(E))) then
3:       back(E) := {p};
4:       while (∃p ∈ (back(E)\sleep(E))) do
5:          let n = next_[E](p);
6:          for all (e ∈ dom(E) such that e ⪍_{E.p} n) do
7:             let E' = pre(E, e);
8:             let u = dep(E, e, n);
9:             if (¬(U_⇒(I_{ē,n̄}, e, n, s_[E'.û]))) then
10:               updateBack(E, E', e, p);
11:               if C(s_[E'.û]) for some C ∈ I_{ē,n̄} then
12:                  add û.p.ê to sleep(E');
13:               else
14:                  updateSleepCS(E, E', e, p);
15:          sleep(E.p) := {x | x ∈ sleep(E), E ⊨ p ⋄ x}
16:             ∪ {x | p.x ∈ sleep(E)}
17:             ∪ {x | x ∈ sleep(E), |x| = 1, m = next_[E](x), U_⇒(I_{n̄,m̄}, n, m, s_[E])};
18:          EXPLORE(E.p);
19:          sleep(E) := sleep(E) ∪ {p};
```

the execution steps associated to those events [10]. Intuitively, two steps p and q are *dependent* if there is at least one execution sequence E for which they do not commute, either because (i) one *enables* the other (i.e., the execution of p leads to introducing q, or viceversa), or because (ii) $s_{[E.p.q]} \neq s_{[E.q.p]}$. We define $dep(E, e, n)$ as the subsequence containing all events e' in E that occur after e and happen-before n in $E.p$ (i.e., $e <_E e'$ and $e' \rightarrow_{E.p} n$). The unconditional dependency relation is used for defining the concept of a *race* between two events. Event e is said to be in race with event e' in execution E, if the events belong to different processes, e happens-before e' in E ($e \rightarrow_E e'$), and the two events are "concurrent", i.e. there exists an equivalent execution sequence $E' \simeq E$ where the two events are adjacent. We write $e \lesssim_E e'$ to denote that e is in race with e' and that the race can be reversed (i.e., the events can be executed in reverse order). POR algorithms use this relation to reduce the number of equivalent execution sequences explored, with SDPOR ensuring that only one execution sequence in each equivalence class is explored.

2.2   State-of-the-Art DPOR with Unconditional Independence

Algorithm 1 shows the state-of-the-art DPOR algorithm –based on the SDPOR algorithm of [1,2],[1] which in turn is based on the original DPOR algorithm of [9]. We refer to this algorithm as DPOR in what follows. The context-sensitive extension of CSDPOR [3] (lines 14 and 16) and our extension highlighted in blue

---

[1] The extension to support *wake-up trees* [2] is deliberately not included to simplify the presentation.

(lines 8–10, 11–13 and 17) should be ignored by now and will be described in Sect. 3.

The algorithm carries out a depth-first exploration of the execution tree using POR receiving as parameter a derivation E (initially empty). Essentially, it dynamically finds reversible races and is able to backtrack at the appropriate scheduling points to reverse them. For this purpose, it keeps two sets at every prefix E' of E: $back(E')$ with the set of processes that must be explored from E', and, $sleep(E')$ with the set of sequences of processes that previous executions have determined do not need to be explored from E'. Note that in the original DPOR the sleep set contained only single processes, but in later improvements sequences of processes are added, so our description considers this general case. The algorithm starts by selecting any process p that is enabled by the state reached after executing E and is not already in $sleep(E)$. If it does not find any such process p, it stops. Otherwise, after setting $back(E) = \{p\}$ to start the search, it explores every element in $back(E)$ that is not in $sleep(E)$. The backtrack set of E might grow as the loop progresses (due to later executions of line 10). For each such p, DPOR performs two phases: race detection (lines 6, 7 and 10) and state exploration (lines 15, 18 and 19). The race detection starts by finding all events e in $dom(E)$ such that $e \precsim_{E.p} n$, where n is the event being selected (see line 5). For each such e, it sets E' to $pre(E, e)$, i.e., to be the prefix of E up to, but not including e. Procedure $updateBack$ modifies $back(E')$ in order to ensure that the race between e and n is reversed. The source-set extension of [1,2] detects cases where there is no need to modify $back(E')$ –this is done within procedure $updateBack$ whose code is not shown because it is not affected by our extension. After this, the algorithm continues with the state exploration phase for $E.p$, by retaining in its sleep set any element x in $sleep(E)$ whose events in $E.p$ are independent of the next event of p in E (denoted as $E \models p \diamond x$), i.e., any x such that $next_{[E]}(p)$ would not happen-before any event in $dom(E.p.x)\setminus dom(E.p)$. Then, the algorithm explores $E.p$, and finally it adds p to $sleep(E)$ to ensure that, when backtracking on E, p is not selected until a dependent event with it is selected. All versions of the DPOR algorithm (except [3]) rely on the unconditional (or context-insensitive) dependency relation. This relation has to be over-approximated, usually by requiring that global variables accessed by one execution step are not modified by the other.

Example 1. Consider the example in Fig. 1 with 3 processes p, q, r containing a single atomic block. Since all processes have a single event, by abuse of notation, we refer to events by their process name throughout all examples in the paper. Relying on the usual over-approximation of dependency all three pairs of events are dependent. Therefore, starting with one instance per process, the algorithm has to explore 6 execution sequences, each with a different happens-before relation. The tree, including the dotted and dashed fragments, shows the exploration from the initial state $z = -2$, $x = -2$. The value of variable z is shown in brackets at each state. Essentially, in all states of the form $E.e$, the algorithm always finds a reversible race between the next event of the current selected process (p, q or r) and e, and adds it to $back(E)$. Also, when backtracking on E, none of the elements in $sleep(E)$ is propagated down, since all events are considered dependent. In the best case, considering an exact (yet unconditional) dependency relation which realizes that events p and r are independent, the algorithm will make the following reductions. In state 6, p and r will not be in race and hence p will not be added to $back(q)$. This avoids exploring the sequence $p.r$ from 5. When backtracking on state 0 with r, where $sleep(\epsilon) = \{p,q\}$, p will be propagated down to $sleep(r)$ since $\epsilon \models r \diamond p$, hence avoiding the exploration of $p.q$ from 8. Thus, the algorithm will explore 4 sequences.

```
p: x = x+1;
q: if (z >= 0) z = x;
r: z = z+1; x = x+1;
```

$I_{\bar{p},\bar{q}} = \{z \le -1\}$
$I_{\bar{p},\bar{r}} = \{true\}$
$I_{\bar{q},\bar{r}} = \{(z \ge 0), (z = x), (z \le -2)\}$

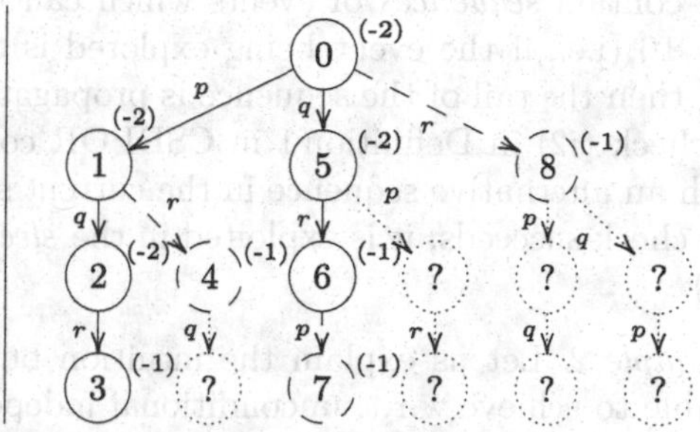

Fig. 1. Left: code of working example (up) and ICs (down). Right: execution tree starting from $z = -2$, $x = -2$. Full tree computed by SDPOR, dotted fragment not computed by CSDPOR, and, dashed+dotted fragment not computed by CDPOR.

3 DPOR with Conditional Independence

Our aim in CDPOR is twofold: (1) provide techniques to both infer and soundly check conditional independence, and (2) be able to exploit them at *all* points of the DPOR algorithm where dependencies are used. Section 3.1 reviews the notions of conditional independence and ICs, and introduces a first type of check where ICs can be directly used in the DPOR algorithm. Section 3.2 illustrates why ICs cannot be used at the remaining independence check points in the algorithm, and introduces sufficient conditions to soundly exploit them at those points. Finally, Sect. 3.3 presents the CDPOR algorithm that includes all types of checks.

3.1 Using Precomputed ICs Directly Within DPOR

Conditional independence consists in checking independence at the given state.

Definition 1 (conditional independence). *Two events α and β are independent in state S, written $indep(\alpha, \beta, S)$ if (i1) none of them enables the other from S; and, (i2) if they are both enabled in S, then $S \xrightarrow{\alpha \cdot \beta} S'$ and $S \xrightarrow{\beta \cdot \alpha} S'$.*

The use of conditional independence in the POR theory was firstly studied in [15], and it has been partially applied within the DPOR algorithm in CSDPOR [3]. Function *updateSleepCS* at line 14 and the modification of *sleep* at 16 encapsulate this partial application of CSDPOR (the code of *updateSleepCS* is not shown because it is not affected by our extension). Intuitively, *updateSleepCS* works as follows: when a reversible race is found in the current sequence being explored, it builds an *alternative* sequence which corresponds to the reverse race, and then checks whether the states reached after running the two sequences are the same. If they are, it adds the alternative sequence to the corresponding *sleep* set so that this sequence is not fully explored when backtracking. Therefore, sleep sets can contain *sequences* of events which can be propagated down via the rule of line 16 (i.e., if the event being explored is the head of a sequence in the sleep set, then the tail of the sequence is propagated down). In essence, the technique to check $(i2)$ in Definition 1 in CSDPOR consists in checking state equivalence with an alternative sequence in the current state (hence it is conditional) and, if the check succeeds, it is exploited in the *sleep* set only (and not in the *backtrack* set).

Example 2. Let us explain the intuition behind the reductions that CSDPOR is able to achieve w.r.t. unconditional independence-based DPOR on the example. In state 1, when the algorithm selects q and detects the reversible race between q and p, it computes the alternative sequence $q.p$ and realizes that $s_{[p.q]} = s_{[q.p]}$, and hence adds $p.q$ to $sleep(\epsilon)$. Similarly, in state 2, it computes $p.r.q$ and realizes that $s_{[p.q.r]} = s_{[p.r.q]}$ adding $r.q$ to $sleep(p)$. Besides these two alternative sequences, it computes two more. Overall, CSDPOR explores 2 complete sequences ($p.q.r$ and $q.r.p$) and 13 states (the 9 states shown, plus 4 additional states to compute the alternative sequences).

Instead of computing state equivalence to check $(i2)$ as in [3], our approach assumes precomputed *independence constraints* (ICs) for all pairs of atomic blocks in the program. ICs will be evaluated at the appropriate state to determine the independence between pairs of concurrent events executing such atomic blocks.

Definition 2 (ICs). *Consider two events α and β that execute, respectively, the atomic blocks $\bar{\alpha}$ and $\bar{\beta}$. The* independence constraints $I_{\bar{\alpha},\bar{\beta}}$ *are a set of boolean expressions (constraints) on the variables accessed by α and β (including local and global variables) s.t., if some constraint C in $I_{\bar{\alpha},\bar{\beta}}$ holds in state S, written $C(S)$, then condition $(i2)$ of $indep(\alpha, \beta, S)$ holds.*

Our first contribution is in lines 11–13 where ICs are used within DPOR as follows. Before executing *updateSleepCS* at line 14, we check if some constraint in $I_{\bar{e},\bar{n}}$ holds in the state $s_{[E'.\hat{u}]}$, by building the sequence $E'.\hat{u}$, where $u = dep(E, e, n)$. Only if our check fails we proceed to execute *updateSleepCS*. The advantages of our check w.r.t. *updateSleepCS* are: (1) the alternative execution sequence built by *updateSleepCS* is strictly longer than ours and hence more states will be explored, and (2) *updateSleepCS* must check state equivalence while we evaluate boolean expressions. Yet, because our IC is an approximation, if we fail to prove independence we can still use *updateSleepCS*.

Example 3. Consider the ICs in Fig. 1 (down left), which provide the constraints ensuring the independence of each pair of atomic blocks, and whose synthesis is explained in Sect. 4.1. In the exploration of the example, when the algorithm detects the reversible race between q and p in state 1, instead of computing $q.p$ and then comparing $s_{[p.q]} = s_{[q.p]}$ as in CSDPOR, we would just check the constraint in $I_{\bar{p},\bar{q}}$ at state ϵ, i.e., in $z = -2$ (line 11), and since it succeeds, $q.p$ is added to $sleep(\epsilon)$. The same happens at states 2, again at 1 (when backtracking with r), and 5. This way we avoid the exploration of the additional 4 states due to the computation of the alternative sequences in Example 2 (namely $q.p$, $r.p$ and $r.q$ from state 0, and $r.q$ from 1). The algorithm is however still exploring many redundant derivations, namely states 4, 5, 6, 7 and 8.

3.2   Transitive Uniformity: How to Further Exploit ICs Within DPOR

The challenge now is to use ICs, and therefore conditional independence, at the remaining dependency checks performed by the DPOR algorithm, and most importantly, for the race detection (line 6). In the example, that would avoid the addition of q and r to $back(\epsilon)$ and r to $back(p)$, and hence would make the algorithm only explore the sequence $p.q.r$. Although that can be done in our example, it is unsound in general as the following counter-example illustrates.

Example 4. Consider the same example but starting from the initial state $z = -1$, $x = -2$. During the exploration of the first sequence $p.q.r$, the algorithm will not find any race since p and q are independent in $z = -1$, q and r are independent in $z = x = -1$, and, p and r are always independent. Therefore, no more sequences than $p.q.r$ with final result $z = 0$ will be explored. There is however a non-equivalent sequence, $r.q.p$, which leads to a different final state $z = -1$.

The problem of using conditional independence within the POR theory was already identified by Katz and Peled [15]. Essentially, the main idea of POR is that the different linearizations of a partial order yield equivalent executions that can be obtained by swapping adjacent independent events. However, this is no longer true with conditional dependency. In Example 4, using conditional independence, the partial order of the explored derivation $p.q.r$ would be empty, which means there would be 6 possible linearizations. However $r.q.p$ is not equivalent to $p.q.r$ since q and p are dependent in $s_{[r]}$, i.e., when $z = 0$. An extra condition, called *uniformity*, is proposed in [15] to allow using conditional independence within the POR theory. Intuitively, *uniform independence* adds a condition to Definition 1 to ensure that independence holds at all successor states for those events that are enabled and are *uniformly independent* with the two events whose independence is being proved. While this notion can be checked *a posteriori* in a given exploration, it is unclear how it could be applied in a dynamic setting where decisions are made *a priori*. Here we propose a weaker notion of uniformity, called *transitive uniformity*, for which we have been able to prove that the *dynamic*-POR framework is sound. The difference with [15] is that our extra condition ensures that independence holds at all successor states for *all* events that are enabled, which is thus a superset of the events considered in [15]. We notice that the general happens-before definition of [1,2] does not capture our transitive uniform conditional independence below (namely property seven of [1,2] does not hold), hence CDPOR cannot be seen as an instance of SDPOR but rather as an extension.

Definition 3. *The* transitive uniform *conditional independence relation, written* $unif(\alpha, \beta, S)$, *fulfills (i1) and (i2) and, (i3)* $unif(\alpha, \beta, S_\gamma)$ *holds for all* $\gamma \notin \{\alpha, \beta\}$ *enabled in* S, *where* S_γ *is defined by* $S \xrightarrow{\gamma} S_\gamma$.

During the exploration of the sequence $p.q.r$ in Example 4, the algorithm will now find a reversible race between p and q, since the independence is not transitively uniform in $z = -1, x = -2$. Namely, *(i3)* does not hold since r is enabled and we have $x = -1$ and $z = 0$ in $s_{[r]}$, which implies $\neg unif(p, q, s_{[r]})$ (*(i2)* does not hold).

We now introduce sufficient conditions for transitive uniformity that can be precomputed statically, and efficiently checked, in our dynamic algorithm. Condition *(i1)* is computed dynamically as usual during the exploration simply storing enabling dependencies. Condition *(i2)* is provided by the ICs. Our sufficient conditions to ensure *(i3)* are as follows. For each atomic block b, we precompute *statically* (before executing DPOR) the set $W(b)$ of the global variables that can be modified by the full execution of b, i.e., by an instruction in b or by any other block called from, or enabled by, b (transitively). To this end, we do a simple analysis which consists in: (1) First we build the call graph for the program to establish the calling relationships between the blocks in the program. Note that when we find a process creation instruction $spawn(P[ini])$ we have a calling relationship between the block in which the spawn instruction appears and P. (2) We obtain (by a fixed point computation) the largest relation fulfilling that g belongs to $W(b)$ if either g is *modified* by an instruction in b or g belongs to $W(c)$ for some block c called from b. This computation can be done with different levels of precision, and it is well-studied in the static analysis field [18]. We let $G(C)$ be the set of global variables evaluated on constraint C in I.

Definition 4 (sufficient condition for transitive uniformity, $U_\Rightarrow$). *Let* E *be a sequence,* I *a set of constraints,* α *and* β *be two events enabled in* $s_{[E]}$, *and* $T = next_{[E]}(enabled(s_{[E]})) \setminus \{\alpha, \beta\}$, *we define* $U_\Rightarrow(I, \alpha, \beta, s_{[E]}) \equiv \exists C \in I :$ $C(s_{[E]}) \wedge ((G(C) \cap \bigcup_{t \in T} W(\bar{t})) = \emptyset)$.

Intuitively, our sufficient condition ensures transitive uniformity by checking that the global variables involved in the constraint C of the IC used to ensure the uniformity condition are not modified by other enabled events in the state.

Theorem 1. *Given a sequence* E *and two events* α *and* β *enabled in* $s_{[E]}$, *we have that* $U_\Rightarrow(I_{\bar{\alpha}, \bar{\beta}}, \alpha, \beta, s_{[E]}) \Rightarrow unif(\alpha, \beta, s_{[E]})$.

3.3   The Constrained DPOR Algorithm

The code highlighted in blue in Algorithm 1 provides the extension to apply conditional independence within DPOR. In addition to the pruning explained in Sect. 3.1, it achieves two further types of pruning:

1. *Back-set reduction.* The race detection is strengthened with an extra condition (line 9) so that e and n (the next event of p) are in race only if they are not conditionally independent in state $s_{[E'.u]}$ (using our sufficient condition above). Here u is the sub-sequence of events of E that occur after e and "happen-before" n. This way the conditional independence is evaluated in the state after the shortest subsequence so that the events are adjacent in an equivalent execution sequence.
2. *Sleep-set extension.* An extra condition to propagate down elements in the sleep set is added (line 17) s.t. a sequence x, with just one process, is propagated if its corresponding event is conditionally independent of n in $s_{[E]}$.

It is important to note also that the inferred conditional independencies are recorded in the happens-before relation to be later re-used for subsequent computations of the $\precsim$ and *dep* definitions.

Example 5. Let us describe the exploration for the example in Fig. 1 using our CDPOR. At state 1, the algorithm checks whether p and q are in race. $U_\Rightarrow(I_{\bar{p},\bar{q}}, p, q, S)$ does not hold in $z = -2$ since, although $(z \leq -1) \in I_{\bar{p},\bar{q}}$ holds, we have that $G(z \leq -1) \cap W(r) = \{z\} \neq \emptyset$. Process q is hence added to $back(\epsilon)$. On the other hand, since $(z \leq -1) \in I_{\bar{p},\bar{q}}$ holds in $z = -2$ (line 11), $q.p$ is added to $sleep(\epsilon)$ (line 12). At state 2 the algorithm checks the possible race between q and r after executing p. This time the transitive uniformity of the independence of q and r holds since $(z \leq -2) \in I_{\bar{q},\bar{r}}$ holds, and there are no enabled events out of $\{q, r\}$. Our algorithm therefore avoids the addition of r to $back(p)$ (pruning 1 above). The algorithm also checks the possible race between p and r in $z = -2$. Again, $true \in I_{\bar{p},\bar{r}}$ holds and is uniform since $G(true) = \emptyset$ (pruning 1). The algorithm finishes the exploration of sequence $p.q.r$ and then backtracks with q at state 0. At state 5 the algorithm selects process r (p is in the sleep set of 5 since it is propagated down from the $q.p$ in $sleep(\epsilon)$). It then checks the possible race between q and r, which is again discarded (pruning 1), since transitive uniformity of the independence of q and r can be proved: we have that $(z \leq -2) \in I_{\bar{q},\bar{r}}$ holds in $z = -2$ and $W(p) \cap G(z \leq -2) = \emptyset$, where p is the only enabled event out of $\{q, r\}$ and $W(p) = \{x\}$. This avoids adding r to $back(\epsilon)$. Finally, at state 5, p is propagated down in the new sleep set (pruning 2), since as before $true \in I_{\bar{p},\bar{r}}$ ensures transitive uniformity. The exploration therefore finishes at state 6.

Overall, on our working example, CDPOR has been able to explore only one complete sequence $p.q.r$ and the partial sequence $q.r$ (a total of 6 states). The latter one could be avoided if a more precise sufficient condition for uniformity is provided which, in particular, is able to detect that the independence of p and q in ϵ is transitive uniform, i.e., it still holds after r (even if r writes variable z).

Theorem 2 (soundness). *For each Mazurkiewicz trace T defined by the happens before relation, Explore($\epsilon, \emptyset$) in Algorithm 1 explores a complete execution sequence T' that reaches the same final state as T.*

4   Automatic Generation of ICs Using SMT

Generating ICs amounts to proving (conditional) program equivalence w.r.t. the global memory. While the problem is very hard in general, proving equivalence of smaller blocks of code becomes more tractable. This section introduces a novel SMT-based approach to synthesize ICs between pairs of atomic blocks of code. Our ICs can be used within any transformation or analysis tool –beyond DPOR– which can gain accuracy or efficiency by knowing that fragments of code (conditionally) commute. Section 4.1 first describes the inference for basic blocks; Sect. 4.2 extends it to handle process creation and Sect. 4.3 outlines other extensions, like loops, method invocations and data structures.

4.1   The Basic Inference

In this section we consider blocks of code containing conditional statements and assignments using linear integer arithmetic (LIA) expressions. The first step to carry out the inference is to transform q and r into two respective *deterministic* Transition Systems (TSs), T_q and T_r (note that q and r are assumed to be deterministic), and compose them in both reverse orders $T_{q \cdot r}$ and $T_{r \cdot q}$. Consider r and q in Fig. 1 whose associated TSs are (primed variables represent the final value of the variables):

$$T_q : z \geq 0 \to z' = x; \qquad T_r : true \to x' = x + 1, z' = z + 1;$$
$$z < 0 \to z' = z;$$

The code to be analyzed is the composition of T_q and T_r in both orders:

$$T_{q \cdot r}: \ z \geq 0 \to x' = x + 1, z' = x + 1; \qquad T_{r \cdot q}: \ z \geq -1 \to x' = x + 1, z' = x + 1;$$
$$z < 0 \to x' = x + 1, z' = z + 1; \qquad\qquad z < -1 \to x' = x + 1, z' = z + 1;$$

In what follows we denote by $T_{a \cdot b}$ the deterministic TS obtained from the concatenation of the blocks a and b, such that all variables are assigned in one instruction using parallel assignment. We let $A \mid_G$ be the restriction to the global memory of the assignments in A (i.e., ignoring the effect on local variables). The following definition provides an SMT formula over LIA (a boolean formula where the atoms are equalities and inequalities over linear integer arithmetic expressions) which encodes the independence between the two blocks.

Definition 5 (IC generation). *Let us consider two atomic blocks q and r and a global memory G and let $C_i \to A_i$ (resp. $C'_j \to A'_j$) be the transitions in $T_{q \cdot r}$ (resp. $T_{r \cdot q}$). We obtain $F_{q,r}$ as the SMT formula: $\bigvee_{i,j}(C_i \wedge C'_j \wedge A_i \mid_G = A'_j \mid_G)$.*

Intuitively, the SMT encoding in the above definition has as solutions all those states where both a condition C_i of a transition in $T_{q \cdot r}$ and C'_j of a transition in $T_{r \cdot q}$ hold (and hence are compatible) and the final global state after executing all instructions in the two transitions (denoted A_i and A'_j) remains the same.

Next, we generate the constraints of the independence condition $I_{q,r}$ by obtaining a compact representation of all models over linear arithmetic atoms (computed by an *allSAT* SMT solver) satisfying $F_{q,r}$. In particular, we add a constraint in $I_{q,r}$ for every obtained model.

Example 6. In the example, we have the TS with conditions and assignments:

$$T_{q \cdot r}: C_1{:}z \geq 0 \quad A_1{:}x' = x + 1, z' = x + 1 \quad \middle| \quad T_{r \cdot q}: C'_1{:}z \geq -1 \quad A'_1{:}x' = x + 1, z' = x + 1$$
$$\phantom{T_{q \cdot r}:} C_2{:}z < 0 \quad A_2{:}x' = x + 1, z' = z + 1 \quad\middle|\quad \phantom{T_{r \cdot q}:} C'_2{:}z < -1 \quad A'_2{:}x' = x + 1, z' = z + 1$$

and we obtain a set with three constraints $I_{q,r} = \{(z \geq 0), (z = x), (z < -1)\}$ by computing all models satisfying the following resulting formula:

$$(z \geq 0 \wedge z \geq -1 \wedge x + 1 = x + 1 \wedge x + 1 = x + 1) \vee$$
$$(z \geq 0 \wedge z < -1 \wedge x + 1 = x + 1 \wedge x + 1 = z + 1) \vee$$
$$(z < 0 \wedge z \geq -1 \wedge x + 1 = x + 1 \wedge z + 1 = x + 1) \vee$$
$$(z < 0 \wedge z < -1 \wedge x + 1 = x + 1 \wedge z + 1 = z + 1)$$

The second conjunction is unsatisfiable since there is no model with both C_1 and C'_2. On the other hand, the equalities of the first and the last conjunctions always hold, which give us the constraints $z \geq 0$ and $z \leq -2$. Finally, all equalities hold when $x = z$, which give us the third constraint as a result for our SMT encoding.

Note that, as in this case $F_{q,r}$ describes not only a sufficient but also a necessary condition for independence, the obtained constraints IC are also a sufficient and necessary conditions for independence. This allows removing line 14 in the algorithm, since the context-sensitive check will fail if line 11 does. However, the next extensions do not ensure that the generated ICs are necessary conditions.

4.2   IC for Blocks with Process Creation

Consider the following two methods whose body constitutes an atomic block (e.g., the lock is taken at the method start and released at the return). They are inspired by a highly concurrent computation for the Fibonacci used in the experiments. Variables **nr** and **r** are global to all processes:

```
fib(int v) {                      res(int v) {
    if (v≤1) {spawn(res(v));}         if (nr>0) {nr=0; r=v; }
    else {spawn(fib(v-1));            else {spawn(res(r+v));
          spawn(fib(v-2));}                 r=0;nr=1;}
}                                 }
```

We now want to infer $I_{\mathrm{fib}(v),\mathrm{fib}(v_1)}$, $I_{\mathrm{fib}(v),\mathrm{res}(v_1)}$, $I_{\mathrm{res}(v),\mathrm{res}(v_1)}$. The first step is to obtain, for each block r, a *TS with uninterpreted functions*, denoted TS_r^u, in which transitions are of the form $C \rightarrow (A, S)$ where A are the parallel assignments as in Sect. 4.1, and S is a multiset containing calls to fresh *uninterpreted functions* associated to the processes spawned within the transition (i.e., a process creation $spawn(P)$ is associated to an uninterpreted function $spawn\_P$).

$T_{\mathsf{fib}}^u \colon v \leq 1 \to (skip, \{spawn\_res(v)\})$
$\qquad v > 1 \to (skip, \{spawn\_fib(v-1), spawn\_fib(v-2)\})$

$T_{\mathsf{res}}^u \colon nr \geq 0 \to (nr' = 0, r' = v, \{\})$
$\qquad nr < 0 \to (nr' = 1, r' = 0, \{spawn\_res(r+v)\})$

The following definition extends Definition 5 to handle process creation. Intuitively, it associates a fresh variable to each different element in the multisets (mapping P' below) and enforces equality among the multisets.

Definition 6 (IC generation with process creation). *Let us consider $TS_{r \cdot q}^u$ and $TS_{q \cdot r}^u$. We define $P = \{\cup s \mid s \in S, \text{ with } C \to (A, S) \in TS_{r \cdot q}^u \cup TS_{q \cdot r}^u\}$. Let P' be a mapping from the elements in P to fresh variables, and $P'(S)$ be the replacement of the elements in the multiset S applying the mapping P'. Let $C_i \to (A_i, S_i)$ (resp. $C'_j \to (A'_j, S'_j)$) be the transitions in $TS_{q \cdot r}^u$ (resp. $TS_{r \cdot q}^u$). We obtain $F_{q,r}$ as the SMT formula: $\bigvee_{i,j}(C_i \wedge C'_j \wedge A_i \mid_G = A'_j \mid_G \wedge P'(S_i) \equiv P'(S'_j))$.*

For simplicity and efficiency, we consider that $\equiv$ corresponds to the syntactic equality of the multisets. However, in order to improve the precision of the encoding we apply P' to S_i and S_j replacing two process creations by the same variable if they are equal modulo associativity and commutativity (AC) of arithmetic operators and after substituting the equalities already imposed by $A_i \mid_G = A'_j$ (see example below). A more precise treatment can be achieved by using equality with uninterpreted functions (EUF) to compare the multisets of processes.

Example 7. Let us show how we apply the above definition to infer $I_{\mathsf{res}(v), \mathsf{res}(v_1)}$. We first build $T_{\mathsf{res}(v) \cdot \mathsf{res}(v_1)}$ from $T_{\mathsf{res}(v)}$ by composing it with itself:

$$nr \leq 0 \to (nr' = 0, r' = v_1, \{spawn\_res(r+v)\})$$
$$nr > 0 \to (nr' = 1, r' = 0, \{spawn\_res(v+v_1)\})$$

and $T_{\mathsf{res}(v_1) \cdot \mathsf{res}(v)}$ which is like the one above but exchanging v and v_1. Next, we define $P' = \{spawn\_res(r+v) \mapsto x_1, spawn\_res(v+v_1) \mapsto x_2, spawn\_res(r+v_1) \mapsto x_3, spawn\_res(v_1+v) \mapsto x_4\}$ and apply it with the improvement described above

$$(nr \leq 0 \wedge nr \leq 0 \wedge 0 = 0 \wedge v = v_1 \wedge \{x_1\} = \{x_1\}) \vee$$
$$(nr \leq 0 \wedge nr > 0 \wedge 0 = 1 \wedge v_1 = 0 \wedge \{x_1\} = \{x_4\}) \vee$$
$$(nr > 0 \wedge nr \leq 0 \wedge 1 = 0 \wedge 0 = v \wedge \{x_2\} = \{x_3\}) \vee$$
$$(nr > 0 \wedge nr > 0 \wedge 1 = 1 \wedge 0 = 0 \wedge \{x_2\} = \{x_2\})$$

Note that the second and the third conjunction are unfeasible and hence can be removed from the formula. In the first one $spawn\_res(r+v_1)$ is replaced by x_1 (instead of x_3) since we can substitute v_1 by v as $v = v_1$ is imposed in the conjunction and in the fourth one $spawn\_res(v_1+v)$ is replaced by x_2 (instead of x_4) since it is equal modulo AC to $spawn\_res(v+v_1)$. Then we finally have

$$(nr \leq 0 \wedge nr \leq 0 \wedge 0 = 0 \wedge v = v_1) \quad \vee \quad (nr > 0 \wedge nr > 0 \wedge 1 = 1 \wedge 0 = 0)$$

As before, $I_{\mathsf{res}(v), \mathsf{res}(v_1)} = \{(nr > 0), (v = v_1)\}$ is then obtained by computing all satisfying models. In the same way we obtain $I_{\mathsf{fib}(v), \mathsf{res}(v_1)} = I_{\mathsf{fib}(v), \mathsf{fib}(v_1)} = \{true\}$.

The following theorem states the soundness of the inference of ICs, that holds by construction of the SMT formula.

Theorem 3 (soundness of independence conditions). *Given the assumptions in Definition 6, if $\exists C \in I_{r,q}$ s.t. $C(S)$ holds, then $S \xrightarrow{r \cdot q} S'$ and $S \xrightarrow{q \cdot r} S'$.*

We will also get a necessary condition in those instances where the use of syntactic equality modulo AC on the multisets of created processes (as described above) is not loosing precision. This can be checked when building the encoding.

4.3   Other Extensions

We abstract loops from the code of the blocks so that we can handle them as uninterpreted functions similarly to Definition 6. Basically, for each loop, we generate as many uninterpreted functions as variables it modifies (excluding local variables of the loop) plus one to express all processes created inside the loop. The functions have as arguments the variables accessed by the loop (again excluding local variables). This transformation allows us to represent that each variable might be affected by the execution of the loop over some parameters, and then check in the reverse trace whether we get to the loop over the same parameters.

Definition 7 (loop extraction for IC generation). *Let us consider a loop L that accesses $x_1, \ldots, x_n$ variables and modifies $y_1, \ldots, y_m$ variables (excluding local loop variables) and let $l_1, \ldots, l_{m+1}$ be fresh function symbol names. We replace L by the following code:*

$$x'_1 = x_1; \ldots; \; x'_n = x_n; \; y_1 = l_1(x'_1, ..., x'_n); \ldots; \; y_m = l_m(x'_1, ..., x'_n);$$
$$spawn(f_{m+1}(x'_1, ..., x'_n)); \quad (only\,if\,there\,are\,spawn\,operations\,inside\,the\,loop)$$

Existing dependency analysis can be used to infer the subset of $x_1, \ldots, x_n$ that affects each y_i, achieving more precision with a small pre-computation overhead.

The treatment of method invocations (or function calls) to be executed atomically within the considered blocks can be done analogously to loops by introducing one fresh function for every (non-local) variable that is modified within the method call and one more for the result. The parameters of these new functions are the original ones plus one for each accessed (non-local) variable. After the transformations for both loops and calls described above, we have TSs with function calls that are treated as uninterpreted functions in a similar way to Definition 6. However these functions can now occur in the conditions and the assignments of the TS. To handle them, we use again a mapping P''' to remove all function calls from the TS and replace them by fresh integer variables. After that the encoding is like in Definition 6, and we obtain an SMT formula over LIA, which is again sent to the allSAT SMT solver. Once we have obtained the models we replace back the introduced fresh variables by the function calls using the mapping P''. Several simplifications on equalities involving function calls can be done before and after invoking the solver to improve the result. As a final remark, data structures like lists or maps have been handled by expressing their uses as function calls, hence obtaining constraints that include conditions on them.

5   Experiments

In this section we report on experimental results that compare the performance of three DPOR algorithms: SDPOR [1,2], CSDPOR [3] and our proposal CDPOR. We have implemented and experimentally evaluated our method within the SYCO tool [3], a systematic testing tool for message-passing concurrent programs. SYCO can be used online through its web interface available at http://costa.fdi.ucm.es/syco. To generate the ICs, SYCO calls a new feature of the VeryMax program analyzer [6] which uses Barcelogic [5] as SMT solver. As benchmarks, we have borrowed the examples from [3] (available online from the previous url) that were used to compare SDPOR with CSDPOR. They are classical concurrent applications: several concurrent sorting algorithms (QS, MS, PS), concurrent Fibonacci Fib, distributed workers Pi, a concurrent registration system Reg and database DBP, and a consumer producer interaction BB. These benchmarks feature the typical concurrent programming methodology in which computations are split into smaller atomic subcomputations which concurrently interleave their executions, and which work on the same shared data. Therefore, the concurrent processes are highly interfering, and both inferring ICs and applying DPOR algorithms on them becomes challenging.

We have executed each benchmark with size increasing input parameters. A timeout of 60 s is used and, when reached, we write $>X$ to indicate that for the corresponding measure we encountered X units up to that point (i.e., it is at least X). Table 1 shows the results of the executions for 6 different inputs. Column Tr shows the number of traces, S the number of states that the algorithms explore, and T the time in sec it takes to compute them. For CDPOR, we also show the time T^{smt} of inferring the ICs (since the inference is performed once for all executions, it is only shown in the first row). Times are obtained on an Intel(R) Core(TM) i7 CPU at 2.5 GHz with 8 GB of RAM (Linux Kernel 5.4.0). Columns G^s and G^{cs} show the time speedup of CDPOR over SDPOR and CSDPOR, respectively, computed by dividing each respective T by the time T of CDPOR. Column G^{smt} shows the time speedup over CSDPOR including T^{smt} in the time of CDPOR. We can see from the speedups that the gains of CDPOR increase exponentially in all examples with the size of the input. When compared with CSDPOR, we achieve reductions up to 4 orders of magnitude for the largest inputs on which CSDPOR terminates (e.g., Pi, QS). It is important to highlight that the number of non-unitary sequences stored in sleep sets is 0 in every benchmark except in BB for which it remains quite low (namely for BB(11) the peak is 22).

W.r.t. SDPOR, we achieve reductions of 4 orders of magnitude even for smaller inputs for which SDPOR terminates (e.g., PS). Note that since most examples reach the timeout, the gains are at least the ones we show, thus the

Table 1. Experimental evaluation

Bench.	SDPOR			CSDPOR			CDPOR				Speed-up		
	Tr	S	T	Tr	S	T	Tr	S	T	T^{smt}	G^s	G^{cs}	G^{smt}
Fib(6)	3k	26k	7.7	1	244	0.1	1	50	0.03	0.12	366	4	0.6
Fib(7)	>13k	>160k	60.0	1	551	0.3	1	82	0.05		>1364	6	1.4
Fib(8)	>8k	>101k	60.0	1	2k	0.7	1	134	0.12		>527	6	3.0
Fib(9)	>4k	>51k	60.0	1	3k	2.8	1	218	0.25		>242	12	7.5
Fib(10)	>2k	>27k	60.0	1	8k	11.5	1	354	0.69		>88	17	14.3
Fib(14)	>10	>3k	60.0	>1	>4k	60.0	1	3k	42.67		>2	>2	>1.5
QS(10)	512	9k	2.6	1	4k	1.0	1	38	0.02	11.99	199	71	0.1
QS(13)	5k	91k	29.5	1	29k	7.9	1	50	0.03		1474	395	0.7
QS(15)	>7k	>157k	60.0	1	115k	42.6	1	58	0.05		>1500	1064	3.6
QS(20)	>4k	>98k	60.0	>1	>148k	60.0	1	78	0.04		>1539	>1539	>5.0
QS(25)	>3k	>96k	60.0	>1	>133k	60.0	1	98	0.06		>1017	>1017	>5.0
QS(200)	>5	>2k	60.0	>1	>87k	60.0	1	798	4.45		>14	>14	>3.7
MS(10)	628	7k	2.9	1	187	0.1	1	42	0.02	0.12	175	6	0.7
MS(30)	>6k	>55k	60.0	1	974	1.0	1	118	0.13		>484	8	4.0
MS(65)	>2k	>16k	60.0	1	3k	3.5	1	258	0.47		>131	8	6.1
MS(100)	>2k	>15k	60.0	>1	>19k	60.0	1	398	0.97		>63	>63	>55.6
MS(150)	>2k	>21k	60.0	>1	>18k	60.0	1	598	2.21		>28	>28	>26.0
MS(220)	>341	>6k	60.0	>1	>5k	60.0	1	878	4.49		>14	>14	>13.1
Pi(7)	6k	49k	16.2	74	2k	0.4	1	23	0.02	0.05	1243	27	5.6
Pi(8)	>10k	>105k	60.0	264	5k	1.7	1	26	0.02		>4616	128	26.9
Pi(9)	>11k	>120k	60.0	2k	19k	7.0	1	29	0.02		>4000	465	108.9
Pi(10)	>10k	>128k	60.0	6k	91k	45.2	1	32	0.02		>3530	2655	683.7
Pi(12)	>9k	>122k	60.0	>7k	>128k	60.0	1	38	0.03		>2400	>2400	>810.9
Pi(20)	>5k	>101k	60.0	>5k	>115k	60.0	1	62	0.09		>723	>723	>454.6
PS(4)	288	2k	0.4	2	41	0.1	1	16	0.01	0.59	72	2	0.1
PS(5)	35k	156k	43.2	8	142	0.1	1	22	0.01		5391	5	0.1
PS(6)	>32k	>141k	60.0	72	2k	0.4	1	29	0.02		>4286	28	0.7
PS(7)	>29k	>130k	60.0	2k	28k	7.5	1	37	0.03		>2858	357	12.3
PS(9)	>25k	>109k	60.0	>11k	>165k	60.0	1	56	0.06		>1053	>1053	>92.9
PS(11)	>23k	>103k	60.0	>9k	>132k	60.0	1	79	0.09		>690	>690	>88.8
DBP(5)	243	8k	2.0	133	4k	1.0	32	193	0.08	0.09	27	14	6.2
DBP(6)	729	33k	8.2	308	11k	3.2	64	386	0.16		53	21	13.3
DBP(7)	3k	134k	36.9	699	32k	10.8	128	771	0.33		113	33	26.2
DBP(8)	>4k	>157k	60.0	2k	91k	36.1	256	2k	0.79		>77	47	41.6
DBP(10)	>6k	>116k	60.0	>4k	>125k	60.0	2k	7k	3.23		>19	>19	>18.2
DBP(12)	>9k	>79k	60.0	>8k	>111k	60.0	5k	25k	15.79		>4	>4	>3.8
BB(6)	924	4k	1.3	215	2k	0.5	64	382	0.91	0.18	2	1	0.4
BB(7)	4k	13k	4.3	580	4k	1.2	128	830	1.49		3	1	0.8
BB(8)	13k	49k	17.2	2k	11k	3.3	256	2k	2.79		7	2	1.1
BB(9)	>41k	>156k	60.0	5k	30k	9.0	512	4k	6.15		>10	2	1.5
BB(10)	>46k	>176k	60.0	12k	81k	23.6	2k	9k	12.50		>5	2	1.9
BB(11)	>44k	>169k	60.0	>44k	>169k	60.0	3k	18k	25.74		>3	>3	>2.4

concrete numbers shown should not be taken into account. In some examples (e.g., BB, MS), though the gains are linear for the small inputs, when the size of the problem increases both SDPOR and CSDPOR time out, while CDPOR can still handle them efficiently.

Similar reductions are obtained for number of states explored. In this case, the system times out when it has memory problems, and the computation stops progressing (hence the number of explored states does not increase with the input any more). As regards the time to infer the annotations T^{smt}, we observe that in most cases it is negligible compared to the exploration time of the other methods. QS is the only example that needs some seconds to be solved and this is due to the presence of several nested conditional statements combined with the use of built-in functions for lists, which makes the generated SMT encoding harder for the solver and the subsequent simplification step. Note that the inference is a pre-process which does not add complexity to the actual DPOR algorithm.

6   Related Work and Conclusions

The notion of conditional independence in the context of POR was first introduced in [11,15]. Also [12] provides a similar strengthened dependency definition. CSDPOR was the first approach to exploit this notion within the state-of-the-art DPOR algorithm. We advance this line of research by fully integrating conditional independence within the DPOR framework by using *independence constraints* (ICs) together with the notion of *transitive uniform* conditional independence –which ensures the ICs hold along the whole execution sequence. Both ICs and transitive uniformity can be approximated statically and checked dynamically, making them effectively applicable within the dynamic framework. The work in [14,21] generated for the first time ICs for processes with a single instruction following some predefined patterns. This is a problem strictly simpler than our inference of ICs both in the type of IC generated (restricted to the patterns) and on the single-instruction blocks they consider. Furthermore, our approach using an AllSAT SMT solver is different from the CEGAR approach in [4]. The ICs are used in [14,21] for SMT-based bounded model checking, an approach to model checking fundamentally different from our stateless model checking setting. As a consequence ICs are used in a different way, in our case with no bounds on number of processes, nor derivation lengths, but requiring a uniformity condition on independence in order to ensure soundness. Maximal causality reduction [13] is technically quite different from CDPOR as it integrates SMT solving within the dynamic algorithm.

Finally, data-centric DPOR (DCDPOR) [7] presents a new DPOR algorithm based on a different notion of dependency according to which the equivalence classes of derivations are based on the pairs read-write of variables. Consider the following three simple processes $\{p, q, r\}$ and the initial state $x = 0$:

p: write(x=5), q: write(x=5), r: read(x). In DCDPOR, we have only three different observation functions: (r, x) (reading the initial value), (r, p) (reading the value that p writes), (r, q) (reading the value that q writes). Therefore, this notion of relational independence is finer grained than the traditional one in DPOR. However, DCDPOR does not consider conditional dependency, i.e., it does not realize that (r, p) and (r, q) are equivalent, and hence only two explorations are required (and explored by CDPOR). The example in conclusion, our approach and DCDPOR can complement each other: our approach would benefit from using a dependency based on the read-write pairs as proposed in DCDPOR, and DCDPOR would benefit from using conditional independence as proposed in our work. It remains as future work to study this integration. Related to DCDPOR, [16] extends optimal DPOR with observers. For the previous example, [16] needs to explore five executions: $r.p.q$ and $r.q.p$, are equivalent because p and q do not have any observer. Another improvement orthogonal to ours is to inspect dependencies over chains of events, as in [17,19].

References

1. Abdulla, P.A., Aronis, S., Jonsson, B., Sagonas, K.: Source sets: a foundation for optimal dynamic partial order reduction. J. ACM **64**(4), 25:1–25:49 (2017)
2. Abdulla, P.A., Aronis, S., Jonsson, B., Sagonas, K.F.: Optimal dynamic partial order reduction. In: POPL, pp. 373–384 (2014)
3. Albert, E., Arenas, P., de la Banda, M.G., Gómez-Zamalloa, M., Stuckey, P.J.: Context-sensitive dynamic partial order reduction. In: Majumdar, R., Kunčak, V. (eds.) CAV 2017. LNCS, vol. 10426, pp. 526–543. Springer, Cham (2017). https://doi.org/10.1007/978-3-319-63387-9_26
4. Bansal, K., Koskinen, E., Tripp, O.: Commutativity condition refinement (2015)
5. Bofill, M., Nieuwenhuis, R., Oliveras, A., Rodríguez-Carbonell, E., Rubio, A.: The barcelogic SMT solver. In: Gupta, A., Malik, S. (eds.) CAV 2008. LNCS, vol. 5123, pp. 294–298. Springer, Heidelberg (2008). https://doi.org/10.1007/978-3-540-70545-1_27
6. Borralleras, C., Larraz, D., Oliveras, A., Rivero, J.M., Rodríguez-Carbonell, E., Rubio, A.: VeryMax: tool description for termCOMP 2016. In: WST (2016)
7. Chalupa, M., Chatterjee, K., Pavlogiannis, A., Vaidya, K., Sinha, N.: Data-centric dynamic partial order reduction. In: POPL 2018 (2018)
8. Clarke, E.M., Grumberg, O., Minea, M., Peled, D.A.: State space reduction using partial order techniques. STTT **2**(3), 279–287 (1999)
9. Flanagan, C., Godefroid, P.: Dynamic partial-order reduction for model checking software. In: POPL, pp. 110–121 (2005)
10. Godefroid, P. (ed.): Partial-Order Methods for the Verification of Concurrent Systems. LNCS, vol. 1032. Springer, Heidelberg (1996). https://doi.org/10.1007/3-540-60761-7
11. Godefroid, P., Pirottin, D.: Refining dependencies improves partial-order verification methods (extended abstract). In: Courcoubetis, C. (ed.) CAV 1993. LNCS, vol. 697, pp. 438–449. Springer, Heidelberg (1993). https://doi.org/10.1007/3-540-56922-7_36
12. Günther, H., Laarman, A., Sokolova, A., Weissenbacher, G.: Dynamic reductions for model checking concurrent software. In: Bouajjani, A., Monniaux, D. (eds.) VMCAI 2017. LNCS, vol. 10145, pp. 246–265. Springer, Cham (2017). https://doi.org/10.1007/978-3-319-52234-0_14
13. Huang, S., Huang, J.: Speeding up maximal causality reduction with static dependency analysis. In: ECOOP, pp. 16:1–16:22 (2017)
14. Kahlon, V., Wang, C., Gupta, A.: Monotonic partial order reduction: an optimal symbolic partial order reduction technique. In: Bouajjani, A., Maler, O. (eds.) CAV 2009. LNCS, vol. 5643, pp. 398–413. Springer, Heidelberg (2009). https://doi.org/10.1007/978-3-642-02658-4_31
15. Katz, S., Peled, D.A.: Defining conditional independence using collapses. TCS **101**(2), 337–359 (1992)
16. Aronis, S., Jonsson, B., Lång, M., Sagonas, K.: Optimal dynamic partial order reduction with observers. In: Beyer, D., Huisman, M. (eds.) TACAS 2018. LNCS, vol. 10806, pp. 229–248. Springer, Cham (2018). https://doi.org/10.1007/978-3-319-89963-3_14
17. Nguyen, H.T.T., Rodríguez, C., Sousa, M., Coti, C., Petrucci, L.: Quasi-optimal partial order reduction. CoRR, abs/1802.03950 (2018)
18. Nielson, F., Nielson, H.R., Hankin, C.: Principles of Program Analysis. Springer, Heidelberg (1999). https://doi.org/10.1007/978-3-662-03811-6

19. Rodríguez, C., Sousa, M., Sharma, S., Kroening, D.: Unfolding-based partial order reduction. In: CONCUR, pp. 456–469 (2015)
20. Valmari, A.: Stubborn sets for reduced state space generation. In: Rozenberg, G. (ed.) ICATPN 1989. LNCS, vol. 483, pp. 491–515. Springer, Heidelberg (1991). https://doi.org/10.1007/3-540-53863-1_36
21. Wang, C., Yang, Z., Kahlon, V., Gupta, A.: Peephole partial order reduction. In: Ramakrishnan, C.R., Rehof, J. (eds.) TACAS 2008. LNCS, vol. 4963, pp. 382–396. Springer, Heidelberg (2008). https://doi.org/10.1007/978-3-540-78800-3_29

CPS, Hardware, Industrial Applications

Formal Verification of a Vehicle-to-Vehicle (V2V) Messaging System

Mark Tullsen[1]([✉]), Lee Pike[2], Nathan Collins[1], and Aaron Tomb[1]

[1] Galois, Inc., Portland, OR, USA
{tullsen,conathan,atomb}@galois.com
[2] Groq, Inc., Palo Alto, USA
leepike@gmail.com

Abstract. Vehicle-to-Vehicle (V2V) communications is a "connected vehicles" standard that will likely be mandated in the U.S. within the coming decade. V2V, in which automobiles broadcast to one another, promises improved safety by providing collision warnings, but it also poses a security risk. At the heart of V2V is the communication messaging system, specified in SAE J2735 using the Abstract Syntax Notation One (ASN.1) data-description language. Motivated by numerous previous ASN.1 related vulnerabilities, we present the formal verification of an ASN.1 encode/decode pair. We describe how we generate the implementation in C using our ASN.1 compiler. We define *self-consistency* for encode/decode pairs that approximates functional correctness without requiring a formal specification of ASN.1. We then verify self-consistency and memory safety using symbolic simulation via the *Software Analysis Workbench*.

Keywords: Automated verification · ASN.1 · Vehicle-to-Vehicle
LLVM · Symbolic execution · SMT solver

1 Introduction

At one time, automobiles were mostly mechanical systems. Today, a modern automobile is a complex distributed computing system. A luxury car might contain tens of millions of lines of code executing on 50–70 microcontrollers, also known as *electronic control units* (ECUs). A midrange vehicle might contain at least 25 ECUs, and that number continues to grow. In addition, various radios such as Bluetooth, Wifi, and cellular provide remote interfaces to an automobile.

With all that code and remotely-accessible interfaces, it is no surprise that software vulnerabilities can be exploited to gain unauthorized access to a vehicle. Indeed, in a study by Checkoway *et al.* on a typical midrange vehicle, for every remote interface, they found some software vulnerability that provided an attacker access to the vehicle's internal systems [4]. Furthermore, in each case,

---

This work was performed while Dr. Pike was at Galois, Inc.

H. Chockler and G. Weissenbacher (Eds.): CAV 2018, LNCS 10982, pp. 413–429, 2018.
https://doi.org/10.1007/978-3-319-96142-2_25

once the interface is exploited, the attackers could parlay the exploit to make arbitrary modifications to other ECUs in the vehicle. Such modifications could include disabling lane assist, locking/unlocking doors, and disabling the brakes. Regardless of the interface exploited, full control can be gained.

Meanwhile, the U.S. Government is proposing a new automotive standard for vehicle-to-vehicle (V2V) communications. The idea is for automobiles to have dedicated short-range radios that broadcast a *Basic Safety Message* (BSM)— e.g., vehicle velocity, trajectory, brake status, etc.—to other nearby vehicles (within approximately 300 m). V2V is a crash prevention technology that can be used to warn drivers of unsafe situations—such as a stopped vehicle in the roadway. Other potential warning scenarios include left-turn warnings when line-of-sight is blocked, blind spot/lane change warnings, and do-not-pass warnings. In addition to warning drivers, such messages could have even more impact for autonomous or vehicle-assisted driving. The U.S. Government estimates that if applied to the full national fleet, approximately one-half million crashes and 1,000 deaths could be prevented annually [15]. We provide a more detailed overview of V2V in Sect. 2.

While V2V communications promise to make vehicles safer, they also provide an additional security threat vector by introducing an additional radio and more software on the vehicle.

This paper presents initial steps in ensuring that V2V communications are implemented securely. We mean "secure" in the sense of having no flaws that could be a vulnerability; confidentiality and authentication are provided in other software layers and are not in scope here. Specifically, we focus on the security of encoding and decoding the BSM. The BSM is defined using ASN.1, a data description language in widespread use. It is not an exaggeration to say that ASN.1 is the backbone of digital communications; ASN.1 is used to specify everything from the X.400 email protocol to voice over IP (VoIP) to cellular telephony. While ASN.1 is pervasive, it is a complex language that has been amended substantially over the past few decades. Over 100 security vulnerabilities have been reported for ASN.1 implementations in MITRE's Common Vulnerability Enumeration (CVE) [14]. We introduce ASN.1 and its security vulnerabilities in Sect. 3.

This paper presents the first work in formally verifying a subsystem of V2V. Moreover, despite the pervasiveness and security-critical nature of ASN.1, it is the first work we are aware of in which any ASN.1 encoder (that translate ASN.1 messages into a byte stream) and decoder (that recovers an ASN.1 message from a byte stream) has been formally verified. The only previous work in this direction is by Barlas *et al.*, who developed a translator from ASN.1 into CafeOBJ, an algebraic specification and verification system [1]. Their motivation was to allow reasoning about broader network properties, of which an ASN.1 specification may be one part, their work does not address ASN.1 encoding or decoding and appears to be preliminary.

The encode/decode pair is first generated by Galois' ASN.1 compiler, part of the *High-Assurance ASN.1 Workbench* (HAAW). The resulting encode/decode pair is verified using Galois' open source *Software Analysis Workbench* (SAW), a state-of-the-art symbolic analysis engine [6]. Both tools are further described in Sect. 4.

In Sect. 5 we state the properties verified: we introduce the notion of self-consistency for encode/decode verification, which approximates functional correctness without requiring a formal specification of ASN.1 itself. Then we describe our approach to verifying the self consistency and memory safety of the C implementation of the encode/decode pair in Sect. 6 using compositional symbolic simulation as implemented in SAW. In Sect. 7 we put our results into context.

2 Vehicle-to-Vehicle Communications

As noted in the introduction, V2V is a short-range broadcast technology with the purpose of making driving safer by providing early warnings. In the V2V system, the BSM is the key message broadcasted, up to a frequency of 10 Hz (it can be perhaps lower due to congestion control). The BSM must be compatible between all vehicles, so it is standardized under SAE J2735 [7].

The BSM is divided into Part I and Part II, and both are defined with ASN.1. Part I is called the *BSM Core Data* and is part of every message broadcast. Part I includes positional data (latitude, longitude, and elevation), speed, heading, and acceleration. Additionally it includes various vehicle state information including transmission status (e.g., neutral, park, forward, reverse), the steering wheel angle, braking system status (e.g., Are the brakes applied? Are anti-lock brakes available/engaged?, etc.), and vehicle size. Our verification, described in Sect. 6, is over Part I.

Part II is optional and extensible. Part II could include, for example, regionally-relevant data. It can also include additional vehicle safety data, including, for example, which of the vehicle's exterior lights are on. It may include information about whether a vehicle is a special vehicle or performing a critical mission, such as a police car in an active pursuit or an ambulance with a critical patient. It can include weather data, and obstacle detection.

3 ASN.1

Abstract Syntax Notation One (ASN.1) is a standardized data description language in widespread usage. Our focus in this section is to give a sense of what ASN.1 is as well as its complexity. We particularly focus on aspects that have led to security vulnerabilities.

3.1 The ASN.1 Data Description Language and Encoding Schemes

ASN.1 was first standardized in 1984, with many revisions since. ASN.1 is a data description language for specifying messages; although it can express relations between request and response messages, it was not designed to specify stateful protocols. While ASN.1 is "just" a data description language, it is quite large and complex. Indeed, merely parsing ASN.1 specifications is difficult. Dubuisson notes that the grammar of ASN.1 (1997 standard) results in nearly 400 shift/reduce errors and over 1,300 reduce/reduce errors in a LALR(1) parser generator, while a LL(k) parser generator results in over 200 production rules beginning with the same lexical token [8]. There is a by-hand transformation of the grammar into an LL(1)-compliant grammar, albeit no formal proof of their equivalence [9].

Not only is the syntax of ASN.1 complex, but so is its semantics. ASN.1 contains a rich datatype language. There are at least 26 base types, including arbitrary integers, arbitrary-precision reals, and 13 kinds of string types. Compound datatypes include sum types (e.g., CHOICE and SET), records with subtyping (e.g., SEQUENCE), and recursive types. There is a complex constraint system (ranges, unions, intersections, etc.) on the types. Subsequent ASN.1 revisions support open types (providing a sort of dynamic typing), versioning to support forward/backward compatibility, user-defined constraints, parameterized specifications, and so-called *information objects* which provide an expressive way to describe relations between types.

So far, we have only highlighted the data description language itself. A set of *encoding rules* specify how the ASN.1 messages are serialized for transmission on the wire. Encoder and decoder pairs are always with respect to a specific schema and encoding rule. There are at least nine standardized ASN.1 encoding rules. Most rules describe 8-bit byte (octet) encodings, but three rule sets are dedicated to XML encoding. Common encoding rules include the Basic Encoding Rules (BER), Distinguished Encoding Rules (DER), and Packed Encoding Rules (PER). The encoding rules do not specify the transport layer protocol to use (or any lower-level protocols, such as the link or physical layer).

3.2   Example ASN.1 Specification

To get a concrete flavor of ASN.1, we present an example data *schema*. Let us assume we are defining messages that are sent (TX) and received (RX) in a query-response protocol.

```
MsgTx ::= SEQUENCE {
  txID  INTEGER(1..5),
  txTag UTF8STRING
}
MsgRx ::= SEQUENCE {
  rxID INTEGER(1..7),
  rxTag SEQUENCE(SIZE(0..10)) OF INTEGER
}
```

We have defined two top-level types, each a SEQUENCE type. A SEQUENCE is an named tuple of fields (like a C struct). The MsgTx sequence contains two fields: txID and txTag. These are typed with built-in ASN.1 types. In the definition of `MsgRx`, the second field, `rxTag`, is the `SEQUENCE OF` structured type; it is equivalent to an array of integers that can have a length between 0 and 10, inclusively. Note that the `txID` and `rxID` fields are *constrained* integers that fall into the given ranges.

ASN.1 allows us to write values of defined types. The following is a value of type `MsgTx`:

```
msgTx MsgTx ::= {
  txID  1,
  txTag "Some msg"
}
```

3.3   ASN.1 Security

There are currently over 100 vulnerabilities associated with ASN.1 in the MITRE Common Vulnerability Enumeration (CVE) database [14]. These vulnerabilities cover many vendor implementations as well as encoders and decoders embedded in other software libraries (e.g., OpenSSL, Firefox, Chrome, OS X, etc.). The vulnerabilities are often manifested as low-level programming vulnerabilities. A typical class of vulnerabilities are unallowed memory reads/writes, such as buffer overflows and over-reads and NULL-pointer dereferences. While generally arcane, ASN.1 was recently featured in the popular press when an ASN.1 vender flaw was found in telecom systems, ranging from cell tower radios to cellphone baseband chips [11]; an exploit could conceivably take down an entire mobile phone network.

Multiple aspects of ASN.1 combine to make ASN.1 implementations a rich source for security vulnerabilities. One reason is that many encode/decode pairs are hand-written and ad-hoc. There are a few reasons for using ad-hoc encoders/decoders. While ASN.1 compilers exist that can generate encoders and decoders (we describe one in Sect. 4.1), many tools ignore portions of the ASN.1 specification or do not support all encoding standards, given the complexity and breadth of the language. A particular protocol may depend on ASN.1 language features or encodings unsupported by most existing tools. Tools that support the full language are generally proprietary and expensive. Finally, generated encoders/decoders might be too large or incompatible with the larger system (e.g., a web browser), due to licensing or interface incompatibilities.

Even if an ASN.1 compiler is used, the compiler will include significant hand-written libraries that deal with, e.g., serializing or deserializing base types and memory allocation. For example, the unaligned packed encoding rules (UPER) require tedious bit operations to encode types into a compact bit-vector representation. Indeed, the recent vulnerability discovered in telecom systems is not in protocol-specific generated code, but in the associated libraries [11].

Finally, because ASN.1 is regularly used in embedded and performance-critical systems, encoders/decoders are regularly written in unsafe languages, like C. As noted above, many of the critical security vulnerabilities in ASN.1 encoders/decoders are memory safety vulnerabilities in C.

4   Our Tools for Generating and Verifying ASN.1 Code

We briefly introduce the two tools used in this work. First we introduce our
ASN.1 compiler for generating the encode/decode pair, then we introduce the
symbolic analysis engine used in the verification.

4.1   *High-Assurance ASN.1 Workbench* (HAAW)

Our *High-Assurance ASN.1 Workbench* (HAAW) is a suite of tools developed
by Galois that supports each stage of the ASN.1 protocol development lifecycle:
specification, design, development, and evaluation. It is composed of an interpreter, compiler, and validator, albeit with varying levels of maturity. HAAW is
implemented in Haskell.

The HAAW compiler is built using semi-formal design techniques and is thoroughly tested to help ensure correctness. The implementation of the HAAW compiler is structured to be as manifestly correct as feasible. It effectively imports a
(separately tested) ASN.1 interpreter which is then "partially-evaluated" on the
fly to generate code. The passes are as follows: An input ASN.1 specification is
"massaged" to a specification-like form which can be interpreted by a built-in
ASN.1 interpreter. This specification-like form is combined with the interpreter
code and is converted into a lambda-calculus representation; to this representation we apply multiple optimization rules; we finally "sequentialize" to a monadic
lambda-calculus (where we are left with the lambda calculus, sequencing operators, and encoding/decoding primitives), this last representation is then transformed into C code. The generated code is linked with a library that encodes
and decodes the basic ASN.1 types.

Moreover, while the HAAW compiler improves the quality of the code generated, we verify the generated code and libraries directly, so HAAW is not part
of the trusted code-base.

4.2   The Software Analysis Workbench (SAW)

The *Software Analysis Workbench* (SAW)[1] is Galois' open-source, state-of-the-
art symbolic analysis engine for multiple programming languages. Here we briefly
introduce SAW, see Dockins *et al.* [6] for more details.

An essential goal of SAW is to generate semantic models of programs independent of a particular analysis task and to interface with existing automated
reasoning tools. SAW is intended to be mostly automated but supports user-
guidance to improve scalability.

The high-level architecture of SAW is shown in Fig. 1. At the heart of SAW
is *SAWCore*. SAWCore is SAW's intermediate representation (IR) of programs.
SAWCore is a dependently-typed functional language, providing a functional representation of the semantics of a variety of imperative and functional languages.

---

[1] saw.galois.com.

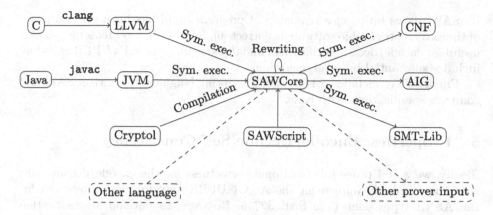

Fig. 1. SAW architecture, reproduced from [6].

SAWCore includes common built-in rewrite rules. Additionally, users can provide domain-specific rewrite rules, and because SAWCore is a dependently-typed language, rewrite rules can be given expressive types to prove their correctness.

SAW currently supports automated translation of both *low-level virtual machine* (LLVM) and *Java virtual machine* (JVM) into SAWCore. Thus, programming languages that can be compiled to these two targets are supported by SAW. Indeed, SAW can be used to prove the equivalence between programs written in C and Java.

SAWCore can also be generated from Cryptol. Cryptol is an open-source language[2] for the specification and formal verification of bit-precise algorithms [10], and we use it to specify portions of our code, as we describe in Sect. 6.

A particularly interesting feature of Cryptol is that it is a typed functional language, similar to Haskell, but includes a size-polymorphic type system that includes linear integer constraints. To give a feeling for the language, the concatenate operator (#) in Cryptol has the following type:

```
(#) : fst, snd, a (fin fst)
  => [fst]a -> [snd]a -> [fst + snd]a
```

It concatenates two sequences containing elements of type a, the first of length fst—which is constrained to be of finite (fin) length (infinite sequences are expressible in Cryptol)—and the second of length snd. The return type is a sequence of a's of length fst + snd. Cryptol relies on *satisfiability modulo theories* (SMT) solving for type-checking

SAWCore is typically exported to various formats supported by external third-party solvers. This includes SAT solver representations (and inverter graphs (AIG), conjunctive normal form (CNF), and ABC's format [3]), as well as SMT-Lib2 [2], supported by a range of SMT solvers.

---

[2] https://cryptol.net/.

SAW allows bit-precise reasoning of programs, and has been used to prove optimized cryptographic software is correct [6]. SAW's bit-level reasoning is also useful for encode/decode verification, and in particular, ASN.1's UPER encoding includes substantial bit-level operations.

Finally, SAW includes *SAWScript*, a scripting language that drives SAW and connects specifications with code.

5   Properties: Encode/Decode Self Consistency

Ideally, we would prove full functional correctness for the encode/decode pair: that they correctly implement the ASN.1 UPER encoding/decoding rules for the ASN.1 types defined in SAE J2735. However, to develop a specification that would formalize all the required ASN.1 constructs, their semantics, and the proper UPER encoding rules would be an extremely large and tedious undertaking (decades of "man-years"?). Moreover, it is not clear how one would ensure the correctness of such a specification.

Instead of proving full functional correctness, we prove a weaker property by proving consistency between the encoder and decoder implementations. We call our internal consistency property *self-consistency*, which we define as the conjunction of two properties, *round-trip* and *rejection*. We show that self-consistency implies that decode is the inverse of encode, which is an intuitive property we want for an encode/decode pair.

The *round-trip property* states that a valid message that is encoded and then decoded results in the original message. This is a completeness property insofar as the decoder can decode all valid messages.

A less obvious property is the *rejection property*. The rejection property informally states that any invalid byte stream is rejected by the decoder. This is a soundness property insofar as the decoder *only* decodes valid messages.

In the context of general ASN.1 encoders/decoders, let us fix a schema S and an encoding rule. Let M_S be the set of all ASN.1 abstract messages that satisfy the schema. Let B the set of all finite byte streams. Let $enc_s : M_s \to B$ be an encoder, a total function on M_s. Let *error* be a fixed constant such that $error \notin M_s$. Let the total function $dec_s : B \to (M_s \cup \{error\})$ be its corresponding decoder.

The round-trip and rejection properties can respectively be stated as follows:

Definition 1 (Round-trip)

$$\forall m \in M_s. dec_s(enc_s(m)) = m.$$

Definition 2 (Rejection)

$$\forall b \in B. dec_s(b) = error \lor enc_s(dec_s(b)) = b.$$

The two properties are independent: a decoder could properly decode valid byte streams while mapping invalid byte streams to valid messages. Such a decoder would be allowed by Round-trip but not by Rejection. An encode/decode pair that fails the Rejection property could mean that *dec* does not terminate normally on some inputs (note that *error* is a valid return value of *dec*). Clearly, undefined behavior in the decoder is a security risk.

Definition 3 (Self-consistency). *An encode/decode pair enc_S and dec_S is self-consistent if and only if it satisfies the round-trip and rejection properties.*

Self-consistency does not require any reference to a specification of ASN.1 encoding rules, simplifying the verification. Indeed, they are applicable to any encode/decode pair of functions.

However, as noted at the outset, self-consistency does not imply ful functional correctness. For example, for an encoder enc_S and decoder dec_S pair, suppose the messages $M_S = \{m_0, m_1\}$ and the byte streams B includes $\{b_0, b_1\} \subseteq B$. Suppose that according to the specification, it should be the case that $enc_S(m_0) = b_0$, $enc_S(m_1) = b_1$, $dec_s(b_0) = m_0$ and $dec(b_1) = m_1$, and for all $b \in B$ such that $b \neq b_0$ and $b \neq b_1$, $dec_S(b) = error$. However, suppose that in fact $enc_S(m_0) = b_1$, $enc_S(m_1) = b_0$, $dec_S(b_0) = m_1$ and $dec_S(b_1) = m_0$, and for all other $b \in B$, $dec(b) = error$. Then enc_S and dec_S satisfy both the round-trip and rejection properties, while being incorrect.

That said, if self-consistency holds, then correctness reduces to showing that either encoder or decoder matches its specification, but showing both hold is unnecessary.

In our work, we formally verify self-consistency and memory safety. We also give further, informal, evidence of correctness by both writing individual test vectors and by comparing our test vectors to that produced by other ASN.1 compilers.

6   Verification

Figure 2 summarizes the overall approach to generating and verifying the encode/decode pair, which we reference throughout this section.

6.1   First Steps

The given SAE J2735 ASN.1 specification (J2735.asn) is given as input to HAAW to generate C code for the encoder and decoder. A HAAW standard library is emitted (the dotted line from HAAW to libHAAW.c in Fig. 2 denotes that the standard library is not specific to the SAE-J2735 specification and is not compiled from HAAW).

We wrote the round-trip and rejection properties (Sect. 5) as two C functions. For example, the round-trip property is encoded, approximately, as follows:

```
bool round_trip(BSM *msg_in) {
  unsigned char str[BUF_SIZE];
  enc(msg_in, str);
```

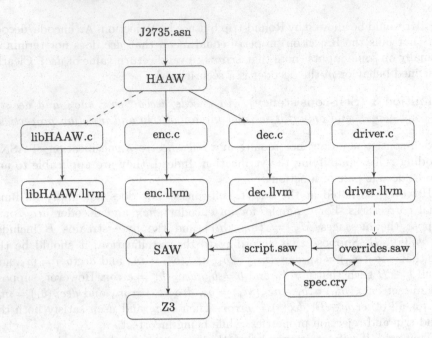

Fig. 2. Code generation and verification flow.

```
    BSM *msg_out;
    dec(msg_out, str);
    return equal_msg(msg_in, msg_out);
}
```

The actual `round_trip` property is slightly longer as we need to deal with C level setup, allocation, etc. This is why we chose to implement this property in C (rather than in SAWScript).

Now all we need to do is verify, in SAWScript, that the C function `round_trip` returns 1 *for all inputs*. At this point, it would be nice to say the power of our automated tools was sufficient to prove `round_trip` without further programmer intervention. This, unsurprisingly, was not the case. Most of the applications of SAW have been to cryptographic algorithms where code typically has loops with statically known bounds. In our encoder/coder code we have a number of loops with unbounded iterations: given such code we need to provide some guidance to SAW.

In the following sections we present how we were able to use SAW, as well as our knowledge of our specific code, to change an intractable verification task into one that could be done (by automated tools) in less than 5 h. An important note: the rest of this section describes SAW techniques that allow us to achieve tractability, they do not change the soundness of our results.

6.2   Compositional Verification with SAW Overrides

SAW supports *compositional verification*. A function (e.g., compiled from Java or C) could be specified in Cryptol and verified against its specification. That Cryptol specification can then be used in analyzing the remainder of the program, such that in a symbolic simulation, the function is replaced with its specification. We call this replacement an *override*. Overrides can be used recursively and can dramatically improve the scalability of a symbolic simulation. SAW's scripting language ensures by construction that an override has itself been verified.

Overrides are like lemmas, we prove them once, separately, and can re-use them (without re-proof). The lemma that an override provides is an equivalence between a C function and a declarative specification provided by the user (in Cryptol). The effort to write a specification and add an override is often required to manage intractability of the automated solvers used.

6.3   Overriding "copy_bits" in SAW

There are two critical libHAAW functions that we found to be intractable to verify using symbolic simulation naively. Here we describe generating overrides for one of them:

```
copy_bits
  ( unsigned char * dst
  , uint32_t *dst_i
  , unsigned char const * src
  , uint32_t *src_i
  , uint32_t const length)
{
  uint32_t src_i_bound = *src_i + length;
  while (*src_i < src_i_bound) {
    copy_overlapping_bits (dst, dst_i, src, src_i, src_i_bound);
  }
  return 0;
}
```

The above function copies length bits from the src array to the dst array, starting at the bit indexed by src_i in src and index dst_i in dst; src_i and dst_i are incremented by the number of bits copied; copy_overlapping_bits is a tedious but loop-free function with bit-level computations to convert to/from a bit-field and byte array. This library function is called by both the encoder and decoder.

One difficulty with symbolically executing copy_bits with SAW is that SAW unrolls loops. Without a priori knowledge of the size of length and src_i, there is no upper bound on the number of iterations of the loop. Indeed, memory safety is dependent on an invariant holding between the indices, the number of bits to copy, and the length of the destination array: the length of the destination array is not passed to the function, so there is no explicit check to ensure no write-beyond-array in the destination array.

Even if we could fix the buffer sizes and specify the relationship between the length and indexes so that the loop could be unrolled in theory, in practice, it would still be computationally infeasible for large buffers. In particular, we would have to consider every valid combination of the length and start indexes, which is cubic in the bit-length of the buffers.

To override copy_bits, we write a specification of copy_bits in Cryptol. The specification does not abstract the function, other than eliding the details of pointers, pointer arithmetic, and destructive updates in C. The specification is given below:

```
copy_bits : dst_n, src_n
            [dst_n][8] -> [32] -> [src_n][8] -> [32] -> [32]
            -> ([dst_n][8], [32], [32])
copy_bits dst0 dst_i0 src src_i0 length = (dst1, dst_i1, src_i1)
  where
  dst_bits0 = join dst0
  src_bits0 = join src

  dst1 = split (copy dst_bits0 0)
  copy dst_bits i =
    if i == length
    then dst_bits
    else copy dst_bits'' (i + 1)
    where
    dst_bits'' = update dst_bits (dst_i0 + i)
                 (src_bits0 @ (src_i0 + i))

  dst_i1 = dst_i0 + length
  src_i1 = src_i0 + length
```

We refer to the *Cryptol User Manual* for implementation details [10], but to provide an intuition, we describe the type signature (the first three lines above): the type is polymorphic, parameterized by dst_n and src_n. A type [32] is a bit-vector of length 32. A type [dst_n][8] is an array of length dst_n containing byte values. The function takes a destination array of bytes, a 32-bit destination index, a source array of bytes, a source index, an a length, and returns a triple containing a new destination array, and new destination and source indices, respectively. Because the specification is pure, the values that are destructively updated through pointers in the C implementation are part of the return value in the specification.

6.4   Multiple Overrides for "copy_bits" in SAW

Even after providing the above override for copy_bits, we are *still* beyond the limits of our underlying solvers to automatically prove the equivalence of copy_bits with its Cryptol specification.

However, we realize that for the SAE J2735 encode/decode, copy_bits is called with a relatively small number of specific concrete values for the sizes of the dst and src arrays, the indexes dst_i and src_i, and the length of bits to copy length. The only values that we need to leave symbolic are the bit values within the dst and src arrays. Therefore, rather than creating a single override for an arbitrary call to copy_bits, we generate separate overrides for each unique set of "specializable" arguments, i.e., dst_i, src_i, and length.

Thus we note another feature of SAW: SAW allows us to specify a set of concrete function arguments for an override; for each of these, SAW will specialize the override. (I.e., it will prove each specialization of the override.) In our case this turns one intractable override into 56 tractable ones. The 56 specializations (which corresponds to the number of SEQUENCE fields in the BSM specification) were not determined by trial and error but by running instrumented code.

It is important to note that the consequence of a missing overrride specialization cannot change the soundness of SAW's result: Overrides in SAW cannot change the proof results, they only change the efficiency of proof finding. If we had a missing override specialization for copy_bits we would only be back where we started: a property that takes "forever" to verify.

This approach works well for the simple BSM Part I. However, once we begin to verify encoders/decoders for more complex ASN.1 specifications (e.g., containing CHOICE and OPTIONAL constructs), this method will need to be generalized.

6.5   Results

A SAW script (script.saw) ties everything together and drives the symbolic execution in SAW and lifts LLVM variables and functions into a dependent logic to state pre- and post-conditions and provide Cryptol specifications as needed. Finally, SAW then generates a SMT problem; Z3 [5] is the default solver we use.

Just under 3100 lines of C code were verified, not counting blank or comment lines. The verification required writing just under 100 lines of Cryptol specification. There are 1200 lines of SAW script auto-generated by the test harness in generating the override specifications. Another 400 lines of SAW script is hand-written for the remaining overrides and to drive the overall verification.

Executed on a modern laptop with an Intel Core i7-6700HQ 2.6 GHz processor and 32 GB of memory, the verification takes 20 min to prove the round-trip property and 275 min to prove the rejection property. The round-trip property is less expensive to verify because symbolic simulation is sensitive to branching, and for the round-trip property, we assert the data is valid to start, which in turn ensures that all of the decodings succeed. In rejection, on the other hand, we have a branch at each primitive decode, and we need to consider both possibilities (success and failure).

7   Discussion

7.1   LLVM and Definedness

Note that our verification has been with respect to the LLVM semantics not the C source of our code. SAW does not model C semantics, but inputs LLVM as the program's semantics (we use CLANG to generate LLVM from the C). By verifying LLVM, SAW is made simpler (it need only model LLVM semantics rather than C) and we can do inter-program verification more easily. The process of proving that a program satisfies a given specification within SAW guarantees definedness of the program (and therefore memory safety) as a side effect. That is, the translation from LLVM into SAWCore provides a well-defined semantics for the program, and this process can only succeed if the program is well-defined. In some cases, this well-definedness is assumed during translation and then proved in the course of the specification verification. For instance, when analyzing a memory load, SAW generates a semantic model of what the program does if the load was within the bounds of the object it refers to, and generates a side condition that the load was indeed in bounds.

Verifying LLVM rather than the source program is a double-edged sword. On the one hand, the compiler front-end that generates LLVM is removed from the trusted computing base. On the other hand, the verification may not be sound with respect to the program's source semantics. In particular, C's undefined behaviors are a superset of LLVM's undefined behaviors; a compiler can soundly remove undefined behaviors but not introduce them. For example, a flaw in the GCC compiler allowed the potential for an integer overflow when multiplying the size of a storage element by the number of elements. The result could be insufficient memory being allocated, leading to a subsequent buffer overflow. CLANG, however, introduces an implicit trap on overflow [12].

Moreover, the LLVM language reference does not rigorously specify well-definedness, and it is possible that our formalization of LLVM diverges from a particular compiler's [13].

7.2   Other Assumptions

We made some memory safety assumptions about how the encode/decode routines are invoked. First, we assume that the input and output buffers provided to the encoder and decoder, respectively, do not alias. We also assume that each buffer is 37 bytes long (sufficient to hold a BSM with Part I only). A meta argument shows that buffers of *at least* 37 bytes are safe: we verify that for all 37-byte buffers, we never read or write past their ends. So, if the buffers were longer, we would never read the bytes above the 37th element.

For more complex data schemas (and when we extend to BSM Part II) whose messages require a varying octet size, we would need to ensure the buffers are sufficiently large for all message sizes.

7.3   Proof Robustness

By "proof robustness" we mean how much effort is required to verify another protocol or changes to the protocol. We hypothesize that for other protocols that use UPER and a similar set of ASN.1 constructs, the verification effort would be small. Most of our manual effort focused on the `libHAAW` libraries, which is independent of the particular ASN.1 protocol verified. That said, very large protocol specifications may require additional proof effort to make them compositional.

In future work, we plan to remove the need to generate overrides as a separate step (as described in Sect. 6.2) by modifying HAAW to generate overrides as it generates the C code.

8   Conclusion

Hopefully we have motivated the security threat to V2V and the need for eliminating vulnerabilities in ASN.1 code. We have presented a successful application of automated formal methods to real C code for a real-world application domain.

There are some lessons to be learned from this work:

(1) Fully automated proofs of correctness properties are possible, but not trivial. The encoding of properties into C and SAWScript and getting the proofs to go through took one engineer approximately 3 months, this engineer had some experience with SAW; we were also able to get support and bug-fixes from the SAW developers. (It also helped that the code was bug-free so no "verification" time was spent on finding counter-examples and fixing code.)

(2) The straightforward structure of the C used in the encode/decode routines made them more amenable to automated analysis (see Sect. 6). It certainly helped that the code verified was compiler-generated and was *by design* intended to be, to some degree, manifestly correct. The lesson is not "*choose* low-hanging fruit" but "*look*, low-hanging fruit in safety critical code" or possibly even "*create* low-hanging fruit!" (by using simpler C).

(3) For non-trivial software, the likelihood of having a correct specification at hand, or having the resources to create it, is quite slim! For instance, to fully specify correct UPER encoding/decoding for arbitrary ASN.1 specifications would be a Herculean task. But in our case, we formulated two simple properties—Round-Trip and Rejection—and by proving them we have also shown memory safety and some strong (not complete, see Sect. 5) guarantees of functional correctness. This technique could be applied to any encode/decode pair.

There are many ways we hope to extend this work:

(1) We plan to extend our verification to the full BSM. This now gets us to more challenging ASN.1 constructs (e.g., `CHOICE`) that involve a more complicated control-flow in the encoders/decoders. We do not expect a proof to be found automatically, but our plan is to generate lemmas with the generated C code that will allow proofs to go through automatically.

(2) Once we can automatically verify the full BSM, we expect to be able to perform a similar fully-automatic verification on many ASN.1 specifications (most do not use the full power of ASN.1). We would like to explore what properties of a given ASN.1 specification might guarantee the ability to perform such a fully-automatic verification.

(3) By necessity, parts of our SAWScript and the verification properties have a dependence on the particular API of the HAAW compiler (how abstract values are encoded, details of the encoding/decoding functions, memory-management design choices, etc.). Currently the authors are working on generalizing this so that one can abstract over ASN.1-tool-specific API issues. The goal is to be able to extend our results to other encode/decode pairs (generated by hand or by other ASN.1 compilers).

(4) Note that the self-consistency property is generic (and has no reference to ASN.1). As a result, we believe our work can be extended to encode/decode pairs on non-ASN.1 data.

Acknowledgments. This work was performed under subcontract to Battelle Memorial Institute for the National Highway Safety Transportation Administration (NHTSA). We thank Arthur Carter at NHTSA and Thomas Bergman of Battelle for their discussions and guidance. Our findings and opinions do not necessarily represent those of Battelle or the United States Government.

References

1. Barlas, K., Koletsos, G., Stefaneas, P.S., Ouranos, I.: Towards a correct translation from ASN.1 into CafeOBJ. IJRIS **2**(3/4), 300–309 (2010)
2. Barrett, C., Fontaine, P., Tinelli, C.: The SMT-LIB Standard: Version 2.5. Technical report, Department of Computer Science, The University of Iowa (2015). www.SMT-LIB.org
3. Brayton, R., Mishchenko, A.: ABC: an academic industrial-strength verification tool. In: Touili, T., Cook, B., Jackson, P. (eds.) CAV 2010. LNCS, vol. 6174, pp. 24–40. Springer, Heidelberg (2010). https://doi.org/10.1007/978-3-642-14295-6_5
4. Checkoway, S., McCoy, D., Kantor, B., Anderson, D., Shacham, H., Savage, S., Koscher, K., Czeskis, A., Roesner, F., Kohno, T.: Comprehensive experimental analyses of automotive attack surfaces. In: USENIX Security (2011)
5. de Moura, L., Bjørner, N.: Z3: an efficient smt solver. In: Ramakrishnan, C.R., Rehof, J. (eds.) TACAS 2008. LNCS, vol. 4963, pp. 337–340. Springer, Heidelberg (2008). https://doi.org/10.1007/978-3-540-78800-3_24
6. Dockins, R., Foltzer, A., Hendrix, J., Huffman, B., McNamee, D., Tomb, A.: Constructing semantic models of programs with the software analysis workbench. In: Blazy, S., Chechik, M. (eds.) VSTTE 2016. LNCS, vol. 9971, pp. 56–72. Springer, Cham (2016). https://doi.org/10.1007/978-3-319-48869-1_5
7. DSRC Technical Committee: Dedicated Short Range Communications (DSRC) message set dictionary (j2735_20103). Technical report, SAE International (20016)
8. Dubuisson, O.: ASN.1 Communication between heterogeneous Systems. Elsevier-Morgan Kaufmann, Burlington (2000)
9. Fouquart, P., Dubuisson, O., Duwez, F.: Une analyse syntaxique d'ASN.1:1994. Technical report, Internal Report RP/LAA/EIA/83, France Télécom R&D, March 1996

10. Galois Inc.: Cryptol: the language of cryptography. Galois, Inc., portland (2016). http://www.cryptol.net/files/ProgrammingCryptol.pdf
11. Goodin, D.: Software flaw puts mobile phones and networks at risk of complete takeover. Ars Technica (2016)
12. Lattner, C.: What every C programmer should know about undefined behavior #3/3. Online blog, May 2011. http://blog.llvm.org/2011/05/what-every-c-programmer-should-know_21.html
13. Lee, J., Youngju Song, Y.K., Hur, C.K., Das, S., Majnemer, D., Regehr, J., Lopes, N.P.: Taming undefined behavior in LLVM. In: Proceedings of 38th Conference on Programming Language Design and Implementation (PLDI) (2017)
14. MITRE: Common vulnerabilities and exposures for ASN.1, February 2017. https://cve.mitre.org/cgi-bin/cvekey.cgi?keyword=ASN.1
15. U.S. Dept. of Transportation: Fact sheet: Improving safety and mobility through vehicle-to-vehicle communications technology (2016). https://icsw.nhtsa.gov/safercar/v2v/pdf/V2V_NPRM_Fact_Sheet_121316_v1.pdf

Continuous Formal Verification
of Amazon s2n

Andrey Chudnov[1], Nathan Collins[1], Byron Cook[3,4], Joey Dodds[1],
Brian Huffman[1], Colm MacCárthaigh[3], Stephen Magill[1(✉)], Eric Mertens[1],
Eric Mullen[2], Serdar Tasiran[3], Aaron Tomb[1], and Eddy Westbrook[1]

[1] Galois, Inc., Portland, USA
stephen@galois.com
[2] University of Washington, Seattle, USA
[3] Amazon Web Services, Seattle, USA
[4] University College London, London, UK

Abstract. We describe formal verification of s2n, the open source TLS
implementation used in numerous Amazon services. A key aspect of this
proof infrastructure is continuous checking, to ensure that properties
remain proven during the lifetime of the software. At each change to the
code, proofs are automatically re-established with little to no interaction from the developers. We describe the proof itself and the technical
decisions that enabled integration into development.

1 Introduction

The Transport Layer Security (TLS) protocol is responsible for much of the
privacy and authentication we enjoy on the Internet today. It secures our phone
calls, our web browsing, and connections between resources in the cloud made
on our behalf. In this paper we describe an effort to prove the correctness of
s2n [3], the open source TLS implementation used by many Amazon and Amazon
Web Services (AWS) products (*e.g.* Amazon S3 [2]). Formal verification plays
an important role for s2n. First, many security-focused customers (*e.g.* financial
services, government, pharmaceutical) are moving workloads from their own data
centers to AWS. Formal verification provides customers from these industries
with concrete information about *how* security is established in Amazon Web
Services. Secondly, automatic and continuous formal verification facilitates rapid
and cost-efficient development by a distributed team of developers.

In order to realize the second goal, verification must continue to work with
low effort as developers change the code. While fundamental advances have been
made in recent years in the tractability of full verification, these techniques
generally either: (1) target a fixed version of the software, requiring significant re-
proof effort whenever the software changes or, (2) are designed around synthesis
of correct code from specifications. Neither of these approaches would work for
Amazon as s2n is under continuous development, and new versions of the code
would not automatically inherit correctness from proofs of previous versions.

© The Author(s) 2018
H. Chockler and G. Weissenbacher (Eds.): CAV 2018, LNCS 10982, pp. 430–446, 2018.
https://doi.org/10.1007/978-3-319-96142-2_26

To address the challenge of program proving in such a development environment, we built a proof and associated infrastructure for s2n's implementations of DRBG, HMAC, and the TLS handshake. The proof targets an existing implementation and is updated either automatically or with low effort as the code changes. Furthermore, the proof connects with existing proofs of security properties, providing a high level of assurance.

Our proof is now deployed in the continuous integration environment for s2n, and provides a distributed team of developers with repeated proofs of the correctness of s2n even as they continue to modify the code. In this paper, we describe how we structured the proof and its supporting infrastructure, so that the lessons we learned will be useful to others who address similar challenges.

Figure 1 gives an overview of our proof for s2n's implementation of the HMAC algorithm and the tooling involved. At the left is the ultimate security property of interest, which for HMAC is that if the key is not known, then HMAC is indistinguishable from a random function (given some assumptions on the underlying hash functions). This is a fixed security property for HMAC and almost never changes (a change would correspond to some new way of thinking about security in the cryptographic research community). The HMAC specification is also fairly static, having been updated only once since its publication in 2002[1]. Beringer et al. [6] have published a mechanized formal proof that the high-level HMAC specification establishes the cryptographic security property of interest.

As we move to the right through Fig. 1, we find increasingly low-level artifacts and the rate of change of these artifacts increases. The low-level HMAC specification includes details of the API exposed by the implementation, and the implementation itself includes details such as memory management and performance optimizations. This paper focuses on verifying these components in a manner that uses proof automation to decrease the manual effort required for ongoing maintenance of these verification artifacts. At the same time, we ensure that the automated proof occurring on the right-hand side of the figure is linked to the stable, foundational security results present at the left.

In this way, we realize the assurance benefit of the foundational security work of Beringer et al. while producing a proof that can be integrated into the development workflow. The proof is applied as part of the *continuous integration* system for s2n (which uses Travis CI) and runs every time a code change is pushed or a pull request is issued. In one year of code changes only three manual updates to the proof were required.

The s2n source code, proof scripts, and access to the underlying proof tools can all be found in the s2n GitHub [3] repository. The collection of proof runs is logged and appears on the s2n Travis CI page [4].

In addition to the HMAC proof, we also reused the approach shown in the right-hand side of Fig. 1 to verify the deterministic random big generator (DRBG) algorithm and the TLS Handshake protocol. In these cases we didn't link to foundational cryptographic security proofs, but nonetheless had specifications that provided important benefits to developers by allowing them to (1)

---

[1] And this update did not change the functional behavior specified in the standard.

check their code against an independent specification and (2) check that their code continues to adhere to this specification as it changes. Our TLS Handshake proof revealed a bug (which was promptly fixed) in the s2n implementation [10], providing evidence for the first point. All of our proofs have continued to be used in development since their introduction, supporting the second point.

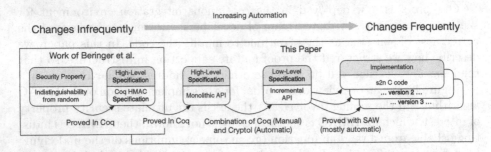

Fig. 1. An overview of the structure of our HMAC proof.

Related Work. Projects such as Everest [8,12], Cao [5], and Jasmin [1], generate verified cryptographic implementations from higher level specifications, *e.g.* F* models. While progress in this space continues to be promising—HACL* has recently achieved performance on primitives that surpasses handwritten C [25]—we have found in our experiments that the generated TLS code does not yet meet the performance, power, and space constraints required by the broad range of AWS products that use s2n.

Static analysis for hand-written cryptographic implementations has been previously reported in the context of Frama-C/PolarSSL [23], focusing on scaling memory safety verification to a large body of code. Additionally, unsound but effective bug hunting techniques such as fuzzing have been applied to TLS implementations in the past [11,18]. The work we report on goes further by proving behavioral correctness properties of the implementation that are beyond the capabilities of these techniques. In this we were helped because the implementation of s2n is small (less than 10k LOC), and most iteration is bounded.

The goal of our work is to verify deep properties of an existing and actively developed open source TLS implementation that has been developed for both high performance and low power as required by a diverse range of AWS products. Our approach was guided by lessons learned in several previous attempts to prove the correctness of s2n that either (1) required too much developer interaction during the modification of the code [17], or (2) where pushbutton symbolic model checking tools did not scale. Similarly, proofs developed using tools from the Verified Software Toolchain (VST) [6] are valuable for establishing the correctness and security of specifications, but are not sufficiently resilient to code changes, making them challenging to integrate into an ongoing development process. Their use of a layered proof structure, however, provided us with a specification that we could use to leverage their security proof in our work.

O'Hearn details the industry impact of continuous reasoning about code in [19], and describes additional instances of integration of formal methods with developer workflows.

2 Proof of HMAC

In this section, we walk through our HMAC proof in detail, highlighting how the proof is decomposed, the guarantees provided, the tools used, and how this approach supports integration of verification into the development work-flow. While HMAC serves as an example, we have also performed a similar proof of the DRBG and TLS Handshake implementations. We do not discuss DRBG further, as there are no proof details that differ significantly from HMAC. We describe our TLS verification in Sect. 3.

2.1 High-Level HMAC Specification

The keyed-Hash Message Authentication Code algorithm (HMAC) is used for authenticated integrity in TLS 1.2. Authenticated integrity guarantees that the data originated from the sender and was not changed or duplicated in transit. HMAC is used as the foundation of the TLS Pseudorandom Function (PRF), from which the data transmission and data authentication shared keys are derived. This ensures that both the sender and recipient have exchanged the correct secrets before a TLS connection can proceed to the data transmission phase.

HMAC is also used by some TLS cipher suites to authenticate the integrity of TLS records in the data transmission phase. This ensures, for example, that a third party watching the TLS connection between a user and a webmail client is unable to change or repeat the contents of an email body during transmission. It is also used by the HMAC-based Extract-and-Expand Key Derivation Function (HKDF) which is implemented within s2n as a utility function for general purpose key derivation and is central to the design of the TLS1.3 PRF.

FIPS 198-1 [24] defines the HMAC algorithm as

$$\mathsf{HMAC}(K, message) = \mathsf{H}((K \oplus opad) \| \mathsf{H}((K \oplus ipad) \| message))$$

where H is any hash function, $\oplus$ is bitwise xor, and $\|$ is concatenation. $opad$ and $ipad$ are constants defined by the specification. We will refer to this definition as the *monolithic* specification.

Following Fig. 1, we use the Cryptol specification language [14] to express HMAC in a form suitable for mechanized verification, first in a monolithic form, and then in an incremental form. We prove high-level properties with Coq [22] and tie these to the code using the Software Analysis Workbench (SAW) [16]. We first describe the proof of high-level properties before going into specifics regarding the tools in Sect. 2.4.

2.2   Security Properties of HMAC

The Cryptol version of the Monolithic HMAC specification follows.

```
hmac k message = H((k ^ opad) # H((k ^ ipad) # message))
```

where H is any hash function, ^ is bitwise xor, and # is concatenation.

The high-level Cryptol specification and the FIPS document look nearly identical, but what assurance do we have that either description of the algorithm is cryptographically secure? We can provide this assurance by showing that the Cryptol specification establishes one of the security properties that HMAC is intended to provide—namely, that HMAC is indistinguishable from a function returning random bits.

Indistinguishability from random is a property of cryptographic output that says that there is no effective strategy by which an attacker that is viewing the output of the cryptographic function and a true random output can distinguish the two, where an "effective" strategy is one that has a non-negligible chance of success given bounded computing resources. If the output of a cryptographic function is indistinguishable from random, that implies that no information can be learned about the inputs of that function by examining the outputs.

We prove that our Cryptol HMAC specification has this indistinguishability property using an operational semantics of Cryptol we developed in Coq. The semantics enable us to reuse portions of the proof by Beringer et. al [6], which uses the Coq Foundational Cryptography Framework (FCF) library [20] to establish the security of the HMAC construction. We construct a Coq proof showing that our Cryptol specification is equivalent (when interpreted using the formal operational semantics) to the specification considered in the Beringer et. al work. The Cryptol specification is a stepping stone to automated verification of the s2n implementations, so when combined with the verification work we describe subsequently, we eventually establish that the implementation of HMAC in s2n also has the desired security property. The Coq code directly relating to HMAC is all on the s2n GitHub page. These proofs are not run as part of continuous integration, rather, they are only rerun in the unlikely event that the monolithic specification changes.

2.3   Low-Level Specification

The formal specification of HMAC presented in the FIPS standard operates on a single *complete* message. However, network communication often requires the incremental processing of messages. Thus all modern implementations of HMAC provide an incremental interface with the following abstract types:

```
init : Key -> State
update : Message -> State -> State
digest : State -> MAC
```

The init function creates a state from a key, the update function updates that state incrementally with chunks of the message, and the digest function finalizes the state, producing the MAC.

The one-line monolithic specification is related to these incremental functions as follows. If we can partition a message m into $m = m_1 \| m_2 \| \dots \| m_n$ then (in pseudo code/logic notation)

$$\mathsf{HMAC}(k, m) = \mathsf{digest}(\mathsf{update}(m_n(\dots(\mathsf{update}\ m_1(\mathsf{init}\ k)))) \qquad (1)$$

In other words, any MAC generated by partitioning a message and incrementally sending it in order through these functions should be equal to a MAC generated by the complete message HMAC interface used in the specification.

We prove that the incremental interface to HMAC is equivalent to the non-incremental version using a combination of manual proof in Coq and automated proof in Cryptol. Note that this equivalence property can be stated in an implementation-independent manner and proved outside of a program verification context. This is the approach we take—independently proving that the incremental and monolithic message interfaces compute the same HMAC, and then separately showing that s2n correctly implements the incremental interface.

Our Coq proof proceeds via induction over the number of partitions with the following lemmas establishing the relationship between the monolithic and iterative implementations. These lemmas are introduced as axioms in the Coq proof, but subsequently checked using SAW.

```
update_empty : forall s, HMAC_update empty_string s = s.

equiv_one : forall m k,
 HMAC_digest (HMAC_update m (HMAC_init k)) = HMAC k m.

update_concat : forall m1 m2 s,
 HMAC_update (concat m1 m2) s = HMAC_update m2 (HMAC_update m1 s).
```

The first lemma states that processing an empty message does not change the state. The second lemma states that applying the incremental interface to a single message is equivalent to applying the monolithic interface. These lemmas constitute the base cases for an inductive proof of equation (1) above. The last lemma states that calling update twice (first with m1 and then with m2) results in the same state as calling update once with m1 concatenated with m2. This constitutes the inductive step in the proof of (1).

The update_empty lemma can be proved by analyzing the code with symbolic values provided for the state s, as the state is of fixed size. The equiv_one and update_concat lemmas require reasoning about unbounded data. SAW has limited support for such proofs. In particular, it has support for equational rewriting of terms in its intermediate language, but not for induction. In the case of the update_concat lemma, a few simple builtin rewrite rules are sufficient to establish the statement for all message sizes. For equiv_one, a proof of the statement for all message sizes would require induction. Since SAW does not support induction, we prove that this statement holds for a finite number of key and message sizes. In theory we could still obtain a complete proof by checking all message sizes up to 16k bytes (the maximum size message permitted by the TLS standard). This may be tractable in a one-off proof, but for our continuously-applied proofs we instead consider a smaller set of samples, chosen to cover all branches in the code. This yields a result that is short of full proof, but still provides much higher state space coverage than testing methods.

Given the three lemmas above, we then use Coq to prove the following theorem by induction on the list of partitions, ms.

```
HMAC key (fold_right concat empty_string ms) =
    HMAC_digest (fold_left (fun (st: state) msg =>
                                    HMAC_update msg st)
                  ms
                (HMAC_init key)).
```

The theorem establishes the equivalence of the incremental and monolithic interfaces for any decomposition of a message into any number of fragments of any size.

2.4   Implementation Verification

The incremental Cryptol specification is low-level enough that we were able to connect it to the s2n HMAC implementation using automated proof techniques. As this is the aspect of the verification effort that is critical for integration into an active development environment, we go into some detail, first discussing the tools that were used and then describing the structure of the proof.

Tools. We use the Software Analysis Workbench (SAW) to orchestrate this step of the proof. SAW is effective both for manipulating the kinds of functional terms that arise from Cryptol, and for constructing functional models from imperative programs. It can be used to show equivalence of distinct software implementations (*e.g.* an implementation in C and one in Java) or equivalence of an implementation and an executable specification.

SAW uses bounded symbolic execution to translate Cryptol, Java, and C programs into logical expressions, and proves properties about the logical expressions using a combination of rewriting, SAT, and SMT. The result of the bounded symbolic execution of the input programs is a pure functional term representing the function's entire semantics. These extracted semantics are then related to the Cryptol specifications by way of precondition and postcondition assertions on the program state.

The top-level theorems we prove have some variables that are universally quantified (e.g. the key used in HMAC) and others that are parameters we instantiate to a constant (e.g. the size of the key). We achieve coverage for the latter by running the proof for several parameter instantiations. In some cases this is sufficient to cover all cases (e.g. the standard allows only a small finite number of key sizes). In others, the space of possible instantiations is large enough that fully covering it would yield runtimes too long to fit into the developer workflow (for example, messages can be up to 16k long). In such cases, we consider a smaller set of samples, chosen to cover all branches in the code.

This yields a result that is short of full proof, but still provides much higher state space coverage than testing methods.

Internally SAW reasons about C programs by first translating them to LLVM. For the remainder of the paper we will talk about the C code, although from a soundness perspective the C code must be compiled through LLVM for the proofs to apply to the compiled code.

Proof Structure. The functions in the low-level Cryptol specification described above share the incremental format of the C program, and also consume arguments and operate on state that matches the usage of arguments and state in the C code. However, the Cryptol specification does not capture the layout of state in memory. This separates concerns and allows us to reason about equivalence of the monolithic and incremental interfaces in a more tractable purely functional setting, while performing the implementation proof in a context in which the specification and implementation are already structurally quite similar.

As an example of this structural similarity, the C function has type:

```
int s2n_hmac_update(struct s2n_hmac_state *state,
                     const void *in, uint32_t size);
```

We define a corresponding Cryptol specification with type:

```
hmac_update : {Size} (32 >= width Size) =>
              HMAC_state -> [Size][8] -> HMAC_state
```

These type signatures look a bit different, but they represent the same thing. In Cryptol, we list `Size` first, because it is a type, not a value. This means that we do not need to independently check that the input buffer (in Cryptol represented by the type `[Size][8]`) matches the size input—the Cryptol type system guarantees it. The type system also sets the constraint that the size doesn't exceed 2^{32}, a constraint set by the C type of `Size`.

We use SAW's SAWScript language to describe the expected memory layout of the C program, and to map the inputs and outputs of the Cryptol function to the inputs and outputs of the C program. The following code presents the SAWScript for the `hmac_update_spec` function.

```
1   let hmac_update_spec msg_size cfg = do {
2       (msg_val, msg_pointer) <- ptr_to_fresh_array msg_size i8;
3       (initial_state, state_pointer) <- setup_hmac_state cfg
4       hmac_invariants initial_state cfg;
5
6       execute_func [state_pointer, message_pointer, msg_size];
7
8       let final_state =
9           {{ hmac_update_c_state initial_state msg_val }};
10      check_hmac_state state_pointer final_state;
11      hmac_invariants final_state cfg;
12      check_return zero;
13  };
```

This SAWScript code represents a Hoare triple, with the precondition and post condition separated by the body (the `execute_func` command), which performs the symbolic execution of the LLVM code using the provided arguments. Lines 2 and 3 are effectively universal quantification over the triple, setting up the values and pointers that match the type needed by the C function. The values `msg_val` and `initial_state` are referenced in both the C code and the Cryptol specification, whereas the pointers exist only on the C side.

Lines 8–10 capture that the final state resulting from executing the C function should be equivalent to the state produced by evaluating the Cryptol specification. Specifically, Lines 8 and 9 capture the output of the Cryptol specification (double curly braces denote Cryptol expressions within SAWScript) and Line 10 asserts that this state matches the C state present in memory at `state_pointer`. This is what ultimately establishes equivalence of the implementation and specification.

The proof is aided by maintaining a collection of state invariants, which are assumed to hold in Line 4 and are re-established in Line 11. These are manual invariants, but they occur as function specifications rather than appearing internal to loops. They only require modification in the event that the meaning of the HMAC state changes.

The `msg_size` parameter indicates how large of a message this particular proof should cover. Because SAW performs a bounded unrolling of the program under analysis, each proof must cover one fixed size for each unbounded data structure or iterative construct. However, by parameterizing the proof, it can easily be repeated for multiple sizes. Furthermore, as described in Sect. 2.3, we also prove in Coq that calling update twice with messages m_1 and m_2 is equivalent to calling it once with m_1 concatenated with m_2. As a consequence, the fixed size proofs we perform of update can be composed to guarantee that the update function is correct even over longer messages.

The `cfg` parameter contains configuration values for each of the six hashes that can be used with HMAC. The configuration values of interest to HMAC are the input and output sizes of the hash block function.

Given the specification of the C function above, we can now verify that the implementation satisfies the specification:

```
verify m "s2n_hmac_update"
    hash_ovs true (hmac_update_spec msg_size cfg) yices_hash_unint;
```

The `"s2n_hmac_update"` argument specifies the C function that we are verifying. `hash_ovs` is a list, defined elsewhere, that contains all of the *overrides* that the verification will use. An override is a specification that will be used in place of a particular implementation function and corresponds to what other tools call *stubs* or *models*. In this case, we've overridden all of the C hash functions, stating assumptions regarding their use of memory and their equivalence to Cryptol implementations of the same hash functions. When the verifier comes across a call to one of these hash functions in the C code, it will instead use the provided specification. The result is that our proof *assumes correct implementation of the hash functions*.

The fact that the structure of the low-level Cryptol specification matches the structure of the C code, coupled with SAW's use of SMT as the primary mechanism for discharging verification conditions, enables a proof that continues to work through a variety of code changes. In particular, changes to the code in function bodies often requires no corresponding specification or proof script change. Similarly, changes that add fields or change aspects of in-memory data structures that are not referenced by the specification do not require proof updates. Changes in the API (e.g. function arguments) do require proof script changes, but these are typically minor. Fixing a broken proof typically involves adding a new state field to the SAW script, updating the Cryptol specification to use that field correctly, and then passing the value of that field into the Cryptol program in the post-condition. If the Cryptol specification is incorrect, SAW will generate counterexamples that can be used to trace through the code and the spec together in order to discover the mismatch.

2.5   Integrating the Proof into Development

Integration with the s2n CI system mostly took place within the Travis configuration file for s2n. At the time of integration, targets for the build, integration testing, and fuzzing on both Linux and OSX already existed. We updated the Travis system with Bash scripts that automatically download and install the appropriate builds of SAW, Z3, and Yices into the Travis system. These files are in the s2n repository and can be reused by anyone under the Apache 2.0 license.

A Travis CI build can occur on any number of virtual machines, and each virtual machine is given an hour to complete. We run our HMAC proofs on configurations for six different hashes. For each of these configurations we check at three key-sizes in order to test the relevant cases in the implementation (small keys get padded, exact keys remain unchanged, and large keys are hashed). For each of those key-sizes we check six different message sizes. These proofs run in an average of ten minutes. We discovered that it's best to stay well clear of the 60 min limit imposed by Travis in order to avoid false-negatives due to variations in execution time.

The proof runs alongside the tests that are present in the s2n repository on every build, and if the proof fails a flag is raised just as if a test case were to fail.

3   Proof of TLS Handshake

In addition to the HMAC and DRBG proofs, we have proved correctness of the TLS state machine implemented in s2n. Specifically, we have proved that (1) it implements a subset of TLS 1.2 as defined in IETF RFCs 5246 [21], 5077 [15] and 6066 [13] and (2) the socket corking API, which optimizes how data is split into packets, is used correctly. Formally, we proved that the implementation *refines* a specification (conversely, the specification *simulates* the implementation). We obtained this Cryptol specification, called the *RFC specification* by examining the RFCs and hand-compiling them into a Cryptol file complete with relevant excerpts from the RFCs. We assume that the TLS handshake as specified in the RFCs is secure, and do not formalize nor verify any cryptographic properties of the specification. In the future, we would like to take a similar approach to that described in Sect. 2.2 to link our refinement proof with a specification-level security proof for TLS, such as that from miTLS [9].

The s2n state machine is designed to ensure correctness and security, preventing join-of-state-machines vulnerabilities like SMACK [7]. In addition, s2n allows increased throughput via the use of TCP socket corking, which combines several TLS records into one TCP frame where appropriate.

The states and transitions of the s2n state machine are encoded explicitly as linearized arrays, as opposed to being intertwined with message parsing and other logic. This is an elegant decomposition of the problem that makes most of the assumptions explicit and enables the use of common logic for message and error handling as well as protocol tracking.

Even with the carefully designed state machine implementation, formal specification and verification helped uncover a bug [10].

Structure of the TLS Handshake State Machine Correctness Proof. The automated proof of correctness of the TLS state machine has two parts (Fig. 2). First we establish an equivalence between the two functions[2] that drive the TLS handshake state machine in s2n and their respective specifications in Cryptol. Again we utilize *low-level* specifications that closely mirror the shape of the C functions. Our end goal, however, is correctness with respect to the standards, encoded in the *RFC specification* in Cryptol. The library implements only a subset of the standards, thus we can only prove a simulation relation and not equivalence. Namely, we show that every sequence of messages generated by the low-level specification starting from a valid initial state can be generated by the RFC specification starting from a related state. The dashed line in Fig. 2 shows at which points the states match at the implementation and specification levels.

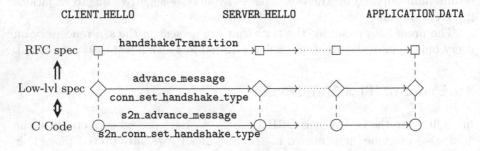

Fig. 2. Structure of the TLS handshake correctness proof

---

[2] s2n_conn_set_handshake_type and s2n_advance_message.

RFC-Based Specification of the TLS Handshake. The high-level hand-shake protocol specification that captures the TLS state machine is implemented in Cryptol and accounts for the protocol, message type and direction, as well as conditions for branching in terms of abstract connection parameters, but not message contents.

We represent the set of states as unsigned 5-bit integers (Listing 1). The state transition relation is represented by a Cryptol function `handshakeTransition` (Listing 2) which, given abstract connection parameters (Listing 3) and the current state returns the next state. If there is no valid next state, the state machine stutters. The parameters determine the transition to take in each state and represent configurations of the end-points as well as contents of the `HELLO` message sent by the other party. We kept the latter separate from the message specifications in order to avoid reasoning about message structure and parsing. We can still relate the abstract parameters to the implementation because they are captured in the connection state. Finally, the `message` function (Listing 4) gives the message type, protocol and direction for every state.

```
type State = [5]
(helloRequestSent : State) = 0
(clientHelloSent  : State) = 1
(serverHelloSent  : State) = 2
// ...
(serverCertificateStatusSent : State) = 23
```

Listing 1: Specification of TLS handshake protocol states

```
handshakeTransition : Parameters -> State -> State
handshakeTransition params old =
  snd (find fst (True, old) [ (old == from /\ p, to)
                            | (from, p, to) <- valid_transitions]) where
  valid_transitions =
    [(helloRequestSent, True, clientHelloSent)
    ,(clientHelloSent,  True, serverHelloSent)
    ,(serverHelloSent, params.keyExchange != DH_anon
                       /\ ~params.sessionTicket, serverCertificateSent)
    // ...
    ,(serverCertificateStatusSent, ~(keyExchangeNonEphemeral params)
    , serverKeyExchangeSent)
    ]
```

Listing 2: Specification of the TLS handshake state transition function. Valid transitions are encoded as triples (*start, transition condition, end*).

```
type KeyExchange = [3]
(DH_anon : KeyExchange) = 0
// ...
(DH_RSA  : KeyExchange) = 5

type Parameters =
{keyExchange : KeyExchange     // Negotiated key exchange algorithm
,sessionTicket : Bit           // The client had a session ticket
,renewSessionTicket : Bit      // Server decides to renew a session ticket
,sendCertificateStatus : Bit   // Server decides to send the certificate
                               //   status message
,requestClientCert : Bit       // Server requests a cert from the client
,includeSessionTicket : Bit}   // Server includes a session ticket
                               //   extension in SERVER_HELLO
```

Listing 3: Abstract connection parameters

```
message : State -> Message
message = lookupDefault messages (mkMessage noSender data error)
  where messages =
    [(helloRequestSent, mkMessage server handshake helloRequest)
    ,(clientHelloSent, mkMessage client handshake clientHello)
    ,(serverHelloSent, mkMessage server handshake serverHello)
    // ...
    ,(serverChangeCipherSpecSent,
      mkMessage server changeCipherSpec changeCipherSpecMessage)
    ,(serverFinishedSent, mkMessage server handshake finished)
    ,(applicationDataTransmission, mkMessage both data applicationData)
    ]
```

Listing 4: Expected message sent/received in each handshake state

Socket Corking. Socket corking is a mechanism for reducing packet fragmentation and increasing throughput by making sure full TCP frames are sent whenever possible. It is implemented in Linux and FreeBSD using the TCP_CORK and TCP_NOPUSH flags respectively. When the flag is set, the socket is considered corked, and the operating system will only send complete (filled up to the buffer length) TCP frames. When the flag is unset, the current buffer, as well as all future writes, are sent immediately.

Writing to an uncorked socket is possible, but undesirable as it might result in partial packets being sent, potentially reducing throughput. On the other hand, forgetting to uncork a socket after the last write can have more serious consequences. According to the documentation, Linux limits the duration of corking to 200 ms, while FreeBSD has no limit. Hence, leaving a socket corked in FreeBSD might result in the data not being sent. We have verified that sockets are not corked or uncorked twice in a row. In addition, the structure of the message handling implementation in s2n helps us informally establish a stronger corking safety property. Because explicit handshake message sequences include the direction the message is sent, we can establish that the socket is (un)corked appropriately when the message direction changes. In future work we plan to expand the scope of our proof to allow us to formally establish full corking safety.

4   Operationalizing the Proof

We have integrated the checking of our proof into the build system of s2n, as well as the Continuous Integration (CI) system used to check the validity of code as it is added to the s2n repository on GitHub. For the green "build passed" badge displayed on the s2n GitHub page to appear, all code updates now must successfully verify with our proof scripts. Not only do the these checks run on committed code, they are also automatically run on all pull requests to the project. This allows the maintainers of s2n to quickly determine the correctness of submitted changes when they touch the code that we have proved. In this section we discuss aspects of our tooling that were important enablers of this integration.

Proof Robustness. For this integration to work, our proofs must be robust in the face of code change. Evolving projects like s2n should not be slowed down by the need to update proofs every time the code changes. Too many proof updates can lead to significantly slowed development or, in the extreme case, to proofs being disabled or ignored in the CI environment. The automated nature of our proofs mean that they generally need to be changed only in the event of interface modifications—either to function declarations or state definitions.

Of these two, state changes are the most common, and can be quite complex considering that there are usually large possibly nested C structs involved (for example, the `s2n_connection` struct has around 50 fields, some of which are structs themselves). To avoid the developer pain that would arise if such struct updates caused the proof the break, we have structured the verification so that proof scripts do not require updates when the modified portions of the state do not affect the computation being proved. Recall that our proofs are focused on functional correctness. Thus in order to affect the proof, a new or modified field must influence the computation. Many struct changes target non-security-critical portions of the code (*e.g.* to track additional data for logging) and so do not meet this criterion. For such fields we prove that they are handled in a memory safe manner and that they do not affect the computation being performed by the code the proof script targets.

In the future, we intend to add the option to perform a "strict" version of this state handling logic to SAW, which would ensure that newly added fields are not modified at all by the portion of the code being proved. Such a check would ensure that the computation being analyzed computes the specified function *and nothing else* and would highlight cases in which new fields introduce undesirable data flows (e.g. incorrectly storing sensitive data). However even such an option would not replace whole program data flow analysis, which we recommend in cases where there is concern about potential incorrect data handling.

A. Chudnov et al.

Negative Test Cases. Each of our proofs also includes a series of negative test cases as evidence that the tools are functioning properly. These test cases patch the code with a variety of mistakes that might actually occur and then run the same proof scripts using the same build tools to check that the tool detects the introduced error.

Examples of the negative test cases we use include an incorrect modification to a side-channel mitigation, running our TLS proofs on a version of the code with an extra call to cork and uncork, a version modified to allow early CCS, as well as a version with the incomplete handshake bug that we discovered in the process of developing the proof. Such tests are critical, both to display the value of the proofs, by providing them with realistic bugs to catch, and as a defense against possible bugs in the tool that may be introduced as it is updated.

Proof Metrics. We also report real-time proof metrics. Our proof scripts print out JSON encoded statistics into the Travis logs. From there, we have developed an in-browser tool that scrapes the Travis logs for the project, compiling the relevant statistics into easily consumable charts and tables. The primary metrics we track are: (1) the number of lines of code that are analyzed by the proof (which increases as we develop proofs for more components of s2n), and (2) the number of times the verified code has been changed and re-analyzed (which tracks the ongoing value of the proof). This allows developers to easily track the impact of the proofs over time.

Since deployment of the proof to the CI system in November of 2016 our proofs have been re-played 956 times. This number does not account for proof re-plays performed in forks of the repository. We have had to update the proof three times. In all cases the proof update was complete before the code review process finished. Not all of these runs involved modification to the code that our proofs were about, however each of the runs increased the confidence of the maintainers in the relevant code changes, and each run reestablishes the correctness of the code to the public, who may not be aware of what code changed at each commit.

HMAC and DRBG each took roughly 3 months of engineering effort. The TLS handshake verification took longer at 8 months, though some of that time involved developing tool extensions to support reasoning about protocols. At the start of each project, the proof-writers were familiar with the proof tools but not with the algorithms or the s2n implementations of them. The effort amounts listed above include understanding the C code, writing the specifications in Cryptol, developing the code-spec proofs using SAW, the CI implementation work, and the process of merging the proof artifacts into the upstream code-base.

5 Conclusion

In this case study we have described the development and operation in practice of a continuously checked proof ensuring key properties of the TLS implementation used by many Amazon and AWS services. Based on several previous attempts to prove the correctness of s2n that either required too much developer inter-action during modifications or where symbolic reasoning tools did not scale, we developed a proof structure that nearly eliminates the need for developers to understand or modify the proof following modifications to the code.

References

1. Almeida, J.B., Barbosa, M., Barthe, G., Blot, A., Grégoire, B., Laporte, V., Oliveira, T., Pacheco, H., Schmidt, B., Strub, P.: Jasmin: high-assurance and high-speed cryptography. In: Thuraisingham, B.M., Evans, D., Malkin, T., Xu, D. (eds.), Proceedings of the 2017 ACM SIGSAC Conference on Computer and Communications Security, CCS 2017, Dallas, TX, USA, 30 October– 03 November 2017, pp. 1807–1823. ACM (2017)
2. Amazon.com, Inc., Amazon Simple Storage Service (s3). https://aws.amazon.com/s3/
3. Amazon.com, Inc. s2n. https://github.com/awslabs/s2n. Accessed Dec 2017
4. awslabs/s2n - Travis CI. https://travis-ci.org/awslabs/s2n
5. Barbosa, M., Castro, D., Silva, P.F.: Compiling CAO: from cryptographic specifications to C implementations. In: Abadi, M., Kremer, S. (eds.) POST 2014. LNCS, vol. 8414, pp. 240–244. Springer, Heidelberg (2014). https://doi.org/10.1007/978-3-642-54792-8_13
6. Beringer, L., Petcher, A., Katherine, Q.Y., Appel, A.W.: Verified correctness and security of OpenSSL HMAC. In: USENIX Security Symposium, pp. 207–221 (2015)
7. Beurdouche, B., Bhargavan, K., Delignat-Lavaud, A., Fournet, C., Kohlweiss, M., Pironti, A., Strub, P.-Y., Zinzindohoue, J.K.: A messy state of the union: taming the composite state machines of TLS. In: 2015 IEEE Symposium on Security and Privacy (SP), pp. 535–552. IEEE (2015)
8. Bhargavan, K., Fournet, C., Kohlweiss, M., Pironti, A., Strub, P.: Implementing TLS with verified cryptographic security, pp. 445–459. IEEE, May 2013
9. Bhargavan, K., Fournet, C., Kohlweiss, M., Pironti, A., Strub, P.-Y., Zanella-Bèguelin, S.: Proving the TLS handshake secure (as it is). Cryptology ePrint Archive, Report 2014/182 (2014). https://eprint.iacr.org/2014/182
10. Chudnov, A.: Missing branches in the handshake state machine, July 2017. https://github.com/awslabs/s2n/pull/551
11. de Ruiter, J., Poll, E.: Protocol state fuzzing of TLS implementations. In: 24th USENIX Security Symposium (USENIX Security 15), pp. 193–206. USENIX Association, Washington, D.C. (2015)
12. Delignat-Lavaud, A., Fournet, C., Kohlweiss, M., Protzenko, J., Rastogi, A., Swamy, N., Zanella-Béguelin, S., Bhargavan, K., Pan, J., Zinzindohoué, J.K.: Implementing and proving the TLS 1.3 record layer. In: 2017 IEEE Symposium on Security and Privacy (SP), pp. 463–482. IEEE (2017)
13. Eastlake III, D.: Transport Layer Security (TLS) Extensions: Extension Definitions. RFC 6066, January 2011
14. Erkök, L., Matthews, J.: Pragmatic equivalence and safety checking in Cryptol, p. 73. ACM Press (2008)
15. Eronen, P., Tschofenig, H., Zhou, H., Salowey, J.A.: Transport Layer Security (TLS) Session Resumption without Server-Side State. RFC 5077, January 2008
16. Galois, Inc.: The software analysis workbench. https://saw.galois.com/index.html
17. Gorelli, M.: Deductive verification of the s2n HMAC code. Master's thesis, Universtity of Oxford (2016)

18. Kaloper-Meršinjak, D., Mehnert, H., Madhavapeddy, A., Sewell, P.: Not-quite-so-broken TLS: lessons in re-engineering a security protocol specification and implementation. In: 24th USENIX Security Symposium (USENIX Security 2015), pp. 223–238. USENIX Association, Washington, D.C. (2015)
19. O'Hearn, P.: Continuous reasoning: scaling the impact of formal methods. In: Logic in Computer Science (LICS). (2018)
20. Petcher, A., Morrisett, G.: The foundational cryptography framework. arXiv:1410.3735 [cs], October 2014. arXiv:1410.3735
21. Rescorla, E., Dierks, T.: The Transport Layer Security (TLS) Protocol Version 1.2. RFC 5246, August 2008
22. The Coq Development Team. The Coq proof assistant, version 8.7.1, December 2017
23. Trustinsoft. PolarSSL verification kit. https://trust-in-soft.com/polarssl-verification-kit/
24. Turner, J.M.: The keyed-Hash Message Authentication Code (HMAC). Federal Information Processing Standards Publication (2008)
25. Zinzindohoué, J.-K., Bhargavan, K., Protzenko, J., Beurdouche, B.: HACL*: a verified modern cryptographic library. In: ACM Conference on Computer and Communications Security (CCS) (2017)

Symbolic Liveness Analysis of Real-World Software

Daniel Schemmel[1]([✉]), Julian Büning[1], Oscar Soria Dustmann[1], Thomas Noll[2], and Klaus Wehrle[1]

[1] Communication and Distributed Systems,
RWTH Aachen University, Aachen, Germany
{schemmel,buening,soriadustmann,
wehrle}@comsys.rwth-aachen.de
[2] Software Modeling and Verification,
RWTH Aachen University, Aachen, Germany
noll@cs.rwth-aachen.de

Abstract. Liveness violation bugs are notoriously hard to detect, especially due to the difficulty inherent in applying formal methods to real-world programs. We present a generic and practically useful liveness property which defines a program as being live as long as it will eventually either consume more input or terminate. We show that this property naturally maps to many different kinds of real-world programs.

To demonstrate the usefulness of our liveness property, we also present an algorithm that can be efficiently implemented to dynamically find lassos in the target program's state space during Symbolic Execution. This extends Symbolic Execution, a well known dynamic testing technique, to find a new class of program defects, namely liveness violations, while only incurring a small runtime and memory overhead, as evidenced by our evaluation. The implementation of our method found a total of five previously undiscovered software defects in BusyBox and the GNU Coreutils. All five defects have been confirmed and fixed by the respective maintainers after shipping for years, most of them well over a decade.

Keywords: Liveness analysis · Symbolic Execution · Software testing
Non-termination bugs

1 Introduction

Advances in formal testing and verification methods, such as Symbolic Execution [10 12,22 24,42,49] and Model Checking [5,6,13,17,21,27,29,30,43,50], have enabled the practical analysis of real-world software. Many of these approaches are based on the formal specification of temporal system properties using sets of infinite sequences of states [1], which can be classified as either safety, liveness, or properties that are neither [31]. (However, every linear-time property can be represented as the conjunction of a safety and a liveness property.) This distinction is motivated by the different techniques employed for proving or disproving such

H. Chockler and G. Weissenbacher (Eds.): CAV 2018, LNCS 10982, pp. 447–466, 2018.
https://doi.org/10.1007/978-3-319-96142-2_27

properties. In practical applications, safety properties are prevalent. They constrain the finite behavior of a system, ensuring that "nothing bad" happens, and can therefore be checked by reachability analysis. Hence, efficient algorithms and tools have been devised for checking such properties that return a finite counterexample in case of a violation [34].

Liveness properties, on the other hand, do not rule out any finite behavior but constrain infinite behavior to eventually do "something good" [2]. Their checking generally requires more sophisticated algorithms since they must be able to generate (finite representations of) infinite counterexamples. Moreover, common finite-state abstractions that are often employed for checking safety do generally not preserve liveness properties.

While it may be easy to create a domain-specific liveness property (e.g., "a GET/HTTP/1.1 must eventually be answered with an HTTP/1.1 {status}"), it is much harder to formulate *general* liveness properties. We tackle this challenge by proposing a liveness property based on the notion of programs as implementations of algorithms that transform input into output:

Definition 1. *A program is* live *if and only if it always eventually consumes input or terminates.*

By relying on input instead of output as the measure of progress, we circumnavigate difficulties caused by many common programming patterns such as printing status messages or logging the current state.

Detection. We present an algorithm to detect violations of this liveness property based on a straightforward idea: Execute the program and check after each instruction if the whole program state has been encountered before (identical contents of all registers and addressable memory). If a repetition is found that does not consume input, it is deterministic and will keep recurring ad infinitum. To facilitate checking real-world programs, we perform the search for such *lassos* in the program's state space while executing it symbolically.

Examples. Some examples that show the generality of this liveness property are: 1. Programs that operate on input from files and streams, such as cat, sha256sum or tail. This kind of program is intended to continue running as long as input is available. In some cases this input may be infinite (e.g., cat -). 2. Reactive programs, such as calc.exe or nginx wait for events to occur. Once an event occurs, a burst of activity computes an answer, before the software goes back to waiting for the next event. Often, an event can be sent to signal a termination request. Such events are input just as much as the contents of a file read by the program are input.

In rare cases, a program can intuitively be considered live without satisfying our liveness property. Most prominent is the yes utility, which will loop forever, only printing output. According to our experience the set of useful programs that intentionally allow for an infinite trace consuming only finite input is very small and the violation of our liveness property can, in such cases, easily be recognized as intentional. Our evaluation supports this claim (cf. Sect. 6).

Bugs and Violations. The implementation of our algorithm detected a total of five unintended and previously unknown liveness violations in the GNU Coreutils and BusyBox, all of which have been in the respective codebases for at least 7 to 19 years. All five bugs have been confirmed and fixed within days. The three implementations of yes we tested as part of our evaluation, were correctly detected to not be live. We also automatically generated liveness violating input programs for all sed interpreters.

1.1   Key Contributions

This paper presents four key contributions:

1. The definition of a generic liveness property for real-world software.
2. An algorithm to detect its violations.
3. An open-source implementation of the algorithm, available on GitHub[1], implemented as an extension to the Symbolic Execution engine KLEE [10].
4. An evaluation of the above implementation on a total of 354 tools from the GNU Coreutils, BusyBox and toybox, which so far detects five previously unknown defects in widely deployed real-world software.

1.2   Structure

We discuss related work (Sect. 2), before formally defining our liveness property (Sect. 3). Then, we describe the lasso detection algorithm (Sect. 4), demonstrate the practical applicability by implementing the algorithm for the SymEx engine KLEE (Sect. 5) and evaluate it on three real-world software suites (Sect. 6). We finally discuss the practical limitations (Sect. 7) and conclude (Sect. 8).

2   Related Work

General liveness properties [2] can be verified by *proof-based methods* [40], which generally require heavy user support. Contrarily, our work is based upon the state-exploration approach to verification. Another prominent approach to verify the correctness of a system with respect to its specification is automatic *Model Checking* using automata or tableau based methods [5].

In order to combat state-space explosion, many optimization techniques have been developed. Most of these, however, are only applicable to safety properties. For example, *Bounded Model Checking (BMC)* of software is a well-established method for detecting bugs and runtime errors [7,18,19] that is implemented by a number of tools [16,38]. These tools investigate finite paths in programs by bounding the number of loop iterations and the depth of function calls, which is not necessarily suited to detect the sort of liveness violations we aim to discover. There is work trying to establish completeness thresholds of BMC for (safety and) liveness properties [33], but these are useful only for comparatively small

---

[1] https://github.com/COMSYS/SymbolicLivenessAnalysis.

systems. Moreover, most BMC techniques are based on boolean SAT, instead of SMT, as required for dealing with the intricacies of real-world software.

Termination is closely related to liveness in our sense, and has been intensively studied. It boils down to showing the well-foundedness of the program's transition relation by identifying an appropriate ranking function. In recent works, this is accomplished by first synthesizing conditional termination proofs for program fragments such as loops, and then combining sub-proofs using a transformation that isolates program states for which termination has not been proven yet [8]. A common assumption in this setting is that program variables are mathematical integers, which eases reasoning but is generally unsound. A notable exception is AProVE [28], an automated tool for termination and complexity analysis that takes (amongst others) LLVM intermediate code and builds a SymEx graph that combines SymEx and state-space abstraction, covering both byte-accurate pointer arithmetic and bit-precise modeling of integers. However, advanced liveness properties, floating point values, complex data structures and recursive procedures are unsupported. While a termination proof is a witness for our liveness property, an infinite program execution constitutes neither witness nor violation. Therefore, *non-termination* proof generators, such as TNT [26], while still related, are not relevant to our liveness property.

The authors of Bolt [32] present an entirely different approach, by proposing an in-vivo analysis and correction method. Bolt does not aim to prove that a system terminates or not, but rather provides a means to force already running binaries out of a long-running or infinite loop. To this end, Bolt can attach to an unprepared, running program and will detect loops through memory snapshotting, comparing snapshots to a list of previous snapshots. A user may then choose to forcefully break the loop by applying one of two strategies as a last-resort option. Previous research into in-vivo analysis of hanging systems attempts to prove that a given process has run into an infinite loop [9]. Similarly to Bolt, Looper also attaches to a binary but then uses Concolic Execution (ConEx) to gain insight into the remaining, possible memory changes for the process. This allows for a diagnosis of whether the process is still making progress and will eventually terminate. Both approaches are primarily aimed at understanding or handling an apparent hang, not for proactively searching for unknown defects.

In [35], the authors argue that non-termination has been researched significantly less than termination. Similar to [14,25], they employ static analysis to find every Strongly Connected SubGraph (SCSG) in the Control Flow Graph (CFG) of a given program. Here, a Max-SMT solver is used to synthesize a formulaic representation of each node, which is both a quasi-invariant (i.e., always holding after it held once) and edge-closing (i.e., not allowing a transition that leaves the node's SCSG to be taken). If the solver succeeds for each node in a reachable SCSG, a non-terminating path has been found.

In summary, the applicability of efficient methods for checking liveness in our setting is hampered by restrictions arising from the programming model, the supported properties (e.g., only termination), scalability issues, missing support for non-terminating behavior or false positives due to over-approximation. In the following, we present our own solution to liveness checking of real-world software.

3   Liveness

We begin by formally defining our liveness property following the approach by Alpern and Schneider [1–3], which relies on the view that liveness properties do not constrain the finite behaviors but introduce conditions on infinite behaviors. Here, possible behaviors are given by (edge-labeled) transition systems.

Definition 2 (Transition System). *A transition system T is a 4-tuple $(S, Act, \rightarrow, I)$:*

- *S is a finite set of states,*
- *Act is a finite set of actions,*
- *$\rightarrow \subseteq S \times Act \times S$ is a transition relation (written $s \xrightarrow{\alpha} s'$), and*
- *$I \subseteq S$ is the set of initial states.*

For $s \in S$, the sets of outgoing *actions is denoted by $Out(s) = \{\alpha \in Act \mid s \xrightarrow{\alpha} s'$ for some $s' \in S\}$. Moreover, we require T to be* deadlock free*, i.e., $Out(s) \neq \emptyset$ for each $s \in S$. A* terminal state *is indicated by a self-loop involving the distinguished action $\downarrow \in Act$: if $\downarrow \in Out(s)$, then $Out(s) = \{\downarrow\}$.*

The self-loops ensure that all *executions* of a program are infinite, which is necessary as terminal states indicate successful completion in our setting.

Definition 3 (Executions and Traces). *An (infinite)* execution *is a sequence of the form $s_0 \alpha_1 s_1 \alpha_2 s_2 \ldots$ such that $s_0 \in I$ and $s_i \xrightarrow{\alpha_{i+1}} s_{i+1}$ for every $i \in \mathbb{N}$. Its* trace *is given by $\alpha_1 \alpha_2 \ldots \in Act^\omega$.*

Definition 4 (Liveness Properties)

- *A* linear-time property *over Act is a subset of Act^ω.*
- *Let $\Pi \subseteq Act$ be a set of* productive *actions such that $\downarrow \in \Pi$. The Π-liveness property is given by $\{\alpha_1 \alpha_2 \ldots \in Act^\omega \mid \alpha_i \in \Pi$ for infinitely many $i \in \mathbb{N}\}$.*

A liveness property is generally characterized by the requirement that each finite trace prefix can be extended to an infinite trace that satisfies this property. In our setting, this means that in each state of a given program it is guaranteed that eventually a productive action will be performed. That is, infinitely many productive actions will occur during each execution. As $\downarrow$ is considered productive, terminating computations are live. This differs from the classical setting where terminal states are usually considered as deadlocks that violate liveness.

We assume that the target machine is deterministic w.r.t. its computations and model the consumption of input as the only source of non-determinism. This means that if the execution is in a state in which the program will execute a non-input instruction, only a single outgoing (unproductive) transition exists. If the program is to consume input on the other hand, a (productive) transition exists for every possible value of input. We only consider functions that provide at least one bit of input as input functions, which makes $\downarrow$ the only productive action that is also deterministic, that is, the only productive transition which must be taken once the state it originates from is reached. More formally, $|Out(s)| > 1 \Leftrightarrow Out(s) \subseteq \Pi \setminus \{\downarrow\}$. Thus if a (sub-)execution $s_i \alpha_{i+1} s_{i+1} \cdots$ contains no productive transitions beyond $\downarrow$, it is fully specified by its first state s_i, as there will only ever be a single transition to be taken.

Similarly, we assume that the target machine has finite memory. This implies that the number of possible states is finite: $|S| \in \mathbb{N}$. Although we model each possible input with its own transition, input words are finite too, therefore Act is finite and hence $Out(s)$ for each $s \in S$.

4   Finding Lassos

Any trace t that violates a liveness property must necessarily consist of a finite prefix p that leads to some state $s \in S$, after which no further productive transitions are taken. Therefore, t can be written as $t = pq$, where p is finite and may contain productive actions, while q is infinite and does not contain productive actions. Since S is a finite set and every state from s onward will only have a single outgoing transition and successor, q must contain a cycle that repeats itself infinitely often. Therefore, q in turn can be written as $q = fc^\omega$ where f is finite and c non-empty. Due to its shape, we call this a *lasso* with pf the *stem* and c the *loop*.

Due to the infeasible computational complexity of checking our liveness property statically (in the absence of input functions, it becomes the finite-space halting problem), we leverage a dynamic analysis that is capable of finding any violation in bounded time and works incrementally to report violations as they are encountered. We do so by searching the state space for a lasso, whose loop does not contain any productive transitions. This is naïvely achieved in the dynamic analysis by checking whether any other state visited since the last productive transition is equal to the current one. In this case the current state deterministically transitions to itself, i.e., is part of the loop.

To implement this idea without prohibitively expensive resource usage, two main challenges must be overcome: 1. Exhaustive exploration of all possible inputs is infeasible for nontrivial cases. 2. Comparing states requires up to 2^{64} byte comparisons on a 64 bit computer. In the rest of this section, we discuss how to leverage SymEx to tackle the first problem (Sect. 4.1) and how to cheapen state comparisons with specially composed hash-based fingerprints (Sect. 4.2).

4.1   Symbolic Execution

Symbolic Execution (SymEx) has become a popular dynamic analysis technique whose primary domain is automated test case generation and bug detection [10–12,15,22,41,42,49]. The primary intent behind SymEx is to improve upon exhaustive testing by symbolically constraining inputs instead of iterating over all possible values, which makes it a natural fit.

Background. The example in Fig. 1 tests whether the variable x is in the range from 5 to 99 by performing two tests before returning the result. As x is the

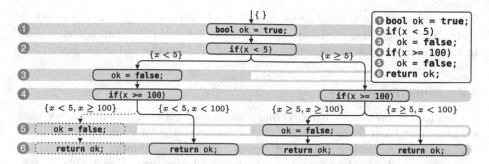

Fig. 1. SymEx tree showing the execution of a snippet with two `ifs`. The variable `x` is symbolic and one state is unreachable, as its Path Constraint is unsatisfiable.

input to this snippet, it is initially assigned an unconstrained symbolic value. Upon branching on x < 5 in line 2, the SymEx engine needs to consider two cases: One in which x is now constrained to be smaller than 5 and another one in which it is constrained to *not* be smaller than 5. On the path on which x < 5 held, `ok` is then assigned `false`, while the other path does not execute that instruction. Afterwards, both paths encounter the branch if(x > = 100) in line 4. Since the constraint set $\{x < 5, x \geq 100\}$ is unsatisfiable, the leftmost of the four resulting possibilities is unreachable and therefore not explored. The three remaining paths reach the return statement in line 6. We call the set of currently active constraints the *Path Constraint (PC)*. The PC is usually constructed in such a way, as to contain constraints in the combined theories of quantifier-free bit-vectors, finite arrays and floating point numbers[2].

Symbolic Execution of the Abstract Transition System. By using symbolic values, a single SymEx state can represent a large number of states in the transition system. We require that the SymEx engine, as is commonly done, never assigns a symbolic value (with more than one satisfying model) to the instruction pointer. Since the productive transitions of the transition system are derived from instructions in the program code, this means that each instruction that the SymEx engine performs either corresponds to a number of productive, input-consuming transitions, or a number of unproductive, *not* input-consuming transitions. Therefore, any lasso in the SymEx of the program is also a lasso in the transition system (the ↓ transition requires trivial special treatment).

To ensure that the opposite is also true, a simple and common optimization must be implemented in the SymEx engine: Only add branch conditions to the PC that are not already implied by it. This is the case iff exactly one of the two branching possibilities is satisfiable, which the SymEx engine (or rather its SMT solver) needs to check in any case. Thereby it is guaranteed that if the SymEx state is part of a loop in the transition system, not just the concrete

---

[2] While current SymEx engines and SMT solvers still struggle with the floating point theory in practice [37], the SMT problem is decidable for this combination of theories. Bitblasting [20] gives a polynomial-time reduction to the boolean SAT problem.

values, but also the symbolic values will eventually converge towards a steady state. Again excluding trivial special treatment for program termination, a lasso in the transition system thus entails a lasso in the SymEx of the program.

4.2 Fingerprinting

To reduce the cost of each individual comparison between two states, we take an idea from hash maps by computing a *fingerprint* ρ for each state and comparing those. A further significant improvement is possible by using a strong cryptographic hash algorithm to compute the fingerprint: Being able to rely (with very high probability) on the fingerprint comparison reduces the memory requirements, as it becomes unnecessary to store a list of full predecessor states. Instead, only the fingerprints of the predecessors need to be kept.

Recomputing the fingerprint after each instruction would still require a full scan over the whole state at each instruction however. Instead, we enable efficient, incremental computation of the fingerprint by not hashing everything, but rather hashing many small *fragments*, and then composing the resulting hashes using bitwise xor. Then, if an instruction attempts to modify a fragment f, it is easy to compute the old and new fragment hashes. The new fingerprint ρ_{new} can then be computed as $\rho_{new} := \rho_{old} \oplus hash(f_{old}) \oplus hash(f_{new})$. Changing a single fragment therefore requires only two computations and bitwise xors on constant size bit strings—one to remove the old fragment from the composite and one to insert the new one. Each incremental fingerprint update only modifies a small number of fragments statically bounded by the types used in the program.

4.3 Algorithm Overview

The proposed algorithm explores as much of the input state as is possible within a specified amount of time, using SymEx to cover large portions of the input space simultaneously. Every SymEx state is efficiently checked against all its predecessors by comparing their fingerprints.

5 Efficient Implementation of the Algorithm

To develop the algorithm presented in the previous section into a practically useful program, we decided to build upon the KLEE SymEx engine [10], with which many safety bugs in real-world programs have been previously found [10,15,41]. As KLEE in turn builds upon the LLVM compiler infrastructure [36], this section begins with a short introduction to LLVM Intermediate Representation (IR) (Sect. 5.1), before explaining how the fragments whose hashes make up the fingerprint can be implemented (Sect. 5.2) and how to track fingerprints (Sect. 5.3). Finally, we detail a technique to avoid as many comparisons as possible (Sect. 5.4).

5.1 LLVM Intermediate Representation

LLVM Intermediate Representation (IR) was designed as a typed, low-level language independent from both (high-level) source language and any specific target architecture, to facilitate compiler optimizations. It operates on an unlimited number of typed registers of arbitrary size, as well as addressable memory. Instructions in IR operate in Static Single Assignment (SSA) form, i.e., registers are only ever assigned once and never modified. The language also has functions, which have a return type and an arbitrary number of typed parameters. Apart from global scope, there is only function scope, but IR features no block scope.

Addressable objects are either global variables, or explicitly allocated, e.g., using `malloc` (cleaned up with `free`) or `alloca` (cleaned up on return from function).

Main Memory (Concrete):	0x01	Address	Value
Main Memory (Symbolic):	0x02	Address	Sym. Expression
Register (Concrete):	0x03	Instruction ID	Value
Register (Symbolic):	0x04	Instruction ID	Sym. Expression
Argument (Concrete):	0x05	(Function ID, Argument Number)	Value
Argument (Symbolic):	0x06	(Function ID, Argument Number)	Sym. Expression

Fig. 2. Six kinds of fragments suffice to denote all possible variants. Symbolic values are written as serialized symbolic expressions consisting of all relevant constraints. All other fields only ever contain concrete values, which are simply used verbatim. Fields of dynamic size are denoted by a ragged right edge.

5.2 Fragments

When determining what is to become a fragment, i.e., an atomic portion of a fingerprint, two major design goals should be taken into consideration:

1. Collisions between hashed fragments should not occur, as they would expunge one another from the fingerprint. This goal can be decomposed further:
   (a) The hashing algorithm should be chosen in a manner that makes collisions so unlikely, as to be non-existent in practice.
   (b) The fragments themselves need to be generated in a way that ensures that no two different fragments have the same representation, as that would of course cause their hashes to be equal as well.
2. Fragment sizes should be as close as possible to what will be modified by the program in one step. Longer fragments are more expensive to compute and hash, and shorter fragments become invalidated more frequently.

Avoiding Collisions. In order to minimize the risk of accidental collisions, which would reduce the efficacy of our methodology, we chose the cryptographically secure checksum algorithm BLAKE2b [4] to generate 256 bit hashes, providing 128 bit collision resistance. To the best of our knowledge, there are currently

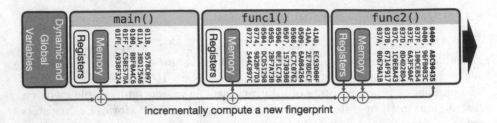

incrementally compute a new fingerprint

Fig. 3. Incremental computation of a new fingerprint. Fingerprints are stored in a call stack, with each stack frame containing a partial fingerprint of all addressable memory allocated locally in that function, another partial fingerprint of all registers used in the function and a list of previously encountered fingerprints. A partial fingerprint of all dynamic and global variables is stored independently.

no relevant structural attacks on BLAKE2b, which allows us to assume that the collision resistance is given. For comparison: The revision control system GIT currently uses 160 bit SHA-1 hashes to create unique identifiers for its objects, with plans underway to migrate to a stronger 256 bit hash algorithm[3].

To ensure that the fragments themselves are generated in a collision-free manner, we structure them with three fields each, as can be seen in Fig. 2. The first field contains a tag that lets us distinguish between different types of fragments, the middle field contains an address appropriate for that type, and the last field is the value that the fragment represents. We distinguish between three different address spaces: 1. main memory, 2. LLVM registers, which similarly to actual processors hold values that do not have a main memory address, and 3. function arguments, which behave similarly to ordinary LLVM registers, but require a certain amount of special handling in our implementation. For example, the fragment $(0x01, 0xFF3780, 0xFF)$ means that the memory address $0xFF3780$ holds the concrete byte $0xFF$. This fragment hashes to $ea58...f677$.

If the fragment represents a concrete value, its size is statically bounded by the kind of write being done. For example, a write to main memory requires 1 byte + 8 byte + 1 byte = 10 byte and modifying a 64 bit register requires $1 \text{ byte} + 8 \text{ byte} + \frac{64 \text{ bit}}{8 \text{ bit/byte}} = 17$ byte. In the case of fragments representing symbolic values on the other hand, such a guarantee cannot effectively be made, as the symbolic expression may become arbitrarily large. Consider, for example, a symbolic expression of the form $\lambda = \text{input}_1 + \text{input}_2 + \ldots + \text{input}_n$, whose result is directly influenced by an arbitrary amount of n input words.

In summary, fragments are created in a way that precludes structural weaknesses as long as the hash algorithm used (in our case 256 bit BLAKE2b) remains unbroken and collisions are significantly less probable than transient failures of the computer performing the analysis.

---

[3] https://www.kernel.org/pub/software/scm/git/docs/technical/hash-function-transition.html (Retrieved Jan. 2018).

5.3 Fingerprint Tracking

When using the KLEE SymEx engine, the call stack is not explicitly mapped into the program's address space, but rather directly managed by KLEE itself. This enables us to further extend the practical usefulness of our analysis by only considering fragments that are directly addressable from each point of the execution, which in turn enables the detection of certain non-terminating recursive function calls. It also goes well together with the implicit cleanup of all function variables when a function returns to its caller.

To incrementally construct the current fingerprint we utilize a stack that follows the current call stack, as is shown exemplary in Fig. 3. Each entry consists of three different parts: 1. A (partial) fingerprint over all local registers, i.e., objects that are not globally addressable, 2. A (partial) fingerprint over all locally allocated objects in main memory and 3. A list of pairs of instruction IDs and fingerprints, that denote the states that were encountered previously.

Modifying Objects. Any instruction modifying an object without reading input, such as an addition, is dealt with as explained previously: First, recompute the hash of the old fragment(s) before the instruction is performed and remove it from the current fingerprint. Then, perform the instruction, compute the hash of the new fragment(s) and add it to the current fingerprint.

Similarly modify the appropriate partial fingerprint, e.g., for a load the fingerprint of all local registers of the current function. Note that this requires each memory object to be mappable to where it was allocated from.

Function Calls. To perform a function call, push a new entry onto the stack with the register fingerprint initialized to the xor of the hashes of the argument fragments and the main memory fingerprint set to the neutral element, zero. Update the current fingerprint by removing the caller's register fingerprint and adding the callee's register fingerprint. Add the pair of entry point and current fingerprint to the list of previously seen fingerprints.

Function Returns. When returning from a function, first remove both the fingerprint of the local registers, as well as the fingerprint of local, globally addressable objects from the current fingerprint, as all of these will be implicitly destroyed by the returning function. Then pop the topmost entry from the stack and re-enable the fingerprint of the local registers of the caller.

Reading Input. Upon reading input all previously encountered fingerprints must be disregarded by clearing all fingerprint lists of the current SymEx state.

5.4 Avoiding Comparisons

While it would be sufficient to simply check all previous fingerprints for a repetition every time the current fingerprint is modified, it would be rather inefficient to do so. To gain as much performance as possible, our implementation attempts to perform as few comparisons as possible.

We reduce the number of fingerprints that need to be considered at any point by exploiting the structure of the call stack: To find any non-recursive infinite loop, it suffices to search the list of the current stack frame, while recursive infinite loops can be identified using only the first fingerprint of each stack frame.

We also exploit static control flow information by only storing and testing fingerprints for Basic Blocks (BBs), which are sequences of instructions with linear control flow[4]. If any one instruction of a BB is executed infinitely often, all of them are. Thus, a BB is either fully in the infinite cycle, or no part of it is.

It is not even necessary to consider every single BB, as we are looking for a trace with a finite prefix leading into a cycle. As the abstract transition system is an unfolding of the CFG, any cycle in the transition system must unfold from a cycle in the CFG. Any reachable cycle in the CFG must contain a BB with more than one predecessor, as at least one BB must be reachable from both outside and inside the cycle. Therefore, it is sufficient to only check BBs with multiple predecessors. As IR only provides intraprocedural CFGs, we additionally perform a check for infinite recursion at the beginning of each function.

6 Evaluation

In this section we demonstrate the effectiveness and performance of our approach on well tested and widely used real-world software. We focus on three different groups of programs: 1. The GNU Coreutils and GNU sed (Sect. 6.1), 2. BusyBox (Sect. 6.2) and 3. Toybox (Sect. 6.3) and evaluate the performance of our liveness analysis in comparison with baseline KLEE in the following metrics: 1. instructions per second and 2. peak resident set size. Additionally, we analyze the impact of the time limit on the overhead (Sect. 6.4). We summarize our findings in Sect. 6.5.

Setup. We used revision aa01f83[5] of our software, which is based on KLEE revision 37f554d[6]. Both versions are invoked as suggested by the KLEE authors and maintainers [10,47] in order to maximize reproducability and ensure realistic results. However, we choose the Z3 [39] solver over STP [20] as the former provides a native timeout feature, enabling more reliable measurements. The solver timeout is 30 s and the memory limit is 10 000 MiB.

We run each configuration 20 times in order to gain statistical confidence in the results. From every single run, we extract both the instructions, allowing us to compute the instructions per second, and the peak resident set size of the process, i.e., the maximal amount of memory used. We additionally reproduced the detected liveness violations with 30 runs each with a time limit of 24 h, recording the total time required for our implementation to find the first violation. For all results we give a 99% confidence interval.

---

[4] In IR there is an exemption for function calls, namely they do not break up BBs.

[5] https://github.com/COMSYS/SymbolicLivenessAnalysis/tree/aa01f83.

[6] https://github.com/klee/klee/tree/37f554d.

6.1   GNU Utilities

We combine the GNU tools from the Coreutils 8.25 [45] with GNU sed 4.4 [46], as the other tool suites also contain an implementation of the sed utility. We excluded 4 tools from the experiment as their execution is not captured by KLEE's system model. Thereby, the experiment contains a total of 103 tools.

Violations. The expected liveness violation in yes occurred after 2.51 s $\pm$ 0.26 s. In 26 out of 30 runs, we were also able to detect a violation in GNU sed after a mean computation time of 8.06 h $\pm$ 3.21 h (KLEE's timeout was set to 24 h). With the symbolic arguments restricted to one argument of four symbolic characters, reproduction completed in all 30 runs with a mean of 5.19 min $\pm$ 0.17 min.

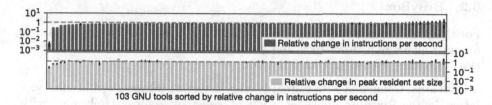

Fig. 4. GNU Coreutils and GNU sed, 60 min time limit. Relative change of instructions per second (top) and peak resident set (bottom) versus the KLEE baseline. Note the logarithmic scale and the black 99% confidence intervals.

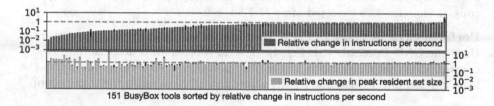

Fig. 5. BusyBox, 60 min time limit. Relative change of instructions per second (top) and peak resident set (bottom) versus the KLEE baseline. Note the logarithmic scale and the black 99% confidence intervals.

We detected multiple violations in tail stemming from two previously unknown bugs, that we reported. Both bugs were originally detected and reported in version 8.25[7] and fixed in version 8.26. Both bugs were in the codebase for over 16 years. Reproducing the detection was successful in 30 of 30 attempts with a mean time of 1.59 h $\pm$ 0.66 h until the first detected violation.

We detected another previously unknown bug in ptx. Although we originally identified the bug in version 8.27, we reported it after the release of 8.28[8], leading

---

[7] GNU tail report 1: http://bugs.gnu.org/24495.

GNU tail report 2: http://bugs.gnu.org/24903.

[8] GNU ptx report: http://bugs.gnu.org/28417.

to a fix in version 8.29. This bug is not easily detected: Only 9 of 30 runs completed within the time limit of 24 h. For these, mean time to first detection was 17.15 h ± 3.74 h.

Performance. Figure 4 shows the relative changes in instructions per second and peak resident set. As can be seen, performance is only reduced slightly below the KLEE baseline and the memory overhead is even less significant. The leftmost tool, `make-prime-list`, shows the by far most significant change from the KLEE baseline. This is because `make-prime-list` only reads very little input, followed by a very complex computation in the course of which no further input is read.

6.2   BusyBox

For this experiment we used BusyBox version 1.27.2 [44]. As BusyBox contains a large number of network tools and daemons, we had to exclude 232 tools from the evaluation, leaving us with 151 tools.

Violations. Compared with Coreutils' `yes`, detecting the expected liveness violation in the BusyBox implementation of `yes` took comparatively long with 27.68 s ± 0.33 s. We were unable to detect any violations in BusyBox `sed` without restricting the size of the symbolic arguments. When restricting them to one argument with four symbolic characters, we found the first violation in all 30 runs within 1.44 h ± 0.08 h. Our evaluation uncovered two previously unknown bugs in BusyBox `hush`[9]. We first detected both bugs in version 1.27.2. In all 30 runs, a violation was detected after 71.73 s ± 5.00 s.

Performance. As shown in Fig. 5, BusyBox has a higher slowdown on average than the GNU Coreutils (c.f. Fig. 4). Several tools show a *decrease* in memory consumption that we attribute to the drop in retired instructions. `yes` shows the least throughput, as baseline KLEE very efficiently evaluates the infinite loop.

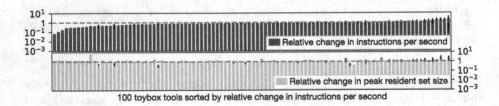

Fig. 6. Toybox, 60 min time limit. Relative change of instructions per second (top) and peak resident set (bottom) versus the KLEE baseline. Note the logarithmic scale and the black 99% confidence intervals.

---

[9] BusyBox `hush` report 1: https://bugs.busybox.net/10421.
   BusyBox `hush` report 2: https://bugs.busybox.net/10686.

6.3 Toybox

The third and final experiment with real-world software consists of 100 tools from toybox 0.7.5 [48]. We excluded 76 of the total of 176 tools, which rely on operating system features not reasonably modeled by KLEE.

Violations. For yes we encounter the first violation after 6.34 s ± 0.24 s, which puts it in between the times for GNU yes and BusyBox yes. This violation is also triggered from env by way of toybox's internal path lookup. As with the other sed implementations, toybox sed often fails to complete when run with the default parameter set. With only one symbolic argument of four symbolic characters, however, we encountered a violation in all 30 runs within 4.99 min ± 0.25 min.

Performance. Overall as well, our approach shows a performance for toybox in between those for the GNU Coreutils and BusyBox, as can be seen in Fig. 6. Both memory and velocity overhead are limited. For most toybox tools, the overhead is small enough to warrant always enabling our changes when running KLEE.

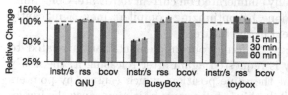
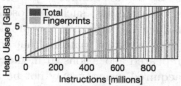

Fig. 7. Changes in instructions per second, peak resident set and branch coverage over multiple KLEE timeouts. Note the logarithmic scale and the black 99% confidence intervals.

Fig. 8. Heap usage of a 30 min BusyBox hush run. The 186 vertical lines show detected liveness violations.

6.4 Scaling with the Time Limit

To ascertain whether the performance penalty incurred by our implementation scales with the KLEE time limit, we have repeated each experiment with time limits 15 min, 30 min and 60 min. The results shown in Fig. 7 indicate that, at least at this scale, baseline KLEE and our implementation scale equally well. This is true for almost all relevant metrics: retired instructions per second, peak resident set and covered branches. The prominent exception is BusyBox's memory usage, which is shown exemplary in Fig. 8 for a 30 min run of BusyBox hush. As can be seen, the overhead introduced by the liveness analysis is mostly stable at about a quarter of the total heap usage.

6.5   Summary

All evaluated tool suites show a low average performance and memory penalty when comparing our approach to baseline KLEE. While the slowdown is significant for some tools in each suite, it is consistent as long as time and memory limits are not chosen too tightly. In fact, for these kinds of programs, it is reasonable to accept a limited slowdown in exchange for opening up a whole new category of defects that can be detected. In direct comparison, performance varies in between suites, but remains reasonable in each case.

7   Limitations

Our approach does not distinguish between interpreters and interpreted programs. While this enables the automatic derivation of input programs for such interpreters as sed, it also makes it hard to recognize meaningful error cases. This causes the analysis of all three implementations of sed used in the evaluation (Sect. 6) to return liveness violations.

In its current form, our implementation struggles with runaway counters, as a 64 bit counter cannot be practically enumerated on current hardware. Combining static analyses, such as those done by optimizing compilers may significantly reduce the impact of this problem in the future.

A different pattern that may confound our implementation is related to repeated allocations. If memory is requested again after releasing it, the newly acquired memory may not be at the same position, which causes any pointers to it to have different values. While this is fully correct, it may cause the implementation to not recognize cycles in a reasonable time frame. This could be mitigated by analyzing whether the value of the pointer ever actually matters. For example, in the C programming language, it is fairly uncommon to inspect the numerical value of a pointer beyond comparing it to NULL or other pointers. A valid solution would however require strengthening KLEE's memory model, which currently does not model pointer inspection very well.

Another potential problem is how the PC is serialized when using symbolic expressions as the value of a fragment (c.f. Sect. 5.2). We currently reuse KLEE's serialization routines, which are not exactly tuned for performance. Also, each symbolic value that is generated by KLEE is assigned a unique name, that is then displayed by the serialization, which discounts potential equivalence.

Finally, by building upon SymEx, we inherit not only its strengths, but also its weaknesses, such as a certain predilection for state explosion and a reliance on repeated SMT solving [12]. Also, actual SymEx implementations are limited further than that. For example, KLEE returns a concrete pointer from allocation routines instead of a symbolic value representing all possible addresses.

8   Conclusion and Outlook

It is our strong belief that the testing and verification of liveness properties needs to become more attractive to developers of real-world programs. Our work provides a step in that direction with the formulation of a liveness property that is general and practically useful, thereby enabling even developers uncomfortable with interacting with formal testing and verification methods to at least check their software for liveness violation bugs.

We demonstrated the usefulness of our liveness property by implementing it as an extension to the Symbolic Execution engine KLEE, thereby enabling it to discover a class of software defects it could not previously detect, and analyzing several large and well-tested programs. Our implementation caused the discovery and eventual correction of a total of five previously unknown defects, three in the GNU Coreutils, arguably one of the most well-tested code bases in existence, and two in BusyBox. Each of these bugs had been in released software for over 7 years—four of them even for over 16 years, which goes to show that this class of bugs has so far proven elusive. Our implementation did not cause a single false positive: all reported violations are indeed accompanied by concrete test cases that reproduce a violation of our liveness property.

The evaluation in Sect. 6 also showed that the performance impact, in matters of throughput as well as in matters of memory consumption, remains significantly below 2× on average, while allowing the analysis to detect a completely new range of software defects. We demonstrated that this overhead remains stable over a range of different analysis durations.

In future work, we will explore the opportunities for same-state merging that our approach enables by implementing efficient equality testing of SymEx states via our fingerprinting scheme. We expect that this will further improve the performance of our approach and maybe even exceed KLEE's baseline performance by reducing the amount of duplicate work done.

Acknowledgements. This research is supported by the European Research Council (ERC) under the European Union's Horizon 2020 Research and Innovation Programme (grant agreement №. 647295 (SYMBIOSYS)).

References

1. Alpern, B., Schneider, F.B.: Verifying temporal properties without temporal logic. ACM Trans. Program. Lang. Syst. **11**(1), 147–167 (1989)
2. Alpern, B., Schneider, F.B.: Defining liveness. Inf. Process. Lett. **21**(4), 181–185 (1985)
3. Alpern, B., Schneider, F.B.: Recognizing safety and liveness. Distrib. Comput. **2**(3), 117–126 (1987)
4. Aumasson, J.P., Neves, S., Wilcox-O'Hearn, Z., Winnerlein, C.: BLAKE2: simpler, smaller, fast as MD5. In: Proceedings of the 11th International Conference on Applied Cryptography and Network Security (ACNS 2013), pp. 119–135, June 2013
5. Baier, C., Katoen, J.P.: Principles of Model Checking. The MIT Press, Cambridge (2008)
6. Ball, T., Podelski, A., Rajamani, S.K.: Boolean and cartesian abstraction for model checking C programs. Int. J. Softw. Tools Technol. Transf. **5**(1), 49–58 (2003)

7. Biere, A., Cimatti, A., Clarke, E., Zhu, Y.: Symbolic model checking without BDDs. In: Cleaveland, W.R. (ed.) TACAS 1999. LNCS, vol. 1579, pp. 193–207. Springer, Heidelberg (1999). https://doi.org/10.1007/3-540-49059-0_14

8. Borralleras, C., Brockschmidt, M., Larraz, D., Oliveras, A., Rodríguez-Carbonell, E., Rubio, A.: Proving termination through conditional termination. In: Legay, A., Margaria, T. (eds.) TACAS 2017. LNCS, vol. 10205, pp. 99–117. Springer, Heidelberg (2017). https://doi.org/10.1007/978-3-662-54577-5_6

9. Burnim, J., Jalbert, N., Stergiou, C., Sen, K.: Looper: lightweight detection of infinite loops at runtime. In: Proceedings of the 24th IEEE/ACM International Conference on Automated Software Engineering (ASE 2009), November 2009

10. Cadar, C., Dunbar, D., Engler, D.: KLEE: unassisted and automatic generation of high-coverage tests for complex systems programs. In: Proceedings of the 8th USENIX Symposium on Operating Systems Design and Implementation (OSDI 2008), December 2008

11. Cadar, C., Ganesh, V., Pawlowski, P.M., Dill, D.L., Engler, D.R.: EXE: automatically generating inputs of death. ACM Trans. Inf. Syst. Secur. **12**(2), 10 (2008)

12. Cadar, C., Sen, K.: Symbolic execution for software testing: three decades later. Commun. ACM **56**(2), 82–90 (2013)

13. Chan, W., Anderson, R.J., Beame, P., Burns, S., Modugno, F., Notkin, D., Reese, J.D.: Model checking large software specifications. IEEE Trans. Softw. Eng. **24**(7), 498–520 (1998)

14. Chen, H.Y., Cook, B., Fuhs, C., Nimkar, K., O'Hearn, P.W.: Proving nontermination via safety. In: Proceedings of the 20th International Conference on Tools and Algorithms for the Construction and Analysis of Systems (TACAS 2014), April 2014

15. Chipounov, V., Kuznetsov, V., Candea, G.: S2E: a platform for in vivo multi-path analysis of software systems. In: Proceedings of the 16th International Conference on Architectural Support for Programming Languages and Operating Systems (ASPLOS 2011), March 2011

16. Clarke, E., Kroening, D., Lerda, F.: A tool for checking ANSI-C programs. In: Jensen, K., Podelski, A. (eds.) TACAS 2004. LNCS, vol. 2988, pp. 168–176. Springer, Heidelberg (2004). https://doi.org/10.1007/978-3-540-24730-2_15

17. Clarke, E.M., Grumberg, O., Hiraishi, H., Jha, S., Long, D.E., McMillan, K.L., Ness, L.A.: Verification of the Futurebus+ cache coherence protocol. Formal Methods Syst. Des. **6**(2), 217–232 (1995)

18. Cordeiro, L., Fischer, B., Marques-Silva, J.: SMT-based bounded model checking for embedded ANSI-C software. IEEE Trans. Softw. Eng. **38**(4), 957–974 (2012)

19. Falke, S., Merz, F., Sinz, C.: The bounded model checker LLBMC. In: ASE 2013, pp. 706–709 (2013)

20. Ganesh, V., Dill, D.L.: A Decision procedure for bit-vectors and arrays. In: Proceedings of the 19th International Conference on Computer-Aided Verification (CAV 2007), pp. 519–531, July 2007

21. Godefroid, P.: Model checking for programming languages using VeriSoft. In: POPL 1997, pp. 174–186. ACM (1997)

22. Godefroid, P., Klarlund, N., Sen, K.: DART: directed automated random testing. In: Proceedings of the Conference on Programming Language Design and Implementation (PLDI 2005), vol. 40, pp. 213–223, June 2005

23. Godefroid, P., Levin, M.Y., Molnar, D.: SAGE: whitebox fuzzing for security testing. ACM Queue **10**(1), 20 (2012)

24. Godefroid, P., Levin, M.Y., Molnar, D.A.: Automated whitebox fuzz testing. In: Proceedings of the 15th Network and Distributed System Security Symposium (NDSS 2008), vol. 8, pp. 151–166, February 2008
25. Gulwani, S., Srivastava, S., Venkatesan, R.: Program analysis as constraint solving. In: Proceedings of the Conference on Programming Language Design and Implementation (PLDI 2008), June 2008
26. Gupta, A., Henzinger, T.A., Majumdar, R., Rybalchenko, A., Xu, R.G.: Proving non-termination. In: POPL 2008, pp. 147–158. ACM (2008)
27. Havelund, K., Pressburger, T.: Model checking Java programs using Java PathFinder. Int. J. Softw. Tools Technol. Transf. **2**(4), 366–381 (2000)
28. Hensel, J., Giesl, J., Frohn, F., Ströder, T.: Proving termination of programs with bitvector arithmetic by symbolic execution. In: De Nicola, R., Kühn, E. (eds.) SEFM 2016. LNCS, vol. 9763, pp. 234–252. Springer, Cham (2016). https://doi.org/10.1007/978-3-319-41591-8_16
29. Holzmann, G., Najm, E., Serhrouchni, A.: Spin model checking: an introduction. Int. J. Softw. Tools Technol. Transf. **2**(4), 321–327 (2000)
30. Holzmann, G.J.: Design and validation of protocols: a tutorial. Comput. Netw. ISDN Syst. **25**(9), 981–1017 (1993)
31. Kindler, E.: Safety and liveness properties: a survey. Bull. Eur. Assoc. Theor. Comput. Sci. **53**, 268–272 (1994)
32. Kling, M., Misailovic, S., Carbin, M., Rinard, M.: Bolt: on-demand infinite loop escape in unmodified binaries. In: Proceedings of the 27th Annual Conference on Object-Oriented Programming Systems, Languages and Applications (OOPSLA 2012), October 2012
33. Kroening, D., Ouaknine, J., Strichman, O., Wahl, T., Worrell, J.: Linear completeness thresholds for bounded model checking. In: Gopalakrishnan, G., Qadeer, S. (eds.) CAV 2011. LNCS, vol. 6806, pp. 557–572. Springer, Heidelberg (2011). https://doi.org/10.1007/978-3-642-22110-1_44
34. Kupferman, O., Vardi, M.Y.: Model checking of safety properties. Formal Methods Syst. Des. **19**(3), 291–314 (2001)
35. Larraz, D., Nimkar, K., Oliveras, A., Rodríguez-Carbonell, E., Rubio, A.: Proving non-termination using Max-SMT. In: Proceedings of the 26th International Conference on Computer-Aided Verification (CAV 2014), July 2014
36. Lattner, C., Adve, V.: LLVM: a compilation framework for lifelong program analysis & transformation. In: Proceedings of the 2nd International Symposium on Code Generation and Optimization (CGO 2004), San Jose, CA, USA, pp. 75–88, March 2004
37. Liew, D., Schemmel, D., Cadar, C., Donaldson, A.F., Zähl, R., Wehrle, K.: Floating-point symbolic execution: a case study in N-version programming. In: Proceedings of the 32nd IEEE/ACM International Conference on Automated Software Engineering (ASE 2017), pp. 601–612, October–November 2017
38. Merz, F., Falke, S., Sinz, C.: LLBMC: bounded model checking of C and C++ programs using a compiler IR. In: Joshi, R., Müller, P., Podelski, A. (eds.) VSTTE 2012. LNCS, vol. 7152, pp. 146–161. Springer, Heidelberg (2012). https://doi.org/10.1007/978-3-642-27705-4_12
39. de Moura, L., Bjørner, N.: Z3: an efficient SMT solver. In: Proceedings of the 14th International Conference on Tools and Algorithms for the Construction and Analysis of Systems (TACAS 2008), pp. 337–340, March–April 2008
40. Owicki, S., Lamport, L.: Proving liveness properties of concurrent programs. TOPLAS **4**(3), 455–495 (1982)

41. Sasnauskas, R., Landsiedel, O., Alizai, M.H., Weise, C., Kowalewski, S., Wehrle, K.: KleeNet: discovering insidious interaction bugs in wireless sensor networks before deployment. In: Proceedings of the 9th ACM/IEEE International Conference on Information Processing in Sensor Networks (IPSN 2010), April 2010
42. Sen, K., Marinov, D., Agha, G.: CUTE: a concolic unit testing engine for C. In: Proceedings of the Conference on Programming Language Design and Implementation (PLDI 2005), vol. 30, pp. 263–272, June 2005
43. Straunstrup, J., Andersen, H.R., Hulgaard, H., Lind-Nielsen, J., Behrmann, G., Kristoffersen, K., Skou, A., Leerberg, H., Theilgaard, N.B.: Practical verification of embedded software. Computer 33(5), 68–75 (2000)
44. The BusyBox Developers: BusyBox: The Swiss Army Knife of Embedded Linux, August 2017, version 1.27.2. https://busybox.net
45. The GNU Project: GNU Coreutils, January 2016, version 8.25. https://www.gnu.org/software/coreutils
46. The GNU Project: GNU sed, February 2017, version 4.4. https://www.gnu.org/software/sed
47. The KLEE Team: OSDI 2008 Coreutils Experiments. http://klee.github.io/docs/coreutils-experiments/. Section 07
48. The toybox Developers: toybox, October 2017, version 0.7.5. http://landley.net/toybox
49. Tillmann, N., De Halleux, J.: Pex-white box test generation for .NET. In: Proceedings of the 2nd International Conference on Tests and Proofs (TAP 2008), pp. 134–153, April 2008
50. Tretmans, J., Wijbrans, K., Chaudron, M.: Software engineering with formal methods: the development of a storm surge barrier control system revisiting seven myths of formal methods. Formal Methods Syst. Des. 19(2), 195–215 (2001)

Model Checking Boot Code from AWS Data Centers

Byron Cook[1,2], Kareem Khazem[1,2], Daniel Kroening[3], Serdar Tasiran[1],
Michael Tautschnig[1,4(✉)], and Mark R. Tuttle[1]

[1] Amazon Web Services, Seattle, USA
tautschn@amazon.com
[2] University College London, London, UK
[3] University of Oxford, Oxford, UK
[4] Queen Mary University of London, London, UK

Abstract. This paper describes our experience with symbolic model checking in an industrial setting. We have proved that the initial boot code running in data centers at Amazon Web Services is memory safe, an essential step in establishing the security of any data center. Standard static analysis tools cannot be easily used on boot code without modification owing to issues not commonly found in higher-level code, including memory-mapped device interfaces, byte-level memory access, and linker scripts. This paper describes automated solutions to these issues and their implementation in the C Bounded Model Checker (CBMC). CBMC is now the first source-level static analysis tool to extract the memory layout described in a linker script for use in its analysis.

1 Introduction

Boot code is the first code to run in a data center; thus, the security of a data center depends on the security of the boot code. It is hard to demonstrate boot code security using standard techniques, as boot code is difficult to test and debug, and boot code must run without the support of common security mitigations available to the operating system and user applications. This industrial experience report describes work to prove the memory safety of initial boot code running in data centers at Amazon Web Services (AWS).

We describe the challenges we faced analyzing AWS boot code, some of which render existing approaches to software verification unsound or imprecise. These challenges include

1. memory-mapped input/output (MMIO) for accessing devices,
2. device behavior behind these MMIO regions,
3. byte-level memory access as the dominant form of memory access, and
4. linker scripts used during the build process.

Not handling MMIO or linker scripts results in imprecision (false positives), and not modeling device behavior is unsound (false negatives).

We describe the solutions to these challenges that we developed. We implemented our solutions in the C Bounded Model Checker (CBMC) [20]. We achieve

H. Chockler and G. Weissenbacher (Eds.): CAV 2018, LNCS 10982, pp. 467–486, 2018.
https://doi.org/10.1007/978-3-319-96142-2_28

soundness with CBMC by fully unrolling loops in the boot code. Our solutions automate boot code verification and require no changes to the code being analyzed. This makes our work particularly well-suited for deployment in a continuous validation environment to ensure that memory safety issues do not reappear in the code as it evolves during development. We use CBMC, but any other bit-precise, sound, automated static analysis tool could be used.

2   Related Work

There are many approaches to finding memory safety errors in low-level code, from fuzzing [2] to static analysis [24, 30, 39, 52] to deductive verification [21, 34].

A key aspect of our work is soundness and precision in the presence of very low-level details. Furthermore, full automation is essential in our setting to operate in a continuous validation environment. This makes some form of model checking most appealing.

CBMC is a bounded model checker for C, C++, and Java programs, available on GitHub [13]. It features bit-precise reasoning, and it verifies array bounds (buffer overflows), pointer safety, arithmetic exceptions, and assertions in the code. A user can bound the model checking done by CBMC by specifying for a loop a maximum number of iterations of the loop. CBMC can check that it is impossible for the loop to iterate more than the specified number of times by checking a *loop-unwinding assertion*. CBMC is sound when all loop-unwinding assertions hold. Loops in boot code typically iterate over arrays of known sizes, making it possible to choose loop unwinding limits such that all loop-unwinding assertions hold (see Sect. 5.7). BLITZ [16] or F-Soft [36] could be used in place of CBMC. SATABS [19], Ufo [3], Cascade [55], Blast [9], CPAchecker [10], Corral [33, 43, 44], and others [18, 47] might even enable unbounded verification. Our work applies to any sound, bit-precise, automated tool.

Note that boot code makes heavy use of pointers, bit vectors, and arrays, but not the heap. Thus, memory safety proof techniques based on three-valued logic [45] or separation logic as in [8] or other techniques [1, 22] that focus on the heap are less appropriate since boot code mostly uses simple arrays.

KLEE [12] is a symbolic execution engine for C that has been used to find bugs in firmware. Davidson et al. [25] built the tool FIE on top of KLEE for detecting bugs in firmware programs for the MSP430 family of microcontrollers for low-power platforms, and applied the tool to nearly a hundred open source firmware programs for nearly a dozen versions of the microcontroller to find bugs like buffer overflow and writing to read-only memory. Corin and Manzano [23] used KLEE to do taint analysis and prove confidentiality and integrity properties. KLEE and other tools like SMACK [49] based on the LLVM intermediate representation do not currently support the linker scripts that are a crucial part of building boot code (see Sect. 4.5). They support partial linking by concatenating object files and resolving symbols, but fail to make available to their analysis the addresses and constants assigned to symbols in linker scripts, resulting in an imprecise analysis of the code.

S^2E [15] is a symbolic execution engine for x86 binaries built on top of the QEMU [7] virtual machine and KLEE. S^2E has been used on firmware. Parvez et al. [48] use symbolic execution to generate inputs targeting a potentially buggy statement for debugging. Kuznetsov et al. [42] used a prototype of S^2E to find bugs in Microsoft device drivers. Zaddach et al. [56] built the tool Avatar on top of S^2E to check security of embedded firmware. They test firmware running on top of actual hardware, moving device state between the concrete device and the symbolic execution. Bazhaniuk et al. [6,28] used S^2E to search for security vulnerabilities in interrupt handlers for System Management Mode on Intel platforms. Experts can use S^2E on firmware. One can model device behavior (see Sect. 4.2) by adding a device model to QEMU or using the signaling mechanism used by S^2E during symbolic execution. One can declare an MMIO region (see Sect. 4.1) by inserting it into the QEMU memory hierarchy. Both require understanding either QEMU or S^2E implementations. Our goal is to make it as easy as possible to use our work, primarily by way of automation.

Ferreira et al. [29] verify a task scheduler for an operating system, but that is high in the software stack. Klein et al. [38] prove the correctness of the seL4 kernel, but that code was written with the goal of proof. Dillig et al. [26] synthesize guards ensuring memory safety in low-level code, but our code is written by hand. Rakamarić and Hu [50] developed a conservative, scalable approach to memory safety in low-level code, but the models there are not tailored to our code that routinely accesses memory by an explicit integer-valued memory address. Redini et al. [51] built a tool called BootStomp on top of angr [54], a framework for symbolic execution of binaries based on a symbolic execution engine for the VEX intermediate representation for the Valgrind project, resulting in a powerful testing tool for boot code, but it is not sound.

3   Boot Code

We define *boot code* to be the code in a cloud data center that runs from the moment the power is turned on until the BIOS starts. It runs before the operating system's boot loader that most people are familiar with. A key component to ensuring high confidence in data center security is establishing confidence in boot code security. Enhancing confidence in boot code security is a challenge because of unique properties of boot code not found in higher-level software. We now discuss these properties of boot code, and a path to greater confidence in boot code security.

3.1   Boot Code Implementation

Boot code starts a sequenced boot flow [4] in which each stage locates, loads, and launches the next stage. The boot flow in a modern data center proceeds as follows: (1) When the power is turned on, before a single instruction is executed, the hardware interrogates banks of fuses and hardware registers for configuration information that is distributed to various parts of the platform. (2) *Boot code* starts up to boot a set of microcontrollers that orchestrate bringing up the rest of the platform. In a cloud data center, some of these microcontrollers are feature-rich cores with their own devices used to support virtualization. (3) The BIOS familiar to most people starts up to boot the cores and their devices. (4) A boot loader for the hypervisor launches the hypervisor to virtualize those cores. (5) A boot loader for the operating system launches the operating system itself. The security of each stage, including operating system launched for the customer, depends on the integrity of all prior stages [27].

Ensuring boot code security using traditional techniques is hard. Visibility into code execution can only be achieved via debug ports, with almost no ability to single-step the code for debugging. UEFI (Unified Extensible Firmware Interface) [53] provides an elaborate infrastructure for debugging BIOS, but not for the boot code below BIOS in the software stack. Instrumenting boot code may be impossible because it can break the build process: the increased size of instrumented code can be larger than the size of the ROM targeted by the build process. Extracting the data collected by instrumentation may be difficult because the code has no access to a file system to record the data, and memory available for storing the data may be limited.

Static analysis is a relatively new approach to enhancing confidence in boot code security. As discussed in Sect. 2, most work applying static analysis to boot code applies technology like symbolic execution to binary code, either because the work strips the boot code from ROMs on shipping products for analysis and reverse engineering [42,51], or because code like UEFI-based implementations of BIOS loads modules with a form of dynamic linking that makes source code analysis of any significant functionality impossible [6,28]. But with access to the source code—source code without the complexity of dynamic linking— meaningful static analysis at the source code level is possible.

3.2   Boot Code Security

Boot code is a foundational component of data center security: it controls what code is run on the server. Attacking boot code is a path to booting your own code, installing a persistent root kit, or making the server unbootable. Boot code also initializes devices and interfaces directly with them. Attacking boot code can also lead to controlling or monitoring peripherals like storage devices.

The input to boot code is primarily configuration information. The runtime behavior of boot code is determined by configuration information in fuses, hardware straps, one-time programmable memories, and ROMs.

From a security perspective, boot code is susceptible to a variety of events that could set the configuration to an undesirable state. To keep any malicious adversary from modifying this configuration information, the configuration is usually locked or otherwise write-protected. Nonetheless, it is routine to discover during hardware vetting before placing hardware on a data center floor that some BIOS added by a supplier accidentally leaves a configuration register unlocked after setting it. In fact, configuration information can be intentionally unlocked for the purpose of patching and then be locked again. Any bug in a patch or in a patching mechanism has the potential to leave a server in a vulnerable configuration. Perhaps more likely than anything is a simple configuration mistake at installation. We want to know that no matter how a configuration may have been corrupted, the boot code will operate as intended and without latent exposures for potential adversaries.

The attack surface we focus on in this paper is memory safety, meaning there are no buffer overflows, no dereferencing of null pointers, and no pointers pointing into unallocated regions of memory. Code written in C is known to be at risk for memory safety, and boot code is almost always written in C, in part because of the direct connection between boot code and the hardware, and sometimes because of space limitations in the ROMs used to store the code.

There are many techniques for protecting against memory safety errors and mitigating their consequences at the higher levels of the software stack. Languages other than C are less prone to memory safety errors. Safe libraries can do bounds checking for standard library functions. Compiler extensions to compilers like gcc and clang can help detect buffer overflow when it happens (which is different from keeping it from happening). Address space layout randomization makes it harder for the adversary to make reliable use of a vulnerability. None of these mitigations, however, apply to firmware. Firmware is typically built using the tool chain that is provided by the manufacturer of the microcontroller, and firmware typically runs before the operating system starts, without the benefit of operating system support like a virtual machine or randomized memory layout.

4   Boot Code Verification Challenges

Boot code poses challenges to the precision, soundness, and performance of any analysis tool. The C standard [35] says, "A volatile declaration may be used to describe an object corresponding to an MMIO port" and "what constitutes an access to an object that has volatile-qualified type is implementation-defined." Any tool that seeks to verify boot code must provide means to model what the C standard calls *implementation-defined behavior*. Of all such behavior, MMIO and device behavior are most relevant to boot code. In this section, we discuss these issues and the solutions we have implemented in CBMC.

4.1   Memory-Mapped I/O

Boot code accesses a device through *memory-mapped input/output* (MMIO). Registers of the device are mapped to specific locations in memory. Boot code reads or writes a register in the device by reading or writing a specific location in memory. If boot code wants to set the second bit in a configuration register, and if that configuration register is mapped to the byte at location 0x1000 in memory, then the boot code sets the second bit of the byte at 0x1000. The problem posed by MMIO is that there is no declaration or allocation in the source code specifying this location 0x1000 as a valid region of memory. Nevertheless accesses within this region are valid memory accesses, and should not be flagged as an out-of-bounds memory reference. This is an example of implementation-defined behavior that must be modeled to avoid reporting false positives.

To facilitate analysis of low-level code, we have added to CBMC a built-in function

```
__CPROVER_allocated_memory(address, size)
```

to mark ranges of memory as valid. Accesses within this region are exempt from the out-of-bounds assertion checking that CBMC would normally do. The function declares the half-open interval [address, address+size) as valid memory that can be read and written. This function can be used anywhere in the source code, but is most commonly used in the test harness. (CBMC, like most program analysis approaches, uses a test harness to drive the analysis.)

4.2   Device Behavior

An MMIO region is an interface to a device. It is unsound to assume that the values returned by reading and writing this region of memory follow the semantics of ordinary read-write memory. Imagine a device that can generate unique ids. If the register returning the unique id is mapped to the byte at location 0x1000, then reading location 0x1000 will return a different value every time, even without intervening writes. These side effects have to be modeled. One easy approach is to 'havoc' the device, meaning that writes are ignored and reads return nondeterministic values. This is sound, but may lead to too many false positives. We can model the device semantics more precisely, using one of the options described below.

If the device has an API, we havoc the device by making use of a more general functionality we have added to CBMC. We have added a command-line option

```
--remove-function-body device_access
```

to CBMC's goto-instrument tool. When used, this will drop the implementation of the function device_access from compiled object code. If there is no other definition of device_access, CBMC will model each invocation of device_access as returning an unconstrained value of the appropriate return type. Now, to havoc a device with an API that includes a read and write method, we can use this command-line option to remove their function bodies, and CBMC will model each invocation of read as returning an unconstrained value.

At link time, if another object file, such as the test harness, provides a second definition of device_access, CBMC will use this definition in its place. Thus, to model device semantics more precisely, we can provide a device model in the test harness by providing implementations of (or approximations for) the methods in the API.

If the device has no API, meaning that the code refers directly to the address in the MMIO region for the device without reference to accessor functions, we have another method. We have added two function symbols

```
__CPROVER_mm_io_r(address, size)
__CPROVER_mm_io_w(address, size, value)
```

to CBMC to model the reading or writing of an address at a fixed integer address. If the test harness provides implementations of these functions, CBMC will use these functions to model every read or write of memory. For example, defining

```
char __CPROVER_mm_io_r(void *a, unsigned s) {
  if(a == 0x1000) return 2;
}
```

will return the value 2 upon any access at address 0x1000, and return a non-deterministic value in all other cases.

In both cases—with or without an API—we can thus establish sound and, if needed, precise analysis about an aspect of implementation-defined behavior.

4.3 Byte-Level Memory Access

It is common for boot code to access memory a byte at a time, and to access a byte that is not part of any variable or data structure declared in the program text. Accessing a byte in an MMIO region is the most common example. Boot code typically accesses this byte in memory by computing the address of the byte as an integer value, coercing this integer to a pointer, and dereferencing this pointer to access that byte. Boot code references memory by this kind of explicit address far more frequently than it references memory via some explicitly allocated variable or data structure. Any tool analyzing boot code must have a method for reasoning efficiently about accessing an arbitrary byte of memory.

The natural model for memory is as an array of bytes, and CBMC does the same. Any decision procedure that has a well-engineered implementation of a theory of arrays is likely to do a good job of modeling byte-level memory access. We improved CBMC's decision procedure for arrays to follow the state-of-the-art algorithm [17,40]. The key data structure is a weak equivalence graph whose vertices correspond to array terms. Given an equality $a = b$ between two array terms a and b, add an unlabeled edge between a and b. Given an update $a\{i \leftarrow v\}$ of an array term a, add an edge labeled i between a and $a\{i \leftarrow v\}$. Two array terms a and b are weakly equivalent if there is a path from a to b in the graph, and they are equal at all indices except those updated along the path. This graph is used to encode constraints on array terms for the solver. For simplicity, our implementation generates these constraints eagerly.

4.4 Memory Copying

One of the main jobs of any stage of the boot flow is to copy the next stage into memory, usually using some variant of memcpy. Any tool analyzing boot code must have an efficient model of memcpy. Modeling memcpy as a loop iterating through a thousand bytes of memory leads to performance problems during program analysis. We added to CBMC an improved model of the memset and memcpy library functions.

Boot code has no access to a C library. In our case, the boot code shipped an iterative implementation of memset and memcpy. CBMC's model of the C library previously also used an iterative model. We replaced this iterative model of `memset` and `memcpy` with a single array operation that can be handled efficiently by the decision procedure at the back end. We instructed CBMC to replace the boot code implementations with the CBMC model using the `--remove-function-body` command-line option described in Sect. 4.2.

4.5   Linker Scripts

Linking is the final stage in the process of transforming source code into an executable program. Compilation transforms source files into object files, which consist of several *sections* of related object code. A typical object file contains sections for executable code, read-only and read-write program data, debugging symbols, and other information. The linker combines several object files into a single executable object file, merging similar sections from each of the input files into single sections in the output executable. The linker combines and arranges the sections according to the directives in a *linker script*. Linker scripts are written in a declarative language [14].

The functionality of most programs is not sensitive to the exact layout of the executable file; therefore, by default, the linker uses a generic linker script[1] the directives of which are suited to laying out high-level programs. On the other hand, low-level code (like boot loaders, kernels, and firmware) must often be hard-coded to address particular memory locations, which necessitates the use of a custom linker script.

One use for a linker script is to place selected code into a specialized memory region like a *tightly-coupled memory* unit [5], which is a fast cache into which developers can place hot code. Another is device access via memory-mapped I/O as discussed in Sects. 4.1 and 4.2. Low-level programs address these hard devices by having a variable whose address in memory corresponds to the address that the hardware exposes. However, no programming language offers the ability to set a variable's address from the program; the variable must instead be laid out at the right place in the object file, using linker script directives.

While linker scripts are essential to implement the functionality of low-level code, their use in higher-level programs is uncommon. Thus, we know of no work that considers the role of linker scripts in static program analysis; a recent formal treatment of linkers [37] explicitly skips linker scripts. Ensuring that static analysis results remain correct in the presence of linker scripts is vital to verifying and finding bugs in low-level code; we next describe problems that linker scripts can create for static analyses.

Linker Script Challenges. All variables used in C programs must be *defined* exactly once. Static analyses make use of the values of these variables to decide program correctness, provided that the source code of the program and libraries used is available. However, linker scripts also define symbols that can be accessed as variables from C source code. Since C code never defines these symbols, and

---

[1] On Linux and macOS, running `ld --verbose` displays the default linker script.

linker scripts are not written in C, the values of these symbols are unknown to a static analyzer that is oblivious to linker scripts. If the correctness of code depends on the values of these symbols, it cannot be verified. To make this discussion concrete, consider the code in Fig. 1.

```
/* main.c */                      /* link.ld */
#include <string.h>               SECTIONS {
                                    .text : {
extern char text_start;             text_start=.;
extern char text_size;              *(.text)
extern char scratch_start;          }
                                    text_size=SIZEOF(.text);
int main() {                        .scratch : {
  memcpy(&text_start,                 scratch_start=.;
         &scratch_start,              .=.+0x1000;
         (size_t)&text_size);         scratch_end=.;
}                                     }
                                  }
```

Fig. 1. A C program using variables whose addresses are defined in a linker script.

This example, adapted from the GNU linker manual [14], shows the common pattern of copying an entire region of program code from one part of memory to another. The linker writes an executable file in accordance with the linker script on the right; the expression "." (period) indicates the current byte offset into the executable file. The script directs the linker to generate a code section called .text and write the contents of the .text sections from each input file into that section; and to create an empty 4 KiB long section called .scratch. The symbols text_start and scratch_start are created at the address of the beginning of the associated section. Similarly, the symbol text_size is created at the address equal to the code size of the .text section. Since these symbols are defined in the linker script, they can be freely used from the C program on the left (which must declare the symbols as extern, but not define them). While the data at the symbols' locations is likely garbage, the symbols' *addresses* are meaningful; in the program, the addresses are used to copy data from one section to another.

Contemporary static analysis tools fail to correctly model the behavior of this program because they model symbols defined in C code but not in linker scripts. Tools like SeaHorn [32] and KLEE [12] do support linking of the intermediate representation (IR) compiled from each of the source files with an IR linker. By using build wrappers like wllvm [46], they can even invoke the native system linker, which itself runs the linker script on the machine code sections of the object files. The actions of the native linker, however, are not propagated back to the IR linker, so the linked IR used for static analysis contains only information derived from C source, and not from linker scripts. As a result, these analyzers

476   B. Cook et al.

lack the required precision to prove that a safe program is safe: they generate false positives because they have no way of knowing (for example) that a memcpy is walking over a valid region of memory defined in the linker script.

Information Required for Precise Modeling. As we noted earlier in this section, linker scripts provide definitions to variables that may only be declared in C code, and whose addresses may be used in the program. In addition, linker scripts define the layout of code sections; the C program may copy data to and from these sections using variables defined in the linker script to demarcate valid regions inside the sections. Our aim is to allow the static analyzer to decide the memory safety of operations that use linker script definitions (if indeed they are safe, i.e., don't access memory regions outside those defined in the linker script). To do this, the analyzer must know (referencing our example in Fig. 1 but without loss of generality):

1. that we are copying &text_size bytes starting from &text_start;
2. that there exists a code section (i.e., a valid region of memory) whose starting address equals &text_start and whose size equals &text_size;
3. the concrete values of that code section's size and starting address.

Fact 1 is derived from the source code; Fact 2—from parsing the linker script; and Fact 3—from disassembling the fully-linked executable, which will have had the sections and symbols laid out at their final addresses by the linker.

Extending CBMC. CBMC compiles source files with a front-end that emulates the native compiler (gcc), but which adds an additional section to the end of the output binary [41]; this section contains the program encoded in CBMC's analysis-friendly intermediate representation (IR). In particular, CBMC's frontend takes the linker script as a command-line argument, just like gcc, and delegates the final link to the system's native linker. CBMC thus has access to the linker script and the final binary, which contains both native executable code and CBMC IR. We send linker script information to CBMC as follows:

1. use CBMC's front end to compile the code, producing a fully-linked binary,
2. parse the linker script and disassemble the binary to get the required data,
3. augment the IR with the definitions from the linker script and binary, and
4. analyze the augmented intermediate representation.

Our extensions are Steps 2 and 3, which we describe in more detail below. They are applicable to tools (like SeaHorn and KLEE) that use an IR linker (like llvm-link) before analyzing the IR.

Extracting Linker Script Symbols. Our extension to CBMC reads a linker script and extracts the information that we need. For each code section, it extracts the symbols whose addresses mark the start and end of the section, if any; and the symbol whose address indicates the section size, if any. The sections key of Fig. 2 shows the information extracted from the linker script in Fig. 1.

Extracting Linker Script Symbol Addresses. To remain architecture independent, our extension uses the `objdump` program (part of the GNU Binutils [31]) to extract the addresses of all symbols in an object file (shown in the `addresses` key of Fig. 2). In this way, it obtains the concrete addresses of symbols defined in the linker script.

```
"sections" : {                      }
  ".text": {                      },
    "start": "text_start",        "addresses" : {
    "size": "text_size"             "text_start": "0x0200",
  },                                "text_size": "0x0600",
  ".scratch" : {                    "scratch_start": "0x1000",
    "start": "scratch_start",       "scratch_end": "0x2000",
    "end": "scratch_end"          }
```

Fig. 2. Output from our linker script parser when run on the linker script in Fig. 1, on a binary with a 1 KiB `.text` section and 4 KiB `.scratch` section.

Augmenting the Intermediate Representation. CBMC maintains a symbol table of all the variables used in the program. Variables that are declared `extern` in C code and never defined have no initial value in the symbol table. CBMC can still analyze code that contains undefined symbols, but as noted earlier in this section, this can lead to incorrect verification results. Our extension to CBMC extracts information described in the previous section and integrates it into the target program's IR. For example, given the source code in Fig. 1, CBMC will replace it with the code given in Fig. 3.

In more detail, CBMC

1. converts the types of linker symbols in the IR and symbol table to `char *`,
2. updates all expressions involving linker script symbols to be consistent with this type change,
3. creates the IR representation of C-language definitions of the linker script symbols, initializing them before the entry point of `main()`, and
4. uses the `__CPROVER_allocated_memory` API described in Sect. 4.1 to mark code sections demarcated by linker script symbols as allocated.

The first two steps are necessary because C will not let us set the address of a variable, but will let us store the address in a variable. CBMC thus changes the IR type of `text_start` to `char *`; sets the value of `text_start` to the address of `text_start` in the binary; and rewrites all occurrences of "`&text_start`" to "`text_start`". This preserves the original semantics while allowing CBMC to model the program. The semantics of Step 4 is impossible to express in C, justifying the use of CBMC rather than a simple source-to-source transformation.

```
#include <string.h>                #include <string.h>

extern char text_start;           char *text_start = 0x0200;
extern char text_size;            char *text_size = 0x0600;
extern char scratch_start;        char *scratch_start = 0x1000;

int main() {                      int main() {
                                    __CPROVER_allocated_memory(
                                      0x0200, 0x0600);
                                    __CPROVER_allocated_memory(
                                      0x1000, 0x1000);
  memcpy(&text_start,               memcpy(text_start,
         &scratch_start,                   scratch_start,
         (size_t)&text_size);              (size_t)text_size);
}                                 }
```

Fig. 3. Transformation performed by CBMC for linker-script-defined symbols.

5 Industrial Boot Code Verification

In this section, we describe our experience proving memory safety of boot code running in an AWS data center. We give an exact statement of what we proved, we point out examples of the verification challenges mentioned in Sect. 4 and our solutions, and we go over the test harness and the results of running CBMC.

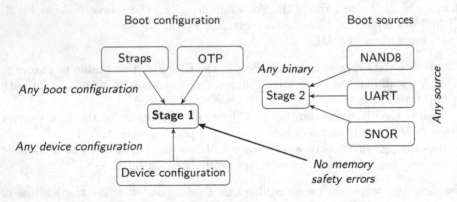

Fig. 4. Boot code is free of memory safety errors.

We use CBMC to prove that 783 lines of AWS boot code are memory safe. Soundness of this proof by bounded model checking is achieved by having CBMC check its loop unwinding assertions (that loops have been sufficiently unwound). This boot code proceeds in two stages, as illustrated in Fig. 4. The first stage prepares the machine, loads the second stage from a boot source, and launches the second stage. The behavior of the first stage is controlled by configuration information in hardware straps and one-time-programmable memory (OTP), and by device configuration. We show that no configuration will induce a memory safety error in the stage 1 boot code.

More precisely, we prove:

Assuming
  – a buffer for stage 2 code and a temporary buffer are both 1024 bytes,
  – the cryptographic, CRC computation, and printf methods have no side effects and can return unconstrained values,
  – the CBMC model of `memcpy` and `memset`, and
  – ignoring a loop that flashes the console lights when boot fails;
then
  – for every boot configuration,
  – for every device configuration,
  – for each of the three boot sources, and
  – for every stage 2 binary,
the stage 1 boot code will not exhibit any memory safety errors.

Due to the second and third assumptions, we may be missing memory safety errors in these simple procedures. Memory safety of these procedures can be established in isolation. We find all memory safety errors in the remainder of the code, however, because making buffers smaller increases the chances they will overflow, and allowing methods to return unconstrained values increases the set of program behaviors considered.

The code we present in this section is representative of the code we analyzed, but the actual code is proprietary and not public. The open-source project rBoot [11] is 700 lines of boot code available to the public that exhibits most of the challenges we now discuss.

5.1 Memory-Mapped I/O

MMIO regions are not explicitly allocated in the code, but the addresses of these regions appear in the header files. For example, an MMIO region for the hardware straps is given with

```
#define REG_BASE          (0x1000)
#define REG_BOOT_STRAP    (REG_BASE + 0x110)
#define REG_BOOT_CONF     (REG_BASE + 0x124)
```

Each of the last two macros denotes the start of a different MMIO region, leaving 0x14 bytes for the region named REG_BOOT_STRAP. Using the builtin function added to CBMC (Sect. 4.1), we declare this region in the test harness with

```
__CPROVER_allocated_memory(REG_BOOT_STRAP, 0x14);
```

5.2 Device Behavior

All of the devices accessed by the boot code are accessed via an API. For example, the API for the UART is given by

```
int UartInit(UART_PORT port, unsigned int baudRate);
void UartWriteByte(UART_PORT port, uint8_t byte);
uint8_t UartReadByte(UART_PORT port);
```

In this work, we havoc all of the devices to make our result as strong as possible. In other words, our device model allows a device read to return any value of the appropriate type, and still we can prove that (even in the context of a misbehaving device) the boot code does not exhibit a memory safety error. Because all devices have an API, we can havoc the devices using the command line option added to CBMC (Sect. 4.2), and invoke CBMC with

```
--remove-function-body UartInit
--remove-function-body UartReadByte
--remove-function-body UartWriteByte
```

5.3 Byte-Level Memory Access

All devices are accessed at the byte level by computing an integer-valued address and coercing it to a pointer. For example, the following code snippets from BootOptionsParse show how reading the hardware straps from the MMIO region discussed above translates into a byte-level memory access.

```
#define REG_READ(addr) (*(volatile uint32_t*)(addr))

regVal = REG_READ(REG_BOOT_STRAP);
```

In CBMC, this translates into an access into an array modeling memory at location 0x1000 + 0x110. Our optimized encoding of the theory of arrays (Sect. 4.3) enables CBMC to reason more efficiently about this kind of construct.

5.4 Memory Copying

The memset and memcpy procedures are heavily used in boot code. For example, the function used to copy the stage 2 boot code from flash memory amounts to a single, large memcpy.

```
int SNOR_Read(unsigned int address,
              uint8_t* buff,
              unsigned int numBytes) {
  ...
  memcpy(buff,
         (void*)(address + REG_SNOR_BASE_ADDRESS),
         numBytes);
  ...
}
```

CBMC reasons more efficiently about this kind of code due to our loop-free model of memset and memcpy procedures as array operations (Sect. 4.4).

5.5   Linker Scripts

Linker scripts allocate regions of memory and pass the addresses of these regions and other constants to the code through the symbol table. For example, the linker script defines a region to hold the stage 2 binary and passes the address and size of the region as the addresses of the symbols stage2_start and stage2_size.

```
.stage2 (NOLOAD) : {
  stage2_start = .;
  . = . + STAGE2_SIZE;
  stage2_end = .;
} > RAM2
stage2_size = SIZEOF(.stage2);
```

The code declares the symbols as externally defined, and uses a pair of macros to convert the addresses of the symbols to an address and a constant before use.

```
extern char stage2_start[];
extern char stage2_size[];

#define STAGE2_ADDRESS  ((uint8_t*)(&stage2_start))
#define STAGE2_SIZE     ((unsigned)(&stage2_size))
```

CBMC's new approach to handling linker scripts modifies the CBMC intermediate representation of this code as described in Sect. 4.5.

5.6   Test Harness

The main procedure for the boot code begins by clearing the BSS section, copying a small amount of data from a ROM, printing some debugging information, and invoking three functions

```
SecuritySettingsOtp();
BootOptionsParse();
Stage2LoadAndExecute();
```

that read security settings from some one-time programmable memory, read the boot options from some hardware straps, and load and launch the stage 2 code.

The test harness for the boot code is 76 lines of code that looks similar to

```
void environment_model() {
  __CPROVER_allocated_memory(REG_BOOT_STRAP, 0x14);
  __CPROVER_allocated_memory(REG_UART_UART_BASE,
                             UART_REG_OFFSET_LSR +
                             sizeof(uint32_t));
  __CPROVER_allocated_memory(REG_NAND_CONFIG_REG,
                             sizeof(uint32_t));
}

void harness() {
  environment_model();
```

```
    SecuritySettingsOtp();
    BootOptionsParse();
    Stage2LoadAndExecute();
}
```

The `environment_model` procedure defines the environment of the software under test not declared in the boot code itself. This environment includes more than 30 MMIO regions for hardware like some hardware straps, a UART, and some NAND memory. The fragment of the environment model reproduced above uses the `__CPROVER_allocated_memory` built-in function added to CBMC for this work to declare these MMIO regions and assign them unconstrained values (modeling unconstrained configuration information). The `harness` procedure is the test harness itself. It builds the environment model and calls the three procedures invoked by the boot code.

5.7   Running CBMC

Building the boot code and test harness for CBMC takes 8.2 s compared to building the boot code with `gcc` in 2.2 s.

Running CBMC on the test harness above as a job under AWS Batch, it finished successfully in 10:02 min. It ran on a 16-core server with 122 GiB of memory running Ubuntu 14.04, and consumed one core at 100% using 5 GiB of memory. The new encoding of arrays improved this time by 45 s.

The boot code consists of 783 lines of statically reachable code, meaning the number of lines of code in the functions that are reachable from the test harness in the function call graph. CBMC achieves complete code coverage, in the sense that every line of code CBMC fails to exercise is dead code. An example of dead code found in the boot code is the default case of a switch statement whose cases enumerate all possible values of an expression.

The boot code consists of 98 loops that fall into two classes. First are for-loops with constant-valued expressions for the upper and lower bounds. Second are loops of the form `while (num) {...; num--}` and code inspection yields a bound on `num`. Thus, it is possible to choose loop bounds that cause all loop-unwinding assertions to hold, making CBMC's results sound for boot code.

6   Conclusion

This paper describes industrial experience with model checking production code. We extended CBMC to address issues that arise in boot code, and we proved that initial boot code running in data centers at Amazon Web Services is memory safe, a significant application of model checking in the industry. Our most significant extension to CBMC was parsing linker scripts to extract the memory layout described there for use in model checking, making CBMC the first static analysis tool to do so. With this and our other extensions to CBMC supporting devices and byte-level access, CBMC can now be used in a continuous validation flow to check for memory safety during code development. All of these extensions are in the public domain and freely available for immediate use.

References

1. Abdulla, P.A., Bouajjani, A., Cederberg, J., Haziza, F., Rezine, A.: Monotonic abstraction for programs with dynamic memory heaps. In: Gupta, A., Malik, S. (eds.) CAV 2008. LNCS, vol. 5123, pp. 341–354. Springer, Heidelberg (2008). https://doi.org/10.1007/978-3-540-70545-1_33
2. AFL: American fuzzy lop. http://lcamtuf.coredump.cx/afl
3. Albarghouthi, A., Li, Y., Gurfinkel, A., Chechik, M.: UFO: a framework for abstraction- and interpolation-based software verification. In: Madhusudan, P., Seshia, S.A. (eds.) CAV 2012. LNCS, vol. 7358, pp. 672–678. Springer, Heidelberg (2012). https://doi.org/10.1007/978-3-642-31424-7_48
4. Arbaugh, W.A., Farber, D.J., Smith, J.M.: A secure and reliable bootstrap architecture. In: 1997 IEEE Symposium on Security and Privacy, 4–7 May 1997, Oakland, CA, USA, pp. 65–71. IEEE Computer Society (1997). https://doi.org/10.1109/SECPRI.1997.601317
5. Arm Holdings: ARM1136JF-S and ARM1136J-S Technical Reference Manual (2006). https://developer.arm.com/docs/ddi0211/latest/
6. Bazhaniuk, O., Loucaides, J., Rosenbaum, L., Tuttle, M.R., Zimmer, V.: Symbolic execution for BIOS security. In: 9th USENIX Workshop on Offensive Technologies (WOOT 15). USENIX Association, Washington, D.C. (2015)
7. Bellard, F.: QEMU, a fast and portable dynamic translator. In: Proceedings of the Annual Conference on USENIX Annual Technical Conference, ATEC 2005, p. 41. USENIX Association, Berkeley (2005)
8. Berdine, J., et al.: Shape analysis for composite data structures. In: Damm, W., Hermanns, H. (eds.) CAV 2007. LNCS, vol. 4590, pp. 178–192. Springer, Heidelberg (2007). https://doi.org/10.1007/978-3-540-73368-3_22
9. Beyer, D., Henzinger, T.A., Jhala, R., Majumdar, R.: Checking memory safety with Blast. In: Cerioli, M. (ed.) FASE 2005. LNCS, vol. 3442, pp. 2–18. Springer, Heidelberg (2005). https://doi.org/10.1007/978-3-540-31984-9_2
10. Beyer, D., Keremoglu, M.E.: CPAchecker: a tool for configurable software verification. In: Gopalakrishnan, G., Qadeer, S. (eds.) CAV 2011. LNCS, vol. 6806, pp. 184–190. Springer, Heidelberg (2011). https://doi.org/10.1007/978-3-642-22110-1_16
11. Burton, R.A.: rBoot: an open source boot loader for the ESP8266 (2017). https://github.com/raburton/rboot
12. Cadar, C., Dunbar, D., Engler, D.R.: KLEE: unassisted and automatic generation of high-coverage tests for complex systems programs. In: Draves, R., van Renesse, R. (eds.) 8th USENIX Symposium on Operating Systems Design and Implementation, OSDI 2008, 8–10 December 2008, San Diego, California, USA, Proceedings, pp. 209–224. USENIX Association (2008). http://www.usenix.org/events/osdi08/tech/full_papers/cadar/cadar.pdf
13. C bounded model checker GitHub repository. https://github.com/diffblue/cbmc
14. Chamberlain, S., Taylor, I.L.: The GNU linker. Red Hat, Inc. (2018). https://sourceware.org/binutils/docs/ld/
15. Chipounov, V., Kuznetsov, V., Candea, G.: The S2E platform: design, implementation, and applications. ACM Trans. Comput. Syst. 30(1), 2:1–2:49 (2012)
16. Cho, C.Y., D'Silva, V., Song, D.: BLITZ: compositional bounded model checking for real-world programs. In: 2013 28th IEEE/ACM International Conference on Automated Software Engineering (ASE), pp. 136–146, November 2013

17. Christ, J., Hoenicke, J.: Weakly equivalent arrays. In: Lutz, C., Ranise, S. (eds.) FroCoS 2015. LNCS (LNAI), vol. 9322, pp. 119–134. Springer, Cham (2015). https://doi.org/10.1007/978-3-319-24246-0_8

18. Cimatti, A., Griggio, A.: Software model checking via IC3. In: Madhusudan, P., Seshia, S.A. (eds.) CAV 2012. LNCS, vol. 7358, pp. 277–293. Springer, Heidelberg (2012). https://doi.org/10.1007/978-3-642-31424-7_23

19. Clarke, E., Kroening, D., Sharygina, N., Yorav, K.: SATABS: SAT-based predicate abstraction for ANSI-C. In: Halbwachs, N., Zuck, L.D. (eds.) TACAS 2005. LNCS, vol. 3440, pp. 570–574. Springer, Heidelberg (2005). https://doi.org/10.1007/978-3-540-31980-1_40

20. Clarke, E., Kroening, D., Lerda, F.: A tool for checking ANSI-C programs. In: Jensen, K., Podelski, A. (eds.) TACAS 2004. LNCS, vol. 2988, pp. 168–176. Springer, Heidelberg (2004). https://doi.org/10.1007/978-3-540-24730-2_15

21. Cohen, E., et al.: VCC: a practical system for verifying concurrent C. In: Berghofer, S., Nipkow, T., Urban, C., Wenzel, M. (eds.) TPHOLs 2009. LNCS, vol. 5674, pp. 23–42. Springer, Heidelberg (2009). https://doi.org/10.1007/978-3-642-03359-9_2

22. Condit, J., Hackett, B., Lahiri, S.K., Qadeer, S.: Unifying type checking and property checking for low-level code. In: Proceedings of the 36th Annual ACM SIGPLAN-SIGACT Symposium on Principles of Programming Languages, POPL 2009, pp. 302–314. ACM, New York (2009)

23. Corin, R., Manzano, F.A.: Taint analysis of security code in the KLEE symbolic execution engine. In: Chim, T.W., Yuen, T.H. (eds.) ICICS 2012. LNCS, vol. 7618, pp. 264–275. Springer, Heidelberg (2012). https://doi.org/10.1007/978-3-642-34129-8_23

24. Synopsys static analysis (Coverity). http://coverity.com

25. Davidson, D., Moench, B., Ristenpart, T., Jha, S.: FIE on firmware: finding vulnerabilities in embedded systems using symbolic execution. In: Presented as part of the 22nd USENIX Security Symposium (USENIX Security 2013), pp. 463–478. USENIX, Washington, D.C. (2013)

26. Dillig, T., Dillig, I., Chaudhuri, S.: Optimal guard synthesis for memory safety. In: Biere, A., Bloem, R. (eds.) CAV 2014. LNCS, vol. 8559, pp. 491–507. Springer, Cham (2014). https://doi.org/10.1007/978-3-319-08867-9_32

27. Dodge, C., Irvine, C., Nguyen, T.: A study of initialization in Linux and OpenBSD. SIGOPS Oper. Syst. Rev. **39**(2), 79–93 (2005). https://doi.org/10.1145/1055218.1055226

28. Engblom, J.: Finding BIOS vulnerabilities with symbolic execution and virtual platforms, June 2016. https://software.intel.com/en-us/blogs/2017/06/06/finding-bios-vulnerabilities-with-excite

29. Ferreira, J.F., Gherghina, C., He, G., Qin, S., Chin, W.N.: Automated verification of the FreeRTOS scheduler in HIP/SLEEK. Int. J. Softw. Tools Technol. Transf. **16**(4), 381–397 (2014)

30. Fortify static code analyzer. https://software.microfocus.com/en-us/products/static-code-analysis-sast/overview

31. Free Software Foundation: Documentation for Binutils 2.29 (2017). https://sourceware.org/binutils/docs-2.29/

32. Gurfinkel, A., Kahsai, T., Komuravelli, A., Navas, J.A.: The SeaHorn verification framework. In: Kroening, D., Păsăreanu, C.S. (eds.) CAV 2015. LNCS, vol. 9206, pp. 343–361. Springer, Cham (2015). https://doi.org/10.1007/978-3-319-21690-4_20

33. Haran, A., et al.: SMACK+Corral: a modular verifier. In: Baier, C., Tinelli, C. (eds.) TACAS 2015. LNCS, vol. 9035, pp. 451–454. Springer, Heidelberg (2015). https://doi.org/10.1007/978-3-662-46681-0_42
34. Harrison, J.: HOL Light theorem prover. http://www.cl.cam.ac.uk/~jrh13/hol-light
35. ISO/IEC 9899:2011(E): Information technology - Programming languages - C. Standard, International Organization for Standardization, Geneva, CH, December 2011
36. Ivančić, F., Yang, Z., Ganai, M.K., Gupta, A., Ashar, P.: Efficient SAT-based bounded model checking for software verification. Theoret. Comput. Sci. **404**(3), 256–274 (2008)
37. Kell, S., Mulligan, D.P., Sewell, P.: The missing link: explaining ELF static linking, semantically. In: Visser, E., Smaragdakis, Y. (eds.) Proceedings of the 2016 ACM SIGPLAN International Conference on Object-Oriented Programming, Systems, Languages, and Applications, OOPSLA 2016, Part of SPLASH 2016, Amsterdam, The Netherlands, 30 October–4 November 2016, pp. 607–623. ACM (2016)
38. Klein, G., Elphinstone, K., Heiser, G., Andronick, J., Cock, D., Derrin, P., Elkaduwe, D., Engelhardt, K., Kolanski, R., Norrish, M., Sewell, T., Tuch, H., Winwood, S.: seL4: formal verification of an OS kernel. In: Proceedings of the ACM SIGOPS 22nd Symposium on Operating Systems Principles, SOSP 2009, pp. 207–220. ACM, New York (2009)
39. Klocwork static code analyzer. https://www.klocwork.com/
40. Kroening, D., Strichman, O.: Decision Procedures - An Algorithmic Point of View. Texts in Theoretical Computer Science. An EATCS Series, 2nd edn. Springer, Heidelberg (2016). https://doi.org/10.1007/978-3-662-50497-0
41. Kroening, D., Tautschnig, M.: Automating software analysis at large scale. In: Hliněný, P., et al. (eds.) MEMICS 2014. LNCS, vol. 8934, pp. 30–39. Springer, Cham (2014). https://doi.org/10.1007/978-3-319-14896-0_3
42. Kuznetsov, V., Chipounov, V., Candea, G.: Testing closed-source binary device drivers with DDT. In: Proceedings of the 2010 USENIX Conference on USENIX Annual Technical Conference, USENIXATC 2010, p. 12. USENIX Association, Berkeley (2010)
43. Lal, A., Qadeer, S.: Powering the static driver verifier using Corral. In: Proceedings of the 22nd ACM SIGSOFT International Symposium on Foundations of Software Engineering, FSE 2014, pp. 202–212. ACM, New York (2014)
44. Lal, A., Qadeer, S., Lahiri, S.K.: A solver for reachability modulo theories. In: Madhusudan, P., Seshia, S.A. (eds.) CAV 2012. LNCS, vol. 7358, pp. 427–443. Springer, Heidelberg (2012). https://doi.org/10.1007/978-3-642-31424-7_32
45. Lev-Ami, T., Manevich, R., Sagiv, M.: TVLA: a system for generating abstract interpreters. In: Jacquart, R. (ed.) Building the Information Society. IIFIP, vol. 156, pp. 367–375. Springer, Boston (2004). https://doi.org/10.1007/978-1-4020-8157-6_28
46. Mason, I.A.: Whole program LLVM (2017). https://github.com/SRI-CSL/whole-program-llvm/tree/master/wllvm
47. McMillan, K.L.: Lazy abstraction with interpolants. In: Ball, T., Jones, R.B. (eds.) CAV 2006. LNCS, vol. 4144, pp. 123–136. Springer, Heidelberg (2006). https://doi.org/10.1007/11817963_14
48. Parvez, R., Ward, P.A.S., Ganesh, V.: Combining static analysis and targeted symbolic execution for scalable bug-finding in application binaries. In: Proceedings of the 26th Annual International Conference on Computer Science and Software Engineering, CASCON 2016, pp. 116–127. IBM Corporation, Riverton (2016)

49. Rakamarić, Z., Emmi, M.: SMACK: decoupling source language details from verifier implementations. In: Biere, A., Bloem, R. (eds.) CAV 2014. LNCS, vol. 8559, pp. 106–113. Springer, Cham (2014). https://doi.org/10.1007/978-3-319-08867-9_7

50. Rakamarić, Z., Hu, A.J.: A scalable memory model for low-level code. In: Jones, N.D., Müller-Olm, M. (eds.) VMCAI 2009. LNCS, vol. 5403, pp. 290–304. Springer, Heidelberg (2008). https://doi.org/10.1007/978-3-540-93900-9_24

51. Redini, N., Machiry, A., Das, D., Fratantonio, Y., Bianchi, A., Gustafson, E., Shoshitaishvili, Y., Kruegel, C., Vigna, G.: BootStomp: on the security of bootloaders in mobile devices. In: Kirda, E., Ristenpart, T. (eds.) 26th USENIX Security Symposium, USENIX Security 2017, Vancouver, BC, Canada, 16–18 August 2017, pp. 781–798. USENIX Association (2017). https://www.usenix.org/conference/usenixsecurity17/technical-sessions/presentation/redini

52. Sen, K.: Automated test generation using concolic testing. In: Proceedings of the 8th India Software Engineering Conference, ISEC 2015, p. 9. ACM, New York (2015)

53. Unified extensible firmware interface forum. http://www.uefi.org/

54. Wang, F., Shoshitaishvili, Y.: Angr - the next generation of binary analysis. In: 2017 IEEE Cybersecurity Development (SecDev), pp. 8–9, September 2017

55. Wang, W., Barrett, C., Wies, T.: Cascade 2.0. In: McMillan, K.L., Rival, X. (eds.) VMCAI 2014. LNCS, vol. 8318, pp. 142–160. Springer, Heidelberg (2014). https://doi.org/10.1007/978-3-642-54013-4_9

56. Zaddach, J., Bruno, L., Francillon, A., Balzarotti, D.: AVATAR: a framework to support dynamic security analysis of embedded systems' firmwares. In: 21st Network and Distributed System Security Symposium (NDSS), February 2014

Android Stack Machine

Taolue Chen[1,6], Jinlong He[2,5], Fu Song[3], Guozhen Wang[4], Zhilin Wu[2(✉)],
and Jun Yan[2,5]

[1] Birkbeck, University of London, London, UK
[2] State Key Laboratory of Computer Science, Institute of Software,
Chinese Academy of Sciences, Beijing, China
wuzl@ios.ac.cn
[3] ShanghaiTech University, Shanghai, China
[4] Beijing University of Technology, Beijing, China
[5] University of Chinese Academy of Sciences, Beijing, China
[6] State Key Laboratory of Novel Software Technology,
Nanjing University, Nanjing, China

Abstract. In this paper, we propose Android Stack Machine (ASM), a
formal model to capture key mechanisms of Android multi-tasking such
as activities, back stacks, launch modes, as well as task affinities. The
model is based on pushdown systems with multiple stacks, and focuses
on the evolution of the back stack of the Android system when interacting with activities carrying specific launch modes and task affinities. For
formal analysis, we study the reachability problem of ASM. While the
general problem is shown to be undecidable, we identify expressive fragments for which various verification techniques for pushdown systems or
their extensions are harnessed to show decidability of the problem.

1 Introduction

Multi-tasking plays a central role in the Android platform. Its unique design, via
activities and back stacks, greatly facilitates organizing user sessions through
tasks, and provides rich features such as handy application switching, background app state maintenance, smooth task history navigation (using the "back"
button), etc [16]. We refer the readers to Sect. 2 for an overview.

Android task management mechanism has substantially enhanced user experiences of the Android system and promoted personalized features in app design.
However, the mechanism is also notoriously difficult to understand. As a witness,
it constantly baffles app developers and has become a common topic of question-
and-answer websites (for instance, [2]). Surprisingly, the Android multi-tasking

---

This work was partially supported by UK EPSRC grant (EP/P00430X/1),
ARC grants (DP160101652, DP180100691), NSFC grants (61532019, 61761136011,
61662035, 61672505, 61472474, 61572478) and the National Key Basic Research (973)
Program of China (2014CB340701), the INRIA-CAS joint research project "Verifi-
cation, Interaction, and Proofs", and Key Research Program of Frontier Sciences,
CAS, Grant No. QYZDJ-SSW-JSC036.

H. Chockler and G. Weissenbacher (Eds.): CAV 2018, LNCS 10982, pp. 487–504, 2018.
https://doi.org/10.1007/978-3-319-96142-2_29

mechanism, despite its importance, has not been thoroughly studied before, let along a formal treatment. This has impeded further developments of computer-aided (static) analysis and verification for Android apps, which are indispensable for vulnerability analysis (for example, detection of task hijacking [16]) and app performance enhancement (for example, estimation of energy consumption [8]).

This paper provides a formal model, i.e., *Android Stack Machine* (ASM), aiming to capture the key features of Android multi-tasking. ASM addresses the behavior of Android *back stacks*, a key component of the multi-tasking machinery, and their interplay with attributes of the activity. In this paper, for these attributes we consider four basic *launch modes*, i.e., standard (STD), singleTop (STP), singleTask (STK), singleInstance (SIT), and *task affinities*. (For simplicity more complicated activity attributes such as *allowTaskReparenting* will not be addressed in the present paper.) We believe that the semantics of ASM, specified as a transition system, captures faithfully the actual mechanism of Android systems. For each case of the semantics, we have created "diagnosis" apps with corresponding launch modes and task affinities, and carried out extensive experiments using these apps, ascertaining its conformance to the Android platform. (Details will be provided in Sect. 3.)

For Android, technically ASM can be viewed as the counterpart of pushdown systems with multiple stacks, which are the *de facto* model for (multi-threaded) concurrent programs. Being rigours, this model opens a door towards a formal account of Android's multi-tasking mechanism, which would greatly facilitate developers' understanding, freeing them from lengthy, ambiguous, elusive Android documentations. We remark that it is known that the evolution of Android back stacks could also be affected by the *intent flags* of the activities. ASM does not address intent flags explicitly. However, the effects of most intent flags (e.g., FLAG_ACTIVITY_NEW_TASK, FLAG_ACTIVITY_CLEAR_TOP) can be simulated by launch modes, so this is *not* a real limitation of ASM.

Based on ASM, we also make the first step towards a formal analysis of Android multi-tasking apps by investigating the *reachability problem* which is fundamental to all such analysis. ASM is akin to pushdown systems with multiple stacks, so it is perhaps not surprising that the problem is undecidable in general; in fact, we show undecidability for most interesting fragments even with just two launch modes. In the interest of seeking more expressive, practice-relevant decidable fragments, we identify a fragment STK-**dominating ASM** which assumes STK activities have different task affinities and which further restricts the use of SIT activities. This fragment covers a majority of open-source Android apps (e.g., from Github) we have found so far. One of our technical contributions is to give a decision procedure for the reachability problem of STK-dominating ASM, which combines a range of techniques from simulations by pushdown systems with transductions [19] to abstraction methods for multi-stacks. The work, apart from independent interests in the study of multi-stack pushdown systems, lays a solid foundation for further (static) analysis and verification of Android apps related to multi-tasking, enabling model checking of Android apps, security analysis (such as discovering task hijacking), or typical tasks in software engineering such as automatic debugging, model-based testing, etc.

We summarize the main contributions as follows: (1) We propose—to the best of our knowledge—the first comprehensive formal model, Android stack machine, for Android back stacks, which is also validated by extensive experiments. (2) We study the reachability problem for Android stack machine. Apart from strongest possible undecidablity results in the general case, we provide a decision procedure for a practically relevant fragment.

2   Android Stack Machine: An Informal Overview

In Android, an application, usually referred to as an *app*, is regarded as a collection of *activities*. An activity is a type of app components, an instance of which provides a graphical user interface on screen and serves the entry point for interacting with the user [1]. An app typically has many activities for different user interactions (e.g., dialling phone numbers, reading contact lists, etc). A distinguished activity is the *main* activity, which is started when the app is launched. A *task* is a collection of activities that users interact with when performing a certain job. The activities in a task are arranged in a stack in the order in which each activity is opened. For example, an email app might have one activity to show a list of latest messages. When the user selects a message, a new activity opens to view that message. This new activity is pushed to the stack. If the user presses the "Back" button, an activity is finished and is popped off the stack. [In practice, the onBackPressed() method can be overloaded and triggered when the "Back" button is clicked. Here we assume—as a model abstraction—that the onBackPressed() method is not overloaded.] Furthermore, multiple tasks may run concurrently in the Android platform and the *back stack* stores all the tasks as a stack as well. In other words, it has a nested structure being a stack of stacks (tasks). We remark that in android, activities from different apps can stay in the same task, and activities from the same app can enter different tasks.

Typically, the evolution of the back stack is dependent mainly on two attributes of activities: *launch modes* and *task affinities*. All the activities of an app, as well as their attributes, including the launch modes and task affinities, are defined in the *manifest file* of the app. The launch mode of an activity decides the corresponding operation of the back stack when the activity is launched. As mentioned in Sect. 1, there are four basic launch modes in Android: "standard", "singleTop", "singleTask" and "singleInstance". The task affinity of an activity indicates to which task the activity prefers to belong. By default, all the activities from the same app have the same affinity (i.e., all activities in the same app prefer to be in the same task). However, one can modify the default affinity of the activity. Activities defined in different apps can share a task affinity, or activities defined in the same app can be assigned with different task affinities. Below we will use a simple app to demonstrate the evolution of the back stack.

Example 1. In Fig. 1, an app ActivitiesLaunchDemo[1] is illustrated. The app contains four activities of the launch modes STD, STP, STK and SIT, depicted

---

[1] Adapted from an open-source app https://github.com/wauoen/LaunchModeDemo.

by green, blue, yellow and red, respectively. We will use the colours to name the activities. The green, blue and red activities have the same task affinity, while the yellow activity has a distinct one. The *main activity* of the app is the green activity. Each activity contains four buttons, i.e., the green, blue, yellow and red button. When a button is clicked, an instance of the activity with the colour starts. Moreover, the identifiers of all the tasks of the back stack, as well as their contents, are shown in the white zones of the window. We use the following execution trace to demonstrate how the back stack evolves according to the launch modes and the task affinities of the activities: The user clicks the buttons in the order of green, blue, blue, yellow, red, and green.

1. [*Launch the app*] When the app is launched, an instance of the main activity starts, and the back stack contains exactly one task, which contains exactly one green activity (see Fig. 1(a)). For convenience, this task is called the green task (with id: 23963).
2. [*Start an* STD *activity*] When the green button is clicked, since the launch mode of the green activity is STD, a new instance of the green activity starts and is pushed into the green task (see Fig. 1(b)).
3. [*Start an* STP *activity*] When the blue button is clicked, since the top activity of the green task is *not* the blue activity, a new instance of the blue activity is pushed into the green task (see Fig. 1(c)). On the other hand, if the blue button is clicked again, because the launch mode of the blue activity is STP and the top activity of the green task is already the blue one, a new instance of the blue activity will *not* be pushed into the green task and its content is kept unchanged.
4. [*Start an* STK *activity*] Suppose now that the yellow button is clicked, since the launch mode of the yellow activity is STK, and the task *affinity* of the yellow activity is different from that of the bottom activity of the green task, a new task is created and an instance of the yellow activity is pushed into the new task (called the yellow task, with id: 23964, see Fig. 1(d), where the leftmost task is the top task of the back stack).
5. [*Start an* SIT *activity*] Next, suppose that the red button is clicked, because the launch mode of the red activity is SIT, a new task is created and an instance of the red activity is pushed into the new task (called the red task, with id: 23965, see Fig. 1(e)). Moreover, at any future moment, the red activity is the only activity of the red task. Note that here a new task is created in spite of the affinity of the red activity.
6. [*Start an* STD *activity from an* SIT *activity*] Finally, suppose the green button is clicked again. Since the top task is the red task, which is supposed to contain only one activity (i.e., the red activity), the green task is then moved to the top of the back stack and a new instance of the green activity is pushed into the green task (see Fig. 1(f)).

3 Android Stack Machine

For $k \in \mathbb{N}$, let $[k] = \{1, \cdots, k\}$. For a function $f : X \rightarrow Y$, let $\mathsf{dom}(f)$ and $\mathsf{rng}(f)$ denote the domain (X) and range (Y) of f respectively.

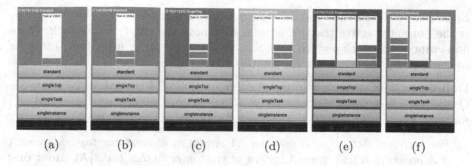

Fig. 1. ActivitiesLaunchDemo: the running example (Color figure online)

Definition 1 (Android stack machine). *An* Android stack machine (ASM) *is a tuple* $\mathcal{A} = (Q, \mathsf{Sig}, q_0, \Delta)$, *where*

- Q *is a finite set of control states, and* $q_0 \in Q$ *is the initial state,*
- $\mathsf{Sig} = (\mathsf{Act}, \mathsf{Lmd}, \mathsf{Aft}, A_0)$ *is the* activity signature, *where*
  - Act *is a finite set of activities,*
  - $\mathsf{Lmd} : \mathsf{Act} \to \{\mathsf{STD}, \mathsf{STP}, \mathsf{STK}, \mathsf{SIT}\}$ *is the launch-mode function,*
  - $\mathsf{Aft} : \mathsf{Act} \to [m]$ *is the task-affinity function, where* $m = |\mathsf{Act}|$,
  - $A_0 \in \mathsf{Act}$ *is the* main *activity,*
- $\Delta \subseteq Q \times (\mathsf{Act} \cup \{\triangleright\}) \times \mathsf{Inst} \times Q$ *is the transition relation, where* $\mathsf{Inst} = \{\square, \mathsf{back}\} \cup \{\mathsf{start}(A) \mid A \in \mathsf{Act}\}$, *such that (1) for each transition* $(q, A, \alpha, q') \in \Delta$, *it holds that* $q' \neq q_0$, *and (2) for each transition* $(q, \triangleright, \alpha, q') \in \Delta$, *it holds that* $q = q_0$, $\alpha = \mathsf{start}(A_0)$, *and* $q' \neq q_0$.

For convenience, we usually write a transition $(q, A, \alpha, q') \in \Delta$ as $q \xrightarrow{A,\alpha} q'$, and $(q, \triangleright, \alpha, q') \in \Delta$ as $q \xrightarrow{\triangleright,\alpha} q'$. Intuitively, $\triangleright$ denotes an empty back stack, $\square$ denotes there is no change over the back stack, back denotes the pop action, and $\mathsf{start}(A)$ denotes the activity A being started. We assume that, if the back stack is empty, the Android stack system terminates (i.e., no further continuation is possible) unless it is in the initial state q_0, We use $\mathsf{Act}_\star$ to denote $\{B \in \mathsf{Act} \mid \mathsf{Lmd}(B) = \star\}$ for $\star \in \{\mathsf{STD}, \mathsf{STP}, \mathsf{STK}, \mathsf{SIT}\}$.

Semantics. Let $\mathcal{A} = (Q, \mathsf{Sig}, q_0, \Delta)$ be an ASM with $\mathsf{Sig} = (\mathsf{Act}, \mathsf{Lmd}, \mathsf{Aft}, A_0)$.

A *task* of $\mathcal{A}$ is encoded as a word $S = [A_1, \cdots, A_n] \in \mathsf{Act}^+$ which denotes the content of the stack, with A_1 (resp. A_n) as the top (resp. bottom) symbol, denoted by $\mathsf{top}(S)$ (resp. $\mathsf{btm}(S)$). **We also call the bottom activity of a non-empty task S as the** *root* **activity of the task.** (Intuitively, this is the *first* activity of the task.) For $\star \in \{\mathsf{STD}, \mathsf{STP}, \mathsf{STK}, \mathsf{SIT}\}$, a task S is called a $\star$-*task* if $\mathsf{Lmd}(\mathsf{btm}(S)) = \star$. We define the *affinity* of a task S, denoted by $\mathsf{Aft}(S)$, to be $\mathsf{Aft}(\mathsf{btm}(S))$. For $S_1 \in \mathsf{Act}^*$ and $S_2 \in \mathsf{Act}^*$, we use $S_1 \cdot S_2$ to denote the concatenation of S_1 and S_2, and ϵ is used to denote the empty word in Act^*.

As mentioned in Sect. 2, the (running) tasks on Android are organized as the *back stack*, which is the main modelling object of ASM. Typically we write a back stack ρ as *a sequence of non-empty tasks*, i.e., $\rho = (S_1, \cdots, S_n)$, where

S_1 and S_n are called the top and the bottom task respectively. (Intuitively, S_1 is the currently active task.) ε is used to denote the empty back stack. For a non-empty back stack $\rho = (S_1, \cdots, S_n)$, we overload top by using $\mathsf{top}(\rho)$ to refer to the task S_1, and thus $\mathsf{top}^2(\rho)$ the top activity of S_1.

Definition 2 (Configurations). *A configuration of $\mathcal{A}$ is a pair (q, ρ) where $q \in Q$ and ρ is a back stack. Assume that $\rho = (S_1, \cdots, S_n)$ with $S_i = [A_{i,1}, \cdots, A_{i,m_i}]$ for each $i \in [n]$. We require ρ to satisfy the following constraints:*

1. *For each $A \in \mathsf{Act_{STK}}$ or $A \in \mathsf{Act_{SIT}}$, A occurs in at most one task. Moreover, if A occurs in a task, then A occurs at most once in that task.* [**At most one instance for each STK/SIT-activity**]
2. *For each $i \in [n]$ and $j \in [m_i - 1]$ such that $A_{i,j} \in \mathsf{Act_{STP}}$, $A_{i,j} \neq A_{i,j+1}$.* [**Non-stuttering forSTP- activities**]
3. *For each $i \in [n]$ and $j \in [m_i]$ such that $A_{i,j} \in \mathsf{Act_{STK}}$, $\mathsf{Aft}(A_{i,j}) = \mathsf{Aft}(S_i)$.* [**Affinities of STK- activities agree to the host task**]
4. *For each $i \in [n]$ and $j \in [m_i]$ such that $A_{i,j} \in \mathsf{Act_{SIT}}$, $m_i = 1$.* [**SIT-activities monopolize a task**]
5. *For $i \neq j \in [n]$ such that $\mathsf{btm}(S_i) \notin \mathsf{Act_{SIT}}$ and $\mathsf{btm}(S_j) \notin \mathsf{Act_{SIT}}$, $\mathsf{Aft}(S_i) \neq \mathsf{Aft}(S_j)$.* [**Affinities of tasks are mutually distinct, except for those rooted at SIT- activities**]

By Definition 2(5), each back stack ρ contains at most $|\mathsf{Act_{SIT}}| + |\mathsf{rng}(\mathsf{Aft})|$ (more precisely, $|\mathsf{Act_{SIT}}| + |\{\mathsf{Aft}(A) \mid A \in \mathsf{Act} \setminus \mathsf{Act_{SIT}}\}|$) tasks. Moreover, by Definition 2(1–5), all the root activities in a configuration are pairwise distinct, which allows to refer to a task whose root activity is A as *the* A-task.

Let $\mathsf{Conf}_{\mathcal{A}}$ denote the set of configurations of $\mathcal{A}$. The *initial* configuration of $\mathcal{A}$ is (q_0, ε). To formalize the semantics of $\mathcal{A}$ concisely, we introduce the following shorthand stack operations and one auxiliary function. Here $\rho = (S_1, \cdots, S_n)$ is a non-empty back stack.

$$\mathsf{Noaction}(\rho) \equiv \rho \qquad\qquad \mathsf{Push}(\rho, B) \equiv (([B] \cdot S_1), S_2, \cdots, S_n)$$

$$\mathsf{NewTask}(B) \equiv ([B]) \qquad\qquad \mathsf{NewTask}(\rho, B) \equiv ([B], S_1, \cdots, S_n)$$

$$\mathsf{Pop}(\rho) \equiv \begin{cases} \varepsilon, & \text{if } n = 1 \text{ and } S_1 = [A]; \\ (S_2, \cdots, S_n), & \text{if } n > 1 \text{ and } S_1 = [A]; \\ (S_1', S_2, \cdots, S_n), & \text{if } S_1 = [A] \cdot S_1' \text{ with } S_1' \in \mathsf{Act}^+; \end{cases}$$

$$\mathsf{PopUntil}(\rho, B) \equiv (S_1'', S_2, \cdots, S_n), \text{ where}$$
$$S_1 = S_1' \cdot S_1'' \text{ with } S_1' \in (\mathsf{Act} \setminus \{B\})^* \text{ and } \mathsf{top}(S_1'') = B;$$

$$\mathsf{Move2Top}(\rho, i) \equiv (S_i, S_1, \cdots, S_{i-1}, S_{i+1}, \cdots, S_n)$$

$$\mathsf{GetNonSITTaskByAft}(\rho, k) \equiv \begin{cases} S_i, & \text{if } \mathsf{Aft}(S_i) = k \text{ and } \mathsf{Lmd}(\mathsf{btm}(S_i)) \neq \mathsf{SIT}; \\ \mathsf{Undef}, & \text{otherwise.} \end{cases}$$

Intuitively, $\mathsf{GetNonSITTaskByAft}(\rho, k)$ returns a non-SIT task whose affinity is k if it exists, otherwise returns Undef.

In the sequel, we define the transition relation $(q, \rho) \xrightarrow{A} (q', \rho')$ on $\mathsf{Conf}_{\mathcal{A}}$ to formalize the semantics of $\mathcal{A}$. We start with the transitions out of the initial state q_0 and those with $\square$ or back action.

- For each transition $q_0 \xrightarrow{\triangleright,\mathsf{start}(A_0)} q$, $(q_0, \varepsilon) \xrightarrow{\mathcal{A}} (q, \mathsf{NewTask}(A_0))$.
- For each transition $q \xrightarrow{A,\square} q'$ and $(q, \rho) \in \mathsf{Conf}_\mathcal{A}$ such that $\mathsf{top}^2(\rho) = A$, $(q, \rho) \xrightarrow{\mathcal{A}} (q', \mathsf{Noaction}(\rho))$.
- For each transition $q \xrightarrow{A,\mathsf{back}} q'$ and $(q, \rho) \in \mathsf{Conf}_\mathcal{A}$ such that $\mathsf{top}^2(\rho) = A$, $(q, \rho) \xrightarrow{\mathcal{A}} (q', \mathsf{Pop}(\rho))$.

The most interesting case is, however, the transitions of the form $q \xrightarrow{A,\mathsf{start}(B)} q'$. We shall make case distinctions based on the launch mode of B. For each transition $q \xrightarrow{A,\mathsf{start}(B)} q'$ and $(q, \rho) \in \mathsf{Conf}_\mathcal{A}$ such that $\mathsf{top}^2(\rho) = A$, $(q, \rho) \xrightarrow{\mathcal{A}} (q', \rho')$ if one of the following cases holds. Assume $\rho = (S_1, \cdots, S_n)$.

$\boxed{\text{CASE } \mathsf{Lmd}(B) = \mathsf{STD}}$

- $\mathsf{Lmd}(A) \neq \mathsf{SIT}$, then $\rho' = \mathsf{Push}(\rho, B)$;
- $\mathsf{Lmd}(A) = \mathsf{SIT}^2$, then

  • if $\mathsf{GetNonSITTaskByAft}(\rho, \mathsf{Aft}(B)) = S_i{}^3$, then $\rho' = \mathsf{Push}(\mathsf{Move2Top}(\rho, i), B)$,
  • if $\mathsf{GetNonSITTaskByAft}(\rho, \mathsf{Aft}(B)) = \mathsf{Undef}$, then $\rho' = \mathsf{NewTask}(\rho, B)$;

$\boxed{\text{CASE } \mathsf{Lmd}(B) = \mathsf{STP}}$

- $\mathsf{Lmd}(A) \neq \mathsf{SIT}$ and $A \neq B$, then $\rho' = \mathsf{Push}(\rho, B)$;
- $\mathsf{Lmd}(A) \neq \mathsf{SIT}$ and $A = B$, then $\rho' = \mathsf{Noaction}(\rho)$;
- $\mathsf{Lmd}(A) = \mathsf{SIT}$ (see footnote 2),

  • if $\mathsf{GetNonSITTaskByAft}(\rho, \mathsf{Aft}(B)) = S_i$ (see footnote 3), then

    * if $\mathsf{top}(S_i) \neq B$, $\rho' = \mathsf{Push}(\mathsf{Move2Top}(\rho, i), B)$,
    * if $\mathsf{top}(S_i) = B$, $\rho' = \mathsf{Move2Top}(\rho, i)$;

  • if $\mathsf{GetNonSITTaskByAft}(\rho, \mathsf{Aft}(B)) = \mathsf{Undef}$, then $\rho' = \mathsf{NewTask}(\rho, B)$;

$\boxed{\text{CASE } \mathsf{Lmd}(B) = \mathsf{SIT}}$

- $A = B$ (see footnote 2), then $\rho' = \mathsf{Noaction}(\rho)$;
- $A \neq B$ and $S_i = [B]$ for some $i \in [n]^4$, then $\rho' = \mathsf{Move2Top}(\rho, i)$;
- $A \neq B$ and $S_i \neq [B]$ for each $i \in [n]$, then $\rho' = \mathsf{NewTask}(\rho, B)$;

$\boxed{\text{CASE } \mathsf{Lmd}(B) = \mathsf{STK}}$

- $\mathsf{Lmd}(A) \neq \mathsf{SIT}$ and $\mathsf{Aft}(B) = \mathsf{Aft}(S_1)$, then

  • if B does *not* occur in $S_1{}^5$, then $\rho' = \mathsf{Push}(\rho, B)$;
  • if B occurs in $S_1{}^6$, then $\rho' = \mathsf{PopUntil}(\rho, B)$;

- $\mathsf{Lmd}(A) \neq \mathsf{SIT} \implies \mathsf{Aft}(B) \neq \mathsf{Aft}(S_1)$, then

---

[2] By Definition 2(4), $S_1 = [A]$.
[3] If i exists, it must be unique by Definition 2(5). Moreover, $i > 1$, as $\mathsf{Lmd}(A) = \mathsf{SIT}$.
[4] If i exists, it must be unique by Definition 2(1). Moreover, $i > 1$, as $A \neq B$.
[5] B does *not* occur in ρ at all by Definition 2(3–5).
[6] Note that B occurs at most once in S_1 by Definition 2(1).

- if $\mathsf{GetNonSITTaskByAft}(\rho, \mathsf{Aft}(B)) = S_i{}^7$,

  * if B does *not* occur in S_i (see footnote 5), then $\rho' = \mathsf{Push}(\mathsf{Move2Top}(\rho, i), B)$;
  * if B occurs in $S_i{}^8$, then $\rho' = \mathsf{PopUntil}(\mathsf{Move2Top}(\rho, i), B)$,

- if $\mathsf{GetNonSITTaskByAft}(\rho, \mathsf{Aft}(B)) = \mathsf{Undef}$, then $\rho' = \mathsf{NewTask}(\rho, B)$;

This concludes the definition of the transition definition of $\xrightarrow{\mathcal{A}}$. As usual, we use $\overset{\mathcal{A}}{\Rightarrow}$ to denote the reflexive and transitive closure of $\xrightarrow{\mathcal{A}}$.

Example 2. The ASM for the ActivitiesLaunchDemo app in Example 1 is $\mathcal{A} = (Q, \mathsf{Sig}, q_0, \Delta)$, where $Q = \{q_0, q_1\}$, $\mathsf{Sig} = (\mathsf{Act}, \mathsf{Lmd}, \mathsf{Aft}, A_g)$ with

- $\mathsf{Act} = \{A_g, A_b, A_y, A_r\}$, corresponding to the green, blue, yellow and red activity respectively in the ActivitiesLaunchDemo app,
- $\mathsf{Lmd}(A_g) = \mathsf{STD}$, $\mathsf{Lmd}(A_b) = \mathsf{STP}$, $\mathsf{Lmd}(A_y) = \mathsf{STK}$, $\mathsf{Lmd}(A_r) = \mathsf{SIT}$,
- $\mathsf{Aft}(A_g) = \mathsf{Aft}(A_b) = \mathsf{Aft}(A_r) = 1$, $\mathsf{Aft}(A_y) = 2$,

and Δ comprises the transitions illustrated in Fig. 2. Below is a path in the graph $\xrightarrow{\mathcal{A}}$ corresponding to the sequence of user actions clicking the green, blue, blue, yellow, red, blue button (cf. Example 1),

$$(q_0, \varepsilon) \xrightarrow{\triangleright, \mathsf{start}(A_g)} (q_1, ([A_g])) \xrightarrow{A_g, \mathsf{start}(A_b)} (q_1, ([A_b, A_g])) \xrightarrow{A_b, \mathsf{start}(A_b)}$$
$$(q_1, ([A_b, A_g])) \xrightarrow{A_b, \mathsf{start}(A_y)} (q_1, ([A_y], [A_b, A_g])) \xrightarrow{A_y, \mathsf{start}(A_r)}$$
$$(q_1, ([A_r], [A_y], [A_b, A_g])) \xrightarrow{A_r, \mathsf{start}(A_g)} (q_1, ([A_g, A_b, A_g], [A_r], [A_y])).$$

Proposition 1 reassures that $\xrightarrow{\mathcal{A}}$ is indeed a relation on $\mathsf{Conf}_{\mathcal{A}}$ as per Definition 2.

Proposition 1. *Let $\mathcal{A}$ be an ASM. For each $(q, \rho) \in \mathsf{Conf}_{\mathcal{A}}$ and $(q, \rho) \xrightarrow{\mathcal{A}} (q', \rho')$, $(q', \rho') \in \mathsf{Conf}_{\mathcal{A}}$, namely, (q', ρ') satisfies the five constraints in Definition 2.*

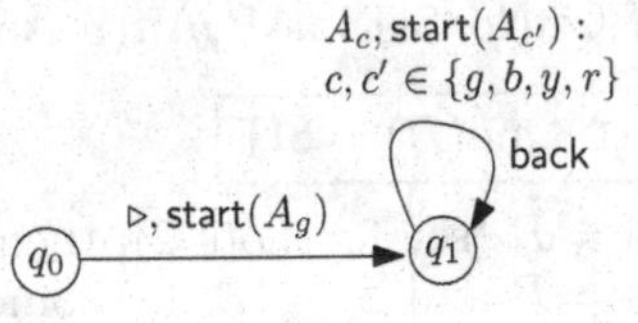

Fig. 2. ASM corresponding to the ActivitiesLaunchDemo app

Remark 1. A single app can clearly be modeled by an ASM. However, ASM can also be used to model multiple apps which may share tasks/activities. (In this case, these multiple apps can be composed into a single app, where a new main activity is added.) This is especially useful when analysing, for instance, task hijacking [16]. We sometimes do not specify the main activity explicit for convenience. The translation from app source code to ASM is not trivial, but follows standard routines. In particular, in ASM, the symbols stored into the back stack are just

---

[7] If i exists, it must be unique by Definition 2(5). Moreover, $i > 1$, as $\mathsf{Lmd}(A) \neq \mathsf{SIT} \implies \mathsf{Aft}(B) \neq \mathsf{Aft}(S_1)$.

[8] Note that B occurs at most once in S_i by Definition 2(1).

names of activities. Android apps typically need to, similar to function calls of programs, store additional local state information. This can be dealt with by introducing an extend activity alphabet such that each symbol is of the form $A(b)$, where $A \in$ Act and b represents local information. When we present examples, we also adopt this general syntax.

Model validation. We validate the ASM model by designing "diagnosis" Android apps with extensive experiments. For each case in the semantics of ASM, we design an app which contains activities with the corresponding launch modes and task affinities. To simulate the transition rules of the ASM, each activity contains some buttons, which, when clicked, will launch other activities. For instance, in the case of $\mathsf{Lmd}(B) = \mathsf{STD}$, $\mathsf{Lmd}(A) = \mathsf{SIT}$, $\mathsf{GetNonSITTaskByAft}(\rho, \mathsf{Aft}(B)) = \mathsf{Undef}$, the app contains two activities A and B of launch modes SIT and STD respectively, where A is the main activity. When the app is launched, an instance of A is started. A contains a button, which, when clicked, starts an instance of B. We carry out the experiment by clicking the button, monitoring the content of the back stack, and checking whether the content of the back stack conforms to the definition of the semantics. Specifically, we check that there are exactly two tasks in the back stack, one task comprising a single instance of A and another task comprising a single instance of B, with the latter task on the top. Our experiments are done in a Redmi-4A mobile phone with Android version 6.0.1. The details of the experiments can be found at https://sites.google.com/site/assconformancetesting/.

4   Reachability of ASM

Towards formal (static) analysis and verification of Android apps, we study the fundamental *reachability* problem of ASM. Fix an ASM $\mathcal{A} = (Q, \mathsf{Sig}, q_0, \Delta)$ with $\mathsf{Sig} = (\mathsf{Act}, \mathsf{Lmd}, \mathsf{Aft}, A_0)$ and a *target state* $q \in Q$. There are usually two variants: the *state reachability problem* asks whether $(q_0, \varepsilon) \xrightarrow{\mathcal{A}} (q, \rho)$ for *some* back stack ρ, and the *configuration reachability problem* asks whether $(q_0, \varepsilon) \xrightarrow{\mathcal{A}} (q, \rho)$ when ρ is also given. We show they are interchangeable as far as decidability is concerned.

Proposition 2. *The configuration reachability problem and the state reachability problem of ASM are interreducible in exponential time.*

Proposition 2 allows to focus on the state reachability problem in the rest of this paper. Observe that, when the activities in an ASM are of the same launch mode, the problem degenerates to that of standard pushdown systems or even finite-state systems. These systems are well-understood, and we refer to [6] for explanations. To proceed, we deal with the cases where there are exactly two launch modes, for which we have $\binom{4}{2} = 6$ possibilities. The classification is given in Theorems 1 and 2. Clearly, they entail that the reachability for general ASM (with at least two launch modes) is undecidable. To show the undecidablity, we reduce from Minsky's two-counter machines [14], which, albeit standard, reveals the expressibility of ASM. We remark that the capability of *swapping the order of two distinct non-SIT-tasks in the back stack—without resetting* the content of any of them—is the main source of undecidability.

Theorem 1. *The reachability problem of ASM is undecidable, even when the ASM contains only (1)* STD *and* STK *activities, or (2)* STD *and* SIT *activities, or (3)* STK *and* STP *activities, or (4)* SIT *and* STP *activities.*

In contrast, we have some relatively straightforward positive results:

Theorem 2. *The state reachability problem of ASM is decidable in polynomial time when the ASM contains* STD *and* STP *activities only, and in polynomial space when the ASM contains* STK *and* SIT *activities only.*

As mentioned in Sect. 1, we aim to identify expressive fragments of ASM with decidable reachability problems. To this end, we introduce a fragment called **STK-dominating ASM**, which accommodates all four launch modes.

Definition 3 (STK-dominating ASM). *An ASM is said to be STK-dominating if the following two constraints are satisfied:*

(1) the task affinities of the STK *activities are mutually distinct,*

(2) for each transition $q \xrightarrow{A,\text{start}(B)} q' \in \Delta$ such that $A \in \text{Act}_{\text{SIT}}$, it holds that either $B \in \text{Act}_{\text{SIT}} \cup \text{Act}_{\text{STK}}$, or $B \in \text{Act}_{\text{STD}} \cup \text{Act}_{\text{STP}}$ and $\text{Aft}(B) = \text{Aft}(A_0)$.

The following result explains the name "STK-dominating".

Proposition 3. *Let $\mathcal{A} = (Q, \text{Sig}, q_0, \Delta)$ be an STK-dominating ASM with $\text{Sig} = (\text{Act}, \text{Lmd}, \text{Aft}, A_0)$. Then each configuration (q, ρ) that is reachable from the initial configuration (q_0, ε) in $\mathcal{A}$ satisfies the following constraints: (1) for each STK activity $A \in \text{Act}$ with $\text{Aft}(A) \neq \text{Aft}(A_0)$, A can only occur at the bottom of some task in ρ, (2) ρ contains at most one STD/STP-task, which, when it exists, has the same affinity as A_0.*

It is not difficult to verify that the ASM given in Example 2 is STK-dominating.

Theorem 3. *The state reachability of STK-dominating ASM is in 2-EXPTIME.*

The proof of Theorem 3 is technically the most challenging part of this paper. We shall give a sketch in Sect. 5 with the full details in [6].

5   STK-dominating ASM

For simplicity, we assume that $\mathcal{A}$ **contains STD and STK activities only**[9]. To tackle the (state) reachability problem for STK-dominating ASM, we consider two cases, i.e., $\text{Lmd}(A_0) = \text{STK}$ and $\text{Lmd}(A_0) \neq \text{STK}$. The former case is simpler

[9] The more general case that $\mathcal{A}$ also contains STP and SIT activities is slightly more involved and requires more space to present, which can be found in [6].

because, by Proposition 3, all tasks will be rooted at STK activities. For the latter, more general case, the back stack may contain, apart from several tasks rooted at STK activities, one single task rooted at A_0. Sections 5.1 and 5.2 will handle these two cases respectively.

We will, however, first introduce some standard, but necessary, backgrounds on pushdown systems. We assume familiarity with standard *finite-state automata* (NFA) and *finite-state transducers* (FST). We emphasize that, in this paper, FST refers to a special class of finite-state transducers, namely, *letter-to-letter* finite-state transducers where the input and output alphabets are the same.

Preliminaries of Pushdown systems. A *pushdown system* (PDS) is a tuple $\mathcal{P} = (Q, \Gamma, \Delta)$, where Q is a finite set of *control states*, Γ is a finite *stack alphabet*, and $\Delta \subseteq Q \times \Gamma \times \Gamma^* \times Q$ is a finite set of transition rules. The size of $\mathcal{P}$, denoted by $|\mathcal{P}|$, is defined as $|\Delta|$.

Let $\mathcal{P} = (Q, \Gamma, \Delta)$ be a PDS. A *configuration* of $\mathcal{P}$ is a pair $(q, w) \in Q \times \Gamma^*$, where w denotes the *content* of the stack (with the leftmost symbol being the top of the stack). Let $\mathsf{Conf}_\mathcal{P}$ denote the set of configurations of $\mathcal{P}$. We define a binary relation $\xrightarrow{\mathcal{P}}$ over $\mathsf{Conf}_\mathcal{P}$ as follows: $(q, w) \xrightarrow{\mathcal{P}} (q', w')$ iff $w = \gamma w_1$ and there exists $w'' \in \Gamma^*$ such that $(q, \gamma, w'', q') \in \Delta$ and $w' = w'' w_1$. We use $\xRightarrow{\mathcal{P}}$ to denote the *reflexive and transitive closure* of $\xrightarrow{\mathcal{P}}$.

A configuration (q', w') is *reachable* from (q, w) if $(q, w) \xRightarrow{\mathcal{P}} (q', w')$. For $C \subseteq \mathsf{Conf}_\mathcal{P}$, $\mathsf{pre}^*(C)$ (resp. $\mathsf{post}^*(C)$) denotes the set of *predecessor* (resp. *successor*) reachable configurations $\{(q', w') \mid \exists (q, w) \in C, (q', w') \xRightarrow{\mathcal{P}} (q, w)\}$ (resp. $\{(q', w') \mid \exists (q, w) \in C, (q, w) \xRightarrow{\mathcal{P}} (q', w')\}$). For $q \in Q$, we define $C_q = \{q\} \times \Gamma^*$ and write $\mathsf{pre}^*(q)$ and $\mathsf{post}^*(q)$ as shorthand of $\mathsf{pre}^*(C_q)$ and $\mathsf{post}^*(C_q)$ respectively.

As a standard machinery to solve reachability for PDS, a *$\mathcal{P}$-multi-automaton* ($\mathcal{P}$-MA) is an NFA $\mathcal{A} = (Q', \Gamma, \delta, I, F)$ such that $I \subseteq Q \subseteq Q'$ [4]. Evidently, multi-automata are a special class of NFA. Let $\mathcal{A} = (Q', \Gamma, \delta, I, F)$ be a $\mathcal{P}$-MA and $(q, w) \in \mathsf{Conf}_\mathcal{P}$, (q, w) is *accepted* by $\mathcal{A}$ if $q \in I$ and there is an accepting run $q_0 q_1 \cdots q_n$ of $\mathcal{A}$ on w with $q_0 = q$. Let $\mathsf{Conf}_\mathcal{A}$ denote the set of configurations accepted by $\mathcal{A}$. Moreover, let $\mathcal{L}(\mathcal{A})$ denote the set of words w such that $(q, w) \in \mathsf{Conf}_\mathcal{A}$ for some $q \in I$. For brevity, we usually write MA instead of $\mathcal{P}$-MA when $\mathcal{P}$ is clear from the context. Moreover, for an MA $\mathcal{A} = (Q', \Gamma, \delta, I, F)$ and $q' \in Q$, we use $\mathcal{A}(q')$ to denote the MA obtained from $\mathcal{A}$ by replacing I with $\{q'\}$. A set of configurations $C \subseteq \mathsf{Conf}_\mathcal{P}$ is *regular* if there is an MA $\mathcal{A}$ such that $\mathsf{Conf}_\mathcal{A} = C$.

Theorem 4 ([4]). *Given a PDS $\mathcal{P}$ and a set of configurations accepted by an MA $\mathcal{A}$, we can compute, in polynomial time in $|\mathcal{P}| + |\mathcal{A}|$, two MAs $\mathcal{A}_{\mathsf{pre}^*}$ and $\mathcal{A}_{\mathsf{post}^*}$ that recognise $\mathsf{pre}^*(\mathsf{Conf}_\mathcal{A})$ and $\mathsf{post}^*(\mathsf{Conf}_\mathcal{A})$ respectively.*

The connection between ASM and PDS is rather obvious. In a nutshell, ASM can be considered as a PDS with *multiple* stacks, which is well-known to be undecidable in general. Our overall strategy to attack the state reachability problem for the fragments of ASM is to simulate them (in particular, the multiple stacks) via—in some cases, decidable extensions of—PDS.

5.1   Case Lmd(A_0) = STK

Our approach to tackle this case is to simulate $\mathcal{A}$ by an *extension* of PDS, i.e., *pushdown systems with transductions* (TrPDS), proposed in [19]. In TrPDS, each transition is associated with an FST defining how the stack content is modified. Formally, a TrPDS is a tuple $\mathcal{P} = (Q, \Gamma, \mathscr{T}, \Delta)$, where Q and Γ are precisely the same as those of PDS, $\mathscr{T}$ is a finite set of FSTs over the alphabet Γ, and $\Delta \subseteq Q \times \Gamma \times \Gamma^* \times \mathscr{T} \times Q$ is a finite set of transition rules. Let $\mathcal{R}(\mathscr{T})$ denote the set of transductions defined by FSTs from $\mathscr{T}$ and $\llbracket \mathcal{R}(\mathscr{T}) \rrbracket$ denote the *closure* of $\mathcal{R}(\mathscr{T})$ under composition and left-quotient. A TrPDS $\mathcal{P}$ is said to be *finite* if $\llbracket \mathcal{R}(\mathscr{T}) \rrbracket$ is finite.

The configurations of $\mathcal{P}$ are defined similarly as in PDS. We define a binary relation $\xrightarrow{\mathcal{P}}$ on $\mathsf{Conf}_{\mathcal{P}}$ as follows: $(q, w) \xrightarrow{\mathcal{P}} (q', w')$ if there are $\gamma \in \Gamma$, the words w_1, u, w_2, and $\mathcal{T} \in \mathscr{T}$ such that $w = \gamma w_1$, $(q, \gamma, u, \mathcal{T}, q') \in \Delta$, $w_1 \xrightarrow{\mathcal{T}} w_2$, and $w' = u w_2$. Let $\xRightarrow{\mathcal{P}}$ denote the reflexive and transitive closure of $\xrightarrow{\mathcal{P}}$. Similarly to PDS, we can define $\mathsf{pre}^*(\cdot)$ and $\mathsf{post}^*(\cdot)$ respectively. Regular sets of configurations of TrPDS can be represented by MA, in line with PDS. More precisely, given a finite TrPDS $\mathcal{P} = (Q, \Gamma, \mathscr{T}, \Delta)$ and an MA $\mathcal{A}$ for $\mathcal{P}$, one can compute, in time polynomial in $|\mathcal{P}| + |\llbracket \mathcal{R}(\mathscr{T}) \rrbracket| + |\mathcal{A}|$, two MAs $\mathcal{A}_{\mathsf{pre}^*}$ and $\mathcal{A}_{\mathsf{post}^*}$ that recognize the sets $\mathsf{pre}^*(\mathsf{Conf}_{\mathcal{A}})$ and $\mathsf{post}^*(\mathsf{Conf}_{\mathcal{A}})$ respectively [17–19].

To simulate $\mathcal{A}$ via a finite TrPDS $\mathcal{P}$, the back stack $\rho = (S_1, \cdots, S_n)$ of $\mathcal{A}$ is encoded by a word $S_1 \sharp \cdots \sharp S_n \sharp \bot$ (where $\sharp$ is a delimiter and $\bot$ is the bottom symbol of the stack), which is stored in the stack of $\mathcal{P}$. Recall that, in this case, each task S_i is rooted at an STK-activity which sits on the bottom of S_i. Suppose $\mathsf{top}(S_1) = A$. When a transition $(q, A, \mathsf{start}(B), q')$ with $B \in \mathsf{Act}_{\mathsf{STK}}$ is fired, according to the semantics of $\mathcal{A}$, the B-task of ρ, say S_i, is switched to the top of ρ and changed into $[B]$ (i.e., all the activities in the B-task, except B itself, are popped). To simulate this in $\mathcal{P}$, we replace every stack symbol in the place of S_i with a dummy symbol $\dagger$ and keep the other symbols unchanged. On the other hand, to simulate a back action of $\mathcal{A}$, $\mathcal{P}$ continues popping until the next non-dummy and non-delimiter symbol is seen.

Proposition 4. *Let $\mathcal{A} = (Q, \mathsf{Sig}, q_0, \Delta)$ be an STK-dominating ASM with $\mathsf{Sig} = (\mathsf{Act}, \mathsf{Lmd}, \mathsf{Aft}, A_0)$ and $\mathsf{Lmd}(A_0) = \mathsf{STK}$. Then a finite TrPDS $\mathcal{P} = (Q', \Gamma, \mathscr{T}, \Delta')$ with $Q \subseteq Q'$ can be constructed in time polynomial in $|\mathcal{A}|$ such that, for each $q \in Q$, q is reachable from (q_0, ε) in $\mathcal{A}$ iff q is reachable from $(q_0, \bot)$ in $\mathcal{P}$.*

For a state $q \in Q$, $\mathsf{pre}^*_{\mathcal{P}}(q)$ can be effectively computed as an MA $\mathcal{B}_q$, and the reachability of q in $\mathcal{A}$ is reduced to checking whether $(q_0, \bot) \in \mathsf{Conf}_{\mathcal{B}_q}$.

5.2   Case Lmd(A_0) ≠ STK

We then turn to the more general case $\mathsf{Lmd}(A_0) \neq \mathsf{STK}$ which is significantly more involved. For exposition purpose, we consider an ASM $\mathcal{A}$ where **there are exactly two STK activities** A_1, A_2, and the task affinity of A_2 is the same as that of the main task A_0 (and thus the task affinity of A_1 is different from that of A_0). We also assume that all the activities in $\mathcal{A}$ are "standard" except A_1, A_2. Namely $\mathsf{Act} = \mathsf{Act_{STD}} \cup \{A_1, A_2\}$ and $A_0 \in \mathsf{Act_{STD}}$ in particular. Neither of these two assumptions is fundamental and their generalization is given in [6].

By Proposition 3, there are at most two tasks in the back stack of $\mathcal{A}$. The two tasks are either an A_0-task and an A_1-task, or an A_2-task and an A_1-task. An A_2-task can only surface when the original A_0-task is popped empty. If this happens, no A_0-task will be recreated again, and thus, according to the arguments in Sect. 5.1, we can simulate the ASM by TrPDS directly and we are done. The challenging case is that we have both an A_0-task and an A_1-task. To solve the state reachability problem, the main technical difficulty is that the order of the A_0-task and the A_1-task may be switched for arbitrarily many times before reaching the target state q. Readers may be wondering why they *cannot* simply simulate two-counter machines. The reason is that the two tasks are *asymmetric* in the sense that, each time when the A_1-task is switched from the bottom to the top (by starting the activity A_1), the content of the A_1-task is reset into $[A_1]$. But this is *not* the case for A_0-task: when the A_0-task is switched from the bottom to the top (by starting the activity A_2), if it does not contain A_2, then A_2 will be pushed into the A_0-task; otherwise all the activities above A_2 will be popped and A_2 becomes the top activity of the A_0-task. Our decision procedure below utilises the asymmetry of the two tasks.

Intuition of construction. The crux of reachability analysis is to construct a *finite abstraction* for the A_1-task and incorporate it into the control states of $\mathcal{A}$, so we can reduce the state reachability of $\mathcal{A}$ into that of a pushdown system $\mathcal{P}_\mathcal{A}$ (with a single stack). Observe that a run of $\mathcal{A}$ can be seen as a sequence of task switching. In particular, an $A_0; A_1; A_0$ *switching* denotes a path in $\xrightarrow{\mathcal{A}}$ where the A_0-task is on the top in the *first* and the *last* configuration, while the A_1-task is on the top in all the *intermediate* configurations. The main idea of the reduction is to simulate the $A_0; A_1; A_0$ switching by a "macro"-transition of $\mathcal{P}_\mathcal{A}$. Note that the A_0-task regains the top task in the last configuration either by starting the activity A_2 or by emptying the A_1-task. Suppose that, for an $A_0; A_1; A_0$ switching, in the first (resp. last) configuration, q (resp. q') is the control state and α (resp. β) is the finite abstraction of the A_1-task. Then for the "macro"-transition of $\mathcal{P}_\mathcal{A}$, the control state will be updated from (q, α) to (q', β), and the stack content of $\mathcal{P}_\mathcal{A}$ is updated accordingly:

- If the A_0-task regains the top task by starting A_2, then the stack content is updated as follows: if the stack does not contain A_2, then A_2 will be pushed into the stack; otherwise all the symbols above A_2 will be popped.
- On the other hand, if the A_0-task regains the top task by emptying the A_1-task, then the stack content is not changed.

Roughly speaking, the abstraction of the A_1-task must carry the information that, when A_0-task and A_1-task are the top resp. bottom task of the back stack and A_0-task is emptied, whether the target state q can be reached from the configuration at that time. As a result, we define the abstraction of the A_1-task whose content is encoded by a word $w \in \mathsf{Act}^*$, denoted by $\alpha(w)$, as the set of all states $q'' \in Q$ such that the target state q can be reached from $(q'', (w))$ in $\mathcal{A}$. [Note that during the process that q is reached from $(q'', (w))$ in $\mathcal{A}$, the A_0-task does not exist anymore, but a (new) A_2-task, may be formed.] Let $\mathsf{Abs}_{A_1} = 2^Q$.

To facilitate the construction of the PDS $\mathcal{P}_\mathcal{A}$, we also need to record how the abstraction "evolves". For each $(q', A, \alpha) \in Q \times (\mathsf{Act} \setminus \{A_1\}) \times \mathsf{Abs}_{A_1}$, we compute the set $\mathsf{Reach}(q', A, \alpha)$ consisting of pairs (q'', β) satisfying: there is an $A_0; A_1; A_0$ switching such that in the first configuration, A is the top symbol of the A_0-task, q' (resp. q'') is the control state of the first (resp. last) configuration, and α (resp. β) is the abstraction for the A_1-task in the first (resp. last) configuration.[10]

Computing $\mathsf{Reach}(q', A, \alpha)$. Let $(q', A, \alpha) \in Q \times (\mathsf{Act} \setminus \{A_1\}) \times \mathsf{Abs}_{A_1}$. We first simulate relevant parts of $\mathcal{A}$ as follows:

- Following Sect. 5.1, we construct a TrPDS $\mathcal{P}_{\overline{A_0}} = (Q_{\overline{A_0}}, \Gamma_{\overline{A_0}}, \mathcal{T}_{\overline{A_0}}, \Delta_{\overline{A_0}})$ to simulate *the A_1-task and A_2-task of $\mathcal{A}$ after the A_0-task is emptied*, where $Q_{\overline{A_0}} = Q \cup Q \times Q$ and $\Gamma_{\overline{A_0}} = \mathsf{Act} \cup \{\sharp, \dagger, \bot\}$. Note that A_0 may still—as a "standard" activity—occur in $\mathcal{P}_{\overline{A_0}}$ though the A_0-task disappears.
  In addition, we construct an MA $\mathcal{B}_q = (Q_q, \Gamma_{\overline{A_0}}, \delta_q, I_q, F_q)$ to represent $\mathsf{pre}^*_{\mathcal{P}_{\overline{A_0}}}(q)$, where $I_q \subseteq Q_{\overline{A_0}}$. Then given a stack content $w \in \mathsf{Act}^*_{\mathsf{STD}} A_1$ of the A_1-task, the abstraction $\alpha(w)$ of w, is the set of $q'' \in I_q \cap Q$ such that $(q'', w \sharp \bot) \in \mathsf{Conf}_{\mathcal{B}_q}$.
- We construct a PDS $\mathcal{P}_{\overline{A_0, A_2}} = (Q_{\overline{A_0, A_2}}, \Gamma_{\overline{A_0, A_2}}, \mathcal{T}_{\overline{A_0, A_2}}, \Delta_{\overline{A_0, A_2}})$ to simulate the A_1-task of $\mathcal{A}$, where $\Gamma_{\overline{A_0, A_2}} = (\mathsf{Act} \setminus \{A_2\}) \cup \{\bot\}$. In addition, to compute $\mathsf{Reach}(q', A, \alpha)$ later, we construct an MA $\mathcal{M}_{(q', A, \alpha)} = (Q_{(q', A, \alpha)}, \Gamma_{\overline{A_0, A_2}}, \delta_{(q', A, \alpha)}, I_{(q', A, \alpha)}, F_{(q', A, \alpha)})$ to represent

$$\mathsf{post}^*_{\mathcal{P}_{\overline{A_0, A_2}}}(\{(q_1, A_1 \bot) \mid (q', A, \mathsf{start}(A_1), q_1) \in \Delta\}).$$

Definition 4. $\mathsf{Reach}(q', A, \alpha)$ *comprises*

- *the pairs* $(q'', \beta) \in Q \times \mathsf{Abs}_{A_1}$ *satisfying that (1)* $(q', A, \mathsf{start}(A_1), q_1) \in \Delta$, *(2)* $(q_1, A_1 \bot) \xrightarrow{\mathcal{P}_{\overline{A_0, A_2}}} (q_2, Bw \bot)$, *(3)* $(q_2, B, \mathsf{start}(A_2), q'') \in \Delta$, *and (4)* β *is the abstraction of Bw, for some $B \in \mathsf{Act} \setminus \{A_2\}$, $w \in (\mathsf{Act} \setminus \{A_2\})^*$ and $q_1, q_2 \in Q$,*
- *the pairs* $(q'', \bot)$ *such that* $(q', A, \mathsf{start}(A_1), q_1) \in \Delta$ *and* $(q_1, A_1 \bot) \xrightarrow{\mathcal{P}_{\overline{A_0, A_2}}} (q'', \bot)$ *for some* $q_1 \in Q$.

Importantly, conditions in Definition 4 can be characterized algorithmically.

Lemma 1. *For* $(q', A, \alpha) \in Q \times (\mathsf{Act} \setminus \{A_1\}) \times \mathsf{Abs}_{A_1}$, $\mathsf{Reach}(q', A, \alpha)$ *is the union of*

- $\{(q'', \bot) \mid (q'', \bot) \in \mathsf{Conf}_{\mathcal{M}_{(q', A, \alpha)}}\}$ *and*

---

[10] As we can see later, $\mathsf{Reach}(q', A, \alpha)$ does not depend on α for the two-task special case considered here. We choose to keep α in view of readability.

– *the set of pairs* $(q'', \beta) \in Q \times \mathsf{Abs}_{A_1}$ *such that there exist* $q_2 \in Q$ *and* $B \in$
$\mathsf{Act} \setminus \{A_2\}$ *satisfying that* $(q_2, B, \mathsf{start}(A_2), q'')$, *and*
$(B(\mathsf{Act} \setminus \{A_2\})^* \sharp \bot) \cap (\mathsf{Act}^*_{\mathsf{STD}} A_1 \sharp \bot) \cap (\mathcal{L}(\mathcal{M}_{(q',A,\alpha)}(q_2))\langle\bot\rangle^{-1}) \sharp \bot \cap \mathcal{L}_\beta \neq \emptyset$,
where $\mathcal{L}(\mathcal{M}_{(q',A,\alpha)}(q_2))\langle\bot\rangle^{-1}$ *is the set of words* w *such that* $w\bot$ *belongs to*
$\mathcal{L}(\mathcal{M}_{(q',A,\alpha)}(q_2))$, *and* $\mathcal{L}_\beta = \bigcap_{q''' \in \beta} \mathcal{L}(\mathcal{B}_q(q''')) \cap \bigcap_{q''' \in Q \setminus \beta} \overline{\mathcal{L}(\mathcal{B}_q(q'''))}$, *with* $\overline{\mathcal{L}}$
representing the complement language of $\mathcal{L}$.

Construction of $\mathcal{P}_A$. We first construct a PDS $\mathcal{P}_{A_0} = (Q_{A_0}, \Gamma_{A_0}, \Delta_{A_0})$, to
simulate the A_0-task of $\mathcal{A}$. Here $Q_{A_0} = (Q \times \{0, 1\}) \cup (Q \times \{1\} \times \{\mathsf{pop}\})$,
$\Gamma_{A_0} = \mathsf{Act}_{\mathsf{STD}} \cup \{A_2, \bot\}$, and Δ_{A_0} comprises the transitions. Here 1 (resp. 0)
marks that the activity A_2 is in the stack (resp. is not in the stack) and the tag
pop marks that the PDS is in the process of popping until A_2. The construction
of $\mathcal{P}_{A_0}$ is relatively straightforward, the details of which can be found in [6].

We then define the PDS $\mathcal{P}_A = (Q_A, \Gamma_{A_0}, \Delta_A)$, where $Q_A = (\mathsf{Abs}_{A_1} \times Q_{A_0}) \cup$
$\{q\}$, and Δ_A comprises the following transitions,

– for each $(p, \gamma, w, p') \in \Delta_{A_0}$ and $\alpha \in \mathsf{Abs}_{A_1}$, we have $((\alpha, p), \gamma, w, (\alpha, p')) \in \Delta_A$
  (here $p, p' \in Q_{A_0}$, that is, of the form (q', b) or (q', b, pop)), [**behaviour of
  the** A_0**-task**]
– for each $(q', A, \alpha) \in Q \times (\mathsf{Act} \setminus \{A_1\}) \times \mathsf{Abs}_{A_1}$ and $b \in \{0, 1\}$ such that
  $\mathcal{M}_{(q',A,\alpha)}(q) \neq \emptyset$, we have $((\alpha, (q', b)), A, A, q) \in \Delta_A$, [**switch to the** A_1-
  task and reach q **before switching back**]
– for each $(q', A, \alpha) \in Q \times (\mathsf{Act} \setminus \{A_1\}) \times \mathsf{Abs}_{A_1}$ and $(q'', \beta) \in \mathsf{Reach}(q', A, \alpha)$
  such that $\beta \neq \bot$,
  - if $A \neq A_2$, then we have $((\alpha, (q', 0)), A, A_2 A, (\beta, (q'', 1))) \in \Delta_A$ and
    $((\alpha, (q', 1)), A, \varepsilon, (\beta, (q'', 1, \mathsf{pop}))) \in \Delta_A$,
  - if $A = A_2$, then we have $((\alpha, (q', 1)), A_2, A_2, (\beta, (q'', 1))) \subset \Delta_A$,
    [**switch to the** A_1**-task and switch back to the** A_0**-task later by
    launching** A_2]
– for each $(q', A, \alpha) \in Q \times (\mathsf{Act} \setminus \{A_1\}) \times \mathsf{Abs}_{A_1}$, $(q'', \bot) \in \mathsf{Reach}(q', A, \alpha)$ and
  $b \in \{0, 1\}$, we have $((\alpha, (q', b)), A, A, (\emptyset, (q'', b))) \in \Delta_A$,
  [**switch to the** A_1**-task and switch back to the** A_0**-task later when
  the** A_1**-task becomes empty**]
– for each $\alpha \in \mathsf{Abs}_{A_1}$, $b \in \{0, 1\}$ and $A \in \mathsf{Act}_{\mathsf{STD}} \cup \{A_2\}$, $((\alpha, (q, b)), A, A, q) \in$
  Δ_A, [q **is reached when the** A_0**-task is the top task**]
– for each $q' \in Q$ and $\alpha \in \mathsf{Abs}_{A_1}$ with $q' \in \alpha$, $((\alpha, (q', 0)), \bot, \bot, q) \in \Delta_A$.
  [q **is reached after the** A_0**-task becomes empty and the** A_1**-task
  becomes the top task**]

Proposition 5. *Let* $\mathcal{A}$ *be an* STK-*dominating ASM where there are exactly two*
STK-*activities* A_1, A_2 *and* $\mathsf{Aft}(A_2) = \mathsf{Aft}(A_0)$. *Then* q *is reachable from the
initial configuration* (q_0, ε) *in* $\mathcal{A}$ *iff* q *is reachable from the initial configuration*
$((\emptyset, (q_0, 0)), \bot)$ *in* $\mathcal{P}_A$.

6   Related Work

We first discuss *pushdown systems with multiple stacks* (MPDSs) which are the most relevant to ASM. (For space reasons we will skip results on general pushdown systems though.) A multitude of classes of MPDSs have been considered, mostly as a model for *concurrent* recursive programs. In general, an ASM can be encoded as an MPDS. However, this view is hardly profitable as general MPDSs are obviously Turing-complete, leaving the reachability problem undecidable.

To regain decidability at least for reachability, several subclasses of MPDSs were proposed in literature: (1) bounding the number of context-switches [15], or more generally, phases [10], scopes [11], or budgets [3]; (2) imposing a linear ordering on stacks and pop operations being reserved to the first non-empty stack [5]; (3) restricting control states (e.g., *weak* MPDSs [7]). However, our decidable subclasses of ASM admit none of the above bounded conditions. A unified and generalized criterion [12] based on MSO over graphs of bounded tree-width was proposed to show the decidability of the emptiness problem for several restricted classes of automata with auxiliary storage, including MPDSs, automata with queues, or a mix of them. Since ASMs work in a way fairly different from multi-stack models in the literature, it is unclear—literally for us—to obtain the decidability by using bounded tree-width approach. Moreover, [12] only provides decidability proofs, but without complexity upper bounds. Our decision procedure is based on symbolic approaches for pushdown systems, which provides complexity upper bounds and which is amenable to implementation.

Higher-order pushdown systems represent another type of generalization of pushdown systems through higher-order stacks, i.e., a nested "stack of stack" structure [13], with decidable reachability problems [9]. Despite apparent resemblance, the back stack of ASM can *not* be simulated by an order-2 pushdown system. The reason is that the order between tasks in a back stack may be dynamically changed, which is not supported by order-2 pushdown systems.

On a different line, there are some models which have addressed, for instance, GUI activities of Android apps. *Window transition graphs* were proposed for representing the possible GUI activity (window) sequences and their associated events and callbacks, which can capture how the events and callbacks modify the back stack [21]. However, the key mechanisms of back stacks (launch modes and task affinities) were not covered in this model. Moreover, the reachability problem for this model was not investigated. A similar model, labeled transition graph with stack and widget (LATTE [20]) considered the effects of launch modes on the back stacks, but not task affinities. LATTE is essentially a finite-state abstraction of the back stack. However, to faithfully capture the launch modes and task affinities, one needs an infinite-state system, as we have studied here.

7   Conclusion

In this paper, we have introduced Android stack machine to formalize the back stack system of the Android platform. We have also investigated the decidability of the reachability problem of ASM. While the reachability problem of ASM is undecidable in general, we have identified a fragment, i.e., STK-dominating ASM, which is expressive and admits decision procedures for reachability.

The implementation of the decision procedures is in progress. We also plan to consider other features of Android back stack systems, e.g., the "allowTaskReparenting" attribute of activities. A long-term program is to develop an efficient and scalable formal analysis and verification framework for Android apps, towards which the work reported in this paper is the first cornerstone.

References

1. Android documentation. https://developer.android.com/guide/components/activities/tasks-and-back-stack.html
2. Stackoverflow entry: Android singletask or singleinstance launch mode? https://stackoverflow.com/questions/3219726/
3. Abdulla, P.A., Atig, M.F., Rezine, O., Stenman, J.: Multi-pushdown systems with budgets. In: Formal Methods in Computer-Aided Design (FMCAD), pp. 24–33 (2012)
4. Bouajjani, A., Esparza, J., Maler, O.: Reachability analysis of pushdown automata: application to model-checking. In: Mazurkiewicz, A., Winkowski, J. (eds.) CONCUR 1997. LNCS, vol. 1243, pp. 135–150. Springer, Heidelberg (1997). https://doi.org/10.1007/3-540-63141-0_10
5. Breveglieri, L., Cherubini, A., Citrini, C., Crespi-Reghizzi, S.: Multi-push-down languages and grammars. Int. J. Found. Comput. Sci. 7(3), 253–292 (1996)
6. Chen, T., He, J., Song, F., Wang, G., Wu, Z., Yan, J.: Android stack machine (full version) (2018). http://www.dcs.bbk.ac.uk/~taolue/pub-papers/ASM-full.pdf
7. Czerwinski, W., Hofman, P., Lasota, S.: Reachability problem for weak multipushdown automata. In: Proceedings of the 23rd International Conference on (CONCUR), pp. 53–68 (2012)
8. Hao, S., Li, D., Halfond, W.G.J., Govindan, R.: Estimating mobile application energy consumption using program analysis. In: Proceedings of the 35th International Conference on Software Engineering (ICSE), pp. 92–101 (2013)
9. Knapik, T., Niwinski, D., Urzyczyn, P.: Higher-order pushdown trees are easy. In: Proceedings of the 5th International Conference on Foundations of Software Science and Computation Structures (FOSSACS), pp. 205–222 (2002)
10. La Torre, S., Madhusudan, P., Parlato, G.: A robust class of context-sensitive languages. In: Proceedings of the 22nd IEEE Symposium on Logic in Computer Science (LICS), pp. 161–170 (2007)
11. La Torre, S., Napoli, M.: Reachability of multistack pushdown systems with scope-bounded matching relations. In: Proceedings of the 22nd International Conference on Concurrency Theory (CONCUR), pp. 203–218 (2011)
12. Madhusudan, P., Parlato, G.: The tree width of auxiliary storage. In: Proceedings of the 38th ACM SIGPLAN-SIGACT Symposium on Principles of Programming Languages (POPL), pp. 283–294 (2011)
13. Maslov, A.N.: Multilevel stack automata. Probl. Inf. Transm. 15, 1170–1174 (1976)
14. Minsky, M.: Computation: Finite and Infinite Machines. Prentice Hall Int., Upper Saddle River (1967)

15. Qadeer, S., Rehof, J.: Context-bounded model checking of concurrent software. In: Proceedings of the 11th International Conference on Tools and Algorithms for the Construction and Analysis of Systems (TACAS), pp. 93–107 (2005)
16. Ren, C., Zhang, Y., Xue, H., Wei, T., Liu, P.: Towards discovering and understanding task hijacking in android. In: Proceedings of the 24th USENIX Security Symposium (USENIX Security), pp. 945–959 (2015)
17. Song, F.: Analyzing pushdown systems with stack manipulation. Inf. Comput. **259**(1), 41–71 (2018)
18. Song, F., Miao, W., Pu, G., Zhang, M.: On reachability analysis of pushdown systems with transductions: application to Boolean programs with call-by-reference. In: Proceedings of the 26th International Conference on Concurrency Theory (CONCUR), pp. 383–397 (2015)
19. Uezato, Y., Minamide, Y.: Pushdown systems with stack manipulation. In: Proceedings of the 11th International Symposium on Automated Technology for Verification and Analysis (ATVA), pp. 412–426 (2013)
20. Yan, J., Wu, T., Yan, J., Zhang, J.: Widget-sensitive and back-stack-aware GUI exploration for testing android apps. In: Proceedings of the 2017 IEEE International Conference on Software Quality, Reliability and Security (QRS), pp. 42–53 (2017)
21. Yang, S., Zhang, H., Wu, H., Wang, Y., Yan, D., Rountev, A.: Static window transition graphs for android. In: Proceedings of the 30th IEEE/ACM International Conference on Automated Software Engineering (ASE), pp. 658–668 (2015)

Formally Verified
Montgomery Multiplication

Christoph Walther(✉) (iD)

Technische Universität Darmstadt,
Darmstadt, Germany
Chr.Walther@informatik.tu-darmstadt.de

Abstract. We report on a machine assisted verification of an efficient implementation of Montgomery Multiplication which is a widely used method in cryptography for efficient computation of modular exponentiation. We shortly describe the method, give a brief survey of the VeriFun system used for verification, present the formal proofs and report on the effort for creating them. Our work uncovered a serious fault in a published algorithm for computing multiplicative inverses based on Newton-Raphson iteration, thus providing further evidence for the benefit of computer-aided verification.

Keywords: Modular arithmetic · Multiplicative inverses
Montgomery Multiplication · Program verification
Theorem proving by induction

1 Introduction

Montgomery Multiplication [6] is a method for efficient computation of residues $a^j \bmod n$ which are widely used in cryptography, e.g. for RSA, Diffie-Hellman, ElGamal, DSA, ECC etc. [4,5]. The computation of these residues can be seen as an iterative calculation in the commutative ring with identity $R_n = (\mathbb{N}_n, \oplus, \mathsf{i}_n, \odot, 0, 1 \bmod n)$ where $n \geq 1$, $\mathbb{N}_n = \{0, \ldots, n-1\}$, addition defined by $a \oplus b = a + b \bmod n$, inverse operator defined by $\mathsf{i}_n(a) = a \cdot (n-1) \bmod n$, multiplication defined by $a \odot b = a \cdot b \bmod n$, neutral element 0 and identity $1 \bmod n$.

For any $m \in \mathbb{N}$ relatively prime to n, some $m_n^{-1} \in \mathbb{N}_n$ exists such that $m \odot m_n^{-1} = 1 \bmod n$. m_n^{-1} is called the *multiplicative inverse* of m in R_n and is used to define a further commutative ring with identity $R_n^m = (\mathbb{N}_n, \oplus, \mathsf{i}_n, \otimes, 0, m \bmod n)$ where multiplication is defined by $a \otimes b = a \odot b \odot m_n^{-1}$ and identity given as $m \bmod n$. The multiplication $\otimes$ of R_n^m is called *Montgomery Multiplication*.

The rings R_n and R_n^m are isomorphic by the isomorphism $h : R_n \to R_n^m$ defined by $h(a) = a \odot m$ and $h^{-1} : R_n^m \to R_n$ given by $h^{-1}(a) = a \odot m_n^{-1}$. Consequently $a \cdot b \bmod n$ can be calculated in ring R_n^m as well because

$$a \cdot b \bmod n = a \odot b = h^{-1}(h(a \odot b)) = h^{-1}(h(a) \otimes h(b)). \qquad (*)$$

© The Author(s) 2018
H. Chockler and G. Weissenbacher (Eds.): CAV 2018, LNCS 10982, pp. 505–522, 2018.
https://doi.org/10.1007/978-3-319-96142-2_30

```
function redc(x, z, m, n:ℕ):ℕ <=
if m ≠ 0
  then let q := (x + n · (x · z mod m))/m in
          if n > q then q else q − n end_if
        end_let
end_if

function redc*(x, z, m, n, j:ℕ):ℕ <=
if m ≠ 0
  then if n ≠ 0
          then if j = 0
                  then m mod n
                  else redc(x · redc*(x, z, m, n, ⁻(j)), z, m, n)
                end_if
        end_if
end_if
```

Fig. 1. Procedures redc and redc* implementing the Montgomery Reduction

The required operations $h, \otimes$ and h^{-1} can be implemented by the so-called *Montgomery Reduction* redc [6] (displayed in Fig. 1) as stated by Theorem 1:

Theorem 1. *Let* $a, b, n, m \in \mathbb{N}$ *with* $m > n > a$, $n > b$ *and* n, m *relatively prime, let* $I = i_m(n_m^{-1})$ *and let* $M = m^2 \bmod n$. *Then* I *is called the* Montgomery Inverse *and (1)* $h(a) = redc(a \cdot M, I, m, n)$, *(2)* $a \otimes b = redc(a \cdot b, I, m, n)$, *and (3)* $h^{-1}(a) = redc(a, I, m, n)$.

By (∗) and Theorem 1, $a \cdot b \bmod n$ can be computed by procedure redc and consequently $a^j \bmod n$ can be computed by iterated calls of redc (implemented by procedure redc* of Fig. 1) as stated by Theorem 2:

Theorem 2. *Let* a, n, m, I *and* M *like in Theorem 1. Then for all* $j \in \mathbb{N}$:[1]

$$a^j \bmod n = redc(redc^*(redc(a \cdot M, I, m, n), I, m, n, j), I, m, n).$$

By Theorem 2, $j + 2$ calls of redc are required for computing $a^j \bmod n$, viz. one call to map a to $h(a)$, j calls for the Montgomery Multiplications and one call for mapping the result back with h^{-1}. This approach allows for an efficient computation of $a^j \bmod n$ in R_n^m (for sufficient large j), if m is chosen as a power of 2 and some odd number for n, because $x \bmod m$ then can be computed with constant time and x/m only needs an effort proportional to $\log m$ in procedure redc, thus saving the expensive $\bmod n$ operations in R_n.

---

[1] Exponentiation is defined here with $0^0 = 1$ so that $redc(redc^*(redc(0 \cdot M, I, m, n), I, m, n, 0), I, m, n) = 1 \bmod n$ holds in particular.

2   About ✔eriFun

The truth of Theorems 1 and 2 is not obvious at all, and some number theory with modular arithmetic is needed for proving them. Formal proofs are worthwhile because correctness of cryptographic methods is based on these theorems.

```
structure bool                        <= true, false
structure N                           <= 0,⁺(⁻:N)
structure signs                       <= '+', '−'
structure Z                           <= [outfix] ⟨ : ⟩(sign:signs, [outfix]| : N)
structure triple[@T1, @T2, @T3]       <= [outfix] < : > ( [postfix]₁ : @T1,
                                         [postfix]₂ : @T2, [postfix]₃ : @T3 )

lemma z ≠ 0 → [x · (y mod z) ≡ x · y] mod z <= ∀x, y, z : N
if{¬ z = 0, (x · (y mod z) mod z) = (x · y mod z), true}
```

Fig. 2. Data structures and lemmas in ✔eriFun

Proof assistants like Isabelle/HOL, HOL Light, Coq, ACL2 and others have been shown successful for developing formal proofs in Number Theory (see e.g. [14]). Here we use the ✔eriFun system[2] [7,10] to verify correctness of Montgomery Multiplication by proving Theorems 1 and 2. The system's object language consists of universal first-order formulas plus parametric polymorphism. Type variables may be instantiated with polymorphic types. Higher-order functions are not supported. The language provides principles for defining data structures, procedures operating on them, and for statements (called "lemmas") about the data structures and procedures. Unicode symbols may be used and function symbols can be written in out-, in-, pre- and postfix notation so that readability is increased by use of the familiar mathematical notation. Figure 2 displays some examples. The data structure bool and the data structure N for natural numbers built with the constructors 0 and $^+$(...) for the successor function are the only predefined data structures in the system. $^-$(...) is the selector of $^+$(...) thus representing the predecessor function. Subsequently we need integers Z as well which we define in Fig. 2 as signed natural numbers. For instance, the expression $\langle$'−', 42$\rangle$ is a data object of type Z, selector *sign* yields the sign of an integer (like '−' in the example), and selector |...| gives the absolute value of an integer (like 42 in the example). Identifiers preceded by @ denote type variables, and therefore polymorphic triples are defined in Fig. 2. The expression <42, $\langle$'+', 47$\rangle$, $\langle$'−', 5$\rangle$> is an example of a data object of type *triple*[N, Z, Z]. The ith component of a triple is obtained by selector (...)$_i$.

Procedures are defined by *if*- and *case*-conditionals, functional composition and recursion like displayed in Fig. 1. Procedure calls are evaluated eagerly,

---

[2] An acronym for "A Verifier for Functional Programs".

i.e. call-by-value. The use of incomplete conditionals like for redc and redc* results in incompletely defined procedures [12]. Such a feature is required when working with polymorphic data structures but is useful for monomorphic data structures too as it avoids the need for stipulating artificial results, e.g. for $n/0$. Predicates are defined by procedures with result type bool. Procedure function[infix] $> (x, y : \mathbb{N}) : $ bool $<= \ldots$ for deciding the greater-than relation is the only predefined procedure in the system. Upon the definition of a procedure, ✓eriFun's automated termination analysis (based on the method of *Argument-Bounded Functions* [8,11]) is invoked for generating termination hypotheses which are sufficient for the procedure's termination and proved like lemmas. Afterwards induction axioms are computed from the terminating procedures' recursion structure to be on stock for future use.

Lemmas are defined with conditionals $if : bool \times bool \times bool \rightarrow bool$ as the main connective, but negation $\neg$ and *case*-conditionals may be used as well. Only universal quantification is allowed for the variables of a lemma. Figure 2 displays a lemma about (the elsewhere defined) procedure mod (computing the remainder function) which is frequently used in subsequent proofs. The string in the headline (between "lemma" and "$<=$") is just an identifier assigning a name to the lemma for reference and must not be confused with the statement of the lemma given as a boolean term in the lemma body. Some basic lemmas about equality and $>$, e.g. stating transitivity of $=$ and $>$, are predefined in the system. Predefined lemmas are frequently used in almost every case study so that work is eased by having them always available instead of importing them from some proof library.

Lemmas are proved with the *HPL*-calculus (abbreviating *Hypotheses, Programs* and *Lemmas*) [10]. The most relevant proof rules of this calculus are *Induction, Use Lemma, Apply Equation, Unfold Procedure, Case Analysis* and *Simplification*. Formulas are given as sequents of form $H, IH \vdash goal$, where H is a finite set of *hypotheses* given as literals, i.e. negated or unnegated predicate calls and equations, IH is a finite set of *induction hypotheses* given as partially quantified boolean terms and *goal* is a boolean term, called the *goalterm* of the sequent. A deduction in the *HPL*-calculus is represented by a tree whose nodes are given by sequents. A lemma ℓ with body $\forall \ldots goal$ is *verified* iff *(i)* the goalterm of each sequent at a leaf of the proof tree rooted in $\{\}, \{\} \vdash goal$ equals *true* and *(ii)* each lemma applied by *Use Lemma* or *Apply Equation* when building the proof tree is *verified*. The base of this recursive definition is given by lemmas being proved without using other lemmas. Induction hypotheses are treated like *verified* lemmas, however being available only in the sequent they belong to.

The *Induction* rule creates the base and step cases for a lemma from an induction axiom. By choosing *Simplification*, the system's first-order theorem prover, called the *Symbolic Evaluator*, is started for rewriting a sequent's goalterm using the hypotheses and induction hypotheses of the sequent, the definitions of the data structures and procedures as well as the lemmas already *verified*. This reasoner is guided by heuristics, e.g. for deciding whether to use a procedure definition, for speeding up proof search by filtering out useless lemmas, etc. Equality reasoning is implemented by conditional term rewriting with *AC*-matching, where the orientation of equations is heuristically established [13]. The Symbolic Evaluator is a fully automatic tool over which the user has no control, thus leaving the *HPL*-proof rules as the only means to guide the system to a proof.

Also the *HPL*-calculus is controlled by heuristics. When applying the *Verify* command to a lemma, the system starts to compute a proof tree by choosing appropriate *HPL*-proof rules heuristically. If a proof attempt gets stuck, the user must step in by applying a proof rule to some leaf of the proof tree (sometimes after pruning some unwanted branch of the tree), and the system then takes over control again. Also it may happen that a further lemma must be formulated by the user before the proof under consideration can be completed. All interactions are menu driven so that typing in proof scripts is avoided (see [7,10]).

✓eriFun is implemented in JAVA and installers for running the system under *Windows, Unix/Linux* or *Mac* are available from the web [7]. When working with the system, we use proof libraries which had been set up over the years by extending them with definitions and lemmas being of general interest. When importing a definition or a lemma from a library into a case study, all program elements and proofs the imported item depends on are imported as well. The correctness proofs for Montgomery Multiplication depend on 9 procedures and 96 lemmas from our arithmetic proof library, which ranges from simple statements like associativity and commutativity of addition up to more ambitious theorems about primes and modular arithmetic. In the sequel we will only list the lemmas which are essential to understand the proofs and refer to [7] for a complete account of all used lemmas and their proofs.

3 Multiplicative Inverses

We start our development by stipulating how multiplicative inverses are computed. To this effect we have to define some procedure $\mathfrak{I} : \mathbb{N} \times \mathbb{N} \to \mathbb{N}$ satisfying[3]

$$\forall x, y{:}\mathbb{N} \ y \neq 0 \wedge gcd(x,y) = 1 \to [x \cdot \mathfrak{I}(x,y) \equiv 1] \, mod \, y \tag{1}$$

$$\forall x, y, z{:}\mathbb{N} \ y \neq 0 \wedge gcd(x,y) = 1 \to [z \cdot x \cdot \mathfrak{I}(x,y) \equiv z] \, mod \, y \tag{2}$$

$$\forall n, x, y, z{:}\mathbb{N} \ y \neq 0 \wedge gcd(x,y) = 1 \to [n + z \cdot x \cdot \mathfrak{I}(x,y) \equiv n + z] \, mod \, y. \tag{3}$$

Lemma 2 is proved with Lemma 1 and library lemma

$$\forall n, m, x, y{:}\mathbb{N} \ gcd(n,m) = 1 \wedge [m \cdot x \equiv m \cdot y] \, mod \, n \to [x \equiv y] \, mod \, n \tag{4}$$

after instructing the system to use library lemma

$$\forall x, y, z{:}\mathbb{N} \ z \neq 0 \to [x \cdot (y \, mod \, z) \equiv x \cdot y] \, mod \, z \tag{5}$$

---

[3] If $x, y, z \in \mathbb{Z}$ and $n \in \mathbb{N}$, then $n|z$ abbreviates $z \, mod \, n = 0$, where $z \, mod \, n = -(|z| \, mod \, n)$ if $z < 0$, and $[x \equiv y] \, mod \, n$ stands for $n|x - y$. $x \, mod \, n = y \, mod \, n$ is sufficient for $[x \equiv y] \, mod \, n$ but only necessary, if x and y have same polarity.

and √eriFun proves Lemma 3 automatically using Lemma 2 as well as library lemma

$$\forall n, x, y, z : \mathbb{N} \; z \neq 0 \wedge [x \equiv y] \, mod \, z \rightarrow [x + n \equiv y + n] \, mod \, z. \qquad (6)$$

Multiplicative inverses can be computed straightforwardly with Euler's ϕ-function, where Lemma 1 then is proved with Euler's Theorem [7,14]. But this approach is very costly and therefore unsuitable for an implementation of Montgomery Multiplication.

```
function euclid(x, y : N) : triple[N, Z, Z] <=
if y = 0
  then ≪ x, ⟨'+', 1⟩, ⟨'+', 0⟩ ≫
  else let e := euclid(y, (x mod y)), g := (e)₁, s := (e)₂, t := (e)₃ in
      case sign(s) of
        '+' : ≪ g, ⟨'-', |t|⟩, ⟨'+', |s| + (x/y)·|t|⟩ ≫,
        '-' : ≪ g, ⟨'+', |t|⟩, ⟨'-', |s| + (x/y)·|t|⟩ ≫
      end_case
    end_let
end_if

function ℑ_B(x, y : N) : N <=
if y ≠ 0
  then let s := (euclid(x, y))₂ in
      case sign(s) of '+' : (|s| mod y), '-' : y − (|s| mod y) end_case
    end_let
end_if
```

Fig. 3. Computation of multiplicative inverses by the extended Euclidean algorithm

3.1 Bézout's Lemma

A more efficient implementation of procedure $\mathfrak{I}$ is based on Bézout's Lemma stating that the greatest common divisor can be represented as a linear combination of its arguments:

Bézout's Lemma
For all $x, y \in \mathbb{N}$ some $s, t \in \mathbb{Z}$ exist such that $gcd(x, y) = x \cdot s + y \cdot t$.

If $y \neq 0$, $\mathfrak{I}_B(x, y) := s \, mod \, y$ is defined and $gcd(x, y) = 1$ holds, then by Bézout's Lemma $[x \cdot \mathfrak{I}_B(x, y) = x \cdot (s \, mod \, y) \equiv x \cdot s \equiv x \cdot s + y \cdot t = 1] \, mod \, y$. To implement this approach, the integer s need to be computed which can be performed by the extended Euclidean algorithm displayed in Fig. 3. This approach is more efficient because a call of $euclid(x, y)$ (and in turn of $\mathfrak{I}_B(x, y)$ given as in Fig. 3) can be computed in time proportional to $(log \, y)^2$ if $x < y$, whereas the use of Euler's ϕ-function needs time proportional to $2^{log \, y}$ in the context of Montgomery Multiplication (as $\phi(2^{k+1}) = 2^k$).

However, $s \in \mathbb{Z}$ might be negative so that $y + (s \, mod \, y) \in \mathbb{N}$ instead of $s \, mod \, y$ then must be used as the multiplicative inverse of x because the carriers

lemma Bézout's Lemma #1 <= ∀ x, y : ℕ
let e := euclid(x, y), g := (e)₁, s := (e)₂, t := (e)₃ in
  case sign(s) of '+' : x·|s| = y·|t| + g, '−' : x·|s| + g = y·|t| end_case   (7)
end_let

lemma Bézout's Lemma #2 <= ∀ x, y : ℕ (euclid(x, y))₁ = gcd(x, y) .   (8)

Fig. 4. Bézout's Lemma

of the rings R_n and R_n^m are subsets of $\mathbb{N}$. We therefore define $\mathfrak{I}_B$ as shown in Fig. 3 which complicates the proof of Lemma 1 (with $\mathfrak{I}$ replaced by $\mathfrak{I}_B$) as this definition necessitates a proof of $[x \cdot y + x \cdot (s \bmod y) \equiv 1] \bmod y$ if $s < 0$.

Bézout's Lemma is formulated in our system's notation by the pair of lemmas displayed in Fig. 4. When prompted to prove Lemma 7, the system starts a Peano induction upon x but gets stuck in the step case. We therefore command to use induction corresponding to the recursion structure of procedure euclid. ✔eriFun responds by proving the base case and simplifying the induction conclusion in case $sign(s) = $ '+' to

$$y \neq 0 \rightarrow x \cdot |t| + g = (x \bmod y) \cdot |t| + g + |t| \cdot (y-1) \cdot (x/y) + |t| \cdot (x/y) \qquad \text{(i)}$$

(where e abbreviates $euclid(y, (x \bmod y))$, $g := (e)_1$, $s := (e)_2$ and $t := (e)_3$) using the induction hypothesis

$$\forall x' : \mathbb{N} \; let\{e := euclid(x', (x \bmod y)), \; g := (e)_1, \; s := (e)_2, \; t := (e)_3;$$
$$case\{sign(s);$$
$$\text{'+'} : x' \cdot |s| = (x \bmod y) \cdot |t| + g,$$
$$\text{'−'} : x' \cdot |s| + g = (x \bmod y) \cdot |t|\}\}$$

and some basic arithmetic properties. We then instruct the system to use the quotient-remainder theorem for replacing x at the left-hand side of the equation in (i) by $(x/y) \cdot y + (x \bmod y)$ causing ✔eriFun to complete the proof. The system computes a similar proof obligation for case $sign(s) = $ '−' which is proved in the same way.

By "basic arithmetic properties" we mean well known facts like associativity, commutativity, distributivity, cancellation properties etc. of $+, -, \cdot, /, gcd, \ldots$ which are defined and proved in our arithmetic proof library. These facts are used almost everywhere by the Symbolic Evaluator so that we will not mention their use explicitly in the sequel.

When called to prove Lemma 8 by induction corresponding to the recursion structure of procedure euclid, ✔eriFun responds by proving the base case and rewrites the step case with the induction hypothesis to

$$y \neq 0 \rightarrow gcd(x, y) = gcd(y, (x \bmod y)). \qquad \text{(ii)}$$

It then automatically continues with proving (ii) by induction corresponding to the recursion structure of procedure gcd where it succeeds for the base and the step case. Lemma 8 is useful because it relates procedure euclid to procedure gcd of our arithmetic proof library so that all lemmas about gcd can be utilized for the current proofs.

For proving the inverse property

$$\forall x, y{:}\mathbb{N} \ y \neq 0 \wedge gcd(x, y) = 1 \rightarrow [x \cdot \mathfrak{I}_B(x, y) \equiv 1] \ mod \ y \tag{9}$$

of procedure $\mathfrak{I}_B$, we call the system to unfold procedure call $\mathfrak{I}_B(x, y)$. VeriFun responds by proving the statement for case $sign(s) =$ '+' using Bézout's Lemma 7 and 8 and the library lemmas

$$\forall x, y, z{:}\mathbb{N} \ z \neq 0 \wedge z \mid x \rightarrow [x + y \equiv y] \ mod \ z \tag{10}$$

$$\forall x, y{:}\mathbb{N} \ y \neq 0 \rightarrow y \mid x \cdot y \tag{11}$$

as well as (5), but gets stuck in the remaining case with proof obligation

$$y \neq 0 \wedge sign(s) = \ '-' \ \wedge \ g = 1 \rightarrow [x \cdot y - x \cdot (|s| \ mod \ y)] \equiv 1] \ mod \ y \tag{iii}$$

where g abbreviates $(euclid(x, y))_1$ and s stands for $(euclid(x, y))_2$. Proof obligation (iii) represents the unpleasant case of the proof development and necessitates the invention of an auxiliary lemma for completing the proof. After some unsuccessful attempts, we eventually came up with lemma

$$\forall x, y, z, u{:}\mathbb{N} y \neq 0 \wedge y \mid (x \cdot z + u) \wedge x \geq u \rightarrow [x \cdot y - x \cdot (z \ mod \ y) \equiv u] \ mod \ y. \tag{12}$$

For proving (iii), we command to use Lemma 12 for replacing the left-hand side of the congruence in (iii) by g, and VeriFun computes

$$\begin{aligned} y \neq 0 \wedge sign(s) = \ '-' \ \wedge \ g = 1 \rightarrow \\ (x \geq g \rightarrow y \mid (x \cdot |s| + g)) \wedge \\ (x < g \rightarrow [x \cdot y - x \cdot (|s| \ mod \ y) \equiv 1] \ mod \ y. \end{aligned} \tag{iv}$$

Now we can call the system to use Bézout's Lemma 7 for replacing $x \cdot |s| + g$ in (iv) by $y \cdot |t|$ causing VeriFun to complete the proof with Bézout's Lemma 8 and library lemma (11) in case of $x \geq g$ and otherwise showing that $x < g = 1$ entails $x = 0$ and $1 = g = gcd(0, y) = y$ in turn, so that $x \cdot y - x \cdot (|s| \ mod \ y)$ simplifies to 0 and $[0 \equiv 1] \ mod \ y$ rewrites to *true*.

It remains to prove auxiliary lemma (12) for completing the proof of Lemma 9: After being called to use library lemma[4]

$$\forall x, y, z{:}\mathbb{N} \ z \neq 0 \wedge z \mid (x - y) \wedge z \mid (y - x) \rightarrow [x \equiv y] \ mod \ z \tag{13}$$

---

[4] At least one of $z|(x - y)$ or $z|(y - x)$ holds trivially because subtraction is defined such that $a - b = 0$ iff $a \leq b$.

for replacing the left-hand side of the congruence in (12) by u, **✔eriFun** computes

$$y \neq 0 \wedge y \mid (x \cdot z + u) \wedge x \geq u \rightarrow y \mid (u - (x \cdot y - x \cdot (z \bmod y))) \quad \text{(v)}$$

with the library lemmas (11) and

$$\forall x, y, z{:}\mathbb{N}\ z \neq 0 \wedge [x \equiv y]\ mod\ z \rightarrow z \mid (x - y) \quad (14)$$

$$\forall x, y, z, n{:}\mathbb{N}\ n \neq 0 \rightarrow [x + y \cdot (z\ mod\ n) \equiv x + y \cdot z]\ mod\ n. \quad (15)$$

We then command to use library lemma $\forall x, y, z{:}\mathbb{N}\ z \neq 0 \wedge x \leq y \rightarrow x \leq y \cdot z$ (with u substituted for x, x for y and $y - (z\ mod\ y)$ for z) after x factoring out, causing **✔eriFun** to prove (v) with the synthesized lemma[5]

$$\forall x, y{:}\mathbb{N}\ y \neq 0 \rightarrow y > (x\ mod\ y). \quad (16)$$

```
function ℑ_N'(x, k:ℕ):ℕ <=
if 2 > k
  then k
  else let h := ⌈k/2⌉; r := ℑ_N'((x mod 2 ↑ h), h); y := 2 ↑ k in
       (2 · r + ((r · r mod y) · x mod y) mod y)
       end_let
end_if

function ℑ_N(x, y:ℕ):ℕ <= if y ≠ 0 then y − ℑ_N'(x, log₂(y)) end_if
```

Fig. 5. Computation of multiplicative inverses by Newton-Raphson iteration

3.2   Newton's Method

Newton-Raphson iteration is a major tool in arbitrary-precision arithmetic and efficient algorithms for computing multiplicative inverses are developed in combination with Hensel Lifting [2]. Figure 5 displays an implementation by procedure $\mathfrak{I}_N$ for odd numbers x and powers y of 2 (where $\uparrow$ computes exponentiation satisfying $0 \uparrow 0 = 1$). Procedure $\mathfrak{I}_N$ is defined via procedure $\mathfrak{I}_{N'}$ which is obtained from [3], viz. Algorithm 2′ *Recursive Hensel*, where however '−' instead of '+' is used in the result term. Algorithm 2′ was developed to compute a multiplicative inverse of x modulo p^k for any x not dividable by a prime p and returns a negative integer in most cases. By replacing '−' with '+', all calcula tions can be kept within $\mathbb{N}$ so that integer arithmetic is avoided. As procedure $\mathfrak{I}_{N'}$ computes the absolute value of a negative integer computed by Algorithm 2′, one additional subtraction is needed to obtain a multiplicative inverse which is implemented by procedure $\mathfrak{I}_N$. The computation of $\mathfrak{I}_N(x, 2^k)$ only requires $log\ k$ steps (compared to k^2 steps for $\mathfrak{I}_B(x, 2^k)$), and therefore $\mathfrak{I}_N$ is the method of choice for computing a Montgomery Inverse.

---

[5] Synthesized lemmas are a spin-off of the system's termination analysis.

However, Algorithm 2′ is flawed so that we wasted some time with our verification attempts: The four *mod*-calls in the algorithm are not needed for correctness, but care for efficiency as they keep the intermediate numbers small. Now instead of using modulus 2^k for both inner *mod*-calls, Algorithm 2′ calculates $mod\ 2^{\lceil k/2 \rceil}$ thus spoiling correctness. As the flawed algorithm cares for even smaller numbers, the use of $mod\ 2^{\lceil k/2 \rceil}$ could be beneficial indeed, and therefore it was not obvious to us whether we failed in the verification only because some mathematical argumentation was missing. But this consideration put us on the wrong track. Becoming eventually frustrated by the unsuccessful verification attempts, we started ✓eriFun's *Disprover* [1] which—to our surprise—came up with the counter example $x = 3, k = 2$ for Lemma 17 in less than a second.[6] We then repaired the algorithm as displayed in Fig. 5 and subsequently verified it (cf. Lemma 20). Later we learned that the fault in Algorithm 2′ has not been recognized so far and that one cannot do better to patch it as we did.[7]

For proving the inverse property (20) of procedure $\mathfrak{I}_N$, we first have to verify the correctness statement

$$\forall x, k{:}\mathbb{N}\ 2 \nmid x \rightarrow (x \cdot \mathfrak{I}_{N'}(x, k)\ mod\ 2^k) = 2^k - 1 \tag{17}$$

for procedure $\mathfrak{I}_{N'}$: We call the system to use induction corresponding to the recursion structure of procedure $\mathfrak{I}_{N'}$ which provides the induction hypothesis

$$\forall x'{:}\mathbb{N}\ k \geq 2 \wedge 2 \nmid x' \rightarrow (x' \cdot \mathfrak{I}_{N'}(x', \lceil k/2 \rceil)\ mod\ 2^{\lceil k/2 \rceil}) = 2^{\lceil k/2 \rceil} - 1. \tag{18}$$

✓eriFun proves the base case, but gets stuck in the step case with

$$k \geq 2 \wedge 2 \nmid x \rightarrow$$
$$(x \cdot (2A + (x \cdot (A^2\ mod\ 2^k)\ mod\ 2^k)\ mod\ 2^k)\ mod\ 2^k) = 2^k - 1 \tag{i}$$

where A stands for $\mathfrak{I}_{N'}((x\ mod\ 2^{\lceil k/2 \rceil}), \lceil k/2 \rceil)$. By prompting the system to use Lemma 5, proof obligation (i) is simplified to

$$k \geq 2 \wedge 2 \nmid x \rightarrow (2B + B^2\ mod\ 2^k) = 2^k - 1 \tag{ii}$$

(where B abbreviates $x \cdot A$) thus eliminating the formal clutter resulting from the *mod*-calls in procedure $\mathfrak{I}_{N'}$. Next we replace $2B + B^2$ by $(B + 1)^2 - 1$ and then call the system to replace B by $(B/C) \cdot C + R$ where $C = 2^{\lceil k/2 \rceil}$ and $R = ((x\ mod\ C) \cdot A\ mod\ C)$, which is justified by the quotient-remainder theorem as R rewrites to $(B\ mod\ C)$ by library lemma (5). This results in proof obligation

$$k \geq 2 \wedge 2 \nmid x \rightarrow (((B/C) \cdot C + R + 1)^2 - 1\ mod\ 2^k) = 2^k - 1 \tag{iii}$$

---

[6] The Disprover is based on two heuristically controlled disproving calculi, and its implementation provides four selectable execution modes (Fast Search, Extended Search, Simple Terms and Structure Expansion). For difficult problems, the user may support the search for counter examples by presetting some of the universally quantified variables with general terms or concrete values.

[7] Personal communication with Jean-Guillaume Dumas.

and we command to use the induction hypothesis (18) for replacing R in (iii) by $C - 1$. ✔eriFun then responds by computing

$$k \geq 2 \wedge 2 \nmid x \rightarrow (((B/C) \cdot C + C)^2 - 1 \bmod 2^k) = 2^k - 1 \qquad \text{(iv)}$$

using library lemmas $\forall x, y, z{:}\mathbb{N} \; y \neq 0 \wedge z \neq 0 \wedge z \mid y \rightarrow [(x \bmod y) \equiv x] \bmod z$ and (5) to prove $2 \nmid (x \bmod 2^{\lceil k/2 \rceil})$ for justifying the use of the induction hypothesis. When instructed to factor out C in (iv), the system computes

$$k \geq 2 \wedge 2 \nmid x \rightarrow ((2^{\lceil k/2 \rceil})^2 \cdot (B/C + 1)^2 - 1 \bmod 2^k) = 2^k - 1. \qquad \text{(v)}$$

We command to use library lemma

$$\forall x, y, z{:}\mathbb{N} \; z \neq 0 \wedge z \nmid x \wedge z \mid y \wedge y \geq x \rightarrow (y - x \bmod z) = z - (x \bmod z) \qquad \text{(19)}$$

for replacing the left-hand side of the equation in (v) yielding

$$k \geq 2 \wedge 2 \nmid x \rightarrow 2^k - (1 \bmod 2^k) = 2^k - 1 \qquad \text{(vi)}$$

justified by proof obligation

$$k \geq 2 \wedge 2 \nmid x \rightarrow$$
$$2^k \neq 0 \wedge 2^k \nmid 1 \wedge 2^k \mid (2^{\lceil k/2 \rceil})^2 \cdot (B/C + 1)^2 \wedge (2^{\lceil k/2 \rceil})^2 \cdot (B/C + 1)^2 \geq 1$$

which ✔eriFun simplifies to

$$k \geq 2 \wedge 2 \nmid x \rightarrow 2^k \mid (2^{\lceil k/2 \rceil})^2 \cdot (B/C + 1)^2 \qquad \text{(vii)}$$

in a first step. It then uses auxiliary lemma $\forall x{:}\mathbb{N} \; x \leq 2 \cdot \lceil x/2 \rceil$ and the library lemmas (11) and $\forall x, y, z{:}\mathbb{N} \; x \neq 0 \wedge z \leq y \rightarrow x^z \mid x^y$ for rewriting (vii) subsequently to $true$. Finally the system simplifies (vi) to $true$ as well by unfolding the call of procedure mod, and Lemma 17 is proved.

When called to verify the inverse property

$$\forall x, y{:}\mathbb{N} \, 2 \nmid x \wedge 2^?(y) \rightarrow [x \cdot \mathfrak{I}_N(x, y) \equiv 1] \bmod y \qquad \text{(20)}$$

of procedure $\mathfrak{I}_N$ (where $2^?(y)$ decides whether y is a power of 2), ✔eriFun unfolds the call of procedure $\mathfrak{I}_N$ and returns

$$y \geq 2 \wedge 2 \nmid x \wedge 2^?(y) \rightarrow (x \cdot y - x \cdot \mathfrak{I}_{N'}(x, log_2(y)) \bmod y) = 1. \qquad \text{(viii)}$$

Now we instruct the system to use library lemma (19) for replacing the left-hand side of the equation in (viii), and ✔eriFun computes

$$y \geq 2 \wedge 2 \nmid x \wedge 2^?(y) \rightarrow$$
$$(x \cdot \mathfrak{I}_{N'}(x, log_2(y)) \bmod y) \neq 0 \wedge y - (x \cdot \mathfrak{I}_{N'}(x, log_2(y)) \bmod y) = 1 \qquad \text{(ix)}$$

using auxiliary lemma $\forall x, y{:}\mathbb{N} \, 2^?(y) \rightarrow y > \mathfrak{I}_{N'}(x, log_2(y))$ and the library lemmas (11), (14) and

$$\forall x, y, z{:}\mathbb{N} \; x \cdot y > x \cdot z \rightarrow y > z. \qquad \text{(21)}$$

Finally we let the system use library lemma $\forall x{:}\mathbb{N} \, 2^?(x) \rightarrow 2^{log_2(x)} = x$ to replace both moduli y in (ix) by $2^{log_2(y)}$ causing ✔eriFun to rewrite both occurrences of $(x \cdot \mathfrak{I}_{N'}(x, log_2(y)) \bmod y)$ with Lemma 17 to $y - 1$ and proof obligation (ix) to $true$ in turn, thus completing the proof of (20).

function $i(x, y : \mathbb{N}) : \mathbb{N} \mathrel{<=}$ if $y \neq 0$ then $(x \cdot {}^-(y) \bmod y)$ end_if

function $h(x, m, n : \mathbb{N}) : \mathbb{N} \mathrel{<=}$ if $n \neq 0$ then $(x \cdot m \bmod n)$ end_if

function $\otimes(x, y, m, n : \mathbb{N}) : \mathbb{N} \mathrel{<=}$ if $n \neq 0$ then $(x \cdot y \cdot \Im(m, n) \bmod n)$ end_if

function $h^{-1}(x, m, n : \mathbb{N}) : \mathbb{N} \mathrel{<=}$ if $n \neq 0$ then $(x \cdot \Im(m, n) \bmod n)$ end_if

function $\Im(x, y : \mathbb{N}) : \mathbb{N} \mathrel{<=}$ if $2^?(y)$ then $\Im_N(x, y)$ else $\Im_B(x, y)$ end_if

Fig. 6. Procedures for verifying Montgomery Multiplication

4   Correctness of Montgomery Multiplication

We continue by defining procedures for computing the functions $i, h, \otimes$ and h^{-1} as displayed in Fig. 6, where we write $i(x, y)$ instead of $i_y(x)$ in the procedures and lemmas. As we aim to prove correctness of Montgomery Multiplication using procedure $\Im_N$ for computing the Montgomery Inverse with minimal costs, $2 \nmid n \wedge 2^?(m)$ instead of $gcd(n, m) = 1$ must be demanded to enable the use of Lemma 20 when proving the statements of Theorems 1 and 2. However, the multiplicative inverses n_m^{-1} and m_n^{-1} *both* are needed in the *proofs* (whereas only n_m^{-1} is used in *applications* of redc and redc*). Consequently procedure $\Im_N$ cannot be used in the proofs as it obviously fails in computing m_n^{-1} (except for case $n = m = 1$, of course). This problem does not arise if procedure $\Im_B$ is used instead, where $gcd(n, m) = 1$ is demanded, because $\Im_B(n, m) = n_m^{-1}$ and $\Im_B(m, n) = m_n^{-1}$ for any coprimes n and m by Lemma 9. The replacement of $\Im_B$ by $\Im_N$ when computing the Montgomery Inverse then must be justified afterwards by additionally proving

$$\forall x, y : \mathbb{N} \; 2 \nmid x \wedge 2^?(y) \rightarrow \Im_B(x, y) = \Im_N(x, y). \tag{22}$$

However, proving (22) would be a complicated and difficult enterprise because the recursion structures of procedures euclid and $\Im_{N'}$ differ significantly. But we can overcome this obstacle by a simple workaround: We use procedure $\Im$ of Fig. 6 instead of $\Im_B$ in the proofs and let the system verify the inverse property

$$\forall x, y : \mathbb{N} \; y \neq 0 \wedge gcd(x, y) = 1 \rightarrow [x \cdot \Im(x, y) \equiv 1] \bmod y \tag{i}$$

of procedure $\Im$ before: ✔eriFun easily succeeds with library lemma (4) and the inverse property (9) of procedure $\Im_B$ after being instructed to use library lemma $\forall x, y, n : \mathbb{N} \; n \geq 2 \wedge n \mid y \wedge gcd(x, y) = 1 \rightarrow n \nmid x$ and the inverse property (20) of procedure $\Im_N$. Consequently $\Im(n, m) = n_m^{-1}$ and $\Im(m, n) = m_n^{-1}$ for any coprimes n and m, and therefore $\Im$ can be used in the proofs. The use of $\Im_N$ instead of $\Im$ when computing the Montgomery Inverse is justified afterwards with lemma

$$\forall x, y : \mathbb{N} \; 2^?(y) \rightarrow \Im(x, y) = \Im_N(x, y)$$

having an obviously trivial (and automatic) proof.

Central for the proofs of Theorems 1 and 2 is the key property

$$\forall m, n, x{:}\mathbb{N} \quad m > n \wedge n \cdot m > x \wedge gcd(n, m) = 1 \to$$
$$redc(x, \mathrm{i}(\mathfrak{I}(n, m), m), m, n) = (x \cdot \mathfrak{I}(m, n) \bmod n) \tag{23}$$

of procedure redc: For proving Theorem 1.1

$$\forall m, n, a{:}\mathbb{N} \; m > n > a \wedge gcd(n, m) = 1 \to$$
$$h(a, m, n) = redc(a \cdot (m \cdot m \bmod n), \mathrm{i}(\mathfrak{I}(n, m), m), m, n) \tag{Thm 1.1}$$

we command to use (23) for replacing the right-hand side of the equation by $(a \cdot (m \cdot m \bmod n) \cdot \mathfrak{I}(m, n) \bmod n)$. The system then replaces the left-hand side of the equation with $a \cdot m \bmod n$ by unfolding procedure call $h(a, m, n)$ and simplifies the resulting equation to *true* with Lemma 2, the synthesized lemma (16) and the library lemmas (5) and

$$\forall x, y, u, v{:}\mathbb{N} \; x > y \wedge u > v \to x \cdot u > y \cdot v. \tag{24}$$

Theorems 1.2 and 1.3, viz.

$$\forall m, n, a, b{:}\mathbb{N} \; m > n > a \wedge n > b \wedge gcd(n, m) = 1$$
$$\to \otimes(a, b, m, n) = redc(a \cdot b, \mathrm{i}(\mathfrak{I}(n, m), m), m, n) \tag{Thm 1.2}$$

$$\forall m, n, a{:}\mathbb{N} \; m > n > a \wedge gcd(n, m) = 1$$
$$\to h^{-1}(a, m, n) = redc(a, \mathrm{i}(\mathfrak{I}(n, m), m), m, n) \tag{Thm 1.3}$$

are (automatically) proved in the same way.

Having proved Theorem 1, it remains to verify the key property (23) for procedure redc (before we consider Theorem 2 subsequently). We start by proving that division by m in R_n can be expressed by $\mathfrak{I}$: We call the system to prove

$$\forall m, n, x{:}\mathbb{N} \; n \neq 0 \wedge m \mid x \wedge gcd(n, m) = 1 \to [x/m \equiv x \cdot \mathfrak{I}(m, n)] \bmod n \tag{25}$$

and **✓eriFun** automatically succeeds with Lemma 2 and the library lemmas (4) and $\forall x, y, z{:}\mathbb{N} y \neq 0 \wedge y \mid x \to (x/y) \cdot y = x$.

As a consequence of Lemma 25, the quotient q in procedure redc can be expressed in R_n by $\mathfrak{I}$ in particular (if redc is called with the Montgomery Inverse as actual parameter for the formal parameter z), which is stated by lemma

$$\forall m, n, x{:}\mathbb{N} \; n \neq 0 \wedge gcd(n, m) = 1$$
$$\to [(x + n \cdot (x \cdot \mathrm{i}(\mathfrak{I}(n, m), m) \bmod m))/m \equiv x \cdot \mathfrak{I}(m, n)] \bmod n. \tag{26}$$

For obtaining a proof, we command to use Lemma 25 for replacing the left-hand side of the congruence in (26) by $(x + n \cdot (x \cdot \mathrm{i}(\mathfrak{I}(n, m), m) \bmod m)) \cdot \mathfrak{I}(m, n)$

causing **✓eriFun** to complete the proof using Lemma 3 as well as the library lemmas (5), (10), (11), (15) and $\forall x, y : \mathbb{N} \ y \neq 0 \to y \mid (x + (y-1) \cdot x)$.

An obvious correctness demand for the method is that each call of redc (under the given requirements) computes some element of the residue class $mod \ n$. This is guaranteed by the conditional subtraction of n from the quotient q in the body of procedure redc. However, at most one subtraction of n from q results in the desired property only if $n + n > q$ holds, which is formulated by lemma

$$\forall m, n, x : \mathbb{N} \ m \cdot n > x \to n + n > (x + n \cdot (x \cdot i(\mathfrak{I}(n,m), m) \ mod \ m))/m. \quad (27)$$

We prompt the system to use a case analysis upon $m \cdot (n+n) > x + n \cdot (x \cdot i(\mathfrak{I}(n,m), m) \ mod \ m)$ causing **✓eriFun** to prove the statement in the positive case with the library lemmas (5) and $\forall x, y, z : \mathbb{N} \ x \cdot z > y \to x > y/z$ and to verify it in the negative case with the synthesized lemma (16) and the library lemmas (5), (21) and $\forall x, y, u, v : \mathbb{N} \ x > y \land u \geq v \to x + u > y + v$.

Now the $mod \ n$ property of procedure redc can be verified by proving lemma

$$\forall m, n, x : \mathbb{N} \ m > n \land n \cdot m > x \land gcd(n, m) = 1 \to$$
$$redc(x, i(\mathfrak{I}(n,m), m), m, n) = (redc(x, i(\mathfrak{I}(n,m), m), m, n) \ mod \ n). \quad (28)$$

We let the system unfold the call of procedure mod in (28) causing **✓eriFun** to use the synthesized lemma (16) for computing the simplified proof obligation

$$m > n \land n \cdot m > x \land gcd(n, m) = 1 \to n > redc(x, i(\mathfrak{I}(n,m), m), m, n). \quad (i)$$

Then we command to unfold the call of procedure redc which simplifies to

$$m > n \land n \cdot m > x \land gcd(n, m) = 1 \land$$
$$(x + n \cdot (x \cdot i(\mathfrak{I}(n,m), m) \ mod \ m))/m \geq n$$
$$\to n > (x + n \cdot (x \cdot i(\mathfrak{I}(n,m), m) \ mod \ m))/m - n. \quad (ii)$$

Finally we let the system use library lemma $\forall x, y, z : \mathbb{N} \ x > y \land y \geq z \to x - z > y - z$ resulting in proof obligation

$$m > n \land n \cdot m > x \land gcd(n, m) = 1$$
$$\land (x + n \cdot (x \cdot i(\mathfrak{I}(n,m), m) \ mod \ m))/m \geq n$$
$$[\ n + n > (x + n \cdot (x \cdot i(\mathfrak{I}(n,m), m) \ mod \ m))/m \land$$
$$\land (x + n \cdot (x \cdot i(\mathfrak{I}(n,m), m) \ mod \ m))/m \geq n$$
$$\to (n + n) - n > (x + n \cdot (x \cdot i(\mathfrak{I}(n,m), m) \ mod \ m))/m - n]$$
$$\to n > (x + n \cdot (x \cdot i(\mathfrak{I}(n,m), m) \ mod \ m))/m - n \quad (iii)$$

which simplifies to

$$m > n \land n \cdot m > x \land gcd(n, m) = 1$$
$$\land (x + n \cdot (x \cdot i(\mathfrak{I}(n,m), m) \ mod \ m))/m \geq n$$
$$\land (n + n) - n > (x + n \cdot (x \cdot i(\mathfrak{I}(n,m), m) \ mod \ m))/m - n$$
$$\to n > (x + n \cdot (x \cdot i(\mathfrak{I}(n,m), m) \ mod \ m))/m - n \quad (iv)$$

by Lemma 27 and to *true* in turn using the plus-minus cancellation.

Now all lemmas for proving the key lemma (23) are available: We demand to use Lemma 28 for replacing the left-hand side of the equation in (23) by $(redc(x, \mathsf{i}(\mathfrak{I}(n,m),m),m,n) \bmod n)$ and to apply lemma (26) for replacing the right-hand side by $((x+n \cdot (x \cdot \mathsf{i}(\mathfrak{I}(n,m),m) \bmod m))/m \bmod n)$ resulting in the simplified proof obligation

$$m > n \wedge n \cdot m > x \wedge gcd(n,m) = 1 \rightarrow$$
$$[redc(x, \mathsf{i}(\mathfrak{I}(n,m),m),m,n) \equiv (x+n \cdot (x \cdot \mathsf{i}(\mathfrak{I}(n,m),m) \bmod m))/m] \bmod n.$$
$$\text{(v)}$$

Then we unfold the call of procedure redc causing the system to prove (v) with library lemma (5).

Having proved the key lemma (23), the proof of Theorem 2

$$\forall m,n,a,j{:}\mathbb{N} \ \ m > n > a \wedge gcd(n,m) = 1 \rightarrow$$
$$(a^j \bmod n) = redc(redc^*(redc(a \cdot M,I,m,n),I,m,n,j),I,m,n) \quad \text{(Thm 2)}$$

(where $M = ((m \cdot m) \bmod n)$ and $I = \mathsf{i}(\mathfrak{I}(n,m),m))$ is easily obtained by support of a further lemma, viz.

$$\forall m,n,a,j{:}\mathbb{N} \ \ m > n > a \wedge gcd(n,m) = 1 \rightarrow$$
$$(m \cdot a^j \bmod n) = redc^*(redc(a \cdot M,I,m,n),I,m,n,j). \quad \text{(29)}$$

When called to use Peano induction upon j for proving (29), ✔eriFun proves the base case and rewrites the step case with the induction hypothesis to

$$m > n > a \wedge gcd(n,m) = 1 \wedge j \neq 0 \rightarrow$$
$$(m \cdot a^{j-1} \cdot a \bmod n) = redc(redc(a \cdot M,I,m,n) \cdot (m \cdot a^{j-1} \bmod n),I,m,n). \quad \text{(vi)}$$

Then we command to replace both calls of redc with the key lemma (23) causing ✔eriFun to succeed with the lemmas (2), (5), (16) and (24).

Finally the system proves (Thm 2) using lemmas (2), (5), (16), (29) and library lemma $\forall x,y,z{:}\mathbb{N} \ x \neq 0 \wedge y > z \rightarrow x \cdot y > z$ after being prompted to use (Thm 1.3) for replacing the right-hand side of the equation in (Thm 2).

5   Discussion and Conclusion

We presented machine assisted proofs verifying an efficient implementation of Montgomery Multiplication, where we developed the proofs ourselves as we are not aware of respective proofs published elsewhere. Our work also uncovered a serious fault in a published algorithm for computing multiplicative inverses based on Newton-Raphson Iteration [3], which could have dangerous consequences (particularly when used in cryptographic applications) if remained undetected.

	Proc.	Lem.	Rules	User	System	%	Steps	mm:ss
$\mathfrak{I}_B(n,m) = n_m^{-1}$	8 (7)	49 (3)	241 (39)	36 (3)	205 (36)	85, 1 (92, 3)	3171	0:19
$\mathfrak{I}_N(n,m) = n_m^{-1}$	10 (9)	76 (3)	368 (59)	59 (3)	309 (56)	84, 0 (94, 9)	6692	1:32
Theorems 1 & 2	20 (12)	116 (3)	547 (78)	96 (6)	451 (72)	82, 4 (92, 3)	9739	2:19

Fig. 7. Proof statistics

Figure 7 displays the effort for obtaining the proofs (including all procedures and lemmas which had been imported from our arithmetic proof library). Column *Proc.* counts the number of user defined procedures (the recursively defined ones given in parentheses), *Lem.* is the number of user defined lemmas (the number of synthesized lemmas given in parentheses), and *Rules* counts the total number of *HPL*-proof rule applications, separated into user invoked (*User*) and system initiated (*System*) ones (with the number of uses of *Induction* given in parentheses). Column *%* gives the automation degree, i.e. the ratio between *System* and *Rules*, *Steps* lists the number of first-order proof steps performed by the Symbolic Evaluator and *Time* displays the runtime of the Symbolic Evaluator.[8]

The first two rows show the effort for proving Lemmas 9 and 20 as illustrated in Sect. 3. As it can be observed from the numbers, verifying the computation of multiplicative inverses by Newton-Raphson Iteration is much more challenging for the system and for the user than the method based on Bézout's Lemma. Row *Theorems 1 and 2* below displays the effort for proving Theorems 1 and 2 as illustrated in Sect. 4 (with the effort for the proofs of Lemmas 9 and 20 included).

The numbers in Fig. 7 almost coincide with the statistics obtained for other case studies in Number Theory performed with the system (see e.g. [14] and also [7] for more examples), viz. an automation degree of $\sim$85% and a success rate of $\sim$95% for the induction heuristic. All termination proofs (hence all required induction axioms in turn) had been obtained without user support, where 6 of the 12 recursively defined procedures, viz. mod, /, gcd, $\log_2$, euclid and $\mathfrak{I}_{N'}$, do not terminate by structural recursion.[9] While an automation degree up to 100% can be achieved in mathematically simple domains, e.g. when sorting lists [7,9], values of 85% and below are not that satisfying when concerned with *automated* reasoning. The cause is that quite often elaborate ideas for developing a proof are needed in Number Theory which are beyond the ability of the system's heuristics guiding the proof search.[10] We also are not aware of other reasoning systems offering more machine support for obtaining proofs in this difficult domain.

---

[8] Time refers to running **√eriFun** 3.5 under *Windows 7 Enterprise* with an INTEL Core i7-2640M 2.80 GHz CPU using JAVA 1.8.0_45.

[9] Procedure $2^7(\ldots)$ is not user defined, but synthesized as the *domain procedure* [12] of the incompletely defined procedure $\log_2$.

[10] Examples are the use of the quotient-remainder theorem for proving (i) in Sect. 3.1 and (iii) in Sect. 3.2 which are the essential proof steps there although more complex proof obligations result.

From the user's perspective, this case study necessitated more work than expected, and it was a novel experience for us to spend some effort for verifying a very small and non-recursively defined procedure. The reason is that correctness of procedure redc depends on some non-obvious and tricky number theoretic principles which made it difficult to spot the required lemmas. In fact, almost all effort was spend for the invention of the auxiliary lemmas in Sect. 4 and of Lemma 12 in Sect. 3.1. Once the "right" lemma for verifying a given proof obligation eventually was found, its proof turned out to be a routine task. The proof of Lemma 17 is an exception as it required some thoughts to create it and some effort as well to lead the system (thus spoiling the proof statistics). Proof development was significantly supported by the system's *Disprover* [1] which (besides detecting the fault in Algorithm 2′) often helped not to waste time with trying to prove a false conjecture, where the computed counterexamples provided useful hints how to debug a lemma draft.

References

1. Aderhold, M., Walther, C., Szallies, D., Schlosser, A.: A fast disprover for √eriFun. In: Ahrendt, W., Baumgartner, P., de Nivelle, H. (eds.) Proc. Workshop on Non-Theorems, Non-Validity, Non-Provability, DISPROVING 2006, Seattle, WA, pp. 59–69 (2006). http://verifun.de/documents
2. Brent, R., Zimmermann, P.: Modern Computer Arithmetic. Cambridge University Press, New York (2010)
3. Dumas, J.: On Newton-Raphson iteration for multiplicative inverses modulo prime powers. IEEE Trans. Comput. **63**(8), 2106–2109 (2014). https://doi.org/10.1109/TC.2013.94
4. Hankerson, D., Menezes, A.J., Vanstone, S.: Guide to Elliptic Curve Cryptography. Springer, Secaucus (2003). https://doi.org/10.1007/b97644
5. Menezes, A.J., Oorschot, P.C.V., Vanstone, S.A., Rivest, R.L.: Handbook of Applied Cryptography. CRC Press Inc., Boca Raton (2001)
6. Montgomery, P.L.: Modular multiplication without trial division. Math. Comput. **44**(170), 519–521 (1985). https://doi.org/10.1090/S0025-5718-1985-0777282-X
7. VeriFun. http://www.verifun.de
8. Walther, C.: On proving the termination of algorithms by machine. Artif. Intell. **71**(1), 101–157 (1994). https://doi.org/10.1016/0004-3702(94)90063-9
9. Walther, C.: A largely automated verification of GHC's natural mergesort. Technical report VFR 17/01, FB Informatik, Techn. Universität Darmstadt (2017)
10. Walther, C., Schweitzer, S.: Verification in the classroom. J. Autom. Reason. **32**(1), 35–73 (2004). https://doi.org/10.1023/B:JARS.0000021872.64036.41
11. Walther, C., Schweitzer, S.: Automated termination analysis for incompletely defined programs. In: Baader, F., Voronkov, A. (eds.) LPAR-11. LNCS, vol. 3452, pp. 332–346. Springer, Heidelberg (2005). https://doi.org/10.1007/978-3-540-32275-7_22
12. Walther, C., Schweitzer, S.: Reasoning about incompletely defined programs. In: Sutcliffe, G., Voronkov, A. (eds.) LPAR-12. LNCS, vol. 3835, pp. 427–442. Springer, Heidelberg (2005). https://doi.org/10.1007/11591191_30

522   C. Walther

13. Walther, C., Schweitzer, S.: A pragmatic approach to equality reasoning. Technical report VFR 06/02, FB Informatik, Technische Universität Darmstadt (2006). http://verifun.de/documents
14. Walther, C., Wasser, N.: Fermat, Euler, Wilson - Three case studies in number theory. J. Autom. Reason. **59**(2), 267–286 (2017). https://doi.org/10.1007/s10817-016-9387-z

Inner and Outer Approximating Flowpipes for Delay Differential Equations

Eric Goubault, Sylvie Putot[✉], and Lorenz Sahlmann

LIX, CNRS and École Polytechnique,
Palaiseau, France
putot@lix.polytechnique.fr

Abstract. Delay differential equations are fundamental for modeling networked control systems where the underlying network induces delay for retrieving values from sensors or delivering orders to actuators. They are notoriously difficult to integrate as these are actually functional equations, the initial state being a function. We propose a scheme to compute inner and outer-approximating flowpipes for such equations with uncertain initial states and parameters. Inner-approximating flowpipes are guaranteed to contain only reachable states, while outer-approximating flowpipes enclose all reachable states. We also introduce a notion of robust inner-approximation, which we believe opens promising perspectives for verification, beyond property falsification. The efficiency of our approach relies on the combination of Taylor models in time, with an abstraction or parameterization in space based on affine forms, or zonotopes. It also relies on an extension of the mean-value theorem, which allows us to deduce inner-approximating flowpipes, from flowpipes outer-approximating the solution of the DDE and its Jacobian with respect to constant but uncertain parameters and initial conditions. We present some experimental results obtained with our C++ implementation.

1   Introduction

Nowadays, many systems are composed of networks of control systems. These systems are highly critical, and formal verification is an essential element for their social acceptability. When the components of the system to model are distributed, delays are naturally introduced in the feedback loop. They may significantly alter the dynamics, and impact safety properties that we want to ensure for the system. The natural model for dynamical systems with such delays is Delay Differential Equations (DDE), in which time derivatives not only depend on the current state, but also on past states. Reachability analysis, which involves computing the set of states reached by the dynamics, is a fundamental tool for the verification of such systems. As the reachable sets are not exactly computable, approximations are used. In particular, outer (also called over)-approximating

© The Author(s) 2018
H. Chockler and G. Weissenbacher (Eds.): CAV 2018, LNCS 10982, pp. 523–541, 2018.
https://doi.org/10.1007/978-3-319-96142-2_31

flowpipes are used to prove that error states will never be reached, whereas inner (also called under)-approximating flowpipes are used to prove that desired states will actually be reached, or to falsify properties. We propose in this article a method to compute both outer- and inner-approximating flowpipes for DDEs.

We concentrate on systems that can be modeled as parametric fixed-delay systems of DDEs, where both the initial condition and right-hand side of the system depend on uncertain parameters, but with a unique constant and exactly known delay:

$$\begin{cases} \dot{z}(t) = f(z(t), z(t-\tau), \beta) & \text{if } t \in [t_0 + \tau, T] \\ z(t) = z_0(t, \beta) & \text{if } t \in [t_0, t_0 + \tau] \end{cases} \quad (1)$$

where the continuous vector of variables z belongs to a state-space domain $\mathcal{D} \subseteq \mathbb{R}^n$, the (constant) vector of parameters β belongs to the domain $\mathcal{B} \subseteq \mathbb{R}^m$, and $f : \mathcal{D} \times \mathcal{D} \times \mathcal{B} \to \mathcal{D}$ is C^∞ and such that Eq. (1) admits a unique solution[1] on the time interval $[t_0, T]$. The initial condition is defined on $t \in [t_0, t_0 + \tau]$ by a function $z_0 : \mathbb{R}^+ \times \mathcal{B} \to \mathcal{D}$. The method introduced here also applies in the case when the set of initial states is given as the solution of an uncertain system of ODEs instead of being defined by a function. Only the initialization of the algorithm will differ. When several constant delays occur in the system, the description of the method is more complicated, but the same method applies.

Example 1. We will exemplify our method throughout the paper on the system

$$\begin{cases} \dot{x}(t) = -x(t) \cdot x(t-\tau) =: f(x(t), x(t-\tau), \beta) & t \in [0, T] \\ x(t) = x_0(t, \beta) = (1 + \beta t)^2 & t \in [-\tau, 0] \end{cases}$$

We take $\beta \in \left[\frac{1}{3}, 1\right]$, which defines a family of initial functions, and we fix $\tau = 1$.

This system is a simple but not completely trivial example, for which we have an analytical solution on the first time steps, as detailed in Example 4.

Contributions and Outline. In this work, we extend the method introduced by Goubault and Putot [16] for ODEs, to the computation of inner and outer flow-pipes of systems of DDEs. We claim, and experimentally demonstrate with our prototype implementation, that the method we propose here for DDEs is both simple and efficient. Relying on outer-approximations and generalized interval computations, all computations can be safely rounded, so that the results are guaranteed to be sound. Finally, we can compute inner-approximating flowpipes combining existentially and universally quantified parameters, which offers some strong potential for property verification, beyond falsification.

In Sect. 2, we first define the notions of inner and outer-approximating flow-pipes, as well as robust inner-approximations, and state some preliminaries on generalized interval computations, which are instrumental in our inner flowpipes computations. We then present in Sect. 3 our method for outer-approximating

---

[1] We refer the reader to [12, 27] for the conditions on f.

solutions to DDEs. It is based on the combination of Taylor models in time with a space abstraction relying on zonotopes. Section 4 relies on this approach to compute outer-approximations of the Jacobian of the solution of the DDE with respect to the uncertain parameters, using variational equations. Inner-approximating tubes are obtained from these using a generalized mean-value theorem introduced in Sect. 2. We finally demonstrate our method in Sect. 5, using our C++ prototype implementation, and show its superiority in terms of accuracy and efficiency compared to the state of the art.

Related Work. Reachability analysis for systems described by ordinary differential equations, and their extension to hybrid systems, has been an active topic of research in the last decades. Outer-approximations have been dealt with ellipsoidal [20], sub-polyhedral techniques, such as zonotopes or support functions, and Taylor model based methods, for both linear and non-linear systems [2,4–6,10,14,17,26]. A number of corresponding implementations exist [1,3,7,13,22,25,29]. Much less methods have been proposed, that answer the more difficult problem of inner-approximation. The existing approaches use ellipsoids [21] or non-linear approximations [8,16,19,31], but they are often computationally costly and imprecise. Recently, an interval-based method [24] was introduced for bracketing the positive invariant set of a system without relying on integration. However, it relies on space discretization and has only been applied successfully, as far as we know, to low dimensional systems.

Taylor methods for outer-approximating reachable sets of DDEs have been used only recently, in [28,32]. We will demonstrate that our approach improves the efficiency and accuracy over these interval-based Taylor methods.

The only previous work we know of for computing inner-approximations of solutions to DDEs, is the method of Xue et al. [30], extending the approach proposed for ODEs in [31]. Their method is based on a topological condition and a careful inspection of what happens at the boundary of the initial condition. We provide in the section dedicated to experiments a comparison to the few experimental results given in [30].

2 Preliminaries on Outer and Inner Approximations

Notations and Definitions. Let us introduce some notations that we will use throughout the paper. Set valued quantities, scalar or vector valued, corresponding to uncertain inputs or parameters, are noted with bold letters, e.g x. When an approximation is introduced by computation, we add brackets: outer-approximating enclosures are noted in bold and enclosed within inward facing brackets, e.g. $[x]$, and inner-approximations are noted in bold and enclosed within outward facing brackets, e.g. $]x[$.

An outer-approximating extension of a function $f : \mathbb{R}^m \to \mathbb{R}^n$ is a function $[f] : \mathcal{P}(\mathbb{R}^m) \to \mathcal{P}(\mathbb{R}^n)$, such that for all x in $\mathcal{P}(\mathbb{R}^m)$, $\mathrm{range}(f, x) = \{f(x), x \in x\} \subseteq [f](x)$. Dually, inner-approximations determine a set of values proved to belong to the range of the function over some input set. An inner-approximating extension of f is a function $]f[: \mathcal{P}(\mathbb{R}^m) \to \mathcal{P}(\mathbb{R}^n)$, such that for all $\boldsymbol{x}$ in $\mathcal{P}(\mathbb{R}^m)$, $]f[(\boldsymbol{x}) \subseteq \text{range}(f, \boldsymbol{x})$. Inner and outer approximations can be interpreted as quantified propositions: $\text{range}(f, \boldsymbol{x}) \subseteq [\boldsymbol{z}]$ can be written $(\forall x \in \boldsymbol{x})(\exists z \in [\boldsymbol{z}])(f(x) = z)$, while $]\boldsymbol{z}[\subseteq \text{range}(f, \boldsymbol{x})$ can be written $(\forall z \in]\boldsymbol{z}[)(\exists x \in \boldsymbol{x})(f(x) = z)$.

Let $\varphi(t, \beta)$ for time $t \geq t_0$ denote the time trajectory of the dynamical system (1) for a parameter value β, and $\boldsymbol{z}(t, \boldsymbol{\beta}) = \{\varphi(t, \beta), \beta \in \boldsymbol{\beta}\}$ the set of states reachable at time t for the set of parameter values $\boldsymbol{\beta}$. We extend the notion of outer and inner-approximations to the case where the function is the solution $\varphi(t, \beta)$ of system (1) over the set $\boldsymbol{\beta}$. An outer-approximating flowpipe is given by an outer-approximation of the set of reachable states, for all t in a time interval:

Definition 1 (Outer-approximation). *Given a vector of uncertain (constant) parameters or inputs $\beta \in \boldsymbol{\beta}$, an outer-approximation at time t of the reachable set of states, is $[\boldsymbol{z}](t, \boldsymbol{\beta}) \supseteq \boldsymbol{z}(t, \boldsymbol{\beta})$, such that $(\forall \beta \in \boldsymbol{\beta})(\exists z \in [\boldsymbol{z}](t, \boldsymbol{\beta}))(\varphi(t, \beta) = z)$.*

Definition 2 (Inner-approximation). *Given a vector of uncertain (constant) parameters or inputs $\beta \in \boldsymbol{\beta}$, an inner-approximation at time t of the reachable set, is $]\boldsymbol{z}[(t, \boldsymbol{\beta}) \subseteq \boldsymbol{z}(t, \boldsymbol{\beta})$ such that $(\forall z \in]\boldsymbol{z}[(t, \boldsymbol{\beta}))(\exists \beta \in \boldsymbol{\beta})(\varphi(t, \beta) = z)$.*

In words, any point of the inner flowpipe is the solution at time t of system (1), for some value of $\beta \in \boldsymbol{\beta}$. If the outer and inner approximations are computed accurately, they approximate with arbitrary precision the exact reachable set.

Our method will also solve the more general robust inner-approximation problem of finding an inner-approximation of the reachable set, robust to uncertainty on an uncontrollable subset $\beta_{\mathcal{A}}$ of the vector of parameters β:

Definition 3 (Robust inner-approximation). *Given a vector of uncertain (constant) parameters or inputs $\beta = (\beta_{\mathcal{A}}, \beta_{\mathcal{E}}) \in \boldsymbol{\beta}$, an inner-approximation of the reachable set $\boldsymbol{z}(t, \boldsymbol{\beta})$ at time t, robust with respect to $\beta_{\mathcal{A}}$, is a set $]\boldsymbol{z}[_{\mathcal{A}}(t, \boldsymbol{\beta}_{\mathcal{A}}, \boldsymbol{\beta}_{\mathcal{E}})$ such that $(\forall z \in]\boldsymbol{z}[_{\mathcal{A}}(t, \boldsymbol{\beta}_{\mathcal{A}}, \boldsymbol{\beta}_{\mathcal{E}}))(\forall \beta_{\mathcal{A}} \in \boldsymbol{\beta}_{\mathcal{A}})(\exists \beta_{\mathcal{E}} \in \boldsymbol{\beta}_{\mathcal{E}})(\varphi(t, \beta_{\mathcal{A}}, \beta_{\mathcal{E}}) = z)$.*

Outer and Inner Interval Approximations. Classical intervals are used in many situations to rigorously compute with interval domains instead of reals, usually leading to outer-approximations of function ranges over boxes. We denote the set of classical intervals by $\mathbb{IR} = \{[\underline{x}, \overline{x}], \underline{x} \in \mathbb{R}, \overline{x} \in \mathbb{R}, \underline{x} \leq \overline{x}\}$. Intervals are non-relational abstractions, in the sense that they rigorously approximate independently each component of a vector function f. We thus consider in this section a function $f : \mathbb{R}^m \to \mathbb{R}$. The natural interval extension consists in replacing real operations by their interval counterparts in the expression of the function. A generally more accurate extension relies on a linearization by the mean-value theorem. Suppose f is differentiable over the interval $\boldsymbol{x}$. Then, the mean-value theorem implies that $(\forall x_0 \in \boldsymbol{x})(\forall x \in \boldsymbol{x})(\exists c \in \boldsymbol{x})(f(x) = f(x_0) + f'(c)(x - x_0))$. If we can bound the range of the gradient of f over $\boldsymbol{x}$, by $[\boldsymbol{f'}](\boldsymbol{x})$, then we can derive the following interval enclosure, usually called the mean-value extension: for any $x_0 \in \boldsymbol{x}$, $\text{range}(f, \boldsymbol{x}) \subseteq f(x_0) + [\boldsymbol{f'}](\boldsymbol{x})(\boldsymbol{x} - x_0)$.

Example 2. Consider $f(x) = x^2 - x$, its range over $x = [2, 3]$ is $[2, 6]$. The natural interval extension of f, evaluated on $[2, 3]$, is $[f]([2, 3]) = [2, 3]^2 - [2, 3] = [1, 7]$. The mean-value extension gives $f(2.5) + [f']([2, 3])([2, 3] - 2.5) = [1.25, 6.25]$, using $x_0 = 2.5$ and $[f'](x) = 2x - 1$.

Modal Intervals and Kaucher Arithmetic. The results introduced in this section are mostly based on the work of Goldsztejn *et al.* [15] on modal intervals. Let us first introduce generalized intervals, i.e., intervals whose bounds are not ordered, and the Kaucher arithmetic [18] on these intervals.

The set of generalized intervals is denoted by $\mathbb{IK} = \{x = [\underline{x}, \overline{x}], \underline{x} \in \mathbb{R}, \overline{x} \in \mathbb{R}\}$. Given two real numbers $\underline{x}$ and $\overline{x}$, with $\underline{x} \le \overline{x}$, one can consider two generalized intervals, $[\underline{x}, \overline{x}]$, which is called *proper*, and $[\overline{x}, \underline{x}]$, which is called *improper*. We define dual($[a, b]$) $= [b, a]$ and pro ($[a, b]$) $= [\min(a, b), \max(a, b)]$.

Definition 4 ([15]). *Let $f : \mathbb{R}^m \to \mathbb{R}$ be a continuous function and $x \in \mathbb{IK}^m$, which we can decompose in $x_{\mathcal{A}} \in \mathbb{IR}^p$ and $x_{\mathcal{E}} \in (dual \, \mathbb{IR})^q$ with $p + q = m$. A generalized interval $z \in \mathbb{IK}$ is (f, x)-interpretable if*

$$(\forall x_{\mathcal{A}} \in x_{\mathcal{A}})\,(Q_z z \in \, pro \, z)\,(\exists x_{\mathcal{E}} \in \, pro\, x_{\mathcal{E}})\,(f(x) = z) \qquad (2)$$

where $Q_z = \exists$ if (z) is proper, and $Q_z = \forall$ otherwise.

When all intervals in (2) are proper, we retrieve the interpretation of classical interval computation, which gives an outer-approximation of range(f, x), or $(\forall x \in x)\,(\exists z \in [z])\,(f(x) = z)$. When all intervals are improper, (2) yields an inner-approximation of range(f, x), or $(\forall z \in]$pro $z[)\,(\exists x \in$ pro $x)\,(f(x) = z)$.

Kaucher arithmetic [18] provides a computation on generalized intervals that returns intervals that are interpretable as inner-approximations in some simple cases. Kaucher addition extends addition on classical intervals by $x + y = [\underline{x} + \underline{y}, \overline{x} + \overline{y}]$ and $x - y = [\underline{x} - \overline{y}, \overline{x} - \underline{y}]$. For multiplication, let us decompose $\mathbb{IK}$ in $\mathcal{P} = \{x = [\underline{x}, \overline{x}], \underline{x} \geqslant 0 \wedge \overline{x} \geqslant 0\}$, $-\mathcal{P} = \{x = [\underline{x}, \overline{x}], \underline{x} \leqslant 0 \wedge \overline{x} \leqslant 0\}$, $\mathcal{Z} = \{x = [\underline{x}, \overline{x}], \underline{x} \leqslant 0 \leqslant \overline{x}\}$, and dual $\mathcal{Z} = \{x = [\underline{x}, \overline{x}], \underline{x} \geqslant 0 \geqslant \overline{x}\}$. When restricted to proper intervals, the Kaucher multiplication coincides with the classical interval multiplication. Kaucher multiplication xy extends the classical multiplication to all possible combinations of x and y belonging to these sets. We refer to [18] for more details.

Kaucher arithmetic defines a generalized interval natural extension (see [15]):

Proposition 1. *Let $f : \mathbb{R}^m \to \mathbb{R}$ be a function, given by an arithmetic expression where each variable appears syntactically only once (and with degree 1). Then for $x \in \mathbb{IK}^m$, $f(x)$, computed using Kaucher arithmetic, is (f, x)-interpretable.*

In some cases, Kaucher arithmetic can thus be used to compute an inner-approximation of range(f, x). But the restriction to functions f with single occurrences of variables, that is with no dependency, prevents a wide use. A generalized interval mean-value extension allows us to overcome this limitation:

Theorem 1. *Let $f : \mathbb{R}^m \to \mathbb{R}$ be differentiable, and $\boldsymbol{x} \in \mathbb{IK}^m$ which we can decompose in $\boldsymbol{x}_{\mathcal{A}} \in \mathbb{IR}^p$ and $\boldsymbol{x}_{\mathcal{E}} \in (\text{dual } \mathbb{IR})^q$ with $p + q = m$. Suppose that for each $i \in \{1, \ldots, m\}$, we can compute $[\boldsymbol{\Delta}_i] \in \mathbb{IR}$ such that*

$$\left\{ \frac{\partial f}{\partial x_i}(x), \ x \in pro \ \boldsymbol{x} \right\} \subseteq [\boldsymbol{\Delta}_i]. \tag{3}$$

Then, for any $\tilde{x} \in pro \ \boldsymbol{x}$, the following interval, evaluated with Kaucher arithmetic, is $(f, \boldsymbol{x})$-interpretable:

$$\tilde{f}(\boldsymbol{x}) = f(\tilde{x}) + \sum_{i=1}^{n} [\boldsymbol{\Delta}_i](\boldsymbol{x}_i - \tilde{x}_i). \tag{4}$$

When using (4) for inner-approximation, we can only get the following subset of all possible cases in the Kaucher multiplication table: $(\boldsymbol{x} \in \mathcal{P}) \times (\boldsymbol{y} \in \text{dual } \mathcal{Z}) = [\underline{xy}, \overline{x}\overline{y}]$, $(\boldsymbol{x} \in -\mathcal{P}) \times (\boldsymbol{y} \in \text{dual } \mathcal{Z}) = [\overline{x}\underline{y}, \overline{x}\overline{y}]$, and $(\boldsymbol{x} \in \mathcal{Z}) \times (\boldsymbol{y} \in \text{dual } \mathcal{Z}) = 0$. Indeed, for an improper $\boldsymbol{x}$, and $\tilde{x} \in pro \ \boldsymbol{x}$, it holds that $(\boldsymbol{x} - \tilde{x})$ is in dual $\mathcal{Z}$. The outer-approximation $[\boldsymbol{\Delta}_i]$ of the Jacobian is a proper interval, thus in $\mathcal{P}$, $-\mathcal{P}$ or $\mathcal{Z}$, and we can deduce from the multiplication rules that the inner-approximation is non empty only if $[\boldsymbol{\Delta}_i]$ does not contain 0.

Example 3. Let f be defined by $f(x) = x^2 - x$, for which we want to compute an inner-approximation of the range over $\boldsymbol{x} = [2, 3]$. Due to the two occurrences of x, $f(\text{dual } x)$, computed with Kaucher arithmetic, is not $(f, \boldsymbol{x})$-interpretable. The interval $\tilde{f}(\boldsymbol{x}) = f(2.5) + \boldsymbol{f}'([2,3])(\boldsymbol{x} - 2.5) = 3.75 + [3,5](\boldsymbol{x} - 2.5)$ given by its mean-value extension, computed with Kaucher arithmetic, is $(f, \boldsymbol{x})$-interpretable. For $\boldsymbol{x} = [2,3]$, using the multiplication rule for $\mathcal{P} \times \text{dual } \mathcal{Z}$, we get $\tilde{f}(\boldsymbol{x}) = 3.75 + [3,5]([2,3] - 2.5) = 3.75 + [3,5][0.5, -0.5] = 3.75 + [1.5, -1.5] = [5.25, 2.25]$, that can be interpreted as: $(\forall z \in [2.25, 5.25]) \, (\exists x \in [2,3]) \, (z = f(x))$. Thus, $[2.25, 5.25]$ is an inner-approximation of range$(f, [2,3])$.

In Sect. 4, we will use Theorem 1 with f being each component (for a n-dimensional system) of the solution of the uncertain dynamical system (1): we need an outer enclosure of the solution of the system, and of its Jacobian with respect to the uncertain parameters. This is the objective of the next sections.

3 Taylor Method for Outer Flowpipes of DDEs

We now introduce a Taylor method to compute outer enclosures of the solution of system (1). The principle is to extend a Taylor method for the solution of ODEs to the case of DDEs, in a similar spirit to the existing work [28,32]. This can be done by building a Taylor model version of the method of steps [27], a technique for solving DDEs that reduces these to a sequence of ODEs.

3.1 The Method of Steps for Solving DDEs

The principle of the method of steps is that on each time interval $[t_0+i\tau, t_0+(i+1)\tau]$, for $i \geq 1$, the function $z(t-\tau)$ is a known history function, already computed as the solution of the DDE on the previous time interval $[t_0 + (i-1)\tau, t_0 + i\tau]$. Plugging the solution of the previous ODE into the DDE yields a new ODE on the next tile interval: we thus have an initial value problem for an ODE with $z(t_0 + i\tau)$ defined by the previous ODE. This process is initialized with $z_0(t)$ on the first time interval $[t_0, t_0 + \tau]$. The solution of the DDE can thus be obtained by solving a sequence of IVPs for ODEs. Generally, there is a discontinuity in the first derivative of the solution at $t_0 + \tau$. If this is the case, then because of the term $z(t - \tau)$ in the DDE, a discontinuity will also appear at each $t_0 + i\tau$.

Example 4. Consider the DDE defined in Example 1. On $t \in [0, \tau]$ the solution of the DDE is solution of the ODE

$$\dot{x}(t) = f(x(t), x_0(t - \tau, \beta)) = -x(t)(1 + \beta(t - \tau))^2, \ t \in [0, \tau]$$

with initial value $x(0) = x_0(0, \beta) = 1$. It admits the analytical solution

$$x(t) = \exp\left(-\frac{1}{3\beta}\left((1 + (t - 1)\beta)^3 - (1 - \beta)^3\right)\right), \ t \in [0, \tau] \tag{5}$$

The solution of the DDE on the time interval $[\tau, 2\tau]$ is the solution of the ODE

$$\dot{x}(t) = -x(t)\exp\left(-\frac{1}{3\beta}\left((1 + (t - \tau - 1)\beta)^3 - (1 - \beta)^3\right)\right), \ t \in [\tau, 2\tau]$$

with initial value $x(\tau)$ given by (5). An analytical solution can be computed, using the transcendantal lower γ function.

3.2 Finite Representation of Functions as Taylor Models

A sufficiently smooth function g (e.g. C^∞), can be represented on a time interval $[t_0, t_0 + h]$ by a Taylor expansion

$$g(t) = \sum_{i=0}^{k}(t - t_0)^i g^{[i]}(t_0) + (t - t_0)^{k+1}g^{[k+1]}(\xi), \tag{6}$$

with $\xi \in [t_0, t_0 + h]$, and using the notation $g^{[i]}(t) := \frac{g^{(i)}(t)}{i!}$. We will use such Taylor expansions to represent the solution $z(t)$ of the DDE on each time interval $[t_0 + i\tau, t_0 + (i + 1)\tau]$, starting with the initial condition $z_0(t, \beta)$ on $[t_0, t_0 + \tau]$. For more accuracy, we actually define these expansions piecewise on a finer time grid of fixed time step h. The function $z_0(t, \beta)$ on time interval $[t_0, t_0 + \tau]$ is thus represented by $p = \tau/h$ Taylor expansions. The lth such Taylor expansion, valid on the time interval $[t_0 + lh, t_0 + (l + 1)h]$ with $l \in \{0, \dots, p - 1\}$, is

$$z_0(t, \beta) = \sum_{i=0}^{k}(t - t_0)^i z^{[i]}(t_0 + lh, \beta) + (t - t_0)^{k+1}z^{[k+1]}(\xi_l, \beta), \tag{7}$$

for a $\xi_l \in [t_0 + lh, t_0 + (l + 1)h]$.

3.3 An Abstract Taylor Model Representation

In a rigorous version of the expansion (7), the $z^{[i]}(t_0+lh,\beta)$ as well as $g^{[k+1]}(\xi_l,\beta)$ are set-valued, as the vector of parameters β is set valued. The simplest way to account for these uncertainties is to use intervals. However, this approach suffers heavily from the wrapping effect, as these uncertainties accumulate with integration time. A more accurate alternative is to use a Taylor form in the parameters β for each $z^{[i]}(t_0+lh,\beta)$. This is however very costly. We choose in this work to use a sub-polyhedric abstraction to parameterize Taylor coefficients, expressing some sensitivity of the model to the uncertain parameters: we rely on affine forms [9]. The result can be seen as Taylor models of arbitrary order in time, and order close to 1 in the parameters space.

The vector of uncertain parameters or inputs $\beta \in \boldsymbol{\beta}$ is thus defined as a vector of affine forms over m symbolic variables $\varepsilon_i \in [-1,1]$: $\beta = \alpha_0 + \sum_{i=1}^{m_j} \alpha_i \varepsilon_i$, where the coefficients α_i are vectors of real numbers. This abstraction describes the set of values of the parameters as given within a zonotope. In the sequel, we will use for zonotopes the same bold letter notation as for intervals, that account for set valued quantities.

Example 5. In Example 1, $\boldsymbol{\beta} = [\frac{1}{3}, 1]$ can be represented by the centered form $\beta = \frac{2}{3} + \frac{1}{3}\varepsilon_1$. The set of initial conditions $\boldsymbol{x}_0(t,\beta)$ is abstracted as a function of the noise symbol ε_1. For example, at $t = -1$, $\boldsymbol{x}_0(-1,\beta) = (1-\beta)^2 = (1 - \frac{2}{3} - \frac{1}{3}\varepsilon_1)^2 = \frac{1}{9}(1-\varepsilon_1)^2$. The abstraction of affine arithmetic operators is computed componentwise on the noise symbols ε_i, and does not introduce any over-approximation. The abstraction of non affine operations is conservative: an affine approximation of the result is computed, and a new noise term is added, that accounts for the approximation error. Here, using $\varepsilon_1^2 \in [0,1]$, affine arithmetic [9] will yield $[\boldsymbol{x}_0](-1,\beta) = \frac{1}{9}(1 - 2\varepsilon_1 + [0,1]) = \frac{1}{9}(1.5 - 2\varepsilon_1 + 0.5\varepsilon_2)$, with $\varepsilon_2 \in [-1,1]$. We are now using notation $[\boldsymbol{x}_0]$, denoting an outer-approximation. Indeed, the abstraction is conservative: $[\boldsymbol{x}_0](-1,\beta)$ takes its values in $\frac{1}{9}[-1,4]$, while the exact range of $\boldsymbol{x}_0(-1,\beta)$ for $\beta \in [\frac{1}{3}, 1]$ is $\frac{1}{9}[0,4]$.

Now, we can represent the initial solution for $t \in [t_0, t_0 + \tau]$ of the DDE (1) as a Taylor model in time with zonotopic coefficients, by evaluating in affine arithmetic the coefficients of its Taylor model (7). Noting $\boldsymbol{r}_{0j} = [t_0 + jh, t_0 + (j+1)h]$, we write, for all $j = 0, \ldots, p-1$,

$$[\boldsymbol{z}](t) = \sum_{l=0}^{k-1}(t-t_0)^l[\boldsymbol{z}_{0j}]^{[l]} + (t-t_0)^k[\overline{\boldsymbol{z}}_{0j}]^{[k]}, \; t \in \boldsymbol{r}_{0j} \qquad (8)$$

where the Taylor coefficients

$$[\boldsymbol{z}_{0j}]^{[l]} := \frac{[\boldsymbol{z}_0]^{(l)}(t_0+jh,\beta)}{l!}, \quad [\overline{\boldsymbol{z}}_{0j}]^{[l]} := \frac{[\boldsymbol{z}_0]^{(l)}(\boldsymbol{r}_{0j},\beta)}{l!} \qquad (9)$$

can be computed by differentiating the initial solution with respect to t ($[\boldsymbol{z}_0]^{(l)}$ denotes the l-th time derivative), and evaluating the result in affine arithmetic.

Example 6. Suppose we want to build a Taylor model of order $k = 2$ for the initial condition in Example 1 on a grid of step size $h = 1/3$. Consider the Taylor model for the first step $[t_0, t_0 + h] = [-1, -2/3]$: we need to evaluate $[\boldsymbol{x}_{00}]^{[0]} = [\boldsymbol{x}_0](-1, \boldsymbol{\beta})$, which was done Example 5.

We also need $[\boldsymbol{x}_{00}]^{[1]}$ and $[\overline{\boldsymbol{x}_{00}}]^{[2]}$. We compute $[\boldsymbol{x}_{00}]^{[1]} = [\dot{x}_0](-1, \boldsymbol{\beta}) = 2\beta(1 - \beta)$ and $[\overline{\boldsymbol{x}_{00}}]^{[2]} = [\boldsymbol{x}_0]^{(2)}(r_l)/2 = [\ddot{x}_0](r_l)/2 = \beta^2$, with $\beta = \frac{2}{3} + \frac{1}{3}\varepsilon_1$. We evaluate these coefficients with affine arithmetic, similarly to Example 5.

3.4 Constructing Flowpipes

The abstract Taylor models (8) introduced in Sect. 3.3, define piecewise outer-approximating flowpipes of the solution on $[t_0, t_0 + \tau]$. Using the method of steps, and plugging into (1) the solution computed on $[t_0 + (i-1)\tau, t_0 + i\tau]$, the solution of (1) can be computed by solving the sequence of ODEs

$$\dot{z}(t) = f(z(t), z(t - \tau), \beta), \text{ for } t \in [t_0 + i\tau, t_0 + (i+1)\tau] \qquad (10)$$

where the initial condition $z(t_0 + i\tau)$, and $z(t - \tau)$ for t in $[t_0 + i\tau, t_0 + (i+1)\tau]$, are fully defined by (8) when $i = 1$, and by the solution of (10) at previous step when i is greater than 1.

Let the set of the solutions of (10) at time t and for the initial conditions $z(t') \in \boldsymbol{z}'$ at some initial time $t' \geq t_0$ be denoted by $\boldsymbol{z}(t, t', \boldsymbol{z}')$. Using a Taylor method for ODEs, we can compute flowpipes that are guaranteed to contain the reachable set of the solutions $\boldsymbol{z}(t, t_0 + \tau, [\boldsymbol{z}](t_0 + \tau))$ of (10), for all times t in $[t_0 + \tau, t_0 + 2\tau]$, with $[\boldsymbol{z}](t_0 + \tau)$ given by the evaluation of the Taylor model (8). This can be iterated for further steps of length τ, solving (10) for $i = 1, \ldots, T/\tau$, with an initial condition given by the evaluation of the Taylor model for (10) at the previous step.

We now detail the algorithm that results from this principle. Flowpipes are built using two levels of grids. At each step on the coarser grid with step size τ, we define a new ODE. We build the Taylor models for the solution of this ODE on the finer grid of integration step size $h = \tau/p$. We note $t_i = t_0 + i\tau$ the points of the coarser grid, and $t_{ij} = t_0 + i\tau + jh$ the points of the finer grid. In order to compute the flowpipes in a piecewise manner on this grid, the Taylor method relies on Algorithm 1. All Taylor coefficients, as well as Taylor expansion evaluations, are computed in affine arithmetic.

Step 1: Computing an a Priori Enclosure.

We need an a priori enclosure $[\overline{z}_{ij}]$ of the solution $z(t)$, valid on the time interval $[t_{ij}, t_{i(j+1)}]$. This is done by a straightforward extension of the classical approach [26] for ODEs relying on the interval Picard-Lindelöf method, applied to Eq. (10) on $[t_{ij}, t_{i(j+1)}]$ with initial condition $[z_{ij}]$. If $[f]$ is Lipschitz, the natural interval extension $[F]$ of the Picard-Lindelöf operator defined by $[F](z) = [z_{ij}] + [t_{ij}, t_{i(j+1)}][f](z, [\overline{z}_{i(j-1)}], \beta)$, where the enclosure of the solution over $r_{i(j-1)} = [t_{i(j-1)}, t_{ij}]$ has already be computed as $[\overline{z}_{i(j-1)}]$, admits a unique fixpoint. A simple Jacobi-like iteration, $z_0 = [z_{ij}]$, $z_{l+1} = F(z_l)$ for all $l \in \mathbb{N}$, suffices to reach the fixpoint of this iteration which

Build by (9) the $[z_{0j}]^{[l]}$, $j \in \{0, \ldots, p-1\}$ that define the Taylor model on $[t_0, t_0 + \tau]$, and Initialize next flowpipe: $[z_{10}] = [z_0](t_{10}, \beta)$ at $t_{10} = t_0 + \tau$
For all $i = 0, \ldots, T/\tau$ do
    For all $j = 0, \ldots, p-1$ do
        Step 1: compute an a priori enclosure $[\overline{z}_{ij}]$ of $z(t)$ valid on $[t_{ij}, t_{i(j+1)}]$
        Step 2: build by (12), (14), a Taylor model valid on $[t_{ij}, t_{i(j+1)}]$
        Using (11), initialize next flowpipe: $[z_{i(j+1)}] = [z](t_{i(j+1)}, t_{ij}, [z_{ij}])$ if
$j < p-1$, $[z_{(i+1)0}] = [z](t_{(i+1)0}, t_{ij}, [z_{ij}])$ if $j = p-1$

Algorithm 1. Sketch of the computation of outer reachable sets for a DDE

yields $[\overline{z}_{ij}]$, and ensures the existence and uniqueness of a solution to (10) on $[t_{ij}, t_{i(j+1)}]$. However, it may be necessary to reduce the step size.

Step 2: Building the Taylor Model. A Taylor expansion of order k of the solution at t_{ij} which is valid on the time interval $[t_{ij}, t_{i(j+1)}]$, for $i \geq 1$, is

$$[z](t, t_{ij}, [z_{ij}]) = [z_{ij}] + \sum_{l=1}^{k-1} (t - t_{ij})^l [f_{ij}]^{[l]} + (t - t_{ij})^k [\overline{f}_{ij}]^{[k]}, \quad (11)$$

The Taylor coefficients are defined inductively, and can be computed by automatic differentiation, as follows:

$$[f_{ij}]^{[1]} = [f]\left([z_{ij}], [z_{(i-1)j}], \beta\right) \quad (12)$$

$$[f_{1j}]^{[l+1]} = \frac{1}{l+1}\left(\left[\frac{\partial f^{[l]}}{\partial z}\right][f_{1j}]^{[1]} + [z_{0j}][f_{0j}]^{[1]}\right) \quad (13)$$

$$[f_{ij}]^{[l+1]} = \frac{1}{l+1}\left(\left[\frac{\partial f^{[l]}}{\partial z}\right][f_{ij}]^{[1]} + \left[\frac{\partial f^{[l]}}{\partial z^\tau}\right][f_{(i-1)j}]^{[1]}\right) \quad \text{if } i \geq 2 \quad (14)$$

The Taylor coefficients for the remainder term are computed in a similar way, evaluating $[f]$ over the a priori enclosure of the solution on $r_{ij} = [t_{ij}, t_{i(j+1)}]$. For instance, $[\overline{f}_{ij}]^{[1]} = [f]([\overline{z}_{ij}], [\overline{z}_{(i-1)j}])$. The derivatives can be discontinuous at t_{i0}: the $[f_{i0}]^{[l]}$ coefficients correspond to the right-handed limit, at time t_{i0}^+.

Let us detail the computation of the coefficients (12), (13) and (14). Let $z(t)$ be the solution of (10). By definition, $\frac{dz}{dt}(t) = f(z(t), z(t-\tau), \beta) = f^{[1]}(z(t), z(t-\tau), \beta)$ from which we deduce the set valued version (12). We can prove (14) by induction on l. Let us denote ∂z the partial derivative with respect to $z(t)$, and ∂z^τ with respect to the delayed function $z(t-\tau)$. We have

$$
\begin{aligned}
f^{[l+1]}(z(t), z(t-\tau), \beta) &= \tfrac{1}{(l+1)!}\tfrac{d^{(l+1)}z}{dt^{(l+1)}}(t) = \tfrac{1}{l+1}\tfrac{d}{dt}\left(f^{[l]}(z(t), z(t-\tau), \beta)\right) \\
&= \tfrac{1}{l+1}\left(\dot{z}(t)\tfrac{\partial f^{[l]}}{\partial z} + \dot{z}(t-\tau)\tfrac{\partial f^{[l]}}{\partial z^\tau}\right) \\
&= \tfrac{1}{l+1}\left(f(z(t), z(t-\tau), \beta)\tfrac{\partial f^{[l]}}{\partial z} + \right. \\
&\qquad\qquad \left. f(z(t-\tau), z(t-2\tau), \beta)\tfrac{\partial f^{[l]}}{\partial z^\tau}\right)
\end{aligned}
$$

from which we deduce the set valued version (14). For $t \in [t_0 + \tau, t_0 + 2\tau]$, the only difference is that $\dot{z}(t - \tau)$ is obtained by differentiating the initial solution of the DDE on $[t_0, t_0 + \tau]$, which yields (13).

Example 7. As in Example 6, we build the first step of the Taylor model of order $k = 2$ on the system of Example 1. We consider $t \in [t_0 + \tau, t_0 + 2\tau]$, on a grid of step size $h = 1/3$. Let us build the Taylor model on $[t_0 + \tau, t_0 + \tau + h] = [0, 1/3]$: we need to evaluate$[\boldsymbol{x}_{10}]$, $[\boldsymbol{f}_{10}]^{[1]}$ and $[\overline{\boldsymbol{f}}_{10}]^{[2]}$ in affine arithmetic.

Following Algorithm 1, $[\boldsymbol{x}_{10}] = [\boldsymbol{x}_0](t_{10}, \boldsymbol{\beta}) = [\boldsymbol{x}_0](t_0 + \tau, \boldsymbol{\beta}) = [\boldsymbol{x}_0](0, \boldsymbol{\beta}) = 1$. Using (12) and the computation of $[\boldsymbol{x}_{00}]$ of Example 5, $[\boldsymbol{f}_{10}]^{[1]} = [\boldsymbol{f}]([\boldsymbol{x}_{10}], [\boldsymbol{x}_{00}]) = [\boldsymbol{f}](1, \frac{1}{9}(1.5 - 2\varepsilon_1 + 0.5\varepsilon_2)) = -\frac{1}{9}(1.5 - 2\varepsilon_1 + 0.5\varepsilon_2)$. Finally, using (13), $[\overline{\boldsymbol{f}}_{10}]^{[2]} = 0.5\dot{f}(\boldsymbol{r}_{10}, \boldsymbol{r}_{00})$, where $\boldsymbol{r}_{i0}$ for $i = 0, 1$ (with $\boldsymbol{r}_{00} = \boldsymbol{r}_{10} - \tau$) is the time interval of width h equal to $[t_{i0}, t_{i1}] = [-1 + i, -1 + i + 1/3]$, and $\dot{f}(t, t - \tau) = \dot{x}(t)x(t - \tau) + x(t)\dot{x}(t - \tau) = f(t, t - \tau)x(t - \tau) + x(t)\dot{x}_0(t - \tau) = -x(t)x(t - \tau)^2 + 2x(t)\beta(1 + \beta t)$. Thus, $[\overline{\boldsymbol{f}}_{10}]^{[2]} = -0.5[\boldsymbol{x}(\boldsymbol{r}_{10})][\boldsymbol{x}(\boldsymbol{r}_{00})]^2 + [\boldsymbol{x}(\boldsymbol{r}_{10})]\beta(1 + \beta \boldsymbol{r}_{10})$. We need enclosures for $x(\boldsymbol{r}_{00})$ and $x(\boldsymbol{r}_{10})$, to compute this expression. Enclosure $[\boldsymbol{x}(\boldsymbol{r}_{00})]$ is directly obtained as $[\boldsymbol{x}_0](\boldsymbol{r}_{00}) = (1 + \beta \boldsymbol{r}_{00})^2$, evaluated in affine arithmetic. Evaluating $[\boldsymbol{x}(\boldsymbol{r}_{10})]$ requires to compute an a priori enclosure of the solution on interval $\boldsymbol{r}_{10}$, following the approach described as Step 1 in Algorithm 1. The Picard-Lindelöf operator is $[\boldsymbol{F}](\boldsymbol{x}) = [\boldsymbol{x}_{10}] + [0, \frac{1}{3}][\boldsymbol{f}](\boldsymbol{x}, [\boldsymbol{x}(\boldsymbol{r}_{00})], \boldsymbol{\beta}) = 1 + [0, \frac{1}{3}](1 + \beta \boldsymbol{r}_{00})^2 \boldsymbol{x}$. We evaluate it in interval rather than affine arithmetic for simplicity: $[\boldsymbol{F}](\boldsymbol{x}) = 1 + [0, \frac{1}{3}](1 + [\frac{1}{3}, 1][-1, -\frac{2}{3}])^2 \boldsymbol{x} = 1 + [0, \frac{7^2}{3^5}]\boldsymbol{x}$. Starting with $\boldsymbol{x}_0 = [\boldsymbol{x}_{10}] = 1$, we compute $\boldsymbol{x}_1 = [\boldsymbol{F}](1) = [1, 1 + \frac{7^2}{3^5}]$, $\boldsymbol{x}_2 = [\boldsymbol{F}](\boldsymbol{x}_1) = [1, 1 + \frac{7^2}{3^5} + (\frac{7^2}{3^5})^2]$, etc. This is a geometric progression, that converges to a finite enclosure.

Remark. A fixed step size yields a simpler algorithm. However it is possible to use a variable step size, with an additional interpolation of the Taylor models.

4   Inner-Approximating Flowpipes

We will now use Theorem 1 in order to compute inner-approximating flowpipes from outer-approximating flowpipes, extending the work [16] for ODEs to the case of DDEs. The main idea is to instantiate in this theorem the function f as the solution $z(t, \beta)$ of our uncertain system (1) for all t, and $\boldsymbol{x}$ as the range $\boldsymbol{\beta}$ of the uncertain parameters. For this, we need to compute an outer-approximation of $z(t, \tilde{\beta})$ for some $\tilde{\beta} \in \boldsymbol{\beta}$, and of its Jacobian matrix with respect to β at any time t and over the range $\boldsymbol{\beta}$. We follow the approach described in Sect. 3.4.

Outer-Approximation of the Jacobian Matrix Coefficients. For the DDE (1) in arbitrary dimension $n \in \mathbb{N}$ and with parameter dimension $m \in \mathbb{N}$, the Jacobian matrix of the solution $z = (z_1, \ldots, z_n)$ of this system with respect to the parameters $\beta = (\beta_1, \ldots, \beta_m)$ is

$$J_{ij}(t) = \frac{\partial z_i}{\partial \beta_j}(t)$$

for i between 1 and n, j between 1 and m. Differentiating (1), we obtain that the coefficients of the Jacobian matrix of the flow satisfy

$$\dot{J}_{ij}(t) = \sum_{k=1}^{p} \frac{\partial f_i}{\partial z_k}(t) J_{kj}(t) + \sum_{k=1}^{p} \frac{\partial f_i}{\partial z_k^\tau}(t) J_{kj}(t - \tau) + \frac{\partial f_i}{\partial \beta_j}(t) \qquad (15)$$

with initial condition $J_{ij}(t) = (J_{ij})_0(t, \beta) = \frac{\partial (z_i)_0}{\partial \beta_j}(t, \beta)$ for $t \in [t_0, t_0 + \tau]$.

Example 8. The Jacobian matrix for Example 1 is a scalar since the DDE is real-valued and the parameter is scalar. We easily get $\dot{J}_{11}(t) = -x(t-\tau)J_{11}(t) - x(t)J_{11}(t - \tau)$ with initial condition $(J_{11})_0(t, \beta) = 2t(1 + \beta t)$.

Equation (15) is a DDE of the same form as (1). We can thus use the method introduced in Sect. 3.4, and use Taylor models to compute outer-approximating flowpipes for the coefficients of the Jacobian matrix.

Computing Inner-Approximating Flowpipes. Similarly as for ODEs [16], the algorithm that computes inner-approximating flowpipes, first uses Algorithm 1 to compute outer-approximations, on each time interval $[t_{ij}, t_{i(j+1)}]$, of

1. the solution $z(t, \tilde{\beta})$ of the system starting from the initialization function $z_0(t, \tilde{\beta})$ defined by a given $\tilde{\beta} \in \boldsymbol{\beta}$
2. the Jacobian $J(t, \beta)$ of the solution, for all $\beta \in \boldsymbol{\beta}$

Then, we can deduce inner-approximating flowpipes by using Theorem 1. Let as in Definition 3 $\beta = (\beta_\mathcal{A}, \beta_\mathcal{E})$ and note $J_\mathcal{A}$ the matrix obtained by extracting the columns of the Jacobian corresponding to the partial derivatives with respect to $\beta_\mathcal{A}$. Denote by $J_\mathcal{E}$ the remaining columns. If the quantity defined by Eq. (16) for t in $[t_{ij}, t_{i(j+1)}]$ is an improper interval

$$]z[_\mathcal{A}(t, t_{ij}, \boldsymbol{\beta}_\mathcal{A}, \boldsymbol{\beta}_\mathcal{E}) = [z](t, t_{ij}, [\tilde{z}_{ij}]) + [J]_\mathcal{A}(t, t_{ij}, [J_{ij}])(\boldsymbol{\beta}_\mathcal{A} - \tilde{\beta}_\mathcal{A})$$
$$+ [J]_\mathcal{E}(t, t_{ij}, [J_{ij}])(\text{dual } \boldsymbol{\beta}_\mathcal{E} - \tilde{\beta}_\mathcal{E}) \qquad (16)$$

then the interval (pro $]z[_\mathcal{A}(t, t_{ij}, \boldsymbol{\beta}_\mathcal{A}, \boldsymbol{\beta}_\mathcal{E}))$ is an inner-approximation of the reachable set $z(t, \boldsymbol{\beta})$ valid on the time interval $[t_{ij}, t_{i(j+1)}]$, which is robust with respect to the parameters $\beta_\mathcal{A}$, in the sense of Definition 3. Otherwise the inner-approximation is empty. If all parameters are existentially quantified, that is if the subset $\beta_\mathcal{A}$ is empty, we obtain the classical inner-approximation of Definition 2. Note that a unique computation of the center solution $[\tilde{z}]$ and the Jacobian matrix $[J]$ can be used to infer different interpretations as inner-approximations or robust inner-approximations. With this computation, the robust inner flowpipes will always be included in the classical inner flowpipes.

The computation of the inner-approximations fully relies on the outer-approximations at each time step. A consequence is that we can soundly implement most of our approach using classical interval-based methods: outward rounding should be used for the outer approximations of flows and Jacobians. Only the final computation by Kaucher arithmetic of improper intervals should be done with inward rounding in order to get a sound computation of the inner-approximation.

Also, the wider the outer-approximation in Taylor models for the center and the Jacobian, the tighter and thus the less accurate is the inner-approximation. This can lead to an empty inner-approximation if the result of Eq. (16) in Kaucher arithmetic is not an improper interval. This can occur in two way. Firstly, the Kaucher multiplication $[J]_{\mathcal{E}}(\text{dual } \beta_{\mathcal{E}} - \tilde{\beta}_{\mathcal{E}})$ in (16), yields a non-zero improper interval only if the Jacobian coefficients do not contain 0. Secondly, suppose that the Kaucher multiplication yields an improper interval. It is added to the proper interval $[z](t, t_{ij}, [\tilde{z}_{ij}]) + [J]_{\mathcal{A}} * (\beta_{\mathcal{A}} - \tilde{\beta}_{\mathcal{A}})$. The center solution $[z](t, t_{ij}, [\tilde{z}_{ij}])$ can be tightly estimated, but the term $[J]_{\mathcal{A}}(\beta_{\mathcal{A}} - \tilde{\beta}_{\mathcal{A}})$ that measures robustness with respect to the $\beta_{\mathcal{A}}$ parameters can lead to a wide enclosure. If this sum is wider than the improper interval resulting from the Kaucher multiplication, then the resulting Kaucher sum will be proper and the inner-approximation empty.

5 Implementation and Experiments

We have implemented our method using the FILIB++ C++ library [23] for interval computations, the FADBAD++[2] package for automatic differentiation, and (a slightly modified version of) the aaflib[3] library for affine arithmetic.

Let us first consider the running example, with order 2 Taylor models, and an integration step size of 0.05. Figure 1 left presents the results until $t = 2$ (obtained in 0.03 s) compared to the analytical solution (dashed lines): the solid external lines represent the outer-approximating flowpipe, the filled region represents the inner-approximating flowpipe. Until time $t = 0$, the DDE is in its initialization phase, and the conservativeness of the outer-approximation is due to the abstraction in affine arithmetic of the set of initialization functions. Using higher-order Taylor models, or refining the time step improves the accuracy. However, for the inner-approximation, there is a specific difficulty: the Jacobian contains 0 at $t = -1$, so that the inner-approximation is reduced to a point. This case corresponds to the parameter value $\beta = 1$. To address this problem, we split the initial parameter set in two sub-intervals of equal width, compute independently the inner and outer flowpipes for these two parameters ranges, and then join the results to obtain Fig. 1 center. It is somehow counter intuitive that we can get this way a larger, thus better quality, inner-approximating set, as the inner-approximation corresponds to the property that there exist a value of β in the parameter set such that a point of the tube is definitely reached. Taking a larger β parameter set would intuitively lead to a larger such inner tube. However, this is in particular due to the fact that we avoid here the zero in the

---

[2] http://www.fadbad.com.
[3] http://aaflib.sourceforge.net.

Jacobian. More generally, such a subdivision yields a tighter outer-approximation of the Jacobian, and thus better accuracy when using the mean-value theorem.

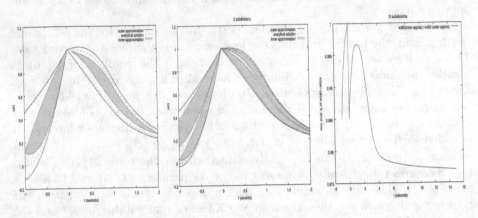

Fig. 1. Running example (Taylor model order 2, step size 0.05)

In order to obtain an inner-approximation without holes, we can use a subdivision of the parameters with some covering. This is the case for instance using 10 subdivisions, with 10% of covering. Results are now much tighter: Fig. 1 right represents a measure $\gamma(x, t)$ of the quality of the approximations (computed in 45 s) for a time horizon $T = 15$, with Taylor Model of order 3, a step size of 0.02. This accuracy measure $\gamma(x, t)$ is defined by $\gamma(x, t) = \frac{\gamma_u(x)}{\gamma_o(x)}$ where $\gamma_u(x)$ and $\gamma_o(x)$ measure respectively the width of the inner-approximation and outer-approximation, for state variable x. Intuitively, the larger the ratio (bounded by 1), the better the approximation. Here, $\gamma(x, t)$ almost stabilizes after some time, to a high accuracy of 0.975. We noted that in this example, the order of the Taylor model, the step size and the number of initial subdivisions all have a notable impact on the stabilized value of γ, that can here be decreased arbitrarily.

Example 9. Consider a basic PD-controller for a self-driving car, controlling the car's position x and velocity v by adjusting its acceleration depending on the current distance to a reference position p_r, chosen here as $p_r = 1$. We consider a delay τ to transfer the input data to the controller, due to sensing, computation or transmission times. This leads, for $t \geq 0$, to:

$$\begin{cases} x'(t) = v(t) \\ v'(t) = -K_p\big(x(t - \tau) - p_r\big) - K_d\, v(t - \tau) \end{cases}$$

Choosing $K_p = 2$ and $K_d = 3$ guarantees the asymptotic stability of the controlled system when there is no delay. The system is initialized to a constant function $(x, v) \in [-0.1, 0.1] \times [0, 0.1]$ on the time interval $[-\tau, 0]$.

This example demonstrates that even small delays can have a huge impact on the dynamics. We represent in the left subplot of Fig. 2 the inner and outer

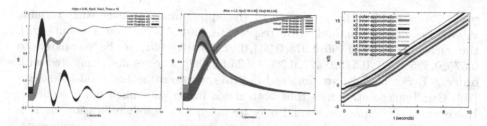

Fig. 2. Left and center: velocity and position of controlled car (left $\tau = 0.35$, center $\tau = 0.2$); Right: vehicles position in the platoon example

approximating flowpipes for the velocity and position, with delay $\tau = 0.35$, until time $T = 10$. They are obtained in 0.32 s, using Taylor models of order 3 and a time step of 0.03. The parameters were chosen such that the inner-approximation always remains non-empty. We now study the robustness of the behavior of the system to the parameters: K_p and K_d are time invariant, but now uncertain and known to be bounded by $(K_p, K_d) \in [1.95, 2.05] \times [2.95, 3.05]$. The Jacobian matrix is now of dimension 2×4. We choose a delay $\tau = 0.2$, sufficiently small to not induce oscillations. Thanks to the outer-approximation, we prove that the velocity never becomes negative, in contrast to the case of $\tau = 0.35$ where it is proved to oscillate. In Fig. 2 center, we represent, along with the over-approximation, the inner-approximation and a robust inner-approximation. The inner-approximation, in the sense of Definition 2, contains only states for which it is proved that there exists an initialization of the state variables x and v in $[-0.1, 0.1] \times [0, 0.1]$ and a value of K_p and K_d in $[1.95, 2.05] \times [2.95, 3.05]$, such that these states are solutions of the DDE. The inner-approximation which is robust with respect to the uncertainty in K_p and K_d, in the sense of Definition 3, contains only states for which it is proved that, whatever the values of K_p and K_d in $[1.95, 2.05] \times [2.95, 3.05]$, there exist an initialization of x and v in $[-0.1, 0.1] \times [0, 0.1]$, such that these states are solutions of the DDE. These results are obtained in 0.24 s, with order 3 Taylor models and a time step of 0.04. The robust inner-approximation is naturally included in the inner-approximation.

We now demonstrate the efficiency of our approach and its good scaling behavior with respect to the dimension of the state space, by comparing our results with the results of [30] on their seven-dimensional Example 3:

Example 10. Let $\dot{x}(t) = f(x(t), x(t - \tau))$, $t \in [\tau = 0.01, T]$, where $f(x(t), x(t - \tau)) = (1.4x_3(t) - 0.9x_1(t - \tau), 2.5x_5(t) - 1.5x_2(t), 0.6x_7(t) - 0.8x_3(t)x_2(t), 2 - 1.3x_4(t)x_3(t), 0.7x_1(t) - x_4(t)x_5(t), 0.3x_1(t) - 3.1x_6(t), 1.8x_6(t) - 1.5x_7(t)x_2(t))$, and the initial function is constant on $[-\tau, 0]$ with values in a box[4] $[1.0, 1.2] \times [0.95, 1.15] \times [1.4, 1.6] \times [2.3, 2.5] \times [0.9, 1.1] \times [0.0, 0.2] \times [0.35, 0.55]$. We compute outer and inner approximations of the reachable sets of the DDE until time $t = 0.1$, and compare the quality measure

---

[4] The first component is different from that given in [30], but is the correct initial condition, after discussion with the authors.

$\gamma(x_1),\ldots,\gamma(x_7)$ for the projection of the approximations over each variable x_1 to x_7, of our method with respect to [30]. We obtain for our work the measures $0.998, 0.996, 0.978, 0.964, 0.97, 0.9997, 0.961$, to be compared to $0.575, 0.525, 0.527, 0.543, 0.477, 0.366, 0.523$ for [30]. The results, computed with order 2 Taylor models, are obtained in 0.13 s with our method, and 505 s with [30]. Our implementation is thus both much faster and much more accurate. However, this comparison should only be taken as a rough indication, as it is unfair to [30] to compare their inner boxes to our projections on each component.

Example 11. Consider now the model, adapted from [11], of a platoon of n autonomous vehicles. Vehicle C_{i+1} is just after C_i, for $i = 1$ to $n - 1$. Vehicle C_1 is the leading vehicle. Sensors of C_{i+1} measure its current speed v_{i+1} as well as the speed v_i of the vehicle just in front of it. There respective positions are x_{i+1} and x_i. We take a simple model where each vehicle C_{i+1} accelerates so that to catch up with C_i if it measures that $v_i > v_{i+1}$ and acts on its brakes if $v_i < v_{i+1}$. Because of communication, accelerations are delayed by some time constant τ:

$$\dot{x}_i(t) = v_i(t) \qquad\qquad i = 2,\cdots,n$$
$$\dot{v}_{i+1}(t) = \alpha(v_i(t-\tau) - v_{i+1}(t-\tau))\ i = 2,\cdots,n-1$$

We add an equation defining the way the leading car drives. We suppose it adapts its speed between 1 and 3, following a polynomial curve. This needs to adapt the acceleration of vehicle C_2:

$$\dot{x}_1(t) = 2 + (x_1(t)/5 - 1)(x_1(t)/5 - 2)(x_1(t)/5 - 3)/6$$
$$\dot{v}_2(t) = \alpha(2 + (x_1(t)/5 - 1)(x_1(t)/5 - 2)(x_1(t)/5 - 3)/6 - v_2(t-\tau))$$

We choose $\tau = 0.3$ and $\alpha = 2.5$. The initial position before time 0 of car C_i is slightly uncertain, taken to $-(i-1) + [-0.2, 0.2]$, and its speed is in [1.99,2.01]. We represent in the right subplot of Fig. 2 the inner and outer approximations of the position of the vehicles in a 5 vehicles platoon (9-dimensional system) until time T = 10, with a time step of 0.1, and order 3 Taylor models, computed in 2.13 s. As the inner-approximations of different vehicles intersect, there are some unsafe initial conditions, such that the vehicules will collide. This example allows us to demonstrate the good scaling of our method: for 10 vehicles (19-dim system) and with the same parameters, results are obtained in 6.5 s.

6   Conclusion

We have shown how to compute, efficiently and accurately, outer and inner flow-pipes for DDEs with constant delay, using Taylor models combined with an efficient space abstraction. We have also introduced a notion of robust inner-approximation, that can be computed by the same method. We would like to extend this work for fully general DDEs, including variable delay, as well as study further the use of such computations for property verification on networked control systems. Indeed, while testing is a weaker alternative to inner-approximation for property falsification, we believe that robust inner-approximation provides new tools towards robust property verification or control synthesis.

Acknowledgments. The authors were supported by ANR project MALTHY, ANR-13-INSE-0003, DGA project "Complex Robotics Systems Safety" and the academic chair "Complex Systems Engineering" of Ecole Polytechnique-ENSTA-Télécom-Thalès-Dassault-DCNS-DGA-FX-FDO-Fondation ParisTech.

References

1. Sandretto, J.A.D., Chapoutot, A.: DynIBEX: a differential constraint library for studying dynamical systems. In: HSCC, April 2016. Poster
2. Althoff, M.: Reachability analysis of nonlinear systems using conservative polynomialization and non-convex sets. In: HSCC 2013, pp. 173–182. ACM (2013)
3. Althoff, M.: An introduction to CORA 2015. In: ARCH 2014 and ARCH 2015, pp. 120–151 (2015)
4. Althoff, M., Stursberg, O., Buss, M.: Reachability analysis of nonlinear systems with uncertain parameters using conservative linearization. In: Proceedings of CDC, pp. 4042–4048 (2008)
5. Bouissou, O., Chapoutot, A., Djoudi, A.: Enclosing temporal evolution of dynamical systems using numerical methods. In: Brat, G., Rungta, N., Venet, A. (eds.) NFM 2013. LNCS, vol. 7871, pp. 108–123. Springer, Heidelberg (2013). https://doi.org/10.1007/978-3-642-38088-4_8
6. Chen, X., Ábrahám, E., Sankaranarayanan, S.: Taylor model flowpipe construction for non-linear hybrid systems. In: RTSS, pp. 183–192 (2012)
7. Chen, X., Ábrahám, E., Sankaranarayanan, S.: Flow*: an analyzer for non-linear hybrid systems. In: Sharygina, N., Veith, H. (eds.) CAV 2013. LNCS, vol. 8044, pp. 258–263. Springer, Heidelberg (2013). https://doi.org/10.1007/978-3-642-39799-8_18
8. Chen, X., Sankaranarayanan, S., Abraham, E.: Under-approximate flowpipes for non-linear continuous systems. In: FMCAD, pp. 59–66. IEEE/ACM (2014)
9. Comba, J., Stolfi, J.: Affine arithmetic and its applications to computer graphics. In: SIBGRAPI (1993)
10. Dang, T., Testylier, R.: Reachability analysis for polynomial dynamical systems using the Bernstein expansion. Reliab. Comput. **17**, 128–152 (2012)
11. Erneux, T.: Applied Delay Differential Equations. Surveys and Tutorials in the Applied Mathematical Sciences. Springer, New York (2009). https://doi.org/10.1007/978-0-387-74372-1
12. Falbo, C.E.: Some elementary methods for solving functional Differential equations (2004)
13. Frehse, G., et al.: SpaceEx: scalable verification of hybrid systems. In: Gopalakrishnan, G., Qadeer, S. (eds.) CAV 2011. LNCS, vol. 6806, pp. 379–395. Springer, Heidelberg (2011). https://doi.org/10.1007/978-3-642-22110-1_30
14. Girard, A.: Reachability of uncertain linear systems using zonotopes. In: Morari, M., Thiele, L. (eds.) HSCC 2005. LNCS, vol. 3414, pp. 291–305. Springer, Heidelberg (2005). https://doi.org/10.1007/978-3-540-31954-2_19
15. Goldsztejn, A., Daney, D., Rueher, M., Taillibert, P.: Modal intervals revisited: a mean-value extension to generalized intervals. In: QCP 2005 (2005)

16. Goubault, E., Putot, S.: Forward inner-approximated reachability of non-linear continuous systems. In: HSCC, pp. 1–10. ACM (2017)
17. Le Guernic, C., Girard, A.: Reachability analysis of hybrid systems using support functions. In: Bouajjani, A., Maler, O. (eds.) CAV 2009. LNCS, vol. 5643, pp. 540–554. Springer, Heidelberg (2009). https://doi.org/10.1007/978-3-642-02658-4_40
18. Kaucher, E.W.: Interval analysis in the extended interval space IR. In: Alefeld, G., Grigorieff, R.D. (eds.) Fundamentals of Numerical Computation. Computing Supplementum, vol. 2, pp. 33–49. Springer, Vienna (1980). https://doi.org/10.1007/978-3-7091-8577-3_3
19. Korda, M., Henrion, D., Jones, C.N.: Inner approximations of the region of attraction for polynomial dynamical systems. In: NOLCOS (2013)
20. Kurzhanski, A.B., Varaiya, P.: Ellipsoidal techniques for reachability analysis. In: Lynch, N., Krogh, B.H. (eds.) HSCC 2000. LNCS, vol. 1790, pp. 202–214. Springer, Heidelberg (2000). https://doi.org/10.1007/3-540-46430-1_19
21. Kurzhanski, A.B., Varaiya, P.: Ellipsoidal techniques for reachability analysis: internal approximation. Syst. Control Lett. 41, 201–211 (2000)
22. Kurzhanski, A.B., Varaiya, P.: Ellipsoidal toolbox. Technical report, EECS, Berkeley, May 2006
23. Lerch, M., Tischler, G., von Gudenberg, J.W., Hofschuster, W., Kramer, W.: FILIB++, a fast interval library supporting containment computations. ACM Trans. Math. Softw. 32, 299–324 (2006)
24. Le Mézo, T., Jaulin, L., Zerr, B.: Bracketing the solutions of an ordinary Differential equation with uncertain initial conditions. Appl. Math. Comput. 318, 70–79 (2017)
25. Nedialkov, N.S.: VNODE-LP—a validated solver for initial value problems in ordinary differential equations. Technical report CAS-06-06-NN (2006)
26. Nedialkov, N.S., Jackson, K., Corliss, G.: Validated solutions of initial value problems for ordinary Differential equations. Appl. Math. Comput. 105, 21–68 (1999)
27. Shampine, L.F., Thompson, S.: Numerical solution of delay Differential equations. In: Gilsinn, D.E., Kalmár-Nagy, T., Balachandran, B. (eds.) Delay Differential Equations, pp. 1–27. Springer, Boston (2009). https://doi.org/10.1007/978-0-387-85595-0_9
28. Szczelina, R.: Rigorous integration of delay differential equations. Ph.D. thesis, Faculty of Mathematics and Computer Science, Jagiellonian University, Krakow (2014)
29. Testylier, R., Dang, T.: NLTOOLBOX: a library for reachability computation of nonlinear dynamical systems. In: Van Hung, D., Ogawa, M. (eds.) ATVA 2013. LNCS, vol. 8172, pp. 469–473. Springer, Cham (2013). https://doi.org/10.1007/978-3-319-02444-8_37
30. Xue, B., et al.: Safe over- and under-approximation of reachable sets for delay Differential equations. In: Abate, A., Geeraerts, G. (eds.) FORMATS 2017. LNCS, vol. 10419, pp. 281–299. Springer, Cham (2017). https://doi.org/10.1007/978-3-319-65765-3_16
31. Xue, B., She, Z., Easwaran, A.: Under-approximating backward reachable sets by polytopes. In: Chaudhuri, S., Farzan, A. (eds.) CAV 2016. LNCS, vol. 9779, pp. 457–476. Springer, Cham (2016). https://doi.org/10.1007/978-3-319-41528-4_25
32. Zou, L., Fränzle, M., Zhan, N., Mosaad, P.N.: Automatic verification of stability and safety for delay Differential equations. In: Kroening, D., Păsăreanu, C.S. (eds.) CAV 2015. LNCS, vol. 9207, pp. 338–355. Springer, Cham (2015). https://doi.org/10.1007/978-3-319-21668-3_20

Author Index